WHAT CAN THEY BE?

These most wonderful, strange and

MYSTERIOUS ANIMALS!

Two in number and of distinct species, found in a CAVE, in the hither-to unexplored Wilds of Africa, in a singularly perfect state of pre-servation, have been secured for a short time only. Mr. Barnum

WILL GIVE ONE THOUSAND DOLLARS

To any naturalist or other person who will correctly classify the WHAT CAN THEY BE? under any species or genus laid down in GOLDSMITH, CUVIER or any other published work on NATURAL HISTORY. These indescribable animals are to be seen at all hours.

Re-engaged for a short time that most extraordinary living NONDESCRIPT, the

WHAT is IT?

The most curious creature in the world, and the most interesting. He seems to be neither a Man, nor a Monkey, but has many of the features and peculiarities of each. He has a bright intelligent eye, is playful as a kitten and every way interesting and pleasing.

THE GRAND AQUARIA

Occupying one of the spacious halls of the Museum, is well stocked with Fish from various Rivers and Seas and is con-stantly receiving new acquisitions of rare and interesting specimens from every part of the globe.

MR. BARNUM will be glad at all times to supply, gratuitously, pictures of curiosities to such visitors as will put them up in conspicuous places. Inquire of the doorkeeper.

New York Herald Job Office, 97 Nassau street, New York.

BUNK

OTHER BOOKS BY KEVIN YOUNG

Nonfiction

    The Grey Album: On the Blackness of Blackness

Poetry

    Blue Laws: Selected & Uncollected Poems 1995–2015
    Book of Hours
    Ardency: A Chronicle of the Amistad *Rebels*
    Dear Darkness
    For the Confederate Dead
    Black Maria
    To Repel Ghosts: The Remix
    Jelly Roll: A Blues
    To Repel Ghosts
    Most Way Home

Editor

    The Hungry Ear: Poems of Food & Drink
    The Collected Poems of Lucille Clifton 1965–2010
    The Best American Poetry 2011
    The Art of Losing: Poems of Grief & Healing
    Jazz Poems
    John Berryman: Selected Poems
    Blues Poems
    Giant Steps: The New Generation of African American Writers

BUNK

The Rise of

Hoaxes, Humbug,

Plagiarists, Phonies,

Post-Facts, and Fake News

Kevin Young

GRAYWOLF PRESS

This publication is made possible, in part, by the voters of Minnesota through a Minnesota State Arts Board Operating Support grant, thanks to a legislative appropriation from the arts and cultural heritage fund, and a grant from the Wells Fargo Foundation. Significant support has also been provided by Target, the McKnight Foundation, the Lannan Foundation, the Amazon Literary Partnership, and other generous contributions from foundations, corporations, and individuals. To these organizations and individuals we offer our heartfelt thanks.

Published by Graywolf Press
250 Third Avenue North, Suite 600
Minneapolis, Minnesota 55401

www.graywolfpress.org

Published in the United States of America
Printed in Canada

ISBN 978-1-55597-791-7

2 4 6 8 9 7 5 3 1
First Graywolf Printing, 2017

Library of Congress Control Number: 2017930117

Cover design: Kyle G. Hunter

Cover art: Charles Eisenmann, "Ashbury Ben The Leopard Boy" and "Old Zip Barnum's What is It," 1885. Harvard Theatre Collection, Houghton Library, Harvard University

Endpapers: Barnum's American Museum handbill, 1860. Harvard Theatre Collection, Houghton Library, Harvard University *for*

R. E. N.

a true friend

Fried ice cream is a reality.

—P. FUNK
Maggot Brain

Alas! Victor, when falsehood can look so like the truth,
who can assure themselves of certain happiness?

—MARY SHELLEY
Frankenstein

The following is based on actual events.
Only the names, locations, and events
have been changed.

—*Anchorman*

I am composing on the typewriter late at night, thinking of today.
How well we all spoke. A language is a map of our failures.
Frederick Douglass wrote an English purer than Milton's. People
suffer highly in poverty. There are methods but we do not use them.
Joan, who could not read, spoke some peasant form of French. Some
of the suffering are: it is hard to tell the truth; this is America; I
cannot touch you now. In America we have only the present tense.

—ADRIENNE RICH
The Burning of Paper Instead of Children

Contents

THREE
Mysteria
A sideshow

BOOK TWO   THE HOAXING OF HISTORY

FOUR
The Vampire's Mirror
Of imposture, forgery & monsters

FIVE
Hack Heaven
Of the journalist & the liar

Charles Eisenmann, "Ashbury Ben The Leopard Boy" and
"Old Zip Barnum's What is It?" 1885.

BUNK

Italian translation and images from the Moon Hoax, ca. 1840.

BOOK ONE

A

HISTORY

OF THE

HOAX

ONE

The

American

Museum

{On the madness of crowds}

Every crowd has a silver lining.
—P. T. BARNUM

GREAT ATTRACTION

JUST ARRIVED AT CONCERT HALL. *1835*
☞ FOR A SHORT TIME ONLY. ☜

JOICE HETH,

NURSE TO

Gen. George Washington,

(The father of our country,) who has arrived at the astonishing age of **161** years! will be seen at Concert Hall, corner of Court and Hanover streets, Boston, for a SHORT TIME ONLY, as she is to fill other engagements very soon. *1835*

JOICE HETH is unquestionably the most astonishing and interesting curiosity in the World! She was the slave of Augustine Washington, (the father of Gen. Washington,) and was the first person who put clothes on the unconscious infant who in after days led our heroic fathers on to glory, to victory and freedom. To use her own language when speaking of the illustrious Father of his country, "she raised him." JOICE HETH was born in the Island of Madagascar, on the Coast of Africa, in the year 1674 and has consequently now arrived at the astonishing

Age of 161 Years!
in 1835

She weighs but forty-six pounds, and yet is very cheerful and interesting. She retains her faculties in an unparalleled degree, converses freely, sings numerous hymns, relates many interesting anecdotes of Gen. Washington, the red coats, &c. and often laughs heartily at her own remarks, or those of the spectators. Her health is perfectly good, and her appearance very neat. She was baptized in the Potomac river and received into the Baptist Church 116 years ago, and takes great pleasure in conversing with Ministers and religious persons. The appearance of this marvellous relic of antiquity strikes the beholder with amazement, and convinces him that his eyes are resting on the oldest specimen of mortality they ever before beheld. Original, authentic and indisputable documents prove however astonishing the fact may appear, JOICE HETH is in every respect the person she is represented.

The most eminent physicians and intelligent men both in New York and Philadelphia, have examined this *living skeleton* and the documents accompanying her, and all *invariably* pronounce her to be as represented 161 *years of age*! Indeed it is impossible for any person, however incredulous, to visit her without astonishment and the most perfect satisfaction that she is as old as represented.

☞ A female is in continual attendance, and will give every attention to the ladies who visit this relic of by gone ages.

She was visited at Niblo's Garden New York, by *ten thousand persons* in two weeks.———Hours of exhibition from 9 A. M to 1 P. M. and from 3 to 10 P. M.—Admittance 25 cents—Children 12½ cents. ☞ Over
1835

"Great Attraction Just Arrived at Concert Hall."
Handbill for Joice Heth exhibition, 1835.

CHAPTER 1

The Age of Imposture

"What the American public always wants is a tragedy with a happy ending." If William Dean Howells was instinctively right when he said this to his fellow novelist Edith Wharton,[1] then the hook of the modern hoax has been to separate the tragedy from that American happy ending. Recently the hoax, at least after the nineteenth century that Wharton and Howells had just seen turn, pretends every tragedy is far worse than it really is—if only to make the scripted ending, no matter how apocalyptic it may be, all the happier. Once the hoax meant to honor, now it embraces horror; once it sought to praise, today the hoax mostly traffics in pain.

Yet across the nineteenth century, the honor and horror of the hoax briefly blended into humor—of a species we might call dark. Nineteenth-century America regularly reveled in the contradictions of what famed showman P. T. Barnum called *humbug*, his many audiences taking pleasure in hoaxing and being hoaxed. What folks wanted was a show—and not necessarily an especially good one. Take the Feejee Mermaid, which Barnum bought and displayed starting in 1842: the exhibit was nothing more than a monkey's upper body—head, arms, torso—sewn together with a fish's tail, looking nothing like the beautiful images used to advertise it. Those who paid to see the humbug surely experienced a number of things, not least of which was a feeling of being fooled, but also a not unpleasant realization at how foolish they had been to be so eager. *How could I have believed in mermaids?* Viewers' betrayal mixed with being humbled, both a wish and a form of curiosity—*curiosities* being Barnum's name for the array of exhibits, freaks, and humbugs presented in his rather elegant American Museum, bought from its former proprietor in 1841.

Of course there would have been a quite different reaction had Barnum marketed his humbug as, say, the "Massachusetts Mermaid." (Turns out he had, in fact, earlier tried out a far less successful "Dorchester Mermaid"!) The advertisement promises exoticness—seen in Barnum's phonetic spelling of the island of Fiji—that both preys on and plays with provinciality. The name Feejee Mermaid also suggests not just where this is found, or what could be found there, but an idea, however subtle, that this "ugly, dried-up, black looking, and diminutive specimen," as Barnum later put it,[2] just might be what passes for a mermaid in that lesser, foreign land. This would only grow worse when he exhibited several actual Fijians and at least one African American as "Figi Cannibals" in 1872, their foreignness (or rather, nativeness) their only freakishness.[3] The Mermaid worked exactly because it provided that mix of shame and superiority that constitutes the humbug.

In his fascinating survey *Humbugs of the World* (1866), Barnum draws a distinction between humbugs and what we might call hoaxes. Barnum objects to *Webster's* definition: "humbug, as a noun, is an 'imposition under fair pretences;' and as a verb, it is, 'to deceive; to impose on.' With all due deference to Doctor Webster, I submit that, according to present usage, this is not the only, nor even the generally accepted, definition of that term."[4] Barnum's mention of Noah Webster is important given Webster's emblematic Americanness—as historian Jill Lepore recounts, in putting out his call for a new dictionary, Webster set out not just to define American usage but to capture "the American language."[5] Sixty-six years after Webster first declared his intention to make a "Dictionary of the American Language," Barnum means to define humbug as an American idea and ideal.

This raises a central question: is there something especially American about the hoax? Where the eighteenth century was the hoax's height in Britain, the nineteenth century starred the United States, so much so that someone at the time called it "the age of imposture."[6] Hoaxing would ironically prove one key way nineteenth-century America sought to establish its bona fides after the fact—just as, a century before, Shakespearean fakes and finds were attempts to claim ancestry and British culture's supremacy. The age of reason gave way to romanticism, which prized truth, originality, mystery, and beauty while also including a bevy of fakers who capitalized on those very things. In contrast, "born in the eighteenth century as an adult," critic Curtis MacDougall writes in his comprehensive 1940 study

Hoaxes, "the United States during the nineteenth century felt the lack of a childhood with its rich memories and cherished traditions."[7] This lack led to a host of hoaxes. There's indeed a powerful, persistent notion that the American character is filled not just with tall tales and sideshows but also with con men and fake Indians, pretend blacks and impostor prophets, with masks and money.

Barnum reaches for "the public" in order to delineate the difference between swindlers, forgers, impostors, cheats, and humbug. "We will suppose, for instance, that a man with 'fair pretences' applies to a wholesale merchant for credit on a large bill of goods. His 'fair pretences' comprehend an assertion that he is a moral and religious man, a member of the church, a man of wealth, etc., etc. It turns out that he is not worth a dollar, but is a base, lying wretch, an impostor and a cheat. He is arrested and imprisoned 'for obtaining property under false pretences' or, as Webster says, 'fair pretences.' He is punished for his villainy. The public do not call him a 'humbug;' they very properly term him a swindler."[8] In contrast, Barnum writes:

> Two actors appear as stars at two rival theatres. They are equally talented, equally pleasing. One advertises himself simply as a tragedian, under his proper name—the other boasts that he is a prince, and wears decorations presented by all the potentates of the world, including the "King of the Cannibal Islands." He is correctly set down as a "humbug," while this term is never applied to the other actor. But if the man who boasts of having received a foreign title is a miserable actor, and he gets up gift-enterprises and bogus entertainments, or pretends to devote the proceeds of his tragic efforts to some charitable object, without, in fact, doing so—he is then a humbug in Dr. Webster's sense of that word, for he is an "impostor under fair pretences." . . .
>
> An honest man who thus arrests public attention will be called a "humbug," but he is not a swindler or an impostor. If, however, after attracting crowds of customers by his unique displays, a man foolishly fails to give them a full equivalent for their money, they never patronize him a second time, but they very properly denounce him as a swindler, a cheat, an impostor; they do not, however, call him a "humbug." He fails, not because he advertises his wares in an *outre* manner, but because, after attracting crowds of patrons, he stupidly and wickedly cheats them.[9]

This is a brilliant distinction: *An honest man who thus arrests public attention will be called a "humbug," but he is not a swindler or an impostor.* It is not the difference, necessarily, between intent and innocence, or a show being exactly as advertised—Barnum's rarely were innocent or as advertised—but whether the show remains worth it once you are already in the door. We can see through Barnum's eyes the ways he, certainly in a self-serving manner, defines the humbug not as fraud, or at least as *simply* fraud. Though dubious in places—fair is false, and false is fair—Barnum also clearly draws a line between humbug and other kinds of hoaxes, from forgery to swindles, that "not a person in the community" confuses with a good show. The question is not whether to humbug or not to humbug, but how to humbug better.

The best, current corollary we have to the dizzying delight of Barnum's many humbugs may be reality television. There, too, we can see a promised spectacle implied as real that quickly turns out to be staged—either relatively subtly (as in television's *The Bachelor*) or not (as in the Feejee Mermaid or *Survivor*). "Reality TV" labels anything from a game show to arranged marriages; from celebrities pretending to be cops or businesspersons or even celebrities to those pretending to be princes or even presidents. More recently, the *Bachelorette* broadcast has incorporated select Twitter posts— none mine, unfortunately—revealing that it's not enough to share our experience of watching silly television virtually, we now must watch ourselves watching. As viewers, we inheritors to Barnum's America tend to feel a mix of *I can't believe I'm watching this* and *I can't believe that person did that* to *I can't wait to see what happens next.*

It would be Barnum who first turned the American invention of the confidence man legit. He did so first in 1835 by using Joice Heth, the black woman he had likely bought for an act in which she pretended to be George Washington's nursemaid, which would have made her over 161 years old. Capitalizing on the growing cult of Washington, Barnum also proved brilliant at making the audience part of the hoax, saying effectively, you're smart, or better yet, you think you're so smart: *come see and decide for yourself.* He made everyone an expert. What reality TV does is make everyone a judge—and not just because "judge shows" are some of the most popular on television. (*Judge Judy* makes a reported sixty million dollars a year, far more than the more prestigious "male-only" job of late-night host.) Courtroom trials also become a different kind of entertainment when swept up in sweeps week, and votes counted without fear of gerrymandering.

Nineteenth-century America's love of humbug allowed the new republic to marvel at its mysteries, question its hypocrisies, and express contradictions of freedom and slavery, exploration and faith. The relatively young nation saw a number of heavy-duty hoaxes and part-time pranks, many of them committed by some of our most beloved writers—Edgar Allan Poe, Mark Twain, practically the entirety of what's called the American Renaissance of the nineteenth century—who questioned truth rather than questing after it. Poe would write of "mystification" and craft an essay in praise of the con he called "diddling" in the 1840s; Herman Melville's *Confidence Man* (1857) helped name a figure growing more familiar. For its part Twain's *Huck Finn* (1885) would mock the very idea of the Lost Dauphin of France that had yielded dozens of pretend contenders to the throne. Soon *Tom Sawyer* would become a verb that means tricking someone to work for you while you sit back and watch.

The very year Barnum showed Joice Heth to an eager public by turns credulous and skeptical, Richard Adams Locke reported on the murder trial of Matthias the Prophet, an event fanned and fed by the inexpensive newspapers known as "the penny press." Born Robert Matthews, preaching an apocalyptic doctrine, Matthias had further renamed himself "the Spirit of Truth." His was yet another American religion founded in "the burned-over district" of the Hudson Valley and western New York, an area of spiritual reawakening that produced Mormonism around the same time and would later in the century yield the Fox sisters, whose communications with spirits (ultimately confessed as fake) spurred on Spiritualism, a movement at the center of several other hoaxes. It also provided an outlet for many other radical sects, notable for their calls for equal rights for women and enslaved Africans.

Yet at the time, Matthias's sensational trial in 1835 for killing one of his followers spawned four different books, including Locke's anonymously issued *Memoirs of Matthias the Prophet, with a Full Exposure of His Atrocious Impositions, and of the Degrading Delusions of His Followers* just two days after his daily reports ran.[10] Matthias had taken over a follower's home to set up a kingdom in his own name, insisting that the wife of the owner was his sexual "spirit match" and marrying her while her husband looked on; he was accused of letting the husband die slowly a few months later (from a broken heart, one might guess) rather than seeking medical help. Certainly Matthias's proclaiming equality while holding himself out as a savior sounds a note familiar to our modern cult leaders. One critic describes Locke's portrayal of Matthias as very much "draped in the portentous gothic tones of one of the horror stories that Edgar Allan Poe was just then beginning to write."[11] Later the same year, Locke would go on to commit one of the most famous hoaxes of the nineteenth century.

The characterizing of Matthias as a charlatan is part of the era's humbug too—the penny press was central to the circus, the metaphoric sign outside announcing its Cannibal King. As an introduction to a reprint of the Moon Hoax has it, the *Sun* and its publisher "had stumbled across an unexpected fact about American society. The New Yorkers of Andrew Jackson's second term did not especially care to read the news. Political life bubbled and fizzed around them constantly anyhow; they had no need of being further informed. The doings of General Jackson or Henry Clay or Louis-Philippe were their own business. Political life was no more important to the New Yorker of 1835 than police court life, and police court life, in fact, was a lot more interesting."[12] Such facts would find life in the deception and reception of the nineteenth-century hoax.

If all this sounds familiar, it is because the transformative advent of the penny press most resembles the current change demonstrated, if not caused, by the Internet. The Web too promised a democratic upheaval, predicated on the notion that freedom could be nearly free; it too soon became filled with sensationalism as news, with support not by sponsors (as earlier papers had) but by advertising (at least at first); it too made court life a kind of politics, addicted to scandal, and politics into a kangaroo court, simply adding "-gate" to every incident; it too implements chaos as a going concern. And like the Internet, the penny press inaugurated by the *Sun*—first popularized by the Matthias scandal and within two years of its start, the best-selling newspaper in the world—was spurred on not by arguments over objectivity or facts but over hoaxes, impostors, vast fictions, con artists, and cheats.

THE CHIMERA

Few people remember that in 1835 men first walked on the moon. That year, however, it was all anyone could talk about—the famed reports in the *Sun* described men with bat wings (*Vespertilio-homo*), unicorns, and biped beavers as viewed on the moon's surface, leading to much speculation and vast newspaper sales in New York and the rest of the relatively new nation. All the city's papers printed extracts or rebuttals; as with our current headline-worthy hoaxes (anyone remember 2009's "balloon boy" hoax?), every outlet had to weigh in. The news of life on the moon spread like riots had the year before, when mobs of white New Yorkers hit the streets looking for blacks, abolitionists, and "amalgamators"—the name given to those who they feared were in favor of race mixing—to intimidate, beat up, or worse.

Needless to say, none of these discoveries on the moon proved true. Locke's Moon Hoax would seem not just a parody of science and faith or a prank on a gullible public but also somehow a transference of some of the energy that led to those riots. Many white readers would rather embrace lunar man-bats than their fellow human beings. As detailed in his book on the Moon Hoax, *The Sun and the Moon*, Matt Goodman writes that Locke, editor of the *Sun*, helped make it the one paper in the city to come out against slavery in a state that, while it no longer sanctioned slavery, by and large supported it in the South and partook of its spoils. No one would mistake the *Sun* for being fully abolitionist; historian Nell Irvin Painter cites noteworthy instances of the *Sun*'s complicitness with slavery. Yet, under Locke the *Sun*'s sometimes antislavery stance in the 1830s was enough for the notorious William Bennett, who ran the fierce competitor the *Morning Herald*, to call it a "drivelling contemporary nigger paper."[13]

With Halley's Comet predicted for 1835, it was an auspicious year. To some that anticipated apparition must have seemed an omen, as well as somehow American: "its reappearance was being awaited with great excitement as well as national pride," Goodman notes, "as this was the first time the comet would ever streak through the skies over the United States."[14] The heavenly body hung over Matthias the Prophet's apocalyptic prophecies and helped make the *Sun*'s celestial claims all the more believable; indeed, the comet was first spotted by U.S. astronomers on the very day Locke launched his Moon Hoax. He had also committed the classic hoax technique of triangulating: the *Sun* purported to merely be reprinting the discoveries of Sir John Herschel, astronomer extraordinaire, from his South African observatory. In the famous Herschel, Locke found a perfect if unaware "coconspirator," as he was not only widely respected but also known to be far away on research and not easily reached. Not just said to be reprints from the *Edinburgh Journal of Science*, the articles went further, claiming to be a report made by Herschel's amanuensis. The result is that the hoax becomes a series of quotes within quotes, hearsay really, from others never quite present.

The Moon Hoax starts simply enough, in one voice—that of the *Sun*—evoking the moon and its mystery:

It is impossible to contemplate any great Astronomical discovery without feelings closely allied to a sensation of awe, and nearly akin to those with which a departed spirit may be supposed to discover the realities of a future state. Bound by the irrevocable laws of nature to the globe on which we live, creatures "close shut up in infinite expanse," it seems like acquiring a fearful supernatural power when any remote mysterious works of the Creator yield tribute to our curiosity. . . .

To render our enthusiasm intelligible, we will state at once, that by means of a telescope of vast dimensions and an entirely new principle, the younger Herschel, at his observatory in the Southern Hemisphere, has already made the most extraordinary discoveries in every planet of our solar system; has discovered planets in other solar systems; has obtained a distinct view of objects in the moon, fully equal to that which the unaided eye commands of terrestrial objects at the distance of a hundred yards; has affirmatively settled the question whether this satellite be inhabited, and by what order of beings; has firmly established a new theory of cometary phenomena; and has solved or corrected nearly every leading problem of mathematical astronomy.[15]

Except for the inhabitation of "the satellite," this account of Herschel's accomplishments and qualifications is true. It is this factitious nature that Locke got exactly right.

He also got the science lingo down. A graduate of Cambridge, Locke was knowledgeable enough to know or pretend to know what he was parroting and skilled enough to invent not just strange things but the official-sounding language surrounding them. He is entirely deadpan, though it is unclear what the exact point of the hoax was—simply to increase sales? to satirize those who believed not only in moon creatures but also the temples they built to presumably the same God?

Certainly there is a piousness to science that Locke seems to be sending up, but there's also the science being used in the name of piousness that the Moon Hoax upends. The mid-1830s mark the rise of eugenics and racialism, with phrenology just one of the many pseudosciences that not only explained but also sought to enact, reinforce, and restrict racial difference. Science, religion, and conceptions of race were yet another triangulation whose results all confirmed each other: the Bible, the stars, even the shapes of heads were enlisted over and over again to prove established prejudices true; objective investigators constantly rediscovered that Negroes, Indians, and other dark races (some of them European, mind you) were indeed still inferior.

The "Great Lunar Astronomical Discoveries" in Herschel's name were similarly hierarchical—Locke's hoax unfolds almost biblically, we soon realize, day by day, as in Genesis. Reading it now we see how each day's discovery by the paper's readers also neatly mirrors the fictional Herschel's nightly observations. Let there be the light of the moon; then the firmaments and valleys, "a lofty chain of obelisk-shaped, or very slender pyramids, standing in irregular groups," cataracts and "innumerable cascades" of water; then the creatures, including moon-bison, and a unicorn "who would be classed on earth as a monster."[16] This may be telling in and of itself—the observations constantly classify and impose earthly assumptions on extraterrestrial beings in a way familiar to contemporary science, especially race science, at least to our ears. Several nights, "being cloudy, were unfavorable to observation." The cloudiness, significantly, was here on earth.

Were such revelations merely wondrous to the readers of 1835? Or readily believed? Certainly they were popular, the *Sun*'s circulation soaring to almost twenty thousand—a remarkable leap considering the penny press as a form hadn't existed till two years before, when the *Sun*'s publisher created it. Before then, newspapers were six cents and chiefly sponsored by political parties. By relying on advertising and circulation the penny papers were able to chart and help invent a new reading public.

News of the "discoveries" became the proverbial talk of the town, with other papers not only reprinting but also confirming the story. Those who debated the articles argued over not whether the series was true but how true; for those who may have suspected it was all a hoax, talk focused on how the trick was achieved rather than exposing it. The story seemed too good, if not to be true then not to be told. The hoax held hints if anyone cared to look—for one, the prestigious and quite real *Edinburgh Journal of Science* from which the excerpts were meant to be taken had folded months before. There was also the question of authorship: like many a hoax, or even straight fiction, the Moon Hoax had appeared not exactly anonymously but pseudonymously.

Still the daily revelations continued, exploring "The Lake of Death" and surrounding extinct volcanoes, including the crater "Endymion" (also the name of Keats's famous poem dedicated to the hoaxer and suicide, Chatterton). The report is here itself in quotation marks, giving the whole a kind of air-quotes quality:

"We found each of the three ovals volcanic and sterile within; but without, most rich, throughout the level regions around them, in every imaginable production of a bounteous soil. Dr. Herschel has classified not less than thirty-eight species of forest trees, and nearly twice this number of plants, found in this tract alone, which are widely different to those found in more equatorial latitudes. Of animals, he classified nine species of mammalia, and five of ovipara. Among the former is a small kind of rein-deer, the elk, the moose, the horned bear, and the biped beaver. The last resembles the beaver of the earth in every other respect than in its destitution of a tail, and its invariable habit of walking upon only two feet. It carries its young in its arms like a human being, and moves with an easy gliding motion. Its huts are constructed better and higher than those of many tribes of human savages, and from the appearance of smoke in nearly all of them, there is no doubt of its being acquainted with the use of fire."[17]

When it came to humanoids on the moon days later, the account was at its most striking:

"We counted three parties of these creatures, of twelve, nine, and fifteen in each, walking erect towards a small wood near the base of the eastern precipices. Certainly they *were* like human beings, for their wings had now disappeared, and their attitude in walking was both erect and dignified. . . . About half of the first party had passed beyond our canvass; but of all the others we had a perfectly distinct and deliberate view. They averaged four feet in height, were covered, except on the face, with short and glossy copper-colored hair, and had wings composed of a thin membrane, without hair, lying snugly upon their backs, from the top of the shoulders to the calves of the legs. The face, which was of a yellowish flesh color, was a slight improvement upon that of the large orang outang, being more open and intelligent in its expression, and having a much greater expansion of forehead. . . . The hair on the head was a darker color than that of the body, closely curled, but apparently not woolly, and arranged in two curious semicircles over the temples of the forehead."[18]

These creatures sound like such a range of racial types that it is hard to know how to read them now. In the racial coding of the day they sound stereotypically black—as noted by Benjamin Reiss in his tremendous book about Barnum and Heth, *The Showman and the Slave*—with Africans and their descendants described as and compared to "orang outangs" (orangutans). I would point out that the creatures' hair is "apparently not woolly," though neither is the hair of people of African descent, but that was how white discourse described black hair almost without deviation in order to indicate its own deviation from the norm. "As if this were not subliminal cue enough," Reiss writes, "Locke concluded with a subtle reference to their childishness and oversexualized nature."[19] So closely observed, so distinct and deliberate, these inverted angels have yellowish flesh, copper hair, and almost as the beast from Revelation, one imagines feet of brass. Locke has crafted a *chimera* in the sense of being both fanciful and false, a combo platter of types. They are amalgams much like those racial ones feared by "the common man" opposed to abolition.

If so, this may only support the question of satire that surrounds the Moon Hoax—though I would insist that intent doesn't make something a hoax or not, Locke's motives appear as complex and varied as "the canvass" of the alleged moon landscape. As an antislavery tract the hoax is too obscure; as racist propaganda it is not obvious enough given the extremes that surrounded it. Phrenology and the rest of the racialist sciences then coming into being in the 1830s were mere allegories in the end, finding one-to-one correlations written on the body that determine the subject's intelligence or preconceived lack thereof.

But wait—there weren't just man-bats on the moon, but also a superior race of beings there. That they lived in the "Vale of the Triads" indicated that they were the third highest of the three kinds of upright beings on the moon. It is tempting to see the lunar humanoids as hierarchical in the ways white eugenicists characterized races on earth, from beaver bipeds (metaphoric Native Americans) to woolly man-bats (Negroes) to this last group, in which "nearly all the individuals in these groups were of a larger stature than the former specimens, less dark in color, and in *every respect* an improved variety of the race." These last are first. "They were creatures of order and subordination."[20]

Subordination is key. The *Sun*'s "discoveries" indicate the moon beings offer a subordination to a higher power, one so complete that they, like God, can only be ascertained by those with the resources, powers, magnification, and import to do so. Whether Locke meant to have these creatures taken as symbolic whites, or just as remarkable discoveries—or to be barely believed at all—the Moon Hoax's popularity certainly owed much to its re-creating on the Moon what many white readers believed could be found at home.

Perhaps, much better: there, on the other end of a telescope, wasn't just life but order, not just extinct craters but vibrant temples, not just sustenance but subordination, not just humanoids but hierarchies.

Even many of those abolitionists who fought for change didn't seek to eliminate hierarchy, just slavery. (Matthias, for his part, promised eliminating both, though in actuality this meant reinstalling himself at the top.) In the Moon Hoax we find creatures as well as coexistence, a lunar den that itself critiqued the earthbound matters in our fallen paradise. Locke had married the fanciful travelogue to that of the outright travel lie, but also to the issues of the day. Not bound by facts, the hoax is free to fabricate feelings and the genres associated with them—it is this artfulness and ambiguity that help explain the Moon Hoax's popularity.

And that popularity cannot be overstated. Within months, Locke's Moon Hoax not only created the most popular newspaper in the world, and practically the very industry of the modern press itself, it also helped galvanize a new, national popular culture. *Moonshine*, a play inspired by the hoax, was performed mere weeks after articles appeared at the renowned, newly rebuilt Bowery Theatre, a venue known for doing topical plays and satires (think a nineteenth-century *Saturday Night Live*). Elsewhere, a life-size cyclorama of the moonscape, its large canvas surely reminiscent of the "canvass" Herschel and his team witnessed, drew many New Yorkers, including Locke himself.[21]

For all its invention, the Moon Hoax also provided an outlet for those previously unserved by the media, but also for the era's shifting sense of truth. "The *Sun* hoax appeared at a time when people did not expect to believe everything they read in the newspapers," Ormond Seavey reminds us in his introduction to the hoax's 1970s reprint. "It is impossible to say how widely or how much they did believe the supposed Supplement. When one examines the contemporary newspaper reaction, one can never separate clearly the believers in the hoax from those who knowingly joined in the deception. . . . It was a time when the tall tale was first recognized as a characteristically American narrative. Both the deadpan teller of the tale and his impassive listeners were conspirators against reality."[22] Readers and newspapermen found in even the Moon Hoax's falseness a metaphor for the times, one that echoes our own.

Was the Vale of Triads also a veil? The unseen is at work here, especially as most subsequent accounts of the hoax fail to mention the Vale dwellers, that superior, lighter race—perhaps because they make clear that race and racialism have plenty to do with the hoax and its success. (For his part, Goodman mistakes these lighter beings for just another kind of man-bat.) Far more reported and repeated are the "almagaman-bats," surely in part because of their stunning visuals in the illustrations that appeared in numerous foreign editions, from Wales to Naples to four editions in France alone. In them, *Vespertilio-homo* seems quite at home on the imagined moon. One practically pirouettes, arms and wings raised, preparing to spin like the earth he was glimpsed from.

DIDDLING

The Moon Hoax's power and popularity may be further indicated by any number of anecdotes: we could mention the way a mob gathered to get the issues of the *Sun* and the new *Discoveries* pamphlet; or how others took credit for the hoax while literally standing in front of Locke, who hadn't yet claimed authorship; or how the rival *Morning Herald* managed to correctly guess and assert Locke as the real author, but then backed down as soon as he wrote a letter not so much denying it as saying it was beneath denying. We could also cite the vast number of unauthorized reprints and translations, or those who fully believed in it—some report over sixty thousand copies being sold, a remarkable number even today. One of the many true yet unbelievable stories involves the news of the discoveries actually reaching Herschel in South Africa in the person of one Caleb Weeks, owner of a menagerie, who promptly provided the astronomer with a copy of the pamphlet; on hearing the news Herschel found himself more fascinated and bemused than angry.

This mix of emotions was the widespread response when the *Sun* finally relented and took responsibility. It seemed to match the ways the nineteenth century in America often said, *I'll show you hoaxing, bigger and better—and though you may know I'm hoaxing you, you'll love it anyway.* Edgar Allan Poe would call this *diddling*—and this poet of the American gothic and inventor of the detective story would offer up praise to hoaxing that remains as important as these other innovations. First published in 1845, Poe's "Diddling Considered as One of the Exact Sciences" suggests a definition that may approach Barnum's humbug:

> Diddling—or the abstract idea conveyed by the verb to diddle—is suf-
> ficiently well understood. Yet the fact, the deed, the thing *diddling*, is

somewhat difficult to define. We may get, however, at a tolerably distinct conception of the matter in hand, by defining—not the thing,
diddling, in itself—but man, as an animal that diddles. . . . A crow
thieves; a fox cheats; a weasel outwits; a man diddles. To diddle is his
destiny. "Man was made to mourn," says the poet. But not so:—he was
made to diddle. This is his aim—his object—his *end*. And for this reason when a man's diddled, we say he's "*done*."[23]

Poe offers up a tricky definition to define such trickery, one fittingly and
playfully twisting in on itself.

More telling may be when Poe writes, "Diddling, rightly considered,
is a compound, of which the ingredients are minuteness, interest, perse-
verance, ingenuity, audacity, *nonchalance*, originality, impertinence, and
grin." This last quality may prove the most important—though the diddler
is "guided by self-interest," certainly "he would return a purse, I am sure,
upon discovering that he had obtained it by an unoriginal diddle"—for the
grin completes the act:

> *Grin:*—Your *true* diddler winds up all with a grin. But this nobody
> sees but himself. He grins when his daily work is done—when his al-
> lotted labors are accomplished—at night in his closet, and altogether
> for his own private entertainment. He goes home. He locks his door.
> He divests himself of his clothes. He puts out his candle. He gets
> into bed. He places his head upon the pillow. All this done, and your
> diddler *grins*. This is no hypothesis. It is a matter of course. I reason
> *à priori*, and a diddle would be *no* diddle without a grin.

It is clear from the examples Poe provides that *true* diddle, like humbug or
the confidence game, is something ingenious yet dishonest, a way of making
merry while also making money. For Poe, often broke, this surely may have
been a metaphor for what he wished he could do—in print at least—in his
many tales and tricks. Poe's diddler sounds a lot like one idea of the writer:
"Your diddler is ingenious. He has constructiveness large. He understands
plot. He invents and circumvents."[24]

Your diddler Poe would commit several hoaxes, and attempt many
more. The title of his *Tales* (1845) indicates Poe's relation to an American
tall-tale tradition still often found in the newspaper. In his other tales and
sketches only published in magazines, Poe provides a good example of the

kinds of tale-telling, confidence men, and humbug found throughout the century. Locke's Moon Hoax, in fact, displaced a hoax Poe had launched just weeks before: his own invented tale of a trip to the moon.

"The Unparalleled Adventure of One Hans Phaall" appeared in the *Transcript* in June 1835. Later Poe would change the last name to Pfaall, its sound further alluding to the danger of such a moon journey with its possible "fall" as well as the "false" quality of the tale itself. Poe was convinced the tale would not only prove a big diddle and deal; he also hoped it would be believed and elicit the kind of attention eventually paid by the public to the Moon Hoax. It was not to be so—and not just because of its appearing in a small-circulation literary magazine just weeks earlier. The piece opens in Holland with high rhetoric and an account of a "hubbub" that turns out to be a hot-air balloon: "It appeared to be—yes! it *was* undoubtedly a species of balloon; but surely no *such* balloon had ever been seen in Rotterdam before. For who, let me ask, ever heard of a balloon manufactured entirely of dirty newspapers?"[25] It would be such newspapers that ultimately led Locke's Moon Hoax to eclipse Poe's, which pleased Poe not one bit.

Indeed, he would charge plagiarism at least privately, which is less odd than you might think for someone who regularly plagiarized. Many plagiarists behave like the cheating husband who's always paranoid about his wife's behavior. Poe's beloved Coleridge ("Of Coleridge I cannot speak but with reverence. His towering intellect! his gigantic power!")[26] also was a plagiarist who would regularly accuse others of literary theft; De Quincey, friend to Coleridge while he was alive, spoke out fiercely against Coleridge's plagiarism after his death, yet was himself a rampant literary robber. Poe the sometime plagiarist may insist the diddle be original, yet several of Poe's other half-hoaxes that followed copied extensively from other books.

Poe's unfinished *Journal of Julius Rodman* (1840) borrows liberally from the 1814 account of the Lewis and Clark expedition; as Goodman also notes of Poe's only novel, *The Narrative of Arthur Gordon Pym* (1838), "Many of the passages that described the South Seas were taken, sometimes virtually word for word, from encyclopedias and earlier travel narratives. All told, as much as one-fifth of the entire book came from elsewhere."[27] It can almost seem that Poe didn't quite recognize how close many of his debts were—then again, Poe was literally in financial debt much of his adult writing life, and in an odd way his plagiarism is a way not only of hiding sources but also of revealing his own learning. His is plagiarizing on a deadline. But that's not enough to explain the ways Poe's plagiarism, as it often is, appears rife with underlying questions of class and legitimacy. It is tempting to read this psychologically, given his having found himself disinherited by his foster father. Plagiarism, we'll learn, often is fraught with issues of origins, parentage, and purloining paternity.

After reading the Moon Hoax, "Poe's first suspicion, characteristically, was literary theft," Ormond Seavey writes.[28] In a letter to a friend on 11 September 1835 about the Moon Hoax, Poe complimented it as "very singular, but when I first purposed writing a Tale concerning the Moon, the idea of *Telescopic* discoveries suggested itself to me—but I afterwards abandoned it. I had, however, spoken of it freely, and from many little incidents and apparently trivial remarks in those *Discoveries*, I am convinced that the idea was stolen from myself."[29] In the end, the timing of the Moon Hoax—appearing just weeks after Poe published "Hans Phaall" in an obscure journal—suggests that, like the double helix, Poe and Locke seem to have discovered the moon nearly simultaneously yet independently.

Because of the success of Locke's *Discoveries*, Poe could not continue the second part of his own hoax, in which he had planned to describe the moon's surface; not only that, Poe now had to deny the charge that it was he who had nicked his idea from Locke. When he reprinted "Hans Pfaall" (spelling now changed) in *Tales from the Grotesque and Arabesque* five years later, Poe felt the need to include a note: "Strictly speaking, there is but little similarity between the above sketchy trifle, and the celebrated 'Moon-Story' of Mr. Locke; but as both have the character of *hoaxes*, (although the one is in a tone of banter, the other of downright earnest,) and as both hoaxes are on the same subject, the moon—moreover, as both attempt to give plausibility by scientific detail—the author of 'Hans Pfaall' thinks it necessary to say, in *self-defence*, that his own *jeu d'esprit* was published, in the 'Southern Literary Messenger,' about three weeks before the commencement of Mr. L's in the 'New York Sun.'"[30] Such defensive verbal gymnastics sound less like his tract on diddling than a diddle itself.

Recall that Poe calls diddling a *science*—a rational practice, achieved through testing and through doubt in much the same way that the con relies on confidence. In a way he is mocking pseudoscience by suggesting a science of falseness. But Poe may as well have meant science fiction, a genre he is often credited with starting—though I think a more accurate start might be Locke's very Moon Hoax. In mentioning their differing tones, Poe inadvertently reveals the largest reason why his is less successful: Poe's story is filled with "banter," easily dismissed; Locke's earnestness, his willingness to take its science as seriously as the fiction (and vice versa) marks the Moon Hoax as the true start of sci-fi. Though rivals with the *Sun*, *New York Herald* editor Bennett's attempt on 5 September to expose Locke as author also put forth a "new species of literature":

> NEW SPECIES OF LITERATURE. — We learn that Mr. R. A. Locke, the ingenious author of the late 'Moon Story' or 'Astronomical Hoax,' is putting on the stocks the frame of a new novel on a subject similar to that of his recent able invention in astronomy. His peculiar and original talent will then be brought out in full relief. His style is nearly as original as his conception. It is ornamented and highly imaginative. He may be said to be the inventor of an entire new species of literature, which we may call the "scientific novel." Sir Walter Scott is the author of the "historical novel," of which he has had many imitators. We have had also crowds of "fashionable novels," but fictitious history, founded on the discoveries and scientific hypotheses of the day, has seldom been attempted until Mr. Locke did so. In fact, Mr Locke has opened a new vein, as original, as curious, as beautiful, as any of the greatest geniuses that ever wrote. He looks forward into futurity, and adapts his characters to the light of science. What, for instance, can be better conceived, than the rapid enthusiasm portrayed in the recent narrative?[31]

Bennett seems awfully prescient—not only in the very hunch that Locke is the author but also in his view of science fiction. "Rapid enthusiasm" would rapidly beget a form about rapidity, sci-fi offering the kind of "fictitious history" it shares with the hoax. The new species spotted on the moon actually meant new forms of fiction on earth.

Poe himself would later describe the Moon Hoax's impact: "The great effect wrought upon the public mind is referable, first, to *the novelty of the idea*; secondly, to the fancy-exciting and reason-repressing character of the alleged discoveries; thirdly, to the consummate tact with which the deception was brought forth; fourthly, to the exquisite *vraisemblance* of the narration."[32] *Vraisemblance* is an apt word, meaning "likelihood"—it speaks of not truth, exactly, but a resemblance to a kind of believability. This is exactly what's missing in the start at least of "Hans Phaall"—which sounds remarkably like the end of *The Wonderful Wizard of Oz* (1900), whose wizard also was labeled a humbug and traveled to fantastic realms via balloon—the tone too excitable and borrowing too many trappings of adventure stories, tall tales, and travel lies to be entirely trusted. Still Poe provides a cross-roads between science fiction and actual science writing, both regularly exploited by the hoax.

He would have more success, however short-lived—and in the *Sun* no less—with a tale now referred to as the Balloon Hoax. Reading both his balloon-based hoaxes now, you can see why Poe's many hoax attempts remained only that—they don't yet have the energy, however melodramatic it may be, of his more gothic tales or of "The Raven," which would be his first runaway success after appearing in January 1845, a busy year for him. (*A crow thieves.*) Yet "Mystification," a little-discussed tale that first appeared in *Tales of the Grotesque and Arabesque* (1840), may help us further understand the continued appeal of diddling to Poe. The voice in it has the trappings of his later gothic stories, the detached narrator relating a kind of contest of wills between two participants: one a bored, completely false baron and the other an earnest man but a fool, banter and earnestness embodied.

A word that occurs frequently in the tale, in many different permutations, is *droll*: the fool cannot understand all he reads, much less that the conversation the baron has around and with him is often poking fun, usually at him; the baron can't help but be droll all the time. Soon the baron somehow gets the earnest man to insult him, then takes rather fake offense and smashes the mirror that held his guest's image. The guest goes home and messages over, through our narrator, a series of missives considering whether he and the baron should duel. (He doesn't seem to realize they have been dueling already.) The baron's response sends the former guest to the bookshelf to read the proper protocol for the duel—in French, natch—and the foolish guest becomes so honored by the baron's manners that the duel is avoided, even if the *jeu* is not. The whole is a "mystification"—the French word that describes something of a prank but also maintaining mystique—that appears here more than *droll* and in many different permutations, including *art mystifique*.

In France, *mystification*—meaning a more prankish, burlesquing literary tradition—emerged in the 1750s, not accidentally around the same time as the words *humbug* and *hoax* in English.[33] That these terms all came into usage during the height of the age of reason suggests the ways that, though hoaxing is as old as writing itself, the trumpeted search for truth and reason in the eighteenth-century Enlightenment was often met by its opposite. This Counter-Enlightenment, as Isaiah Berlin has named it, was more interested in the irrational—as such, the very age of reason constitutes one golden age of the hoax, with Poe's Age of Imposture another—just as our so-called age of information has been met by an equally forceful "age of misinformation" and a slew of new hoaxes. Of hoaxes, there is never a shortage—but it's also true that the weather of a particular time and place can influence what grows during a drought of facts. It is that weather the hoax measures.

The most useful definition of *mystification* may come from the reveal at the end of Poe's tale—an ending far less dramatic than in "The Tell-Tale Heart" or "The Cask of Amontillado" but suggestive of those haunting tales to come. The narrator describes the baron's book having "language . . . ingeniously framed so as to present to the ear all the outward signs of intelligibility, and even of profundity, while in fact not a shadow of meaning existed."[34] Poe's "Mystification" suggests one should know what one reads and should not pretend to know, which makes you not only a buffoon but also a balloon susceptible to the puncturing buffooneries of others. Is the baron then a writer-diddler, tricking his readers in ways Poe sometimes wished to? Or is that just a lot of hot air? Serving as a messenger between the parties in (and in parts of) the story, Poe's narrator foreshadows the weary, observant standoffish tone found in *The Great Gatsby*'s Nick Carraway—if Gatsby is an evocation of American self-invention, Fitzgerald's narrator-neighbor may be his real achievement, capturing a detached American determinism, wearily hurtling toward the abyss while wryly watching from the guesthouse. Neither a fake nor a true believer be, suggests Fitzgerald.

Neither a buffoon nor a baron be, Poe almost quoths. Yet the narrator of "Mystification" does admire his friend the baron for the artfulness of his hoaxing: "The beauty, if I may so call it, of his *art mystifique*, lay in that consummate ability (resulting from an almost intuitive knowledge of human nature, and a most wonderful self-possession,) by means of which he never failed to make it appear that the drolleries he was occupied in bringing to a point, arose partly in spite, and partly in consequence of the laudable efforts he was making for their prevention. . . . The adroitness, too, was no less worthy of observation by which he contrived to *shift the sense of the grotesque from the creator to the created*—from his own person to the absurdities to which he had given rise."[35] Shifting "the sense of the grotesque from the creator to the created": no one before Poe defined the hoax better, almost offhandedly pointing out its pleasures and perils.

Is the hoax an art? A science, like diddling? Or a habit, if not an addiction, like plagiarism? Poe would find himself party to all three. It is a shifting grotesque that's Poe's ultimate accomplishment, his ability in these science fictions and mini-hoaxes to say something not just in the American language but about America. The horror Poe would innovate would soon infect the hoax itself, providing a parade of pain.

Taken together, *Tales of the Grotesque and Arabesque* create a vast template—even a temple—of belief and believability, a mix of science fiction and fact, a factitiousness that would give rise to a particular American voice. Poe's grotesques and arabesques invented the American narrator as an American not just in tone but talk. From such a diddling stance would come the horror and detective stories Poe soon would invent, shifting the grotesque from the creator to what he created: namely, a sturdy, yet shifting, and sometimes shifty, American voice. As Poe wrote in the preface to *Tales of the Grotesque*, "If I have sinned, I have deliberately sinned."[36]

After he died, incoherent and penniless, in Baltimore, Poe's final city now honors him in myriad ways, including naming its football team the Ravens. But perhaps it's less a sign of honor than of the modern hoax's horror that when the U.S. cycling team cheated—gulled, mystified, hoaxed—their way to their seven straight Tour de France victories from 1999 to 2006, they regularly referred to EPO, used in the vampiric practice of blood doping, by a code name: *Poe.*

CHAPTER 2

The Freaks of Dame Fortune

The con, like the hoax or humbug, is typically only half glimpsed. As Gary Lindberg writes in *The Confidence Man in American Literature*, "The confidence man is a covert cultural hero for Americans. He occupies a central place in our popular mythology; yet not many of us would want to acknowledge this fact when stated so bluntly, and that is why we don't notice his centrality. What the con man represents about us can only be seen obliquely, in the discrepancies between our ideals and our conduct."[1] These discrepancies remained especially extreme in mid-nineteenth-century, middle-class American life. If Victorian England experienced what one book calls "the age of equipoise," America in the nineteenth century was not only an Age of Imposture but one of rampant hypocrisy. The con man revealed a cultural comfort with this hypocrisy or discrepancy—as in Barnum—while also expressing a cultural conflict.

Nowhere did nineteenth-century America's hypocrisy show itself, and hide itself, more completely than in chattel slavery. In a young country dedicated to liberty, here was a "peculiar institution" that the Constitution could not speak of clearly, but euphemized instead. The near-daily battles in the penny press provide but one example of the contortions necessary to justify the bondage of fellow human beings. For his part, Richard Adams Locke had set his Moon Hoax not just in the black of outer space but in the perceived darkness of Africa, which to most of the *Sun*'s readers may have seemed just as distant, hostile, and in need of saving. It would prove symbolic not only of slavery but also of salvation that Locke's Herschel was viewing space, both for real and for hoax, from the Cape of Good Hope—the populated moon's surface was seen by many readers as a sign of Providence, of connection with a God who, in His wisdom, had made the universe hospitable. This missionary moon stood in direct contrast to a view of Africa as heathen jungle to be tamed, Christianized, colonized, bested, bought. One group of missionaries would inquire of the real Herschel about sending Bibles to the lunar residents.[2]

Indeed, the chief subject, the very bugaboo, circulating along with the penny papers was slavery. This affected the Moon Hoax directly, as Michael Goodman notes, for within a few weeks the *Sun* offered a "curious apologia for the moon series: it had provided a welcome respite from the nationwide conflict over slavery."[3] This wasn't so much an admission as an ironic deflection: "Most of those who incredulously regard the whole narrative as a hoax, are generally enthusiastic in panegyrizing not only what they are pleased to denominate its ingenuity and talent, but also its useful effect in diverting the public mind, for a while, from the bitter apple of discord, the abolition of slavery; which still unhappily threatens to turn the milk of human kindness into the rancorous gall. . . . Who knows, therefore, whether these discoveries in the moon, with the visions of the blissful harmony of her inhabitants which they have revealed, may not have had the effect of reproving the discords of a country which might be as happy as a paradise!"[4] The Moon Hoax proved less a telescope seeing far afield than a mirror or microscope on a country that aspired to paradise.

This looking was also a way of looking black. In recalling the Moon Hoax decades later, and the humbug more generally, Barnum resorts to questions of blackness. No wonder: just at the same time as the Moon Hoax and the Heth humbug, in part through the penny papers and other forms dependent on the hoax, the United States began to consolidate its broader pop culture, shot through with metaphors of blackness and exacted through the appropriation of African American culture and of actual black bodies. It is no accident that just around this time blackface began to take hold as America's first popular culture. The broader pop culture then emerging proved deeply individual yet one in which rank still mattered—a culture that proclaimed Jacksonian democracy but regularly denied its ideals to its poorest and most disenfranchised. In such an atmosphere black humanity would be not only denied but also debated, displayed, and demonized: by the North, which had slaves but displaced its beliefs onto a South that it by and large supported and depended on; and by a whites-only blackface minstrelsy that would be seen not only as entertainment but also as somehow accurate, real-to-life. Heth was both stolen and symbolic—much like Jim Crow, the character white performer Thomas D. "Daddy" Rice said he borrowed from a black slave that marked the advent of blackface minstrelsy. Could the development of mass media lead to mass history? Or just mass hysteria?

As critic Ben Reiss details in *The Showman and the Slave*, Barnum had a shifting relationship to his first hoax. It was, after all, what spurred him on into a life of humbug, courting the crowd; it also made clear his ability to turn any kind of press to his advantage, manipulating and anticipating every angle. In Providence, Rhode Island, where it proved convenient, Reiss writes, Barnum and his agents made it seem as if Heth was somehow part of an abolitionist cause, raising money to free the rest of her family. When newspaper rumors spread that she had not really been Washington's nurse-maid, was *not even real*—was in fact an automaton—Barnum used the controversy to garner more publicity.

One crucial part of the case remained not how Heth came to be but how she came under Barnum's exhibition—was she bought, like the slave she was raised as and still likely was? A handbill from the time announces her as "born in the Island of Madagascar, on the Coast of Africa, in the year 1674 and has consequently now arrived at the astonishing Age of 161 Years!"[5] Or with the contract Barnum purchased from another exhibitor who had proved less successful with the same act, did Barnum in effect lease her sideshow services? The answer would seem to be: bought and sold. In 1835 Barnum and his team traveled Heth all over the Northeast, displaying the blind black woman in locales like Niblio's Gardens that however fancy, were also informal—visitors not only observed Heth but felt free to ask her questions and touch her in order to connect with someone connected to the first president. "Indeed it is impossible for any person, however incredulous, to visit her without astonishment and the most perfect satisfaction that she is as old as represented," one advertisement related. Later, her wide "exposure" would seem to have hurt the elderly Heth, who died in 1836 after her workaday winter.

Heth's end and afterlife predict how much the modern hoax would become about pain and its performance. Barnum would order Heth's body autopsied in a huge surgical theater, charging fifty cents admission to what turned out to be a sold-out show. Barnum parlayed the doctor's unsurprising conclusion that she was not actually 161 years old but of ordinary advanced age into the sale of more papers and as proof of his first successful humbug.

It would be none other than Locke who got a journalistic exclusive to report on the autopsy.

The fierce rivalry between the penny papers, and their fascination with slavery and arguing over categories, Barnum would take as his advantage. As Reiss notes, Barnum's partner in the endeavor, one Lyman, soon sold a story in all senses to the *Sun*'s rival the *Herald*, proclaiming Heth had indeed been bought by Barnum—but only after whipping the woman who he well knew was not as old as claimed. Lyman claimed she was lazy; while easily bribed, booze only went so far: in fact, Lyman said Barnum had taught Heth her whole act. Such a tale was meant only to emphasize Barnum's wit and power, and his humbug's brilliance. Barnum had supposedly removed Heth's teeth to make her appear older than she was. Reiss fruitfully reads Barnum's shifting stories in ways both historical and psychological, noting that only later, when a story of slavery seemed less than savory, would Barnum turn from such banter to earnestness, claiming now that he had been hoodwinked like all the rest.

All this is to say that Barnum's positioning of Heth sits exactly at the center of the Age of Imposture. As H. M. Paull writes in his essential study *Literary Ethics*, "The early part of the nineteenth century might be called the era of the practical joke; which, when it took a literary form, was perhaps less reprehensible than in its other manifestations."[6] However we name it, this new era with the con man as its archetype could be said to counter the previous age of revolution—an American-spurred and Enlightenment-raised age in which the self was seen as necessarily natural, even unalienable, like its rights. While "in the Revolutionary period, the 'unadorned public man' who was free from the ostentations and chimeras of affected public life became the ideal," critic Eric Fretz writes, "by the mid-nineteenth century the ideal of the unadorned private man had given way to the reality of the public confidence man, or painted woman, who concealed or transformed his or her private nature in the construction of a public identity."[7] To further understand this nineteenth-century Age of Imposture we might also consult the compelling work of Karen Halttunen, whose *Confidence Men and Painted Women* (1986) explores the "conduct manuals" and fashion magazines of the nineteenth century—think of a kind of after-school special for the new middle-class self—that warned against and pictured, often literally, the perils facing newcomers who were easily tricked in the wicked city.

One of these newcomers surely was old-timer Joice Heth. Accordingly, Barnum's first impulse in his postmortem account of his first popular hoax was not to mourn but to publicly celebrate conning the willing crowds—and carving Heth's body—all of which he owned, living or dead. Fretz's championing "Barnum [who] exhibited both himself and his freaks as commodities in an era of exhibitionism that privileged appearance over essence"[8] ignores the fact that Barnum's exhibitionism was also a warning, much like the conduct manuals were. On the one hand, Barnum advertised for an audience to come and touch history via the hand (and breast) that nursed "little Georgie" Washington; on the other, his show warned that if you fall too far out of line or are born wrong, you too might be a freak, put on notice and on display, even dissected. For audiences, visiting the Heth show or autopsy was a way of embracing while also distancing themselves from its humbug.

If blackface is indeed what Ralph Ellison called an exorcism whites performed for the sin of slavery, Heth's display was fraught with blackness, a spell of the highest order. In the section titled "Personal Reminiscences" that opens *Humbugs of the World*, Barnum makes almost explicit the connection between blackness, blacking, and blackface. Taking care to reemphasize that "a man may, by common usage, be termed a 'humbug,' without by any means impeaching his integrity," Barnum describes how "when the great blacking-maker of London despatched his agent to Egypt to write on the pyramids of Ghiza, in huge letters, 'Buy Warren's Blacking, 30, Strand, London,' he was not 'cheating' travellers upon the Nile. His blacking was really a superior article, and well worth the price charged for it, but he was 'humbugging' the public by this queer way of arresting attention." He then returns again to this "blacking" a page or two later:

Speaking of "blacking-makers," reminds me that one of the first sensationists in advertising whom I remember to have seen, was Mr. Leonard Gosling, known as "Monsieur Gosling, the great French blacking-maker." He appeared in New York in 1830. He flashed like a meteor across the horizon; and before he had been in the city three months, nearly everybody had heard of "Gosling's Blacking." . . . The newspapers teemed with poems written in its praise, and showers of pictorial handbills, illustrated almanacs, and tinseled souvenirs, all lauding the virtues of "Gosling's Blacking," smothered you at every point.

The celebrated originator of delineations, "Jim Crow Rice," made his first appearance and Hamblin's Bowery Theatre at about this time. The crowds which thronged there were so great that hundreds from the audience were frequently admitted upon the stage. In one of his scenes, Rice introduced a negro boot-blacking establishment. Gosling was too "wide awake" to let such an opportunity pass unimproved, and Rice was paid for singing an original black Gosling ditty, while a score of placards, bearing the inscription, "Use Gosling's Blacking," were suspended at different points in this negro boot polishing hall.[9]

Barnum goes on to celebrate Gosling's ingenuity, despite his losing his fortune and gaining it again, at which he "snapped his fingers in glee at what unreflecting persons term 'the freaks of Dame Fortune.'" What's being delineated isn't just blackface but race and selling; and the selling of race.

Freaks, fortune, advertising, humbug, blacking: all provide a kind of subterranean autobiography for Barnum, far more telling than his various autobiographies begun in 1855, the same year Whitman's *Leaves of Grass* fashioned a different yet also shifting American self. It also could be revealing in other ways, providing an unauthorized and unacknowledged autobiography of America. Barnum could be obliquely describing Heth and her exhibition in his account of "blacking," a phrase he repeats enough times ad nauseum to reproduce the effect of the original advertising; but he also is revealing that no matter the stage, Jim Crow or Joice Heth provides a black stand-in that ultimately is an advertisement for the white self. Heth made Barnum famous; though he made her famous too, it was only as a kind of come-on to his greater successes to follow.

You could call Heth a "ballyhoo" or brief sampling of the freaks to come in order to get the American public in the hoax's revolving door. "The ballyhoo or 'bally' gives the crowd enough of a taste of the real thing to stimulate their appetite for more, which could be satisfied inside the tent," as critic Ronald E. Ostman reminds us. "The bally consists of a free show outside the sideshow tent to attract a crowd and to convince them that what is inside will be even more elaborate, spectacular, and irresistible."[10] As the Heth tour continued into 1836, the act got more and more complicated, though not necessarily sophisticated—hinting at all the American balderdash that haunts us today. By not just relying on or inventing experts, but making experts of his audience, Barnum tapped into American democracy at its most primal, as well as American hypocrisy at its height. In Heth's case, a living then dead embodiment of such conflict, this often meant Barnum marshaled the forces of abolition to support the exhibition of his likely slave.

A contemporary 1835 pamphlet, issued anonymously but attributed to Barnum, casually protests Heth's enslavement, then describes how she was passed down from Washington's family to others and "from that time she has followed by legal succession, the branches of the family down to the present time."[11] It describes her conversion then says that to be converted is blessed. "She has outlived all her descendants save five, and they are her great grand-children, who are now held in bondage by a highly respectable gentleman of Kentucky, who has generously offered to set them free on being paid two-thirds they cost him. This work, together with what may be collected from her exhibition, after deducting expenses, is expressly for that purpose, and will be immediately done whenever there can be realized the sum sufficient to do it. . . . It is designed that they shall be instructed in the glorious truths of the gospel, so as to become fully qualified to teach their poor unfortunate race the true way to future happiness."[12] At least, happiness with expenses deducted.

Barnum would also manage to make Heth's death and dissection the scene of supposed science, just as he had relied on her myth: all was shot through with commerce. Heth, you could say, was yet another mermaid after his Feejee one—half woman, half beast, breasts bared. In his study *The Inhuman Race* (1997), Leonard Cassuto notes the ways the "racial grotesque" modulates between being a view of a dehumanized, racialized other—for those labeled as freaks and displayed for merely being in their native garb—while also constantly reminding us that labeling others in such a way also threatens the labelers' humanity. "Every culture has its grotesque," he writes. Shifting the sense of the grotesque from the creator to the created, the grotesque in America centered on black figures starting in the nineteenth century as a way not just to claim them uncivilized but to create civilization, and conceive of a new nation.

Amidst such a burgeoning, contradictory culture, a young slave named Isabella could follow Matthias the prophet, in whose false paradise she at least glimpsed a notion of freedom that later would help her make her own way as a spiritual leader—in a land where African American men, to say nothing of women, would soon be denied the vote—a land where that selfsame Isabella would change her name to Sojourner Truth, the former slave turned suffragist and feminist abolitionist challenging the nation's hypocrisies in person, in shadow, and in act.

Simultaneously celebrated and denigrated, often through the very body she supposedly nurtured and wet-nursed with, Heth stands as one of a long line of black women forced to prove their *womanity*. Where the metaphoric (and frequently literal) white crowd often saw the black man as a savage and animal, the black woman was not quite that. Besides a mummy and "a living skeleton," Heth's being called an automaton—an animated thing that raises questions of whether it's alive or not—means she is decidedly without a soul.[13] When accused of being a man at an 1858 rally, Truth proved she was a woman by baring her breasts—a sign of fierceness but also of nurture and nation. Doesn't Truth's act align her not just with the bare-chested image of Liberté embattled yet nurturing a newborn nation, but also with the Madonna nursing what Christians see as the world's salvation?

Heth's breasts, regularly commented on like the Feejee Mermaid's, fit the idea if not the image of the mammy. Traditionally pictured as large, sturdy and asexual, female yet antifeminine (because not white, corseted, or thin), the mammy emerges after the Civil War both as a sign of nostalgia and as a way of managing the guilt over those domestics who continued to manage many white houses. The northern black maid, especially in cinema, was and is often still pictured as a kind of businesslike figure, a helpmate who's integral but not integrated, a silent figure of seriousness and sign of affluence left uncommented on. In contrast, the southern mammy, especially of the early half of the twentieth century, would be represented in white productions as all backtalk and full of sass.[14] Heth combined and prefigured the two in one black body.

Heth's exhibit connects her not just to the freak show but also to the long history of black people on parade, from the auction block to the menagerie, from the first Africans captured and brought as slaves to Jamestown in 1619 to Ota Benga, shown in the Bronx Zoo as a pygmy savage in 1906. Across the nineteenth century, black women regularly got taken apart in public and in death: Millie-Christine, the performing conjoined twins, born into slavery and forcibly examined in life by self-appointed doctors obsessed with whether "The Carolina Twins" had two vulvas or one; Saartje Baartman, the so-called Hottentot Venus on display naked in life, in death her dissected genitalia housed in a jar in the Musée d'Homme ("Man" clearly understood to be white and male). The so-called American school of anthropology made its image, if not its name, off such displays—not only naked pictures of Millie-Christine still circulating but also founder Louis Agassiz's 1850 trip to the Carolinas to study and photograph enslaved African Americans. The resulting nude, rather pornographic photographs of unclothed male and female slaves were later uncovered at Harvard, then the center of the field.[15]

Not that there wasn't resistance, both literal and symbolic: referring to herself often as "I," Millie-Christine would embrace her labels as a singu-

lar freak and the "8th Wonder of the World." Eventually she won her freedom and refused further examination from such doctors; a success in show
business, she would go on to buy the plantation she was born on, and died
there peacefully.

Writing on Barnum and Heth, Ben Reiss argues that Heth becomes
representative of the "open body": a grotesque not in a degenerative sense
but still a racial grotesque in stark contrast to the classical one of George
Washington, who remains ever idealized, aquiline, closed. But what if
the body is not simply open, implying some generous resistance, but *opened*?
In Heth's case and the case of black women of the nineteenth century—and
arguably the centuries since—this opened quality remains literal. Such dis-
sections only prove a manifestation of the myriad public examinations and
symbolic vivisections-in-print during their lifetime.

NONDESCRIPT

If black men are still regularly turned to for fakery, then black women are
subject to kinds of *freakery*.[16] The fact that *freak* remains a shifting term in
black culture—naming a popular dance in the 1970s, and sometimes used
in lieu of "fuck" but more often a gendered term for a "loose woman," or a
painted one—indicates the ways the term still has currency. It also shows
the ways black men too often become complicit in or commit such depictions. Men can *get freaky with you* or sing about it; women are mere freaks
whose best option is to embrace it: *I want a freak in the morning a freak in
the evening just like me*. This isn't to say that the word can't sometimes be re-
claimed, as it regularly was by circus folk, who used and often didn't mind
the label, or at least saw it as a mere role. After all, *freak*, as one sister of color
reminded me, echoes the word *free*. Yet typically, those men who display
freakery, or are freaks displayed—like the late Michael Jackson in his hyperbaric chamber—are quickly read as feminized, painted, and unnatural.[17]

Black writers, especially black female poets, have written brilliantly
about such surgical and symbolic theaters—ones that predicted the theaters of hysterics to come and revealed that funeral rites are just one more
right denied African Americans. Books from Elizabeth Alexander's classic
The Venus Hottentot (1990) to Natasha Trethewey's *Thrall* (2012) and Robin
Coste Lewis's *The Voyage of the Sable Venus* (2015) take on questions of what
it means to be taken apart in public, often having one's privates shown publicly too. Alexander's title poem turns the pen into a scalpel with which to

examine Georges Cuvier, the French scientist who dissected Baartman's body (and who was Louis Agassiz's mentor). I'm not sure which is more damning in the poem, the self-indicting voice of Cuvier in the first part of the poem, or the second part, where Baartman is given a voice to contradict the view of her as simply a freakish phenomenon. In the end it is Cuvier—whom Poe once translated and liberally borrowed from in ghostwriting a textbook on mollusks—who suffers. Biologist and historian of science Stephen Jay Gould calls Poe on Cuvier "part name lender, part literary man, and part plagiarist"; Alexander goes further and takes Cuvier and his racist assumptions apart. The naturalist is dissected metaphorically by "The Venus Hottentot," his abstracted interior scooped out like shellfish, her poem fantasizing a direct reversal of circumstance: "his black heart / . . . on a low / shelf in a white man's museum / so the whole world could see / it was shriveled and hard, / geometric, deformed, unnatural."[18] Such unnaturalness fights notions of natural history.

"History is bunk," Henry Ford would offer. From one angle, he was right inasmuch as Barnum and others used bunk to connect the audience to a history—usually a grand, American one—that it desperately wished were true. Barnum's brilliance was to understand that wish to see America great again, yet again. But Barnum, the Prince of Humbug, also remained deeply connected to an assembly line of assumptions, crafting an image of the black body symbolically and literally disassembled before the audience's eyes.

The term *bunk* was itself born of conflict and race, coined in 1820 from the floor of the Sixteenth Congress when a North Carolina representative continued to filibuster for the Missouri Compromise that made Missouri a slave state: though the question had been called, he said he had to give speech *for* or *to* Buncombe, his home county.[19] "Buncombe" got changed to *bunkum*, then shortened to *bunk*, giving name to that species of fakery, unnecessary flattery, and politicking phoniness that barely believes what it says. Or worse, comes to believe its bunk never stunk.

For Barnum, naming provided much of the power of a show: he knew using exotic terminology and quoting invented experts promised his audience a world they might not otherwise get to see. His early touring exhibitions and popular American Museum gave audience members a sense of traveling without leaving their assumptions, of touring without being tourists. This is one of the hoax's chief gambits. Above all Barnum offered reassurance: even as he let the audience glimpse freaks and curiosities beyond category, visitors got to leave whole, entertained while offered proof of their being higher up on the scale of humanity.

It would be in the notorious exhibition he called "What is It?" that Barnum would dress a black man in animal hides that proved a symbolic *dress*—meaning both a woman's garment and slang for castration.[20] Just months after the publication of Darwin's *Origin of Species* in 1860, intrigued visitors would enter to find the answer to the exhibit's question: a black man they were invited to see as a, or as *the*, so-called missing link in evolution. The *New York Mercury*'s description of the Prince of Wales's visit to the show provides one measure of the figure, "whose humiliating likeness to mankind has led certain muddled philosophers to insinuate that he is an idiotic negro. Only a single glance from the bright and very intelligent eyes of the creature is necessary to disprove this absurd guess, while it adds to our bewilderment when we would trace a brute genealogy for him."[21] It is an indication of how the century's views on race didn't free up but only hardened, the Negro gone from handmaid to inhuman in a genealogy of brutishness— Heth could be many things, a curiosity, a machine, almost an animal, but she wasn't quite an *It*.

With the emphasis purposefully not on the "is" but the "It," Barnum advertised the man he called "What is It?" as a *nondescript*. The term was actually taken from the newly formed field of natural history, used by the likes of Charles Willson Peale in his groundbreaking museum that, at the end of the eighteenth century, helped legitimate and invent museums as institutions, transforming them from private cabinets of curiosities to veritable public entities. As seen in the first gift to Peale's museum, the fish labeled "A curious Non-descript Fish . . . termed by those who caught it a paddlefish,"[22] *nondescript* in Peale's day meant a specimen as yet unclassified in terms of exact species—not one that sat outside known species altogether, unclassifiable.

The continuum between Peale's Museum and Barnum's American Museum was quite literal: Barnum would purchase and scatter Peale's exhibitions by the middle of the nineteenth century. Soon Peale's devotion to science and "rational amusement" and Enlightenment ideals—he had fought prominently in the American Revolution—became dispersed too, with Barnum not so much highlighting science as conscripting or cannibalizing it. The American Museum. at least till it burned down for the second and final time, would be shaped by Barnum until, despite its entertainments, it more resembled the deterministic, racialist "Museums of Man" of the day.

Now, I've seen pictures of "What is It?," and the performer, William Henry Johnson, looks very much like a person. In no way does he resemble his depictions in the papers of the time or in the advertisements for

Barnum's American Museum, hunched over as the requisite cannibal or fitting his billing as "The Monkey-Man," an indistinct racial grotesque in an artificial jungle landscape. This is true even of photographs by the famed Mathew Brady and others in which Johnson's hair has been cut into tufts at the crown of his head to emphasize his head's shape, suggesting he was microcephalic. Later photographs would seem to question this, helping us understand how even the photograph, that allegedly reliable document, is shaped, framed, constrained.

That Barnum, twenty-five years after his Heth beginnings, months after Darwin's revolutionary theory, and on the eve of the Civil War, would draw a direct line between blackness and the "Missing Link," between primitivism and primates, still shocks—though it might not surprise. At first blush at least, such ideas of skull size and savagery couldn't be more different from Peale's stated mission "to show the progress of arts and science, from the savage state to the civilized man; displaying the habits and customs of all nations."[23] Barnum sought to display "What is It?" as a specimen of inferiority in order to stoke American and white superiority; he further suggested these were one and the same. With the exception of Heth's hoax and her "afterlife" in the surgical theater and Bowery Theatre, no exhibition retained the troubling power of this iteration of Barnum's bunk.

"What is It?" produced an array of publications and publicity, including the usual studio portraits and pamphlets as mementos to accompany the freak show. But Johnson was just as often viewed in a cage. Such captivity extended to handbills for Barnum's American Museum, picturing "What is It?" beside "The great living Black Sea Lion" or literally beneath an albino family of "White Negroes, or Moors" and "What Can They Be? These most strange and MYSTERIOUS ANIMALS! Two in number and of distinct species, found in a cave in the hither-to unexplored Wilds of Africa."[24] Barnum's is not so much Africa as any exotic, far-off region in need of taming (this remains true even when he sometimes claimed "What is It?" came from the wilds of California). As in an advertisement for "What is It?" found in the trusty *New York Herald* on 19 March 1860, the exhibit's original capture provided not just an allegory for slavery but also what passed for natural history:

This nondescript was captured by a party of adventurers who were in search of the Gorilla. While exploring the River Gambia, near the mouth, they fell in with a race of beings never before discovered. They were six in number. They were in a PERFECTLY NUDE STATE, roving about among the trees and branches, in the manner common to the Monkey and Orang Outang. After considerable exertion the hunters succeeded in capturing three of these oddities—two males and a female. All of them were forwarded to this country, but, unfortunately, two of them sickened and died on the voyage across. The present one is the only survivor. When first received here his natural position was ON ALL FOURS, and it has required the exercise of the greatest care and patience to teach him to stand perfectly erect, as you behold him at the present moment. But a few weeks have elapsed, in fact, since he first assumed this attitude and walked about upon his feet.[25]

Conflating the language of evolution and exploration, Barnum's racial grotesques ultimately met the broader culture where it lived, or at least where it dreamed and hoaxed. Corrupting Poe's trickster arabesques, Barnum took what in Poe's hands was proto-science fiction and managed to link it to the pseudoscience that Darwin's book meant to combat. Barnum, ever the innovator, was only the first to see that the theory of evolution could be co-opted to suggest its opposite.

"What is It?" became renamed Zip sometime in the 1870s, likely after the blackface minstrelsy character Zip Coon. A pamphlet called *The Life of Zip* published circa 1884, whose rose-colored paper cover image redefines grotesque, claims he was from Australia—the lost land that similar freak show exhibits such as the Wild Australian Children were claimed to be from. Despite declaring its being "as correct a history of this person as it is possible," the promotion quickly abandons personhood in describing the capture of this creature—naked and on all fours—this time in the bush by Barnum's agent, revolver in hand. "It was here noticed that this creature was of a dark color; but the actual hue could only be determined after a thorough washing." This darkness is contagious toward the audiences who see "it": "Thousands went to see it then, and thousands go to see it to-day, but are still in as much darkness as ever, in regard to the true history of this wonderful being."[26] It is hard to imagine an image somehow more grotesque than that of the *nondescript*, but it's true that by including him in the "inhuman race," Barnum's earlier depictions of Johnson at least managed to be somewhat ferocious. Ever a freak, Zip now was merely furry.

Yet as a pioneer of the exhibit that sideshow folk termed "pinhead," Johnson did have a lengthy and successful career, continuing well into the twentieth century, when he often appears more clownlike. By his death in

1926, Johnson was called the "dean of freaks," enjoying what critic Robert Bogdan calls "the longest successful career of any of the sideshow attractions." Johnson's reported last words to his sister indicate how he was well aware of his role: "Well, we fooled 'em for a long time, didn't we?" Ultimately Zip was estimated to have been viewed by over a hundred million people—and his pop culture descendants can be found in popular comics such as namesake Zippy the Pinhead and comedy routines like *Saturday Night Live*'s Coneheads, who hail from faraway France.[27]

An 1885 photograph by Eisenmann, a studio that regularly captured circus folk, depicts "Old Zip Barnum's What is It" alongside "Ashbury Ben The Leopard Boy Age 17 years."[28] The image remains especially powerful in its difference from the nondescript degradations from just a quarter century before: Johnson looks almost regal, furry suit notwithstanding, "ZIP" across his waist like a prize belt; the pair defiantly eyes the camera, boxing gloves on as in the promotional photos of Andy Warhol and Jean-Michel Basquiat posed as pugilists for their groundbreaking collaborations show a century later. Ben even has Basquiat's early, blond mohawk haircut! The image is literally reversed—ZIP appears backward on his belt—but if you look closely, Johnson has an image of George Washington pinned to his chest as if it were a war medal. The photograph offers a reversal of Heth's fate, Johnson literally attaching himself to the Father of Our Nation to offer himself up as his own foundational figure.

STARS OF THE EAST

In Barnum's "What is It?" we can see how an eighteenth-century Counter-Enlightenment, with its mistrust of science and history of hoaxes, could actually join with the Enlightenment and its love of systems to spawn the pseudosciences of the nineteenth century—particularly those that sought to create not just taxonomies but hierarchies between the races. The chain of being was just that. Here is humbug's true trouble—where the hoax had always appealed to a kind of Counter-Enlightenment, providing an irrational, often fearsome sublime, it now relied on the trappings of rational thought to do so, employing *vraisemblance* to suggest racism as a scientific, "natural position."

This went beyond diddling as science into hoaxing as a ritual redolent of race. But I've come to realize the hoax regularly steps in when race rears its head—exactly because it too is a fake thing pretending to be real.

Take the exhibition typically known as the Circassian Beauty. This act, crafted by Barnum in 1864, played into the violent history of the Caucasus region—then undergoing massive unrest—not to mention America's own upheavals. As Linda Frost writes in her study *Never One Nation*, Barnum first hit on a scheme to find "a Circassian girl" after going bankrupt in the 1850s and having to sell his beloved American Museum. Solvent just a few years later and buying back the property, he privately sent his agent to a Turkish market to buy "a beautiful Circassian girl if you can get one very beautiful."[29] Told to pay up to five thousand dollars in gold for one, double that for two, the agent returned without a Beauty but not without a cover story: instead of buying a girl, he claimed to have rescued one from being sold. The Circassian Beauty was born.

The truth apparently is that an ordinary American woman walked in looking for a job and ended up having her hair "mossed" and frizzed out by Barnum; whatever her background, this woman, whom Barnum renamed Zalumma Agra, "Star of the East," became a popular part of his show. Agra's costumes and backstory became a routine other exhibitors would follow, creating a constellation of popular Circassian Beauties whose acts—complete with unlikely names filled with Zs and *cartes de visite* for sale at the show—would continue up to the turn of the twentieth century. Zalumma Agra, Zobeide Luti, Zoe Meleke, Zera Zangritta, Zula Zelick, and Zoe Zuemella, "Circassian Queen": such names were meant to reference the so-called origins of the white race in the Caucasus region.

Freakery met fakery: while "What is It?" represented the depths of blackness and evolution, the Circassian Beauty remained a freak mainly because she represented the height of white beauty under threat of swarthy violence. As described in an 1868 *Biographical Sketch*, pitched for sale at shows, "the Circassian girl, Zalumma Agra . . . presents a type of humanity, so rare in this country, that since its discovery, but two or three individuals of her race have ever visited its shores." The pamphlet goes on to mention the Circassians as refugees from "the terrible ravages of the Russians" driven "into the dominions of the Sultan of Turkey"—this is mostly accurate—saying, "we believe there is no instance of any of their race having voluntarily left their native homes."[30] Yet Barnum hadn't invented the Circassian as the ideal of beauty; as scholar Nell Irvin Painter traces in *The History of White People*, that white ideal was already long established by the early nineteenth century. Rather, Barnum's innovation was to pair this ideal to politics, to stitch the Circassian's Beauty's costume together with barely concealed questions of sex, race, and longing. In this, the Circassian Beauty resembles less show business humbug than hoax.

The racial types Barnum referenced first got defined during the Enlightenment but didn't harden till later. Naturalists such as Johann Friedrich

Blumenbach sought to classify people along with, say, plants; Blumenbach's short thesis *On the Natural Variety of Mankind* (1775) would divide the world into five races, including Ethiopian, Mongolian, and American (or black, yellow, and red).[31] On the eve of the Declaration of Independence announcing "all men are created equal," Blumenbach establishes not just categories but clear hierarchies that would only deepen. "Blumenbach's idea of five varieties gained acceptance," Painter recounts, but it wasn't until his book's third edition and "his introduction of aesthetic judgments into classification in 1795 that [he] gave us the term 'Caucasian.'" In seeking the origins of the white race, Blumenbach settled on Caucasia, where Circassia can be found; here, near the Black Sea, he also assigned the origin of all humanity. "Skin color, not heretofore the crucial factor for Blumenbach, had risen to play a large role. He now sees it necessary to rank skin color hierarchically, beginning, not surprisingly, with white," Painter writes. "Believing it to be the oldest variety of man, he puts it in 'the first place.'"[32] Imagine his surprise that scientists today agree the first *Homo sapiens* emerged from Africa and race doesn't have any scientific basis.

Artificial as they are, Blumenbach's racist categorizations remain with us—even gracing our pro football teams, some of whom still claim *redskin* means something honorific and American. But just as Blumenbach's third edition was all the more racist than his first, and the degradations of "What is It?" far worse than Heth's, the racial categories begun in the eighteenth century—exactly around the advent of the modern hoax—only grew more rigid over the course of the nineteenth century and Barnum's career. Soon black people would be debated widely, and proved regularly, to be an entirely separate species.

By 1864 the Circassian lady's assumed beauty would quite literally stand in contrast to the "natural cannibals," *Negritos*, "wild children," and fake Fijians regularly displayed by Barnum, often on the same bill, and meant to be seen as the bottom of the evolutionary rung. Not to mention What is It?, who wasn't allowed to reach that high. Yet while decidedly attractive, and by decree white, the Circassian Beauty's appearance is more likely to our eyes to resemble a light-skinned black woman with an afro. How many of these Circassian Beauties were actually black girls making themselves over, learning sword swallowing and snake handling and other tricks that eventually became a standard part of the routine, navigating a quite different Black Sea in order to presume whiteness? To scholar Sarah Lewis, "The Circassian Beauties unconsciously anticipated a 1960s statement of black empowerment and self-possession. Their performance of supposed white racial purity became a figurative interrogation exposing the fragility of the claim," especially given their frequently African American–looking features.[33]

The "moss" hairstyle integral to the Circassian Beauty doesn't so much confound rigid racial categories as prove their arbitrariness and the pleasure Barnum and his audience took in visiting—and violating—them. The sideshow and the hoax both offer an aesthetic of uncertainty—one that helped reconcile unease. "Probably less anxious than desirous," Frost writes, "these spectators of Barnum's were presented with images of a conflated and contradictory bondage, a spectacularized slavery that incorporated elements of racial purity, physical desirability, and sexual availability."[34] Dressed as they were in silken costumes of blooming pantaloons and shoulder- or cleavage-baring blouses, how much of the exotic appeal of these declared beauties comes from being a so-called white girl who looks black? The Circassian Beauty's foil, the tragic mulatto or octoroon—that is, a black girl who looks white—had similarly conjured up stock sexual storylines still very much with us. Her colorful stockings showing in cartes de visite, sometimes posed in a corset, the exotic Circassian Beauty stood—or more often reclined—somewhere between the Orientalist odalisque and near-white freak.

The Circassian Beauty story always suggested slavery—not only "white slavery" at the hands of the Turks claimed to have imprisoned her, but Barnum's initial wish to buy a beauty.[35] The Circassian Beauty's whiteness threatened by dark Turks provided a proxy for American slavery, a conflict literally then dividing the nation. She expressed yet displaced the ways slavery in the United States remained sexually violent, especially against black women, while explicitly embodying the opposite. "In her role as a symbol of endangered-yet-rescued whiteness," Frost notes, "the Circassian slave mirrored white Northern representations of the white American woman herself, potentially endangered by the 'dark' and savage forces suddenly 'unleashed' in the South."[36]

As a measure not only of Barnum's but also racialism's resilience, the Circassian Beauty trend took hold until at least the turn of the twentieth century, when it began to fade out—or found its way into the common imagery of the time, such as Bellocq's photographs of mixed-race prostitutes in Storyville, Circassian in all but name. But the fabricated, race-baited term *Caucasian* persists, still used in legal terminology and in common parlance. The confusion even makes its way into the likes of the Boston Marathon bombing of 2013, when the presumed killers came from the Caucasus region.

The Tsarnaev brothers were literally Caucasian, but fail to conform to our common conceptions of whiteness, which, by Job, ain't Muslim or disenfranchised.[37] But *Caucasian* doesn't signify a place or an actual origin—not only is the term inaccurate, it is directly descended from racist eugenics. To avoid using it, as I have learned to, is to understand where words and people actually come from.

Dressed up like science, or pseudoscience, the hoax reveals the ways in which it is another form of wish fulfillment. As detailed in volumes such as Stephen Jay Gould's *Mismeasure of Man*, prominent nineteenth-century and even twentieth-century scientists like Cuvier regularly falsified results and faked data to preserve notions of race and white superiority; to a man they may be said to have "[begun] with conclusions, peered through their facts, and came back in a circle to the same conclusions."[38] In that science called diddling, this meant less peering than staring: in the humbug of What is It? and the Circassian Beauty, a new nation saw that its contradictions might be resolved, not in faking ancestors (as the Enlightenment-era hoax had) or raising up a republic (as Heth did) but in demonizing, or at least displaying, its darkest doubles. That was the nineteenth century's lesson, learned again and again—and ultimately tested in the provocateur persona of Mark Twain, Melville's *Confidence Man*, Hawthorne's black veil, and others of the American Renaissance who, borrowing blackness, followed in Poe's hoaxing, haunted footsteps.

What was "It" and what could "It" be? Once upon a time the hoax tried to prove to the reader, or rediscover, a culture thought lost—or to shore up the worth of tradition. *Join us*, the hoax said. A lost Gaelic poet, fabricated classicism, an unknown Shakespeare play: such were the hoaxes of the eighteenth century in England, when the successful hoax confirmed a culture's wishes. A century later and an ocean away, Barnum didn't simply evoke or resort to the basest assumptions of his day—though often he did—his genius was to turn these into questions, spectacle as speculation. *Is she or isn't she?* Visitors to Barnum's American Museum or various exhibits walked away as curious as they came in; he gave them a genuine fake, a dishonest good time. Barnum offered up the chance to see and *not* believe, perfecting a potent, American cocktail of doubt and danger, desire and delight.

CHAPTER 3

Splitfoot

The hoax without a witness is not a hoax but an idea. Voyeuristic as it is, the hoax demands an audience; you cannot craft a hoax no one sees. In this I disagree with those who feel the only hoaxes we know of are the failed ones. The hoax is not a hoax because it is hidden—it has little need to hide—but because it proclaims itself mightily. The con man needs the mark to believe; the hypnotist needs the skeptic who stands up at a sudden snap of her fingers; the magic trick or fake faith healer both require doubt and then unfailing faith. The hoaxer too craves an audience, whether in publicity meant to draw us into further humbug or as an end unto itself. The famed photographs two young girls took of the so-called Cottingley fairies in the English countryside, for instance, would only became a hoax when they went from gifts their parents gave at Christmas to supposed evidence about the world; the pictures' appeal to Spiritualism, that homegrown American religion, made them inheritors of an American tradition of belief and fakery that P. T. Barnum had only perfected.

Yet Barnum would regularly debunk hoaxes—at least ones not his own—even testifying against a hoax in open court in 1869. Providing a different kind of circus, that year saw a scandalous trial about "spirit photography," a Civil War–time invention and manifestation of Spiritualist beliefs that galled Barnum enough that he had offered a hefty five-hundred-dollar reward for anyone who could produce a genuine picture of spirits to his satisfaction. Three years earlier Barnum spent the entire second section of his *Humbugs of the World* debunking Spiritualists, devoting fourteen chapters to the endeavor.¹ Readers might be forgiven for thinking Barnum exposed, so to speak, spirit photography and its believers because he was envious he hadn't thought of the con first.

Invented by William Mumler, spirit photography began in the early 1860s, not accidentally a time of great national crisis and mourning. The con hid a conflict: as the Civil War raged, Mumler claimed his camera could capture ghosts and spirits of the dead that the naked eye couldn't see. He soon enjoyed a steady stream of customers despite his high price of ten dollars per picture. (In contrast, admission to Barnum's American Museum in 1860 cost just a quarter.) One of the most famous spirit photographs would be Mumler's portrait of Mary Todd Lincoln being embraced and comforted by the "spirits" of the late president and one of their departed sons in 1872. The face of this grieving mother of three dead sons, still wearing mourning clothes years after the president's assassination in 1865, retains an enigmatic look that the Mona Lisa might have envied. The dowager Lincoln's spirit photograph represents not just the wishes of an unwell, grieving woman— who would write friends and near-strangers that she was staying alive only because of her remaining child, Robert—but a fragile country's concerns.

Mrs. Lincoln had first become engaged with Spiritualist causes after the death of the Lincolns' second son, Willie, from childhood illness. "A very slight veil separates us, from the 'loved & lost,'" she wrote a friend on the Fourth of July 1865, and "though unseen by us, they are very near."² This manages to sum up the Spiritualist cause succinctly; spirit photography literally capitalized on this belief, providing "scientific proof" at a time when science (and pseudoscience) was on the rise. This is the problem: the spirit photograph captured spirits as well as an audience; such pictures do not require a ghost but the grieving. And, of course, cash.

Spiritualism had begun in 1848 with the three Fox sisters in the same "burned-over district" of western New York as the Second Great Awakening and other homegrown religions such as Mormonism and the Shakers. The region also gave rise to many other utopian communities, like the cult of Matthias: it was a time, and place, of utopian yearnings. The two youngest Fox sisters, ages fourteen and eleven, claimed to have heard a series of knocks in their home—apparently from the spirit of a dead drifter once buried in the house. Moreover, the sisters said they (and only they) could interpret these "rappings." Visitors flocked to and paid for séances held by the girls, and soon the Fox sisters began to take the show on the road, starting the proceedings by saying *Here, old Splitfoot, do as I do.*

Spiritualism quickly spread into a large movement, catching on in England and Europe, the whole guided by mediums who in turn often had their own "spirit guides." Like its spin-off theosophy, Spiritualism was founded by women and remained a female site of influence: both belief systems provided a realm in which women did not have to serve a patriarchal church; instead, history could serve them and move through them as seers. How else might one commune with Lincoln, or with "spirit Indian guides" who suggested a native-born future, than through an American religion? The ethereal, dark double found in the spirit photograph—to say nothing of the chemical double of the photograph itself—revealed belonging, connection, and, above all, power.

This power was succeeded and countered in the nineteenth century by the theater of the hysteric, whose tone and talk still dominate our current era. The constant panics, rampant imagined ailments, and ill-advised overreactions—the hoax's petri dish—would only grow in that century, when hysterics and hoaxes filled medical theaters. The difference was the dark: the mesmerist's trance, the Spiritualist's séance, the hysteric's patented grand mal seizures all enacted unstated beliefs that the hoax sought out too. Hysteria, for instance, had long been thought a psychological state believed to stem from a physical one (diagnosis: womanhood), when the truth is the opposite—hysteria is a physical symptom bearing witness to a psychological trauma. In much the same way, the hoax and Spiritualism regularly claimed physical proof for what were really only psychological wishes or fears. Again and again over the nineteenth century we see the occult claim to be scientific and dubious science claim to have almost occult insight.

Yet Spiritualism was also connected to other radical American movements like abolitionism and women's suffrage; it was no coincidence that the Seneca Falls movement for women's rights first met in the "burned-over district" in the same year as the Fox sisters' first rappings. As recounted by historian Ann Braude in her *Radical Spirits*, Spiritualism "held two attractions that proved irresistible to thousands of Americans: rebellion against death and rebellion against authority."[3] Spiritualism proved a great equalizer, as Mitch Horowitz points out in *Occult America*, for "spirit communication was open to anyone, anytime. If two teenage girls could reach the otherworld, it stood to reason that *everyone* could. It was a completely egalitarian take on the supernatural, with newspapers and publicity-hungry investigators ready to spread the word."[4] Spiritualism embodies the American paradox: democratic yet elite; accessible to all but reliant on a chosen few; dedicated to group performance but also to self- or spirit help. Spirits may be all around us, but they require a—usually paid—medium to see.

Spiritualism's beliefs not only seem compatible with forms of conjure black slaves had brought with them from Africa; they also connect to a long history of the occult in the former colonies. Freemen and Freemasons alike sought forms of power through occult means, with Spiritualism providing a form of otherworldly and earthly rebellion for black people, especially before the Civil War. Black figures like Paschal Beverly Randolph wrote dozens of articles and books about Spiritualism (which he later denounced) and "sex magick" (which he practiced); Harriet E. Wilson, the first black woman to write and publish a novel in the United States, as scholar P. Gabrielle Foreman has discovered, went on not just to manufacture and market "Mrs. H. E. Wilson's" hair potion but also to become a Spiritualist "trance medium."[5] Some have even said that Mrs. Lincoln's interest in Spiritualism was spurred on by Elizabeth Keckley, her black dressmaker and confidante—whose 1868 memoir *Behind the Scenes; or, Thirty Years a Slave and Four Years in the White House* told of their relationship—though that seems rather spurious.[6] Keckley did, however, serve as something of a "medium" for Mrs. Lincoln, whose reprinted letters and reminiscences in *Behind the Scenes* help us know more about the First Lady's troubled life. Keckley also inspired what's less a satire than a full-blown hoax later in the year: *Behind the Seams* (1868), written by "A Nigger Woman Who Took in Work from Mrs. Lincoln and Mrs. Davis," not only sends up Keckley but also pretends to be by her. "My name is Betsey Kickley," it opens, "and I am a most extraordinary nigger." Really written (and copyrighted) by one D. Ottolengul, the volume questions Keckley's authorship and her very humanity. The N-word recurs over seventy-five times in only two dozen pages.

Harriet Wilson's pioneering novel with the ironic title *Our Nig; or, Sketches from the Life of a Free Black* from 1859 tells a complex, autobiographical tale of her precarious freedom, as the title page has it, "In a Two-Story White House, North / Showing That Slavery's Shadows Fall Even There." The narrative indicts northern abolitionists as nowhere as radical as they declared, or as Spiritualism might suggest. "Our Nig" is, in Wilson's words, "watched by kidnappers, maltreated by professed abolitionists, who didn't want slaves at the South, nor niggers in their own houses, North. Faugh! to lodge one; to eat with one; to admit one through the front door; to sit next one; awful!" The title character marries a "professed fugitive," who eventually turns out to be a charlatan who "left her to her fate—[then] embarked

at sea, with the disclosure that he had never seen the South, and that his il-
literate harangues were humbugs for hungry abolitionists." Wilson here indicts not just slavery but also the antislavery movement—her critique of
abolitionists, as well as her assault on the North's near-servitude, likely hurt
her chances at the selfsame antislavery lecture circuit that her husband, in
the novel and in real life, had humbugged his way into. This also may help
explain why Wilson wasn't known as a literary pioneer until her rediscovery
and authentication in the 1980s by scholar Henry Louis Gates.[7]

In her last chapter, "The Winding Up of the Matter," Wilson goes on
to mention her protagonist's new entrepreneurship, which coincides with
Wilson's actual one: "Providence favored her with a friend who, pitying her
cheerless lot, kindly provided her with a valuable recipe, from which she
might manufacture a useful *article* for her maintenance. This proved a more
agreeable, and an easier way of sustenance."[8] Though here she only hints at
what would soon be marketed as "Mrs. H. E. Wilson's Hair Regenerator,"
the very name and honorific title suggest other generative forces and sus-
taining pleasure after a life of pain. The word *article* suggests both writing
and potion, indeed writing *as* potion. Whether snake oil of hair products
or the snake charming of Spiritualism, Wilson's potions are potent means
of power—ones that remain, strictly speaking, distinct from the hoax. "It
Is No Humbug! Try It & See!" Mrs. Wilson's ads declare.[9] Her preemptive
strike against humbug is as invested in exposing phonies as Barnum is (at
least those not his own). But Wilson also recognizes the ways humbug involves the occult thing called race.

Scholars have now uncovered that Wilson would serve as what she called
"a labourer in the spiritual ranks" for at least two decades after the death
of her child, founding a short-lived lyceum or a Spiritualist Sunday school,
arguing on behalf of (and sometimes with) the cause, and promoting the
ways the Spiritualist "platform" at least advocated, in her words, "no bond,
no sect, no creed, no dogma and no caste."[10] Wilson's spiritual practices also
join a literary continuum, especially in poetry, with later poets such as W. B.
Yeats, Ted Hughes, and James Merrill engaging spirits and mysticism in
their practice and Lucille Clifton recording "Messages from the Ones," her
own powerful, as-yet-unpublished epic, from spirit writings received over a
century after Wilson's debut.

We must draw a distinction here between private belief and public: it
is the desire not for faith but for proof that leads to Spiritualism's forms
of fraud. I do not doubt someone's individual experiences with the spirit

realm—there are still mysteries—and I am not so much interested in exposing Spiritualism as a belief system as I am in tracing accusations of malfeasance made at the very time of the movement's heyday. As Barnum puts it in
Humbugs of the World, "If people declare that they privately communicate with
or are influenced to write or speak by invisible spirits, I cannot prove that they
are deceived or are attempting to deceive me—although I believe that one or
the other of these propositions is true. But when they pretend to give me communications from departed spirits, or tie or untie ropes—to read sealed letters, or to answer test-questions through spiritual agencies, I pronounce all
such pretensions ridiculous impositions, and I stand ready at any time to prove
them so, or to forfeit five hundred dollars, whenever these pretended mediums
will succeed in producing their 'wonderful manifestations' in a room of my se-
lecting, and with apparatus of my providing."[11] Though many Spiritualists apparently shared with Barnum the idea of money as a religion, no medium or
spirit photographer ever met Barnum's bet.

Spiritualism eventually fell victim to confession—or sabotage, if you
were a follower. One of the Fox sisters, Margaret, revealed publicly in 1888
that the rapping was merely the younger two cracking their toes loudly, demonstrating such "spirit raps" in an auditorium of over two thousand people
with her sister Kate among them. It would not be the first or the last time
that confession and exhibition became one, furthering the confession as
an essential extension of the hoax. Spiritualists denounced Margaret—and
though she later recanted, Spiritualism became more dismissed too, despite
persisting, however diminished, into the next century, as measured by the
celebrated creator of detective Sherlock Holmes, Sir Arthur Conan Doyle,
and his many books on the subject. He would publish *The New Revelation*
and *The Case for Spirit Photography* in 1918 alone.[12]

Conan Doyle would blame the Fox sisters' confession on confusion, or
coercion, but the first Spiritualist exposure had in fact happened decades
before. When many of Mumler's allegedly dead subjects turned out to be
alive and well in Boston, the spirit photographer, who had moved his studio
to Manhattan—naturally on Broadway—was arrested and tried for fraud in
1869. Calling him "Mumbler," the *New York Daily Tribune* described a marshal's experience in having "Mumbler" procure a picture of him with his late
father-in-law: "The double picture was taken, and as far as the Marshal's
face was concerned, was a very passable one, but the likeness of the father-
in-law was a most dismal failure; and although spectral and ghostly enough
to have been a veritable emanation from the spirit land, bore not a ghost of

a resemblance to the deceased gentleman." He was still required to ante up ten dollars: "He was told that the price had been so fixed because 'the spirits did not like the throng, and that to exclude the vulgar multitude the price was fixed at the high rate,' &c."[13] Mumler was arrested soon after.

At Mumler's trial Barnum not only offered testimony for the prosecution but, in order to show how easily such effects as double exposure or treated negatives could be faked, also went so far as to re-create such "spirit" effects in a portrait showing Lincoln emerging from his unsplit skull. Spiritualists came to Mumler's aid—after all, on trial was not just Mumler, or his wife, who worked as a medium, but the whole movement. After media attention and lively testimony on both sides, the judge ultimately acquitted Mumler, saying he believed there was fraud but citing lack of evidence. Mumler continued to take his pictures, capturing Mrs. Lincoln a few years later, and spirit photography carried on as an esoteric art well into the twentieth century.

Like the hoax, spirit photography does reveal something, though not exactly what its believers may wish. Rather than a ghost emerging from the sitter or from the medium in the room—or made visible through the medium of photography itself—spirit photography captures the spirit of the age. It takes hindsight rather than second sight to see the ways such images expose beliefs as prepared and fixed as Mumler's glass negatives were. These are all in a sense "psychographs," as photos of occult phenomena made without a camera came to be called—the hoax is almost always a trick disguised as a wish. Or is it a wish achieved through a trick? The real revelation may be just whose wish it is.

SUMMERLAND

Spirit photographs are about second chances, not second sight. Such images provide just the most obvious entry in what critic Ann Douglas calls "the domestication of death," the "contemporary consolation literature" that only increased over the course of the nineteenth century. "Spiritualism in its most generalized and most specific senses was a manifestation of a complex retransfer of force from the living to the dead, from the apparently strong to the apparently weak," she writes. "If you cannot make converts among the living, declare them among the dead. Death must become, not exactly life, but a controlled extension of the feelings, and property rights, of the living."[14] You could go further and say that white mediums and their believers like Mrs. Lincoln were concerned with the dead, whereas black mediums were typically concerned with the living—being property once themselves.

Spirit photographs too connect to transcendentalism, the American movement that, despite its name, focused less on the supernatural than on nature. As Neil Harris writes in his biography of Barnum, "The Transcendental deprecation of art, when compared to nature, led to an emphasis on literalism and imitation which came perilously close, at times, to trickery."[15] Citing Emerson—"I now require this of all pictures, that they domesticate me, not that they dazzle me"—Harris inadvertently suggests the ways spirit photographs managed to both domesticate and dazzle, merging the everyday and the extraordinary in their images of the alleged dead. That they did so using trickery made them all the more American.

The Summerland, as Spiritualists termed the afterlife, offered up in Douglas's formulation a "colonization of heaven," a place that the newly powerful could access and interpret. The ghosts in spirit photographs, too, almost always good, remain something like today's benevolent guardian angels, who do not resemble any aspect of the sexless, immortal, avenging heralds from the Bible.[16] The effect resembles the "heaven tourism" found in more recent fare like *The Boy Who Came Back from Heaven* (2010), one of a string of books that have enjoyed tremendous popularity as well as strong condemnation from many strict Christians, with the one who named the phenomenon calling it "pure junk, fiction in the guise of biography, paganism in the guise of Christianity."[17] The Summerland too offered a more accessible heaven, one to be found by individuals without the interference of doctrine or damnation; in Spiritualism, as in heaven tourism, there is no hell to distract from the uplift. This proves particularly odd given that Mr. Splitfoot suggested none other than a cloven-hoofed devil or at least satyr. It is almost as ironic as the fact that the boy who in truth suffered a paralyzing accident and "came back from heaven" in a popular book written by his father—a book that the boy and his religious mother have since disavowed as "one of the most deceptive books ever"—bears the family name Malarkey.

Two aspects of spirit photography have only become more prevalent in hoaxes today: pretending contact, even conjuring, with famous people who are dead and thus cannot defend themselves or deny the meeting; and making falsehoods that are claimed to be real, especially about people of color, who are somehow expected to spend all their time defending themselves. The hoax seeks fame and to defame, often at the same time. These poles of the hoax persist, suggesting its cleft, splitfoot nature in which the ethereal double is almost always a dark one.

Spirit photographs don't just bring forth late loved ones but also Indians and other racial figures in their most clichéd form, one familiar to the hoax. One of Mumler's photographs of a young medium, "Master Herrod with the Spirits of Europe, Africa, and America" (1870–72), is found right beside Mary Todd Lincoln's in a noteworthy album of 112 spirit photographs that preserve many of our images by Mumler.[18] The proximity is symbolic: even in the spirit realm, in the supposed manifestations of the sitter and viewer and photographer, race rears its ghostly head (or in this case, heads). In another of Mumler's photographs, featuring well-known medium Fanny Conant, her "white Indian" spirit guide comes through, as described by Mumler in his 1875 memoir: "On developing the negative there appeared the form of a young girl, bearing the features of a white person, but dressed in Indian costume, with feathers on her head, large rings in her ears, while encircling her neck was a chain, to which was attached a charm of crescent shape, which was shown to Mrs. Conant by 'Vashti' (the spirit-girl,) a few evenings previous to her sitting for the picture."[19] Which may explain how Mumler knew how to add it.

Spiritualist mediums or their hoaxers are not prescient enough to imagine a spirit world that doesn't conform to ours. In the Summerland, Natives still look like Natives—the obvious stock racial types found in many spirit photographs are proof of their fakery as much as the still-living Bostonians were. Unfortunately, even Harriet Wilson, seeking solidarity or following Spiritualist convention, regularly invoked "Indian guides" while serving as a "colored medium."[20] In the case of Vashti, Mumler gives us a sensationalized backstory of how the jealousy of an "Indian wife" toward her husband, "Big Buffalo," and his new white wife was enough to turn the spirit-girl white while in utero. Most hoaxes have equally otherworldly ambitions, no matter if it's just to get us to see something too good and thus believed. Every blur is proof positive.

Yet why couldn't a new technology capture what the eye cannot measure? Spiritualism had from the onset claimed it was scientific, with its messages seen as "spiritual telegraphs."[21] Other photography at this time, such as Eadweard Muybridge's famous sequence of a horse running—which proved once and for all that all four of a horse's feet left the ground during a gallop—provided ways of seeing beyond human sight. Why couldn't spirit photography seek something beyond sight but well within the human heart: a wish for life beyond life? The difficulty remains that spirit photography isn't just a collaboration with the medium in both senses, but also with the sitter, who serves both as audience and as unwitting coconspirator.

The hoax's ghost story always seeks widespread exposure, and only afterward can we see its dark doubling clearly. But as with spirit photography, are the believers of any hoax innocent victims, or complicit perpetrators? Or, no matter their innocence, false witnesses? One of the hoax's difficulties is that it doesn't distinguish between such states. Believers like Conan Doyle—whose books of spirit photographs, it should be said, look far less haunting or convincing than Mumler's a half century before—relentlessly sought to show a scientific explanation for why such processes worked, when proof of faith is not just a paradox but a tautology.

The enemy of faith is not doubt but proof—especially when it leads to blind belief. It is the search for hard evidence, for seeming scientific confirmation, that aligns occult practices like spirit photography with pseudoscience and unreason. Even as ghosts, the spirits of Africa and America found in Mumler's photographs resemble the hierarchy of the races found in contemporary journals of phrenology and pseudoscientific tracts, arrayed around the white subjects to whom they are subjected. The difficulty with any hoax is that it provides proof for those who already believe; exposed later, the hoax reveals beliefs the hoaxers themselves may not have been aware of. While the hoaxing in spirit photography was still honorific, soon the ghosts, like the hoax itself, would feature far more horror.

THE WHITE SHADOW

It may only be from the vantage point of the unprecedented violence of the First World War that the crises and hypocrisies of the nineteenth century, whether Victorian or Jacksonian, slavery or the Civil War, seem like innocence. But the Fox sisters were matched by another hoax in the early part of the twentieth century—one also committed by young ladies related to each other—whose results would feed the last incarnation of the Spiritualist cause in the longest-held hoax of the twentieth century.

Cousins Elsie Wright and Frances Griffiths were only sixteen and ten when they took photographs with fairies—well, actually several fairies and one gnome—in the English countryside near Elsie's house in Cottingley in 1916. Wright's father then developed two photographs, taken with a Midg camera, in his home darkroom. "The fairies are on the plate—they are on the plate!" Elsie is said to have exclaimed upon seeing them.[22] Though Elsie's father didn't believe the images genuine, the Wrights gave the pictures as Christmas gifts; these made their way to a theosophy group, likely because of the girls' mothers, who each had an interest in the movement.

Founded in 1875, theosophy had extended Spiritualism further into "spiritual science," seeking evidence for spiritualistic phenomena alongside a history of Western esoteric beliefs. Founder Madame Blavatsky was regularly accused of fraud, imposture, and inventing her Indian (from India) mentors. Still, theosophy's most lasting characteristic may be its embrace of Asian philosophy, which would find its way in far more daily and artistic ways in the twentieth century, fascinating writers like Yeats and T. S. Eliot.[23] The girls' pictures caused quite a stir, being used in lectures by noted theosophists such as E. L. Gardner and ultimately finding their way to Arthur Conan Doyle. A longtime convert to the Spiritualist cause, Conan Doyle believed in the photographs just as he did in other doctrines of communicating with the dead, vibrations, and ectoplasm—beliefs surely intensified by the death of his beloved son from injuries sustained and pneumonia contracted during the Great War. The cover of Conan Doyle's *The New Revelation* indicates the emotional stakes: "In this time of terrible loss, the question of immortality has become the burning question of the days."[24] He would invent another detective, Professor Challenger, who would investigate occult phenomena in a series of novels, after first appearing in *The Lost World* in 1912.

Conan Doyle published "the evidence for fairies" in the 1920 Christmas number of the popular *Strand* magazine—the issue became a sensation, selling out within days. The article added two more photographs of the "little folk" taken by the girls with a newly supplied camera. Indeed a whole industry sprang up around the images, including Conan Doyle's *The Coming of the Fairies* (1921), which reprinted his *Strand* article and offered further proof. "The series of incidents set forth in this little volume represent either the most elaborate and ingenious hoax every [*sic*] played upon the public, or else they constitute an event in human history which may in the future appear to have been epoch-making in its character."[25] Just because the former proved true—the photographs are a hoax—doesn't mean the latter isn't true too. The photographs simply mark the end, rather than the start, of an epoch.

The Cottingley fairy photographs, as they came to be known, offered far more than evidence. "The recognition of their existence will jolt the material twentieth-century mind out of its heavy ruts in the mud, and will make it admit that there is a glamour and a mystery to life," Conan Doyle wrote in *The Coming of the Fairies*.[26] The book now appears far less logical, or elementary, than the creator of Sherlock Holmes might suggest. Whenever huge gaps inevitably appear in the evidence, Conan Doyle turns to what might be called spectral evidence to paper them over: "To the objections of photographers that the fairy figures show quite different shadows to those of the human our answer is that ectoplasm, as the etheric protoplasm has been named, has a faint luminosity of its own, which would largely modify shadows."[27] Read now, what such spiritualist pieces put forth as confirmation is clearly just a hunch, and what's more, all hunches are forms of confirmation. This is one advantage of believing in an "invisible world": anything seen is proof; anything unseen, more proof.

If the girls had youth to explain their initial actions, their innocence was not just presumed but proof for those who hardly needed convincing— both that the girls were too young (and lower class) to possibly fake anything and that their youth gave them the ability to see things others could not. Gardner writes to Doyle in June of 1920 that "these nature spirits are of the non-individualized order and I should greatly like to secure some of the higher. But two children such as these are, are rare, and I fear now that we are late because almost certainly the inevitable will shortly happen, one of them will 'fall in love' and then—hey presto!!"[28] Gardner intimates not only that sexuality would change the girls' abilities but also that there are "higher orders" of fairies. Might someone of a higher class than "a mechanic's family of Yorkshire" have seen them?

The many voices alongside Doyle's published in *The Coming of the Fairies* continually reemphasize the "honesty" and "simplicity" of the working-class family, meant as a backhanded compliment. The pseudonyms Conan Doyle chose for the *Strand* account are telling: he renames the family "the Carpenters," evocative of both honest work and Christian faith; Elsie is "Iris," and the youngest, Frances, "Alice," suggesting a Wonderland just beneath her feet. The very promise the fairies hold out can be practically glimpsed in the photos themselves: "What joy is in the complete abandon of their little graceful figures as they let themselves go in the dance! They may have their shadows and trials as we have, but at least there is a great gladness in this demonstration of their life." These are much the same pastoral folk J. R. R. Tolkien would allegorize as Hobbits decades later to provide comfort during yet another war. "These little folk who appear to be our neighbours, with only some small difference of vibration to separate us, will become familiar. The thought of them, even when unseen, will add a charm to every brook and valley and give romantic interest to every country walk," Conan Doyle forecasts.[29]

As with Barnum's Circassian Beauties, the fairy photographs offered up not just innocence but innocence—and whiteness—in jeopardy. One supporter wrote to Conan Doyle: "It occurs to me that the whiteness of the fairies may be due to their lack of shadow, which may also explain their somewhat artificial-looking flatness."[30] The fairies' seemingly undisputed shadowlessness (it's the ectoplasm, stupid) provided a visual metaphor redolent of innocence. The Cottingley fairies suggest another race, one beyond race, which is to say, whiteness ever more purified.

The girls' innocence is also convenient. "I argued that we had certainly traced the pictures to two children of the artisan class, and that such photographic tricks would be entirely beyond them," Conan Doyle says to a skeptic. Almost offhandedly Conan Doyle mentions that Elsie worked a few months for a photographer, running errands and "spotting," but he is so busy spotting fairies himself that he dismisses this experience as unlikely "to teach a fourteen-year-old girl how to 'fake' a plate."[31] It is troubling how untroubled the true believers were. When he takes the negatives to Kodak laboratories to verify, and they rule there is no superimposition "or other trick" in the processing, it never occurs to Conan Doyle that it was in the staging, not the shooting or developing, that the girls faked the fairies.

Over sixty years after taking the photographs, the cousins confirmed what many suspected: the fairies were simply traced drawings cut out and posed with the girls in the countryside. In the "gnome" picture, in fact, a hatpin can be seen; Conan Doyle had said it was a belly button. A 1978 book first revealed the fairies' source image for the drawings as *Princess Mary's Gift Book*—a children's anthology that ironically also included a Conan Doyle story.[32] Still, despite regular questions in the press, it took till 1982 for the pair to confess their hoaxing to the journal the *Unexplained*: "partly to play a prank on grown-ups who sneered at the idea that fairies could be seen, but who cheerfully perpetuated the myth of Santa Claus, they conspired to produce fairy figures that they could photograph convincingly."[33] Surely the girls also enjoyed the secret yet public power these photographs provided, which is not to say money—selling wildly, the photographs' copyright remained not with the girls or the family but the Spiritualists, materialist in at least this sense.

Looking at the Cottingley fairies today it is hard to see the photos as anything but fake, much less credit that they were ever believed. But hoaxes prove that believing is seeing. For Conan Doyle, as for those who accepted the photographs fully or simply read of them in the *Strand*, the fairies are proof not only of the character of two young girls but also of the time.[34] In a century as young as their makers, or fakers, is it no accident that the fairies, copied from a book of French fashions, were dressed au courant? Though that should have been a tip-off to the wary, for the audience it was surely a comfort to know fairies not only fluttered among them in a world changing at the newly described speed of light but also dressed like they did—or even much better. If spirit photography helped a grieving, divided nation deal with the Civil War, then the Cottingley fairy hoax helped believers cope both with the destruction of the First World War and the devastation of the influenza epidemic that followed in its wake. The photographs suggest nothing less than a mix of fairy sophistication and girl-like innocence that soon enough the flapper would simultaneously embody and destroy.

The Cottingley photographs do actually capture two worlds, just not those of the fairies and our own. While spirit photography had merged the death cult of American Victorians with the cult of ladyhood, turning the so-called Angel in the House into a friendly ghost, the Cottingley fairy photographs connect such ladyhood to an Edwardian, late-empire notion of childhood—a time newly romanticized by a West that had once viewed childhood as practically nonexistent. This connection is in large part visual. For, hazy around their edges, the Cottingley fairy photographs resemble nothing less than the images of Julia Margaret Cameron, whose blurred but beautiful photographs from the 1860s and 1870s often captured staged fairies and costumed children in a late-Romantic fog that the Cottingley photos embrace and perpetuate.

Linked to the artistic group the Pre-Raphaelites, Cameron took por-traits of the most learned British figures of her time, from poet Alfred Tennyson to the very Sir John Herschel unwittingly drafted to help along the Moon Hoax. "Mrs. Cameron is making endless Madonnas and May Queens and Foolish Virgins and Wise Virgins and I know not what be-sides," wrote Tennyson's wife, Emily. "It really is wonderful how she puts her spirit into people."[35] Cameron's are spirit photographs of a different sort: even while depicting death, as in the famous painting of the death of Ophelia, the Pre-Raphaelites framed a hazy, pastoral, laudanum-like vi-sion. What's more, their radical views remained tied, at least visually, to a romantic idealized Europeanness reliant on the blackamoor peering from the edge of the picture or just out of frame; the blackamoors and *japonisme*, Orientalism and coded racialism found in Pre-Raphaelite paintings only make the whiteness all the more stark.

A generation later, the Cottingley photographs also can't help but capture a similar, metaphoric "white shadow." Not just the fairies but the girls themselves are framed by what critic Robin Bernstein calls racial innocence, a notion that began "by the mid-nineteenth century, [when] sentimental culture had woven childhood and innocence together wholly. Childhood was then understood not as innocent but as innocence itself; not as a symbol of innocence but as its embodiment. The doctrine of original sin receded, replaced by a doctrine of original innocence. This innocence was raced white."[36] Over and over again, hoaxes from the Circassian Beauty to the pretend Indian will invoke whiteness alongside "original innocence" as a kind of unoriginal sin; the hoax in fact would seem dependent on such racial innocence as a substitution for the truth.

For by the late nineteenth century, Counter-Enlightenment superstition and Enlightenment rationalism had infected each other in a fin de siècle, rosy-cheeked romanticism—a kind of double exposure in which pseudoscience and what we'll come to call *pseudospirituality* got spliced together with the reactionary eugenics of Europe and America. All this was the hoax's hunting ground, whiteness offset by a symbolic black ground.

"Can these be thought-forms?" Sir Arthur asks about the fairies at one point. While he means to suggest mere thoughts caused the pictures to develop, Conan Doyle inadvertently suggests how the fairy photographs acted as wish fulfillment. He himself viewed the fairies as a kind of gateway drug—if people believed these pictures, then perhaps they'd believe in other occult phenomena he was more deeply invested in. Certainly too the fairies helped him connect not just to his lost son but also to his artist father, Charles Doyle, who had provided the images for the first Sherlock Holmes stories and painted numerous fantastical landscapes filled with fairies—a fact rarely recounted in relation to the Cottingley hoax.[37] Given that Charles Doyle's constant images of fairies continued even when he was institutionalized in the asylum where he would die, it is perhaps more understandable why Conan Doyle barely mentions him; or might the son's silence be because his father depicts fairies not as fair but brooding, in a dark style veering toward the grotesque?

Predisposed, Conan Doyle insists fairies are both benevolent and actual, selling them in a fashion: "these people are destined to become just as solid and real as the Eskimos." Of course, it is the making of real people into myth—or the Inuit into the slur "Eskimo"—that is the problem. Conan Doyle makes the fairies figures of ethnography and exploration, invoking Americanness: "When Columbus knelt in prayer upon the edge of America, what prophetic eye saw all that a new continent might do to affect the destinies of the world?"[38] Conan Doyle suggests how much the fairies are an essential, even pleasant, part of empire. The hoax often was too.

The problem isn't simply racism or colonialism but that the very method Conan Doyle uses—indeed, some of the same evidence—closely resembles the pseudoscience of racism and eugenicist efforts still very much with us. Inadvertently the girls themselves suggested as much when Frances sent one of the photos to her pen pal in South Africa, where she had spent her early childhood: "Elsie and I are very friendly with the beck Fairies. It is funny I never used to see them in Africa. It must be too hot for them there."[39] Much like those who believed the Moon Hoax a sign of Providence, the Cottingley fairies reveal how the human need for belief was matched by a pseudoscientific rationale for it—one dependent on race. The effort seemed particularly American, even in its expatriate, English, or imperial forms.

Conan Doyle's unlikely friend, Harry Houdini, the great escape artist, spent his life debunking Spiritualists, objecting to their exploitation of the grieving in large part because of his own grief over his mother's death. How much of the appeal of his act, filled with straitjackets and chains, was his reenacting a metaphoric escape from the asylums and madness of the age or the shackles of slavery barely past? Houdini would regularly denounce séances, clairvoyants, and spirit photographs that sought to profit off pain. Houdini was in this way Barnum's inheritor, a master of illusion who debunked the illusions of others. But where Barnum did so for publicity in a very public time, Houdini did so for private ones—revealing that illusion and truth aren't always enemies and that grief, whether personal or a nation's, needn't require simple comfort. The fake "feel good" culture proved no better than the "feel bad" one that dominates today.

But is believing a hoax, promulgating what you genuinely think true, as troubling as starting one? Conan Doyle does not insist that the Cottingley fairies depict his world—or another, invisible one—but *the* world. His desire for the photos to "jolt the material twentieth-century mind out of its heavy ruts in the mud" and "make it admit that there is a glamour and a mystery to life," would seem in its own way grotesque.[40] The Cottingley fairies don't so much replace race as displace it. Much like in *Peter Pan*'s Neverland, populated by its own fairies and "Indians," lost boys and "picanninies," the hoax's fantasies are not so far away.

While Conan Doyle did acknowledge some of Houdini's debunkings, he claimed Houdini was genuinely a medium and simply lying about it.[41] Still, the two improbably remained friends—even after Houdini's exposé *A Magician Among the Spirits* (1924) that dared take on Conan Doyle—at least till Conan Doyle claimed to have communicated with Houdini's dead mother. In truth, after hoping and failing to communicate with his beloved dead, Houdini left a secret code with his wife in case he could communicate with her from beyond. After his untimely death in 1926 from a botched feat, despite her holding a decade's worth of séances, he never did.

Harry Houdini showing the ease of faking a spirit photograph of Lincoln, 1925.

CHAPTER 4

Bearded Ladies

Was Abraham Lincoln a Spiritualist? The title of Nettie Colburn Maynard's 1891 memoir of her life as "a trance medium" indicates the continued fascination with the assassinated president, whose cult would eventually surpass that of George Washington. A kind of girl wonder and Spiritualist prodigy, Maynard had actually attended to Mrs. Lincoln during the presidency, conducting a series of séances to search the spirit realm for the Lincolns' late son Willie; President Lincoln himself apparently attended one of these sessions, though likely only to watch over his bereft wife's well-being. Maynard not surprisingly makes the most of these executive occasions, going so far as to suggest that her presence and prescience helped with the Emancipation Proclamation.

The publisher's preface to Maynard's book strikes a note that will become familiar to us in introductions to more modern hoax memoirs: "The statements contained in this volume regarding him [Lincoln] are given to the public for the reason that they are not less true than surprising; and being so, they must see the light." Such convoluted grammar, neither true nor surprising, is the métier of hoaxes—as is the reassurance that "what is here written is truth, fact, *history*, and what is more, no man should question them."[1] Yet Maynard's "nonfiction" book doesn't merely mirror other hoaxes; it also directly forecasts a hoax from the 1920s, when a mother-and-daughter team created a series of letters between Lincoln and his supposed childhood sweetheart, Ann Rutledge, a figure whose own import grew with the slew of Lincoln biographies at the start of the twentieth century. This is no coincidence: the hoax, in its modern incarnations, attempts to reconcile horror with history.

In the summer of 1928, one Wilma Frances Minor wrote to the prestigious *Atlantic Monthly* about inheriting letters from the late president. "Miss Minor said her mother obtained them from Frederick Hirth who got them from his sister, Elizabeth Hirth, who got them from Sally Calhoun, who got them from Matilda Cameron, friend of both the alleged correspondents."[2] Such convoluted provenance, or trail of ownership, should have been a tip to the credulous editors, but the *Atlantic* optioned and serialized articles by Minor about "Lincoln, the Lover" for a thousand-dollar advance, four thousand dollars due upon publication—terms generous even now. The first of three monthly installments, in December 1928, was simply called "The Discovery"; the piece was accompanied by a breathless note by editor Ellery Sedgwick, of the prominent Sedgwick family who later brought us Andy Warhol's muse Edie:

> If there is one life of which the American people wish to know everything, it is Abraham Lincoln's. And it is probable that no life in history has been studied with more eager care than his. Historians, students, collectors, lovers of his name, have for three generations followed his every footstep, run down a thousand false trails and a hundred true ones, uncovered all that letters, recollections, tradition, even rumor, had to tell. And in all that career, already in our ears half legendary, there is no chapter which seemed more utterly closed, or which most of us, men and women, have more eagerly desired to open, than the idyll of New Salem, the love of Abraham Lincoln and Ann Rutledge. Historians have for the most part passed it over as casual fancy of boy and girl. The romancers have had a truer inspiration, but, in the absence of tangible facts, a vague tradition was but slender nourishment for the imagination.[3]

Such conditions—an "absence of tangible facts," "a thousand false trails and a hundred true ones," and an overwhelming desire for proving a vague, imagined tradition—are the stuff of the hoax.

"The confidence man makes belief," critic Gary Lindberg writes. The hoax differs in that it *exposes* belief. Readers, the editors first and foremost among them, desired a Lincoln not just romantic but Romantic; he was meant, in these new revelations, also to be deeply spiritual (whether that meant in terms of Spiritualists or Christians, who both wished to color him faithful). Poet Carl Sandburg—the only person to win a Pulitzer in two categories, including for his six-volume biography of Lincoln—spent a day with the alleged archive and pronounced, "These new Lincoln letters seem entirely authentic—and preciously and wonderfully co-ordinate and chime with all else known of Lincoln. Students of Lincoln's personal development will prize and love them for several known reasons and for intangible and inexplicable reasons."[4] Such intangibles help make the inexplicable believable.

The hoax was built for Sandburg, if not literally, then because it stems from his biography's lyrical fancies and their promoting of the Rutledge myth. "Ann Rutledge lay fever-burned. Days passed; help arrived and was helpless," he writes in *Abraham Lincoln: The Prairie Years* (1926). "Moans came from her for the one man of her thoughts. They sent for him. He rode out from New Salem to the Sand Ridge farm. They let him in; they left the two together and alone a last hour in the log house, with slants of light on her face from an open clapboard door. It was two days later that death came." Sandburg fed the myth, like a fever, but the wider American audience also craved a love story, especially one leaned on to explain the president's lifelong depression. "Lincoln sat for hours with no words for those who asked him to speak to them. They went away from him knowing he would be alone whether they stayed or went away."[5] In the face of the inexplicable, audiences will settle for unbelievable.

This includes the *Atlantic*'s editors. While the very size of this "new storehouse of Lincoln material"—filled with letters, books "containing marginalia of intensest interest, including the Bible given him by Ann herself, bearing her own and Lincoln's signature," "the most natural and human of diaries kept by Ann's cousin and bosom friend, Matilda Cameron," and even "touching examples of Ann Rutledge's needlework, and a silver pin which Lincoln salvaged from the barrel which yielded him a treasure-trove of books"—should have proved a red flag, it instead provided a red cape waved in front of an overeager bull. "What a collection!" Sedgwick exclaims. "Here is the human Lincoln, before the sterility of his deification."[6]

Of course, if it weren't for Lincoln's deification, such items would not have assumed the quality of relics. Despite analyzing the paper to find "no suggestion of pulp!," Minor's letters were filled with metaphoric pulp. Neither "passionate" nor "real," Lincoln's mash notes were almost immediately proved forgeries, and amateurish ones at that, complete with references to nonexistent parcels of land and poor handwriting and spelling. Sandburg himself issued an about-face just a day after his authentication.[7] Undaunted, even defiant, Sedgwick continued to serialize "Lincoln the Lover" for two more months, ignoring almost every expert he consulted; many who began to voice their doubts, feeling the Minor material minor, Sedgwick would dismiss. "In a long life I've never seen a man more impervious to reason," wrote the historian who finally broke the case for good.[8] Barnum's idea of the audience as expert, above all other experts, continued.

Sedgwick's "Discovery" claimed that "the chain of descent of the documents is through a series of well-identified persons" and "is a chain of actual flesh and blood." But it was more a spirit that guided the letters: eventually confronted, Minor and her mother confessed that the letters were not authentic; rather, they had channeled all the voices, from Lincoln to Rutledge, with the mother serving as a trance medium. "I would die on the gallows that the spirits of Ann and Abe were speaking through my Mother to me, so that my gifts as a writer combined with her gifts as a medium could hand in something worthwhile to the world," Minor's sworn confession read.[9] The confession's awed tone matched poetic histories like Sandburg's that surely inspired the hoax—and that editors used to confirm details. The hoax, as is often the case, existed in a feedback loop, the confessions only furthering the gambit.

What the "Lincoln letters" and Minor's confession do suggest, as with spirit photography decades before, is a certain pleasure, however incomplete, in exposure. The same was true in Barnum's time, when hoaxes, while not harmless, still were centered on wonderment—or wondering. The Minor affair suggests the way in which, by the early part of the twentieth century, hoaxes went from humbug to romance, and eventually to horror—like the term *freak* itself. Soon both history and the freak would become merely the province of experts.[10]

We might measure this change in the freak, and all those who follow after Barnum—who lived a long, adventurous, and in the end prosperous life, dying in 1891 at age eighty—by his most immediate inheritor to the heights of humbug, Robert L. Ripley. Started in 1919, Ripley's "Believe It or Not!" was not actually a question but an exclamation and exhortation: we are meant to believe. That belief proved telling in a modern world fascinated by what Ripley called his "queeriosities."[11] For, even as he displayed them in his columns and collections, Ripley refused to call freaks by name: "I only deal in oddities. Not freaks," he would tell the *New Yorker*. "He thinks the word 'freak' has an unpleasant connotation and insists that the two-headed fishes, human pincushions, fork-tongued ladies, eyeless infants, four-footed chickens, and three-headed calves to which he has drawn international attention are not freaks. 'An oddity is a high-class freak,' he once said guardedly, when pinned down."[12]

This seems an oddly American phenomenon, the growing gap between what is meant and what is said. Many a euphemism today stems from commerce (*downsizing*), misplaced or overweening or patronizing politeness (*bless her heart*), squeamishness (*restroom* rather than *toilet*), or all of the above (take *casket* instead of *coffin*, an American funeral directors' invention, continuing the "domestication of death"). While changing terminology can represent, and hope to effect, a change in attitudes, in the case of *freak*, this is not exactly the case—as the freak became less acceptable to the American public over the twentieth century, those wondrous individuals became seen less as God-given miracles or medical marvels and more as diseased beings in need or correction or elimination. The freak show would become threatened too. "A sense of the Freak show as an unworthy survival of an unjust past spread everywhere in the early twentieth century," Leslie Fiedler writes in his groundbreaking study *Freaks*, "so that for a while it seemed as if those of us now living might well represent the last generations whose imaginations would be shaped by a live confrontation with nightmare distortions of the human body."[13] Despite his tone here, Fiedler means to praise the freaks in ways Ripley doesn't.

Taken from the Latin for "portent," *prodigy* for centuries had been equated with *monster*, yet neither term meant something horrific. Rather, Western thought viewed the birth of prodigies and monsters as natural wonders, sure signs of God's creation. "Monstrous births, the signs of God's wrath, were also considered miracles, indications of God's power over nature," critic Paul Semonin reminds us.[14] The body, that once-sacred site, by the time of Ripley at least, became mere flesh and blood, not divine will where God's will was written. "Though still an oracle, the extraordinary body was transferred from the public gaze to the sequestered scrutiny of experts by the mid-twentieth century. Thus the wondrous monsters of antiquity, who became the fascinating freaks of the nineteenth century, transformed into the disabled people of the later twentieth century," writes Rosemarie Garland Thomson in her essential book *Extraordinary Bodies*. "The extraordinary body" of the freak "moved from portent to pathology."[15]

What Garland Thomson does not quite say, but implies, is the way this view of the "disabled" body would become a view of the body more generally.

This is especially true for the female body—ever in need of fixing, medicalized, born or bosomed bad, never quite right. No longer a temple, or only that, these days the body is not popularly a mere vessel for the soul: instead, it has become a thing to be endlessly improved, obsessed over, or abandoned—which may prove the same thing. *Letting yourself go* is about weight and no longer about ecstasy.

No longer meaning a body marveled at and feared, a *prodigy* instead became a youthful genius who was admired and raised up before being declared washed up. There would be few second acts in modern American lives, just three-ring circuses; the modern hoax would embrace spectacle too. Soon, across the twentieth century, the prodigious acts once found in the circus and the dime museum—a tame monstrousness—left polite society, at least publicly. The menagerie of bearded ladies, dog boys, pinheads, and so-called freaks once a regular part of family entertainment in places like Barnum's American Museum (at least until it burned down in 1865) were now exiled to the sideshow—and the very idea of the museum would change to mean a repository of art and high culture.

The modern circus had aspirations too: big tops like Barnum's Barnum & Bailey partnership in the 1880s shifted focus, adding exotic animals and smiling clowns to the exoticized people—prodigies or freaks or foreigners—in whom Barnum had specialized. Denuded, the bearded ladies left the center ring. Western culture had walked this tightrope between freakery and fakery for centuries but now presumed not to do so in public. By the start of the twentieth century it was society, not the monster, that had become less wild.

The big tent actually was in this way smaller, demoting "freaks" to the midway or county fair while the prodigious acts that had once shared a roof got sent further afield, to vaudeville—to say nothing of burlesque. Burlesque, which once meant high mockery or low satire, by the turn of the twentieth century came to name a strip show strictly for adults. Like vaudeville, burlesque was also tied to blackface minstrelsy, providing a name for its final act of "after-pieces" and comic opera. The black mask was but a burnt cork away.

Though he may have been reluctant to say *freak*, Ripley would hardly refrain from listing the countries he had visited in a kind of visual colonialism "near the entrance of his Odditorium at the [1933 Chicago] World's Fair, along with two large photographs showing him in the company of a Papuan cannibal chief and a monkey man in India."[16] For as the freak disappeared, race in general and blackness specifically provided American culture a permanent freak—persisting both as extravagant spectacle and as something anyone white with greasepaint might manage.

We have lingered here over the freak because *freaks, like fakes, are not born but made*. This is true no matter whether they are born with the qualities once judged marvelous: as critic Robert Bogdan succinctly puts it, "A freak was defined not by the possession of any particular quality but by a set of practices, a way of thinking about and presenting people with major, minor, and fabricated physical, mental, and behavioral differences."[17] These are not freaks of nature but what Susan Stewart calls "freaks of culture."[18] Their roles, we should be reminded, are not and never were the same as their persons—Bogdan helps us understand that there's a difference between an extremely tall person and a giant, the latter proving a role complete with performances both self- and other inflicted.

With what we might call the secularizing of the *prodigy* in the West as well as the formalizing of the museum over the nineteenth century, the modern hoax followed suit. Once, in the eighteenth century, the hoax meant to honor; later, the hoax in the Age of Imposture aspired to humor till it became a form of romance, whether that meant love or horror. This tension is what we find at the beginning of the twentieth century, when the ghosts were gone yet fairies could still frolic, Lincoln could become a lover, natives were nowhere and everywhere, and the modern—including the modern hoax—was made.

JOLLY SAVAGES

"On or about December 1910 human character changed," Virginia Woolf would declare.[19] Woolf, who happened to be nineteenth-century photographer Julia Margaret Cameron's grandniece, would not only help bring about modernism but also dare to give it a start date. Instead of December 1910, Woolf could well have dated the start of the modern era to earlier in the year and the celebrated *Dreadnought* hoax that took place on 7 February. Donning fake beards, blackface, and turbans, Woolf and three other soon-to-be members of the eventual Bloomsbury group, including her brother Adrian Stephen, impersonated the emperor of Abyssinia and his suite. Managing to board the famed British battleship *Dreadnought*, the group had two members who pretended to be their guides—essentially posing as themselves. As the leader of the half dozen hoaxers wrote in a letter that only came to light over a hundred years later, "I was so amused at being just myself in a tall hat—I had no disguise whatever and talked in an ordinary friendly way to everyone—the others talked nonsense. We had all learned some Swahili: I said they were 'jolly savages' but that I didn't understand much of what they said."[20] "A rum lingo they speak," one of the junior officers grumbled under his breath, but the ship's naval officers, who happened to include a cousin of the woman then still named Virginia Stephen, failed to recognize the blackface troupe as anything but genuine.[21] The crew toured the retinue around, welcoming them with a red carpet and sending them on their way in a carriage—with luck, before their beards fell off.

Soon after, the story of the hoax broke with much embarrassment to the proud British navy, with threats—including of caning—issued by embarrassed officers, including the cousin. Most who learned of it later, however, including the captain, thought it a fine prank. Woolf and her husband, Leonard, later published her brother's account, *The "Dreadnought" Hoax*, at their Hogarth Press in 1936. Having originally posed as an interpreter, Adrian Stephen now offered further interpolation: "By the time we reached the *Dreadnought* the expedition had become for me at any rate almost an affair of every day. It was hardly a question any longer of a hoax. *We were almost acting the truth*."[22]

Why did these future members of the modernist movement darken their skin, speak "gibberish fluently," pretending it was Swahili, and board the primary guardian of the British fleet? Why show up at His Majesty's Ship, the very symbol of empire, masquerading as "black"—or at least blackened—and in the case of the future Virginia Woolf, male? Even as a burlesque, the "*Dreadnought* hoax" enacts a truth not just about those they fooled but about the hoaxers themselves. Savages in the hoax are always jolly.

By the time of the *Dreadnought* escapade, blackface was regularly used in the United States by ethnic white immigrants, who once would have been labeled less than white, as a way of becoming quintessentially American. Like those blackface minstrels before them, the hoaxer and the hoaxes' embrace of blackface meant they could become something not just new but foreign, not just foreign but American, not just American but literally black.

This view may best be called *exoticist*—a way of both wanting the foreign and finding it wanting. The exoticist often insists she is actually native, even if that means playing at it; the exoticist not only takes in what Edward Said terms Orientalism, conceiving the "Orient" as something against which the West defines itself, but also connects these ideas across other formalized kinds of exoticism, from blackface to redface. All are tied to desire. Exoticists rely on race mainly in opposition, playing foreign in order to contend, or content themselves, that they belong. Nothing can be more American than wearing blackface or redskin; nothing more British than donning a dark beard and turban. While not always white, the exoticist is always at home.

In boarding the most prominent of the British fleet, emblem of its soon-fading empire, the "jolly savages" showed up the British Empire while also making fun of an Abyssinia where royalty was only an illusion. What the Dreadnoughts spoke was the language of the hoax—elemental, bearded, gibberish as native tongue. Like the hoax, it was contagious: one of the "Swahili" phrases they reportedly uttered, *Bunga-Bunga*, would become "public catchwords for a time, and were introduced as tags into music-hall songs and so forth," Adrian Stephen writes.[23] A glance at the proverbial Internets reveals that *Bunga-Bunga* has been renewed by disgraced former Italian prime minister Silvio Berlusconi as a term for his sex parties, taken from a common racist joke; the familiar exoticist combination of racism and sex keeps on ticking.

The hoaxers' referring to "Abyssinia" and not Ethiopia indicates some of the hoax's worldview, for Abyssinia, casting its spell, was often misspelled, a sign that more than often it was made up. Abyssinia especially worked this way because of its legendary status in literature. From Samuel Johnson's *Prince of Abissinia* (1759) to Coleridge's "Kubla Khan" (1798)—with its

> damsel with a dulcimer
> In a vision I once saw:
> It was an Abyssinian maid,
> And on her dulcimer she played,
> Singing of Mount Abora[24]

—to pose as Abyssinian royalty was to invoke the stuff of English imagination. Abyssinia was a place believed exactly because it was so often spoken of but so rarely seen. Yet the *Dreadnought* hoax occurred just as Ethiopia was becoming a force in the new world in both senses—while the "Ethiopian" remained the lowest of pseudoscience's racial categories, Ethiopianism named a burgeoning Pan-African movement then at its height in America. Ethiopia became a symbolic home for the progressive "New Negro," black writers invoking an Ethiopian homeland the way the Harlem Renaissance would Africa soon after, and that Rastafarian culture would take up further. That the *Dreadnought* hoaxers would misspell the land as "Abbysinia" in a telegram to the commander of the Home Fleet, a clue the commander surely should've caught, also indicates that the country being conjured was only an idea—a backdrop, or a black one—an abyss.[25]

The photographs of the *Dreadnought* hoax, our main means of knowing what the cohort looked like, are as staged as the hoax itself. The studio shots taken that day encapsulate the empire's descent from Victorian to Edwardian to soon-to-be-war-torn Britain, a parody of power.[26] The whole affair wouldn't have worked as well as a hoax if it were completely convincing; the fake beard must be obvious, if only after the fact. Just as male-to-female drag doesn't seek to transform its performer into an actual woman but rather play with the illusion of femininity, especially of its excesses, the dark makeup the hoaxers wore proved homage and parody in one.

The hoax also honored Adrian Stephen and de Vere's earlier prank at Oxford, pretending to be the "Sultan of Zanzibar" in blackface and spoofing the mayor. Already gone from local to international, might the *Dreadnought* hoax put us in mind of another group of white folks who also darkened their skins and boarded a ship to disrupt and mock the British Empire a century or so before? The Boston Tea Party had announced a revolution, but also an American aesthetic of "redface" that was simultaneously stolen and native-born; the *Dreadnought* hoax announced a change in human character as well as in the character of the hoax itself. This change was predicated on race—or at least its pretense.

This is to say that the *Dreadnought* hoax managed something peculiarly American. For while the blackamoor had been a tradition in British culture since at least Shakespeare, the figure had proved so invisible as to be tragic, trapped in dark skin, a role, or in shadows at the side of the painting's frame. The Dreadnoughts' blackface more resembled America's, and its aspiration as the first national popular culture. If blackface from its start in the 1830s had been one of the things white Americans had used to signal their nativeness, now the Dreadnoughts used it to signal their foreignness—pretending to be foreign powers while pretending to be themselves.

Blackface remains exoticist and offensive as a practice not just because of its long tradition of mocking black selfhood, sexuality, and speech, but because of its assertion that black people are whites merely sullied by dark skin. Such a view was central to the formation of race, with religion or so-called science seeing the "Ethiopian" as degraded and devolved from whites.

"Can the Ethiopian change his skin, or the leopard his spots? *then* may ye also do good, that are accustomed to do evil": pseudoscience and society's conflation of the Ethiopian and evil, skin and permanence, blackness and irredeemable nature would find regular justification in this Bible verse from Jeremiah.[27] Indeed, the biblical Adam and Eve origin story would often prove the only argument *against* the theory of blacks being a separate species, even as chapter and verse were cited to justify slavery too.

Blackness across the eighteenth and nineteenth centuries soon became a mere disease, Negroes descended not from Adam or even the fabled "mark of Cain" but degenerated from corrupted environment, atavistic savagery, or worse. One prominent American Philosophical Society member, writing to Thomas Jefferson, supposed the resulting "black color (as it is called)" of those "known by the epithet of negroes" as "Derived from the Leprosy."[28] (Jefferson didn't exactly disagree.) Might, however obliquely, the *Dreadnought* hoaxers' faked Ethiopia also be referring to the leopard's spots, blackness an epithet they could simply scrub off?

MEMOIRS OF ****

If race in our modern sense began in the Enlightenment, the hoax helped it along. For the hoax during the age of reason centered on race but in a different sense—at least on the surface. Back then the hoax sought to raise up the origins of "the race" as in tribe or nation, as found in some of the most noteworthy hoaxes in English: William-Henry Ireland's forging Shakespeare in the 1790s in an attempt to establish British literary bona fides and connection to the Bard; or Thomas Chatterton's seeking poetic legitimacy by crafting a fake poetic lineage, inventing a fifteenth-century predecessor, Rowley, and fabricating his own "olde" English. Chatterton had modeled his hoax on an equally popular hoax from earlier in the eighteenth century, James Macpherson's synthetic versions of alleged, long-lost poet Ossian, first published in 1760. Both hoaxes offered early instances of the hoax's artificial languages, a trend that would continue. Macpherson, taking actual Gaelic fragments, had added spurious verses and then fabricated a proud backstory for Homeric ancestor Ossian that involved his finding an ancient manuscript.[29] The resulting *Fragments of Ancient Poetry, Collected in the Highlands of Scotland, and Translated from the Gaelic or Erse Language* was not only thought genuine for years but also spurred on a slew of fogbound, mythic poetries of a type regularly called "Ossianic"—a mood both misty and misty-eyed, an almost macho sentimentality that the hoax continues to invoke today.

Seven years after his suicide by arsenic poisoning when he was not yet eighteen, Chatterton's *Poems Supposed to Have Been Written at Bristol by Thomas Rowley and Others, in the Fifteenth Century* appeared in 1777. (Such titles don't just sound long to our ears, but more like a hedge.) Chatterton would soon come to be admired by the Romantic poets who viewed his Rowley poems, whatever their true origin, as essential, and who saw his teenage suicide as a form of martyrdom in a nation that wouldn't recognize true genius.[30] He was both marvelous and monstrous, thus unable to live.

Coleridge would publish his "Monody on the Death of Chatterton" in 1794, decrying his country as a way of claiming it; Wordsworth famously referred to Chatterton as "the marvellous Boy" in 1807; Keats would pledge his *Endymion* "to the memory of Thomas Chatterton" in 1818; three years later, Shelley would dedicate his elegy *Adonais* to Keats after *his* young death, while also invoking Chatterton. This lineage wasn't all male—the first poem to Chatterton I can locate is "Elegy on Mr. Chatterton" (1787) by Ann Yearsley, "a poetical milk-woman," also from Bristol, who claimed, as Coleridge would, Chatterton as a local ancestor lost.[31] Yearsley found in Chatterton what Chatterton would have to fake in Rowley. Bristol could travel in both time and space: Coleridge's biographer Richard Holmes describes his "Monody" as a kind of time travel, with one version imagining Chatterton resurrected for Coleridge's planned yet never-realized journey to America to form a utopian community of "Pantisocrats" along the Susquehanna. "Coleridge's version of the emigration scheme, has at times, almost a science-fiction quality," Holmes writes. Coleridge "imagines creating a time-warp to enable the young Bristol poet to accompany the Pantisocrats: *O Chatterton! that thou wert yet alive! / Sure thou would'st spread the canvass to the gale.*"[32] Such idealism, like time travel, inevitably fails.

In raising up the race, hoaxers like Ireland, Chatterton, and Macpherson meant to champion native excellence—whether that meant Stratford, Bristol, or Scotland—even if they had to fake it. Yet the longest standing of the "early modern" hoaxers, George Psalmanazar, used race in a more modern, and exoticist sense: he spent decades, from 1704 till his death sixty years later, impersonating "a gentleman from Formosa" in public and in publications. Likely a white Frenchman, Psalmanazar required no makeup at all to make up whatever he wanted about his so-called native land, now known as Taiwan. His acting "foreign"—eating raw meat and the like—was enough to convince his Enlightenment audiences. Psalmanazar befriended Samuel Johnson, was asked to lecture at Oxford, and ultimately was received at court; his famed and fake *History and Geographical Description of Formosa* (1704) became a definitive text, so much so that any accurate reports of the island were denounced as fake. With various spellings given for his name, some with as many as six *a*'s, Psalmanazar successfully maintained his ruse for much of the eighteenth century. His fraud was so complete we still don't know his real name.

If his hoaxing didn't chart an actual island, he did help provide a map for the hoax of the twentieth century and beyond. Like the *Dreadnought* hoaxers would, Psalmanazar spoke in a made-up language he pretended was his native tongue—a tongue that inevitably says more about our idea of natives than its speaker. Psalmanazar would go on to translate Anglican litanies and the Lord's Prayer into this fake Formosan; like his *Description* as a whole, his translations flattered the Anglican cause, which helps explain Psalmanazar's popularity in Britain. First the fame, then the defaming: the book's first section, "Travels and Conversion," is really politics disguised as religion, existing chiefly to authenticate and distract us from the second section with its outrageous claims of Jesuit immorality and Formosan customs ("wherefore they Sacrifice Infants to the Sun, and Beasts to the Moon and Stars"), laws ("chiefly design'd against the Papists, who worship the Crucifix"), and images of temples and altars (including "the Gridiron upon which the hearts of the young Children are burnt").[33] Psalmanazar mostly seeks to convert readers to believe in him—his adopted name, taken from *psalm*, suggested reverence.

Psalmanazar's influence extends to his confession that was "Written by himself / In order to be published after his Death." Psalmanazar's *Memoirs of* **** would inspire not only other hoaxes upon its publication in 1764 but also the modern memoir itself. That's because that definitive Enlightenment figure Rousseau's own 1782 *Confessions* were directly influenced by faker Psalmanazar, in style at least; in turn, the *Confessions* are generally credited with establishing our modern notion of the memoir, complete with a focus on salacious detail still with us today.[34] "I cannot better begin this melancholy account of my former life, vile and abominable as it hath been, and blended with such mixture of the most unaccountable pride, folly, and stupid villainy, in opposition to reason, religion, and all checks of conscience, till almost to the thirtieth year of my age, than by humbly acknowledging the infinite mercy of God," Psalmanazar writes.[35] Psalmanazar's over-the-top tone Rousseau would make his own. Though it parrots melancholy, the tone sounds almost triumphant; you might say the modern memoir, true or false, started right here. Certainly in its asterisks, lacunae, shifting names, and "opposition to reason," Psalmanazar's memoir anticipated the pseudonymous, spinning, and redacted quality of the modern hoax.

It also confirms the modern hoax's connection to that white lie, race: Psalmanazar's pale, seemingly un-Asian coloring he explained away as his being from the Formosan higher classes, who lived underground. This made use of older notions of race dependent on environment—ones familiar to the age of reason that established our current racial categories but saw them as not quite as deterministic as they would become over the nineteenth century. Soon what were once neutral or more or less descriptive Linnaean taxonomies became chains of being; then explanations of inferiority for people labeled black, yellow, brown, and red; and then the very justification for slavery or slaughter. By the end of the nineteenth century "Ethiopians" not only were depicted as a lesser race but as a separate and unequal species, a fact detectable even in Negro skulls.

This was true for another faker found in Bristol: Princess Caraboo, who, two days after April Fools' Day, 1817, "*outlandished* her general attire" with her hair in a turban and a shawl "loosely and tastefully put on, in imitation of the Asiatic costume," and was found wandering delirious. Partly by pointing to the *chinoiserie* that one of her soon-to-be hosts had in her house, she managed to pantomime that she was from the island nation of Javasu in the Indian Ocean: "Her father's country she called Congee (*China*)—her own island, from whence she was taken, she called Javasu, and that of her mother the Maudins (*Malay*.) She described her mother's teeth as being blackened, her face and arms painted, and that she wore a jewel at her nose, with a gold chain from it to the left temple." Upon hearing her fake language, complete with a made-up alphabet, one man even pretended that he knew it and started echoing her in it. Local families welcomed her, as did newspapers grateful for the intrigue—one letter writer supposed that "although entirely unacquainted with any single character of her writing, I have deemed her more resembling a *Circassian*; her countenance, her complexion and her manners, favour such a supposition; and probably her appearance here may be connected with the Corsairs who have been hovering about our coast." All told the ruse, an accidentally collective endeavor, lasted for several months until a former neighbor from Devonshire identified her portrait as one "MARY WILLCOCKS, alias BAKER, alias

BAKERSTENDHT." The princess was sent on her way to America no less, land of the free and the con.

Between Psalmanazar and Caraboo we can see the change, which is not to say advance, in the European and American view of race. With Psalmanazar, we are hearing the language of an age of exploration and of enlightenment, garbled and made up though it may be; from Caraboo, we hear the dark rumblings of empire, echoed back by the culture at large. The princess provided an up-close exoticist experience both strange and all too familiar, saying she worshipped "Allah Tallah" and that "the Boogoos (*Cannibals*) were black. That when they took white prisoners, they cut off their heads and arms, and roasted them by a fire, round which they danced, and then eat them."[36] Her accounts of being "bought" and stolen speak to the slave trade then very much alive internationally, displacing it to "copper-coloured" slavers—the exact opposite of Western history—all while exploiting the panic over white slavery. Even the term *outlandished* suggests her method—and the hoax's—committing to the outlandish in order to find her way into a community that, as with the Dreadnoughts, more or less resembled her own. Authenticating not just herself but what her British hosts already had obtained from, and expected of, the East, Caraboo the Circassian Beauty senses and sets patterns for the hoax and for the hierarchies to follow, from cannibalism to color. These would only solidify in the racialized pseudoscience of the rest of the nineteenth century.

But in the eighteenth century race was not as strictly associated with skin color, which is why Psalmanazar could deal in the newly formed types of race without their visual trappings. It was enough for Psalmanazar to play Rousseau's "noble savage" to be believed, for his *Description* to picture white elephants on his tiny imagined island. The emblem of this changing sense of race and skin found its emblem in the "leopard boys" and "piebald families" of blacks with albinism (born without melanin) or vitiligo (loss of pigment in patches) regularly seen on display during the eighteenth and nineteenth centuries. Whether exhibited in the 1790s in the Bartholomew Fair in England, in Peale's museum in the newly formed United States, or Barnum's American Museum, this "White Negro" provides what critic Charles D. Martin calls "the haunting figure of the doppelgänger, the mimic that masters its master"[37]—a black body that could turn (or turn out) white. This view of race would give way to one decidedly American, changing from a figure of wonder, much like the White Negro and other freaks would, to one of natural history.

Jefferson wrote on the White Negro as an "anomaly of nature" in his *Notes on the State of Virginia* (1785), mentioning one among his slaves.[38] (It's unclear if they are *his* in other ways.) Jefferson and other Enlightenment-era Americans—which is not to say enlightened—argued over the piebald figures found on stages and on plantations, stoking a fascination with the fantasy, or fear, of black becoming white. The question was skin: Would improved conditions eventually help the Negro turn white? Was blackness a disease, like leprosy, to be cured? "Whether the black of the negro resides in the reticular membrane between the skin and scarf-skin, or in the scarf-skin itself; whether it proceeds from the colour of the blood, the colour of the bile, or from that of some other secretion, the difference is fixed in nature, and is as real as if its seat and cause were better known to us," Jefferson wrote.[39] Soon the White Negro went from an anomaly for Jefferson, as part of a miscellany for Peale, to another kind of nondescript for the likes of Barnum, who exhibited his own Leopard Boys and "White Negroes, or Moors" well into the 1860s. Displaying the piebald body was a way of airing out anxieties of black contamination while testing and applauding the notion that maybe all that dirty, undesirable black could simply wash off. Perhaps doing so could alleviate the guilt of slavery better than blackface might.

All these encounters of race in Europe and America were part of the exploration that anticipated and accompanied supposed enlightenment. White explorers brought back such wonders as piebald boys and natives of elsewhere and placed them on display. We should here, as Percy G. Adams does in his lively *Travelers and Travel Liars*, draw a distinction between the travelogue that crafts imagined journeys to fanciful lands or the moon—which readers in earlier centuries read with both wonder and skepticism, a kind of accepted humbug—and far more troubling "travel liars," who crafted realistic yet false accounts of real places based on trips they never took. "The eighteenth century is unique in the wholesale production of this variety of fictitious travel literature, the kind that because it was designed to be believed should be separated completely from that other prolific variety of the period, the imaginary travel accounts, such as the fantastic, the utopian, the lunar literature, which were not intended to fool the general reader," Adams writes.[40] Rather, the travel liars' "pseudo voyages that were designed to make the public believe them real" were not concerned "with the use of the marvelous to amuse and instruct but with the employment of deception for the sake of money, pride, or a point of view."[41] This is the very stuff of the hoax.

Psalmanazar's *Description* would go further in suggesting to more than one reader early science fiction—not to mention the fictions found in the very racial categories whose science or self-evident nature we were meant to believe. The persistence of such inaccurate yet too often inescapable racial categories testifies less to their accuracy than to the codification of exploration, colonization, and empire. It is Psalmanazar's manipulation of these categories and anxieties that mark him as the forerunner of the modern hoax and mean that the very age of reason was one golden age of the hoax: the supposed age of information is yet another, its contradictions creating what I call our current Age of Euphemism.

Of course the exoticist idea of the travel liar (autocorrect: *traveliar*) did not end with ship-bound exploration. Barnum made this clear: if you couldn't claim you had journeyed somewhere undiscovered, you could instead wonder with the audience if the specimen standing before the audience came from somewhere far off, exotic, wild. "It seems that the fake ethnographer bears a closer resemblance to the true ethnographer than the latter would care to admit," Justin Stagl reminds us in *A History of Curiosity*.[42] By the end of the nineteenth century, no longer would race mean geography as difference—with *monstrous* as an extra category filled with giants, Lilliputians, and other "prodigies" or wonders—but biology as destiny. This exoticist, ethnographic impulse would continue down through the twentieth century to this day.

Do so many hoaxes involve race—indeed, seem to require race in order to properly function—because race is the ultimate white elephant? Or is it that only in the narrative of race in America does the outrageous seem not only possible but also inevitable, has happened and will again?

GIRL WONDERS

Where Enlightenment hoaxes sought to honor the ancestors, however invented, the nineteenth century had begun to like its hoaxes like it liked its poets: tragic. Linked in early death, indeed birthed by it, the Romantic image of the poet as tortured genius was one the hoax nursed. Hoaxing proved crucial to Romantic ideals—the Romantic insistence on originality, a relatively new concept that took inspiration as its aim, is exactly what the hoax undermines yet relies on. An unease with the idea of the writer as unique visionary would manifest itself again and again: in any number of Romantic "spuriosities"; in Coleridge's infamous serial plagiarism; in Byron's vampire writings, indeed his very legend as author, with its stories of horror and superstition; and in such gothic productions as Mary Shelley's *Frankenstein*, with its cautionary tale of authoring the undead. Shelley's eponymous character is a prodigy in the modern, creative sense who crafts a prodigy in the older, monstrous one—this is yet one more explanation of her novel's subtitle, *The Modern Prometheus*.

It would be horror, and pain over pleasure, that would dominate the twentieth century, both in the genius and in the hoax. The genius or governing spirit of the modernism that emerged by the 1890s and peaked in the 1920s was progress. Such change was not one way: just as the Enlightenment saw the Counter-Enlightenment, modernism was met by antimodernism; both saw their share of hoaxes. Such ongoing tensions in the culture between freedom and its opposite were often emblematized in society's body, whether that meant the looser silhouette of the flapper, the broken bodies of the young men and women of the Great War, or the knock-kneed, akimbo dance of Josephine Baker in the wildly popular La Revue Nègre. In the U.S., the changes were further met by the temperance movement, led by women and often tied to Spiritualism, which had fought for Prohibition for over fifty years. Though they won the day in 1919 the teetotalers ultimately lost the war on that nefarious drug, drink—and the suffragists who fought for the vote relented to win it mainly for white women in 1920. The public pleasures of the Roaring Twenties, "the gaudiest spree in history" as F. Scott Fitzgerald put it, would soon be overshadowed by the hangover of the Depression.[43] While changing gender roles seemed the most obvious example of such societal shifts, all would be shot through with race just as the hoax was. Woolf's blackened, bearded-lady hoax prefigured as much.

The modern era's combinations of ladyhood and looseness, black and white, innocence and intelligence, prohibitions against pleasure and exile from all concerns, found their most potent symbol in the "girl wonder." Such female prodigies frequently recur in the 1910s and 1920s, almost as if the young century itself needed literary celebrities its own age. In contrast to the flapper or the suffragette, the girl wonder helped bridge the new and the old, nostalgia for the ideal of Victorian or pioneer childhood and a fear of and fascination with an uncertain future.

In this girl wonders could be said to be emulating the bearded lady herself, whose performance had long been costumed and "customed" as an elegant Victorian lady. "Except for the beards, these women represented the quintessence of refined respectable womanhood," writes Bogdan in *Freak Show*. "A favorite photographic prop" for a bearded lady was her husband, often bearded too. The beard seemed to represent not only oddity but also a kind of wild Victorianism that, untended, could grow. Yet the bearded lady's success was ultimately tied to exposure from the start: in 1853 Barnum's "Swiss Bearded Lady," who went by Madame Josephine Clofullia—note the reinforced ladyhood, French title and all—was publicly accused by a visitor to the American Museum of being an impostor, and really a man. Insulted by the accusation, Barnum took Madame Josephine to doctors who certified her femaleness, gaining much press and sending attendance through the roof. Of course the whole thing had been humbug, the accuser paid by Barnum as part of the stunt.[44] Accusations of humbug helped further fame and defamation simultaneously.

The image of the girl wonder was equal parts sophisticated and old-fashioned, emblematic of late nineteenth-century sentimentalism even as she morphed into an It Girl representative of the Jazz Age.[45] Such sentimentality had already led to what critic Ann Douglas controversially called the "feminization of American culture" over the nineteenth century—a process conducted not just by women but also by liberal male ministers, and one in which temperance, I would argue, played a major part.[46] So did racial innocence, which had emblematized both sentimentality and American "progress" at least since Little Eva's death scene in Harriet Beecher Stowe's *Uncle Tom's Cabin*. Whether characterized as actress, poetess, authoress, or genius—and even "geniusess"—the girl wonder proved fleet-footed and fleeting. If she would counter the world-weary Lost Generation in the public imagination, suggesting a lost world of childhood innocence preserved in the "pixie cut," the girl wonder also seemed primed for the hoax, helping its transition from humor to horror.

The first girl wonder of the twentieth century may well be Peter Pan. From the start, the boy who named J. M. Barrie's modern fairy tale was portrayed by an actress who depicted his perennially young body in flight. This may suggest less boy-played-by-girl than the feeling twenty-first-century poet Tricia Lockwood remembers from growing up: "I consistently felt myself to be not male or female, but the 11-year-old gender: protagonist."[47] The boy who won't grow up provided a permanent emblem of innocence: first in the onstage play, where Wendy and her siblings return home from Neverland; later in the illustrated book *Peter Pan in Kensington Gardens* (1906), in which Neverland is nowhere in sight, the action occurring in the park where children who've fallen out of their prams live; and ultimately in a stand-alone novelization, *Peter and Wendy* (1911), that most resembles the show and story best known today.[48] The nostalgia Peter's youthfulness engendered contrasts sharply in the play with Wendy, who can't help but return home—and can't help but grow old.

Barrie would become quite familiar with hoaxes, being accused of one when he provided a preface to *The Young Visiters* (1919), a novel replete with misspellings said to have been written by a mere child of nine. Despite the young author's photograph as frontispiece and a reprinted manuscript page, many assumed that Barrie had written the charming book in a child's voice, a charge that still comes up. But *The Young Visiters* is genuine—its author, Daisy Ashford, who was older when the book was published, went on to write several other books. None could compete with the praise for her debut, which the *New York Times* called "quite the most humorous thing that ever found its way into print."[49] The book's comedy comes from its youthful attempt to mimic, and mock, the society novel: "Well said Mr Salteena lapping up his turtle soup you have a very sumpshous house Bernard."[50]

The string of acclaimed female prodigies who took hold in the public imagination reveals the contradictions and dangers facing the girl wonder. Foremost among these is Barbara Newhall Follett, who published her first novel with Knopf in 1927, when she was only twelve years old. This was actually a second effort, as an earlier version she had typed herself was lost in a house fire when she was nine. Encouraged by her father and mother, who had homeschooled her, Follett's resulting book, *The House without Windows; and Eepersip's Life There* became a publishing sensation. The author soon became a figure of wonder, not just in her tale—which is wondrous too, at least in its beginnings. Follett would go on to write another book just a year later, *The Voyage of the Norman D.; as Told by the Cabin-Boy*—this last meaning Follett herself. She had just turned fourteen. This far scarcer volume tells the tale of her trip with her mother, Helen Follett, whom her husband soon announced he was divorcing for a younger woman.[51] Follett would travel farther afield with her mother, who wrote her own children's books about their trips; still, the all-but-abandoned family struggled, with Barbara working on the occasional magazine piece along with "Lost Island," a book that would never be published in her lifetime. Unfortunately, that lifespan is unknown: after an argument with her husband in December 1939, Follett left their home "with $30 and a notebook" and, much like her character Eepersip, simply disappeared. Though not a hoax, Follett's story remains a mystery couched in tragedy, the hoax's favorite domain.

But is the prodigy ever allowed to grow up? Must she remain, like Peter

Pan, forever young? In providing an answer, the case of Opal Whiteley resembles a hoax all the more. Oregon-born Whiteley's early career seems be the blueprint for the modern girl prodigy: writing poems and fairy tales as a young girl, she set off to Hollywood to seek fortune and child stardom that never came. Along the way she gave lectures to women's groups, preached the Word, self-published a book of poetry, *The Fairyland around Us*, at the age of twenty-two, and took pictures dressed as an obligatory "Indian." According to the *New Yorker*, "The press called her a genius; she called herself the Sunshine Fairy. Her popularity stemmed from her avoidance of the dryness of science; she was more of a charismatic mystic,"[52] indicating her connection to pseudospirituality, one of the modern hoax's specialties. One photograph advertising a nature lecture depicts her as an almost supernatural gamine with butterflies alighting upon her. The image actually puts one in mind of certain cigarette cards from the 1890s, giveaways resembling our baseball cards: ones printed by the Kimball Company included ethnic types like Circassians, as well as series of butterflies identified by their scientific names that are actually beautiful young women sporting butterfly wings. Opal's butterflies even resemble the faked Cottingley fairy photographs from a few years before, the wings a special effect a studio added later.

Opal followed *Fairyland* with *The Story of Opal* (1920), first serialized in the *Atlantic* by the same Ellery Sedgwick who would buy the hoax Lincoln letters a few years later. Though she was twenty-three at the time, Whiteley said *Story* was not a memoir of childhood but the literal reconstruction of a diary kept when she was six or seven years old, scribbled on scraps of paper and pieces of bark, often in code. What she said her foster mother or stepmother or evil stepsister had torn asunder, Whiteley now literally pieced back together. Photos show her putting together "the decimated diary" while on retainer from editor Sedgwick and the *Atlantic*, appearing like nothing so much as Henri Matisse surrounded by his paper cutouts while composing his late masterpieces. Some have suggested that Sedgwick was swayed by the appearance of Daisy Ashford's *Young Visiters* on the bestseller list.

It appears doubtful now that any of the pieces were genuine. It is one thing for a young child to craft a whimsical story, as Follett, Ashford, and Opal's first book had done; it's another for the girl wonder to claim a youthful diary kept in its own nearly indecipherable code. This can certainly seem the gibberish of the hoax and not merely, as the subtitle would have it, "the journal of an understanding heart." The quite precious prose extends to the lengthy prefatory list of "Characters in the Narrative" that renames the animals and vegetation in the nature around Whiteley after a canon of literary, historical, and hoax references, including "William Shakespeare, an old gray horse with an understanding soul" and "Thomas Chatterton Jupiter Zeus, a most dear velvety wood-rat." As with the Lincoln letters, the sheer size of the cache actually argues against genuineness: as Ted Weeks, who joined the *Atlantic* after Opal's debacle, remembered it, "a lawyer friend of mine estimated it must have taken the stepmother a week of angry tearing to fill that trunk."[53]

Like many modern hoaxes, such surrounding prefatory and explanatory material hints at invention even as the narrative relies on presumed pain. Whiteley's pain is mainly administered by "the mamma," or foster mother, her language supposedly maintaining childhood spelling and grammar:

> Most times I don't know what I get spanked for. And I do like to know, because if I did have knows what I was spanked for, I'd be real careful about doing what it was again, if it was not helping folks of the fields and woods. I have to do that no matter how many spanks I do get for it. But there is so much joy in the woods and does help spank feels to hurt not so much.[54]

If we were Ann Douglas, we might say the diary's hatred of the mother was symbolic of the desire in the 1920s to rebel against the matriarchal impulses that "feminized" nineteenth-century American culture and gave way to the girl wonder in the first place.

Those who believe in the book's genuineness suggest that Whiteley may have been autistic, which might help explain the diary's precision and precociousness for a six-year-old—yet even this says more about our contemporary labels, and corresponding medicalization of difference, than it does about girl wonders. True or false, Whiteley's case speaks to the split—or *splitfoot*—nature of the prodigy. On one hand, the prodigy describes what we all could be, or become. On the other, the prodigy is a figure of nostalgia, a wonder in the original sense of being born special, or at least unique. This nostalgia is not only personal, but in the West, cultural, reminding us of a former time when the freakish prodigy spoke to a fascination with, but ultimately a fear of, wonder. The figure's uncommon monstrosity is not only desired but just as quickly destroyed.

Whiteley's story is a fairy tale of the kind we've grown used to, both in our lives and in the hoax, which makes easy use of the classic fairy tale's moral and its menaced mood. Opal said she was only adopted by the Whiteleys and was really the lost daughter of Prince Henri of Orléans, a familiar fairy tale fantasia. "The mamma" in *The Story of Opal* becomes a symbolic stepmother who regularly beats her, literally over spilt milk. If Opal's own success story was too good to be believed, then her *Story* was too bad.

After causing an initial sensation, the book would lapse out of print a year later. Later in the decade Whiteley did travel to India, where she apparently charmed a maharaja and offered dispatches from the road. Her end, though far off, proved less than happy—by the Second World War, suffering from delusions, Whiteley was placed in an asylum in England where she died almost fifty years later at ninety-four. Her gravestone bears both "Opal Whiteley" and "Françoise Marie de Bourbon-Orléans," the name she settled on as her real one.

ADVENTURE GIRL

While in some ways deeply modern, the girl wonder, like the bearded lady before her, remained oddly traditional. (Much the same can be seen in our more popular reality television shows, such as *The Bachelor*, in which women are called "ladies" and given roses while being offered "fantasy suites" for intimate nights with their suitors.) As bearded ladies were "typically pictured striking feminine poses in elegant surroundings, wearing fashionable dresses and with their hair done in the latest style," according to Bogdan,[55] the girl wonder would vacillate between a pretend Nativeness amidst nature and an extreme whiteness surrounded by borrowed wings that suggested her own innocent nature. The girl wonder relied on such tensions between perceived masculinity and femininity, the past and the current day, fake and real, occupying a different stage than the bearded lady but playing a similar role.

This can be found in faux-naif poet Fern Gravel, "the gentlest of hoaxes" by James Norman Hall, the coauthor of *Mutiny on the Bounty* who published old-fashioned rhyming verse as if a nine-year-old prodigy. Hall set his hoax not only in the Iowa of his childhood but also just after the turn of the century, predicting the height of the girl wonder but also heightening her innocence. Written in Tahiti, Hall's poetry was exoticist in reverse—*Some day, people will travel / To see the home of the poetess, Fern Gravel*—crafting an effect that was both popular and believed, despite or actually because of the crudity of the verses. "We have found the lost Sappho of Iowa!" crowed the

New York Times, responding, in verse no less, to Gravel's *Oh Millersville!* in 1941.[56] Every one of these characterizations—lost, midwestern, Sappho—was playful and nostalgic, sure, but recognized above all Fern's status as strange outlier, an improbable prodigy. She was unreal not just because she was made up but because she seemed a foregone (and bygone) conclusion.

Not long after Fern Gravel was supposed to have existed, the girl wonder would become viewed as another kind of freak, sharing with the so-called armless and legless wonders of the nineteenth and early twentieth centuries the notion that they were "'wonders' not so much for what they did as for the simple fact that they violated people's expectations of what they could do," as Bogdan puts it.[57] Often viewed as helpless, the girl wonder became legless and armless in a symbolic sense. Any overcoming of their births—femaleness *as* malady—became a sign as it was for legless wonders of "their moral worth." In this way the girl wonder, no matter how aggrandized, was still a monster in both senses.

At first glance, screen actress Joan Lowell's memoir *The Cradle of the Deep* (1929) provides the pleasure of an adventure tale and a primer on the prodigy. Beautifully illustrated throughout, Lowell's seafaring chronicle tells the story of her being raised from infancy at sea—complete with unlikely events such as her father the captain stopping a water spout by shooting it with a rifle from half a mile away. Had she studied the success of Barbara Newhall Follett and her seafaring tale from the year before? Or the fakery of Miss Minor and her Lincoln mash notes? *Cradle* quickly hit the best-seller list with an advertised first run of seventy-five thousand copies, becoming a Book-of-the-Month Club selection amidst talk of a movie.

Cradle takes up the symbolic beard long found in the island adventure, using it to spin a seafaring yarn. It's the beard of the pirate and of the shipwreck, a symbol of masculinity and wildness: Whitman's wild bearish pose as one of the roughs and Tennyson's sitting for Julia Margaret Cameron as the wizard Merlin. Yet Lowell doesn't pretend to be a boy who won't grow up; she's a girl among male sailors who teach her how to. "A bucko captain and his Bible charted for Joan the mysteries of sex," one ad reads. While Wendy from *Peter Pan* has a dog for a nanny, Lowell writes that she "learned about women" not from a nursemaid but nurse sharks.

Assigned to review the book, writer Lincoln Colcord, who actually was born at sea, spotted right away its many maritime errors. Irita Van Doren, the book editor of the *New York Herald Tribune,* took Colcord to the publisher's offices to quiz the author, and Lowell very nearly attacked him. Colcord would say later she didn't threaten to fight him, as the *New Yorker* reported; rather, she lunged toward his face, relenting only "when she had advanced to within a few feet of me" and "looked me over scornfully from head to foot. 'Oh,' she exclaimed in a voice of withering contempt, 'if you weren't so *old*!'"[58] The book was revealed to be nautical nincompoop, and even Lowell's claims of being related to the noted Lowell family of American letters proved false—she was really one Helen Joan Wagner of Berkeley.[59]

Lowell's genius was to update the role of the prodigy to that of the ingenue. Where the prodigy implied the past—which quickly impinged upon the young writer whose best days remained behind her—the ingenue instead could, indeed must, stay young as long as possible, emblematic of the future. The term *ingenue* stems from *ingenuous*, once meaning "native-born" or "free"; Lowell's hoax was rather disingenuous. Much like the story of her swimming around potential agents' yachts when she first pitched her book, her book is a publicity stunt. It is this fame-hungry, stunt-filled future that dogs us now, with too many starlets to chart.

For Simon & Schuster, which started as a concern publishing crossword puzzles, *Cradle* was one of their first attempts to go legit, and they stood by their sensation even as her fish story unraveled. (*Ripley's Believe It or Not!* was their other best seller at the time.) Though the book club offered refunds, most people kept their copies, apparently happily humbugged. One of the several editions of *Cradle* I own—the second edition consisting of 25,000 *copies published the same month as the first*—bears a laid-in letter from Captain Harry W. Crosby, owner of the Crosby Direct Line Ferry Company in Washington State, who penciled this largely unpunctuated note:

> I believe it is mostly true. The Alaska part is every word true. I have met her father and his mate. . . . This girl has spent many years aboard ship but not on the Cain she must have been in a small trading schooner with her father in the South Seas. . . . I was talking with a US inspector in Seattle Capt. Hutchersons He sailed with Joan's father His mate also He says Joan is a Excellent navigator He tells me he believes the Book is true Except as to travels and ships.

Lowell is an excellent navigator—but of the rocky seas of fame and notoriety, which she early on perceived as the same thing. The kinds of support this trusting captain offers, despite his being a seafaring sort, are familiar to other, more landlocked readers—the leagues between a book being "every word true" and "true except as to travel and ships" is exactly the area our Joan pretends to be working in. Her brilliance was to assert there is no difference between pretending and aspiration.

Lowell tells a tale so unbelievable she dares us *not* to believe any of it— we want to find a connection to the telling, a family resemblance either to her, her famous adopted name, or the truth she claims. Setting out in search of every word's being true, we settle for "mostly true." Who cares that she got the name of the ship wrong, and claimed it burned and sank when it was in fact still docked safely in California? It is a brilliant form of hoaxing that, if she did not pioneer, then she certainly perfected: creating clear falsehoods the reader, like a fact-checker, can catch, in order that the other lies, let stand, might be believed.

Cradle would spawn a terrific parody by Corey Ford that also became a best seller. *Salt Water Taffy; or, 20,000 Leagues Away from the Sea* (1929) underscores the hoax's stereotypical literary qualities by using only slightly more blatant blackface images for natives on its satirical endpapers: Lowell's "Dance of the Virgins on No Men Atoll" becomes "Kawa Me Back to Old Virgin-ny." Lowell's work has further inspired artwork, including the recent work of Becca Albee, who has created performances based on Lowell in collaboration with her historian father, who owns the very scrapbook kept by the debunker Colcord.[60]

Lowell signals a new world in which the hoax wouldn't be so much cathartic as an act whose mask was not easily shed. To underscore this, in 1934 she narrated a film, *Adventure Girl*, reportedly based on her discredited memoir—nowadays it would be the reality show a star signs up for after her (usually sex, and often self-aware) scandal. A contemporary review sums up the effort: "Joan Lowell's autobiography, *Cradle of the Deep*, taxed one's credulity. Her picture, *Adventure Girl*, which is being shown at the Rialto, does not tax it: it demands its complete surrender."[61] Lowell practically invented film as a form of authentication after the fact—something all too familiar these days, when the reel defeats the real.

This ocular proof is another aspect of the modern hoax, which can seem in its photographic or filmic reenactments a form of distancing from not just experience but also the truth. "Here again some fine photography and many interesting scenes of the Guatemalans and their country lose most of their effectiveness through Miss Lowell's insistence upon the 're-enactment' of her adventures," the *New York Times* would write. "These include her near burning at the stake by a mob of natives (most of whom are smiling amusedly) and what amounts to a comedy chase. Miss Lowell's purpose in making the cruise was to answer those who were skeptical concerning her autobiography."[62]

Lowell's stance of narrating, reenacting, and sensationalizing her own life has become familiar now given our movies, selfies, and reality television. Her brilliance in her mondo-style film with its stock footage and staged natives was to combine all these in ways Barnum might've admired—answering doubts about her being a hoaxer by filming yet another travel lie. *Thanks, Gunga Din!* to quote Lowell speaking to a native. While it discriminates in all the important ways, blackface or the travel lies in hoaxes such as Lowell's book and film do not bother to distinguish between nativeness—whether of the South Seas or the American South, India or American Indians. Such attitudes mean to prepare us for Lowell's stealing native gold through trickery, mistrust, and violence against the Indigenous population in the movie. As with the Cottingley fairies and *Dreadnought* photographs, film, whether still or moving, exposes more than it seeks to conceal.

With *Cradle*, Joan Lowell captured the spirit of the Roaring Twenties, as well as its end. Her hoaxes prove her a beard of the first order, if a different kind; it is the beard as a kind of put-on, a risqué macho the *Dreadnought* hoaxers first imagined for the century. As an "unghost-written autobiography," as the book's promotional material puts it—a phrase implicating autobiography more generally—*Cradle* manages to forecast the ghostly use of imagination not as an extension of experience but as a balm against it. This aghast stance is no longer rare in our time, when people refer to "nonfiction memoir" as if there's any other kind.

Perhaps it is enough to say that Lowell actually wrote a sequel to her first hoax. Despite other published reports I've read, it is in fact her 1933 book *Gal Reporter* that forms the basis for *Adventure Girl*. Never discussed and hard to find today, *Gal Reporter* recounts Lowell's job after her disgrace—though her fall is only hinted at, it is there nevertheless, like the second part of *Don Quixote*, when he's famous because everyone has read the first book in between. Nervous in the newsroom, largely because she's afraid of her cohort sensing the controversy from the first book, she sets out on a voyage with her father—*again*, we might say except Lowell knows that we know that *Cradle* was a pure, or impure, fabrication. Reversing typical trends, instead of writing a memoir *after* a hoax, Lowell wrote her memoir, fake as it was, before her jaunt as journalist.

Her hoax's sequels, its parodies too, became mere extensions of Lowell's career. Though she didn't write much after *Gal Reporter,* she went on to publish *Promised Land* in 1952 about her later life in Brazil, before dying in Brasilia in 1967. She in many ways came to live abroad the life she first concocted at home. Changed from girl to gal, Lowell was the first to see the ways we would use new media to constantly narrativize our lives not just to strangers but also to ourselves. She would in this way become what one writer calls "the grandmother of the memoir fabricators."[63] She's the most famous hoaxer you've never heard of.

Charming, if strange, Lowell's hoax might still have all the makings of a minor masterpiece—or at least a children's cult classic—if it didn't veer into the familiar romance of race. As the hoax so often does, not to mention the seafaring tale more generally, *Cradle* must find itself some natives. They are as ever: bereft wet nurses and lustful virgins, incompetent chiefs and supposed (if unbelievable) cannibals. But does Lowell's book take up such stock settings and characteristics of nativeness—let's call them accusations—to satisfy the predetermined form of a hoax? Her improbable yet predictable, unlikely yet unavoidable natives are all part of the typical hoax package, yet too often part of the actual travelogue too. "Strange cities, weird islands, foreign people, high caste and low. I learned life in the raw, and therefore learned the truth," Lowell would maintain long after the hoax was revealed.[64] To have left out such clichéd elements would have aroused suspicion much earlier that her book was fake.

After viewing the "Dance of the Virgins" on some island in "the South Seas where Joan, the Captain's Daughter, was rocked in the Cradle of the Deep," a young, pretend Lowell back on the ship smothers her body in grease to give it "a glorious shine that would rival any I saw on the island. . . . I pounded on a rain barrel for a tom-tom." Stopped only by her father the captain from reenacting the native scene she's just observed, Lowell says the next morning she "stood by him wrapped up in a flag," expecting a "licking" for misbehaving. Instead, "He reached up to his book shelf and took down an illustrated copy of Dante's *Inferno,* and opened it to the illustrations of women burning in fire in hell. I was cured. I would never be a dancer!"[65] Old Glory and hellfire won't stop Lowell from dancing around the truth.

The exoticist impulse—combining Orientalism, imperialism, racism, and sex—doesn't just see the other as existing only for the self, but strains to convince us that even at home, to themselves, the native or the Negro is a stranger. And usually naked at that. This is far from the radical notion of a modernism that saw the other as a distant yet inseparable self—*Je est un autre*—but rather views the other as never knowable. In the tradition of "traveliars" like Psalmanazar, it is no accident that such popular pastorals take place on islands. Like Peter Pan's Neverland, the "island" is ultimately internal and existential: whether the place being written about is geographically an island or not, the hoax conceives of its locale as a metaphoric isle in order to more easily fly its conquering flag. It's a place of shadow but also where one can lose one's shadow. So many fantasies and hoaxes from the early part of the twentieth century center on ships and islands that they can seem spawned by those shared symbols of isolation and accidental discovery. As the Americas were to Columbus and his inheritors, these are lands considered deserted simply because there's no one white inhabiting them. The blackface such places inspire, their contagious nativeness, happens so frequently that it's become an essential part of the hoax.

It is in this light—or dark—that the girl wonder's racial innocence is thrown into relief. The "redskins" native to Neverland consist of the "Piccaninny tribe"; Tiger Lily, "the belle of the Piccaninnies," is meant to be an Indian, but was played in 1924 by Asian actress Anna May Wong in the first filmed version.[66] Such undifferentiated coloredness, from Indian to Asian to "picaninny," marks Neverland not just as an outpost of the realm of Wonder but also as party to the same deep-seated, exoticist divisions found in the hoax. The hoax is less an exorcism, as Ralph Ellison described blackface, and more a séance—resurrecting long-standing views in a new guise.

To the exoticist, all hoaxes look alike. The *Dreadnought* hoax, like the nineteenth century's before it and Joan Lowell's after, helps us realize that while they pretend to travel, whether afar or through the ether, hoaxes are really about home.

TWO

Neverland

❊⟨On race & other popular delusions⟩❊

*One can be, indeed one must strive to become, tough and philo-
sophical concerning destruction and death, for this is what most
of mankind has been best at since we have heard of man. (But
remember: most of mankind is not all of mankind.) But it is
not permissible that the authors of devastation should also be
innocent. It is the innocence which constitutes the crime.*

—JAMES BALDWIN
The Fire Next Time

Opal Whiteley costumed as an "Indian," 1918.

CHAPTER 5

Cowboys & Aliens

Like the con, the modern hoax now happens with such regularity, and has such a rehearsed set of responses, that its form has almost become formulaic. If related to that American invention the confidence game, the modern hoax now resembles the long con instead of short cons like the shell game or three-card monte. In his fabulous 1940 study, *The Big Con*, David W. Maurer outlines the slang and the structure of the confidence game, as well as its evolution at the start of the twentieth century. As Maurer describes it, the newly invented long con has a "roper," who brings in the mark, and the "inside man," who works the mark once the mark has been brought in. The big leap forward in the long con was the development in the 1910s of "the store," a semipermanent set of displays meant to mirror a stockbroker's shop, gambling hall, or bookie's window, to wow and woo the mark.[1] If around this same time human character changed, so did the hoax.

No longer would the con man pretend to be a loner, a disgruntled employee seeking to stick it to the Man—in truth the inside man—all the while playing the mark's only friend. Modern con artists get marks to believe they are beating not just the house but the *system*. Such a change, perfected at the start of the twentieth century, preyed not only on the greed of marks but also their need to get ahead. This provided the modern con the ultimate advantage: the mark could be brought to the store over and over, milked for money, a coconspirator simply on a losing streak. Hubris proves as effective a lure as money.

For the hoax the symbolic "store" is the stock set of images, race and gender stereotypes, grotesques and fake horrors, that get returned to again and again. This too is practically scripted: as Luc Sante notes in his introduction to a reissue of *The Big Con*, the con itself is ritualized, featuring "the roper and the inside man, whose roles are as archetypal as Punch and Judy, or Mr. Tambo and Mr. Bones in minstrelsy." British and American, such archetypes enact racial and sexual, if not violent, fantasies. Indeed, Punch and Judy, or blackface minstrelsy, use violence or race as a frequent cover for questions of gender and sex. The hoax is not far behind, substituting ritual for reality. "The big con can also be considered as a form of theater . . . staged with minute naturalistic illusionism for an audience of one, who is moreover enlisted as part of the cast," Sante writes.[2] The hoax widens this cast, asking for our confidence and cooperation.

Yet while the long con, when done right, need never have to end, the hoax is all about its discovery, hinted at all along. Hindsight is the hoax's best light. The hoax is rather a kind of coded confession, revealing not only a deep-seated cultural wish but also a common set of themes—or feints or strategies—that add up to a ritual. This is why we often are not just fooled, but made fools of, by the hoax—indicted by its revelations, not of what's true but of what we truly believe.

The modern hoax, filled with hints and ironies and practically premonitions, is almost begging to be caught—perhaps because once revealed the hoax is only getting started. Exposed, the hoaxer or plagiarist predictably resorts to a script as familiar as the long con. Let's call it the Five Stages of Grift: first, denial, denial, denial; next, redirection; then, admission of a lesser crime, the error excused away as stemming from haste or emotional turmoil or a claim of "parody"; then, in the face of overwhelming evidence, a full if halfhearted confession meant to redeem, though inevitably dogged by some of the same difficulties with telling the truth that got the hoaxer (or politician) here in the first place. What inevitably follows, last in the hoax script, is the publication of a new novel—or a book-length confession—or the combo platter, the reprinting of the disgraced fake "memoir" now with "novel" in small type below the title. Such books now end as they began, with a plea.

Though it often insists on innocence, often as a pervasive, inevitable state, the hoax really believes no one is innocent. This may be something the hoax shares with pornography, which regularly plays with innocence—teacher's pets and schoolgirl uniforms being de rigueur—only to suggest that innocence is just a guise, a sheer layer of clothing, a lusty librarian's hair in an updo.

Pornography is the Victorian era's underbelly, its elaborate underthings notably used to highlight its secrets. The gothic got the overcoats, porn the garters: they came together in the tortured Victorian iconography of real-life yet unsolved Jack the Ripper and nightmarish Dr. Jekyll and Mr. Hyde. Primitiveness is a mere potion away.

Letting your hair down in porn is not just a form of relaxation, or signal of privacy, but a transformation from prude to playmate more immediate and powerful than Superman in a phone booth. The hoax can resemble porn too in that both forms are hyperreal, less interested in revelation than in being revealing. In both so much is faked—the bodies too these days— that they need to constantly remind you they are real. Reality needn't always insist on itself; in fact, to be reality, it mostly mustn't. Nowadays, *realness*— with its "reality shows" and social spectacles—reminds us of itself far too often, providing a further fog from which only reality can wake us.

Yet pornography is pornography because it should *not* be seen. This has been the argument against the category called pornography since its coining in the mid-nineteenth century: that porn doesn't affect the judger, necessarily, who is mature enough (and rich and male enough) to handle it. Even as it anticipated its audience, pornography was invented as a category in the Victorian era to be a private thing, not public—at least till recently, when it is far aboveground, if not mainstream (so much so that *Playboy* for a time went the other way, eliminating full frontal nudity, coyness the new vanguard). Or was porn always a public view of privates? The definers of pornography seek to limit it not for themselves, but on behalf of those more innocent and corruptible. Perversion, not to mention sex, was regularly perceived as happening somewhere else: "Spanish fly," a "French letter," "the English disease," all are euphemisms that designate distance, if not xenophobia. Our age has only perfected and furthered this trend, with a proliferation of euphemisms for sex and for the race of those having it on websites too numerous to mention.

After being revealed, the hoaxer may still claim there's part of the culture that cannot be known, that doesn't exist except for her interpretation, *so she had to make it up*. But the fact remains: when a hoaxer takes on the identity of a Native person or Aborigine, "half-breed" or "half-caste"; when she pretends she is from the ghetto or a drug addict or a princess from Javasu; when he says he was a concentration camp survivor who watched hungry children chew their own fingers; when he fakes being a white-skinned Formosan or a truck-stop transsexual hooker: hoaxers erase those their story purports to represent. If we think a people incapable of language and without origins, the hoaxer says, why do we need an original language? Surely my fake one will do.

Like the modern hoax, the modern circus not accidentally parallels the start of pornography as a distinct category in the Victorian era: one means the extraordinary body on display; the other the ordinary body, frequently gargantuan, on extraordinary display. This is the main difference between earlier hoaxes and our current ones: once the hoax meant to glorify; now it wishes to horrify.

PILGRIMS OF THE WILD

Its own kind of circus, the hoax offers a kind of double exposure, a metaphoric spirit photograph. Exposure in a very real sense is especially relevant for those hoaxers who pretend to be Native American or First Nations members from Canada, not to mention the vast array of "pretendians" gracing our silver screens, spirit tintypes, and slanted stages. Or was the hoax always just a skin game?

The American Indian had become by the twentieth century a regular sideshow attraction, whether at the fairgrounds or the nickelodeon, fit only for a cage or a stage. For shows like Buffalo Bill's Wild West, which ran from the 1880s to the 1910s, the possessive was important: Wild Bill Cody's West became the white audience's. The Wild West show's reenactments of Indian attacks toured both home and abroad, providing a living display of the Manifest Destiny that whites had invoked to justify expansion in America and even across Europe. Always popular, the show gained special notoriety at the 1893 World's Fair, or Columbian Exposition, in Chicago, appearing outside the fair's "White City" that gave us the debut of the Ferris wheel, "cannibalistic Samoans," and a "Dahomey Village" of sixty-nine "native warriors." Adding to this was the first appearance of a woman paid to pretend to be Aunt Jemima: it was a banner moment for fakes and freaks. As critic Robert Bogdan convincingly argues, "The Columbian Exposition contributed to the growth and popularization of the freak show in many ways," setting the precedent of ethnological exhibits at world's fairs and beyond.[3] This tradition of exhibition as ethnography leads directly to bizarre productions like the misguided flop *The Lone Ranger* from 2013: in the film Johnny Depp's Tonto is trapped in a natural history museum, safe and unsound amid the panoramas and tableaux, telling not his Native story but the masked man's. *Who's this "we," Kemosabe?* The real mask for Tonto and the Lone Ranger is a white one.

Besides reinforcing notions of the West as a continuous battle and justifying Native displacement and death, the Wild West show also cemented the figure of the imaginary Indian—a decidedly Plains Indian look, complete with war bonnet—that would prove dominant in popular thought and in the broader West ever since. This did not mean that Buffalo Bill didn't include actual Indigenous people, such as Sitting Bull—just that, like the buffalo hunted nearly to extinction by the early twentieth century, the Natives the show depicted meant to represent a way of life that was slipping away. For his part, Buffalo Bill had spent his early career bragging about killing both Indians and buffalo, having been nicknamed after what he sought to conquer. The show's advertisements made this explicit, billing it not as entertainment but as an "object lesson," not reenactment but history. As Jonathan D. Martin has reconstructed, even before they could see the show, visitors in Chicago first had to go through the "Indian Camp" that pretended to be authentic; there would then be a "race of races" in order of perceived evolution and sophistication, starting with Indians, then gauchos, then whites, then Cody himself. A chronology of scenes from "The Primeval Forest" onward through "The Rifle as an Aid to Civilization" would climax with a proclaimed reenactment of the Battle of Little Bighorn, or Custer's last stand, with Cody and his "Rough Riders" arriving a moment too late to save the day. It would be from Buffalo Bill's troupe that Teddy Roosevelt took the name of his conquering army of soldiers in the Philippines, making the colonial circle complete.[4] The hoax likewise pretends to evolve from spectacle to horror to history, from past to the present, with racial categories and extinction remaining first and foremost.

The Columbian Exposition exposed the ways the twentieth century would be obsessed with *wildness*, and its end. The American century went beyond displaying ordinary native peoples—or fabricating "wild men" like Barnum's "Wild Men of Borneo" and "The Wild Australian Children," who in truth had developmental disabilities—into displaying and keeping live native people in zoos or anthropology departments. The exoticist eye did not exactly differentiate between various native states: the Congolese tribesman Ota Benga would first appear in the Louisiana Purchase Exhibition of 1904 (alongside "dog-eating" native Filipinos) before being housed two years later in the primate display at the Bronx Zoo; Ishi, billed as "the last wild Indian," native to what's now California, would spend the rest of his life in the Anthropology Museum at Berkeley starting in 1911. Zoos could be human too. These notorious cases further linked native exhibition and extinction in the public's eye and mind. In both instances the extinction, practically promised by their labels, was literal, with Ishi dying from unknown diseases he was most certainly not immune to and Benga committing suicide, both in 1916. Against tribal dictates, doctors not only dissected Ishi but kept his brain until it was repatriated to his people nearly a century later. Before then, his brain "lived" in the Smithsonian, captive even after death.

What all this captured, besides actual people, is the racism of science and the science of racism. Filled with freaks of culture, these "human zoos," we must remember, were family entertainments—ones that excluded the people on display from the so-called family of man. The idea may help us understand how troubling the display of natives has been; how trumped up and tied to "natural history" when actually it's neither. The hoax remains content to be ogled, or better yet, to do the ogling.

Hoaxes have their own unnatural history in figures like Grey Owl, who, starting in the 1920s, wrote articles and books on his First Nations upbringing, toured and testified as a famous conservationist, and became revered as an exemplar of his people. Claiming to be the son of a Scotsman and an Apache woman—or Ojibwe, the story kept changing—Grey Owl did live among the Ojibwe in Ontario, often serving as a tracker and guide, trading furs and pelts with whites, and fathering at least one child with a Native woman. Yet as those he lived among well knew, none of this made him Native. Grey Owl was really born well off and white as Archibald Belaney in Britain, where he had grown up under the spell of the dime novel Indian he would later become in the Americas.

While serving as a guide in Canada, he met the First Nations woman, Anahareo, who would become his wife and the symbolic muse of his books, which he began publishing in the United States and Britain starting with *The Men of the Last Frontier* (1931). With the publication of *Pilgrims of the Wild* (1934) and the children's book *Sajo and the Beaver People* (1936), Grey Owl gave up trapping and became a famed environmentalist. Returning to Britain wearing fabricated, unearned war bonnets and garbled Indian garb, he spoke to sold-out crowds about nature and saving the beaver, his favorite endangered cause. In writing to his editors at Scribner's, which would include the famed Maxwell Perkins, Grey Owl preemptively included a "life history of myself, written in the third person" to combat "more than one accusation brought against me that I have a ghost writer" and rumors that he was not who he said he was: "I am not at all anxious for publicity, but a lot that is unwelcome is being handed out, and if I am to be known at all, I want to be known, on this Continent at least, for what I am proud of being—a woodsman of the old school, partly of Indian blood, with an Indian training and background."[5] His books too invoke disappearing ways of life: he speaks of a "last frontier," after all; invoking "the wild," Grey Owl promoted the very wildness Barnum hawked and humbugged decades before. Always pseudoscientific, the fake was pseudospiritual now too.

The *pseudospirituality* the twentieth century exhibited, often literally, would regularly center on the notion of the Native, whether the American Indian or any Indigenous people. Such a free-floating primitivism renders Natives or Negroes mere symptoms or symbols—angelic beings or brutish demons, childlike wonders or ancient freaks. It is this "inhuman" character that the hoax made off with and made use of.

On his extensive lecture tours, Grey Owl—or Wa-sha-quon-asin, as he sometimes called himself—powerfully mirrored back the combination of exhibition and extinction that white audiences came to expect in representations of Indigenous peoples. *How*, he'd say, like a Saturday matinee Indian, which is pretty much what he was, finally realizing the dreams he had while growing up in a stuffy, well-heeled Victorian home. (The greeting is not in fact Ojibwe or Apache.) On tour, he visited the two spinster aunts who raised him after first his father and then his mother abandoned him as a child; the trio, dining out at the nicest hotel in town, must have appeared to onlookers like a strange grouping rather than the motley affinity that makes up any family.[6] As it had proved for whites for centuries before, pretending to be Indian helped make him, if not deeply Native, then all natural and new.

After another lucrative tour, Grey Owl returned to the Canada he claimed as home and died rather suddenly in 1938 from "pneumonia aggravated by drink and physical exhaustion." The end of his reputation happened just as quickly: the very next day he was exposed as a fraud by the *North Bay Nugget*, which had held the story till his death; his friend and British publisher Lovat Dickson would publish *Half-Breed*, a detailed exposé, a year later. (Anahareo, who wrote her own fascinating memoir, claimed she hadn't known his true identity.) Grey Owl had kept his hair and skin dyed to conform to a "half-breed" background: his causes and his story became tainted by the same brush. But there's always a "cause" behind the hoax, a message that the fake messenger fails to realize his fraud actually testifies to.

There has been some recouping of Grey Owl's reputation with the environmentalism and "back to the land" movements of the 1960s and 1970s; he would become, by 1999, the subject of a so-so Richard Attenborough biopic starring Pierce Brosnan. Yet, in the end, Grey Owl wasn't a tour guide of the wilderness or an ambassador to the Great North but a guide on how to fake effectively. To render him as an environmentalist ahead of his time, or his hoax as somehow honoring Native ways, is to ignore the ways in which Grey Owl's very ideas of extinction and "the Wild" are tied up not only with each other but also with white stereotypes about Indigenous peoples. They all stoke the suspicion that Natives are just fake whites.

There's another danger with the hoax: actual issues of value, of conservation and change, become extinct instead. Grey Owl touted his conservationist cause as not just inherently worthy but in need of Indianness to be more effective. Much like the physical image he projected, Grey Owl's Nativeness—and his being able to write despite it, as he offensively reemphasized—are the chief thing he stresses about himself. In films and in person Grey Owl would invite all comers into his house, which was sponsored by the National Parks of Canada—a home shared with his beavers quite literally, as it enclosed part of their dam and water—providing tourists with exactly what they wished for, likely because he was a tourist himself. Grey Owl's short films now appear just another kind of skin flick.[7]

No wonder his name came to grace outdoor catalogs of all things Indian well into the 1950s: his wasn't ever a cause so much as a costume. I have begun to see his pictures and books, sold the way circus folk and Circassian Beauties did their cartes des visite, cabinet cards, and freak show "pitch pamphlets," as no different from any other sideshow ballyhoo: advertisements meant to entice, and often trick, us rubes. Grey Owl too was selling a fantastical past—but where so-called freaks (who often didn't mind the term) sought to deliver entertainment, they often were who they said they were. This is reinforced by the fact that circus folk had names for fake sideshow acts: "gaffs."[8] Grey Owl's gaff promised dire warnings, suffering, guilt, and a bleak future, all of which his high-tone audiences apparently wanted to hear. In photos, to appear more authentically Indian, he scowled.

The frightful future that Grey Owl predicted was not chiefly for himself, nor even the Wild, but for the hoax, which from here on out mostly offered a potent, modern mix of fantasy and fear.

GOING NATIVE

The hoax warns us without warning and informs us without informing; it welcomes us into its arms, where, though it says we have nothing to worry about, it gives voice to our fears and fantasies as unremittingly real. Art can do this too, but it needn't always insist it is real to do so. The hoax, like pornography, shows us what we didn't always know we want, just as the acts it depicts are all an act. There are other, far dirtier jobs the hoax has in mind.

Pornography actually provides the template for several modern hoaxes, from *I, Libertine* (1956) to *Naked Came the Stranger* (1969), books whose very titles inspired their hoaxes. But in the case of Tim Barrus, who wrote several fake memoirs under the made-up Indian name "Nasdijj" in the early part of the twenty-first century, the transformation from porn to hoax proves literal. Before suddenly becoming Navajo, Barrus, born white, had for years written gay porn.

Titles from this earlier incarnation include *Mineshaft* (1984), whose cover and opening lines prove explicit even for the gay pulp genre, and *My Brother, My Lover* (1985), first published by the influential Gay Sunshine Press, which issued a hardcover deluxe edition. The first chapter of *Mineshaft*, named after a real-life S & M club, claims to be about honesty while repetition undermines it: "We are both very honest. And gay. Very gay. You cannot be more gay than we are. Gay, gay, gay." The back cover sets up the book as not just exploring a demimonde—that would be familiar to the genre at least—but also exposing a wider gay world that's somehow false: "It was a strange world filled with strange people, with weird drag queens, bars that catered to the seamier elements, flesh that was pierced and ringed, leather fetishes combined with sadistic practices. Could he find his *true identity* in a gay world gone mad? Did he want to?"[9] Writing in the 1980s, Barrus arrives rather late on the scene to resort to the 1960s practice of gay porn condemning its same-sex pleasures as neurotic and "mad"—or to employ the pretense and disdain of so-called white-jacketed pulps that pretended to be clinical studies of a "twilight world" gone wrong, never mind if what they described felt so right. In the end the book suggests there may be a false way to be gay—though coming long enough after the sexual and gay revolutions, it does so, a cynic might say, only in order to establish a taboo it could then turn right around and violate.

Soon Barrus would reinvent himself by claiming to be Native American, not just with a pseudonym but an entire assumed identity. He took pictures, signed books, and accepted prizes as "Nasdijj," an imaginary Indian who duplicates the dark double found throughout American letters. Critic Leslie Fiedler, a pioneer of cultural studies, has written of this dark double in his classic *Love and Death in the American Novel* (first published in 1960). There he argues that the American novel, afraid of adult (hetero)sexuality, instead depicts its conflicts in homosocial male–male relationships, from *The Last of the Mohicans* to *Moby-Dick* to much of Hemingway. Later, Fiedler would write profoundly about the ways these racial conflicts were not merely confined to fiction: "In our very lives, we have come to repeat this pattern, individual biography recapitulating cultural history. Born theoretically white, we are permitted to pass our childhood as imaginary Indians, our adolescence as imaginary Negroes, and only then are expected to settle down to being what we really are: white once more. Even our whiteness, however, threatens to become imaginary."[10] Impostors such as black pretender Rachel Dolezal, who darkened her skin, twisted her hair, and served as a regional NAACP head, suggest such racial imaginaries are still in play. Inhabiting the Native or the Negro, whether living as or imagining oneself as one, proves a white rite of passage—not to mention a plain old right.

You could say this movement from imaginary Native to imaginary Negro to imaginary whiteness best describes the shifts in our American gothic. Jean-Jacques Rousseau's influential eighteenth-century idea of the "noble savage" had sought Enlightenment among the more natural, human state—one that his fellow Europeans might emulate. Yet the American colonists and criminals shipped from Britain frequently saw the land like they did its original people: as savage and in need of ennobling, or at least taming. Where Europe had the medieval ruin as the inspiration for the gothic and its largest symbol of moral decay, "Gothicism took hold so readily in the American imagination because it replaced the ruling class with the savage figure as chief adversary to settlers in the New World," John Cooley writes in *Savages and Naturals*.[11] The noble savage suggested ruin as a path to be avoided and a symbol to be embraced, fates that befell the Indian.

It wasn't just a whites-only racial innocence that developed by the nineteenth century but a corresponding idea of unavoidable racial ruin: first in the doomed Indian; then "the black" for whom darkness was both unforgivably permanent and reassuringly removable. That this American gothic involved Native Americans seen as childlike (continuing a Calvinist notion of children born inherently tainted with sin) and African Americans often rendered as children in peril (which is to say, as never quite being children) makes this more pointed and poignant. Such ideas remain hard to shake, and impinge on our daily lives—or shall we say daily deaths?—as with black and Indian children tried as if adults or simply shot practically on sight. It happens enough that we might say we've all been hoaxed.

The very idea of the double is suggested by the gothic: "Always present in the Gothic is this: two things that should have remained apart—for example, madness and science; the living and the dead; technology and the human body; the pagan and the Christian; innocence and corruption; the suburban and the rural—are brought together, with terrifying consequences,"[12] critic Gilda Williams notes. More often than not, the hoax doesn't collapse these dualities in one body, as the gothic monster or Jekyll-and-Hyde does, but externalizes them in all manner of dark doubles. "Double stories seem to proliferate when people sense an unnegotiable divide between the true or natural self and society, between nature and culture," Mark Edmundson writes in *Nightmare on Main Street*.[13] In America, as in the hoax, this divide was represented over and over again by race.

The hoax exploits this divide, and invents others, its doubles multiplying far beyond any capacity to comprehend or doubt. The novel, also spawned around the same time as the gothic in the early eighteenth century, embraced the double too—but where the novel had the sense and sensibility *not* to call such doublings reality, and the gothic delighted in its decided artifice, the hoax pretends its dark double is not only real but representative. The brutal blacks, painted Indians, apocalyptic Aborigines, and frenzied females of the hoax we are meant to believe. The hoax's divisions are always long, and wide, profiting off the fragments and fractures of society and proliferating in times of tension. Operating in the gap between what we wish and what we fear, the hoax renders rumors real.

PLAYING INDIAN

If not as a tale of terror, or ruin, American culture often recast the "encounter" between Europeans and Natives—or the master and slave—as a love story. As with the untrue legend of a romance between Joseph Smith and Pocohantas, "the new dream begins with the old, in fact, presupposes it; but it goes further, for it not only imagines joining with Indian or Negro in pseudo-matrimony, or being adopted by some colored foster-father, but being reborn as Indian or Negro, *becoming the other*,"[14] Fiedler notes.

With all this in mind, Barrus's move from gay porn to redface is not so vast a distance. One of the earliest and most important gay pulps, and by many counts still the best-selling one ever, is *Song of the Loon* (1966), a book of love or at least sex between a white man and an Indian one on the frontier. Written under the pseudonym Richard Amory (get it?), the book spun off a trilogy—all told, nearly a third of all gay men read the book in the

1960s and 1970s, some have declared.[15] The book's back cover announces "a mystical blend of elements from Hudson's Green Mansions, J. F. Cooper's Leatherstocking tales, and the works of Jean Genet. What evolves is unique and inimitable . . . an unforgettable fantasy."[16] As this suggests, *Song of the Loon* remains well aware that it's fantasy, "a gay pastoral": "The author wishes it clearly understood that he has, unfortunately, never known or heard of a single Indian remotely resembling Singing Heron or Tlasohkah or Bear-who-dreams," a small prefatory note points out. "He has taken certain very European characters from the novels of Jorge de Montemayor and Gaspar Gil Polo, painted them a gay aesthetic red, and transported them to the American wilderness."[17] This wilderness, of course, resided well inside.

Yet Barrus's books, even when admittedly fiction, were always about fakery, with realness as only an effect and wildness their motivator. The doubling of *My Brother, My Lover*, whose contents prove more literary than its title, is in some ways a prelude to Barrus's later literary works, such as *Anywhere, Anywhere* (1987) and *Genocide: The Anthology* (1988), which extends its Orientalist fantasies into an unsteady mix of fantasy and fear, science fiction and gothic, romanticizing the various genocides he claims to be protesting. It is hard to render the tricky typography of the book's chapter openings, which mask the mundaneness of the stereotypical content:

EVERYTHING WAS PROGR
AM. JIA WAS FROM A SUBO
RDINATE SYSTEM OF NEO
SCENE PLANETS THAT HAD
ORIGINALLY BEEN SEEDE
D BY A RACE OF NOW MYT
HIC EARTH-HUMANS, FIE
RCE, EDUCATED, AND FU
LL OF RELIGION. HUMAN
S WHO HAD ONCE BEEN

called oriental.

Lowercase though it may be, the character Jia's Asianness is central: his "system revolved around three exploding clusters of intermediary suns whose collective name was Asia. His dark quiet features were handsome, almost delicate. His attentive almond eyes were wise and beautiful beyond his years. . . . Jia had no age. He simply was. It was a mathematical concept as Asian as his soul."[18] Barrus keeps the "darkness" of his double simultaneously literal and symbolic; characters are Asian to their soul, even or especially in the book's science fiction sections, by turns sexual or asexual, punished and punisher—in short, irretrievably Other. This is familiar territory for the hoax and the exoticist. Barrus's is a poetics of pain, the yellowface but preface to the redface to come.

In *Anywhere, Anywhere* Barrus would further hint that he himself had been a Vietnam veteran. The book may be labeled fiction, yet like many a hoax, the allure is that its stories may be all too real, mere coded confessions—so much so that when "Nasdijj" was finally debunked it would have to be repeatedly said that Barrus wasn't really a vet. Is this studied ambiguity the author's or the audience's fault? Certainly if he had pretended at military service, he would not be alone—*Stolen Valor*, a fascinating book by military scholars B. G. Burkett and Glenna Whitley, charts this phenomenon of phony veterans, especially surrounding Vietnam. *Stolen Valor*'s extensive catalog of pretend veterans with their thrift-shop Purple Hearts and false stories of "covert ops," influenced by movies and imaginary shared trauma—with the character Rambo as a "touchstone for pretenders, a pattern to follow consciously and unconsciously"[19]—too well applies to *Anywhere* to be completely ignored. Rambo is not only a lost warrior but a symbolic white-Indian survivalist, greased up in militant blackface, out for revenge. In hindsight, *Anywhere* is Barrus's first sortie into a falsified self.

By equating struggles and identities, Barrus crosses that wide line between saying all humanity is shared and enters into the inhumaneness of erasing individual histories. "FIRST the Native American was quarantined/detained AND THEN he was infected." Barrus's seeming nonfictional recounting of other detention camps and forms of quarantine links gay history with Angel Island's troubled one—as a site for unjustified quarantine of Asian immigrants, often for years, off the California coast. In other hands this connection could have proved interesting, especially at the onset of AIDS activism and the real threat of quarantine—yet in discussing inhumane conditions it is strange how inhumane the prose is too, making the Native the social site of suffering. Even here Nasdijj cements the hoax's relation to pulp, and porn, which both titillate and caution; like porn, the goal of the hoax is to see just how long you can keep it up. Barrus's only innovation was to skim off the pulp from the porn, retaining its sadistic and masochistic elements, drawing first blood. From here on out his would be misery as pornography.

With Nasdijj, almost all aspects of the modern hoaxer come to the fore, scouting a familiar trail: a motive, if not financial, then of previously elusive "success"; plagiarizing another's pain; suffering as a form of salvation; extreme physical grotesquerie bordering on the gothic; even the Romantic idea of the prodigy and early death that will come to dominate the hoax. If "youth in peril" is a popular move not just confined to the hoax, Nasdijj marries it to the fake memoir with its frequent "white Indians" and "redskins." "The more he wrote, the more awful a life he revealed," Andrew Chaikivsky wrote in *Esquire* after the truth was revealed.

Nasdijj first came to national attention by writing to *Esquire* claiming to be Native American and seeking publication of more Native voices—at least his. "In the entire history of *Esquire* magazine, you have never once published an American Indian writer. This oversight is profound. I am a Navajo writer who has written (enclosed) an article about the death of my son from fetal alcohol syndrome. FAS is an issue of concern to Native Americans. It should be an issue of concern to white people, too."[20] This critique-as-solicitation led to *Esquire*'s publishing him—the resulting article won acclaim in 1999 as a finalist for a National Magazine Award and ultimately led to a book deal with Houghton Mifflin the next year.

In his debut memoir, *The Blood Runs Like a River Through My Dreams* (2000), Nasdijj describes a life of caring for a dying adopted son, while also dropping hints at his hoaxing: "I wonder if criminal mischief is a misdemeanor. They say criminals are always attracted back to the scene of the crime. I drive away. Repelled." Like Barrus's hinted-at vet status, *Blood* and its two sequels make the Native a bright red symbol of suffering—though impersonating a veteran is a federal crime, and impersonating Indians an American tradition dating from at least the Boston Tea Party. Though it supported the publication of *Blood*, the publishing house must have grown weary of rumblings that something was amiss, or of Nasdijj's increasingly erratic behavior even when winning prizes, as Houghton Mifflin would not publish either of the sequels. Both went on to decreasing sales before Matthew Fleischer exposed Nasdijj in an *LA Weekly* article called "Navahoax" in 2006.

Though *Blood*'s author bio claims "'Nasdijj' is Athabaskan for 'to become again,'" this is literally nonsense—the word Nasdijj is "gibberish," as one Native speaker describes it to Fleischer. Such brazen fauxness does more than just hint at the author's hoax—and it should be said, reads more stereotypically Middle Eastern or "East Indian" than American Indian; rather, it contains the strange suggestion that the Navajo language is itself false. Like

Tonto's faux Native English, the hoax regularly says language too can be made up, signifying that there may well have been no language there to begin with. Call it *English-ish*: "Nasdijj," in his bio and his very (and very made-up) name, is a direct descendant of earlier hoaxes with their faux languages, from Psalmanazar's fake, eighteenth-century Formosan and Princess Caraboo's ludicrous pseudo-lingo from the made-up island Javasu in the nineteenth century; to the "Swahili" and "rum lingo" found in Virginia Woolf's *Dreadnought* hoax. All studiously avoid elements of the actual language they are meant to speak, largely because their talk isn't intended to represent a tongue so much as replace it.

Given that most people would hate to be represented as talking a certain way they feel they don't, much less being mistaken for being from a neighborhood they're not actually from, it's strange how blasé we can be about the otherizing of others. I've seen posts saying the reaction to Nasdijj was merely from oversensitive Native Americans—one blog calls such critics "often low-blood-quantum people springboarding themselves into fame and (they hope) fortune," a description more suited to Barrus than his critics.[21] As such comments indicate, at stake here is *blood*: the system of "blood quantum," or the quantification of how Indian a person is based on traceable ancestry, seeks what one scholar friend notes is the opposite of the "one drop rule" applied to blacks.[22] One drop of blood is enough to make you and yours black for eternity; if Native, you must track your bloodlines back and prove you have more than enough blood to qualify. Both rules, not just social but governmental and legal, reveal the elaborateness and seeming arbitrariness of disenfranchisement.

In the short first chapter of Barrus's *Blood*, the word *Navajo* appears well over a dozen times. Nasdijj's car, named Old Big Wanda, is described as somehow indigenous: "That pickup is of the earth." It is a bit like reading certain male authors, who, writing in the voice of a woman inevitably have her go on and on about her bosom and newly found body; or the book written in blackface that continually refers to the narrator's brown skin. (Sorry, I mean "mocha.") Self-consciousness is the only consciousness such characters possess. While it is fine to write as someone else—and at times powerful and necessary—it requires skill and ethical considerations, even if writing about one's own family. These self-conscious descriptions surrounding a supposedly unique existence provide a clue to that existence's unbelievability.

If that weren't enough, Nasdijj is the only one with a seemingly "Native" name—all the other Navajo people mentioned in the book bear names like Mary Potato and Tommy Nothing Fancy, as if they are extras from some fantasy novel or children's story (say, Carl Sandburg's *Rootabaga Stories*) in which people are named for their whimsical or pedestrian or scary qualities. This is one of the most troubling aspects of Nasdijj's tales, already meant to be troubling—he adopts not only Tommy but allegedly Indian ways of naming, made colorful and decidedly colored.

These ways he also stole. Actual Native writers, especially Sherman Alexie, had been saying well before Nasdijj's first book was published that he was a fake—what's more, Nasdijj is himself a double drawn directly from Alexie.[23] As Alexie wrote in *Time* magazine after Nasdijj became widely exposed, Alexie was born hydrocephalic and required surgery in infancy that left him prone to seizures like Nasdijj's made-up son; he had, in fact, earlier published a story based on this for *Esquire* magazine, the very place Nasdijj had accused, wrongly it turns out, of never publishing Native writers. That Alexie's story went on to be gathered in *Best American Short Stories 1994* and became the basis of the acclaimed film *Smoke Signals* (1998) suggests that *Esquire*'s editors if not readers should have been wary or at least aware of Nasdijj's derivative Nativeness. "Nasdijj's stories also bear uncanny resemblance to the works of N. Scott Momaday, Leslie [Marmon] Silko, and especially Michael Dorris, whose memoir *The Broken Cord* depicts his struggle to care for his adopted FAS-stricken Native Alaskan children," the *LA Weekly* exposé would say later.[24]

Yet few outside the Indigenous community seemed interested in hearing about Nasdijj's nicking. Alexie describes his feelings about being ripped off: "Angry, competitive, saddened, self-righteous and more than a little jealous that this guy was stealing some of my autobiographical thunder, I approached Nasdijj's publishers and told them his book was not only borderline plagiarism but also failed to mention specific tribal members, clans, ceremonies and locations, all of which are vital to the concept of Indian identity. They took me seriously, but they didn't believe me."[25] This is the infectious and dangerous quality of the hoax, another of its harms: the true stories in all senses—Alexie's is a fictionalized autobiography, after all—that the hoax makes use of end up not quite heard.

Nasdijj gives not only his own adopted (or stolen) identity fetal alcohol syndrome but also his adopted son: "Tommy was the one thing I did that was good and didn't fail. The rest of it is ephemeral. The fetal alcohol syndrome was a reality. I gave him happiness and joy and fishing tackle and trucks and dogs."[26] Nasdijj resorts to reinforcing "reality" like his supposed Navajo-ness over and over, saying, "My Indian wife and I took Tom into our hearts and into our home when he was brand spanking new. The particulars are irrelevant. Infants are like freight trains."[27] Does he mean that they come roaring into your lives? Or that if you wait long enough another will come along?

Certainly Nasdijj has a number of other dark doubles running through his books, freighted and fraught, their contents obscure, characters' names emblazoned on their sides like a boxcar. Mary Potato is, of course, an alcoholic who "could have been my mom" mainly because she is drawn from the same stock images as his Native falling-down-drunk mother, who marries Nasdijj's "cowboy father." It quickly becomes clear Barrus is playing Cowboys and Indians—or more pointedly, as in the steampunk film from 2011, *Cowboys & Aliens*. The movie's title is a pitch masquerading as a title (and actually was conceived that way, the concept made into a comic book explicitly to be sold to Hollywood).[28] There cannot be a movie called *Indians & Aliens* because that would be redundant. Though there are actual Native Americans, both as actors and characters, in the movie—including one of the leads from Alexie's film *Smoke Signals*—as with the Wild West show the Indians in *Cowboys & Aliens* too easily become figures of alienation even in their own land:

> Mary Potato was a Navajo, too. She looked like a Navajo. I never did ask to see her papers. Why would I? It was none of my business. Mary Potato could say she was anything. She could have been a Kickapoo for all I knew. I did not care one way or the other what tribe she was from. If she wanted to claim she was a Navajo, then let her.[29]

It is hard not to see this as anything but a coded confession, or rather, bald-faced justification on Nasdijj's part—belonging to the tribe, whether of writer or Indian, is simply a claim, a look, a paper we needn't see, a truth that can never be told or found out.

This is mere prelude to the array of "mongrels" and "half-breeds" typical to the fake memoir. Nasdijj's very truck is "a mongrel migrant vehicle, and it is owned by a mongrel migrant."[30] What's reiterated over and over by Nasdijj is the essential impossibility of such a bicultural and biracial identity, its inherent tragedy. The book's front flap copy says as much: "While Nasdijj struggles with his impossible status as someone of two separate cultures, he also remains a contradiction in a larger sense: he cares for those who often shun him, he teaches hope though he often has none for himself, and he comes home to the land he then must leave." Why, at the millennium's turn, is biracial status rendered "impossible"? Is being a living Indian always a contradiction in a society set on extinction? Where good = dead, such an "impossible status" represents a body at war. Not the cultural, internal kind W. E. B. Du Bois wrote of, invoking his powerful phrase "double consciousness"—that, in the end provides a fruitful double vision and is, above all, a *consciousness*. Instead, like all such "half-breeds," Nasdijj's identity is reduced to the unconscionable eugenicist view—sterile, reactive, paradoxical, pretend, predetermined.

It is important to note that not simply Nasdijj but also his big-time publisher offers up such beliefs. The flap copy is one of many places on a book where a publisher, often in collaboration with the author, positions the book; it is text that in its very authorlessness means to establish authority. Here, we see publisher and author speak in one voice. This is why it is so important to find the actual books, especially in early or first editions, because such bios, prefaces, and disclaimers inevitably change. I regularly discuss such material aspects of the hoax because they are part of the book as object and experience—despite what e-book sellers wish, the book begins far before its guts and contents, which are not merely text but typography, design, packaging, and beauty. The book is where the author exists not just as a single vision but in a collaboration with culture.

This may explain why Barrus invents an adopted sick son, designed to die—he needs a handy figure of extinction, which for him and for much of Western culture, means Native. Again and again, Nasdijj returns to loss— "How do you divorce loss from rage?" he asks of no one. Later, when Tommy Not Really returns as a ghost, which he had been all along, he says, "We're lost again." This lostness is a way of speaking of both what isn't there and what never was, couched as a permanent condition of the Native. "And the wind sings go, go. The ghostly laughing voices of the Navajo."[31]

Go, go becomes a refrain throughout the book, said by ghastly Tommy upon his return. After a while, the refrain began to remind me of the *Go Go Gophers*, that late-1960s cartoon in reruns when I was little, the gophers being two excitable, bucktoothed Indians. Airing during episodes of *Underdog*, that designation could have applied to them: yet while they usually resisted or at least competed with the coyote cavalry, if they got the upper hand it was always temporary and foolishly, all while saying things like "Whoopee Doopee! You-um genius!"

What I watched back then in my pj's looks quite different now, though the now hard-to-find episodes haven't changed. This is exactly how the hoax can speak true: underscoring shared, assumed beliefs, greenlighted by committee. It isn't so much that Nasdijj is yet another example of going native, but that the Native is always going. Though ostensibly a sign of resistance to extinction, the Go Go Gophers—like all fake Indians—too readily serve as its embodiment, going, going but not yet gone.

INDIAN CAMP

Once a fairy tale, the hoax is now a ghost story, told to scare us and simultaneously express our fears. After Nasdijj too was gone, unmasked at last, *Esquire* would discover that Barrus may have actually had an adopted son— one white and not Indian, yet apparently with severe mental difficulties. Rather than the boy's having died, Barrus and his first wife returned him to the state. "The memories of having to give up a child are like arrows in your heart," he tells the magazine in his own voice. After he relates the story of surrendering custody, the reporter senses that out of the many unbelievable stories that preceded it, this one may be true. "By the end of the story, Barrus can hardly speak. For me, it is unlike anything else he's told me about himself these last few days; it is a story of shame and failure. It is almost the opposite of Nasdijj's version (*Anyone could have given him hospitals. I was not anyone. I was Tommy Nothing Fancy's father*); it is the story of the father who abandoned his son."[32] The true story apparently wasn't enough, but was also too much.

While on one hand a way of plotting, quite literally, an escape plan—in a form as melodramatic as "faking my own death"—there seems even more at stake in killing the son off. In Nasdijj, the early deaths kept on coming: another false foster son, "Awee," this one with AIDS, in *The Boy and the Dog Are Sleeping*; and two years later in *Geronimo's Bones* a brother (though not a lover) with the unlikely moniker Tso, short for "The Smarter One." Barrus-as-Nasdijj writes, "Geronimo always seemed somehow to be our third and silent brother," though Geronimo is less a historic figure than the name of a game the two brothers play as an excuse for fantasy: "In my world, the stories are real. I am from a world where those stories imbued our lives with extraordinary vividness. The vividness was reality."[33]

To doubt such a belief, Nasdijj says, is to doubt not just imagination but reality, which he insists is the same thing. Though I believe strongly the imagination can remake reality, this does not make them synonymous, thank goodness. This is especially true in *Geronimo's Bones*, which recounts, often graphically, Nasdijj's being regularly sexually abused by his fake father—including on the night of his made-up mother's death. "Surrealistic accounts of forcible incest by his father read less like rape and more like luke-warm trysts," to quote *LA Weekly*'s article "Navahoax." "Though incestuous rape may be difficult to trump, perhaps even more disturbing is Nasdijj's ten-dency to sexualize teenage boys." It would seem, as he went on, Nasdijj and erotica-era Barrus began merging. But "Navahoax" points out that there's al-ways been a sexual connotation to all Barrus's work. His recent work with boys at risk for AIDS—including a film on his website featuring beautiful boys, some bound, others bloody—celebrates and eroticizes the boy hustler while claiming to advocate for male sex workers. Another speaks of "young boys doing sex work" and not wanting to exploit them, then asks them to "show me your life." The voyeuristic effect gives a retrospective creep factor to Nasdijj's young characters or the putative author as a child in peril and pain.

Now that Nasdijj is no longer, Barrus would return to writing under his real name (though not publishing, except online). His latest efforts are al-most an Internet "catfish" in reverse—instead of creating many online pro-files using different names to lure us in, Barrus has one name yet many sites. To try to track down or simply trace all Barrus's posts is to travel through the trends and shaky afterlife of the Internet—from blogspot to Tumblr to vari-ous charity calls-for-funds and pop-up art spaces. The most characteristic aspect of most any blog is a first few enthusiastic posts, followed by a large gap and a post explaining why the person hasn't posted, and a public inten-tion to post again—usually followed by silence. For Barrus, his posts, like his silences, often unleash the kinds of wrath found in all his books, lead-ing to lengthy rants and, in a bitter irony, someone who has taken up one of Nasdijj's lapsed domain names to use to track and mock Barrus's newer post-ings. Rather than an archive, the Internet is a site of extinction.

Childhood finds its way into one of Barrus's last publications written under his own name before he "became again." "The article he published in *Gray's Sporting Journal* in 1996 under his own byline was palmed off as the true story of how Barrus, a young boy growing up in Key West, sailed to Cuba with his grandfather and fished with Ernest Hemingway," writes Andrew Chaikivsky in a later piece in *Esquire*. "Barrus never fished with Hemingway. He doesn't remember anyone at the magazine ever asking him if it was true or not. It wasn't true, and he seems completely unbothered by it."[34] By claiming Hemingway, Barrus was claiming a connection to the past and Papa and to literature itself. Hemingway would sometimes play soldier (though he really was one), matador, revolutionary, but he was also an actual journalist, drawing fairly clear borders between fiction and non. The writers who followed, especially male writers, would often struggle with Hemingway's style and his lifestyle, mistaking one for the other—and many, from Clifford Irving to James Frey to Barrus, would eventually turn to hoaxing to find their way. Rather than kill off the literary father, who had taken his own life, they more often sought to secret him away, or say through various fictions—rather than through writing fiction—that they had actually met.

Hoaxing Hemingway also seems apt for the soon-to-be Nasdijj because Hemingway's own work, especially in the early Michigan stories like "Indian Camp," embraced or explored Nativeness. Fiedler writes, "If the frontiersman was a mock Indian, and the Western movie star a mock frontiersman, what is Hemingway but the White Indian twice removed?"[35] This removal has a double meaning: all the genocide, "removals," disease, decimation of life and culture visited on the Indigenous people of the Americas we can only wish were a hoax.

"When American life is most American it is apt to be most theatrical," Ralph Ellison wrote, thinking of the Boston Tea Party. "Americans began their revolt from the English fatherland when they dumped the tea into the Boston Harbor masked as Indians, and the mobility of the society created in this limitless space has encouraged the use of the mask for good and evil ever since. As the advertising industry, which is dedicated to the creation of masks, makes clear, that which cannot gain authority from tradition may borrow it with a mask."[36] Cue that iconic image of an Indian crying at the sight of waterways and land covered in litter, trash thrown at his feet, in one of the most famous commercials of the last century: "Keep America Beautiful."[37] Turns out the icon in question, for years thought to be named Iron Eyes Cody, wasn't really Native either, though he had pretended to be for decades. I imagine he ordered his warbonnets and mocs from the Grey Owl impostor catalog.

The ad for that first Earth Day in 1971 was true at least in ways that could easily apply to the hoax: *People start pollution. People can stop it.*

1956
INDIAN CRAFT
SUPPLIES

GREY OWL INDIAN CRAFT CO.

4518 - SEVENTH AVENUE

(between 45th & 46th streets)

BROOKLYN 20, N.Y.

◆

TELEPHONE-GE-6-3287

"Grey Owl Indian Craft Supplies catalog, 1956."

CHAPTER 6

Blood Nation

Are our nonfiction writers these days just fiction writers who missed the mark? Used to be our finest fiction writers were failed poets—Hemingway, Faulkner, Joyce. "I'm a failed poet," William Faulkner told the *Paris Review* in 1956. "Maybe every novelist wants to write poetry first, finds he can't and then tries the short story which is the most demanding form after poetry. And failing at that, only then does he take up novel writing."[1] With hoaxers, fiction appears not another way to reach the truth, but a failed one. By this reasoning, nonfiction doesn't mean "not quite fiction," never rising to fiction's level, but *non* as in "not as good as." Yet actual nonfiction is meant to reveal what's true; the hoax only reveals what we *wish* were true.

No wonder that these days memoir is a form under siege. In a small-print author's note on the copyright page of *Loose Girl: A Memoir of Promiscuity* (2008), Kerry Cohen inadvertently indicates what's wrong with the memoir today:

> This book is a work of nonfiction. I have changed most names and identifying details. I have also, at times, combined certain characters to allow for narrative sense. I have tried to recount the circumstances as best I remember them, but memory can be a faulty device. Facts are important, but I believe that even more important than the facts is truth. I trusted truth to guide me as I wrote. Jack Kerouac once said, "Everything I wrote was true because I believed what I saw." So it is for this book.

Such prefatory notes, indicating the degree of fiction found in a memoir's pages, have become necessary in the wake of writer James Frey's best-selling blowout, his come-to-Oprah moment when he revealed what careful readers suspected even before Oprah picked his memoir *A Million Little Pieces* for her Book Club in 2005: much of his so-called nonfiction was made up. If Frey's televised admission in 2006—the very month Nasdijj was exposed— proved a kind of religious confession, then the real penance has been paid ever since by the memoirists who followed, for whom fact-checking has become a ritual purification and the disclaimer a Hail Mary pass praying for brisk sales to help make it rain.

Truth is the goal of the memoir—or at least its many authentications. Such devices are ways of gaining trust in a mistrustful but too-trusting world. And yet such a disclaimer comes up against the problem encountered by any fabricator coming clean: "To tell you the truth, I am a liar." The liar's paradox has become the memoirist's mantra, indicated by *Loose Girl*'s strategic separation of facts from truth; and its unapologetic reliance on memory as re-created facsimile rather than any strict recounting of verifiable events. Like the name of the memoir that arguably started the modern memoir craze, Mary Karr's *The Liars' Club* (1995), the title *Loose Girl* seems to play with the notion of truth, interrupted.[2] But as Karr makes clear in *The Art of the Memoir* (2015), she's not at all ambiguous about truth: "In cheating the public, hucksters cheat themselves out of their real stories. James Frey must've fought to get sober before *A Million Little Pieces*; just not in the ways he alleged. No doubt he suffered like hell, but he somehow deluded himself that his real misery wasn't bad enough—or maybe his real character wasn't macho enough, or nice enough to warrant scrutiny. . . . Surely his true story would've been worth a read."[3]

Almost all hoaxers, once discovered, go on to write a novel—when it turns out they were writing a novel all along. "Memoirs by ordinary people have been with us for a long time," Robin Hemley reminds us in *A Field Guide for Immersion Writing*, his lively defense of the memoir. "But in my parents' day, they used to be known as 'first novels.'"[4] It is fine to write fiction labeled as such, of course, no matter how apparently autobiographical. Yet in her preface, Cohen seems to forget that no matter what claims he made for it later, Kerouac called what he wrote fiction. To quote Steve Almond from his 2011 "brief inquiry into the fake memoir," "The Heroic Life": "Every time one of these memoirs gets debunked, writers and critics debate what constitutes non-fiction. Often, there's an argument put forward about something called 'emotional truth,' which is supposed to provide moral cover for lying. My definition of creative non-fiction is simple. It is *a radically subjective account of events that objectively took place.* The moment you start making up events that you know did not take place, you're doing another sort of work. It's called fiction."[5] *Work* seems just the right word: fiction is not just a label but a technique, a way of finding not freedom from truth but a freedom in truths told a different way. To claim there is no line between fiction and non- is not a matter of opinion but laziness.

You could say the memoir is a promiscuous form. The novel, the memoir's direct antecedent, is omnivorous—a form that cannibalizes other forms, from letters to hymnals to confessions themselves. The confusion the memoir has caused is actually one over form—for despite what its recent practitioners seem to think, the memoir is a form, not a genre. It is a way of saying, not a way of being. In trying to expand the memoir from a form into a genre like the broader field of nonfiction, the authors of memoir often mistake its strengths—hard facts ennobled by the fluid, specific act of memory—as characteristics not to be championed so much as ignored. As a result, instead of flirting with fiction, as almost all writing does, the memoir flirts with the truth.

LITTLE PIECES

Few I know in the publishing world were surprised when James Frey's *A Million Little Pieces* (2003) was revealed to be, shall we say, embellished. The word on the bookish Brooklyn street was that he had originally shopped the book as fiction—but that agents or publishers said what he'd written would sell better if labeled as nonfiction. (Frey later would confirm this story in his final interview with Oprah Winfrey in her last week of broadcasting in May 2011.) Judging by the relatively modest success of his subsequent novels, that thinking may well have been right.

What's most true about hoaxers is that once they lie, or hoax, or plagiarize, they rarely do it only once: fiction's addictive. If faked authenticity is the engine, and money the goal, the chief by-product of these make-believe memoirs is *truthiness*—an idea actually discussed in the Oprah "trial" of Frey. Though it started as a joke, Stephen Colbert's term *truthiness* remains useful because it indicates both distance from the truth and reliance on the appearance of it. "It used to be, everyone was entitled to their own opinion, but not their own facts. But that's not the case anymore. Facts matter not at all. . . . Truthiness is 'What I say is right, and [nothing] anyone else says could possibly be true.' It's not only that I *feel* it to be true, but that *I* feel it to be true. There's not only an emotional quality, but there's a selfish quality."[6] Though fetishizing the truth, the memoir is not in fact particularly interested in it. Like gangsta rap, its long-lost twin born around the same time, the contemporary memoir's chief note is tragic, the "shock" of a hard-knock life substituting for its lessons; both forms share a need for "realness" over truth, for feelings over facts. But only the memoir has pretensions not just to realness but reality.

The nature—or should I say artifice—of the photograph may provide one good way to view the modern memoir. "Fixing," "dodging," "touching up": all have long been part of the process and history of photography, not to mention spirit photography. We can see this on the very cover of *Love and Consequences: A Memoir of Hope and Survival* (2008), by "Margaret B. Jones," revealed to be a hoax right after publication (and just a week after the fake Holocaust memoir *Misha* was exposed). Jones is not just a pseudonym or "false name" but a false identity—"Jones," really one Margaret Seltzer, represents Seltzer's wish to be an orphaned white child (or rather, a half-white, half-Native one) raised by a black foster family in South Central L.A. There she could grow up an ostensible gang member.

The front cover of *Love and Consequences* is itself a fiction: an older black woman is pictured standing with her arm around a young white child who looks into the distance, the woman looking only at her. Both have their backs to us. The cover doesn't so much announce the book as signal one of the most familiar types in American iconography: the mammy. Dating like Aunt Jemima from the nineteenth century, the mammy or black domestic with her white charge only ended as a widespread image with the insistence of Black Arts in the 1960s—a famous painting from the time pictures Aunt Jemima with a machine gun with a side of flapjacks—here she returns, an unwelcome figure of nostalgia and somehow hope. The only difference here is that on Seltzer's cover the mammy is not oversized—heft being a symbol of Mammy's nurturing yet asexual, sassy yet nonthreatening nature—suggesting not her southern but her urban, cinematic helpmeet.

A glance at the back flap of *Love and Consequences* finds that the cover image is a composite, a convenient fiction. The image is at least two separate but seemingly equal ones, placed together by a designer. It reminds me of how the editors of *Time* magazine, rather than find one of the many mixed-race folks who actually walk the earth, created an "Eve" of their own via computer manipulation for a 1993 cover story.[7] Electronic miscegenation, it would seem, was acceptable; actual race mixing, not so much. This, despite the fact that mixing is exactly the thing Jones the fictional character claims she is the product of—the frisson of mixing is the thrill she provides through her narrative, further suggested by the fake photograph with its altered, but in no way alternative, image.

We may remember the way *Time* also darkened O. J. Simpson's face and mug shot after his arrest in 1994,[8] where his blackness was literally reinforced—the ultimate five o'clock shadow—in ways that Seltzer's whiteness is reinforced in the book. The whiteness Seltzer intimates and maintains, constantly contrasted with her supposed South Central surroundings, is her own. She cannot imagine writing of an all-black world, her "memoir of hope and survival" seems to say, so she inserts herself into one, inventing a personal past that didn't exist to explain what does.

With many of these books, you need not be a book insider to sense their falsehoods—you need only be a reader. Frey's *A Million Little Pieces* opens with him on a plane covered in blood from a broken nose and knocked-out teeth on his way to rehab, this at a time when airport security was at its height; Seltzer's book opens with her supposedly being relocated for some unnamed reason from a white family to a black one despite long-standing prejudices, not to mention laws, that ensure Native children are not easily removed from reservations or their families. The opening gambits in many famous hoaxes fail to pass a simple smell test.

Believability, however, is not what such books are after. The fake memoir doesn't just stretch plausibility; it traffics in extreme versions of supposed reality because anything less might cause us to stop and second-guess—the reader can't afford to stop and ask whether *plausible* means "apparently valid" or "giving a deceptive impression of truth." Instead, we are too busy being shocked and awed (or schlocked and *aww*-ed). Modern hoaxers obey the magician's mantra: distraction is the better part of any trick's power.

I wasn't swayed by either Frey's or Seltzer's book before each was revealed to be a fake. I recall picking up *A Million Little Pieces* in a bookstore, having heard that it was a publishing phenomenon; finding it dubious at best, I put it back down. With Seltzer/Jones it was far more extreme. My local NPR station interviewed her when the book came out, just before the jig was up, and after hearing only a few responses, I told my wife, who'd been listening along, that it sounded like the corniest, *Boyz n the Hood*–era set of clichés about gang life I had ever heard. Sure enough, when days after she was exposed by her sister—who recognized her from a glowing article in the *New York Times* Real

Estate section, no less—it turns out Seltzer had assembled her alter ego, much as Frey had, from every outrageous image of that gangsta-esque era.

At least Frey's name was true. "Jones," called yet another name, Bree, in the book, was a total fiction; so was "Big Mom," the alleged black woman who raised her. Anyone with any ear for African American vernacular knows the phrase "Big Mom" just don't sound right—the nickname's two blunt syllables are awkward and inelegant, two things black vernacular doesn't much go in for. What's more, Seltzer appears to have directly borrowed the name "Big Mom" and much about her alleged Indian identity from actual Indigenous writer Sherman Alexie's novel *Reservation Blues*. Scratch a hoaxer, you often sniff a plagiarist.

Once, the point of memoir or nonfiction like James Baldwin's or Joan Didion's was to say, *Look at me* as a way of saying *Look at us*. "I am the man, I suffered, I was there," to quote Whitman, as James Baldwin did as an epigraph for his second novel, *Giovanni's Room*—a book written in the voice of a white man wrestling with his sexuality. The mask too is as American as lynching. Those memoirists who once asked "Who am I?" saw themselves not just as American but as the whole of America. Today's memoir all too often says, *Look at me and look no further*. Worse, it says, *Looky what happened to me*. And if it didn't happen, why not make it up?

The fabrications of the literary hoax nearly always make the authors more interesting or tougher or bolder than they really are—*worser*, you could say. Frey says he was imprisoned for four months rather than in jail for mere hours, claims hard time when he served none. Never does a Seltzer say, *Life wasn't so bad*. Never does a "Nasdijj" claim, *You know, I get by*. Frey and Seltzer and Nasdijj up the tragic only to increase ego, or sales, or readership. Consider this interview with Frey by Amazon.com before the exposure:

Q: What book has had the most significant impact on your life?

A: Tao te Ching by Lao Tsu. Completely changed how I think, behave, live my life. Nothing else comes close.

Q: You are stranded on a desert island with only one book, one CD, and one DVD—what are they?

A: The book would be the Tao te Ching, the CD would be some compilation of love songs from the 70's and 80's, and the DVD would be highlights from the history of the Cleveland Browns.

Q: What is the worst lie you've ever told?

A: No way I can answer that.

The motto of the make-believe memoir is fibbing only with the point of helping someone else get through a similar struggle—which becomes the measure of the book's real "truth." Even Frey's invoking his love of the Tao, which may be a belief he truly holds, allies him with ancient wisdom. But no gang members stepped forward to ask Seltzer for her representation or help, no prisoners for Frey's. The real sin may be that these fake memoirs are nothing more than "self-help," designed to advance their authors' careers while disguised as inspiration for others.

Take the example of Frey's narrative about Lilly, a fellow addict he supposedly falls in love with in rehab who later kills herself. The events of Lilly's death, told in *A Million Little Pieces* and the sequel, *My Friend Leonard* (2005), are so generic as not to be believed. The style of Frey's writing isn't simply to mimic reality but to create an alternative one by distracting us—in part by mimicking older versions of tough-guy reality patented by Hemingway. Frey is channeling "realism," not reality.

But where Hemingway had the good taste to call even his clearly autobiographical novels fiction, saving his adventures for his life in almost a manic pursuit of "material," Frey gives us no such relief. Rather, Lilly's actual death falls prey to his hoaxing eye. If Frey is still to be believed after his confession, it is not whether she killed herself that he fabricated, but simply how. In his 2006 interview with Oprah after being exposed, he indicated he fabricated to protect Lilly—yet the real reason seems to be that Frey is not producing genre fiction but genre memoir in which drug addicts die and in certain ways. Though the real Lilly supposedly cut her wrists, Frey confessed that he changed the method of death to hanging to make her "unidentifiable." He conflates making someone "unidentifiable" with changing her actual identity. The sad result is that this poor woman's certain death becomes instead a figure of distressing doubt.

Fake memoirists plagiarize another's pain—as if that were the only way to empathize with it. Critic Daniel Mendelsohn, writing in the *New York Times* about Frey, Seltzer, and the concurrent, disturbing trend of fake Holocaust memoirs, reminds us that "in each case, then, a comparatively privileged person has appropriated the real traumas suffered by real people for her own benefit—a boon to the career and the bank account, but more interestingly, judging from the authors' comments, a kind of psychological gratification, too."[9] The fake memoir conflates recounting and inventing pain with its cure. In truth, it provides a placebo effect.

Frey makes his approach to pain manifest—he is its victim and its martyr—by claiming to have had two root canals without painkillers. Oprah challenges his truthfulness, stating, "My dentist said that could not have happened. And I said, 'Oh no. It happened. He told me it happened.'" She receives a typical nondenial denial:

> FREY: I mean, once I talked to the person at the facility about it, you know, the book had been out for nine months. We'd already done a lot of interviews about it. . . . Since that time I've struggled with the idea of it . . .
> OPRAH: No, the *lie* of it. That's a lie. It's not an idea, James. That's a lie.[10]

Winfrey's reply, if memory serves me better than it has Frey, was met with applause.

PRISON BREAKS

Fake memoirists regularly craft figures in their books that continue to express certain ideas about race—namely, stereotypes, damn lies, and statistics. Frey's *My Friend Leonard* begins:

> On my first day in jail, a three hundred pound man named Porterhouse hit me in the back of the head with a metal tray. I was standing in line for lunch and I didn't see it coming. I went down. When I got up, I turned around and I started throwing punches. I landed two or three before I got hit again, this time in the face. I went down again. I wiped blood away from my nose and my mouth and I got up I started throwing punches again. Porterhouse put me in a headlock and started choking me. He leaned toward my ear and said I'm gonna let you go. If you keep fighting me I will fucking hurt you bad. Stay down and I will leave you alone. He let go of me, and I stayed down.
>
> I have been here for eighty-seven days.[11]

Knowing this is entirely fabricated, Frey having been in jail mere hours, our questions may be less for Frey than about Porterhouse and his imaginary punches: *Can you blame him for them?* Also, since Frey was never in prison, how can his sequel exist, much less open with a character he met in confinement? His friend Leonard, like his imaginary friend Porterhouse, is Frey's alter ego, or rather, his egotism altered and made real.

The disingenuousness extends to Porterhouse's race—which is never mentioned, though clearly he is black. Frey strains not just credulity but his attempts to remain "color-blind" by not coming out and saying so. His reluctance is implied as another sign of his blunt prose, styled as reality but really a confirmation of his stereotypes about race. If Frey were telling the truth, he'd tell us Porterhouse was cooked up—black and blue. Instead, a few pages later, his figment—"His real name is Antwan, but he calls himself Porterhouse because he says he's big and juicy like a fine ass steak"—asks Frey to read to him for three hours a day. "In the past twelve weeks we have worked our way through *Don Quixote*, *Leaves of Grass*, and *East of Eden*. We are currently reading *War and Peace*, which is Porterhouse's favorite."[12] Even in captivity, Frey is a social worker, an ex-alcoholic abolitionist teaching the poor brute about words and peace. Frey relies on listing classics of fiction and poetry—*Huck Finn* must be next on the list—that he never read to a prisoner in a jail he never was in so he might borrow some gravitas. Once hurt personified, Porterhouse now plays Boy Friday to a heroic Crusoe, rescued by Frey's very presence. Porterhouse's mythic blackness comes complete with illiteracy—he is a porter, after all. What are we to make, two-hundred-odd pages later, when Frey twice has characters, including Leonard, his friend and father figure, order a porterhouse—cooked well? Porterhouse, with Frey on his side.

You can't make this stuff up. Except that Frey can, mixing the statistical and seeming truthful in the way truthiness loves best: "Most of the prisoners are in for long stretches and will most likely never be free. If they are ever free, they will be more dangerous than they were before they were imprisoned. They could give two fucks about rehabilitation, they need to survive. To survive they need to replace their humanity with savagery. Porterhouse knows this, but wants to remain human for as long as he can."[13] The real reason Frey recites the "facts" of prison life straight out of Stereotypes 101 is to maintain the veneer he needs, the very appearance of nonfiction, of *remaining human*. Like the travel liar, he gives us what we expect any intrepid exoticist explorer to find there, even if that means something savage, barely human.

Rather than documentary, Frey's and Seltzer's hoaxes and the fake memoir more generally owe much to the "mondo" films of the 1920s to the 1950s. In mondo, naturalist footage and stock special-effects footage met with fiction-filled stories about "strange places," like "deepest Africa," all presented as real—a cinematic tradition that could be said to have begun with the 1922 film classic *Nanook of the North* (and carried over into Joan

Lowell's mondo-hoax *Adventure Girl* over a decade later).[14] One of the first twenty-five films honored in the Library of Congress's film registry, *Nanook* may still resonate, but what it inspired is a kind of visual colonialism—everything in the lens was leveled, made equal or equally unworthy of extended study, whether human or animal, fact or fiction, suggesting little distinguished the two.

By the 1960s, mondo films soon gave way to exploitation films that didn't rely on stock footage or documentary style in order to be "true" but that used the guise of real stories to allow them to explore taboo subjects for profit. Women in prison, drug addiction, nudism, the ghetto: all these topics the films conjured as fad or pressing dangers in order to exploit them for profit. In such a light, Frey's and Seltzer's works are rather late projections in the history of Blaxploitation cinema, borrowing their narrative techniques as a signal of the narrative crisis they found themselves in. This millennial narrative crisis, which we'll return to, is both symptom and cause of our current Age of Euphemism.

But Frey and Seltzer reenact something else besides an age-old story of exploitation and our current era of euphemism: namely, an intimacy of black language and experience that, with Seltzer at least, lurks on every page. Opening *Love and Consequences* at random finds this passage:

> I didn't let his words sting me; I expected it. Really, I didn't know much about making [drug] deliveries, except that it paid better than selling weed. I took a step closer to him and looked right at him. That's what my brothers had taught me. Always make people take you seriously. "What you mean, homie? I'm perfect. Who would ever suspect me?"[15]

Part of the forger's pleasure is parading her forgery. In hindsight, hoaxes provide clues to the lies that can be found in the lie itself or its cover-up, a trail of crumbs we both are and aren't meant to follow. If this passage, despite the poor prose, reads now as a not-so-subtle confession of Seltzer's lying, it is furthered by "black dialect," a fiction that Seltzer's introduction makes clear is integral to her faux memoir. She writes, "Please do not confuse the use of slang and my replacing *c*'s with *k*'s as ignorance or stupidity." I'm not sure whose ignorance she means—that of fake black speakers, or her own? It is clearly Seltzer who's ignorant of black speech and who needs to be schooled:

He thought about it for a minute, then laughed again. "Aiight, sho nuff, you right. Ima take a chance on you. You meet me here tomorrow morning befo skool. You go ta skool, right?"

"Sometimes." I shrugged my shoulders and gave him a half smile. He laughed again. The high school graduation rate, though it varies somewhat from neighborhood to neighborhood, in South Central, hovers somewhere around fifty percent.[16]

The gap between the narrator's "Standard English" and her use of slang is not the only thing strained. In this, Seltzer's book is all too familiar—this is what dialect always meant, often literally inscribed on the very photograph of the mammy, or provided by whites as substitutes for or simulacra of black speech. Hollywood actress Louise Beavers, for instance, famously had to go to a dialect coach to be taught how to talk in her many mammy roles. But, as Hattie McDaniel, the first (but not the last) black actress to win an Oscar for playing a maid, said, "I'd rather get paid $700 a week for playing a maid than $7 for being one."

Meanwhile, neither Seltzer's story nor her vernacular is believable, resorting to the clichéd distortion of Black English taken not from life but from plantation novels and exploitation cinema. Rather than a living language, these are the broad strokes of speech misheard, language as a bunch of missteps learned nowhere near "skool"—when in truth the vernacular is a varied, vivid commentary on language itself. Hence the old joke: You know the difference between a dialect and a language? *An army.* Or at least a gang.

If the cover of Seltzer's *Love and Consequences* doesn't clue us in that few to no black people seem to have weighed in on the book's publication in its years-long journey from pitch to print, the writing ought to. And if bad slang isn't enough to raise our doubts, then the prefatory note is. Seltzer refers to the book's language, not its reality—though you could say in the fake memoir, like the fake travelogue before it, both are one and the same. Such caveats are forms of authenticity foisted upon black authors for centuries, traced in books like Robert Stepto's *From Behind the Veil*, with writers from Phillis Wheatley to Paul Laurence Dunbar on down required to seek or append such authenticity (even as others protest such conditions).[17] Seltzer goes ahead and appropriates this precondition for the black writer!

Turning each "c" to "k" indicates more than spelling. Such *English-ish* indicates a philosophical view. The book puts it this way in its "Author's Note on Language, Dialect, and Kontent":

My words and views were learned in the dirt and desolation of South Central Los Angeles. The streets where I grew up were run by the laws of the local gangs. Their laws shaped what we wore, how we talked, and how we navigated the city. When one resident of the urban core asks another where they live, the response often includes not only a street name but also which gang claims that area as its turf. I do now see that there is no difference between Bloods and Crips. We are all the same, the problems and conditions we all face are the same. We were just born into different neighborhoods. My particular street, however, was ruled by the mighty Blood Nation. You will see that re-flected in the language and vision of the book.

Please do not confuse the use of slang and my replacing *c*'s with *k*'s as ignorance or stupidity. I choose to write as we chose to speak in the world of my childhood. A world where Bloods and Crips have such a deep-seated hatred for each other that Bloods smoke bigarettes and Crips celebrate C-days rather than B-days (birthdays). I do it in order to offer up the whole story.[18]

I will spare you the almost unreadable "eye dialect" that follows. All such dialect juxtaposes against "Standard English" in her own voice, making the spoken dialogue a mask only for her, not for those she writes of. Seltzer renders language as merely a function of race, gang status, poverty, and other consequences—such talk invents nothing on its own.

In contrast, actual African American Vernacular English is genera-tive above all else. It is preservative and persevering; coded, recontextu-alizing, and cryptic; youth-oriented, difficult, and self-conscious; ironic and dangerous. Seltzer's language, rather, is "kliché"—it is ventriloquism on a high scale, one in which black folks are commonly used to express "the truth" or realness without thought of the consequences on them as actual people. Symbolized, and thus simplified, in this situation it is only the white author who manages to get out of the ghetto—or prison, if you are Frey—that she herself made. A video Seltzer recorded in character as Jones, apparently for her publisher, speaks with a fake black dialect that would be hilarious if it wasn't troubling, or so familiar. This white-on-black voice is the borrowed language of tragedy, found loudest on TV: "Violence in LA is like the smog, you just learn not to see it," she says. "It's like being a Palestinian suicide bomber—like, when you're born into it, when you're caught up into it, and your ego and pride, it makes perfect,

perfect sense. We used to say growing up, I'm not from America, I'm from South Central, L.A."

The trailer ends with a title card saying, "Her senior year of high school, Jones applied to college, something none of her friends and siblings had done. She didn't tell anyone she'd applied until after she was accepted. She later graduated from the University of Oregon."[19] Her video and her book bio both mention Seltzer's success at the University of Oregon, which she never really graduated from, as a measure of her escaping the milieu in which she found herself. Seltzer has to make this up too, not just out of habit but so her tale ends as all such tales do, with triumph.

Our age's reliance on memoir is also an overreliance on "memory," rather than history, on the imminently subjective rather than the immanent or verifiable. Biography, whether of the self or of another, though interested in the past, is actually a function of the present—it often seeks to understand the present through the past. We are drawn in biographies most to those figures who help explain our times (past presidents), or those rarities for whom our times shed light on theirs (usually lesser-known figures who have now moved to the center of our cultural conversation). These days the memoir has a distant relation to the past, taking a kind of dramatic irony that is overdetermined yet unexplored: *Here's how horrible I once was; let me tell you how hard I had it.*

Or maybe the issue is that there is no distance at all. This may be the memoir's chief appeal. Such books aren't concerned with reflection so much as with fetishizing the despair they chronicle. In some ways, they don't reenact the experience—unlike a poem, which, to quote Robert Lowell, "*is* an event, not a record of an event."[20] Rather, they reenact their denial and render the unusual or unique as exotic. Intimacy is promised, not just by the memoir's subject matter but its style. Frey's style, his lack of quotation marks— just like Seltzer's preponderance of apostrophes in her book's bad dialect—is a form of rendering reality more "real." Their entire books are in air quotes.

Fiction would seem Frey's main addiction, to paraphrase the *Smoking Gun*, the online magazine that first documented Frey's fraud. When confronted by the facts, Frey protested, claiming that the questions the magazine posed to him were the "latest attempt to discredit me. . . . So let the haters hate, let the doubters doubt, I stand by my book, and my life, and I won't dignify this bullshit with any sort of further response."[21] Bullshit and haterade are a powerful combo and seem to lead the hoaxer into delusions of grandeur—*I stand by my life*—and illusions of grand truths.

What's stranger to me are many readers' responses to such revelations, symbolized by Oprah's initial response after Frey's book had publicly been called into question. Frey showed up with his mother (how rogue!) to defend himself on *Larry King Live*. Calling in unexpectedly, Oprah said, "I feel about *A Million Little Pieces* that although some of the facts have been questioned—and people have a right to question, because we live in a country that lets you do that, that the underlying message of redemption in James Frey's memoir still resonates with me. And I know that it resonates with millions of other people who have read this book and will continue to read this book." Is this the equivalent of *If it feels real, it is*? Though later Winfrey would recant this statement, the power of that initial attitude—feeling as fact, feeling *over* fact—is a theatrical and "therapeutic" one familiar to anyone in the Western world of the twenty-first century.[22]

The idea that "James wrote the real deal" is still found years later on comments posted after the *Smoking Gun* article. "I get that readers felt duped by his embellishments," reads one comment, "but I have to say, who cares? He still wrote the book, I think the only crime in art is plagiarism and that's just not the case here." Legions of readers, knowing that Frey falsified his memoir, still persist in saying the book is truthful, or that truth doesn't matter. Mary Karr diagnoses this oxymoron well: "In an off-kilter paradox, our strange cynicism about truth as a possibility has permitted us to accept all manner of bullshit on the page."[23] What's at stake for true believers is nothing less than their feelings—a book "feels real," so it must be, a tautology that may be the best definition of truthiness.

The notion that the hoax merely meant to help suggests hoaxing is the *only* way to help. This false-prophet complex, the latest version of the savior complex, may help explain why hoaxers like Frey defend their hoax nearly to the end, only relenting as the evidence mounts and the court of public opinion turns against them. Any stonewalling as part of the stages of grift is quickly succeeded by the hoaxer's typical defense that no one got hurt—though a hoax is never a victimless crime, if such things even exist.

Still, the language of the legal system seems particularly apt, as it is the basis of the opening of both Frey's and Seltzer's hoaxes—both protagonists are taken from home by officials, left captive among blacks and Porterhouses. They are taken in, and so are we. Many hoaxes depend on liberal pieties (*Everyone's OK! Blacks can learn too!*), as well as conservative spin (*Ketchup is a vegetable*), for their effect. The problem here isn't merely one of speech, or representation, which is troubling enough. Instead it's the mix of these large, unwieldy, and inherited fictions—black mammies, bad dialect, and drugs, oh my!—with the statistical impulse, the two being more closely related than we might think.

The desire to fib about Seltzer's supposed experience mirrors her wish to "skool" us on the horrors of black life. That socioeconomic statistics could provide the basis of her fictions fails to see the ways in which statistics too contain fictions, can distort, and aren't a referendum on an actual life as lived—just as slang isn't. Whose consciousness is she raising here? The ignorant drug dealers'? Or that of the reader—presumed white, and not from South Central—who needs to be reminded how different things are there? *Are we not men? What's in your heart, brother?* There is, Seltzer implies, no there there.

STRANGE DELIVERANCES

It isn't so much the travelogue, whether fake or real, as it is the captivity narrative that's Seltzer's and Frey's true antecedent. *I will tell you about these people, I lived amongst them, dancing with wolves, and have learned not only their language and their habits but also their promise for hope and survival.* This is one clue as to why Seltzer makes her Jones alter ego part Native: as a way of both belonging and not belonging, seeking kinship with a story seemingly as old as America, that of triumph over hardship.

Published from the seventeenth to the nineteenth centuries, captivity narratives bear lengthy titles that easily could be the subtitles of Frey's and Seltzer's books, not to mention the modern memoir more generally: *Memoirs of Odd Adventures, Strange Deliverances, etc.*; or, *A True History of the Captivity and Restoration of*; or, perhaps my favorite, Cotton Mather's *Humiliations Follow'd with Deliverances.* Like the modern memoir, captivity narratives are accounts of life "in the wild"; they imply (or infer) sexual violence; they are also ultimately conversion tales, their salvation *Taken in Substance from Her Own Mouth,* as one title has it. The captivity narrative's mix of piety and self-pity—*A faithful Narrative, of the Many Dangers and Sufferings, as well as Wonderful and Surprizing Deliverances*—becomes more and more familiar the more hoaxes you read. Only faithfulness is now missing, at least where the truth is concerned.

The hoax doesn't borrow the captive's "faithful narrative" but rather its effects. The fake memoir adopts the captivity narrative's extreme ways of experiencing the body not always permitted in a society that was fully American but not yet the United States. In *Captured by Texts,* critic Gary L.

Ebersole describes the captives in this way, inadvertently echoing the protagonist of the modern memoir, from Frey's fake one to Cheryl Strayed's actual travelogue *Wild* (2013): "Captives are human beings in extremis, that is, in situations of grave danger and heightened vulnerability. They are suddenly carried into an alien world and cut off from the normal support systems of family, friends, church, and the larger society in which they had lived. They are abruptly and rudely faced with an immediate threat not only to their physical survival but also to their psychological and sociocultural integrity and identity."[24] Suffering, alienation, the body in pain, redemption: all this found its form in the "white Indian."

This "white Indian," or European settler changed by capture or willing life among the Natives, symbolizes what Ebersole calls the "mixture of fascination and dread" that captivity (and return) held for those on an American frontier. Not only was the white Indian arguably a big part of the popularity of captivity narratives across the centuries, when more than three hundred such narratives found their way into print; the figure also is embodied in fictional characters such as Natty Bumppo, Jeremiah Johnson, and even Katniss Everdeen, protagonist of the *Hunger Games*, who all embrace symbolically Native, woodland ways and, in turn, craft their own legends.[25] Identifying with the American soil means answering a call to return to nature as nation, pointing out the savagery of the present day.

Yet the fake memoir goes further—turning the white Indian caught between cultures into the "half-breed" who is part Native American and part white by birth, a "mixture of fascination and dread" no longer symbolic but literal. Long before *Love and Consequences*, this "half-breed" could be found in any number of hoaxes by pretend Natives, from Grey Owl, as we've seen, to *The Education of Little Tree* (1976), a fake memoir about yet another half-white, half-Indian child that made many school reading lists before being revealed as a hoax. Unfortunately it can still be found on syllabi and in many bookstore Native American studies sections, bought and sold as genuine. Written by Asa Earl Carter, a former Ku Klux Klan member and speechwriter for segregationist George Wallace who penned the infamous "Segregation today, segregation tomorrow, segregation forever" speech (not to mention the novel that became the film *The Outlaw Josie Wales*), *Little Tree*'s continued publication and film adaptation assert not Native humanity but innate strangeness, couched as inherent difference: "Me and Grandpa thought Indian."[26] This statement may seem like honoring Indigenous culture, but it reinscribes a romanticized racialism; its authority comes from asserting faux-Indian ways in a child's voice, to be taken at redface value. In fact, the main character's "half-breed" status—of a kind played to the hilt in the 1970s by the likes of Cher or by Burt Reynolds in his early film appearances—would be symbolic of such books being half-truths themselves, if they weren't fiction entirely.

The hoax's claim of Native heritage is a claim for unimpeachable origins. While it may seem odd for a Klansman to ventriloquize in this way, doing so feeds a nativist impulse. Such claims are widespread, appropriating an outlaw Nativeness that ultimately ends in "aboriginal-face," whether red or brown or black. The white Indian, though surrounded by doom—from *The Last of the Mohicans* to *The Hunger Games*—is triumphant, however fragile her victory. In contrast, bound by blood, cursed by birth, in-betweenness embodied, the half-breed is forced by fate into something far worse.

The colonials saw the "New World" and its natives as alien in order not to think of themselves as alien. Yet I can't help thinking of the displaced nature of the hoax as related to the captivity narratives: after all, American slavery is absent from these tales. It is strange to come across literally hundreds of narratives of captivity that seem to look westward, which here means, look away from the capture, sale, breeding, beating, and enslaving of Africans in the Americas that began soon after the captivity narratives do. In much the same way, the memoir never seems to recognize its direct ancestor in the captivity narrative—or its kissing cousin in the exoticist tales of so-called white slavery that took the captivity narrative's place. This despite the fact that, as Ebersole writes, "in captivity (as in war) one's body is experienced in more fundamental ways than previously." He speaks of the narrative in ways that easily apply to the modern memoir:

> The body is also known more immediately than before as a boundary of fundamental exchanges: severe hunger and thirst reveal the integrity of the body to be fragile and dependent upon the intake of nourishment; at the same time, the body is experienced extruding blood, pus, bile, entrails, embryos, dashed brains, excrement, and vomit. Moreover, in the world of the alien Other, strange sights, sounds, odors, and tastes assault the captive's senses, while dreams, flashbacks, hallucinations, and uncontrollable screams, sighs, tears, and tremors emerge from inside.

In such situations, the body is a painful register of the shattered or porous boundaries of inside and outside, self and other, past and present.[27]

Seltzer wants us to believe she's a "Blood." In his trilogy of fake memoirs, faux-Navajo Nasdijj presents reservation life as one filled with doom and bodies in pain, stressing his membership in the blood nation in his very titles, for example, *The Blood Runs Like a River Through My Dreams* and *Geronimo's Bones*. In much the same way, Frey needs us to believe his pus-filled past and his dentistry without painkillers in order for us to see how out of bounds he is in the present.

Humiliations Follow'd with Deliverances: body fluids also distract us from how fluid the hoax is with the truth, neither faithful nor really narrative. Instead, like the captivity narrative, "such stories are never objective or neutral accounts; they are always structured and informed in specific ways in order to give a shape and a meaning to the captivity," Ebersole writes. And what is captivity without meaning? That would be like a fake memoir without redemption.

Once Frey's hoax began to unravel, just weeks after supporting his appearance on *Larry King Live*, Oprah brought Frey to her show (along with his publisher, Nan Talese) in order to defend or deny what he could no longer claim was the truth. There Frey "came clean"—something demanded of public figures, at least since Watergate, as part of an unspoken pact with the public in the Age of Euphemism. The cover-up is worse than the crime, the saying goes—but what if the cover-up, like the hoax's faux innocence, *is* the crime?

What Frey in the end has produced is not just falsehood but a multitude of other, smaller Freys for whom truth is almost always relative. The fact that one of his lies was about the suicide of an actual woman and the death of two others goes by the wayside. According to *The Smoking Gun*,

> In addition to these rap sheet creations, Frey also invented a role for himself in a deadly train accident that cost the lives of two female high school students. In what may be his book's most crass flight from reality, Frey remarkably appropriates and manipulates details of the incident so he can falsely portray himself as the tragedy's third victim. It's a cynical and offensive ploy that has left one of the victims' parents bewildered. "As far as I know, he had nothing to do with the ac-

cident," said the mother of one of the dead girls. "I figured he was taking license . . . he's a writer, you know, they don't tell everything that's factual and true."

For Frey, the accident and the girl's death are collateral damage, like the truth. Why wouldn't the mourning mother conclude that fabricating facts is something writers just do?

The death here is one not just of truth but of art.

Gone is the idea that something made up, unreal or surreal, could move us. Instead, readers insist that the thing that isn't real *is*: that if it affects them it can't be affected; that they cannot have real feelings about made-up things. It's no accident that Frey's made-up memoirs lack indentations—they are typeset like "poems," borrowing a lyric, left-handed-margin look as if to insist on their own marginalization, suggesting that any variations from the truth come from a kind of poetic license. Frey doesn't just pretend to tell the truth but has pretenses of poetry; as such, Frey's "lyricism" cultivates poetry as meaning "filled with fiction," with pretensions toward literature. Indeed, the most troubling, standard defense of the hoaxer may be the literature defense, as in this prefatory note accompanying later reprints of Frey's book:

> This book is a combination of facts about James Frey's life and certain embellishments. Names, dates, places, events, and details have been changed, invented, and altered for literary effect. The reader should not consider this book anything other than a work of literature.

This is less a disclaimer than a bold claim. The label *literature*, once a mark of excellence or significance—or at the very least an earnest wish for it—is now nothing more than an effect, a feeling, window dressing.

Millions of copies sold can't be wrong, it says, suggesting that what happens within the pages of literature doesn't matter. After all, poetry—and now prose—can't make anything happen. This has the numbing effect of saying that what happens outside the covers of a book doesn't matter either. Yet what if this place others call spun or alien or unreal is actually your home? What if you are the parents of those deceased girls that Frey claimed to know but really didn't? What if you are the imaginary Indian, or Porterhouse's poor unthought-of mother, never allowed to defend against the hoax or ghost or spook that Frey created?

In defending the truth against the hoax, we are in fact defending the imaginary—preserving the possibility that make-believe can make claims on our emotions but not our facts, that the truth is as actual as a tree yet can be as abstract and verifiable as the DNA that makes it up. To quote from Marianne Moore's "Poetry," poetry is made up of "rawness and / that which is on the other hand / genuine"—literature too comes not from mere false-hoods or simple facts, but from raw, genuine life.

Time passes, too, and things that once seemed outrageous fictions seem suddenly real. People forget, the made-up memoir seems to say, so why not get started now? Maybe the modern hoax memoir is not meant to conjure memory but to help readers forget pain by supplanting it with a pretend pain far *worser* than they might could imagine. Like Frey's claiming not to have taken anaesthetic when getting a root canal, the fake memoir is a form of numbing through extremis.

All these distractions and disclaimers can help dull our own radar. These days we are too afraid to call out charlatans: *Everyone's entitled to his own opinion*, we hear, or my least favorite, *It is what it is*. Meanwhile, the useful saying *All isn't what it seems*, seems to have fallen by the wayside. What it seems is all it is.

In a brilliant spoof of Frey's fake memoir, Steve Almond crafts a fake but somehow probable future obituary for Frey. Taking some of its power from the knowledge that obits for the famous are often composed in advance with only the final details of death added before running, "Controversial Author and Cultural Icon Found Dead" uses humor to upend the conventions of the fake memoir and confession, and our own cycle of zero worship and hero worship and back again. Almond imagines Frey living in Las Vegas as "ringmaster of a literary circus, in which exotic dancers and trained animals enacted passages from classic novels." The show (called *Book 'Em, Jimmy!*) closed within a month. The fake obituary further reports that his eldest son, Malcolm X Frey, published "a searing memoir"—*Freyed at the Edges*—that claims the washed-up writer was a "sexual predator who routinely made his children watch him do squats and who ate entire roasted turkeys in one sit-ting." Frey sued his son for defamation, Almond tell us, and settled after an agreement "to include a disclaimer in future editions, noting that portions of the book were fictionalized."[28]

Calling *bullshit* isn't easy. Liars especially don't like being lied about. Which is why Almond uses bullshit to combat bullshit. Which is why Oprah's initial takedown on her show—an icon taking down a pretender to her throne—was all the more remarkable. And why, some years later, it was so puzzling to watch her engaging Frey over two days in a one-on-one interview in 2011, during the final week of broadcasting her famous show. Instead of before a studio audience, Frey gets Oprah back to what appears to be his room, as if in an act of on-camera seduction. The episodes showcase Frey's farmed-out fictions such as *I Am Number Four*, suggesting his creating an author mill were somehow innovative. Truth is, the fake memoir always held out the author as an aggregate, a mere idea. By the end of the broadcast, Oprah is apologizing to Frey, as one might to a manipulative lover, for her previous anger at his bad behavior.

All is forgiven. What's old is a novel again.

"Are They Ambassadors from Mars."
Photograph advertising the
Muse Brothers, 1926.

Chapter 7

Lost Boys

Whenever a fake memoir is exposed, there's this notion—an assumption, really—that the trouble is merely a question of category, something solved simply by relabeling. Why not just call the faked thing fiction and be done with it? Hoaxers themselves provide the biggest resistance to this idea: in an elaborate defense, writer Norma Khouri bristles against the suggestion that her 2003 bestseller, *Forbidden Love*, a memoir of a so-called honor killing eventually shown to be fabricated almost completely, is "more of a novel."

"No," she says flatly. "When you take a true story and you're changing all the characters, dates, the characterizations, blah blah blah, you've got *faction*—fact and fiction, that's what it is."[1] As an example she then mentions best seller *The DaVinci Code*, an acknowledged fiction that, like *Forbidden Love*, happens to bear an enigmatic woman on the cover but also, we realize, shares the belief that the whole world in fact represents something else. Like many a conspiracy theorist, Khouri substitutes the profound discovery that the world has meaning with the notion that the world is one giant code in need of cracking. Or in her case, maintaining.

The conspiracy and the hoax share an equally elaborate dance, the former accusing the world not only of hoaxing but also of covering it up. The hoax instead offers advocacy. Khouri says that by writing *Forbidden Love* she intended to shine a light on the actual phenomenon of honor killing. But as noted by Jordanian journalist Rana Husseini, who is largely credited with drawing attention to honor killings, Khouri's fake book hurt the cause.[2] Not only do exaggerating numbers and fabricating victims as Khouri did distract from the real issues, doing so allows otherwise good people to discount such events altogether—managing to insult those working on the real issue, not to mention placing the victims in very real danger. As Husseini points out, Khouri not only makes such killings far too commonplace, she also assigns the Middle East a kind of totalitarian sexism that may comprise a popular but not accurate view. Women in Jordan can in fact walk down the street without a man and needn't always wear a veil. Khouri's is a view that wouldn't allow for a female journalist like Husseini to exist, while also claiming the existence of certain things that Jordan doesn't actually allow, like the unisex hair salon Khouri claims she owned. Khouri even gets the direction the river flows in her supposedly native city wrong.[3]

The reason the hoaxer, once revealed, remains resistant to changing the label from nonfiction to fiction—not to mention some few who say such distinctions don't matter—is because any power of the prose (I first wrote *pose*) gets lost when rendered unreal. And unreality is exactly the point. Saying *this is fiction* after the fact doesn't provide the temporary pleasure that not knowing which category the writing belonged to might have at first—a blurring that early novels such as *Robinson Crusoe* played with somewhat but on which the hoax relies. Unlike a novel, the hoax feigns certainty yet depends on doubt, so much so that it might be said to colonize it. Above all, we realize afterward that the hoax was not simply reliant on what was on the page, on the screen, or in person, but rather on our own assumptions, now laid bare.

"The American religion—so far as there is one anymore—seems to be doubt," Mary Karr writes. "Whoever believes the least wins, because he'll never be found wrong."[4] And yet this doubt, which has only increased lately, has led not to less hoaxing but more. This is because the hoax doesn't represent the vagueness or difficulty of truth but our unending desire for belief.

BORDERS MEAN NOTHING

Khouri has stumbled upon one true fact: there's a *factional* quality essential to the hoax, if only because the hoax breeds factions, distrust, elaborate fictions. The Middle East has become just another place for such factioning to occur, whether providing an exotic place Americans can visit safely and sexually via their computer (as with Amina Arraf, the "Gay Girl in Damascus"); somewhere they can save (as in the fabrications of Greg Mortenson's *Three Cups of Tea*); or a ground target to be conquered by one man with a rifle (as in the quickly withdrawn fantasy about the Benghazi terrorist attacks, *The Embassy House*). Indeed it proves significant that Khouri, though born in Jordan, was raised in Chicago—for her memoir seems particularly American in its aspirations and social divisions.

The television news magazine *60 Minutes* would debunk both *The Embassy House* and *Three Cups*—the latter by Mortenson, founder of the Central Asian Institute, whose altruism was allegedly stoked by his time stranded in a Pakistani village—though not always exactly how the news show intended. Following leads suggested by Jon Krakauer's own exposé, *Three Cups of Deceit* (2011), reporter Steve Croft doggedly pursued Mortenson and his charity, which it turns out had used donated funds to support its founder's travel and book sales. Krakauer writes that Mortenson's stories about his Pakistani ordeal "are an intricately wrought work of fiction presented as fact. And by no means was this an isolated act of deceit."[5] Yet with *Embassy House*, *60 Minutes* correspondent Lara Logan fell for and practically encouraged a hoaxer's claims in 2013 that he had been an eyewitness, indeed a hero, during the attack on the embassy in Benghazi; truth was, he was nowhere near the compound. The show would be forced to issue a rather reluctant and halfhearted apology for taking the patent lies of an admitted liar—ones used for decidedly partisan purposes—at face value.

Both cases represent factions of belief, any accuracy overwhelmed by an agenda. The credited ghostwriter for *Three Cups*, David Oliver Relin, hints as much in his preface, revealing that Mortenson's "fluid sense of time made pinning down the exact sequence of many events in this book almost impossible" and that "supposedly objective journalists are at risk of being drawn into his orbit, too."[6] To know him, Relin says, is to become not a reporter but an advocate, his story too good to check. "The astonishing, uplifting story of a real-life Indiana Jones" the *Three Cups* paperback advocates or advertises—making these one and the same. We shan't forget that Jones more often went in search of treasure than truth. In contrast, Krakauer compares Mortenson to James Frey, then says Frey never did bilk a charity.

In Khouri's case, writing a book about a made-up killing and pretending to be a political refugee may provide the perfect cover for her being on the lam from fraud charges. The documentary *Forbidden Lies* from 2007 reveals that she may have literally stolen the identity of a former neighbor in Chicago, along with hundreds of thousands of dollars. Khouri continues to isolate and insult those on her supposed side, including the filmmaker, who had called the book "a novel" at first as a way of defending and explaining it.

When Khouri finally takes an onscreen lie detector test to prove she's being truthful, a siren ironically blares ominously in the background; later she will say the noise is what altered her results. Offhandedly in one clip Khouri asks, "Do you want the truth or what I said?"

The strange contemporary case of Amina Arraf, the so-called Gay Girl in Damascus, may help us pull together the various strains of the hoax we've traced across the eighteenth and nineteenth centuries but that are still very much with us: the exoticist and the travel liar; the Circassian Beauty as the figure of desire; violence and the séance; the captivity narrative; the sideshow, the bartered body, and the bearded lady. Arraf's case provides a beard that, while not exactly a cover for sexuality, is certainly consumed by it. For there's yet another meaning of *beard*: like a merkin, the "beard" is a man or woman who provides sexual cover, metaphoric fake facial hair for what lies (and tells lies) beneath. It can mean a person who provides cover for a sexual dalliance, such as the platonic escort who accompanies a mistress to a public event that her married lover might be at; or may mean a date or even a life partner who serves as a heterosexual cover for someone who's gay or lesbian. The beard is not the same thing as a hoax, though it may be its ready accomplice.

Gay Girl in Damascus is a blog that began appearing in early 2011 with posts by Arraf, a self-described Syrian American lesbian. The title said it all. The website quickly grew in popularity and Arraf began several relationships with lesbian political activists, one of whom considered Amina her long-distance girlfriend. When Arraf disappeared a few months later, in the midst of the uprising that became known as the Arab Spring, the Internet flooded with a campaign to learn her whereabouts. "I have been on the telephone with both her parents and all that we can say right now is that she is missing," Amina's cousin posted in her absence.[7] "Free Amina Arraf" posters began appearing online, bearing a motto presumably taken from one of her many vaguely profound quotes—"borders mean NOTHING when you have WINGS"—and suggesting just how fast her story had spread. The region's unrest and uprisings meant that concerned readers and activists well aware of the region's troubles wanted to hear from Amina.

But the inspiring Syrian American lesbian turned out to be a Georgia-born white man, Tom MacMaster. As the *Washington Post* would reveal, MacMaster for several years had used Amina as a fake online profile (sometimes called a "sock puppet") primarily in online forums—he did so, he said, in order to "have a discussion about the real questions" in the Middle East.

Later, in what passes for an apology, MacMaster would say that the blog started "innocently enough" and just "got out of hand"—the questions that must have seemed a distant fantasy for a married graduate student abruptly became a key story in a region front and center in world affairs. When faced with how to end the hoax, MacMaster decided to have Amina kidnapped, claiming bizarrely that he thought that might end interest in her case. His wife, who apparently hadn't known of his other life, was as shocked as the rest of us.

MacMaster's own backstory has a familiar ring to that of other hoaxers: he was a publishing failure who had written pieces in his own voice, and a novel, but these efforts met with little success. "MacMaster posted on different websites and listservs as Amina and suddenly he found himself with an 'extremely full and vivid character,'" NPR reported. "He wrote a backstory for her and started writing a novel based on her. As a way to flesh the character out, he created profiles of Amina on different social networking sites to create a 'depth of character.' He used Amina's profile, he said, so he could snoop around sites that MacMaster couldn't. And he was living the character so much, he would walk into restaurants and know immediately, what Amina would like on a menu and what she wouldn't like."[8] To keep up his hoax, MacMaster had to invent a whole cast of characters, from a loving Arab father ("My father, the hero") to cousins and friends. "Amina kept growing. And I kept trying to 'kill' her," he would say. Failure is one of the hoax's main muses.

It turned out that not just Amina's but MacMaster's innocence was merely an act. It is the innocence, as presumptive as his all-consuming and all-assuming whiteness, that constitutes the crime. The idea that for MacMaster the kidnapping wouldn't cause alarm and might be an exit strategy seems as unbelievable as anything else in the whole affair. One begins to think, as with Nasdijj and other hoaxers with their dying children, that all these kid wonders—not to mention Arabs or lesbians or girl wonders—are invented for the express purpose of being killed off. The Arab proves for MacMaster just another kind of blackface or redskin, electric with extinction.

The mock kidnapping also provided a kind of exoticist fantasy—a fetishistic cliché borrowed from white slavery panics of a century before, the very ones that had informed Barnum's Circassian Beauties. It reveals the hoaxer as not only a desk-bound exoticist but also a cultural and sexual tourist, the bad-girl wonder turned into an Internet star: an American story if ever there was one. The hoaxer's typical exoticist mix of desire and danger is borne out by the "memoir" MacMaster had half-shopped around earlier, claiming to be merely the emissary on behalf of Arraf, who'd written it. A woman he had been in contact with posted the thing online and I had the foresight (or is it schadenfreude?) to download it. Having read what I could, I can report it's a hot mess—Orientalist and exoticist, depicting the Middle East as a place of secret sexuality, white slavery as a white fantasy that would do the Circassian Beauty proud.

It's also confession built on the notion of confession and lies that, we're told, Amina herself provides: "This isn't a fairy tale or an Arabian night's tale; instead, what I've written down is a 'True History,' of everything that happened (and most of it is true) with only minor embellishments, conflations, name-changes (to protect the guilty), and a few event [*sic*] made up out of whole cloth (do recall that I—as well as some others involved—am an Arab and, if you've read much of the current, how shall we say it, more 'Orientalist' press, you'll know that it's axiomatic that Arabs are unreliable and prone to lie (if not to lie prone), so, if you buy that whole reasoning— and why not? It is the dominant paradigm—you'll expect me to lie at every turn. I won't but what'll it matter?"[9] MacMaster uses Amina's invented Arab stereotypes—ones he's perpetuated—against her, saying she won't lie, except a little, though you think it'll be a lot. She won't *lie prone*, either— she'll only pun in order to protect the guilty, which is, we soon realize, MacMaster himself. As if we didn't get the point, the manuscript is called "A Thousand Sighs, and a Sigh: An Arab American Education," though it could be called *A Million Little Yawns*. It is as tasteless as it is talentless.

Like a yawn, the hoax is contagious. MacMaster's unveiling also revealed another pretend lesbian, this one Bill Graber, "a retired Ohio military man and construction worker" also married to a woman. Under the name "Paula Brooks," Graber had helped found a news website LezGetReal, a popular forum for progressives and lesbians. After being exposed just days after MacMaster, Graber too pled advocacy—not realizing that supporting a cause does not necessarily mean pretending to be its very center, or that doing so is a form of the exact privilege the cause may be trying to speak out against. Do people who watch "girl-on-girl" porn really think they are pro-lesbian? The idea of fake lesbians, too, has always been conflated with the "Oriental"—sexy harems and poetesses have a long history of being fantasized and fantabulated by male writers, much like in *Songs of Bilitis* (1894), by Pierre Louys, who at least wrote with a wink, mixing Ossianic fabulism and exoticist erotica in pretending to be a lost lesbian Greek poet.[10] "What the hell is it with straight men and lesbian fantasies?" the female managing editor of LezGetReal wrote in an editorial note; comments alone ran to dozens of pages and the site crashed from all the activity. "Personally, the idea that Tom and Bill were flirting with each other in their personas as lesbians is too funny."[11]

While claiming advocacy, hoaxers really exhibit self-interest. Often this is because there is only the self to support their false claims; any revelations only provide further opportunities for details and forgery. Though no one had met her, Arraf's Facebook page was a very real "who's who of the Syrian opposition movement"[12]—in fact, the confusion over Arraf's identity continued for longer than it might have because online pseudonyms were commonly used within the Arab uprising to hide activists' real identify and protect against reprisal. The advocacy MacMaster's Amina Arraf claimed not only put real bloggers in the Middle East and Syria in jeopardy, but its revelation suggested that the online postings of those who helped foment the uprisings were somehow fake too. The Syrian government seized on the exposing of Amina to say the Arab Spring was simply crafted, or instigated, by carpetbagging foreigners.

In answering questions about his feelings after his first full-fledged stories on LezGetReal, MacMaster stumbles across one "real reason": "When I got a first couple initial media bites, I was extremely flattered and impressed with myself that here I had written something that was fictional but it was getting taken seriously and treated as a real event. It appealed to my vanity that here I am, I'm so smart, I can do this."[13] Of course, the person asking him was none other than "Paula Brooks."

But can you explore real issues as a fake character? Yes, it's called acting. Or fiction. But acting is *not* a method of engaging with the actual world, just as pretending to know what a character might eat does not a novel make—much less make that make-believe real. MacMaster mistakes backstory for the real story—or for real talent—and his creation for Pygmalion when it's really Pinocchio. Is knowing what your character would order the same as challenging the world order? Does feeling like you are Paula Brooks excuse Graber from using her not just as a beard but a fake one?

Once unmasked, MacMaster posted to his/her blog: "A Hoax that got way out of hand. I never meant to hurt anyone." Of course, he hurt not only the cause but also the real people who believed in it. His hoax's domino effect was made clear when NPR spoke to Arraf's would-be girlfriend Sandra Bagaria, who had helped publicize Amina's disappearance and tried calling "Amina" in Syria repeatedly and got no answer. (Her search is now dramatized in a fascinating 2015 French-language documentary, *The Amina Profile*.) Later, MacMaster-as-Amina would blog a response to the missed connection: "We will have a free Syria and a free nation; it is coming soon. The revolution will succeed and we will rise above sectarianism, despotism, sexism, and all the dead weight of these years of bitterness, of division and partition, of oppression and of tyranny. We will be free!"[14] It is only on the guys-only stage MacMaster has set up that the clichés of Amina appear revolutionary.

It should be no surprise to find in her "fake novel," modeled as a memoir, that Arraf is a biracial symbol of displacement. Her mother's being white helps her serve as a kind of mixed-girl wonder. "Maybe half of me is from here and everything else is confusion between those two sides, the stranger and the native, the believer and the infidel."[15] These stark dichotomies and bothersome biracials of course are the only options, ones the hoax reenacts again and again, without the complexity of lived lives or of full-fledged fiction. The true love these hoaxers have is with their characters, which is to say themselves. It will become a familiar pattern in the hoax as we go on.

All this has been made all the more easy by the Internet, the "fireside traveler" or travel liar having been replaced by the desktop one. The *Gay Girl* blog is now squirreled away somewhere like Amina was; LezGetsReal bears no trace of the controversy. For the Internet is a bit of a travel liar itself—an unreal place where real things happen. Quickly we've learned that the Web is far more pseudonymous than anonymous, as we first supposed; online our names have simply been changed to a number, an IP address, protocol and code. Hoaxes, especially online, prove that almost anything, from our lives to our loves, on repeat can be made unreal.

The hoax not just expresses a fantasy but also records a fantasy sold, and most importantly bought, even by the hoaxer herself, as true. It's not just a wish, but a cure for that wish—a curse—it's facepaint you wear, if only for a while. "People want to believe," MacMaster would say. What he doesn't seem to realize is that, unlike Amina Arraf, MacMaster is people too: his willingness to believe his own story is one more sign that the hoax's first victim may be the hoaxer.

BEDS ARE BURNING

Though first published in the United States as *Honor Lost*, *Forbidden Love* achieved its greatest prominence—and best-seller status—in Australia.

Norma Khouri claimed to have fled Jordan only after her friend's murder at the hands of male relatives; she then landed in Greece, where she said she wrote her book in Internet cafés. This made-up backstory, barely "faction," had real-world results as she was awarded political refugee status by Australia, where she eventually settled. In fact, Khouri had immigrated while young to the United States, where her book was more influential than salesworthy—some say it helped spur along the Iraq War, with honor killings cited by U.S. Republican powers that be as a sign of the need for military action.

Writing in the *New York Times*, Iain McCalman describes the Khouri phenomenon in her adopted home of Australia, noting her "pronounced American accent" as central to her appeal:

> Having sold more than 200,000 copies here, *Forbidden Love* has by Australian standards been a runaway best seller, and Ms. Khouri has become a star. It's not hard to see why. She is a compelling public performer, and her book had all the ingredients of a romance novel in chador, but with the extra cachet of truth. Nowadays the allure of "the reality effect" is a worldwide phenomenon, a reaction, perhaps, to the excesses of postmodern relativism, which made us squint at mirages. . . .
>
> *Forbidden Love* was also well timed: it caught the powerful eddies of anxiety and xenophobia churned up in Australia—as much as in the United States—by the tragedies of 9/11 and the Bali nightclub bombing. We were primed to believe any enormity of Muslim males, and Norma Khouri, as an insider, confirmed our prejudices. . . . We were secretly proud that Norma Khouri had chosen to live with us on the periphery of the world.[16]

This periphery may be exactly why Khouri, on the lam and on the make, came to the antipodes. Hers is an American tale, not just because of her Chicago accent or because the book was first published stateside, but in *Forbidden Love*'s willingness to see the world in us-them terms. Displacing race to Australia or Arabia or Asia, as many American hoaxers do, only highlights the way the hoax itself is a form of displacement. Much as in reports of cannibalism, the modern hoax always happens somewhere just over the horizon, the next valley over. The hoax's fears are ultimately part of its fantasy; it means to have its fake and eat it too.

The purported story of an American who learns Aborigine ways on walkabout, Marlo Morgan's *Mutant Message Down Under* is also defined by displacement. The outlandish book tells of the middle-aged, midwestern, suburban, and white author's months-long sojourn in the Australian Outback with an Aborigine "tribe," as she puts it. The Kansas City–based Morgan writes that the group she calls "the Real People" are "without racism"—though she never specifies racism against whom, which helps us know the racism she means is just a feeling, not a system of subjugation that the Aborigines have faced (and resisted) for centuries. Hers is a "pretendian" tale exported from the United States to Australia, fake native pseudo-spirituality and all, hoaxing as an invasive species.

"Australia is a country of immigrants," the Australian critic David Brooks writes. "It is also a country in which the literary hoax has had a particular force and vitality. Such a force and vitality, in fact, that one is tempted to see some sort of connection between them, and to speak of Australia as a hoax culture, even a hoax nation."[17] This has been true for not just its immigrants but its exports too, from the nineteenth century on, like the "professional savages" taken from actual Australian Aborigines or Barnum's so-called Wild Australian Children, who were really just microcephalic from Ohio, hyped as another, otherwise undiscovered race.[18] "Remember, this is the country of the duck-billed platypus," as novelist Peter Carey has a character describe Australia in *My Life as a Fake* (2003), based on the famed Ern Malley hoax.

Malley was a fake poet crafted by two Australian writers to spoof and trick the progressive poets of the day affiliated with *Angry Penguins* magazine. Not only did the hoax work, leading to the publication of a special issue devoted to Malley, but editor and publisher Max Harris was subsequently arrested and tried for obscenity. It's worth restating—Harris was arrested and tried *for the objectionable meaning of nonsense poems from a fake poet*. The meaningless had become filled with meaning, not just for those Angry Penguins who felt Ern Malley heroic but to those authorities who saw in nonsense obscenity, a hoax spun into the most serious kind of satire. Harris's defense was to stand by the poems. He would not be alone—Malley has since been jokingly called the best poet Australia has produced, and this from Australians. "When you are cut off from the rest of the world, things are bound to develop in interesting ways."[19] As in Barnum's day, Australia remains in the Western imagination a wild, far-off place, one where American showmen and hoaxers might exploit evolution, experimentation, or race.

In such a light, *Mutant Message* is as much part of an Australian tradition as it is an American success story: starting out in 1991 as a self-published book with illustrations by the author's daughter, these early efforts have the homemade look, odd capitalization (in all the dialogue), and tacky "fanciness" (or fancy tackiness) of a teenager's poetry. One early cover baldly depicts the kind of contrasts the book will revel in: a creepily rendered older white lady looks straight at us, with an iconic, grizzled, older black face looking off into the distance.[20] We know from his blank, black stare that the elder is wise, anonymous, and all but empty, while the lady, presumed to be the author, grins at us almost conspiratorially, a true diddler. Word-of-mouth success and sales (mostly to New Age clients) led to several self-published editions (often with different covers so it's hard to determine which is a true first) and ultimately a sale to HarperCollins in 1994 for at least $1.6 million.[21] Such a remarkable advance, plus a movie deal optioned for a similar price, would be realized—*Mutant Message* stayed on the best-seller list for nearly a year and spawned a sequel. I've seen figures that Morgan earned up to tens of millions from her "messages."

At first, readers might expect the "mutants" of the title to mean indigenous Australians but her twist is that it's those like her who are Mutants. It's never clear who comes up with this term within the book, or if *Mutant* means "Western" or "non-Aborigine," but we'll overlook that as we're meant to. Though the term *Mutant* may have originated as a sense of critique—reminiscent of slurs of "Die, Mutie!" from early *X-Men* comics from the 1960s—by the end the alliterative echo with her initials lets us know the *Mutant Message* is both heroic and Marlo Morgan's alone. She has been selected to deliver the message from this lost or last tribe she calls "the Real People"; needless to say, such realness, or, better yet, reality effect is a clue that the book is made up.

Not that Morgan has fessed up—though once she did, apologizing over the phone to outraged Aborigine leaders who had gathered to protest at the movie studio planning a film version, she later tried to rescind or at least downplay her admission. First sold as nonfiction, the book got relabeled as fiction, however halfheartedly, by the time of the trade edition. As a note "From the Author to the Reader" puts it:

> This was written after the fact and inspired by actual experience. As you will see, there wasn't a notebook handy. It is sold as a novel to protect the small tribe of Aborigines from legal involvement. I have

deleted details to honor friends who do not wish to be identified and to secure the secret location of our sacred site.

I have saved you a trip to the public library by including important historical information. I can also save you a trip to Australia. The modern-day Aboriginal condition can be seen in any U.S. city, dark-skinned people living in their section of town, well over half on the dole. The employed ones work in menial jobs; their culture appears lost, like the Native American, forced onto designated soil and forbidden for generations to practice all sacred ways.

What I can't save you from is the *Mutant message!*[22]

Why we would want to be saved from the library, one of our culture's sacred sites, is beyond me.

The dark-skinned dole. Besides drawing broad equivalences between vastly different histories, the author's note inadvertently indicates that the fading art of diary keeping may be one key reason today's memoirs bear so little detail. "Diarists never have control over what comes next in their texts. They write with no way of knowing what will happen next in the plot, much less how it will end," the foremost philosopher of the diary and autobiography, Philippe Lejeune, writes. "The future is pitiless and unforeseeable. You do not have any elbow room with the future. And the present—the diarist's subject matter—immediately objects to anything that smacks of invention."[23] Without the present tense of the journal, not to mention journalism, we have an increasingly loose connection with what actually happened—so much so that we regularly claim it may not exist.

In this mixed message, Morgan's conflation of "saving" and "selling" is telling. Morgan claims to be not just the messenger for Aborigine people but their savior—it is "*our* sacred site"—a false prophet conflating the book's selling with its secrets. Both she claims as a form of protection. The conflation continues in the book's epigraphs: two in later trade editions come from Native Americans, hinting at where she actually took much of the mythology she ascribes to Aborigine culture. Another epigraph from "Elder Regal Black Swan," invoking one of the most sacred symbols of Aborigine culture while quoting a figure fabricated by the book itself: "The only way to pass any test is to take the test," he sorta says. "It is inevitable."

The Elder and all Indigenous people in the book perform that impossible pidgin, *English-ish*, familiar to the hoax. Morgan's faux Aborigines are not even native speakers of their own language, one she fails to learn: at least

Psalmanazar or the *Dreadnought* hoaxers had the courtesy to make up a fake language, but her native tongue has no name, nor names for things.[24] "My words are in English" she says, "but their truth is voiceless."[25] Such vagueness extends to Ooota, Morgan's guide. "Ooota said something to the group, and each person said something to me," she writes. "They were telling me their names. The words were very difficult for me, but luckily their names meant something. Names are not used in the same way that we would use 'Debbie' or 'Cody' in the United States, so I could relate each person to the meaning of the name, instead of trying to pronounce the word itself." Their names aren't just translations but bald illustrations, rather like those by her daughter of the Real People found in early editions but tellingly removed from later versions. (Presumably, these are not drawn from life.) "Our group contained Story Teller, Tool Maker, Secret Keeper, Sewing Master, and Big Music, among many others."[26] The result can feel like some bloated Justice League from the future, when the comic book company runs out of creative names and just provides prosaic descriptions of their powers. After this, Morgan is given the label "Mutant" by Ooota (the one person with a name instead of a label), a term she understands as "some significant change in basic structure, resulting in a form of mutation and no longer like the original." This could mean the hoax itself.

By making herself a mutant, Morgan means to co-opt both science and wonder. Yet another name for "freak," *mutant* is a term seemingly modern, clinical, and thus more respectable, but really marks the continued displacement of the freak from a thing of wonder to a thing of science, pseudo or not, that occurs over the twentieth century. On the surface such a change was its own kind of aggrandizement—when in truth "mutant" made being a freak even less of a choice, exchanging wondrous fate for faulty genetics. More importantly, mutation is Morgan's mad-scientist method, taking sacred Aborigine beliefs and splicing them with broad superstitions about Indigenous people—rendered indistinguishable the world over—in order to suit her exoticist purposes.

DO YOU COME FROM A LAND DOWN UNDER?

When I once asked poet Les Murray, one of Australia's premier poets, why the continent-nation was prone to hoaxes, he answered in large part it was a way of not taking things too seriously; the Australian hoax, which is to say hoaxes originating in Australia, seems both a way of reveling in the country's isolation while also fighting, if not parodying it.[27] Ern Malley would seem this way, mocking the modern while a way of becoming more so. Yet lately, just as the American hoax has, the Australian hoax has grown more cynical, if not sinister: "In recent times, though, Australian literary hoaxes have been motivated not by satire, but its opposite—the desire to manufacture stories and identities that conform to marketable fashions," Iain McCalman argues. "In 1995, Helen Darville won a swag of literary awards for a quasi-historical novel about the Holocaust in the Ukraine that gained extra force from her assumed identity as Helen Demidenko. A real-life Serbian immigrant, Streten Bozic, found it easier, however, to get published as an Aboriginal named B. Wongar, as did a Sydney taxi driver, Leon Carmen, who produced a heartfelt memoir called *My Own Sweet Time* written in the guise of an Aboriginal woman called Wanda Koolmatrie."[28] What McCalman doesn't quite say is that all these hoaxes are about racial or ethnic questions; they are in this way further examples of how the modern hoax has changed radically by being more explicit racially.

The hoax set in Australia, usually American in origin and in intent, does much the same. In *Mutant Message*, the narrative begins with Morgan being practically abducted by natives after Ooota picks her up in a jeep under the pretense of giving her an award; after being driven for many kilometers she meets the group, who right away perform a sacred ritual (presumably for the stranger's benefit), throw all her clothes in a fire, and then take her on walkabout. It's quickly clear that her clothes are by the same tailor as the proverbial emperor's.

Simultaneously earthy and otherworldly, all-natural and supernatural, the Real People walk four months in the Outback barely eating; they reveal to Morgan all their secrets though never in their own language; their shit literally don't stink. Quite conveniently she's made the Real People anti-materialistic, sidestepping any ethical issues when later not supporting them with her millions. Of course, the fact that she pocketed any money isn't very Real People of her. Then again, maybe they are called "Real People" after the early 1980s television show by that name that helped pioneer reality television. The show that gave us Byron Allen and Peter Billingsley (later star of *A Christmas Story*) as a kid reporter also provided popular entertainment that, despite its name, makes its subjects neither real nor quite people.

These so-called Real People prove the perfect source—Miss Mutant is sworn to spread the message, yet never reveal them. Left unexplained is exactly why Morgan was chosen for such a role, though hints persist. "The summons came because it appeared to them I was crying for help. I was found to have pure intent. . . . I was found acceptable and worthy of learning the knowledge of the true relationship of humans to the world we live in, the world beyond, the dimension from which we came, and the dimension where we shall all return. I was going to be exposed to the understanding of my own beingness."[29] The "I" here is overwhelming: the Aborigines exist only to reveal Morgan's own being, serving as mere mediums for her message.

Morgan is the "white Indian" from captivity narratives mashed up for a New Age—or for science fiction. Narration like this would not be out of place in the sci-fi film *Avatar*: "I was told the plants and trees sing to us humans silently, and all they ask in return is for us to sing to them. . . . Each morning the tribe sends out a thought or message to the animals and plants in front of us. They say, 'We are walking your way. We are coming to honor your purpose for existence.' It is up to the plants and animals to make their own arrangements who will be chosen." Morgan's is a Neverland where water is not a necessity ("They believe Mutants have many addictions, and water is included") nor is food really ("They walked the blazing Australian Outback, knowing each day they would receive bountiful blessings of the universe. The universe never disappointed them").[30] This may simply seem a magical fantasy, or a harmless allegory for what she believes about the universe; Morgan isn't crafting a fantasy of the self, however, but of the other—in its millions sold and dozens of foreign editions, many readers believe this book is not just about her but also about actual Aborigine life. Ironically, this is especially true because of her claim of fiction: why would she lie about lying?

Morgan describes herself as—or rather has the ever loyal Ooota call her—a "female healer" back in her own society. Though reports indicate Morgan was really only a salesperson for ti-tree oil in the United States and briefly a volunteer at an Australian pharmacy (where she never had enough time to go away for months on walkabout), this unexplained faux-physician role is partnered with stunners like, "In fact, I am certain, there has never been a doctor anywhere, at any time, in any country, at any period in history, who ever healed anything. Each person's healer is within."[31] When one of the group falls and suffers a compound break, "Medicine Man" and "Female Healer" simply "talk" to the bone. Female Healer then takes a tube that had gathered "large clots of blood passed by the women" and uses its "black tar" to "cement the jagged edges of the wound together. She literally tarred them into place, smearing it all over the offending surface. There was no bandage, no binding, no splint, no crutch, and no sutures."[32] If only the book weren't just one giant crutch.

As others have pointed out, Morgan never encounters any other Aborigine people—or any other people period—in her travels. The Outback is as empty as her hand, a biblical desert, half-baked. Yet *Mutant Message*'s Outback fails as a symbol too: it's the Outback according to the steakhouse chain, which too is an American invention (though of course the Real People don't actually eat). Borrowing her setting from the prop department of the *Crocodile Dundee* films, metaphorically using Outback Steakhouse for craft services, Morgan wishes to create her own Mutant franchise. This seems the only good reason that her sequel *Message from Forever* was later reissued as *Mutant Message from Forever*, advertising "10 Messages of Aboriginal Wisdom," including "3. Before Birth You Agreed to Help Others."[33]

All this is made even more offensive by Morgan's implying she has a profound sense of the Aborigine belief system called the Dreaming. "This term refers to a complex system of beliefs, knowledge, and law," as one reference work defines it, knowing the term *the Dreaming* is merely a translation of an idea—one Morgan transmogrifies. "Each Aboriginal language group has its own word for this corpus of beliefs, and in no instance is the word 'dreaming' a literal translation of the universal experience to dream. Rather, the Dreaming describes the period, stories, and mythology telling of the creation era when the ancestral beings came to or arose from the earth and/or seas and commenced their activities." These activities, as I understand the Dreaming, affected the formation of the world: "With the coming of the ancestral beings, the landscape began to take form and shape: every action they performed left its mark." Yet the Dreaming is not past—it is still ongoing, as "through conception, ritual, and day-to-day life, the Dreaming is continually reanimated in the present and projected into the future," a time some have described as "*everywhen*."[34] It isn't that the Dreaming or the Aborigine people are timeless, or without time, rather that time and the Dreaming are still happening.

Instead, the Real People manage to sleep differently from other people, never actually dreaming: "They believe the reason Mutants dream at night is because in our society we are not allowed to dream during the day."[35]

Between their silence, "timelessness," and telepathy, "messages were being relayed between people twenty miles apart."[36] The fake people Morgan invents have need of her: if she can't read their minds yet, it's only a matter of time that she will speak for them in ways only hinted at when she started telling her fable to her New Age customers. As with other hoaxes, like *Forbidden Love*—or *Misha*, whose story of surviving the Holocaust with wolves was unmasked as a hoax in 2008; or the lady claiming to have been raised by monkeys dutifully if dubiously reported in 2013—the tale takes over the narrative.[37] In the end it isn't so much a story as a sales pitch, one those who "buy" it aren't always being asked to believe, though mostly are. The books themselves pose a kind of faith healing, tarring over doubt.

The advantage of such an absolute stance is that any doubt about or questioning of the book can be cast as a lack of imagination or empathy on the skeptic's part:

> Mental telepathy was something I sensed the people back home would find difficult to believe. They could easily accept that humans around the world were cruel to each other, but would be reluctant to believe there were people on earth who are not racist, who live together in total support and harmony, who discover their own unique talent and honor it as well as honor everyone else. The reason, according to Ooota, that Real People can use telepathy is because above all they never tell a lie, not a small fabrication, not a partial truth, nor any gross unreal statement. No lies, at all, so they have nothing to hide.[38]

It doesn't take a mind reader to see this as a coded confession of Morgan's own faking.

Needless to say the Real People's hiddenness (while having nothing to hide) is a great cover for Morgan's own fabrications: "one may conclude either that I am guilty of aiding these people in not conforming with the law, or that because I have not produced the actual tribal members, I am lying and the people do not exist."[39] Door number two please. Invisibility is yet another one of their powers, after all. Though pitched as one big compliment to the Real People with their superhuman mutant powers, powers like telepathy sidestep history and government-based policies against Aborigines—from obliterating and banning their culture to taking away children in what's known as the Stolen Generation. Her Real People are noble savages in an ostrich reality.

There's an undertone throughout the book that the Real People are unfinished, mere raw material—not just primitive, but in process—a process that only Morgan can complete. She can become one after all only through a simple ceremony, on the hoof, skin darkening, dye-job growing out. A copy of the self-published edition that I own is inscribed by the author: *Love from the Outback People and Marlo Morgan*. The "Outback People" may come first but Morgan means to have the last word.

DREAMWORLD

Morgan's illusions sold well across the globe—*except* in Australia, where they would be demonstrably untrue, if more obviously offensive. But Morgan's popularity speaks to her connections to a number of millennial narratives popular at the time she was writing—her Real People are exactly the kind of doomsday cult that would come to dominate the 1990s.

Such millennialism is but one example of the narrative crisis of the 1990s, a crisis in the stories we tell ourselves that has influenced, if not caused, the steady stream of hoaxes we've endured ever since. We may see this fin de siècle phenomenon as the start of the Age of Euphemism, with its endless wars and commensurate hoaxes. Which came first, the hoax or the war? The crime or the cover-up? The fakers or the pseudospirituality they peddle?

Though *Mutant Message* fails even as a kind of pseudospiritual allegory, that's the only way now to read it in anything but a fury. "Another fantasy of disappearing Aborigines," as one critic describes Morgan's book, calling it "a bizarre apotheosis" of cultural tourism. "Remembering and forgetting Aboriginality and whiteness . . . may well be dangerous ventures connected as they are to obscure histories of Aborigines 'holding' utopian promise for non-indigenous people."[40] The Real People provide just this tantalizing but brutalizing foreignness—a paradise not so much unreal as ethereal. In their end, the Real People's very impermanence means that any challenge they might offer modern life actually proves less pointed—after all, they won't be around for us to reckon with.

The hoax continues to be obsessed with extinction, and not just its own. This is one more reason hoaxes recruit unbelievable Natives, imaginary Indians, and pretend blacks—to reinforce the ways that the hoax is not about fact or fiction but fear. In describing typical depictions of Aborigines by whites, critic Deborah Bird Rose (who's white and not originally from Australia) might have been speaking of *Mutant Message*: "Europeans most frequently construct Aborigines as emblems: persons are envisaged as signs which signify European-defined Aboriginality. Their art, their archaeological remains, their concepts of the sacred, and their physical presence are

appropriated to fuel images of national identity. Shadowy but essential figures in Australian mythology, Aborigines have been represented as intrinsic
to Australia's past and largely irrelevant to its future."[41] Morgan's narrative
ends with the group in a cave where wall paintings not only depict their beliefs but predict everything from UFOs to Morgan's birth. Speaking for the
rest of the Justice League (including Time Keeper, Memory Keeper, Peace
Maker, and Kin to Birds), The Elder declares in comic-book language: "We,
the tribe of Divine Oneness Real People, are leaving planet Earth. In our
remaining time we have elected to live the highest level of spiritual life: celibacy, a way to demonstrate physical discipline. We are having no more children. When our youngest member is gone, that will be the last of the pure
human race."[42] The Real People tell her their secrets because, sexless, race-
less, homeless, dreamless, and foodless, they are already extinct.

Morgan makes Aborigine extinction into a literal superpower: further
in the cave is a set of rooms, including a "jeweled chamber" that serves as
"a classroom where the art of disappearing is taught. The Aboriginal race
has long been rumored to vanish into thin air when confronted with danger. Many of the urban-dwelling natives say it was always a hoax. Their
people were never able to do superhuman feats. But they are wrong."[43] This
underground cave, with its modern primitivism, also suggests that Morgan
has not only tapped into the practically perennial millennialism found in
the hoax, but in the alien abduction stories that also peaked in the 1990s.
In *Hystories: Hysterical Epidemics and Mass Media*, Elaine Showalter writes
of such abduction stories as one of a number of rampant fin de siècle epidemics, from multiple personality disorder to Satanic ritual abuse—all of
which are at the center of many a hoax, we'll soon learn.

Alien abduction stories only started in the late 1940s—I would add,
only after the *War of the Worlds* hoax broadcast in 1938—growing until, as
Showalter writes, "in the 1970s, alien abduction stories were so common that
abductees organized conventions." Still, such stories were inconsistent; it was
only in the 1980s that the stories become set in stone, scrubbed of inconsis-
tencies into what one self-described ufologist calls the "common abduction
scenario matrix." Nowadays, "the contemporary abduction hystory [or hysterical history] is extremely conventionalized, an aspect credulous journalists as well as professionally invested ufologists take as the strongest evidence
for its reality and legitimacy."[44] Such a mass-marketed matrix is exactly what
should make us suspicious, its copyability and stock characters its least believable aspects. But these conventioneers now call themselves *Experiencers*.

Besides functioning as contemporary captivity narrative, *Mutant Message* taps into the typical alien abduction story, the Real People proving the ultimate otherworlders and she a herald of a superior race.[45] We are way beyond the typical excuses of "inner truth" versus actual truth—not just because it is apparently okay to lie about natives of anywhere as long as they're not you, but because Morgan makes the Real People foreign to the land of their birth. To the exoticist all native sons are strangers, all native daughters concubines or Circassian Beauties or female eunuchs, all natives less outlandish than outlanders. Any praise is a form here of erasure, not just of customs but lives—indeed, the exoticist seeks to blur any distinctions between the two just as they do with fact and fiction. Fantasy is the real issue, the Real People fitting into Showalter's conviction that "abduction scenarios closely resemble women's pornography. . . . The abductees, however, seem particularly uneasy about sex."[46] Morgan embodies exactly this tension between abduction fantasy and apocalyptic testimony found in alien abduction narratives.

Morgan doesn't just exploit Australia's seeming isolation or American provinciality and ahistoricalness, she provides their fullest expression. Her reenacting ongoing themes of alienation and lostness traditionally associated with Australia may help further explain her book's popularity, at least beyond that nation. Found across the sea (pitched to Americans or at least non-Australians, never having an Australian publisher) and ending under the earth (in a giant cave), the Real People are enlisted as coconspirators in their own destruction. Though they appear to critique "mutantkind," their assured celibacy lets Morgan protect her white ladyhood and also to keep them from being fully human—they are merely humanoid, passionless, which explains why they won't be around to tattle on her in the future.

Morgan's Outback is Never Neverland, a place where dreams and fairy folk meet Native "redskins" rendered unreal: "Truly, someone in this world had their value system in the wrong place, I concluded, but I didn't think it was these primitive people here, in the so-called never-never land of Australia."[47] The Outback actually used to be referred to as "the Never Never," as in the title *We of the Never Never*, a 1908 book by a white woman in the Northern Territory of Australia. Sometimes referred to as a novel, it too presents itself as a nonfiction chronicle with a list of characters as types, from "The Maluka, The Little Missus, The Sanguine Scot, to "a few black 'boys' and lubras." It does, however, include photographs of its landscapes, ones found "away Behind the Back of Beyond, in the Land of the Never-Never; in that elusive land with an elusive name—a land of dangers and hardships and privations yet loved as few lands are loved—a land that bewitches her people with strange spells and mysteries, until they call sweet bitter, and bitter sweet."[48]

Of course, Australia is more often referred to as (or abbrieviated into) another fantastical place: *Oz*. There, the Wizard is someone who pretends to be far more powerful than he is. But Oz is also a rather complex place anyone can visit and get lost. Never Neverland requires an Edwardian idea of innocence and native role play to be seen; it is an island that sits past a star directly opposite Aboriginal *everywhen*.

Fortunately, unlike Morgan's Never Never, the Aborigine people are neither voiceless nor projected. Morgan was actually (or arguably) writing at a time of a resurgence of Aboriginal culture and population; a generous reading of the book might say it was a response to such changes, if it didn't remain so insistent on being unaware of them. In fact, many Aborigine groups offered coordinated resistance to Morgan's fiction. Founded in 1987 to protect and promote Western Australian Aborigine artists, the Dumbartung Aboriginal Corporation issued a ninety-page-plus report on the book, describing how "the origins of our culture are as Ancient as the Earth. . . . Our people suffered the forced colonisation of our Country 200 years ago by the British. Many of our people were killed by organised and authorised massacres. Many deaths were the result of introduced diseases. Water holes were poisoned as the ruthless obsession for land by the Colonists continued. As a result of the Native Welfare Act and its enforcement on Aboriginal People during the 1800s and early 1900s, many families were subject to enforced separation, sacred sites were desecrated and people were dispossessed from the land and were prevented from practising Tribal Customs. Many Aboriginal people suffered the humiliation of having to apply for citizenship rights to their own Country!"[49] Now Morgan says they need not eat.

How do you apply for rights to Never Neverland? The Dumbartung Aboriginal Corporation and others protested in the United States and Japan while Morgan toured there to stop her hoax from spreading unchecked or at least unchallenged. Successful in getting the movie stopped—the corporation says even New Age follower Shirley MacLaine, who was offered the lead in the movie version of Morgan's own reincarnation, refused it— Aborigine leaders weren't able to get Morgan to deliver on a promise to issue her spoken apology in writing.[50] The author maintained the same kinds of nondenial denials that she gave to the *Seattle Times* in 1997: "I did go on walkabout. The people do all the things I say, including the man with a broken leg who is healed enough to walk on it the next day. Everything that I say happened did happen. Nothing in the book is embellished. It's fiction because of what I left out, not what I put in."[51] Morgan's sins are only omissions, and those aren't even sins.

Such omissions do become visible in the difference between early self-published editions and the HarperCollins one. The changes aren't all to make it *more* of a novel; rather, inaccuracies that revealed its falseness, like her using a quarter to call from a payphone once she emerges from walkabout when Australia has no quarters (and presumably she no pockets), got fixed too. Why does a novel need be factually "corrected"?[52] Apart from fixing her aggrandized bio, perhaps the biggest change to later editions was adding a subtitle, *A Woman's Journey into Dreamtime Australia*, that only made Morgan's role more central to the message. The New Age publisher, scared off from reprinting because of factual problems, would have gone further— the scuttled title *Walkabout Woman: Messenger for the Vanishing Tribe* tells you all you need know about the book's true concerns.

Mutant Message represents a subtle but significant shift in our culture in which the art of fiction is less a mask or marketing tool than a concealed weapon. As JT LeRoy will, we shall learn soon enough, Morgan's "fiction" relies on alleged autobiography in every aspect of the hoax, from interviews to the writing itself—all while claiming otherwise whenever convenient or confronted. With Morgan, even her fiction is a fiction.

CHAPTER 8

The Time Machine

If the "novel" part of *Mutant Message* sounds in no way new, it is because it participates in the popular genre of the lost-race novel. Datable at least from H. Rider Haggard's *King Solomon's Mines* (1885), H. G. Wells's *The Time Machine* (1895), and Arthur Conan Doyle's *The Lost World* (1912), such a lost-race or lost-world theme remains a frequent one in literature. Whether found on earth or under it, over the ocean or leagues beneath the sea, the newly discovered race is primitive or supernatural, humanoid or alien. Often the lost race is friendly, but not for long; always the lost world remains anachronistic, animalistic, out of time. It is no accident that this genre sprang up as race was both becoming codified and the hoax was making its transition from humor to romance to horror: for race, often lost, operated in much the same way as the hoax, looking backward and forward at the same time.

Lost-race novels split Jean-Jacques Rousseau's "noble savage" into separate but unequal noble and savage groups—typically welcoming natives pitched against another, less-than-human race. The idea only makes clearer just how Rousseau was influenced by hoaxer Psalmanazar a century before, whose Formosa contrived a brute, aboveground population and pale, underground elite. (Psalmanazar was, of course, of the latter, highest caste.) Psalmanazar's hoax was not just fake history but early science fiction; indeed, it sought to combine the two, in what we might call *science faction*: a way of making the hoax seem realistic even as it embraces the romance of race.

It is no accident that these lost-race elements began appearing at the end of the nineteenth century just as an earlier age of exploration, which had given way to imperialism, began to see empire's end. Combining the "going native" trope from the age of exploration with the travel liar tradition, the codification of racialist science with the confusion of race's fictions, the lost-race novel reveals the ways its precedents are underpinned with imperialism. The lost-race novel, after all, usually involves gold or some other discovery that would get the expedition going. For Haggard's *She* and *King Solomon's Mines*, the site of the lost race was Africa; for the *Lost World*, South America; for the time machine, its undiscovered country was the future.

Race in a sense was a time machine: an invention whose users could go backward and forward in time, rewriting an unlikely past and forecasting a deterministic future. The hoax did much the same, keyed to race along the way. The time machine also suggests this book's method from here on out—journeying back and forth across the history of the hoax in order to trace the hoaxing of history. By jumping around the hoax's history a bit— our DeLorean time machine set to the 1890s, then tracing our way back to the more recent past—we might look ahead to what the millennium, and the rest of our Age of Euphemism, might bring. A hint: our age will realize even more hoaxes, grown only *worser*.

THE LOOT OF THE LAND

The genius of the description of the time machine in Wells's first novel was in using scientific elements to glimpse earth's future; its continued popularity testifies to how it anticipated the theories of relativity and modern notions of history found in the twentieth century. If the start of the eighteenth-century age of exploration also meant the advent of the novel in English, then the end of such "discoveries" in the nineteenth century actually saw the rise of science fiction—often set in the terra incognita of Australia. As I. F. Clarke describes in his thorough bibliography of science fiction, *The Tale of the Future*, "From the time of More's *Utopia* it had been common practice for writers to locate their ideal states or their satires in imaginary lands. Storms, shipwreck or marooning were stock devices used to increase the credibility of the imaginary voyage and to explain the narrator's arrival in Lilliput or Atlantis. . . . Thus, the blank spaces on the map coincided with the need for a neutral zone in which the propagandist could give shape to his hopes or fears; and when Captain Cook discovered Australia and ended forever the legend of *Terra australis incognita*, the same need for a neutral zone made the propagandists look elsewhere."[1] This zone was, of course, never neutral, nor was it uninhabited. Yet to the British who violently colonized it, Australia offered up a symbol of the terra incognita that in turn accrued to its oldest human inhabitants, marking them as "unknown," if not "unknowable"—despite the fact that Aborigines can trace their roots back forty thousand years. This outlandish notion of unknowability is the hoax's native soil.

Barnum and the dime museum had proved pioneers here too—pitch books and invented performer backstories had long made use of lost-race notions, as with Barnum's Wild Australian Children, said to have been found in the bush. Other showmen adopted similar techniques to describe acts like the famed Wild Men of Borneo, "Waino and Plutano"; a pamphlet about them opens by wading into the muddle of race: "Borneo is an Island so large that England, Ireland and Scotland might be set down in the middle of it. The interior of this vast Island is a dense forest, inhabited by a race of humanity, very little different from the animal creation, which is known to travelers as *Negritos*. Yellowish in color, and undersized, they hold no intercourse with semi-civilized tribes, such as their neighbors, the *Dyaks*, or the *Bugis*, who both differ from Malays of Borneo. They dwell in inpenetrable obscurity."[2] The "wild men," like the Wild Australian Children, were really from Ohio.

Not just inverting the colonial act—in which England actually set itself down on, and upon, other islands from Ireland to Australia—this travel lie insisted the Wild Men are not only less than human but black to boot. ("Wild Man of Borneo" soon became a nickname for the orangutan, whose supposed resemblance to Negritos was regularly evoked in racist tracts, which is to say, science.) The wildness of Borneo, like Fiji or Australia before it, became a given—and synonymous with blackness. While Manifest Destiny, imperialism, and white supremacy asserted that anything and anyone might be tamed, Barnum and his exoticist ilk pioneered the hoax notion that *anybody could be made wild*.

By the end of the nineteenth century, white writers regularly set lost-race novels in Australia, less a continent than a place out of time. This even remained true for those actually born in Australia, like Melbourne's William Sylvester Walker, who wrote under the name "Coo-ee." Walker's lost-race novels include *From the Land of the Wombat* (1899), *The Silver Queen* (1908), and *What Lay Beneath* (1909), typically characterizing Indigenous people as freakish foreigners while describing whites as the land's rightful owners. *What Lay Beneath*, published as part of an "Indian and Colonial Library," opens with a chapter called "The Loot of the Land" that's indicative of Marlo Morgan's later hoax—not to mention the hoaxes of Joan Lowell and other travel liars—making the combination of colonialism, conquest, and even Australian-"Indianness" especially obvious.[3] *Negrito*-tude was all about.

Walker's work, like Morgan's, circles a familiar storyline of the lost white child in the Australian landscape, a lively subgenre dating back to the middle of the nineteenth century. Such a "lost in the bush" myth becomes an embodiment of what critic Elspeth Tilley calls a *terra nullius* of Australia where "unsafe (unsettled) space . . . is contained, incorporated, and altered."[4] Morgan, for instance, proves herself both a lost babe in the wilderness and a lost adult, youthful in contrast to her timeless tribe, themselves nullified and unearthly. With Walker's *Silver Queen* the mix of lust, land, and whiteness is placed front and center, the protagonist encountering "The Mysterious Tribe" who "weren't niggers, but light-coloured people. Not half-castes, even, but some sort of breed nearly white." Later, they are described as "so fair in complexion as to give the impression that they were not aboriginals at all, but a cast-away tribe of European origin."[5] The frontispiece of *Land of the Wombat* declares "WE CAME ACROSS A GIRL ALMOST WHITE," notably depicting her topless—rare in a prudish era, unless of course, the subject is "almost white."[6] This is the ultimate exoticist fantasy, the corollary of the lost white child: *the white tribe found.*

Like the white Indian, this imaginary indigenous whiteness is a form of nativism, which is to say empire; as with the Circassian Beauty, the thrill is of pure whiteness set among blackness, sexualized, endangered, on display. The lost-race novel further suggests empire as a lost cause, and concentrates a panic also found in the high dudgeon of the hoax. *Mutant Message* may seem genius in just this way: whenever called on the carpet for her gross misrepresentations of actual Aborigine beliefs or Australian geography, Morgan's response takes its cues from the explorers or doctors at the start of "lost world" novels, whose pet theories and avant-garde science may be mocked and thought of as quackery but soon enough they will prove the world wrong! No wonder it's named a *mutant* message and labeled a novel—not to protect anyone but to take part in the lost race's long-standing scheme of hybrid humanoids found in a lost world.

The mutant is a modern freak, but where the freak was a role assigned as well as chosen, the mutant is an aberration—a freak not simply medicalized but also pathologized. It is in this way an apt metaphor for the modern hoax. Morgan's "Outback" and "DownUnder," in early editions rendered by her as one word, like Neverland, are no different from Psalmanazar's fake Formosa. All these intrepid travel liars are not lost; the land they "discover" is. Hoaxers picture these conquered places as empty of people—except from those who are excessively dark and primitive and silent. The threat, of course, is not that a hoax like Morgan's makes "Real People" real, but that hoaxes render real people unreal. This is a danger passed down from the lost-race novel to the very idea of race itself.

AMERICAN GOLGOTHA

The idea of two distinct races found in the lost-race novel was also familiar from nineteenth-century science—or what passes for it. At the middle of the century, in the midst of the Age of Imposture, the debate about the origins of the races was divided chiefly between those who saw in the "Ethiopian" race a not-so-pale imitation of whites, degenerated from the Creator's vision of Adam and Eve; and those such as influential thinker Louis Agassiz, who argued that the races, meaning black and white (and sometimes red), were created separately. Though it violated biblical dictates, this increasingly accepted notion of "polygenesis" helped to explain Negro and Indian inferiority and justify slavery and dislocation. In discussing, and ultimately dissecting, the "science" of race, evolutionary biologist Stephen Jay Gould writes of Agassiz: "No man did more to establish and enhance the prestige of American biology during the nineteenth century."[7] Innovator of the American idea of science, convener of the first graduate program, fundraiser and founder of Harvard's comparative zoology department, Agassiz believed "the blacks" not even human, and along with his fellow experts in natural history and craniometry, altered the scientific record to help prove it.

Agassiz becomes the ultimate "lost race" explorer, seeking to find an originating lost white tribe and a separate black ancestor that does not exist. All such racial rankings, their own form of hoax, have done worlds of harm. Is there any hoax more dangerous than this?

By embracing polygeny after his studies with Cuvier and other prominent naturalists in Europe, the Swiss-born Agassiz both put American science on the map and managed to insinuate himself American by adopting a chiefly homegrown doctrine. Writing of the scene at the time, Gould describes how "a collection of eclectic amateurs, bowing before the prestige of European theorists, became a group of professionals with indigenous ideas and an internal dynamic that did not require constant fueling from Europe. The doctrine of polygeny acted as an important agent in this transformation; for it was one of the first theories of largely American origin that won the attention and respect of European scientists—so much so that Europeans referred to polygeny as the 'American school' of anthropology."[8] This so-called American school led by Agassiz was founded on racialist ideas and bad science, its polygenesis dependent on widely accepted biases and now-disproved studies. Not that "monogeism" had a higher view of black humanity—it merely sought to align its beliefs with Christian views of creation from Adam and Eve, believing lesser races degenerated from superior whites. The trick for all such supposed sciences was explaining how black people had become the inferior subjects they undoubtedly were now and whether they might be rehabilitated.[9] Slavery thankfully offered itself as the best solution to both theories.

Central to the culture, Agassiz was a regular associate of the Transcendentalists and America's literati, as critic Louis Menand recounts in *The Metaphysical Club* (2001). "It is an indication of how commanding a presence Agassiz was in Boston in the years before the [Civil] war that the Saturday Club—the literary dining and conversation society of which he was a founding member, and whose participants included Emerson, Hawthorne, Longfellow, Whittier, [John Amory] Lowell, Sumner, and [Oliver Wendell] Holmes, all at the peak of their fame—was popularly referred to as Agassiz's Club."[10] Agassiz would not be the only member wrestling with race: not only would Longfellow write his *Song of Hiawatha* in 1855, the same year as Whitman's *Leaves of Grass*, but Emerson also published a chapter on "Race" in 1856 as part of his book *English Traits*. The whole is a confused and confusing affair, Emerson initially arguing with race science ("Who can call by right names what races are in Britain?") then establishing tendentious race theories of his own to describe the superiority of England. "It is race, is it not? that puts the hundred millions of India under the dominion of a remote island in the north of Europe. Race avails much, if that be true which is alleged, that all Celts are Catholics and all Saxons are Protestants; that Celts love unity of power, and Saxons the representative principle. Race is a controlling influence in the Jew, who, for two millenniums, under every climate, has preserved the same character and employments. Race in the negro is of appalling importance."[11]

In ways Agassiz surely influenced, Emerson devotes an appalling number of chapters to describing the "ability," "manners," and "truth" of those he terms "Saxons." He trumpets Celtic influence, then excludes the Irish ("an inferior or misplaced race") and Scottish (with their "rapid loss of all grandeur of mien and manners"), effectively trying to delineate and delimit whiteness, which remains ever more subdivided—as whiteness will. It is no surprise that Emerson ends up with the familiar lost-race fiction of two races on an undeserted island: England houses "the Norman . . . [who] has come popularly to represent in England the aristocratic, and the Saxon the democratic principle."[12] Both Norman and Saxon descend from the Scandinavian, whom he sometimes mislabels Northman or Nordic, Teutonic or Caucasian; most importantly, "both branches of the Scandinavian race are distinguished for beauty." He is a mere step away from that deadly fiction, Aryan: "When it is considered what humanity, what resources of mental and moral power the traits of the *blonde race* betoken, its accession to empire marks a new and finer epoch, wherein the old mineral force shall be subjugated at last by humanity and shall plough in its furrow henceforward. It is not a final race . . . but a race with a future." He says "the ruling passion of Englishmen in these days is a terror of humbug," anticipating the hoax's future terror.[13]

Above all Emerson pits an ambiguous, contradictory yet heroic, white "North" against an unspoken South. His Anglophilia ironically critiques American slavery (Britain had already abolished the practice) while celebrating the English virtues of New England.[14] Yet Emerson also anticipates the genealogical claims of southern whites who similarly willed and humbugged their way to Anglo-Saxon supremacy. If Agassiz made his name in the American North, Agassiz found his fame in the South, especially in Charleston, South Carolina. Here his lectures devolved from a belief in a unified view of race in his Lowell Lectures at Harvard, to saying what he hadn't said, or couldn't quite say, before: "There are upon earth different races of men, inhabiting different parts of its surface, which have different physical characters; and this fact . . . presses upon us the obligation to settle the relative rank among these races." He saw questions of racial rank not as "mock-philanthropy and mock-philosophy" but as fact—which of course turned out to be faction and pseudoscience, not far from lost-race novels that envisioned races under the earth's surface.[15]

The popularity of Agassiz's lectures was intimately tied to the kinds of judgments Americans grew used to making, entertained by exhibits and lyceums alike. "Though many people did not actually understand the scientific theories espoused in public lectures, they nonetheless found the debates and objects of science fascinating. People were learning a new language—the language of modernism—and they wanted to use it. At the sideshow, museum exhibit, public lecture, or demonstration you could test your knowledge, see if you could spot the humbug, and at the same time perhaps have a little fun." Critic Molly Rogers is here writing in the context of Barnum's Feejee Mermaid, which toured Charleston in January 1843, just a few years before Agassiz would go South starting in 1846.[16] Four years later Agassiz returned to photograph African American slaves nude and half-dressed to test his ethnological theories and claims.

For well over a century these photographs were themselves lost. Found in the attic of Harvard's Peabody Museum of Archaelogy and Ethnology in 1976, the daguerreotypes were labeled with the enslaved people's (first) names, their putative owners, and their assumed tribes. Such information labels them further—and further away from the white masters who claimed them, the photographer who captured them, the professor who sought them out, and those who left them in that attic, less in a time machine than a time capsule.[17] Nineteenth-century doctors, many self-appointed, would not only claim expertise but use the fact—or fiction—of expertise to frame and defame their subjects much as the modern hoax would. Barnum would gussy up arguments over his exhibits with pretend natural historians: the Feejee Mermaid was accompanied by one Dr. Griffin, really a coconspirator, who would testify "about his life as an explorer and his theories on zoology." Barnum well knew that it mattered less what the expert actually said than how the expert framed the show, leaving room for the audience: "America's appetite for the peculiar was matched only by its desire *to know*, to obtain knowledge that ostensibly paved the road to mastery—and who did not want to be a master of the modern world?" as Rogers puts it. Even the name "Dr. Griffin" suggested hybridity, the gryphon a mythological beast who served as "guardian of hidden gold mines," she notes.[18] I would go further and remind us that in the South "griffin" also labeled a racial mixture, another name for a "mulatto"—but even lower on the evolutionary ladder.

Such intimations of racial mixing might help explain why fake Dr. Griffin's explanation of the Feejee Mermaid went over less well in the South. In Charleston especially, the visit of the obvious hybrid was met with much resistance, being publicly declared a humbug—and a poor one at that. Once again, the debate circled around not exactly whether the artifact was genuine but whether it was good; anything seen as not trying to convince would be insulting. The main concern was the Mermaid's *look*: meaning both its *appearance*, symbolizing the race mixing expressly verboten but clearly undertaken by white men, usually the very ones who disparaged it; and the audience *looking* at the hoax and seeing how it worked. In much the same way, white debates over the origins of the black race were another kind of humbug, black inferiority a foregone conclusion: just look at them.

Agassiz had first found his "South" heading from Harvard to Philadelphia, the city of Brotherly Love in which he found little. Instead, he encountered Negroes, and repulsion, as he wrote to his mother:

> I can scarcely express to you the painful impression that I received, especially since the feeling that they inspired in me is contrary to all our ideas about the confraternity of the human type [*genre*] and the unique origin of our species. But truth before all. Nevertheless, I experienced pity at the sight of this degraded and degenerate race, and their lot inspired compassion in me in thinking that they really are men. Nonetheless, it is impossible for me to repress the feeling that they are not the same blood as us. In seeing their black faces with their thick lips and grimacing teeth, the wool on their head, their bent knees, their elongated hands, their large curled nails, and especially the livid color of the palm of their hands, I could not take my eyes off their face in order to tell them to stay far away. . . . What unhappiness for the white race—to have tied their existence so closely with that of negroes in certain countries! God preserve us from such a contact![19]

In Philadelphia Agassiz also met his biggest future collaborator in Samuel George Morton. Sharing the then-common yet incorrect belief that not only race but also intelligence could be detected in skull size, Morton had assembled the world's largest collection of over six hundred skulls nicknamed "The American Golgotha."[20] "The most famous anthropologist of his day," according to Menand, Morton initially "had made his name by analyzing the fossils brought back by Lewis and Clark"—but exploration once again gave way to colonization. Morton's two famed books, *Crania Americana* (1839) and *Crania Aegyptiaca* (1844), focused on the skulls of Indigenous Americans and those looted from Egyptian tombs, respectively; using measurements with white pepper seed and later lead shot, Morton ranked the races, with whites at the top, "Americans" (that is, Native Americans) in the middle, and Negroes (including African Americans, Hottentots, and Australian Aborigines) naturally at the bottom.[21] Morton's resulting ranking of the races, seen as objective and scientific, remained in textbooks well past Darwin and the debunking of polygeny; the persistence of his divisions of race can be found today in such long-held notions as Egyptians and "Hindus" being "Caucasian"; or the unfortunate use of "Mongoloid," thankfully on the decline, to mean Down syndrome. Gould reminds us that this last racialized label, seen as a racial reversion, was applied by Dr. Down himself.

Gould also helps us understand how the fad for biological determinism regularly recurs, even today: "The reasons for recurrence are sociopolitical, and not far to seek: resurgences of biological determinism correlate with episodes of political retrenchment, particularly with campaigns for reduced government spending on social programs, or at times of fear among ruling elites, when disadvantaged groups sow serious social unrest or even threaten to usurp power."[22] We might be said today to be in yet another recapitulation of such theories: after Gould's debunking of the "hereditarian interpretation of IQ," and the racial distortions of *The Bell Curve* at the millennium's end—another height of the hoax—the trend continues. Consider the Yale law professor, Amy Chua, who wrote the controversial 2011 best seller *Battle Hymn of the Tiger Mother*, about raising children under what she called Asian traditions; her follow-up book is on the superiority of—surprise, surprise—her and her coauthor husband's races (Asian and white/Jewish), making her initial article, "Why Chinese Mothers Are Superior," literal and pseudoscientific. Or, take *A Troublesome Inheritance* by the so-called science writer from the *New York Times* Nicholas Wade, describing rather unscientifically the ways in which blacks and Asians are inferior, and whites like him superior. Both of these prominent pseudoscientific books, by nonexperts in the field as always is the case, are from 2014. Many a hoax has been built on less.

Needless to say, the provenance of Morton's stolen skulls was as dubious as Agassiz's assertion that he could tell the tribal origins of Negroes just from physical characteristics. What's more, Morton inevitably and regularly fabricated his numerical results in favor of black inferiority: "Morton's summaries are a patchwork of fudging and finagling in the clear interest of controlling a priori convictions," Gould writes. "Yet—and this is the most intriguing aspect of the case—I find no evidence of conscious fraud; indeed, had Morton been a conscious fudger, he would not have published his data so openly." By reanalyzing Morton's numbers, Gould helps us understand how the hoax can happen, and catch hold—less through "conscious fraud" than an unconscious process now called confirmation bias, once called racism. "The prevalence of *unconscious* finagling . . . suggests a general conclusion about the social context of science. For if scientists can be honestly self-deluded to Morton's extent, then prior prejudice may be found anywhere, even in the basics of measuring bones and toting sums."[23] If the hoax has taught us anything, it is that intent in the end doesn't matter—and that once peeled away, the mask or skin of the hoax reveals a skull that can be made to say whatever the hoaxer wishes.

Race wasn't so much a time machine as literally stuck in time. Adhering to Morton's theories allowed Agassiz to discount mutation and what would become known as evolution: "Agassiz didn't think that plants or animals had multiplied, migrated, and mutated over time; it was awkward to have to make an exception for human beings."[24] By the time of his lectures in Charleston in 1847, Agassiz could declare, "The brain of the Negro is that of the imperfect brain of a 7 month's infant in the womb of a White."[25] Black people weren't even people; not just childlike, a familiar attitude, they were premature, embryonic whites. (African Americans are, of course, "the Negro," definitive, while the indefinite article of "a White" leaves white people individualized and exemplary.) In America, and the South, Agassiz could encounter racial difference and not only study but subjugate it. No more fossils and fish as once was his field: it was no less than the United States he was providing a natural history of, but also for. As he had in his Philadelphia encounter, he observed life without realizing or at least admitting that he was altering his observations and not, as science is supposed to, letting the evidence speak. The photos, like skulls, remain silent, not even grinning.

THE DISINTEGRATION MACHINE

Agassiz might put us in mind of Professor Challenger from Conan Doyle's *Lost World* decades later—he too was a professor with a quack theory who went South, and ultimately to South America, in order to prove his crackpot ideas on the types—*genres*—of man. Both in his trip to South Carolina and in an 1865 expedition to Brazil, Agassiz took pictures, made specimens, and collected skulls to fit his theories. Future father of psychology William James, who accompanied Agassiz to Brazil as his student, describes the way the naturalist and his systems sought to fight evolution: "I don't yet understand him very well," James wrote his brother Henry. "His charlatanerie is almost as great as his solid worth; and it seems of an unconscious childish kind that you can't condemn him for as you wd most people. He wishes to be too omniscient." Charlatanerie and science bled into omniscience, not just for Agassiz's set ideas about creation but also for his expansive views of self. As Menand writes, "His science wasn't theoretical and his theory wasn't scientific."[26]

This marked a whole genre. Decades later Conan Doyle, trained as a doctor, could mimic not just logic in Holmes but science in Challenger— and later, pseudoscience and pseudospirituality. Challenger became a mouthpiece for Conan Doyle's Spiritualist beliefs in the 1920s in fictions like *The Land of Mist* or *The Disintegration Machine*. Not that he hadn't used Professor Challenger as a double before: upon the first serialization of *The Lost World* in 1912, Conan Doyle disguised himself as his character, beard and all, and had pictures made that were meant to run alongside his fiction as if real. The prop exploration party was included too. Though on the one hand a harmless lark, the familiar identification of the author with his hero, the effort stands in contrast to Conan Doyle's distancing from Holmes; and suggests the ways in which the fake could infect science, and vice versa.

Conan Doyle's era extended science's discoveries, separating not just races but other hominids—as in Piltdown Man, who supposedly provided a connection between humanoids and *Homo sapiens*. First uncovered near Conan Doyle's home in 1912 and called "the earliest Englishman" by one champion, Piltdown Man proved the British first in scientific discovery; it also showed that the origins of the human race could be "found in England, right in the heart of the British Empire, where any thinking human being knew early man must have evolved," putting "England right at the top of the evolutionary tree of early man."[27] It took several decades to prove Piltdown Man a hoax, its skull altered physically in the ways that Agassiz et al. had altered their skulls' measurements semiconsciously. That some have thought (it appears wrongly) that Conan Doyle was in on the Piltdown hoax only hints at the connection between science and the spirit—or, better yet, pseudoscience, pseudospirituality, and the hoax. Or is it the connection between the hoax of Piltdown, the fiction of *The Lost World*, and the wish of photography?

The times held other strange discoveries meant to reveal entirely separate races, including giants. These included the giant fish found in Alabama at the time of Agassiz; and the Cardiff Giant, uncovered on a New York farm by two workers in 1869, and declared to be the petrified remains of a lost race. Really a hoax crafted by one George Hull, the ten-foot-high figure was carved out of gypsum, providing a parody of the pseudoscience that would have us believe giants once lived (a belief far more plausible apparently than black people being people; we will come to "giant Negroes" soon enough). The farm owner charged admission and the giant from Cardiff became the ultimate native—extinction personified, and petrified. Barnum reportedly offered the astronomical sum of fifty thousand dollars for the giant, and when refused, simply made his own fake and claimed it was the real one.

Giants had long lent a sense of stature in the popular imagination, either to the people said to be descended from them; or those conquered peoples who mythified their conquerors as being literal giants. The giant too was a sideshow staple whose stature continues in our sports, where the mythic and the conquered meet. Again, the giant gave us freaks not of nature but of culture, recognizing our insufficient categories of taxonomy, which had sought to answer age-old questions of what it means to be human. But giants also serve as metaphors for the hoax itself. Three kinds of hoaxes, six types of liars, seven deadly unoriginal sins: any taxonomy of the hoax, while mimicking science, also tends to keep the unruly, factitious form of the hoax far more regulated than it actually is. The hoax has much more in common with cryptozoology, those mythic animal hoaxes found in Barnum and beyond, from his Feejee Mermaid and the Cardiff Giant to the faked Bigfoot footage and Loch Ness monster photographs in the 1970s TV show *In Search Of* that kept me up nights as a kid. Those who wish to reduce the hoax to mere taxonomy try to resolve the paradox of our being affected by things that are patently untrue by displacing blame from our beliefs to categories or to the hoaxers themselves. Turns out that the frequent monsters of the hoax, as Curtis MacDougall reminds us, are not a question of zoology but of psychology.

And psychology not only was at work in the American school of anthropology—with its white desire for a homegrown excellence, a mock philosophy, to help explain the nation's own superiority and its colored peoples' inferiority—but also in the new field of psychology that would come to debunk notions like intelligence being detectable in the skull itself. Darwin's *Origin of Species* would sweep away Agassiz and his willful theories (though many stay with us, morphed into Social Darwinism), and Freud would take care of the rest. Darwin himself would read Agassiz's lectures on Brazil—which include the mad-scientist notion that there were glaciers once in Brazil—writing, "I was very glad to read it, though chiefly as a psychological curiosity."[28] The subconscious explained race better than any skull could.

ARE WE NOT MEN?

H. G. Wells's second novel *The Island of Dr. Moreau* (1896) revels in the romance of race while well aware of the lost cause and the lost empire. Like Joseph Conrad's *Heart of Darkness*, which it resembles and precedes by a few years, *Moreau* is the last gasp of the Victorian era with a fin de siècle flair, one of the many things that has helped it persist in film and other versions for well over a century. The book is a time machine in this way: *Moreau* looks ahead but also deeply evokes its moment. To look at it is to grasp the heights of fiction and just how derivative hoaxes can be. And to see how a focus on race puts at jeopardy one's humanity.

Dr. Moreau is descended from the more famous Victor Frankenstein, yet he is no tortured hero, nor an artist, much less a "victor." (Hoaxer Marlo Morgan could be a latter-day Dr. Moreau if she hadn't also been pretending to be a doctor.) The narrator Edward Prendick's repulsion on first seeing Moreau's Beast People—what the 1977 film version felicitously calls "manimals"—is couched in clear racial terms reminiscent of Agassiz. One Ape Man (alternately called Monkey Man, conflating the two species) is described as "of a moderate size, and with a black negroid face"; others are described unflatteringly, animalistically, as somehow Jewish. All are "grotesque caricatures of humanity": "I had paused half way through the hatchway, looking back, still astonished beyond measure at the grotesque ugliness of this black-faced creature. I had never beheld such a repulsive and extraordinary face before, and yet—if the contradiction is credible—I experienced at the same time an odd feeling that in some way I *had* already encountered exactly the features and gestures that now amazed me." Serving as a manservant to Prendick's other host on the island, "the black," as he's called, is familiar because likely crafted from a bear—but also because he is described in terms familiar to the century that sought to marry, or should we say genetically engineer, race to science, and pervert evolution by its opposite.

All this matters because of other matters—the hoax taking race for granted as scientific, and scientific romance, as Wells's early novels are called, making use of hoax techniques. Like many a travel liar narrative and novel before it, *Moreau* is framed as the discovered writings of a shipwreck survivor—and filled with contradictions made credible. They are the age's: Prendick is repulsed by the vivisection, though mostly of what he believes are men, that Moreau performs; he feels himself above Moreau the mad scientist but in many ways resembles him, especially after the madman's death.

Prendick soon learns that it isn't that the Beast People are human merged with animals; rather they are animals made more than animals through knife and will.

Though it means to evoke evolution, *Moreau* also easily fits the popular pseudoscientific model of degeneration that in the 1890s meant to explain everything from mental illness to women's rights (or lack of them) to race.[29] Even at the time this seemed a direct response to the disorienting speed of modernity at the fin de siècle; our current Age of Euphemism offers another such response. By the 1890s, technology would transform society rapidly: long-distance calling, gramophones, player pianos, popular sheet music, and disc recordings, were all pioneered; the voice changed utterly, the song suddenly separated from the self. This could be one definition of the modern condition. The modern poem helped along this transformation, and helped chart the change: in the 1890s, Dickinson's first poems appeared posthumously in three volumes, as did Whitman's deathbed edition of *Leaves of Grass* in 1892; Stephen Crane would publish *Black Riders*, while innovator Paul Laurence Dunbar crafted a protomodernism whose black selves and songs were double. His refrain *We wear the mask* could serve as modern motto. Other changes in voice emerged, in music especially, with the blooming of the blues, the advent of jazz, and the presence of ragtime and Tin Pan Alley all suggesting other syncopations and even realms.

The 1890s also saw a number of other crises we might label lyrical: hysteria; new fin de siècle narratives like psychoanalysis; and a resurgence of Spiritualism. All these last kinds of lyrical crises the modern hoax took advantage of.

Not that the 1890s only brought advances. Always lesser, now not even human: the theory that "environmental influences caused a 'degeneration' away from a primordial form to create the different racial varieties in the world," as critic Nancy Stepan summarizes it, even informed the hoax and humbug; degeneration, Sander Gilman observes, now meant "the Jew," who would regularly be characterized, as Moreau's monsters were, as black too. Even the literal madwoman in the asylum or metaphoric one in the attic was seen as reverting to a more primitive evolutionary stage.[30] Extensions of these regressive views didn't simply inform or express prejudices but led quite directly to eugenics, later sterilization efforts, and genocides, not to mention the Nazi views of "degenerate art and music"—whose emblem was part Jew, part Negro, part Gypsy, and all jazz.

This conflation was visual: by the 1930s, Nazi propaganda would depict the mentally ill alongside modern art, offering their shared fractured faces as evidence of deep disturbance fit only for extinction. The degenerate would be the freak not just medicalized but eugenicized; the degenerate people and art deemed as such would be destroyed. Or auctioned off at a profit. Ironically the 1937 *Degenerate Art* show that the Nazis staged as an abject lesson in modernism's perils drew over two million visitors, making it far more popular than the official exhibition of German art held at the same time. In some ways, the Nazis would lament in the mentally ill the very thing the surrealists praised in the hysterics and modernists embraced in African and Oceanic art. But rather than a contorted, impure face, the modernists—American or Irish, European or African, Caribbean or African American—saw the power of the mask and of the mad, whose mug shots resemble nothing so much as the long-lost enslaved people of Agassiz, defiantly looking back.[31]

This mask is the monster's and the hoax's; and monsters prove popular. *Moreau* and its film adaptations reveal colonialism's power not just on the colonized but on the colonizer: after all, the House of Pain may be what the manimals fear, but it's where the Doctor lives. And dies. The first film adaptation of Moreau and by far the best, *The Island of Lost Souls* (1932) portrays Moreau as his own kind of dictator, genetically and socially engineering his islanders in ways that speak to the then-rising tide of Nazism, the Holocaust to come. The film also introduces a woman as a potential love interest—who might be a beast person, we're not yet sure—a lead the other *Moreau* films would follow. (To see the later films is to see the devolution of an idea, as the plot becomes more elaborate and less effective, the woman's role ever more rote.) Here named Lota, she is referred to in posters and credits as the Panther Woman in case you missed the point. In the stark chiaroscuro of expressionist horror and pre–Motion Picture Production Code forthrightness, Lota exemplifies the big hair and skimpy outfits of the exoticist ideal, descended from the Circassian Beauty—desirable and desirous, native yet naive. Native-born and typecast, she is Shakespeare's Miranda and Caliban in one, literally drowning the book the shipwrecked protagonist reads to help him get off the isle.

The Panther Woman not only suggests, but lusts after, miscegenation. The lost-race novel, like the Circassian Beauty, regularly evokes interracial sex under threat of violence and slavery; most lost-race novels use the cover or threat of interspecies blending to suggest the charge, in all senses, of race. When used today, a term like *miscegenation* is almost always rendered in invisible quotes in order to convey its status as a racist yet real taboo against "race mixing." But are we aware that "miscegenation" also comes from a hoax? The 1864 pamphlet *Miscegenation*, which coined the word, was meant not just to satire those voting for Republican candidates like Lincoln, but scare them—its race-baiting suggested that the entire party saw race mixing as acceptable and indeed required. "The word is spoken at last. It is Miscegenation—the blending of various races of men—the practical recognition of the brotherhood of all the children of the common father."[32] Issued anonymously, the hoax put forth nonracist ideas to serve practical racist ends; denounced from the floor of Congress, the pamphlet became political fodder, as intended—though it did not succeed in changing the presidential election. But the hoax in its modern form is often political, which is to say, a mix of propaganda and power.

To use the term miscegenation unironically today is to miss the ways the hoax can have consequences for our language. For his part, P. T. Barnum wrote about *Miscegenation* as a delightful piece of humbug, not because it worked but because who would ever be fool enough to believe blacks and whites were equal? By such a rationale, Barnum suggests, the pamphlet's discussions of the physiological equality of the white and colored races and the superiority of mixed races should have been as much a tip-off to its absurdity as its proclaiming "the doctrine of human brotherhood should be accepted in its entirety in the United States."[33] The ultimate point may be that race as defined by others, especially racialists and racists, is in fact a hoax.

Miscegenation—the term and the text—further names a fear wrapped in a fantasy. *You made me a thing*, shouts Bela Lugosi's Sayer of the Law into the camera before Moreau's creations turn against him. Prendick will resort to saying that Moreau is not really dead—is resurrected now in the sky, looking over the Beast People—in order to control them. Attempting to flee Moreau's compound, he urges the Beast People to rebel: "'You who listen,' I cried, pointing now to Moreau, and shouting past him to the Beast Men, 'you who listen! Do you not see these men still fear you, go in dread of you? Why then do you fear them? You are many.'" But such foment won't last long. Reading *Moreau*, we realize that for the narrator to have reacted calmly to the black figure on the ship he's been rescued on would be to ignore not just centuries of racist rhetoric but the Romantic and Victorian eras wherein race was a science. The same would prove true for the hoax, helping explain Jorge Luis Borges's description of *Moreau* as an "atrocious miracle."[34]

The manimals famed cry "Are we not men?" echoes the nineteenth-century black abolitionist cry of "Am I not a man and brother?" The 1977 film version makes its plantation setting quite clear, with Moreau strung up after his death like a lynch victim above the conflagration. The refrain may put us in mind of the influential 1978 debut by the band Devo, where "Are we not men?" serves as part of the chorus of "Jocko Homo." The answer is D-E-V-O, which stands for "de-evolution," a kind of cosmology the Ohio band developed to describe the degraded world around them, even making masks like those in *Lost Souls*, an acknowledged influence, to embody and perform their own feelings of alienation. The ideas of the film merged with the antievolutionary, pseudospiritual claims of the 1925 pamphlet *Jocko-Homo Heavenbound* that Devo's Mark Mothersbaugh found sometime in 1970, and de-evolution was born.

Given the retrograde and regressive tendencies all around them, such devolution seemed self-evident: attending Kent State, at least one founding member of Devo was in the crowd when National Guardsmen fired upon peaceful demonstrators on 4 May 1970; in interviews, the band has since spoken of the killings as galvanizing their worldview. Devo's brilliance was to see, in both *Lost Souls* and *Jocko-Homo*, how an idea could degrade in all senses—and past all sense—and that even degeneration, which had passed for science a century before, could generate art. In describing personal Houses of Pain, the abject could become a metaphor for a modern life. "Whip It" becomes more a commentary on the whip *Lost Souls'* Moreau wields like a slavemaster; Devo will instead *whip it good*.

The *Moreau* novels and films showed what the hoax already hinted at: that there are always two races that are lost, meaning not just the discovered natives but also the white discoverers. We must not forget that the colonizer's DNA would be utterly altered by the colonial experiment. No wonder the first American edition of Wells's *Moreau* bears the subtitle: *A Possibility*.

AMBASSADORS FROM MARS

Scientific romance, like science faction, implicates not just the past but the past's ideas of the future—exactly where the hoax would seek to live. Even in the nineteenth century this future centered on Mars, where lost races could be found according not just to sci-fi but supposed science. After providing the names we still use for the "seas" on Mars, in 1877 astronomer Giovanni Schiaparelli described "canali" spotted on the surface, meaning *channels* in Italian. The term was misinterpreted—willfully it would seem—as "canals," suggesting less natural phenomena than structures built by presumed Martians. What NASA itself calls "a detour in the history of Mars exploration" began.[35]

Mars exploration had its origins in *Gulliver's Travels*, whose parody of Psalmanazar discussed Mars's moons in a fashion that would turn out to be fairly accurate. The exploration would continue in the belief not just in Martians but in the subdivision of them into races—as seen in American novelist Edgar Rice Burroughs and his John Carter novels first serialized in 1912. A Confederate soldier during the Civil War, Carter travels time and space to the red planet whose natives call "Basoom." He is lost-race explorer and conqueror in one, going on to marry Mars royalty, and, like Superman in reverse, gaining power from its different gravity. The idea that Mars requires a conqueror and bore ancient life finds its way in more recent productions such as the 1990 movie *Total Recall* with its amnesiac rogue agents and lost race of Martian mutants, unsubtly called "freaks." (The dyspeptic 2012 reboot quite comfortably moves the action from Mars to "The Colony" Australia, implying they are equally foreign.)

The most famous Mars novel remains Wells's *War of the Worlds* (1898), which imagined a Martian invasion of Earth. Wells apparently meant *War of the Worlds* as a metaphor for colonialism: what would it meant for Britain to be colonized, invaded, as the British Empire had done across the globe? This too took the 1890s as crucial to a human future:

> No one would have believed in the last years of the nineteenth century that this world was being watched keenly and closely by intelligences greater than man's and yet as mortal as his own: that as men busied themselves about their various concerns they were scrutinised and studied, perhaps almost as narrowly as a man with a microscope might scrutinise the transient creatures that swarm and multiply in a drop of water. . . . At most, terrestrial men fancied there might be other men upon Mars, perhaps inferior to themselves and ready to welcome a missionary enterprise. Yet across the gulf of space, minds that are to our minds as ours are to those of the beasts that perish, intellects vast and cool and unsympathetic, regarded this earth with envious eyes, and slowly and surely drew their plans against us. And early in the twentieth century came the great disillusionment.[36]

If American audiences, especially in the subsequent *War of the Worlds* movies, took the alien invasion more as a metaphor for the Cold War or for more earthbound conflicts in the Middle East, it was only as a way to prove their strength as resisters, Cowboys vs. Aliens, revolutionaries till the end.

The same could not be said of the hoax that originated from a different Welles. Orson Welles had long proved a trickster of sorts, at least since his Mercury Theatre company's performance of *War of the Worlds*, the 1938 radio version that exploited broadcast radio, not to mention a frightened and gullible public. The result was a mass hysteria by listeners who thought it was a live news account of an actual Martian invasion. By some estimates nearly a third of the millions who heard the CBS broadcast believed it. More recent studies may downplay the number of panickers, but this fails to grasp the cultural impact: police stations were swamped and phone lines jammed; many are the accounts of folks trying to flee on the highway to who knows where they thought was safe or arming themselves in preparation for the end. In retrospect, the panic the hoax inspired speaks to a larger unease in a country on the brink of World War II—an unease that the radio play's scriptwriter, Howard Koch, would later dramatize in his screenplay for *Casablanca*.[37] But war will center hoaxes more and more, as we'll see.

Much of the radio play's success is structural, taking a lesson from the nineteenth-century humbug, surrounding its shock with banality that felt like facts: in short, *science faction*. The "panic broadcast," as Koch later labeled his adaptation, is structured as a series of interrupted broadcasts and news reports. "Ladies and gentlemen, I have a grave announcement to make," the radio announcer says. "Incredible as it may seem, both the observations of science and the evidence of our eyes lead to the inescapable assumption that those strange beings who landed in the Jersey farmlands tonight are the vanguard of an invading army from the planet Mars."[38] In the radio play any skeptics about the attack are soon vaporized by Martian heat rays, which must've only helped to bring listeners along.

But the apocalyptic mood, often found in the modern hoax, spoke to something larger. "If our radio play had portrayed the Martians as arrivals on a friendly mission, I suspect our audience would have been less ready to accept the drama as something actually happening," Koch writes. This was the horror of the hoax, now coming home. By setting the invasion in the real town of Grovers Mill, New Jersey, Koch subtly invoked the fictional all-American "Grovers Corner" from *Our Town*—and a threat most American. "We tend to assign to others our own fears and aggressions. Hence it was natural for the Michigan farmer who believed he saw one of the objects hovering over a swamp on his land to run into his house for his shotgun instead of making some more hospitable gesture," Koch adds.[39] One gets the feeling that today's reaction would be much the same, except the farmer might wield an assault rifle.

The War of the Worlds also reminds us that the hoax isn't necessarily intentional but based on the audience and its belief. The broadcast was the day before Halloween, after all, that time when we dress up (and as) our fears. "Isn't there anyone on the air?" the broadcast would ask before intermission, actually followed by a station identification, one of many, which indicated this was a radio drama. But few heard that. "Isn't there anyone . . . ?" Welles faced much outcry about the broadcast till several newspapers held that it proved our unpreparedness for a real war. "'Mars Panic' Useful" read one headline; "They have proved how easy it is to start a mass delusion," wrote an influential columnist.[40] Might we also say that the panic was about the mass delusion of race, however displaced to Mars?

For the idea of a Mars Invasion simply transformed the two races of the lost-race genre, dividing the world into human and Martian. And in a world where *human* too often meant *white*, the threat could be interpreted not just as coming from the blackness of space but the blackness of its earthly population. *Mars wants our women.* This was a going concern in America at least since Benjamin Franklin wished for whites to increase "their numbers" in 1751: "While we are, as I may call it, scouring our planet, by clearing America of woods, and so making this side of our globe reflect a brighter light to the eyes of inhabitants in Mars or Venus, why should we . . . darken its people? Why increase the Sons of Africa, by planting them in America?"[41] Yet the "space race" was black too—not only in the folk explorations of Native Americans and African Americans, who had long viewed visitations to and from the stars and the Red Planet as part of their cultural inheritance, but the Afrofuturistic notion in everyone from Sun Ra to P. Funk and Lil Wayne, who see space as a place of further freedom from earthbound concerns. The freak too pitched aliens as the ultimate outsiders: take the black albino Muse Brothers, first kidnapped as children in the 1890s and, as "Eko and Iko," put onstage as Barnum had piebald families before them; later they would find out the truth and their mother sued the circuses—and won. Still they continued in sideshows and the Barnum & Bailey Circus as White Ecuadoran cannibals or dreadlocked "Ambassadors from Mars" till the last brother's death in 2001.[42] They embody the entwined fates of freaks, especially black ones, made mutant or Martian, across the last century.

The lost-race novel time-traveled forward to Mars and back to the winged heels of the Moon Hoax and Poe's failed ones. *Vraisemblance* is exactly what Wells realized in *Moreau* and Welles perfected on the radio. Grafting the travel narrative and lost-race novel to contemporary science, just as Dr. Moreau had his Beast People, H. G. Wells also seems to realize that *not* to have included pseudoscience in his book would have made the fiction too obvious. What else was racialist eugenics, especially in its grotesqueries, but "scientific romance"? Fiction took this lesson from the hoax: that race is an essential and seductive part of the romance.

THE LOST WORLD

A related Romantic impulse is found among modern anthropologists, for whom the idea of discovering a lost tribe dovetails a bit too neatly with the science fiction of discovering a lost race. Depending on one's point of view, such a tribe provides a rebuke to modern life and its devolution; the primitive "lost tribe" also held out a glimpse of our so-called modern civilization's evolutionary past. Enter the Tasaday, a group of people in the Philippines revealed to the outside world in 1971. The group's existence was widely reported, on the American evening news no less, and was eventually featured in journalist John Nance's popular book *The Gentle Tasaday: A Stone Age People in the Philippine Rain Forest* (1975). Though a world and, as the subtitle declared, centuries away, the Tasaday provided an American story in terms of publicity and its appeal to various social forces at play in realpolitik, if not reality.

It seems clear that the Tasaday gave Americans a dark if hopeful double for Vietnam. As writer Robin Hemley traces in his fascinating *Invented Eden*, the Tasaday meant very different things to different people, whether Filipino pride; political fodder for the Marcos dictatorship; or providing a welcome symbol for both humanity's origins and our innate goodness. This primitive race seemed far advanced than supposed civilization. Much was made of the idea that the Tasaday had no word for *war*. Yet was the whole thing a hoax?

"Lost tribe simply means new tribe," wrote one of the first anthropologists invited in to observe the Tasaday; another of his team more pointedly said, "Technically, there is no such thing as a lost tribe but only more isolated than other known tribes."[43] Soon, as in the Heisenberg uncertainty principle, mere observation changed what was being observed. From the onset of their "discovery," the Tasaday were both observed and overlooked by those who said they'd protect them—any reasoned response to their "lostness" would soon come to be lost. As Hemley details, Manuel Elizalde Jr., the charismatic minister of indigenous cultures under Philippines dictator Ferdinand Marcos, could be benevolent or dictatorial in turn. Known as Manda, Elizalde became known to the Tasaday fondly as Momo' Dakel. Manda had as many contradictions as names: he wished to keep the Tasaday sheltered, then let actor Gina Lollobrigida and famed aviator Charles Lindbergh fly in by helicopter to visit.

"A lifetime closely related to fields of aviation has left me familiar with traveling through space," Lindbergh writes in his foreword to Nance's *The Gentle Tasaday*. "Jumping onto a treetop platform in the Tasaday rain forest gave me the strange but similar sensation of traveling through time." The contradictions of the case of the Tasaday can be found in someone like Lindbergh—a notorious anti-Semite and near Nazi, Lindbergh later became an ardent environmentalist fascinated with so-called primitive people. In a sense this too was a perverse extension of Nazism, which found in degeneration a pseudoscientific justification for genocide but maintained a fascination with racial purity and primitiveness. "Somehow I must strike a balance between the civilized and primitive. It was a balance that both the Tasaday and I were seeking from opposite directions," Lindbergh writes.[44] This balance may have been swayed by Lindbergh's constant companion in the book's photographs: a machine gun. Nance's book pictures the Tasaday in loincloths surrounded by guns wielded by their supposed guardians and next to helicopters, that symbol of the Vietnam War, wincing from the rotor blades' winds. Such exoticist contradictions of Stone Age and civilized, lostness and preservation, of good primitives and bad, are found in the "lost race" narrative—not to mention in the modern notion of the hoax, something that by the 1980s the Tasaday were accused of being. This too was a form of time travel: while the 1970s wished to find a group beyond the reaches and plagues of modernity, the wearied and wary 1980s didn't buy it, political and social disillusionment wrought by the likes of Vietnam and Watergate having seen everything corruptible, if not already corrupt.

But the story of the Tasaday demonstrates that in the uncovering of a supposed hoax, few escape unscathed. The Tasaday prove too much of a mirror: each advocate or hoax proponent saw what he or she wanted to see in them, whether a sign of governmental corruption, with the Tasaday paid to pretend to be natives wearing leaves; or pure innocence misunderstood by those hoax proponents, often foreign journalists, who hadn't actually viewed their homes in person. It is remarkable the number of people who derided the Tasaday as fake who hadn't visited the sites they claimed didn't exist. This harks back to anthropology's advent in Agassiz, whose studies proved less time travel than travel lies.

"Whether the Tasaday story is purely scientific or purely journalistic is debatable," Hemley writes. "It tends to be a disconcerting mix of the two."[45] Hemley's journey becomes clearly one about seeing what he's shown, and of interpreters who shade speech to suit their points. "The journalists were satisfied, but they'd ignored the crucial problems of the Tasaday story: the fluidity of language, the impossibility of translation, the ways in which our imaginations combust with events to create fantasies and conspiracies, the ways in which we can be manipulated by our own expectations as much as by the machinations of others."[46] Here is the *half-hoax*, the modern condition in which bunk is believed, mistranslation reigns, and truth be not so much damned as not bothered with. It is we who are lost.

Hemley concludes that, as one anthropologist cautioned at the outset, *lost* simply does mean *isolated*—though the Tasaday were likely not as isolated as originally assumed, they still are not a hoax created by Manda or Marcos. The Tasaday knew other groups and sometimes interacted with them—indeed, this is how they were brought to Manda's attention, through someone who had taught them a few different foodways—though this is exactly why deniers view the whole as a hoax. Any inaccuracy in the initial findings is seen as further proof of a conspiracy rather than reality's complexity, or the flawed nature of observation.

It is when a hoax or, for that matter, science claims purity, racial or otherwise—when the stories start to sound conventionalized, clichéd, consistent, pure in their way—that we should be most skeptical. The truth is messy; real people are complicated; much as we might wish it, isolation is nearly impossible. *For it is the very notion of the lost tribe that is false.*

The notion of the lost tribe also implies that if only such people knew modernity, they would certainly choose it; it dovetails too neatly with the "last of his race" rhetoric around folks like Issa or Ota Benga, on display in "human zoos" and soon dead. Hemley's account mentions a number of lost groups nearly destroyed by their encounter with well-meaning anthropologists—if with the Tasaday this shifted slightly, what awaited them was not civilization but de-evolution. Whether trying to understand the Tasaday or uncover them as a hoax, either effort meant dragging them from their homes or making them stay in them in order to prove their existence. Such testimony became literal—in a near-impossible proposition, several had to publicly testify to who they were at a government hearing. *Are we not men?* A few who once said that Manda had forced them to wear leaves and pretend to be a "lost tribe" would later say it was because in exchange for such testimony companies promised them money they never received. The Tasaday represent not the broken promise of their Stone Age-ness, but a series of promises broken to them. How to preserve a culture now disturbed?

One kept promise, ironically it would seem, was from Manda, who shortly after the Tasaday first were observed, declared the whole area a preserve. This was likely meant to protect them from very real oil and logging interests that regularly destroy rain forests in that region, but was interpreted by many as a sign of hiding the tribe he'd faked into being. Did Manda say the Tasaday should wear leaves to fool the world, or simply to let them know their native garb was acceptable and to be proud of who they were? Was he urging them to be what he wanted or for them to be themselves? Fights over the Tasaday being a hoax or not seem more about the arguers.

The case of the Tasaday is a cautionary tale, not just of the perils of being labeled a hoax but of serving as anyone else's realness. This is especially a problem because whatever we think of them, the people called Tasaday aren't merely imaginary, but actual flesh and blood. As Morgan's "Real People" or any of fiction's so-called lost races or anthropology's "lost tribes" suggest, being called the conscience or living past or reality for all humanity is less than desirable—especially because someone soon will surely seek to change your reality for you.

That conquering cultures and colonizers have often employed the hoax to understand such realities might not be surprising—in this way the hoax is an exercise in ideology. But whose? Unlike more bald-faced forms of propaganda, the successful hoax mystifies its many sources, at least at first, hiding its ideology—though often in plain sight.

See, here's the thing—the regular world, the ordinary world, the light that just now is so remarkable is, in fact, mostly enough, but in the hands of a real artist all this can become extraordinary, can become more than it is, but also what it is. Words or screens or images cannot make the world more real, but they can make it more beautiful or terrifying, recognizing its everyday, atrocious miracles. This is accompanied, perhaps insisted upon, by our wish for whimsy, for fantasy, for the unreal to take us away. But what we lately endure is not actual fantasy that takes the world as its starting point and may, in the end, change that world—rather, we have a life so dependent on reality but insistent on its falseness that even daily life remains constantly full of affect. This is the danger of bunk.

Hoaxers wound the world and then say, see how the world is wounded? They say the whole world is fake and then say they are all that's real. Such behavior they share with cult leaders, whether Jim Jones and his People's Temple or the millennial Heaven's Gate followers. It's no accident that Morgan's Real People are apocalyptic cultists: whenever such a group insists its reality is the only one, that reality inevitably becomes more and more extreme, ending the only way it can, in extinction. The result is not only deadly but deadening.

There are still mysteries. This is exactly why we cannot abandon investigation, or science—but true investigation often admits when it isn't exactly sure. It recognizes, as Stephen Jay Gould does, that "science must be understood as a social phenomenon, a gutsy, human enterprise, not the work of robots programed to collect pure information."[47] Investigation also isn't afraid to say when something's suspicious, but doesn't mistake all suspicion for guilt.

Good nonfiction reveals what happened; fiction what might have: the hoax instead undermines both art and the self, oddly reducing each to autobiography even as it performs its fakery. It often does this through the exotic other, or a dark double, all of which only reinforces the self as superior to all others. Real art invents, which is to say, takes into the self things that aren't it—or aren't obviously, at least—making claims on us that are its own. Such claims are not based on autobiography or backstory or, strictly speaking, money; this last too often seems the hoaxer's and the plagiarist's chief aim, even if that doesn't explain away all these factions, nor their harm. Though it speaks of other things, including shared, unstated beliefs, the hoax ultimately reveals the hoaxer.

THREE

Mysteria

❋a sideshow!

starring JT LeRoy

with guest appearances by
Lance Armstrong
Disneyland Paris
Sybil
& Many Faces of Eve❋

There's a quality of legend about freaks. Like a person in a fairy tale who stops you and demands that you answer a riddle. Most people go through life dreading they'll have a traumatic experience. Freaks were born with their trauma. They've already passed their test in life. They're aristocrats.

—DIANE ARBUS

"Darkest Africa" exhibit, Century of Progress World's Fair in Chicago, 1933–34. Most of the so-called African natives were actually natives of Chicago.

CHAPTER 9

The Heart Is Deceitful

The hoax wends its way through the world as any other American tourist might, journeying from Fiji to the Moon, Australia to the Middle East, deepest New England to darkest England and reddest Mars. But in the spirit of the travel liar, the hoax pretends to go much farther and encounter much *worser.* No wonder the hoax regularly invokes Africa, a place the West has traditionally rendered as indistinguishable from tragedy and considered undistinguished generally—viewed not as a continent but a nation, not a nation-state but a state of mind. By the middle of the twentieth century, the term "'Zulu' came to be the generic name for American circus workers who dressed as Africans," with sideshows themselves regularly called "Nig Shows": such terminology not only erodes any distinction between country or culture but insists on its opposite.[1]

Besides Zulus and Pygmies, both of whom whites would regularly place on display, the chief "tribes" or "country" seen as synonymous with Africa would be the Congo, its perceived passivity and primitiveness matched only by its violence. What Abyssinia had been to the eighteenth and nineteenth centuries, Congo became for the twentieth century and even the twenty-first: a realm of supreme darkness. This monstrous effect echoes in names like King Kong (who is Afro-Asiatic blackness personified, or animalized) and in productions like Michael Crichton's *Congo* (1980), a novel that would become a remarkably strange B movie in 1995. *Congo* fits the lost-race genre to a *T,* with friendly, talking apes versus violent, mutated, "light-skinded mulatto" ones, as my biracial friend and I jokingly called them when we sought out the movie on opening weekend. In 2016 a white actress self-published a book about her gap year in Zambia, which clearly contains elements of hoax—mentioning "jungle" where there is only savanna and claiming genocide in a country that has instead housed refugees. She would call the book *In Congo's Shadow*, despite its not being set there, to better signal danger and darkness.[2] Here as elsewhere the "Congo" is a mere exoticist idea, an unstable, borderless place to be argued over while pillaged and half-hoaxed from. *Why are you going to Africa?* one person asks Laura Linney's character in *Congo* the movie; her answer, *To find something I lost.*

This same lost, unreal Congo is name-checked in "Flower Hunting in the Congo" by JT LeRoy, the last thing published under that name before revealed to be a hoax. The article purports not only to be an account of LeRoy undertaking the activity of the title—another sales pitch as story—but to be doing this alongside real-life writer and MacArthur genius William T. Vollmann. "And here we are in the jungles of the Congo, a place of massive dangers, lured by passion. Perhaps to get away from the constant drain of my own, I have succumbed to the hypothetical passion of another."[3] LeRoy could be describing his (or her) own hoax, of course—but in this piece LeRoy couldn't simply fake meeting, as hoaxes often do, his literary father. Such an encounter must be displaced to the Congo—a place where anything can happen, complete with extra-wild wildlife, obligatory shouting native soldiers, white saviors, and "a flower that is in severe danger of extinction."

It reminds me of the old African proverb: it takes a village to fool a village. Modern hoaxers from Tom MacMaster to Margaret B. Jones don't just make up just one person, or themselves, but a whole host of invented family members, counselors, friends, and doctors—an entire entourage—to keep the lie going and apparently also the impostor. In the elaborate case of JT LeRoy, it was a woman named Laura Albert who became a multitude, portraying a prodigy who, the story went, had endured an almost unspeakable childhood, including abuse and neglect and prostitution. The boy named LeRoy had not only survived but also managed to write three books inspired by his life, charming the literary establishment and becoming an outsider-hero—simultaneously girl wonder and poster boy for various causes. "You'll need handkerchiefs and Novocain to get through his new book," musician Tom Waits said of LeRoy in a 2001 interview for *Vanity Fair*. "It is a golden diving bell crawling through the shark-infested waters of his childhood. He is the witness to all the tales that go on in the dark, and for all of us, long may he have the courage to remember."[4]

Waits's article was accompanied by a photograph of someone supposed to be LeRoy, taken by Mary Ellen Mark. Known for her books *Indian Circus* (1993) and *Falkland Road: Prostitutes of Bombay* (1981), Mark, working in the tradition of the late Diane Arbus, would seem in one shot to marry the sideshow photograph to the history of the freak in its physical and ethnographic forms. These are forms LeRoy would also exploit. As one circus animal trainer told Mark, "You feed animals, they live with you, stay with you, and die with you. Everything that is on two feet is very immoral, but animals are not innocent."[5] Danger and innocence, treachery and death, all became part of the sideshow that was JT LeRoy, P. T. Barnum's brief heir.

DOPING

Following Barnum's lead, attractions like the dime museum took up the exotic banner quite literally, continuing well into the twentieth century—efforts like Hubert's Museum in Times Square persisted until the 1960s, bringing the sideshow inside. "If, as your mother would say, you didn't know what to do with yourself, you would do it as Hubert's Museum," Diane Arbus would mourn once the place closed. Such dime museums resembled their close cousin vaudeville, both of which share an ancestor in the freak shows and their talkers—only rubes called them "barkers"—who urged crowds to come see the sights. Hubert's talker, manager, and later owner was Charlie Lucas, a black performer who'd got his start playing native in fake African shows like the notorious "Darkest Africa" exhibit at the 1933 Century of Progress World's Fair in Chicago; there he spoke "gibberish" as a chief named Wu Foo, garbed in ostrich feathers and spears from a costume shop.[6] In this show, which was billed as "educational," Lucas must have swallowed more than just fire. Going solo, for years afterward he perfected an act advertised as a "dance of love," billed as Wofoo alongside his wife, the snake handler Princess Wago. Both now made Hubert's their own.

Lucas would also be instrumental in introducing Arbus to some of her earliest photographic subjects, including Congo the Jungle Creep and Jack Dracula, the Marked Man, both stars at Hubert's along with exotic dancers, the Handless Sharpshooter, a "Cheating Death" electric chair, and William Durks, who had painted a third eye where his nose should be—Arbus not only shot him but nicknamed him the Man from World War Zero.[7] Covered in tattoos, Mr. Dracula was less a vampire than "a privileged exile," a self-made freak—something JT LeRoy would aspire to. LeRoy's very name meant to suggest freakish royalty, reminiscent of Arbus's declaration, "Freaks were born with their trauma. They've already passed their test in life. They're aristocrats."[8] Arbus was chastised, by Susan Sontag especially, of exploiting her subjects—but this seems to miss the ways that Arbus spent much time at Hubert's or backstage at drag shows, and what's more, the way her subjects themselves, aristocratic in their traumas, look back at her camera. Arbus asks more of us, and the freak, than her critics suggest: "What if we couldn't always tell a trick from a miracle? If you've ever talked to somebody with two heads you know they know something you don't."[9]

The amazing thing about the two or three heads who made up JT LeRoy may be how well the tricks in his name worked, and for how long. The list of those caught up in the act, or by it, reads like a who's who of a certain brand of American royalty: one writer calls LeRoy "the darling of a certain demimonde of the damned; Gus Van Sant, Courtney Love, Madonna, Winona Ryder, Marianne Faithfull, Tatum O'Neal and Garbage's Shirley Manson were all whooping high hosannas about this damaged, cross-dressing naïf."[10] Writers like Mary Karr and Mary Gaitskill all appeared with LeRoy; Madonna, Faithfull, and other rock stars reached out to or wrote for him; fiction writer Dennis Cooper helped encourage LeRoy very early on, and O'Neal and Lou Reed would perform in his stead, JT being too shy to read. I too want only celebrities to read my work. Either aloud or to themselves—I'm not picky.

Rumors swirled for years that JT LeRoy was not who he (sometimes becoming a she) claimed to be. (I will maintain here the quite binary pronouns the hoax iself used.) Such doubts were all but confirmed by Stephen Beachy in his fine example of investigative journalism, "Who Is the Real JT LeRoy?" in *New York* magazine in 2005. Though the piece stops just short of a damning answer—the title is still a question—it began to uncover LeRoy, who "claimed to have bounced around truck stops, through youth shelters and rehab, and to be a junkie. In interviews, JT would claim to be spreading the rumors himself that Dennis Cooper or the director Gus Van Sant was the real JT LeRoy; he suggested that this was the defense mechanism of an abused child, a web of arrows pointing in multiple directions to protect the writer from public exposure. The one irrefutable aspect of his story was that he had an incredible knack for self-promotion. Every other aspect, a mounting pile of evidence suggests, is part of an elaborately wrought fiction."[11] Beachy compares the LeRoy to contemporary con artists as well as eighteenth-century hoax poet Chatterton; despite the revelations, Albert and others around her maintained LeRoy was real. Winona Ryder oddly claimed onstage that she'd met JT years before, outside the San Francisco Opera—was she lying or so consumed by the lie that she believed she'd seen a ghost?

Soon the whole story unraveled: in January 2006, the very same month that James Frey and Nasdijj were exposed, the *New York Times* offered a more complete "unmasking," revealing that Albert's sister-in-law Savannah Knoop had portrayed LeRoy in person for at least five years. But who wrote the books? Albert's life partner Geoffrey Knoop, who had witnessed and participated in the hoax under the nickname Astor, confirmed a month later that the voice heard in phone conversations, and in the books themselves, was actually Albert's. (They would, needless to say, have broken up by then.) By March, when Jack Boulware recounted the full history of the hoax in *Salon*, many of those who had first stood by LeRoy—believing him real, or if a hustle, a good one—now reported feeling betrayed. To read such slow-motion dehoaxing is to see the layers pulled back: not on an artichoke to find its heart but on an onion without a center. Whether raw or poorly cooked, it leaves a bad taste in the mouth.

The success of the act had led LeRoy to write for venues such as the *New York Times*, which earlier in 2005 paid him to visit Disneyland Paris (née Euro Disney). LeRoy wasn't an imaginary friend but a mascot of sorts, the kind found in Disneylands all over the world. But where Disney's live characters are never allowed to break character, with LeRoy the breaks were the character. The result is a madcap travel lie, a nonexistent LeRoy writing as if he's traveling with Albert, Geoffrey Knoop, and their son. "Our 8-year-old, Thor, cowers beneath us—his parents, Astor and Speedie, and me, a surrogate brother, sister, wannabe parent—as we form a shield between him and the miniature cubes [of cheese] pounding down on us. This is France, so it was only a matter of time till the cheese blasted us; we didn't expect it at the Tour de France, though."[12] That's right: LeRoy went to Paris and ended up watching now-admitted cheater Lance Armstrong win his seventh Tour in a row.

Armstrong had already spent the years since his first victory in 1999 denying frequent allegations of doping, saying repeatedly he never used performance-enhancing drugs. "I've said it for seven years. I have never doped," he would repeat for more years than that on shows like *Larry King Live*, one of many publicity stops where his outrage was palpable, downright reliable, his disdain and pure shock almost contagious. This even made its way into pop culture like *Dodgeball: A True Underdog Story*, where he makes a cameo that's creepy in its shaming: *So what are you dying from that's keeping you from the finals? Well I guess if a person didn't quit when the going got tough, they wouldn't have anything to regret for the rest of their life.* The rubber bracelets he began as part of his Livestrong charity haloed his wrist and that of at least fifty-five million other believers by 2005 alone.[13]

It is clear now that Armstrong was never clear. Armstrong wasn't the best rider in the world, it turns out, but the best at cheating: he engineered and oversaw a sophisticated set of protocols designed to fool tests, bullying his fellow riders so they too participated—or were out, their loss—and using the U.S. Postal Service, a sponsor, to help make it happen. (Poor Sheryl Crow.) Even his urine, always an issue in public and in depositions, has fallen under a cloud of suspicion. His fellow cyclists, several of whom won the Tour de France after Armstrong's retirement, would soon get caught doping and go through the familiar routine for the hoaxer—outrage, multiple denials, and, in the face of mounting evidence, confession.

As with JT LeRoy, looking back and knowing any vehement denials are simply lies, it is hard to watch Armstrong's growing outrage and disgust without confronting our own. At first, he'd deny his own miracles, writing in his second autobiography, "There was no mystery and no miracle drug that helped me win that Tour de France in 1999, I explained to Floyd"— Floyd Landis, the rider who rode and doped with Armstrong, his heir apparent and later his undoing.[14] But by 2005 when Armstrong won the Tour while LeRoy supposedly looked on, Armstrong had the hubris to say from the championship dais, "Last thing I'll say for the people who don't believe in cycling—the cynics and skeptics—I'm sorry you can't dream big and I'm sorry you don't believe in miracles."[15] The crowd applauded, the Arc de Triomphe visible in the distance behind him. For Armstrong, atrocious miracles became a kind of currency—part of the story he told, a prototypical American tragedy with a happy ending.

Armstrong's grit was our gravy. He insisted for years that we take his wins at face value, a sign of his not doping, all while, like LeRoy, he urged his illness and recovery as profound metaphors for success and triumph— exercising the American dream. For Armstrong, whose cancer was real— unlike LeRoy, whose AIDS came and went—cancer became an excuse too. Why would I dope when I had cancer? he'd ask of no one. In truth, he began doping not after but *before* his treatment. His admission of as much in the hospital while recovering from cancer surgery would become the centerpiece of a lawsuit whose depositions—Armstrong ever defiant, still lying— would years later help lose him his crowns.

The very notion that Armstrong never tested positive was false: throughout his winning streak, he had several times tested positive for various performance-enhancing drugs and either bullshitted or backdated, bullied or bribed his way out of the charges. In glaring conflicts of interest, he gave large sums to testing agencies such as the World Anti-Doping Agency; he even tried to do so to the U.S. Anti-Doping Agency, which eventually uncovered him. He set up a charity that has certainly helped many, but, given its being built on Armstrong's hoaxing, is it now dirty money? Is Armstrong a person divided: on the one hand, charitable and giving back, and on the other, taking, telling lies, and talking trash about those who told the truth? Or did he craft a charity as the perfect cover for his continued cheating?

"You keep doing your job as Frankenstein," said dogged reporter David Walsh, describing Armstrong's pact with his Italian doping doctor, "and I'll be the best monster you've ever created."[16] Such monstrousness is resilient, drug resistant, you could say. This too should be familiar, as the hoax often preys on its own: where the exoticist once made use of native tribes, now the hoaxer is as likely to appeal to tribalism and our sense of belonging. I wonder: were we collectively fooled because we wanted to believe, or did we believe because we so wanted to be fooled?

With Armstrong we wanted to trust his lies, I think, because that meant our loved ones might not only survive cancer but, unbelievably, come back to win not one, not two, but seven yellow jerseys in the Tour de France. Talker and sideshow act in one, Armstrong promised a resurrection: the freak as a sign of wonder again, miracles his drug. His American fans didn't want success but dominance; not just narrow victory but records smashed, lungs genetically superior, hills overcome barely breathing hard, sweat commingled with blood drawn, doped, and put back in the body. Such vampirism has grown familiar, as the modern hoax prefers monstrousness that it turns romantic.

Fame hungry, defamed, ours has become the vampire's wish—not just to live forever but to live really well while we do. It isn't enough for LeRoy to survive; he must become famous and more. With LeRoy, as with Armstrong, we encounter the hoax at its worst: intimate and ill, though not exactly in the way it appears to be.

PRE-MILLENNIAL TENSION

LeRoy and his hoax cohort came to fame in the mid- to late 1990s, a time filled with millennialism, on the one hand, and euphemism, on the other. From journalistic fabulists like Stephen Glass and Jayson Blair, to James

Frey, Margaret B. Jones, "Nasdijj," Lance Armstrong too: all these phonies on either side of the millennium now appear to be key entries in our era's mistaking the self for the story. It is a crisis we will find more and more, leading directly to our Age of Euphemism.

Albert the mastermind's own narrative crises cast her as a fairy tale orphan and protagonist. If she is to be believed, as a teen in New York City, Albert was actually institutionalized a few times and ultimately ran away. Granted, she only made it to the East Village; there, though Jewish, she fell in with a scarily bigoted skinhead crowd before moving to San Francisco, where she would soon meet and move in with "Astor," Geoffrey Knoop. (Together they have a son, called Thor in public, one fiction I'll maintain.) Having moved there a bit after Albert's arrival, I can attest that in addition to wannabes, actual artists, great booksellers, part-time belly dancers, strippers, and sexual renegades, San Francisco sometimes had, glimpsed mostly from afar, neo-Nazi skinheads. It was as if they were drawn to what they hated, which wouldn't make them the first; this too is a rehearsal for our attraction to hoaxers and their hurt, whether given or felt.

Together Albert and Knoop would start bands with names like Daddy Don't Go and, later on, Thistle, a kind of late-grunge concern. To hear the *New York Times* tell it, the couple were "unfulfilled rock musicians who concocted the character of JT Leroy [*sic*] to gain access first to literary circles and, later, to celebrities."[17] JT was said to be the lyricist (and later would have songs written about him by the likes of Shirley Manson from Garbage, and collaborate with Billy Corgan of the Smashing Pumpkins). Soon Albert would appear at gigs as Speedie, claiming to be JT's social worker, putting on what she herself calls "this annoying, singsong Cockney accent, so you wanted to slap her."[18] The persona Speedie invokes is not just Speedy Gonzales voiced by Looney Tunes master Mel Blanc but also the sidekick of DC comic book hero the Green Arrow: no matter how it's spelled, Speedie is a sidekick's name. No wonder Albert would later say it was second-tier hero Aquaman that she had a mad, safe crush on as a kid.

Albert's arrival in San Francisco also parallels the rise and pride of sex workers in the City by the Bay. "In the early 90s, San Francisco was the G spot of the nation's sex scene," journalist Jack Boulware writes. Albert herself became a phone-sex worker, and "came alive most when interacting with people over the phone. She didn't just talk on the phone, she worked it. Her role-playing skills made her a natural in the sex world."[19] Albert's phone roles, like her most successful one later on, consist of rather broad types—

country bumpkins, stereotypical black women—not so much doppelgängers as gangs of ladies she could imitate. "I could do every accent under the sun. I would be Asian, Russian, German, Swedish, Southern, all the clichés," she'd say later.[20]

When I moved there in 1991 for the summer, and later returned for two years starting in 1992, San Francisco was the kind of place where a week-day matinee for Richard Linklater's *Slackers* was totally packed. You could see acid jazz five nights a week, and hip-hop almost as much; sushi was fast food and if you shot pool you had to obey unwritten rules: *No slop.* You had to call it. Few young folks got a job then in yet another recession, so why not live where you wanted, if not how, and work somewhere while finding your way? Back there and then you could easily meet people but not always get to know them. Evenings, at bars like the Elbo Room or later the Latin American Club (which had once been one), I'd meet people and when asked shyly admit I was a poet; they'd enthusiastically reply, *So am I!* But I'd soon learn they hadn't published anything, or really written anything either. Still it provided a kind of camaraderie, if a tentative one. Soon they'd form a band, or become milliners, or have an exhibition in a café, or quit the West Coast entirely and head home and soon you realized for them this was a va-cation, bohemia merely a waystation. Later I would learn terms like *trusta-farian*; I'd regularly have to remind friends of the difference between being broke and being poor whenever they'd declare they were the latter.

The Summer of Love being long over, that first winter was so cold I could see my breath in my unheated kitchen, which seemed some kind of metaphor: if they hadn't exactly grown up, San Francisco's hippies had grown aggro. It was a time where you can picture someone like Albert start-ing to forge not just a persona but an act, and not just an act but a whole scam, based on what someone not quite her supposedly wrote. She seems pre- and post-techie San Francisco in a nutshell: a place not with people but roles, all too often interchangeable. Was *slacker* just another word for *change-ling*? Your doppelgängers might become better at being you than you.

JT, short for "Jeremiah Terminator," turned out to be an act played not just by Savannah Knoop, Geoffrey's half sister—who was recruited after LeRoy's first book was published—but by other temporary JTs before her, mostly androgynous street kids tracked down and sent to meet famous writers like Gaitskill. As Albert said later, "Geoff and I got in the car and started driving up and down Polk Street, and I saw a boy I'd never seen be-fore. He was nineteen and he was slight, blond, blue-eyed—perfect. I said to him, You want to make fifty bucks, no sex? He said, Sure. I just told him not to talk, just say hello to a woman named Mary, get freaked out, and leave. I took him to the café. Mary Gaitskill was sitting there. The kid walked up to her, said, Hi, I'm Terminator, and he handed her some vinegar and chocolate—things I brought to give her as gifts. She said, Hi, glad to meet you, and when the kid ran off, I sat down. I was there as Speedie, and we talked."[21] For her part, Gaitskill says she always suspected something was up, even telling the London *Independent* as early as 2001, "Even if it turned out to be a hoax, it's a very enjoyable one."[22]

Start to finish, however, it would be Albert who would play LeRoy on the phone, substituting gender for sex. Albert, as Speedie or "Emily Frasier" or what have you, would travel with JT, who would have insisted on such an escort. Later on, newfound friends like Carrie Fisher would warn Savannah-as-JT in person—or unwittingly, Albert-as-JT over the phone—about the creepy hanger-on Speedie. Being told she was bad news for her own invention had to hurt. No matter if, as one friend said of Albert, "she craved the limelight, but she didn't really want all the attention," Albert was shut out of the start-up she herself founded.

LeRoy's bio and writing offered a frisson of connection to some real (and real-to-life) scary shit that others on the West Coast wrote about, whether that's Cooper early on; director Gus Van Sant, whom LeRoy would come to work with, earning a writing credit on *Elephant*, his retelling of the Columbine shootings; or William Vollmann, recruited unknowingly at the end. This absorbent quality is LeRoy's surest strategy. Cooper would later say he initially spoke with LeRoy in part because "he was very much like one of my characters, so I was interested."[23] But the holy hustler canonized by Cooper and Van Sant had long been a familiar trope by the time Albert began writing as him-becoming-her. Albert less contributed to queer lit than co-opted it, starting with the basic sexual hustler or the husband-forced-housewife and adding a bit of stereotypical southern spice.

No wonder that the original track Albert and "Jeffrey Kaos" recorded as Daddy Don't Go for the album *Cyberorgasm 2* sounds like one more fantasy of domination/transvestism frequently found in under-the-counter sleaze paperbacks of the 1960s. As Beachy notes, "The scenario involves Laura calling Kaos her little girl, her little boy, a cock-tease, a whore, and suggesting she'll pimp him out, enacting a relationship so similar to JT's descriptions of his relationship with his mother, Sarah, that it is startling."[24] This notion of author as pimp is both derivative and disturbing. *Hustler* might mean the way writers have to scramble to make it; "Literary Hustler" is the term Beachy uses for LeRoy in his article, after all. There are black vernacular meanings of hustler too, indicating more a striver, or "baller," than a pimp in a literal sense (though *pimp* too has become a commonplace metaphor for a badass). A term vague enough to name a hard-core men's magazine, *hustler* certainly describes what let Albert cozy up to stars, but it's also what prevents her from stopping lying. Hustling is addictive, and hard to quit.

Worse, *pimp* seems to describe Albert's relationship to Savannah Knoop, who would eventually provide JT's body and image—it is she who is doing the rather unconvincing impression of LeRoy in Mark's photograph—and who says in her own postexposure memoir, *Girl Boy Girl* (2008), that she never was paid all that much. LeRoy's first book, *Sarah*, had eight years earlier used a blurry image borrowed from Cooper as the author photo—things moved from there to needing a physical person for photo ops and appearances. "There were starting to be rumors that he was not real, so I knew I needed to supply a body," says Albert about her need to go from JT as just a pseudonym to a presence.[25] Albert's wish "to supply a body" sounds convincing, if creepy—simultaneously the wish of a murderer and the detective tracking down a murder victim. This wish for a body separate from a self would seem consistent with those I know who've been abused. It is also, disturbingly, the abuser's wish—for a body to make one's own, selfish need justifying and nullifying any sense of another person.

Albert would get her sister-in-law addicted to the role, a call girl-boy-girl asked to play JT at the drop of a hat—or at the wearing of one, with a blond wig and sunglasses, soon LeRoy's uniform. One critic calls it "Warholian," an entire aesthetic reduced to a wig. Albert's Speedie and Savannah Knoop's LeRoy would travel the world in an uneasy duo—or rather, trio, with LeRoy coexisting between them. The prose would go further. If Albert enacted among adults a power she couldn't have as a child, it is also true that JT, who had supposedly been pimped out by his own mother, is an idea and image Albert came to pimp out too. She served up LeRoy, the teen prodigy, as a body for others to ogle—to photograph and be photographed with—but that ultimately hid in not-so-plain sight.

HYSTEROGENIC ZONES

The difficulty isn't simply that Albert hoaxed those eager to believe, but that LeRoy received years of support, and often money, from those touched by his backstory: a wonder boy with a horrific past of abuse and truck-stop prostitution, and, at least initially, afflicted with HIV. (This last eventually just faded away.) Dennis Cooper, who always thought something was amiss, still said about the final revelation of the hoax: "I know I was being lied to; I just thought I knew when." LeRoy's famed literary agent, Ira Silverberg, first supported the writer after the revelations but came to feel that "to present yourself as a person who is dying of AIDS in a culture which has lost so many writers and voices of great meaning, to take advantage of that sympathy and empathy, is the most unfortunate part of all of this." Silverberg would go further, saying, "A lot of people believed they were supporting not only a good and innovative and adventurous voice, but that we were supporting a person."[26]

While extreme, LeRoy's story appears extremely familiar, sounding an awful lot like the infamous hoax committed by Anthony Godby Johnson mere years before. A teenager with AIDS, Johnson began calling people in the early 1990s, befriending sympathetic gay writers like Armistead Maupin and the tremendous Paul Monette. Johnson had reportedly been adopted by a social worker named Vicki; she was the only one ever to see "Tony," who, though desperately sick, would talk by phone for hours, detailing his harrowing childhood suffering at the hand of his family's Satanic cult.

Monette would eventually die of AIDS, but not before putting the boy in touch with contacts who helped get Johnson's book, *A Rock and a Hard Place: One Boy's Triumphant Story*, published in 1995. Even television's Mr. Rogers got roped into lending his name to the publication—and in print far larger than the alleged author's. After he read the book in galleys with its foreword by Monette, Maupin blurbed it and asked to make contact with the boy and his guardian. A friendship bloomed.

By all accounts, Tony was a tremendous conversationalist. One night in 1993, as later reported by Tad Friend in the *New Yorker*, Maupin got a call from Vicki, who told him "Tony might not live through the night and was curled up in a ball, asking for Armistead. 'I waited with tremendous anxiety as she passed the phone to him,' Maupin said. 'Tony's voice was small, and he was breathing with great difficulty. I thought, My God, this child is going to die while I'm talking to him. . . . I told Tony, finally, that I loved him. He said it really helped him, and I felt heroic. I went to sleep feeling that I alone, my voice, had made that kind of difference in a child's life.'" Tony would regularly be about to die, or be victimized by the Satanists whose ritual abuse had given him AIDS. Many a famed figure, from Mickey Mantle to Keith Olbermann to novelist Tom Robbins, would counsel Tony through his perpetual pretend death sentence.

This was millennialism as illness. "Tony has become a symbol of modern victimhood," Friend writes, "his body torn apart by the most appalling end-of-the-millennium traumas—child abuse and AIDS. Their depredations eventually robbed Tony of his left leg, his spleen, a testicle, and the sight in one eye. Yet, even as he became bedridden from recurrent pneumonia, his character sparkled."[27] After months of extensive phone calls with Vicki and Tony, Maupin traveled to see him several times only to be told at the last minute that Tony was too sick to see him. He eventually grew suspicious, finding no hospital records, nor any others, for Johnson. Soon the *New Yorker* and elsewhere revealed that "Vicki" was really Joanna Victoria Fraginals, who not only made up Tony but also provided his voice. To this day she has still never admitted to hoaxing.

Maupin would go on to dramatize all this in *The Night Listener*, his 2000 novel based on his experience with Johnson. Though Geoffrey Knoop would say Johnson was the inspiration for LeRoy, Albert later acted as if she didn't know of Johnson's case despite the similarities. Certainly Tony Godby Johnson is only the most obvious example of the hoax meeting mass hysteria, with a Satanic "pedophile ring" invoked as excuse for Vicki's various deceptions and the lack of documentation surrounding her young ward. Johnson, and later LeRoy, revel in just this kind of paranoia, a pop hysteria, which like any such outbreak, isn't easily contained.

There's a way in which the LeRoy hoax not just exhibits some of the symptoms of hysteria but embodies its whole history, from disturbing display to displaced protest about female power. Albert's is a medical theater of one (or two). Might the hoax, so often obsessed with pain and dying—in a sense, hypochondriac—ultimately prove hysteric too?

As critic Joan Acocella reminds us in her brilliant book *Creating Hysteria*, "Hysteria is the appearance of physical symptoms (typically, convulsions, paralyses, strangulation, breathing problems, numbness, pain) or psychological symptoms (anxiety, emotional outbursts, 'spells')—or both—in the absence of any evident organic cause. This is the crux of the disorder: the patient is sick and the doctor doesn't know why. ('Mysteria,' one nineteenth-century specialist called it.) The other critical fact about hysteria is that it has almost always been viewed as a woman's disorder." Though causes varied, hysteria's root was often viewed as physical: the uterus (as memorialized in our term "hysterectomy") or the nerves. In short, the ultimate cause of hysteria was womanhood itself. "From women's sexuality it was not far to go to women's moral weakness—their natural deceitfulness, their immaturity—as a further source of hysteria," Acocella writes. "The link between women and hysteria thus became a tautology. Women developed hysteria not because of some external factor, such as the apportionment of power in society, but simply because they were women. 'As a general rule, all women are hysterical,' wrote the French physician Auguste Fabre in 1883."[28] Another would say the hysteric is quote-unquote a more womanly woman. The absurdity of this should not go unremarked—especially as it persists in large and small ways—and may be exactly in some way what Albert created LeRoy to combat over a century later. The stories Albert published under LeRoy's name (she would surely say wrote *as* him) might earn far more respect for being taken from experience, however awful, than as hysteric imaginings.

Hysteria has always been about, or threatened by, invention. Many studies have sussed out the tensions found in this mental condition—one of whose symptoms was believed to be a propensity to lie—which was often dismissed as ridiculous but that the influential nineteenth-century physician Jean-Martin Charcot took seriously and sought to find an origin for in the body. Called the "Napoleon of Neuroses," and the acknowledged founder of neurology, Charcot ruled over the Salpêtrière, the Parisian medical asylum that had long held women, often against their will, since before the French Revolution.[29] After some key medical discoveries, including identifying what's now known as amyotrophic lateral sclerosis, or ALS, Charcot sought to classify hysteria in much the same way as he had other physical diseases, starting in the 1870s; indeed, he would define the disorder and distinguish it "from epilepsy in particular and from all other mental disorders."[30] By the late nineteenth century he had turned the Salpêtrière into a large-scale operation, as it were, the campus housing up to five thousand women and a bakery—and, most importantly to hysteria's hype, a photography studio.

Charcot's techniques soon became orthodox, his Tuesday lectures in the Salpêtrière's amphitheater legendary: his medical theater was exactly that, bringing in some "grand hysterics," soon well known in their own right, for experts and the public to view. Before a captive audience, Charcot's near-captives performed rather ritualized scenes of hysteria—with phases Charcot labeled *epileptoid, clownism, attitudes passionnelles*, and "so-called terminal delirium, the painful phase during which hysterics 'start talking,' during which one tries to stop the attack, by every possible means,"[31] as

Georges Didi-Huberman writes. Treatment meant frequent use of a primitive clamping device to administer external "ovarian compression," a remedy sometimes asked for by the hysterics themselves. Over time, it's clear that the hysterics would respond to the expectations of the doctors, not to mention the images of hysteria that decorated the medical theater and later circulated in the media. Theirs was a different kind of ballet.

This is not to say that the patients, nearly all women, weren't ill—just that they also frequently suffered from childhood abandonment, unwanted sexual advances, poverty, and abuse. Was the Salpêtrière a continuation or an escape from their previous lives? Patients like Augustine and Blanche (not exactly their real names) now found themselves at the center of not only the famed doctor's attentions but also the culture's. Visitors would speak of their attacks in artistic terms; later, modern dance and the surrealists would draw direct inspiration from the hysterics' movements and mood, with André Breton calling hysteria "the greatest poetic discovery of the late nineteenth century."[32] Freud would famously visit the Salpêtrière in the 1880s and eventually craft his theories of the mind from Charcot, the Salpêtrière, and the patients themselves. He soon would set out to find—or make—his own hysterics.

Charcot's *grand hystérie* was popularized by photographs, all quite dramatic: Augustine can be found in a popular series of *Iconographies*, appearing from the 1870s until the 1890s, when hysteria was at its height. After extensive case studies, illustrations of hypnotism, and *zones hystérogènes*, the volumes literally pictured the women's *hystéro-épilepsie*; the *Iconographies* also sought to link historic events, like witches, to hysteria, rendering hysterics almost supernatural. In one plate, labeled "Léthargie," Augustine is depicted rigidly stretched, unsupported, between two chair backs as if levitating off a magician's table; others give us "Crucifixion" and "Ecstasy" without a sense of their own fictions. The effect is something like the spirit photograph: both picture something not quite there that the sitter or photographer or viewer wished to see. Other plates depict "Délire Érotique," "Attitude Provoquée," "Menace," "Catalepsie: Suggestion," and "Mockery."[33] The LeRoy hoax would seem to cycle through all these phases in turn, ending, one suspects, with the *blépharospasme hystérique* or "hysterical wink." Like the Salpêtrière's hysterics, LeRoy too was overphotographed, creating, as the hoax and hysteria often do, a feedback loop of attention and invention. Hysteria helps Albert explain LeRoy, as well as his beloved monster-mother Sarah, not to mention Albert's reasons for fabricating them both: illness, temperament, immaturity, biology, attention, feigned ecstasy. As with hysteria, JT's symptoms are society's.

What was behind this earlier hysteria for hysteria? "Hysteria became a hot topic in medical circles during the 1880s and 1890s," writes scholar Elaine Showalter, "when feminism, the New Woman, and a crisis in gender were also hot topics in the United States and Europe. Fin-de-siècle feminism coincided with the pseudoscientific discourses of race degeneration: degenerationists believed that women's activism—particularly the fight to be admitted to universities and to enter the professions—led to a decline in marriage and a falling birth rate. Women, they argued, were cultivating their brains but neglecting their biology. . . . The New Woman, one English journalist wrote, 'ought to be aware that her condition is morbid, or at least hysterical.'"[34] These constantly regenerating conditions of race and gender would also hold sway in the culture wars, memoir craze, and narrative crisis of the 1990s, contributing to our age's proliferation of hoaxes.

After many attempts, Augustine finally escaped from the Salpêtrière while disguised, as Albert would be a century later, as a man.

SYBILS

In their very symptoms the Salpêtrière's hysterics offered a protest, however indirect: feeling voiceless, numb, or scripted, these fragile women manifested mutism, immunity to pain, and catalepsy in turn. Hysterics were sometimes suggested to have occult, predictive powers, like a sybil or oracle. Another characteristic of hysteria was dermatography, or skin easily written on with a stylus, the letters sometimes raised there readable for weeks.[35]

Albert also overwrote, taking yet another narrative for LeRoy's own, one suggesting a form of mass hysteria that became epidemic in the 1980s and 1990s: multiple personality disorder. Originally found in the literature as a medical rarity, the modern multiple personality phenomenon started with *The Three Faces of Eve* (1957) and was further popularized by *Sybil* (1973), both best sellers made into extremely popular movies about a woman—always a woman—with the disorder. "Eve, however, was merely the John the Baptist of multiple personality," Acocella writes. "The Christ was 'Sybil Dorsett,' a Columbia University graduate student who in 1954, at age thirty-one, turned up in the office of a psychoanalyst named Cornelia Wilbur and stayed for eleven years. In 1973 this case became the subject of a mass-market book, *Sybil*, by the journalist Flora Rheta Schreiber."[36] Acocella,

Showalter, and others examine and indict the phenomenon, abbreviated as MPD, which not only spread through popular culture but also was reinforced, if not caused, by the very therapy meant to cure it. This proliferation may best be symbolized by the actress Joanne Woodward earning an Oscar for split-personality housewife Eve in the movie based on the book, and later playing Sybil's therapist, Dr. Wilbur, in the TV movie.

The doctor in these stories, as with Charcot, became not only a healer but the hero. This idea Albert seems to have carried into her own stories, both in those she told about JT and then those she had JT himself tell, saying LeRoy was born when "I would sneak out to a pay phone and call hotlines all over the United States making up new stories—always as a boy—to relieve my torment."[37] Eventually she found a psychiatrist named Terrence Owens (who is apparently real): "We had a half-hour phone conversation every day, and I built my life around that. It was the only time I felt alive. . . . I called him as a boy named Jeremiah. He was thirteen at the time, and he was from West Virginia. At first I didn't really know much about him. As with my other characters, I wouldn't know who was talking until the person spoke through me. He would reveal himself to me, I would let it unfold, and I would go to that other world, which was much better to me than my own world, which I hated. I never thought, My God, this isn't true. It felt more alive and more true to me than any of the things in my world."[38] What of *the* world? one wonders.

It must have been awfully tempting for Albert to portray both the patient and the savior shrink, not to mention the superstar they created together. This too was derivative: Dr. Wilbur didn't "realize" Sybil's many personalities simply by discovering them but also by helping create them; the audiotapes of Sybil's therapy, often enhanced with "truth serums," leading questions, and suggestive hypnosis, prove chilling in their coercion.[39] Here were a mad scientist's mutants made real. Wilbur not only named "multiple personality disorder" but also encouraged its multiplying in patients—personalities that therapists by the 1980s would regularly coach, ask for, practically beg to emerge—as well as a broader society for which MPD provided a kind of diagnosis and balm.

If Dr. Jekyll and Mr. Hyde encapsulated a Victorian conception of a divided self, one civilized yet untamed, and hysteria evoked an evolving fin de siècle sexuality, MPD provided a metaphor for our increasingly fractured modern existence. MPD also suggested the fracture—and factioning—that would find its way into the hoax. "Looking at literary and social history suggests that for over a century, multiplicity has offered women a way to express forbidden aspects of the self," Showalter argues.[40] Where the Salpêtrière suggested women as repressed and suppressed, the MPD movement saw their narratives as taking back power—ironically through claiming powerlessness.

By the 1980s, the nineteenth-century medical theater—where Barnum had once butchered and ballyhooed bodies both black and female, and where Charcot displayed grand hysterics—had morphed into television's talk-show stage, where hosts hawked tales of otherwise unverified cannibalism, vile murders of unrecorded babies, and witness-free wooded Satanic rituals, never stopping to ask, *Is this true?* Much less, *Is this believable?* The feedback loop of pop psychology and pop culture unleashed an epidemic of MPD sufferers for whom one "alter" was not enough—some patients displayed well over one hundred, including animals and inanimate objects.

MPD joined Satanic ritual abuse (known as SRA; nothing sounds more "medical" or official than an acronym) and UFO abduction stories as part of the controversial recovered memory movement. To doubt such testimony or memory, the thinking went, was to deny the childhood abuse that was presumed to be the condition's root cause; yet with MPD, much like with the hysterical belief in now-disproved cabals of Satanic and pedophile rings in every suburban oasis, the condition only showed up *after* therapy. In their devastatingly methodical critique of the methods and motives of often untrained recovered memory therapists, Richard Ofshe and Ethan Watters discuss how "these authors, wanting to sell more books, and therapists, hoping to find more converts, have intentionally created symptoms that would spark some level of recognition in everyone but at the same time exclude no one. A cynic might accuse these authors of intentionally using what are sometimes called 'Barnum' statements; that is, observations used by fortune-tellers and con men that sound specific to the individual hearing them but acutally describe a large percentage of the population."[41] There was a Barnum quality to both the promised spectacle and the vague beliefs of SRA that approaches the hoax. In much the same way that UFO sightings began only after Orson Welles's *War of the Worlds* hoax aired—a sign of influence, not accuracy—the overarching familiarity of MPD and SRA narratives takes as much from movies, and from the previous accounts themselves, as from any actual experience. The robes in Satanic rituals appear rented.

In the Satanic panic of the 1980s, no case looms larger than that of the McMartin Preschool, a California day care center where accusations by one disgruntled (and unstable) parent ballooned into outrageous stories of children being forced to witness infanticide, ritual murders, cannibalism, and more. In his tremendous *We Believe the Children*, Richard Beck chronicles the way therapists and untrained investigators led young children into testimony that reflected and reified then-popular fantasies and fears of Satanism, infecting and dividing the once-peaceful California town—the resulting court case would become the longest and most expensive criminal trial in U.S. history.[42] But the McMartin Preschool case was just the most prominent example of how such witch hunts spread to law enforcement agencies, which spent valuable resources and time investigating wild Satanic claims; needless to say, of the tens of thousands of human sacrifices claimed, none were found.[43] Charges against those who ran the preschool were ultimately dropped after seven years of trials yielded no convictions.

The Satanic panic proved particularly American—a pseudospiritual crisis masking a sexist and classist one. By the end Beck's assertion that the real culprit was a fear of women's working outside the home—when in fact child sexual abuse mostly occurs at home—becomes hard to deny. But such mass panics frequently center on sex and sex roles: as a reminder that such hysterias aren't yet behind us, we need only look to Amanda Knox, whose case still divides viewers into those who think she was railroaded by an incompetent Italian justice system and those who still believe she murdered her roommate, according to prosecutors, in an elaborate Satanic ritual.[44] However we feel about the case, it should be said that the media coverage hints at the "crime" of female sexuality. Knox's tabloid nicknames "Angel Face" and "Foxy Knoxy," taken from an online profile, are the Madonna/whore complex writ as large as the headlines that carry them. It makes "Eve White" and "Eve Black," as the original split-personality popstar "Eve" called two of her alters, seem almost quaint—if still suggestive of the dark double traced through our literature and pop culture since at least the nineteenth century.

Like hysteria often does, MPD proved a further manifestation of a fin de siècle apocalyptic anxiety the hoax makes fast friends with. In dissecting the various hysterias of the 1990s, from MPD to SRA, Elaine Showalter sees a recurrent millennialism: "Like the witch-hunts of the 1690s, the mesmerism craze of the 1790s, or the hypnotic cures of the 1890s, the hysterical syndromes of the 1990s clearly speak to the hidden needs and fears of a culture. We are still dealing with the projection of sexual fantasy and real or imagined guilt, with malice and with genuine confusion."[45] Where the male messiah can proclaim the world's end and himself a prophet of it, the female prophet is more often treated like Cassandra, disbelieved yet still on display.

It is hard not to see Sybil too as a hoax, especially now that we know she was coached in her many personalities and that Sybil herself was often aware of her own performance of pathology. When both the ghostwriter and therapist went on the highbrow Dick Cavett talk show in the 1970s, writer Flora Rheta Schreiber said, "Tragically it isn't a hoax—it would be much better for Sybil."[46] Yet recent revelations, including the book *Sybil Exposed* (2011), indicate the ways all three collaborated, colluded even, to maintain not just the illness but the story, with its lucrative, outlandish qualities. The doctor-patient-writer triad made her diagnosis into a best seller, with over six million copies sold. Certainly the doctor in *Sybil*, as well as its writer, Schreiber, both directly benefited financially from Sybil's story, and had little incentive to make her story less sensational—nor to cure her fully.

As with JT LeRoy, Sybil became an identity not just for Sybil herself but also for those around her—not to mention those disaffected who would go on, after similar sets of suggestions, so-called truth serums, and recovered memories, to claim widespread abuse. MPD, as in other incidents of mass hysteria, followed the therapy meant to treat it—any medical centers that set up clinics or whole hospital wings dedicated to treatment would soon see cases of it explode. "The disorders follow the doctors," Showalter reminds us.[47] Sybil's pseudonym suggests her power as predictor and prophecy—in this case of hundreds of now-withdrawn cases of MPD and SRA, but also our Age of Euphemism when illness has become an identity.

Luckily, the MPD epidemic is nearly eradicated—with most of the related court cases of SRA now overturned—the diagnosis diminishing exactly as insurance money for it dried up. MPD has since vanished from the *Diagnostic and Statistical Manual of Mental Disorders*, replaced by the term *dissociative identity disorder*. The chief lobbyist for such a change is Dr. David Spiegel, son of a doctor who saw Sybil when her regular doctor was not able to—the father, in fact, hadn't fully believed the diagnosis at the time. Spiegel fils stresses that multiple personality disorder is actually a misnomer—the problem for such suggestible patients being not too many selves but not quite enough: "You have not more than one but less than one personality."[48] Hysteria is not merely imagined; rather, its symptoms do not necessarily have a physical cause but a psychosomatic one.

Not a sign of more imagination but of less, hoaxes regularly take advantage of the hysteric mood and its method, contagious to the core. "After entertaining the mainstream of popular culture, hysterical syndromes multiply as they interact with social forces such as religious beliefs, political agendas, and rumor panics," Showalter writes, suggesting what's at stake in the hoax too. "Traditional enemies or social scapegoats become part of the scenario, further fueling fears. The longer the epidemic continues, the greater the participants' need to believe it is genuine. In a sense, they feel their honor and integrity are at stake."[49] Just as in mass hysterias, now euphemized as "conversion events," symptoms surface in self-contained groups and closed communities—exactly where the hoax finds its prey. True treatment of hysteria means avoiding belittling symptoms, but also not encouraging them.

But we constantly collude with the hoax. Like Charcot, we the audience unintentionally fall for hysterias tailored just for us; like MPD's media-obsessed, paranoid, and poorly trained therapists, we encourage hoaxes with Barnum statements and expectations of unreality, finding and reinforcing what we are looking for. The crisis the hoax exemplifies is a narrative one—just as the chief treatment advocated for MPD and recovered memory abuse became telling a good, "therapeautic story," one in which "the therapist plays the role of ghost writer or editor in eliciting and shaping the patient's story," we serve as the hoax's midwife, handmaiden, and ghostwriter.[50] Hysteria is a private story made public, even performative, expressing a social need; the hoax moves the other way, a public narrative pretending (or performing) to be private. This is its power, and its harm.

The hoax is not measured by its maker, or intent, or its level of faking, but by its harm. The hoax isn't an illness though its factitiousness can induce suffering and inure us to the suffering of others. The problem isn't that the fabulists, fabricators, phonies, and frauds of our time change actual experience or embellish it, making these received, tampered-with images the only relevant experience—though we need better facts, we need better fictions too—but that by not risking imagining anything new, hoaxes actually diminish experience as not big enough to sustain us.

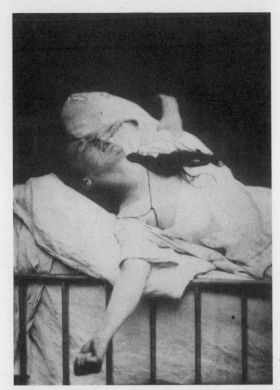

The "Crucifixion" stage
of hysteria, *Iconographie
photographique de la
Salpêtrière*, vol. 2, 1878.

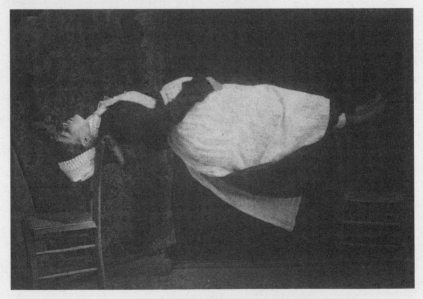

Augustine in the "Léthargie" stage, *Iconographie photographique
de la Salpêtrière*, vol. 3, 1879–80.

CHAPTER 10

Eve Black

Like hysteria before it, multiple personality disorder remained primarily a white woman's affliction—and one particularly American. For the woman known as Eve, in real life a white housewife from still-segregated Georgia, her personalities Eve White and Eve Black sublimate race while relying on old coded dichotomies like evil and good, sin and innocence, black and white.[1] Speaking with a more pronounced southern accent, Eve Black's singing black rock and roll such as "Sixty Minute Man" is meant to be symptomatic of her wildness; her third alter, a plain "Jane" who came to dominate the other personalities, suggests an invisible Tarzan, Boy, and Cheetah too. Eve's tortured Garden of Eden became a tamable jungle.

Yet following the narrative medical account that Charcot innovated, Freud perfected, and the hoax would make off with, the original 1957 account by her doctors describes Eve White as exactly *colorless*: "This neat, colorless young woman was, she said quietly, twenty-five years of age. In a level, slightly monotonous voice she described the severe headaches from which she had suffered now for several months and for which she had been unable to obtain relief."[2] What might name the contagious hysteria of those American white and colorless women after the midcentury, pleading many selves, while at the same time the country's long-standing divisions, black and white, separate and unequal, were collapsing? It may not be too much to say that Eve's divided selves are the country's.

To ask it another way, can there be a black hysteric? Or is hysteria just another aspect of femininity regularly denied black women? There is of course no larger mass hysteria in American history than the epidemic of racism. This too is part of the hoax, and hard to dehoax from; and could be said to be part of the origins of the discovery of the subconscious. For what has remained more unconscious, even now, than the privilege and pain accorded race?

The history of understanding the unconscious began in earnest with mesmerism in the eighteenth century—exactly coinciding, I would add, with the height of the early modern hoax. It would become the stuff of charlatans, but also of the modern idea of mind. Following Mesmer's lead, "very gradually over the course of the nineteenth century, there were reports of a bizarre variation on somnambulism, in which the patient went back and forth between two wholly different states of consciousness, often for long periods. The first detailed medical report of what was then called 'double consciousness' was published in 1816," Joan Acocella writes. "Then from the 1870s to the end of the nineteenth century—that is, at the same time as the hysteria outbreak—there was a small rash of such cases. . . . Double consciousness locked in with the study of hypnosis and also with the late nineteenth-century vogue for spiritualism, and like those other two factors, it fed and was fed by the romantic cult of the irrational. A literature of the double was born."[3] This double was often dark, literally and symbolically.

Might we see in some way W. E. B. Du Bois's embrace of *double consciousness* in a wholly different way as the ultimate literature of the double? In his essential *The Souls of Black Folk* (1903), Du Bois meant double consciousness to describe the fate of African Americans who ever feel this "twoness," living "behind the veil" but also knowing and having to reckon with Americanness and whiteness. Is there at work here a kind of subconscious echoing of the literature of the somnambulist? He too means to understand a modern mind. In this way *Souls of Black Folk* is another kind of diagnostic account.

As such, we might say that Du Bois is also the conscience of the twentieth century, just as he proves prescient about the twenty-first. For if Du Bois forecasts that the "problem of the twentieth century will be the problem of the color line," his echoes of nineteenth-century hypno-hysteric-spiritualist culture also suggests that a subconscious often centers on, and suppresses, race. This repression was expressed in popular culture on the one hand by the race melodrama; on the other, by the hoax.

In JT LeRoy we find both. Despite feints toward an identity radical in terms of gender or class, LeRoy's work was in effect a throwback to a century before. More girl wonder than prodigy, LeRoy becomes something like a *male hysteric*, a phenomenon both Charcot and Freud theorized and even treated but, problematically, never seemed to popularize. We might also say JT LeRoy casts himself as a *nondescript*, that term redolent of classifications and hierarchies—and at least since Barnum, race.

From its first page, LeRoy's debut novel, *Sarah* (2000), unites the race melodrama and the gothic to express the horror of the modern hoax:

> Glad holds the raccoon bone over my head like a halo. 'I have a little something for your own protection,' he says, leaning down over me so close that I can't help but stare up at the brown patches of skin that mottle the pure whiteness of his face.
>
> 'Glad, you look like you're sharecroppin' out your own private patch of cancer,' some of the lot lizards would tease him. But I know the truth of it. Glad told me himself. It's the Choctaw in his blood. That's why he's got good medicine. That's why he's a good pimp for a lot lizard to have.
>
> 'These patches of brown be the In'ian in me, making themselves known,' he tells me over a trucker special breakfast at The Doves Diner: a huge mound of hollandaise eggs and thick-as-a-Bible persimmon pancakes.[4]

Here is a combo platter of all the clichés the hoax can muster, from the "white Indian" and "half-breed" to the bad and black dialect of the fake memoir to the cancer specter, all with a supposedly new breed of sexuality and faux southernness poured on "thick-as-a-Bible." LeRoy's is a nostalgia that romanticizes pain and split personalities, channeling Spiritualism and MPD as pseudoscience and its double, pseudospirituality—all the while making use of the dichotomies of blackness and its opposite.

Such racial marking is a way of trying to claim southernness by someone who isn't. The lot lizards may seem unusual or profound in the high literature to which LeRoy has pretensions—to wit, the first edition of *Sarah* comes with an attached ribbon bookmark—but in hindsight the racial elements and sexual stances seem mere gimmicks. So too the emblem of the raccoon penis bone known as a baculum, given by "Glad" to the narrator but that Albert herself would stock up on and sell online. The curved bone seems designed for wearing around hipster necks; the one I tracked down is signed "JT LEROY" in smudged ink. It is a perfect metaphor, of course, getting Hollywood to wear decorative boners in a town that insists on measuring whoever's is symbolically the biggest. Like Lance Armstrong's yellow Livestrong bracelets, LeRoy's baculums are totems worn to indicate that I, too, belong to the tribe.

The whole (or castrated) thing is meant to suggest a southern gothic. Albert picked the name "LeRoy" as a kind of royal, southernesque name, claiming he was from West Virginia, which is debatably more Appalachian than southern—and certainly not the Deep South. The distinction seems lost on Albert, whose books rely on a shared geographic ignorance on the part of a presumed audience. It reminds me of the joke from *Seinfeld* when Jerry Seinfeld (playing a fictionalized version of himself) complains about his newly converted dentist (played by Bryan Cranston), who he's convinced has converted to Judaism just for the jokes. When the priest he's confessing to asks if it offends him as a Jewish person, Seinfeld responds, *No—it offends me as a comedian.* LeRoy's southernness does not so much offend me as a sometime southerner with exclusively southern roots; it offends me as a writer.

Not that there weren't signs early on. Before the revelations, an "essay" LeRoy published in the *Oxford American* seemed to at least one writer clearly not southern, though entirely gothic. John Nova Lomax recalls reading the beginning of LeRoy's "Coal Miner Mother," which opens

> I remember my momma, Sarah, stripping in the pole clubs to the song "There He Goes" by Loretta Lynn.

"I groaned," Lomax writes. "I knew immediately that this story was not going to have much to do with Lynn, and from there, the Southern Gothic clichés mounted, each more preposterous than the last." Lomax took the extra step of writing to (now deposed) editor Marc Smirnoff and to LeRoy about the "preposterous, uncorroboratable tale, wherein one of the only two businesses mentioned by name did not check out" and received back within hours an "e-mailed dollop of mushy condescension" from someone claiming to be LeRoy's assistant "Nancy," who is "confident" she can speak for him:

> If you were to look at J.T.'s works, you would find that all of them are published as fiction, even those pieces that are very close to his actual experiences. This is because J.T. doesn't really believe in the concept of true fact and true fiction. The way he sees it, any event that occurs is subject to interpretation from the person involved with it. Two people

may be in the exact same situation but take entirely different memories away from it, depending on what they bring to the table and their own personality. Likewise, a writer always weaves parts of his/her life experiences, opinions, thoughts, small noted details, in short, everything that they are and have been, into their writing. It would be unnatural not to do that.

So, you see? No true fact or fiction.

"Nancy" then offers to publish Lomax in an issue of the *Best Music Writing* she—I mean LeRoy—was editing.

Unswayed, Lomax ends his piece in the *Houston Press* by suggesting LeRoy's piece is a hoax, recounting that Smirnoff replied with the kinds of justifications that perpetuate hoaxes while dismissing newspaper fact-checking as quaint: "We have different practices," Smirnoff said. "And this was a literary experiment at a literary magazine, and maybe that's not something you're comfortable with. More power to you. A *literary* experiment in a *literary* magazine."[5] Again with the literature defense. Both the hoaxer's and the editor's responses seem to me about power: exercising it in the name of literature, or dismissing it in the name of someone more famous than you. Despite "LeRoy's" claim in correspondence with the *Oxford American* that "I publish all my stories as fiction anyways," the essay label reinforces how instead of simply writing fiction labeled as such LeRoy claimed that there is "no true fact or fiction"—a hoax worldview if ever was one. "Everything I do or say is fiction," LeRoy had written in response to the magazine's fact checkers, who let the piece stand not seeming to grasp that the hoaxer meant it literally.[6]

Like his Congo, also described in a quote-unquote essay, LeRoy's South is not global but internal: call it "South Virginia," where Savannah Knoop mistakenly told someone she-disguised-as-LeRoy was from. South Virginia may be invented but its borders are closely guarded and governed by others. Where Neverland took its children from real to fake, from the nursery to make-believe, South Virginia—like an idealized "Dixie" more generally—went the other way, a fake thing that's pretending to be real. In LeRoy's case, South Virginia not only doesn't exist, it's not all his own—belonging in part to Breece D'J Pancake, the late West Virginia writer from whom LeRoy borrowed style and more. The result is reminiscent of what Flannery O'Connor mocked as "the School of Southern Degeneracy"—to Albert and her ilk, one implies the other.

Albert crafted LeRoy as a kind of grotesque body to relieve and relive the torment. For noted critic Mikhail Bakhtin writing on Rabelais, the actual grotesque is not a satire but a celebration of unruly life; O'Connor would call it an admission of original sin. "The grotesque body, as we have often stressed, is a body in the act of becoming," Bakhtin writes. "It is never finished, never completed; it is continually built, created, and builds and creates another body. Moreover, the body swallows the world and is itself swallowed by the world." This may at first seem to be LeRoy in a nutshell (or nuthouse), perpetually reinvented, especially when Bakhtin writes, "The essential role belongs to those parts of the grotesque body in which it outgrows its own self, transgressing its own body, in which it conceives a new, *second body*: the bowels and the phallus. These two areas play the leading role in the grotesque image, and it is precisely for this reason that they are predominantly subject to positive exaggeration, to hyperbolization; they can even detach themselves from the body and lead an independent life, for they hide the rest of the body, as something secondary."[7] Instead of "secondary," can this body be a literal second body?

The tension here is between the body as something wondrous or prodigious, as the freak had once been, and the body as something trapped, even prodigal, as the freak became. *I needed to supply a body*: a mother herself, Albert's desire for a body for JT to inhabit was the exact opposite of most creations, and of birth itself, in which physicality precedes language. Instead, as with the spirit photograph or the hysteric, the photographic image demanded a body to follow, and to fit into. The carnivalesque she crafted is far more the spectacle of the sideshow, of voyeurism as an unexplored value that no camera can contain. Photographs of LeRoy are spirit photographs, circus portraits, and anthropological studies in one. Read in this way, the books become an afterthought, the sideshow pamphlets sold at the show by another Cannibal King.

Like the hoax, across the twentieth century the grotesque has gone from a form of humor to its current horror. As O'Connor put it, "In nineteenth-century American writing, there was a good deal of grotesque literature which came from the frontier and was supposed to be funny; but our present grotesque characters, comic though they may be, are at least not primarily so."[8] The immortality that LeRoy seeks is of a far lesser order, the kind Bakhtin cautions against, "in which only the inappropriate is exaggerated"; such a world "is only quantitively [*sic*] large, but qualitatively it is extremely poor, colorless, and far from gay."[9] The result is less grotesque than gross. This wanting to be a boy (because of patriarchal power) who wants to be a girl (because the act wasn't actually convincing) turns out is not anarchic, nor is it colored or merry, but remains relentlessly hierarchical, binary, and "far from gay." Certainly it was read as such—in critical and queer ways—by the actual trans hustlers and street kids who felt betrayed by LeRoy's revelation.[10]

"I can't get enough attention to heal me," Albert admitted after the hoax was exposed. The whole endeavor remains oddly anorectic yet cannibalistic. Savannah Knoop, who played LeRoy, goes on to describe Albert's and her own struggles with food in ways that echo the hoax more generally, with its symbolic body dysmorphism; like the hoax itself, the eating here is less re-ordered than disordered, less a love of Rabelaisian excess than binging and purging, not quite wigging out.

JT LeRoy is a foreign body, never inhabited fully and thus unable to be taken apart. Not that LeRoy doesn't try: the writer Ayelet Waldman, who used to talk with JT on the phone after her husband, fellow writer Michael Chabon, got sick of the bluff, describes how "It was during one of these conversations that I came to my conclusion that JT was, in fact, a fraud. At some point, apropos of nothing, he told me that since we'd last spoken he had gone ahead and had that sex-change operation he'd been think-ing about. . . . 'Really?' I asked. 'I thought they made you go through some elaborate hormonal process before they let you have the final surgery.' 'Nah,' he said. 'I'd done so much damage to my penis, hacking away at it. It was no big deal just to take off the stump.'"[11]

Waldman says such absurdities made her aware something was being pulled—wool, a leg—and went along happily. Nothing wrong with being fake: the phallus, always symbolic and in that way distinct from an ac-tual penis—*a penis is a phallus but a phallus is not a penis*—is often fake. But LeRoy describes a kind of unreality beyond the realm of the believable: the hoax body, always on display, is here neither gargantuan nor dismembered but ever eroding. The hoax craves power, then hacks away at it.

INTERVIEW WITH A VAMPIRE

It took a fall 2006 interview in the *Paris Review*—notably classified as an "Encounter" and not part of the journal's prestigious Art of Fiction series—for Laura Albert to finally confess publicly that she had written the LeRoy books. The issue's incredible cover features a childhood photograph of Albert in a T-shirt that reads *I want to be me!* Albert says she'd been hoaxing since sixth grade:

> There was this one guy that everyone really liked, but no one could speak to him on the phone because they'd giggle too much. So one day, with the other girls listening, I called him using a Swedish accent, and he fell for it. I kept calling him—and the other girls didn't know this. I made up a whole character, Katrin. I went to the library to research Sweden, and I studied Swedish to make sure my accent was right. . . .
>
> Our phone relationship went on for months. It got really elaborate. And then, one day I met him, as Katrin's friend Laura, and we started to hang out together. . . . And I felt for this guy, in the way that you do when you're twelve, where it's safe. It was very real, and it had taken me over. I didn't know how to stop it, but I realized it had to end. So I discovered this kind of cancer that could develop pretty fast, and I gave that to Katrin, and one day when the boy called the house, I told him that Katrin had died.
>
> The next morning the boy's mother showed up at our door. The boy's family was upset, and they wanted to know what had happened. And my mother was like, What the fuck are you talking about? I remember hearing them talking in the other room, and feeling heartbroken. I hadn't meant for any of this to happen.[12]

The interviewer moves on to another question without comment.

Albert here stakes claim to being the original catfish, predating even Tony Godby Johnson or the 2010 documentary that gave us the term. But such a story is itself dubious: reporter Nancy Rommelmann, who grew up in the same neighborhood as Albert, writes that she was childhood friends with the boy crush who was Albert's first love/victim.

> How long, I ask [the crush, Ray], did the calls with Katrin last? "First of all," he says, "it wasn't Katrin, it was Katrina. The calls are going on a couple of weeks, and then she tells me she has leukemia, and she's going to die within the year. And I'm feeling really bad. It made me feel terrible. You know, when you're 13, you want to change the world, and I couldn't." . . . When I ask what happened when Katrina died, Ray doesn't know what I mean. Then he says, "Nancy, you just made

me remember. I got a message on my answering machine right before I got married, 10 years ago, saying, 'Katrina died.'"

Ten years ago?

"Yeah. I didn't know what that meant until you just brought this up," he says. As for Katrina having a death scene back in 1978, Ray says, it didn't happen.[13]

Nor is it true that the whole neighborhood mourned. "Katrina just went back to Europe or faded away or something," Ray told Rommelmann. "She'd told me she was in America because the medical treatment was better, which is pretty clever. But for everyone to suffer and wonder what happened, that is fucked up."[14] Just as innocence is for Nasdijj and advocacy for Marlo Morgan, it is the confession, with Albert, that compounds the crime.

In his *Famous Impostors* (1910), the creator of *Dracula*, Bram Stoker, reminds us that "any statement regarding one's own birth is manifestly not to be relied on."[15] So too the birth of a hoax: JT LeRoy was said to be born on Halloween, a hint if ever there was one, of the hoax and its horror. Albert's birth seems the thing of myth too. "I was born with a fever," Albert says to her *Paris Review* interviewer. "My mother was in labor at the Brooklyn Hospital for three days and she almost died. It was election day, and because of me, my mother didn't get to vote. It was also the Day of the Dead."[16] Between the mention of three days and the day of the dead, Albert mythifies her own birth as a rebirth, filled with near death and feverishness—the vampire's domain. It seems apt then that Dracula's birth in Stoker's fiction was followed a decade later by the writer's study of impostors: as we've seen, the hoax and horror have been linked since at least Poe.[17] Both the vampire and the hoaxer seek to live, and long, off another's stoked pain.

Given her sustained hoaxing, anything Albert says about her rough childhood may seem hard to believe now. This is part of the problem. The hoax makes the truth sound untrue, or unsure—but a few other articles and court case testimony by Albert, unless perjured, of course, seem to corroborate that she was the unfortunate victim of actual childhood sexual abuse. To the *Paris Review* interviewer she says this abuse started at the hands of her mother's boyfriends, "an ongoing cast of characters" she goes on to list: "an Indian called Strong Horse who had done time for murder, Stanley the manic depressive, Motorcycle Bob, and on and on."[18] Even when she tells what approximates the truth, Albert crafts a kind of fairy tale—a grotesque that makes any reality hard to believe. This is the danger of drawing yourself as a cartoon and then calling it autobiographical.

Despite what contestants on reality TV dating shows seem to think, fairy tales don't just offer happy endings. Rather they provide coded forms of violence and blood, danger and beauty, in order to express society's anxieties and storify them for its children. In a short but significant essay, critic Leslie Fiedler describes two of these Western anxieties as "getting married" and "not being eaten." Fiedler also traces our printed popular literature to its roots in the oral fairy tale—as opposed to high literature and scripture, which by the Victorian era had both become canonized in a near-religious sense. Popular literature was always something that could be, indeed needed to be, added to. Writing in 1973, Fiedler appears prescient regarding the continued and even renewed popularity of our own vampire and living-dead tales "in a time like our own when cannibalism, especially in the form of vampirism, has become again a compulsive theme of popular literature, indeed a central feature of mass culture in general." Like the hoax, in fact alongside it, such horror stories survive and resurface, again and again.

Albert turns to the fairy tale—and later, explicitly, fable—to try to render life as myth. A noble goal, perhaps, but one that mistakes the terror for the tale. "Such stories normally treat not the eating of noble enemies by their conquerors . . . or of the hero-father by his rival sons (as analyzed by Freud in *Totem and Taboo*), but the very reverse of the latter: the eating of children by parent-surrogates, which is to say, the inhibition of the future by re-incorporation of what has already been separated from its past by the pangs of birth. One metaphorical name for this is 'incest,' one 'cannibalism.' In the world of myth, they become finally a single terror," Fiedler writes.[19] In the hoax of JT LeRoy—and then the confession of Albert—the terror may be multiple but is not dissimilar. "I feel an ache, a fierce piercing ache somewhere. My hand feels damp. I raise it to my eyes and see blood. Everything dissolves to black," LeRoy writes in *Sarah*, describing what appears to be a scalping.[20]

The sexless, age-defying LeRoy isn't Peter Pan so much as the crocodile whose stomach is a ticking clock, threatening to devour us all. A devouring death, and its opposite, immortality, has in fact long been part of the fairy tale. "This is the underlying fable of *Dracula*," Fiedler writes, "and in that book it is made clear that incest-cannibalism is forever in vain; since the aging suckers of young blood do not themselves become immortal, merely 'un-dead.'"[21] Destruction, blood, and betrayal—often by blood relatives—

engulf LeRoy not because they're mythic but because they express Albert's narrative of her life, one in which she didn't "mean for this to happen."

JT LeRoy expresses the horror that makes up the modern hoax, which is horror of a disintegrating self. This isn't a wish for an "adult fairy tale," as is sometimes said of LeRoy, if only because fairy tales are already for adults.[22] Nor is it a "punk fairy tale"—the subtitle of a Brazilian musical about him!—that LeRoy works. Rather, LeRoy combines nearly all the ideas of the hoax. From fake memoir to "false novels," imposture to the shifting self, forgery and the plagiarism of pain, LeRoy represents the modern hoax's apogee, its contagiousness and contagion. While prosaically embodying the gender bending of *Peter Pan* as well as its desire for everlasting youth, LeRoy ultimately seeks to borrow the fairy tale and its vampire descendants exactly because they are popular. Created within a few years of each other, Count Dracula and Peter Pan are linked by immortality; a century on but light-years behind, LeRoy wishes to conflate the monster's immortality with literature's.

UNDERGROUND, INC.

Our current age's narrative crisis arose when audiences began to mistake grotesqueries for reality, television talk for truth, hysteria for history, and spectacle for nature—that is, something beyond human nature. The grotesque has become the hoax's mood and its method. This may be the most powerful part of LeRoy's books, marrying as they do survivor's guilt to the zombie's hunger, the fairy tale's fear to the truck stop's: in looking into the vampire's mirror we see only Albert, winking hysterically back. The problem with all these dark doubles is not just that they substitute fantasy for reality but also that they render reality two-dimensional, like our screens. All this may be good for tales, or television, or perhaps for JT LeRoy, but it falls rather flat when we learn that the terror of "reality" is only a special effect.

Such a special effect we could call the gothic. Here's the chief distinction between the hoax and the gothic: while the gothic revels in our societal taboos like birth and death, the hoax reveals and exploits our deep-seated social divisions of gender and race, North and South, young and old, not to mention those between the self and the author. Those who forget this last distinction are especially in danger of being hoaxed themselves.

Take the movie *The Heart Is Deceitful Above All Things*, based on LeRoy's 2001 book, which had the misfortune—or good luck, depending—to get released right when LeRoy's true identity was revealed in 2006. (It was a banner year for the hoax, bringing us revelations of Margaret Seltzer, James Frey, and several Holocaust hoaxes.) Carrying the tagline "Behind the greatest hoax of our time is the heartbreaking story that started it all," the film was directed by and starred Asia Argento, an Italian actress who along the way would become lovers with LeRoy (or at least his body double, Savannah Knoop). Argento's father is a famed Italian horror director known for schlock like *Deep Red* and a Warholian *Frankenstein*; no wonder *The Heart Is Deceitful* turns out to be a horror movie, though I'm not sure it is of a kind I can watch. Advertising "The seductive tale of JT LeRoy" seems the wrong word for a story of abuse.

Reviewer Manohla Dargis takes the film, and the books, to task as sexploitation: "A scene of child rape (a JT LeRoy specialty) isn't just ghastly, it's also *grotesque*. Such exploitation, of course, is what puts books like *Sarah* and *The Heart Is Deceitful Above All Things* on best-seller lists. Given publishing's seemingly endless appetite for memoirs filled with sexual sob stories and kinks, a JT LeRoy was inevitable. . . . That the prose is as tedious as the stories are outrageous mattered not at all, compared with such lovingly rendered degradation."[23] Dargis means grotesque in its most typical, not Rabelasian, sense of *gross*; this is a gothic both Italian and southern, those lands where the gothic mood has especially taken root. Film critic Anthony Lane also cites LeRoy's gothic in his damning review of the movie:

> What is awful about Jeremiah being beaten by one of his mother's admirers, for example, is not the deed itself, which the camera attends in gratuitous proximity, but the helpful air of acceptance with which, some time later, he offers a leather belt to the *next* man, fully expecting to be punished for his sins. As for the scene in which he sits in the car, at night, clawing firmly at his cheeks and replying, to his mother's inquiry, 'I'm digging myself out,' I hope never to watch it again. That line is in the book, but LeRoy, who overwrites in the way that some people overdress, spoils it by strapping on an extra phrase: 'I shout past the loud buzzing in my head, 'I'm digging myself out!' and watch clean, cold shafts of sun shadows rip into my flesh.' This is what I think of as *auto-gothic*, and whether Laura Albert (if she was, indeed, the guilty party) meant it as a parody of fashionable angst or whether LeRoy's prose really was the best that she could muster is, in the end, beside the point.[24]

By *auto-gothic*, Lane means, I have come to think, not just an autobiographical gothic but the gothic on autopilot, a self-propelling prophecy.

Such auto-gothic also suggests the self as a grotesquerie, a gothic of one—no matter if LeRoy's self was multiple exactly as an overcompensation for less. This notion of the self would at first seem a radical, roomy one Whitman might admire, or a shifting selfhood that conforms more closely to our postmodern notions, but in using the language of possession and pseudospirituality, Albert actually relies on overdetermined ideas of the author as a solitary prodigy and doomed genius dying young. The doomed prodigy and the vampire share the ominous sense of how the dead, in a fashion, remain alive—gone too soon but preserved forever, for good or ill.

Albert exposed becomes not the child protagonist, girl wonder, or prodigy, as LeRoy himself promised, but the ultimate Evil Stepmother—to LeRoy sure, but also to the very idea of "faction" or fake fiction. All this doesn't mean that LeRoy wasn't real, or more than real, for Albert at least. Feeling possessed, dispossessed—all these were pseudospiritual excuses that Albert, and in a way, LeRoy himself, wrought. This is the American art of reinvention made mystical, the occult as cult: as with hoax spirit photographer Mumler before her, the effort landed her in court. Sued for fraud by the movie company who optioned the rights to a LeRoy book, Albert said of her persona in court, "He was my respirator. He was my channel for air. To me, if you take my JT, my Jeremy, my other, I die."[25] Albert also told the court that, after Savannah Knoop played LeRoy in person, "She became JT. It's like a trinity. We experienced it. It was as if he would leave me and enter her—I know how it sounds."[26]

Film and its ocular proof remain important to the hoax, especially to its revelation: a list of those never-completed films based on books revealed as hoaxes is long indeed, including most all the biggies, from James Frey and JT LeRoy, to Nasdijj and Joan Lowell's original film deal itself. Film preproduction often causes a hoax to be exposed because of cinema's far different scale of money (and liability), as well as attendant publicity—but the chief cause of exposure might chiefly be because of film's collaborative nature. Partners and producers of films have more motivation and financial incentive to discover what some readers usually suspect; in most of these cases, suspicious producers hastened the hoaxes' ends.

If it took time for Albert to fully "come out" and discuss in public her part in the hoax, it is perhaps because of her supposed need to breathe, but also because she might have sensed that what for her was a life raft to others was a sinking ship. The court saw it that way, awarding over $350,000 in the breach-of-contract case to the film company that thought it was hiring LeRoy—who managed to "sign" the contract, despite not existing. Checks were cut to an "Underdog, Inc." The copy of *Sarah* I tracked down is also signed, somewhat—in a generic, childlike hand on the publishers' bookplate to be placed in the book. But the author's name appears clearly misspelled: *LreRoy*. As a note included with the book claims, surely if not assuredly written by a handler—"Nancy," or I can only hope, Speedie herself—"This is LeRoy's 'left-hand' signature—he plays with both hands and both genders!!"[27] But LeRoy is no profound gender play but a familiar parlor trick, less a self-contained double than a two-bit hustle. If a resurrection, it is resurrection as theater, like those faith healers promise. An underdog ink.

The hoax relies on extremes of illness, trauma, and unreality in order to achieve those effects that the patient they symbolize made literal. Good art works the other way around, taking what's happened—the real and the given—and making metaphor from, out of, and beyond it. The problem with the hoax is not falseness posing as reality, but a reliance on layer after layer of re-created reality, altered documents, fake accents, Barnum statements, and nonexistent people—"all the clichés"—that lead to an unrelenting sameness. Albert's innovation as hoaxer was to tweak this slightly into an *unrelenting difference*: abuse, prostitution, raccoon penis bones, and more.

Albert is in fact attempting her umpteenth comeback, this time precipitated by the limited release in 2015 of the less than sympathetic documentary *The Cult of JT LeRoy* (and a more favorable one reliant on her interviews in 2016). After viewing the powerful footage, the question remains not just why create another body, but why subject that body to the most abject deprivation and abuse? How do the people seen humming around Knoop-as-LeRoy feel about things now? And how long till my order of "Books, Bones, Stickers, & more!" arrives? Looking back at the sideshow that was JT LeRoy, no one seems to be having anything close to fun. It's a party of—and to—pain.

As our gender roles change and expand and are challenged—which they have many times before, we should note—we should not forget the pleasure of gender, whether as something simply to be played with or ignored. Certain Native American groups had as many as five different genders. Yet binaries of gender and race are LeRoy's boon companions, whether expressed as North or South, Native or non, black or white, trans or not.[28] Despite all her talk of unconsciousness, and identification, Albert and her

LeRoy hoax betray themselves as essentialist while merely skin deep. Far from freeing, bound like her sister-in-law's breasts, the role Albert created for JT LeRoy was ultimately more complex and confining than the metaphoric closet.

The more I see and learn of LeRoy, the more I've come to find Savannah Knoop's role as the part-time voice and body the only interesting if not necessarily radical one. LeRoy's books wear on you—they haven't aged well, not just because they speak to their moment but because so much of them was not on the page. *It's the same words!* some protest once a hoax is revealed. But to pretend books are the same after a hoax is revealed ignores what's overemphasized in any hoax: the author. If they had been issued anonymously, LeRoy's books would never have been as successful; the gig needed a body because the crime, which is not to say its confession, called for one.

In a 2010 event at the storytelling series the Moth, viewable online, an unmasked Laura Albert came to tell her story—devolving from once telling stories as JT LeRoy now to telling stories about making him up—and described her creation, almost offhandedly, as an "avatar."[29] By *avatar*, it seems clear Albert does not mean an earthly incarnation of the divine but rather is clearly influenced by James Cameron's blockbuster film by that name. As in Cameron's 2009 epic, which earned more money than any other film before it, her avatar is a borrowed body, alien and artificially grown. Or maybe it's that Laura Albert was a sybil—in using *avatar* she anticipates the stock photos and tiny icons our personalities have become, those images bizarre or borrowed or constantly changing that mark our messages and tweets and log-ins. *Did you forget your password?* Once avatar used to be something larger than us, unearthly. Now, only sometimes, our avatar is us.

Whether as an image or an author, JT LeRoy never reaches this higher level, mistaking, as many of us did when younger, potential for art. As the hoax wore on, and off, LeRoy wrote less and got photographed more. Albert willed her way into the good graces of people who felt betrayed, not by her writing—as Truman Capote did when he exposed the secrets of high society in his infamous and incomplete roman à clef—but by lying to their faces after. The revelations keep coming: not only had Albert faked LeRoy's phone voice but all along she'd recorded almost every call, including with LeRoy's shrink. That these Nixonian tapes are now part of a 2016 "documentary" has only reignited her victims' despair.[30] LeRoy's output waned as the fame grew, showing how much LeRoy wasn't just a proxy but a ploy. The inevitable trilogy petered out, each book smaller and less ambitious, from

novel to short stories to what might generously be called a novella to magazine "essays." It would appear that the alter ego was more about ego after all.

While on the one hand Albert's frustration with headlines such as
"Fake Fiction Writer" seem understandable—there's a way in which a fiction writer already implies fake—it's also true that the persona of JT and the
writing aren't separate exactly because Albert made them that way. *Sarah*
is dedicated "to Sarah" as if she's real, not just based on someone who is;
LeRoy would not only write fake fictions but also review books, visit Disney
Europe, and hire themselves out for nonfiction gigs. If a Frankenstein
monster, LeRoy offered a critique of his creator that the creator could not
withstand.

Albert would say she always intended to kill JT off—like any other
monster, you might say—but just couldn't. Were Albert-as-JT's frequent
pleas of suicide a way of ending the hoax or simply scams to court more
pity? Should we be thankful that those who listened to JT saved a life, even
if not the one they thought they were saving? The hoax muddies the waters
around us all—but in reading about actual deaths that "JT" would respond
to, or about Paul Monette's death from AIDS during the Anthony Godby
Johnson debacle, Albert's hoax becomes more and more troubling. Did she
drop the HIV from JT's bio in order to "live it up"? For Albert, the tragedy
wasn't in spite of the work; it was a form of it.

We know there's a strict pact with autobiography, in which the writer
and the persona on the page are pretty much the same; while always there
even when unstated, often this pact is made quite explicitly, through various
prefaces and attestations. But there is, we must remember, a fiction pact—
not just that fiction writers will tell us when they are lying but that *they will
lie only about the really important stuff.* Novelist Elena Ferrante, whose pseudonymity sought the opposite of personal fame, puts it slightly differently:
"Sometimes we tell ourselves lovely tales, sometimes petty lies. Falsehoods
protect us, mitigate suffering, allow us to avoid the terrifying moment of serious reflection, they dilute the horrors of our time, they even save us from
ourselves. Instead, when one writes one must never lie. In literary fiction
you have to be sincere to the point where it's unbearable, where you suffer
the emptiness of the pages."[31] I would say that the pact art makes is not that
it always speaks truthfully, but that when it lies, it lets us in on that too. This
traditionally might include the bio on the back of the book or the name on
the front; as in Ferrante, it might also mean making use of near truths, or
exploiting the fallacy that all writing is autobiography. But it doesn't mean

license to lie in interviews or to readers about such poignant and powerful things as child abuse or AIDS or even how the books came to be written.

This pact is a transfer of the very trust we take from fairy tales or stories told at bedtime. We expect these to be invented, even terrifying, and take great pleasure in make-believe as children. But we don't expect the story-teller, mother or father or other figures, to turn out not to be what she or he or they say they are. The anxiety over this is actually found in the fairy tales themselves, with their wolves disguised as grandmothers, killers described as fathers, mothers left absent or replaced by evil stepmothers.

If autobiography "is a mode of reading as much as it is a type of writing," as critic Philippe Lejeune has argued,[32] then fiction is a way of reading too—and of living. This may further explain why so many hoaxers who wrote memoirs that were really fiction, or fictions they hinted were memoirs, won't relabel their books once discovered. As such hoaxers well intuit, if you promote the idea among readers that your fiction was merely a thin veil, after being exposed not only does the author become unreliable but the writing does too. Like the strip-mall psychic whose claims seem merely laughable once deturbaned, hair filled with static, the writer whose sleight of hand gets revealed appears less a magician than a charlatan, and not a very charming one. Any tricks seem mere trickery. We know from unreliable narrators, but the hoax suggests not so much an "unreliable author" as that there's no other kind. For all its drama, the auto-gothic and its president and client JT LeRoy are filled with self-abuse.

What we can best say about Albert is that she sought to be a "genuine fraud," not a phony one. But an artist is not (or not only) a bullshit artist. Just as with those who knew him—and her, and them—it becomes hard with JT LeRoy, as with the hoax more generally, to know just what to believe, much less trust, in the end. And with the hoax, the end is always nigh.

Circassian Beauty with Standing Man, c. 1880s.

BOOK TWO

THE

HOAXING

OF

HISTORY

FOUR

The

Vampire's

Mirror

❦{Of imposture, forgery & monsters}❧

A forgery is always worse than it looks.
—ELIOT WEINBERGER

26 Argynnis cybele

Cigarette card, Kimball Company, ca. 1890s.

CHAPTER 11

Butterfly Books

The history of the hoax is chiefly the hoaxing of history: a forgery pretending it has one, inevitably better and older than it really is; the plagiarist or impostor or spirit photographer insisting that no history exists *except what I say there is*. As we move forward from the hoax's varied history into the ways the hoax makes use of history, we move from the spirit photograph as the emblem of the past as never dying to that of the forgery—that object that insists it once was alive. These days history pretends to be all the more personal, taking on the kinds of trauma and wild backstory that would do any fake memoirist proud. Forgeries seek not only to have a convincing history but also to change History—witness the Hitler Diaries or any number of Holocaust hoaxers who don't merely connect personal history to public history, as the modern memoir has, but seek to have the personal supersede the public record.

It's my history, the forger claims—I can lie if I want to.

Just as hysteria follows doctors, almost as if they were its cause, forgeries follow experts. Many a hoax—from forged paintings to outright fictions, the "Lincoln the Lover" letters and that famed, fake missing link, Piltdown Man—has passed the inspection of a bevy of credulous authenticators. It is hard to pull off a forgery without someone, or a crew of someones, testifying to its authenticity. "As long as there are fakers, there have to be experts," Orson Welles argues in his fascinating film *F for Fake*. "But if there were no experts, would there be any fakers?" P. T. Barnum let the audience imagine themselves expert; modern hoaxers hold themselves out as experts. By not just showing what's fake but how, Welles means to trump them all.

A good forger goes beyond merely presenting a forged or faked Picasso to craft further documents that authenticate the fake's existence. The same goes for literary forgery, which fakes a backstory as well as a document—providing a collaboration between present and past, the hoaxer and the audience—something meant to fool, make a fool of, or make money from (usually all three). One dare not challenge this history; you may miss out on a great deal, moneywise, if you do. For the forger, like other hoaxers, seeks to make the audience complicit—not to mention rich. It's this last quality—of money as history—that courses through the forgery and leaves the audience seeming especially vulnerable, simultaneously victims and volunteers. Behind every forger is a thwarted historian.

Famed bookman Robert A. Wilson makes a useful distinction between forgeries and fakes: one is an invention, the other is an imposture. "Forgeries may be defined as spurious productions of books or pamphlets that never actually existed, as opposed to fakes which are conscious reproductions of items made at a later date with the intention of deception."[1] This should sound familiar: most of the hoaxes we've looked at, from fake memoirs to travel fabulism, have meant making things up that never happened, abstracted inventions—"fakes" in Wilson's terminology. Forgery helps us understand how the modern hoax shifted from exoticists faking the Other to impostors forging a self.

The best confession of forgery may actually be *Frankenstein*. Published anonymously by a young Mary Shelley in 1818, it is no hoax but a novel remarkably modern in form and outlook, one about the art of making and fabricating. Subtitled *The Modern Prometheus* after the Greek god who stole fire for humankind, the question becomes who's the Prometheus? Is the one liberating humanity the man named Frankenstein or his creation? Or are one or both false gods? The book's modernity is also monstrous: there's a sinking sense that the melancholy, creative stifling, and suffering of the book doesn't belong to Victor Frankenstein alone, but to his time, and now ours. Turning our attention to the hoax as forgery, we confront a monster that is neither silent nor inarticulate but that has its own life that speaks back.

While the myth of *Frankenstein*—popular enough that the title character's name has become conflated with his creation—is about "male birth" as a primal destructive force, it is also about crafting a kind of false life whose true name is harm. The conflation of maker and monster mirrors that of the author and her book, which have contaminated each other to the point that it can be hard to distinguish one from the other. (It has even led some to question Mary Shelley's authority over her text.[2] Such deauthorizing accusations are depressingly commonplace against female authors, I have found.) What's more, the notion of a "Frankenstein" might describe the hoax here and now: half alive and half true, constantly resurrected, deadly and deadly serious.

Victor refers to his creation as "my own vampire, my own spirit let loose from the grave, and forced to destroy all that was dear to me."[3] The monster himself is incredibly articulate and goes on to take over the narrative for a lot of the book, speaking of the pain of being and of being born, cursing his "creator." Creator and monster are authors of each other, we're told; the monster's "growing up" involves his realization of the pain of existence. Critic Sady Doyle not only defends Shelley's creation, she sees it as "revenge" for the suicide of Shelley's half sister, Fanny, abused for being "illegitimate" and who "tore her own name off her suicide note. 'You will soon forget there was ever such a creature as.' Frankenstein's monster has no name." The very name Frankenstein, Doyle points out, might descend from Frances, Fanny's given name.[4] Whatever its origins, Frankenstein is as obsessed with innocence and redolent of its opposite—guilt or shame—as the hoax is. As if to highlight this, Peter Carey's My Life as a Fake is a horror story about a forger whose creation comes to life; modeled after Australia's Ern Malley poetry hoax that invented an unsung working-class poet who died young, Carey's novel takes a quote from Frankenstein as its epigraph: "I beheld the wretch—the miserable monster whom I had created. He held up the curtain of the bed; and his eyes, if eyes they may be called, were fixed on me."[5]

The monster's chapters in Frankenstein are certainly ones of insurrection. Slavery is never far from the mind of a reader, or the monster—one of the book's many powers is to make those roles, slaver and slave, reader and monster, shared for a time. The result is a cautionary tale about manmade institutions—and I do mean men—and justifications for the invention of oppression, echoing the dangers of the hoax. We could call Frankenstein the grotesque's revenge, the monster giving voice to, and indicting, all those hoax creations, from James Frey's Porterhouse and Nasdijj's Mary Potato, to Marlo Morgan's Real People and the unreal JT LeRoy, whose creators made them not just up but less than human. In her fascinating study Black Frankenstein, Elizabeth Young (no relation) illumines the way that the idea of Frankenstein crisscrossed the Atlantic, becoming a sympathetic allegory of the slave while also a critique of oppression.[6] After all, slavery was the real monster of the Americas.

Victor Frankenstein as forger suggests the self as divided, heralding the dark double that found its way into allegorical fictions like *Dr. Jekyll and Mr. Hyde*; into American literature more broadly; and especially into the modern hoax. In this way, he's the hoax personified, the forger and the expert, too, who believe it into being. But Mary Shelley's masterpiece also implies, in its gothic way, that the self—not the autobiography or psychobiography or history, but the inalienable self—could be faked. Or worse, had become fake already. And that this modern, forged, Frankensteined self, expressed through forgery and the hoax, surely spells doom.

BUTTERFLY BOOKS

The formula of using the personal to obscure rather than illuminate history may be found at large in the long career of poet and once-best-selling novelist Frederic Prokosch—a career that spans much of the twentieth century. In the early 1930s, Prokosch printed a set of undeniably beautiful pamphlets—at times containing his own poetry, but mainly the work of those he admired, from then-living W. H. Auden and T. S. Eliot to the late Hart Crane and Emily Dickinson. Later called the "butterfly books" because of their gorgeous colorful handmade paper covers, these small chapbooks—some literally matchbook size—Prokosch would use to curry favor, gifting authors their own poems that he picked and published. Entreating letters inevitably asked the recipients to sign and return a few copies. Many did—and the books, always with artificially reduced limitations, became ever more rare and valued.

Take the colophon, the paragraph that explains how a book was printed, accompanying Prokosch's printing of *Two Poems* (1935) by T. S. Eliot:

> Twenty-two copies . . . printed for the author: five on Arches, numbered 1–5; five on Normandie, numbered I–V; five on Bremen, numbered a–e; five on Brussels parchment, numbered A–E; and two on red Florentine, numbered x and xx.[7]

Prokosch used the original butterfly books as a way of writing himself into that sacred space, a literary community. If he couldn't write his way into modernism, he'd gift it. Even the colophon misled—the books are not actually printed "for the author" but for Prokosch. Still, Eliot signed his copy of *Two Poems* to regift it to someone else.[8]

The butterfly books were the gift that kept on giving. In 1968 Prokosch sought to sell a complete set of them; it had after all been several decades since the success of his debut novel, *The Asiatics*, published in 1935. Though labeled fiction, the best seller was regularly taken as an actual guide of sorts to Asia—a place Prokosch had never visited. He wouldn't, of course, be the first to invent villages and villagers, rituals and rescues in a far-off "Orient," but while he never claimed the book was accurate or realistic—it is Asiatic, not Asian—its success was bound up with familiar exoticist notions. At the time, the book was praised by everyone from André Gide, who called it "an authentic masterpiece," to Albert Camus and Eliot himself. The gift, I guess, worked.

He would return to this faked Asia for his second book, *Seven Who Fled* (1937), also a best seller. Certainly not everyone saw it as realistic; the *New York Times* reviewer made clear that "this Central Asia of Prokosch's is no actual place upon the surface of the earth. Like Xanadu, like Arcadia, like Atlantis or Aea or Poictesme, it is a phantom manufactured by a restless mind."[9] In their fashion, Prokosch's butterfly books and his "Asiatic" novels all realized the desirability of the exotic and proved that rarity could be cultivated and captured, mounted like a butterfly. Nothing necessarily wrong with such phantom Neverlands, I suppose, but as with Psalmanazar and other travel liars, the exoticist shares the forger's tools: bringing the exotic close as well as implying that there's no reality there besides what I make. The forger's fabulism is always for sale.

The problem isn't necessarily that Prokosch has invented someone—or three or four someones—but that he invented something not at all new. The Western vogue for Asian subjects, in yellowface and fiction, is at least a century old—not accidentally, as old as modernism itself, which took much inspiration from the East. The more nefarious versions of this continually make their way into the hoax, whether in the yellowface of the made-up poet known as Yasusada, or the most recent entry, hoax Chinese poet Yi-Fen Chou. Hoaxes often include a faked poem, especially a forged one—it would seem a way of establishing literary bona fides, both for the forger and the pretend subject, as we shall see. But that unlikely genre, the poetry hoax, continues to provide some of the more entertaining gambits, often by skewering prevailing tastes and literary pomposity. Since at least the *Spectra* hoax of 1916 or the Ern Malley hoax of 1944, the poetry hoax with its mocking mask has both helped make the world modern and made fun of modernity. What few of the poetry hoaxers could have counted on is their antimodern poetry's appeal for modernism. The hoax is a monster; and monsters prove popular.

Poetry hoaxes also reveal that the hoax, even as forgery, is not just about money but also about the same kinds of social divides that haunt other hoaxes. This is true of Hiroshima survivor Araki Yasusada, whose poems first began appearing in the mid-1990s, culminating in a "special supplement" of the noted *American Poetry Review* as "Doubled Flowering: From the Notebooks of Araki Yasusada." A few months later the journal *Lingua Franca* would help reveal the author to be a hoax, prompting a couple of reactions: Arthur Vogelsang, the editor at *APR* who had published the poems, called them a "criminal act"; another professor of Japanese literature dismissed them as "just Japanized crap."[10] Between those who thought it a horrible betrayal and those who thought it just bad poetry—as if there's a difference—emerged supporters of the effort, who dipped into the grab bag of "hoaxcuses," poetic license among them, to praise the hoax.

A book also called *Double Flowering* gathered all this material, pro and con, in an attempt to turn the typical hoax casebook into a vehicle to get big. Though he's never quite admitted it, Kent Johnson, whose name the book is copyrighted under, seems to have written the entire Yasusada oeuvre. The book's many appendices claim that the Yasusada poems were actually written by yet another Japanese author whose pseudonym was "Tosa Motokiyu"; Motokiyu happened to be Johnson's roommate along with Javier Alvarez, and "in entrusting his works to us, Motokiyu instructed us to acknowledge publicly, after his death, that the Yasusada manuscript is a fictional creation. At the same time, he directed us never to reveal his legal name."[11] Bio notes indicate Yasusada was supposed to have died in 1972 from complications of radiation "after a long struggle with cancer"; his wife and youngest daughter died in the atomic bombing, and another child "perished less than four years later from radiation sickness."[12] A lone surviving son supposedly found the documents now gathered in his name. Like most other modern hoaxes the Yasusada poems are predicated upon suffering; more than anything else, such suffering is what helps define it as a hoax.

Yasusada's fake biography swallows everything in sight, his poetry included. Though it cannot save him, this fake bio—in which Yasusada was said to be influenced by postmodern Western poets, philosophers, and artists, including Jack Spicer, Roland Barthes, and Robert Smithson—does expose both the faker and the fake. Smithson for one only began working after Yasusada supposedly died from cancer. While in some ways a planted hint, the fact remains that the hoax only works if we believe, as Johnson seems to, that there is no avant-garde in Japan and so Yasusada of course must identify with a Western one. Readers initially ignored such anachronisms because Yasusada flatters American and European artistry even as he offers a story of survival, however short lived. Or is it we who think this? Citations by Yasusada of books by white guy experimental poets mean to compliment not only Yasusada but the so-called avant-garde—the gadget's lone genius is the way he both mocks and manages to compliment the cool kids, secretly wanting to be one of them.

Both Yasusada and his alleged inventor Motokiyu are dead for all the reasons seen in other hoaxes—for convenience—as well as for a connection to the *poète maudit*. Yasusada regularly makes use of American clichés about Japanese culture, placing them in the native speaker's mouth: "The sake-shop hisses with its pleasures, all boiled up. / Here the young are speaking of virility and all the hidden forms."[13] Hidden forms, hissing pleasures: the poems' self-consciousness ("And then he said, there is a language and I made it") fails to save them, indicating as it does that no experiences, especially Asian ones, are possible besides those mediated by others.

This suffering also is deeply exoticist. Perhaps the best response to Yasusada comes from a group including Juliana Chang, Walter K. Lew, Tan Lin, Eileen Tabios, and John Yau: "Like most hoaxes, Johnson's is fueled mainly by the potential for self-gain. And like all hoaxes it is complex—his act of yellowface at once plays into an existing and apparently vigorous orientalist fantasy, exposes American ignorance of both Japanese poetry and recent Japanese history, and levels a critique against an experimental writing community to which the author also seeks to ingratiate himself."[14] This complexity depends on the apparatus around the poems—what we might, if generous, call the Yasusada archive, as critic Marjorie Perloff does—not to mention the poems themselves, flying the flag of Western influence. To quote Chang and her cohort, "Yasusada represented the emblematic Other, removed from historical time, a creature of myth. Thus the 'hoax' demonstrates something very real: that the myth of the Other refuses to die."[15]

No wonder Yasusada continues to resurrect as if in a horror movie's endless sequels, spawning other poetry projects and critical responses. It also turns out the poems had earlier incarnations: as poet and essayist David Wojahn uncovered, Johnson published three poems "From the Notebooks of Ogawara Miyamora" under his own name that he "later reprinted under Yasusada's name, including one alleged to be Yasusada's final poem, written on his deathbed."[16] It would seem that when those failed to get widespread attention Johnson created the elaborate layers that don't just maintain the fiction of Yasusada but mystify his identity. Johnson apparently even cited

Yasusada in his own dissertation. Yet Johnson writes, "The Yasusada is not an egotistical gesture; it is a profoundly selfless one: a creative act of pure transference and an insistent abdication of any personal claim that might have resulted in worldly advantages."[17] Worldly advantages? He does realize that this is poetry, right? There's a chilling way the hoax invites us not to believe in it so much as to believe in nothing. This will grow more and more familiar in a half-hoax world.

The problem's not that Yasusada isn't real so much as the poems require their fiction to be read at all; and any hoax's framing fictions are what's first to disappear when finally exposed. All his feints signal not self-consciousness but a dispersal of its evidence—in a letter, Yasusada (via Motokiyu) signs off, "Good bye. Here is my image. I am sincere"[18]—the result proving less a hoax than a "horcrux," that invention from *Harry Potter* whereby the villain who shall not be named hides his corrupted soul in objects scattered across the world. What's worse, Yasusada's fake tale of Western influence on Japanese poetry actually reverses the real story of literary modernism. For it was Asian culture, particularly Chinese and Japanese poetry and Noh drama, that helped give rise in the West to a poetry of image, elision, and precision from Amy Lowell to Ezra Pound to Yeats. Though often rendered as a purification (or rejection) of romanticism, Western modernism might be said to be nothing more than reckoning with influences and advances from Asia as well as Africa.

Ignoring Asian modernism altogether, the Yasusada archive ignores the confluence of cultures much like the phantom poet's only author image, a blurry photograph resembling a combination of photostat and woodcut that Eliot Weinberger described as "what appeared to be the blurred xerox of a xerox of a mug shot of some low-level yakuza." This might prove interesting if the work wasn't so decidedly stereotypical and quote-unquote Japanese: Johnson's gnomic lines suggest the broad yet familiar sound of portent, resolutely foreign, looking less like poems than the shorthand cribs provided to English translators. Weinberger calls this "the style, not of Japanese poetry, but of American translations of Japanese poetry"; Wojahn calls it "translationesque."[19] We might just call it *English-ish*, found in other hoaxes from the *Dreadnought* hoax to JT LeRoy. Kent Johnson's pomo apparatus just adds up to a new kind of interpretive, and interpolated, pidgin.[20] For "the Yasusada," whether in its concerns or its apparatus, is not about turning Japanese but about whiteness.

Much the same could be said of Yi-Fen Chou, only the most recent entry in the yellowface tradition. As we learned upon the publication of *The Best American Poetry 2015*, Yi-Fen turned out to be an alias of white writer Michael Derrick Hudson, who confessed in his bio note that "after a poem of mine has been rejected a multitude of times under my real name, I put Yi-Fen's name on it and send it out again. As a strategy for 'placing' poems this has been quite successful for me. The poem in question . . . was rejected under my real name forty (40) times before I sent it out as Yi-Fen Chou," he admits. "As Yi-Fen the poem was rejected nine (9) times."[21] The poem itself, "The Bees, the Flowers, Jesus, Ancient Tigers, Poseidon, Adam and Eve," is laden with coded confession, as most forgeries are: "My life's spent / running an inept tour for my own sad swindle of a vacation / until every goddamned thing's reduced to botched captions / and dabs of misinformation in fractured, / not-quite-right English." Hudson's revelation, his hoax's "not-quite-right English," was greeted with immediate and widespread outrage. *Jezebel*'s headline is typical: "If You're a White Man Who Can't Get Published Under Your Own Name, Take the Hint."[22] Yet despite what Hudson's "strategy" seems to suggest and his own numbers belie, publishing isn't filled with brown, red, and yellow hordes. But Yi-Fen Chou is not about numbers or names; it is about whiteness that seeks privilege however and wherever it wishes, regularly insisting on its ability to be anything at all—especially nonwhite. "They Pretend to Be Us While Pretending We Don't Exist," Jenny Zhang wrote in response to the case.[23] To add insult to imaginary, it turns out that Hudson even borrowed the name from a real person he knew. Such impositions on and of people of color, forged as well as fake, simultaneously erase race and privilege it above all—especially the hoaxer's own.

With Prokosch, Hudson, and others, the impetus for the hoax is less a desire for success than a fear of failure. Four years after the first 1968 auction of the butterfly books at Sotheby's, Prokosch sold another set—which were always "unauthorized originals" of a kind—along with a number of recent forgeries he pretended to have printed decades before. Quickly the antiquarian bookseller who bought the books grew suspicious and enlisted bibliographic specialist Nicolas Barker to investigate; Barker quickly proved that the materials, both the paper and the typefaces, were of recent vintage. This is not very hard to ascertain: I find that the later books, while similar at a glance, do not maintain the same sheen of age or elegance or paper; it is hard not to think Prokosch wanted to get caught. When confronted with the fact of his fiction, he stalled and avoided, pleading with Barker, who planned to publish a newspaper or magazine story on the case, to hold his story. "It is difficult for me to know how I can apologize to you for this silly and irresponsible business of my 'mendacious' poetry pamphlets," he said in a half apology to the bookseller-buyers. "What then seemed a merely mischievous prank I now recognize as totally idiotic and irresponsible."[24] This does not mean the deception was unique, even for Prokosch.

Going beyond printing unauthorized versions of actual poems, he went on to publish and presumably write at least one fake poem he attributed to Gertrude Stein. This is especially strange because Prokosch had actually met Stein, whom he now claimed had given him an unpublished work that he had brought out as a deluxe pamphlet. Yet given Stein's thoroughness—Robert A. Wilson describes how "being convinced of her own genius and immortality from the very beginning, she preserved every scrap of paper she ever received—every letter, card, note, and household bill, right down to the bills for the clipping and grooming of her pet poodle"[25]—chances of there being no record of the poem's composition prove quite slim.

What's more, the poem *Lily* sounds nothing like Stein, that poet who influenced not just poetry but, through Hemingway's (and her own) very Stein-ness, prose. Here's the forged poem in its entirety:

Gone is Lily
Where she goes
Lily's secret
No one knows

Weep for Lily
All who must
All that's lovely
Falls to dust

Lily's gone
And where she goes
In her hat
There is a rose

Red the rose
In Lily's hat
Lily's gone
And that is that

This is not Stein but a Frankenstein. As if to overcompensate, the copy of the simple four-page book held at Yale's Beinecke Library—a single page folded—is signed by Prokosch not once but four separate times, not including the autograph on his bookplate. The copy also includes a note on "Printing Data," confirming its actual 1969 printing in Paris; he also indicates a few other collections that the book might be found in, including that of Nicolas Barker, his chief tormentor.[26] *Lily*'s secret everyone knows: like forgeries often do, *Lily* insists it's a "signature" piece in order to protect against doubt, must announce its value loudly while it obscures its provenance, all in order to further establish value. If it can't be a signature piece of Stein's, it can be over-signed by Prokosch. Ironically, Prokosch's fakes have now become pricey, their manufactured scarcity serving them better than that of Beanie Babies.

But why pick Stein to connect himself to? In doing so, Prokosch gets to impersonate a far better writer, not to mention someone who's essentially out of the closet (or at least never was really in it); someone who managed, despite being lesbian and Jewish, to survive the war in Vichy France; someone who was the exemplary expatriate, managing in exile to remain quintessentially American and to return triumphant on a stateside book tour for *The Autobiography of Alice B. Toklas*. Such acceptance Prokosch could only wish for, and hoaxes prove the ultimate wishful thinking.

Prokosch's story about the poem also contained a prank: he would go on to explain that he sold the manuscript of *Lily* to one Peter Vredenbergh, whose fate, like many forgeries, involves a shipwreck; he "died in California somewhere in 1940 or thereabouts. I last saw him getting on the boat in Seville in October 1939, and was told much later that he had died." As Prokosch's biographer indicates, "No such person as Peter Vredenbergh existed," except as a character in Poe's 1838 *Narrative of Arthur Gordon Pym*. There, Pym narrates, "Early this morning we had the misfortune to lose a man overboard. He was an American named Peter Vredenburgh, a native of New York, and was one of the most valuable hands on board the schooner. In going over the bows his foot slipped, and he fell between two cakes of ice, never rising again."[27] Later in the same passage, the crew spots a great quantity of albatrosses—symbolic of the hoax's Romantic yearnings.

UNDER THE WINTER MOON

Prokosch sought in the hoax a popular, and popularizing, form. To read Prokosch's books, or about his life as in Robert M. Greenfield's biography

Dreamer's Journey, is to witness someone trying over and over again to capture his original acclaim. Appearing in 1941 on the cover of the *New York Times Book Review* for his third novel, Prokosch, "the mystic, the visionary, the poet who so often utters his scorn for 'the mad materialists,'" would not only receive praise there from Harold Strauss but "the familiar Prokosch" could still be spoken of as essential reading: "One has come to expect Prokosch to use startling forms, or no form at all."[28]

Most of his later novels failed to attract notice, his poetry less, and as Prokosch went on he began more and more to engage forgery as an idea and even as a way of making art. Employing pseudonyms, ghosting books for others, penning novels allegedly written in the voice of someone else, his fabulisms grew closer and closer to taking over reality. In a kind of bridge-burning act, Prokosch submitted a novel titled *Under the Winter Moon* under the name Teresa Brooke to his longtime publisher Doubleday after they'd dropped him. "It is highly unlikely that the mere formality of submitting a novel under a pseudonym deceived anyone at the firm for very long," Greenfield notes. "It suited all parties to let the matter rest, however, and both sides cultivated a silence."[29] After Doubleday rejected it, someone else took up the publishing effort.

One of Prokosch's final novels—though not his last fiction—would be *The Missonghili Manuscript* (1968), structured as a diary of Byron's last days. Complete with allegedly lost manuscripts, destroyed originals, copies of copies, the novel's structure doesn't just play with the idea of forgery, Prokosch's Byron invokes it throughout. Prokosch, as usual, was chasing a trend—George Gordon, Lord Byron's influence was on the rise at this time, as measured by his memorial at long last being added to Westminster Abbey in 1969, his scandalous past having kept him from Poets' Corner for a century and a half after his death. Prokosch's first sale of the forged butterfly books occurred soon after the publication of his Byron book.

In this Prokosch would follow the many forgeries that dogged Byron's life and tomcatting reputation, not to mention those that continued after his death. Critic James Soderholm reminds us that "Byron's first full-fledged fan," Caroline Lamb, "wrote her vow of affection for her poet-love by practicing the sincerest and the most bedeviling form of flattery" when "in early January 1813 Lamb forged a letter to herself from Byron in order to obtain his favorite portrait of himself—the Newstead miniature—from John Murray, his publisher."[30] Lamb pretends Byron's the ultimate seducer as a way of seducing him. Prokosch similarly saw his forgery as an act of seduction—not just for an intimate audience but a broader one. It must have proved irresistible to try to capture some of the Byronmania that had swept England and made George Gordon into Lord Byron, the prototypical rock star. Doing so connected him not just to the history of the hoax but to the vampire tale.

The first full-length vampire story in English was *The Vampyre* (1819), based on a fragment by Byron but written by Byron's physician, John Polidori. Yet the book had its first life as a hoax. Polidori traveled with Byron to Switzerland in 1816, along with what poet Galway Kinnell calls a "malaise à trois"—Percy Bysshe Shelley, his wife, Mary Shelley, and her step-sister Claire, who after also being involved with Shelley, would bear Byron's child. This was during the 1816 "Year without a Summer," whose worldwide gloom was brought on by a volcano eruption the year before; famously, the group one day held a ghost story parlor game that would change the course of literature, ultimately leading to Mary Shelley's *Frankenstein*. In Byron's case, he managed that summer to write the fragment "The End of My Journey," an eerie story that would become the basis of Polidori's *Vampyre*.[31] That unsunny season would see a reincarnation, or shall we say revenant, of the recurring gothic impulse that the hoax would tap into as it too grew more obsessed with horror.

Polidori's vampiric "Lord Ruthven" is modeled after Byron, whose time in Italy had been precipitated in part by his fleeing not altogether unfounded rumors of an incestuous relationship with his half sister. Indicting the gentry more generally, *The Vampyre* was the first tale to codify the vampire as a nobleman, critic Richard Davenport-Hines argues, forecasting the ways Irish writer Bram Stoker's *Dracula* (1897) would comment on the fading strengths of the British Empire. Dracula's skin is not only undead but über-white, suggesting a nocturnal, robber baron royalty that the vampire regularly glamorizes. An unscrupulous publisher exploited Byron's infamy as well, bringing out *The Vampyre* attributed to "The Right Honourable Lord Byron"; the publisher's half-hoax worked, with the pamphlet selling thousands under Byron's name and going through five imprints in the first edition. "Soon Goethe—to the bafflement of critics ever since—pronounced 'The Vampyre' some of Byron's best work," one critic writes.[32] Although Polidori, and Byron, would quickly come forward and correct the misattribution by the middle of the edition, the book would remain a kind of dark double for Byron.

Byron himself would have a further double in the form of a pretend descendant. Calling himself Major George Gordon de Luna Byron—his very name suggesting the moon, with connotations of "lunacy" and vampirism—this impostor claimed after Byron's death to be the son of Byron and a Spanish countess. Given Byron's bad-boy reputation, it seemed somewhat plausible. Writing to one of Byron's old friends, the impostor gave a lengthy account of his pretend pilgrimage retracing Byron's travels "from the city of the Sultan to the Pyramids and Cataracts of the Nile; from Mount Ararat to the mouth of the Ganges."[33] He was posing as another kind of gentleman vampire, an exoticist at home in the hoax. "Major Byron" went on to cause a minor crisis in the study of the romantics after supplying forgeries published as genuine in *Letters of Percy Bysshe Shelley, with an Introductory Essay by Robert Browning* in 1852.

For a diagnosis of the hoax more broadly we might refer to a doctor's contemporaneous account of "Vampyrism," also from 1852, in *Popular Superstitions and the Truths Contained Therein*: "It is a strange world. The ills we fear are commonly not those which overwhelm us."[34] The hoaxer works on and with just these fears. For there is a gothic quality to hoaxes, especially impostures and plagiarism—not just ideas of ruin and ruination but a set of orphan narratives that reinforce our anxieties about legitimacy and originality. Impostors like Major Byron and JT LeRoy a century and a half later craft new names and assume royal titles to derive legitimacy from the patriarchy in different ways and for different reasons: one searches for a royal patrimony and lineage; the other for a male voice, a "le roi" to address the patriarchy from within. Prokosch used Byron for both kinds of legitimacy, all the while viewing him as something of a sexual outlaw or at least rebel, another dark twin. Prokosch, a noteworthy tennis player, was always good at doubles.

Prokosch had begun the butterfly books in 1932 as an act of seduction toward Auden, whom he'd previously sent a nude photograph of himself along with an admiring letter. When he sent a similar package, as it were, to Stephen Spender, his biographer relates that he became the butt of gossip, culminating with Auden's "Letter to Lord Byron" in its seemingly pointed lines about "Sometimes containing frank demands for cash, / Sometimes sly hints at a platonic pash, / And sometimes, though I think this rather crude, / The correspondent's photo in the rude."[35] Byronic forgery may prove a kind of version of Romantic (if not Romanesque) passion—but was one impetus for Prokosch's forgery what his biographer calls his "double life" as a semicloseted gay man?

Certainly Prokosch, in letters at least, regularly alludes to a kind of double life, or dark past. "With all the surface 'respectability,' diplomatic and scholarly and illustrious social contacts, my real life has been subversive, anarchic, vicious, lonely, and capricious," he wrote a friend in 1963:

I have spent my life alone, utterly alone, and no biography of me could ever more than scratch the surface. . . . My real life (if I ever dared to write it!) has transpired in darkness, secrecy, fleeting contacts and incommunicable delights, any number of strange picaresque escapades and even crimes, and I don't think that any of my "friends" have even the faintest notion of what I'm really like or have any idea of what my life has really consisted of.[36]

Was Prokosch's self-described secrecy just a form of fakery that prepared him for another? Were his forgeries a form of hiding far more? Or is his invoking "darkness" a way of suggesting opacity as a tactic? Critic Nicholas de Villiers writes of opacity as a way of refusing the inquiries into sexual preference and a rejection of the notion of the closet—requiring gay people to be open about their identity can be as pernicious as outing.[37] But Prokosch's opacity seems an ominous come-on, a way of not so quietly confessing—promising a menace he only wishes he could deliver, albatrosses circling. This is self-dramatization rather than exploration—while on one hand a coded confession of his forgery, and on the other an admission of his somewhat-secret sexuality that society still punished as a crime, his haunted hinting sounds more like the declarations of revenge that forgers retrospectively claim as their motivation, blaming the world for their silence. Prokoksch regularly lied about ordinary biographical details, such as his birth and background, wanting to be European like his father; his forgery is not a continuation of his sexuality but a confirmation of his much-commented-upon love of guises.

In contrast, Prokosch's fellow gay exiles in Italy after the war would be rather open sexually, especially in their writing. In his lively *Memoirs of an Aesthete* (1971), Harold Acton recalls the scene in postwar Rome, which included Tennessee Williams, Gore Vidal, and Prokosch. While Vidal had already written 1948's *The City and the Pillar*, "which he informed me was a pioneer among homosexual novels," Acton wrote, "Tennessee Williams was obsessed with sexual frustration and its deviations but at least he treated it in a poetical manner." For Acton, who had actually spent time in China, Prokosch doesn't fare nearly as well: "Prokosch, whose writings, *genre génie*, fell short of his perfervid imagination, had the dark good looks of an advertiser for razor blades, but I was told he was a tennis champion."[38] Prokosch's work seems to meet the fate of the forger who, busy copying the style of others, regularly ends up stunted in his or her own artistic growth.

For his part, Vidal himself knew Prokosch's work and read it avidly as a teen, long before meeting him. In reviewing Prokosch's memoir *Voices* years later, he would not only compare Prokosch's early fame (and looks) to Byron's, he would offer his fiction high praise: "García Márquez would not write the way that he does if Prokosch had not written the way that he did. At a time when the American novel was either politically *engagé* or devoted to the homespun quotidian, Prokosch's first two novels were a half-century ahead of their time."[39] Another longtime fan of Prokosch's, Isaac Bashevis Singer, wrote presciently that "pondering about Prokosch and his fate, I have come to the conclusion that he is himself in a way at fault for being so woefully neglected. He has not cared to husband his natural riches. . . . His roots are in this land. If Prokosch, like Faulkner, had limited his creative energies to one milieu, one region, he would certainly be counted today among the pillars of American literature."[40] Instead, Prokosch remained on the lam, not just self-exiled in Europe but forging as a form of hiding.

He looked, Vidal writes, "more like a pirate than a writer."

OTHERWISE

Even as a forger Prokosch couldn't achieve fame. Rather than the newspaper scandal about his forgeries Prokosch feared, Nicolas Barker's strictly scholarly reference work *The Butterfly Books: An Enquiry into the Nature of Certain Twentieth Century Pamphlets* took a decade and a half to appear—far enough from the initial forgeries that the impact was far less felt than it otherwise might have been. Not one to miss a chance to appear in print, Prokosch would provide the epilogue to Barker's belated book.

Barker's title is an homage to John Carter and Graham Pollard's *Enquiry into the Nature of Certain Nineteenth Century Pamphlets* (1934), which notably uncovered one of the most famous book forgers of the nineteenth century, Thomas J. Wise.[41] (The 1934 *Enquiry* in turn referred to Edmond Malone's famous *An Inquiry into the Authenticity of Certain Papers and Instruments Attributed to Shakespeare* from 1796, an exposé of Shakespeare forger William-Henry Ireland.)[42] Like Mark Hofmann, the more recent forger of Dickinson and Mormon materials, Wise was also a bookseller, collector, and bibliographer, using his status as all three to support his misdeeds. He served as forger, fencer, and authenticator at once, retrospectively becoming the most notorious forger of the nineteenth century.

While he never did confess before his death in 1937, Wise never rebutted the charges raised by the *Enquiry* either; given his silence, his most ardent early supporters waned. The *Enquiry* has been widely praised for its evenhanded tone, textual comparisons, and its groundbreaking use of forensic science and comparison of paper and fonts, with the results revealing that many of Wise's pamphlets were not produced till decades after the supposed publication dates.[43] Since then, it has come out that he likely had an accomplice—or two. Starting as early as 1887, Wise et al. made facsimiles of existing books then altered them into fakes; next Wise began fabricating new books he said were old, claiming he either bought the special material from aging authors or entreated them to give him.

Holding himself up as expert, he would list books that didn't exist in his bibliographies of almost every figure of nineteenth-century British literature, from Ruskin to Thackeray, Tennyson to the Brownings, then miraculously locate them, providing unbelievable "finds" to clients only too happy to buy what they thought genuine. (Some current booksellers still persist in using him as a reference on legitimate items, when all of Wise should be considered corrupt.) Not only was he well positioned as a book dealer, he also focused on writers at the height of their fame but not necessarily their powers. Wise would borrow the con job and plagiarist's technique, befriending the previous generation of aging geniuses and their scholars, making himself a middleman more central to the authors' lives than he truly was—and even getting them to sign spurious documents or using his correspondence to later support his claim that he got the rarities directly from them. No wonder his day job was as a seller of commodities, mostly oil for perfumes and artificial flavorings.

Wise boldly forged the most famous love poems of the age, Elizabeth Barrett Browning's *Sonnets from the Portuguese*, and had been so convincing that he'd fooled Robert Browning into authenticating a forged pamphlet of his late wife's powerful antislavery poem, "The Runaway Slave at Pilgrim's Point," which Wise claimed had first appeared separately in 1849. Of all the poems to fake, it seems ironic that Wise would select "Runaway Slave" to place early on in the British Museum, where he began donating and thereby authenticating his entire "Ashley Street" collection in 1888. If such a venerable institution held the pamphlets, who could doubt them or him? In truth, "Runaway Slave" had begun its life as an abolitionist tract sold presumably for, or at, fund-raising events, the poem taking on the voice of the runaway in question—the poem's subtle treatment of the woman's rape by her white owners, and later her killing the resulting child à la Toni Morrison's

Beloved a long century later, remains deeply moving. To make this in any way ring false, as Wise's forgery does, and to make it a thing of private commerce rather than public protest, is to desecrate the poem's memory. Wise attempts to turn it to forge not just history but a prophecy: the poem's status as separate booklet would seek to resolve the long-standing contradictions and Barrett Browning's unease at her family's owning slaves in their native Jamaica.

The false bloodlines via Wise of "Runaway Slave" offer oblique comment on both the dead slave child's birth (and death) and also the poet's own, as Barrett Browning was often suggested to be Creole, if not of African descent herself. Once again the hoax met race. Not that John Carter and Graham Pollard, authors of the *Enquiry*, are sensitive to such questions: one of their sources of discovering Wise's forgeries is an illustration they and they alone call "Thackeray's Nigger Boy," whose change in appearance after the original reveals all. "There is is a noticeable breakage of lines in the more heavily shaded portions of the design, particularly on the faces of the nigger boys and the shadows behind them."[44] Broken blackness gives you away every time.

Like Frankenstein's monster, forgeries are the ultimate fugitives—even in their materials. The famed twentieth-century art forger Tom Keating's paintings often contained taunting messages in the underpainting—if ever examined by X-ray or other modern means they would reveal their fakery. All forgeries bear their own confessions, barely buried.

The public confessions of a forger should be met with suspicion too. Rather than being repentant after the revelation of his forgeries, Prokosch's hoaxes only grew bolder. In his last book, *Voices* (1983), purporting to be a memoir of his childhood and life abroad, Prokosch becomes something like Woody Allen's Zelig, absorbing history in lieu of personality; or the proverbial Forrest Gump, happening to be in exactly the right place, with Stein or Auden or Joyce or other greats, during their every significant discovery. Better yet, Prokosch's fake adventures supersede the famous folks he encounters. Like Wise before him, Prokosch forges a connection to the geniuses of a generation before, peddling intimacy as much as influence.

Call it a "suburban legend": the forger is always fortunate, doesn't just discover a Da Vinci but *the* Da Vinci. He unearths not just Shakespeare fragments but, if you're teenaged William-Henry Ireland, a previously unknown Shakespeare play, *Vortigern and Rowena*, which he then had to write himself; finds not just any poem by Barrett Browning but her most political and famed. Smart is the forger who specializes in minor works, but forgers by and large are less wise than they are Wise. Prokosch too is ever fortunate. Prokosch writes in *Voices* that at Cambridge he invites a don to tea who of course turns out to be A. E. Housman, who asks our young squire, "Is your air of simplicity just a part of your cunning, or is your cunning just an aspect of your inner simplicity?"[45]

Such encounters we both want to believe and often later repeat without confirmation—much like the fortuitous meeting between Dickens and Dostoevsky, an anecdote that became repeated widely without basis, even appearing in official biographies, until revealed to be a hoax committed by a self-described "rejected scholar."[46] Might what art historians call *connoisseurship* protect us against cunning? Can good taste sniff out a bad hoax? It is hard to know, especially given how many an expert has authenticated many a forgery. All it takes to succeed is the forger producing something aimed at the predisposed tastes of the expert collector or curator in question: the art expert who theorizes Vermeer's lost religious phase soon finds himself presented with not just one but many. In much this way Prokosch pitched *Voices* perfectly to Vidal. Still, connoisseurship—science too—is actually what uncovered Prokosch's butterfly books. What we need, then, is more gut—that Spidey sense that might help us when our head and our heart have lost our way—and a better understanding of the science of seeing.

Not just for money or revenge or fame, Prokosch hoaxes above all to alter the historical record, placing himself at its center. (He also forges Europe as the "center of culture" exactly when it had begun to shift to the Americas, ignoring Africa and Asia ultimately.) He did so first with the genuine butterfly books through their beseeching beauty; and later with *Voices* and his forgeries, which he once revealed even extended to forged signatures in genuine pamphlets. Certainly this work's willingness to embrace the in-between, never true nor false, would seem a monster that the forger finds familiar, if not family. The effort is reminiscent of what the fake Dostoevsky once wrote about what Dickens didn't actually say: "There were two people in him, he told me: one who feels as he ought to feel and one who feels the opposite. From the one who feels the opposite I make my evil characters, from the one who feels as a man ought to feel I try to live my life."[47]

The hoax is less a collaboration than a confabulation—mostly provided by the hoaxer, but the rest filled in by the viewer or reader, who's flattered following Barnum's lead, as expert. We might have to revise our view slightly from here on out: the hoax doesn't so much hold a mirror up to nature, or up to the hoaxer, as it holds a mirror up to its audience. And the hoax imagines that audience to be wide.

FIFTY CENTS   FEBRUARY 21, 1972

TIME

CON MAN OF THE YEAR

**Clifford
Irving
by
Elmyr
de Hory**

Special Section: A Guide to Nixon's China

"Con Man of the Year," *Time* magazine cover, 1972.

CHAPTER 12

Spruce Goose

Forgery is sometimes spoken of admiringly, especially given the art forger's skills of mimicry that can literally be on display. As its title implies, Jonathon Keats's *Forged: Why Fakes Are the Great Art of Our Age* argues in favor of fakery as a vital form of creativity. "Art and forgery are two sides of the same conversation," says Keats, "and what they can tell one another is potentially profound."[1] Copying a painting requires skill, whereas the copying of literary work takes little besides a pen or keyboard, a scanner or a photocopier. Both the modern con artist's and the forger's appeal stems from the popular belief that they may in fact be *artistes manqué*, artists without an art form, frustrated like we all may feel.

The forger especially can develop a delusion of his genius that not just the audience but he himself falls for. Or is a forged painting just a different form of plagiarism? "Fakes are contemporary portraits of past styles. No great talent is required, just a modicum of handiness and some art-critical acuity," writes art critic Peter Schjeldahl, arguing against those who see no harm in forgeries. "A forger needn't master the original artist's skill, only the look of it. Indeed, especially in a freewheeling mode like Abstract Expressionism, a bit of awkwardness, incidental to the branded appearance, may impress a smitten chump as a marker of sincerity—even as something new and endearing about a beloved master."[2] Like the vampire, who breeds with a bite, the forgery needs an original to copy from—not so much questioning our notions of originality as devouring them. No wonder the term for stealing in old-school hip-hop is *biting*.

Still we might agree with Jonathon Keats that the look of forgery, or our view of it, has changed: "The meaning of forgery was as different in the Renaissance—and as foreign to contemporary culture—as the 16th-century meaning of art. In fact, forgery and art are deeply interrelated. They reflect the same societal interests, and they have always evolved together. The modern Western response to forgery is anxiety. The mood of modern Western art is anxious."[3] But here Keats and I part ways. Because while I think the hoax produces anxiety, or reproduces it in the case of the forgery, it should be clear that the hoax itself is a kind of anxiety—a symptom, even a hysteria—surrounding questions of origins and the truth, suffering and redemption, innocence and righteousness and race.

In his essential book *On Art and Connoisseurship*, critic Max J. Friedlander provides one of the most succinct arguments about forgery. Though he is thinking of forged works of art, he could easily mean the written or lived hoax: "The forger is an impostor and a child of his time, who disowns the method of vision which is natural to him. . . . Oscillating between uneasy cautiousness and brazenness, afraid lest his own voice may grow too loud and betray him, he succumbs to the prejudices of taste that belong to his own period the moment he will give 'beauty.' His pathos sounds hollow, theatrical and forced, since it does not spring from emotion."[4] This we have already found true with fake memoir, which quickly can seem kitsch, and with "fake fiction," those novels disguised as memoirs. Both roam far from the origins of the novel in English, which began as a memoir pretending to be real.

After all, "beauty" is constructed, and time-stamped. We know instinctively that beauty changes, but it's hard for us to see our time's standards that we more or less share. Any age's dominant style is necessarily invisible, and invisibility is the forger's ultimate goal too. Yet in seeking to go undetected, forgers often mistake their time's standards for those of their past subjects, resulting in anachronisms and oddball elements: each forgery is a time machine that unknowingly yet willfully alters the past. "Deliberation and consciousness reveal themselves in artistic form as lack of life or else hesitation," Friedlander writes. The results bear none of what he calls the "decisiveness of the original work."[5]

I am reminded of a truism that surprised me when I learned it years ago, namely, that it's easier (or at least more common) for art forgers to forge those artists who have the most distinctive of styles. It goes hand in hand with the fact that the most valuable part of an artist's work is the most easily identifiable, or typical: the odder corners of an artist's work fetch less. When folks look at a Warhol, or look to buy one, they want a canonical example (though he's perhaps one of the few popular enough that any Warhol will do). As once-successful biographer turned forger Lee Israel details in her 2008 confession, *Can You Ever Forgive Me?*, she gave book dealers and autograph collectors "classic" versions of famous authors; her Dorothy Parker sounds like Parker because it's merely copied, or because it's a distillation of Parker's style for style's, and sale's, sake. Israel the forger was a stylist; she specialized in racy postscripts to actual letters. What's more, "my success as a forger was somehow in sync with my erstwhile success as a biographer: I had for decades practiced a kind of merged identity with my subjects; to say I 'channeled' is only a slight exaggeration."[6] The forger, like the con man, shows us what we want to see; a forger's confession, we realize, does this too.

The forger, like the hoaxer more broadly, substitutes style for substance (consider Frederic Prokosch) and distractions for decisiveness (see Margaret B. Jones); a certain blandness, at least in person, rather than boldness (Tom MacMaster); relies on familiarity rather than the force of recognition that comes with the truly new. Such derivativeness, dullness, and indecisiveness—which ironically can look like a kind of surety, forged as it is in retrospect—remain one thing when characteristic of an artwork. But the hoax uses these same bland means to craft a strict backstory about race. This backstory, often a black one, is not based on nuance or chance, things at work in any life—or any artwork—but on a stock set of images smoothed over by retelling. Consider the ways that, say, former 2016 presidential candidate Ben Carson required the stories of how bad he was—stabbing friends, being a rageaholic, even plagiarizing papers while in college—to conform to a stock jail-to-Yale narrative. When his veracity was questioned, he attacked the messenger because for him, the messenger was the message. *Worser* would be much better. We find the forgery too is about image in lieu of story. Such behavior will only grow *worser* as we go on.

Once exposed, the hoax doesn't wear well and tends to look ridiculous quickly: it can be hard to believe anyone ever thought the awkward painting was a Vermeer; or thought that the pleather journals of recent vintage were actually Hitler's; or that anyone believed that white girl with the faux-ghetto accent really had been a member of a black gang. "After being unmasked every forgery is a useless, hybrid and miserable thing," Friedlander writes.[7] Perhaps hoaxes are less hybrid monsters than fabricated "cryptids"— that name for supposedly unfound species, like Sasquatches and the Loch

Ness monster, whose fake evidence for their existence is still hard to unsee once revealed.

Race proves yet another mythic beast hard to disprove once believed, elusive yet fearsome, leaving its tracks everywhere—especially all over the hoax.

FAKE!

Most hoaxes aren't meant to stand on their own—much less forever—they are plagiarisms of another's strong style, shortcutting the personal struggle that characterizes great art, not to mention plagiarizing another's pain. Ironically, it is exactly because of this that "fakes are arguably the most authentic of artifacts," Jonathon Keats writes. "Certainly, they're the most candid, once the dissimulation has been detected."[8] Given that forgeries often come with a backstory meant to shore up belief, when the forgery is revealed, its—and our—assumptions are revealed too. For this reason, the forgery lasts only forty years, Friedlander argues—or two generations. Nowadays, as with computers, these generations—or is it degenerations—happen faster and faster.

Exactly because of its ever-shortening half-life, forgery offers up a kind of *unauthorized autobiography*. This goes beyond Prokosch's "unauthorized originals" or a forger painting or Israel writing "in the style of": these days, forgery, always overreliant on biography, has instead become a metaphor for modern life itself. Certainly that was one principle behind the Howard Hughes hoax masterminded by Clifford Irving. Irving was a midlist novelist, whose previous book *Fake!* (1969) was nonfiction about "the greatest art forger of our time," Elmyr de Hory, a book intended to make Irving great too. When sales of *Fake!* weren't up to expectations, Irving turned to Hughes, one of the richest people alive and a famous recluse, unseen in public for over a decade. The results may signal a key start of our Age of Euphemism.

As an enigma, Hughes was the perfect subject but also the perfect cover: Irving would phone his longtime editor in 1971 and say Hughes had written him to say he liked *Fake!*, paying himself a compliment, as forgers often do, on the way to getting paid. As proof, Irving penned (or penciled) a handwritten letter from Hughes, writing later that his "Hughes would be the supreme egotist. He would begin every possible sentence in his letters to me with the pronouns *I* and *My*."[9] Irving modeled his capital letters, and Hughes's signature, on images from a recent *Newsweek* article.

After reading the letter, his friend and editor at McGraw-Hill took the bait. Contract in hand, Irving set about concocting not a biography but an autobiography in Hughes's voice, with Hughes unburdening himself to the unlikely Irving. Ably assisted by his good friend Richard Suskind and his then-wife, Edith, halfway through the writing Irving asked not only for a bigger advance but also for separate checks, totaling $750,000, to be cut to "H. R. Hughes." The half-baked plan called for the Swiss-born Edith to cash the checks in a Swiss bank; all it would take would be those initials on a proper passport. Irving would forge the signature on that too. Discounting Wall Street's frauds, the gamble was one of the boldest and highest-paying hoaxes of the twentieth century. Irving's talent was to turn forgery from a blue-collar, painted, and often painful endeavor into a white-collar crime.

The result was a near-epic *Autobiography of Howard Hughes*. The block-buster book and deal were announced with much fanfare—and immediately met by strident denials from Howard Hughes's camp. Yet Hughes himself remained nowhere to be seen. What does Irving do in the face of growing suspicion? *Press the bet*, he says, taking a lesson from the craps table, letting it ride. The publishing date approaching, Irving held fast, telling everyone from McGraw-Hill to his lawyer that the biography was legit, and it was just Hughes being Hughes by denying it all. This "pressing" is one way of dealing with the press, and was effective enough to buy him more time and far more support. Hughes himself would break his years-long silence by calling into a speakerphone press conference on 7 January 1972, in an effort to turn the tide: "This must go down in history. I only wish I was still in the movie business because I don't remember any scripts as wild or as stretching of the imagination as this yarn has turned out to be," Hughes told the room of reporters interviewing his disembodied voice. "This episode is just so fantastic that it taxes your imagination to believe that a thing like this could happen."[10] The press conference itself was fantastical, a parody of Hughes's appearance before Congress to keep his company afloat decades earlier. Still McGraw-Hill remained stalwart—clinging to the contract signed by Irving in Hughes's hand, they believed they had paid their money to Hughes and somehow he'd gotten cold feet.

It wasn't money that undid Irving but love. Who was that mysterious lady captured on Swiss security cameras? news outlets and the authorities wondered. When it turned out to be Irving's wife, Edith, pretending to be "Helga Hughes," the jig was up. The book was already in proofs before the ultimate proof against Irving was revealed. Irving's case was not helped by his longtime mistress Nina van Pallandt's admitting publicly he was with her in the Caribbean when he claimed to be with Hughes. Van Pallandt had learned that Irving, in his other travels to support the illusion of meeting Hughes all around the world, picked up a comely scuba-diving instructor who now was enjoying her fifteen minutes of infamy, posing for newspapers in scuba gear or with the hit soundtrack from *Shaft*; he'd cheated on his mistress, and now she was furious. Evidence mounting, reporters swarming, the book was canceled a week before its release date and any finished copies pulped.

Soon after, *Time* named Irving "Con Man of the Year" in a February 1972 cover story. The magazine commissioned the cover from now-known forger Elmyr de Hory, who signed it *Elmyr*—the single name with which he would eventually sign his own, "authorized fake" paintings. You could call this his first genuine fake. During his decades-long forgery career, Elmyr had more often signed them *Matisse* or *Picasso* (though he strenuously maintained against all common sense that it was his coconspirators who would add those in). Elmyr's very signature reminds us that the story of a forger is also one of not just collaboration or confabulation but collusion: middlemen and coconspirators usually ripping off the actual forgers; and an audience who can't get enough cheap masterpieces to match the couch.

To wit, if Howard Hughes is Irving's creation, in large part so is Elmyr. (The critic Keats goes so far as to say that Irving's made-up Hughes is ironically far more accurate than his Elmyr.) In retrospect Irving's *Fake!* finds him casing the joint, figuring out the form of the fake in order to do one himself—and to provide justification ahead of time. "All the world loves to see the experts and the establishment made a fool of," he says. *Fake!* also tells a story of failure, which is to say, a story about the genesis of almost any hoax. Irving and McGraw-Hill may have had high hopes for *Fake!* but so did Elmyr, who was to share in the profits.

The story Elmyr tells (and has Irving tell on his behalf) is that of the refugee, who like the spy remains beyond simple right and wrong: homeless, stateless, without proper papers, Elmyr appears to feel no qualms buying old paper, or using paper excised from the backs of old books, to forge his paintings. The refugee blues are often written thus. Just as the spy is the ultimate sanctioned plagiarist—stealing files, copying paper surreptitiously—what troubles us in the hoaxer we instead excuse (or used to) in the refugee, who must bribe or bilk or steal across borders during war in order to flee persecution, death, or worse.

Shortly after *Fake!* was published but before the Hughes hoax was re-vealed, Irving declared that "the important distinction to talk about when talking about the genuine quality of a painting is not so much if it is a real painting or a fake—it's whether it's a good fake or a bad fake."[11] He told this onscreen to the filmmaking giant Orson Welles on Ibiza, presumably as part of a film Welles was making on Elmyr that quickly became about Irving. For even as he was taping his interview with Welles, Irving was al-ready busy concocting his own fake. All these layers of hoaxing became the subject of Welles's *F for Fake* (1973), his late cinematic masterpiece that sees the twists and turns of charlatanism as both a subject for cinema and one of its past incarnations. After all, the movies only make you think you are watching something moving, a mere trick of the eye, reminding us that an illusion can move you.

Just as Welles had taken his notoriety from his "panic broadcast" of *War of the Worlds* to Hollywood to make *Citizen Kane*, a film about a great man's even greater self-delusions, Welles would look back over his career in what he called the "film essay" that is *F for Fake*.[12] He notes his influence in that the advent of UFO sightings can be traced to his radio broadcast—not due as much to Area 51, he suggests, as AM radio. The very notion of myste-ria begins at home, Welles knew well. Yet our wish to experience illusion is not the same as a wish for illusion to be true. Cinema reminds us of that—shown at an editing board, Welles in *F for Fake* quite literally stops the film several times, constantly conveying to us that his film is constructed. The movieola or editing deck is its own time machine. Just as he embraces illu-sion, he destroys it, Welles making clear that "for the next hour everything in this film is strictly based on the available facts," a promise he keeps. At least with his fingers crossed.

Welles is trying to help us see that reality may not be enough. Certainly few filmmakers, who make their living painting with light, would say so. "Reality—it's the toothbrush waiting for you at home," Welles says onscreen. Just because it's true, he means, don't make it art. He shows us behind the curtain to remind us we need the curtain. Welles's film about fakery, what he later termed a "fake confessional,"[13] insists on a yearning for more than real-ity, as seen in his incredible reverie about the cathedral at Chartres during one montage. Having seen that structure myself, the spires and Gothic vaults that the anonymous builders of that monument to the spirit crafted, I am tempted to agree with Welles's statement that "maybe a man's name doesn't matter that much." It is this yearning, Welles suggests, that cannot be falsified.

Irving instead comes to see it all as a cosmic joke: "The great faker of the twentieth century becomes a modern folk hero for those who have a lot of larceny in ourselves but don't have the opportunity or courage to express," he says in the trailer for *F for Fake*. He is speaking of Elmyr, at least ostensibly. Irving appeared more shocked than anyone that his own "caper"— taking money from a publisher for a project that didn't exist, then having his wife cash the checks for hundreds of thousands of dollars in her native Switzerland—was actually, legally, fraud. When they came to arrest him, his first reaction was, *For what?*

All Irving's accounts of the hoax reiterate the partialness of knowledge as well as our partiality in trusting those who've passed our tests. The publishers insist on a handwriting analysis of not just one but several letters Irving forged: all pass as genuine. Editors at McGraw-Hill and at *Life* magazine, to which the serial rights were sold, regularly take as definitive proof ephemera like postmarks; unlike scientists, they and we proceed less from doubt than from surety. Irving's brilliance may lie in just this realization that he can beat the experts, as he manages to time and time again—by preying not on their fallibility but on their blinding need to believe. Many were fooled, including a tough journalist who once met Hughes decades ago and is asked to verify whether the autobiography itself was genuine. Only Hughes could have talked that way, declares the *Time* magazine reporter, one of the last to interview Hughes before his seclusion—if he believed otherwise, he would also have to accept that he didn't know Hughes as well as he thought.

Irving exploited Barnum's trick of allowing everyone to be an expert by regularly giving the book's publishers, lawyers, agents, and editors occasion to feel they themselves had verified a piece of information—a turn of phrase or mention that they recognized would convince them of exactly what we know now is not true. Repeating a lie in two different places would count as verification. The hoax has as unwilling collaborators a whole host of those who transubstantiated mere suggestion into fact. In much the same way that a fake Vermeer needn't resemble a real one, just a prior forgery—one conditioning us for the other—Irving provided a Hughes that people didn't know but felt they did. Or wished to. Those who'd met Hughes or had dealings with him felt most strongly that no one could've made up what Irving had, in fact, invented.

Not that he acted, so to speak, alone. Just as with JT LeRoy, it took a trio to conduct the Howard Hughes hoax—and the revelation of Hughes's "autobiography" also spawned a trilogy of confessions. After a rushed-out hardcover book written about the case by British reporters, Irving and his writing partner Suskind published a quickie mass-market paperback of their own with the awkward title *Clifford Irving: What Really Happened; His Untold Story of the Hughes Affair* (1972); the book was later reprinted as *Project Octavio* (1976) and finally as *The Hoax* (1981) under Irving's name alone.[14] This retitling is especially strange because all three books are the same, down to the typesetting, except for a few updated paragraphs at the end. The confessions are themselves collaborations; at one point in *Project Octavio*, named after the code the publisher uses to refer to the Hughes book, Irving refers to himself and Suskind as "Irvkind."

The chutzpah and teamwork involved remain impressive—from the start Irving told his coconspirators that if his longtime publisher McGraw-Hill ever found out, they would simply view it as a caper and rerelease the book as a novel or "unauthorized biography." As the evidence mounted against them, and the hoax unraveled in public, it never seemed to occur to the hoaxers that it would become state's evidence. The Hughes affair, in fact, signaled a shift from the dynamic, dark doubles of the fake memoir to the troubled trio of impostors we lately see more and more. The terrible threes also found their way into a love triangle with Edith, Clifford, and his baroness van Pallandt, who'd sung for years in a popular folk duo, Nina and Frederik, with her soon-estranged husband.[15] Irving's continued affair with Nina threatened his marriage and kids and the hoax, as it seemed to be behind some of Irving's more brazen behavior. Once Nina learned of his dalliance with his scuba instructor she apparently lied to the grand jury that she didn't know about the hoax in order to clear her name; she went on to write her own fast-tracked tell-all, *Nina*. Like its fellow hoaxes the Howard Hughes hoax was contagious, its many actors kissing and mostly telling.

The whole Hughes affair proves yet another conquest—a Romantic one, but an affair nonetheless—the con artist a kind of macho pick-up artist. Not surprising, then, that "The Autobiography" concocts a meeting between Hughes and Ernest Hemingway, Irving's literary Papa, or that he describes these passages as pure collaboration—or collusion. The result is a passion play with first Irving playing Hughes, then Suskind. "We were on the road to a unique creation, a remarkable man telling a remarkable life story; all the more remarkable because it was based on fact and yet we had the freedom and power to infuse fact with the drama of fiction."[16] Unfortunately, after their first go at the fake meeting, the tape recorder wasn't on. They do another take, a "second rambling version of Howard's fictitious thirteen-year relationship with Papa Hemingway," a tall tale that, reprinted in *Project Octavio*, runs for over sixteen pages. If Irving couldn't meet Hemingway on literary grounds, he'd go in disguise: first as "Hughes," then later as Hughes assuming yet another fake identity, "George Garden." Papa's almost immediate welcome in Cuba to this fake-Hughes-cum-Garden is meant for Irving, who like his literary cohort and his hoax brethren, wrestles with Hemingway's reputation in ways big and small, actual and fictional.

Despite such details, Keats calls the late Suskind a "hack biographer," rendering him irrelevant.[17] By denying the duo's clear collaboration, the author of *Forged* buys into the very notion his thesis seeks to undo: the author or painter or forger as a Romantic, singular, godlike authority. To call Suskind an "accessory" is to view him in a legal sense only. Suskind is the ultimate ghost, then, the kind of writer who can disappear into a role—not to mention from sight. But maybe that's it: while perhaps there's a simple or legal reason, Irving and ultimately Keats cannot recognize Suskind as coauthor because his very presence as *ghost* points out too many others. Suskind often wrote not just as Hughes but as Irving—yet Suskind's name is removed from the final iteration of *The Hoax*. Irving himself is ghosting Hughes's story: his biggest accomplishment (and payday) as a writer comes from an illusion. Or is it a delusion?

To write instead of "Irvkind"—that "cryptid," or mythic beast, like Bigfoot barely seen—is to confront the idea of collaboration, and to realize that even the best forgers are deeply derivative, "collaborating" with a required original. Any beauty is borrowed.

It's striking in retrospect how short yet how involved the Hughes affair really was: it took just over a year to go from concoction to phone call to fat contract to press release to near publication to exposure. Still, *The Autobiography* managed an eerily convincing job, embodying Hughes so completely that it appears some of what they stumbled into proved true—but then a false prophet can get something right now and again. "Some of the material which we invented out of the whole cloth was later checked by *Time-Life*'s experienced staff of researchers," Irving writes. "We had decided to have Howard's father, a rough-cut *bon vivant* race around Houston in a 1920 35-horsepower Peerless." Several "old-timers in the Houston area" confirm it with the fact-checker, with a slight correction: it was a 1902 model rather than a 1920.[18] Peerless itself, *The Autobiography* concocts a character so complete and unruly—for whom quixoticness was almost a core philosophy—that the most outrageous claim became "something Howard would do." The more contrary the better. "Nothing was too outrageous," Irving tells Suskind while they're writing. "'The wilder the story,' I explained to Dick, 'the deeper their need to believe it. And of course, it's less checkable.'"[19] The real Hughes's written denials were taken as further proof that it must be true.

If Hughes had brought some of this on himself through his extreme hermit-like behavior, not to mention his cheapness and much-discussed germophobia, it was up to Irving and Suskind to suss it out and make it a quintessential American story, one that resonated with others. Their Howard Hughes was the Great Gatsby before the fall, or better yet, a Citizen Kane without a "Rosebud"—the ineffable, innocent thing searched for and unfound. "He gave me a prune," Suskind says, inventing an exchange with Hughes. The proferred organic prune becomes a totem—in the film version of *The Hoax* a funny one, while in the actual affair it serves as a kind of MacGuffin, a fake-out meant to hide just how unreal Irving and Suskind's story is. It is nice touch despite the fact, as the prune at least knows well, the two are full of shit.

Who wouldn't want to pretend to be a billionaire ladies' man who literally soared above the crowd? At least until his folly—like the real Hughes's all-wooden "Spruce Goose," the largest plane ever built—made it airborne only a few moments before sinking. Hughes became "a mouthpiece for all the opinions which Dick [Suskind] and I had only occasionally voiced in our own books—because who, after all, was interested in the philosophical meanderings of a couple of journeyman writers?" It isn't so much that Irving listens to Hughes tell of his life as Hughes is made to listen to Irving's. A hint at Irving's inner state is found in *Project Octavio*, as Irving (or his ghost) writes:

> I saw that I had lived for too long as a man deliberately projecting an image of contentment. I was not content, and I doubted that I could ever achieve that state before I was old and unburdened of mundane desire. The objects of desire were illusion; their attainment gave only ephemeral satisfaction. The risk itself provided the sense of being alive. . . . Men climbed Himalayan mountain peaks "because they were there"—and for me, the hoax "was there." I had formulated my own challenge and that was motive enough. . . . The means were the end. I could turn my back on the challenge and I knew without a doubt that

I would be a wiser man for having done so. It was an aberration—in one sense, highly civilized; in another, deeply primitive.[20]

This half-civilized, half-primitive state, while perhaps the human condition, also aptly names the hoax's natural level. Self-destructive, it is a matter of life *and* death, of illusion and desire, a state of mind where wishes are unchecked and checks are cashed by a wigged wife pretending to be a billionaire's stand-in.

Irving hoaxes not because the hoax is there, but to prove *he* is.

UNAUTHORIZED AUTOBIOGRAPHY

What Suskind via Irving via Hughes really stumbled upon is what might be called "an unauthorized *auto*biography"—the autobiography written by someone besides the self. More than ghostwritten, this form has grown only more familiar since the Hughes affair, found in books like Jamaica Kincaid's *Autobiography of My Brother*; the form might be said to begin with the Enlightenment's Samuel Johnson as told by Bosworth, but its modern exemplar surely is Gertrude Stein's audacious *The Autobiography of Alice B. Toklas*, a praise song to the self she writes in her life partner's voice.

Might an autobiography best be described—or achieved—as the art of writing about the self as if it belongs to someone else? This is certainly the approach Salman Rushdie takes in his *Joseph Anton* (2012), the remarkable and true account of his years spent, chiefly in hiding, under the Ayatollah Khomeini's fatwa for *The Satanic Verses*. Rushdie's fate is not to bow to fate, to try, under the death sentence of state-sponsored terror, in the midst of incredible pressure and unrelenting threat, to craft a life. Revisiting a technique also found in Henry Adams's posthumously published *Education*, Rushdie writes the book in the third person, suggesting how the fatwa forced him not only out of his home but out of his very name. He must invent an alias for the security team to refer to him by: his choice, using the first names of Joseph Conrad and Anton Chekov, would give his memoir its title. Rushdie came to despise the nickname "Joe" his code name led to.

From another angle—a skewed cubist one, say, as in a Picasso as painted by Elmyr—Irving's *Autobiography of Howard Hughes* more resembles its offspring, such as *Dutch* (1999), the official and notorious biography of Ronald Reagan by Pulitzer Prize–winning writer Edmund Morris. In order to describe an elusive, public figure, Morris turned to fictional techniques, inventing and inserting himself as a figure in Reagan's past who observes events such as his saving lives as a lifeguard. In an attempt to reach the future president nicknamed "Dutch," Morris too had to invent meetings or at least encounters between author and subject; he would later say it was because Reagan was an unknowable cipher.

Such an idea is one the Hughes *Autobiography* pioneers—though it also finds itself not chiefly in the company of the hoax memoir but more in the tradition of the pretend biography of a fake person. Simply put, it is a spy story: the film *The Hoax* makes this espionage literal, with a whole new conspiracy subplot that claims the hoax led to exposing the Watergate break-ins. "There's a James Bond setup here that's out of the worst possible detective novel you could ever read," Irving would say in a *60 Minutes* interview, revealing his real motives while still peddling that the *Autobiography* was real.[21] As befits Bond, the book's setting is also an international, island-hopping, jet-set one—Irving and sometimes Suskind live on Ibiza and meet in the resorts of the new world, from Oxaca, St. Thomas, Florida, Las Vegas, and California, where they supposedly interview Hughes himself. (Like any other travel liar's, their hoax centers on islands.) The Hughes affair marks the exact moment in the culture when the image of the artist changed: once part of a transnational, transient, urban bohemia, the artist now was the member of an exiled, broke, but high-flying baronage, ripe for the hoaxing.

Unlike the *Autobiography of Howard Hughes*, which Irving appears to have accepted will define him, Irving does not claim *Spy*, his 1969 book written with Herbert Burkholz the same year as *Fake!* Never mentioned in his bios, or in his accounts of the Hughes affair published shortly after, *Spy* may not merit a mention because it reveals Irving's fascination with outright deception and treason far more than does *Fake!* For the spy represents what Irving is unable to fully admit: the danger of his hoax, of capture and certain jail and perhaps worse; and the question of morality. One he's in denial of and the other he has pretensions to. Also, to speak of the spy is to confess betrayal of those who once trusted you. Irving's editor Beverly Loo and his initial lawyer Marty Ackerman, both believing this was only a contract dispute and taking his side against increasingly wary publishers at McGraw-Hill and *Life* magazine, are only two of those he personally betrayed. Irving spends little or no time talking about the fallout, instead reveling in the caper.

There had always been spies, of course, but the spy changed after the Second World War. If the spy had been a mistaken identity for the writer since the Romantics, when Coleridge was suspected of being one, the spy soon became the chief keeper and spiller of secrets. The postwar path the American writer would follow matches the spy's almost exactly: once a lone wolf, now part of the pack, the creative writing MFA degree would become another newly coined anagram, like the CIA. (This connection many would say is literal, with recent yet unfounded claims that the Iowa Writers' Workshop was established by the CIA.) As double agents, forgers and plagiarists go further than poets might, using old paper to create false histories and cover up any crimes. The spy, like the hoaxer, cannot not admit that by fabricating another's life—a sanctioned plagiarist stealing files, copying texts, licensed not just to kill but to lie—she risks losing hers. Secret agents, like refugees, preserve their identities at the risk of life and limb if caught, but also at the risk of something resembling a self.

Such battles would-be writer Quentin Rowan reenacts in his debut spy novel, *Assassin of Secrets*. As revealed the week it was published in November 2011, the novel written under the pseudonym Q. R. Markham turns out to be nearly completely plagiarized—I repeat, it appears to include *nothing original*—with only the names changed to protect the guilty. A remarkable thirty-three examples of passages from other sources occur in the book's first thirty-five pages alone.[22] Rowan's setting *Assassin* in 1967 helps him borrow the atmosphere of the era, as well as to steal more easily from the unparalleled spy books of the time. Even his derivativeness is derivative—he took his pen name from James Bond, though not from the Bond books by Ian Fleming but from a sequel written by Kingsley Amis.[23] Plagiarism becomes several things for Rowan, from macho overcompensation to denial; later he would call it "a strange schizophrenic form of gambling" to seeing the book "as my 'last shot' " to "people pleasing."[24] Despite, or perhaps because of, his many self-diagnoses, Markham's plagiarism is an addiction above all. In a much quoted and maligned piece three weeks after being uncovered, Rowan's "Confession of a Plagiarist" used the language of addiction on The Fix, a website with recovery at its center. The best comment about his confession is also the first: "Good essay. Who wrote it?" For the plagiarist, like the forger, the unimaginable extent of the crime is its best form of protection.

The Autobiography remains the biggest hoax (and one of the richest) of the last century not only because of the enigma of Hughes or its near success but also because it takes in all the ways one can hoax, from imposture to plagiarism to forgery. It makes use of all then-current forms of technology to do so, from phone calls and cables, tape recordings to photocopies. Like

Watergate, or plagiarism, Irving's is a kind of internal espionage. Reading *Project Octavio* or the full *Autobiography of Howard Hughes*, which Irving has now released as an e-book, we must confront the idea that Irving's innovation was based not on forgery, which we might admire—or fraud, which we might forgive—but on wholesale theft of another manuscript. For the faux Hughes autobiography makes off with the work of Noah Dietrich, Hughes's onetime right-hand man, whose book in progress in a strange but apparently true twist Dietrich's agent unwittingly asked Irving to review while he happened to be visiting Irving's family. After making a copy and, later, copying from it, Irving told the agent it was worthless in order to forestall the competition. Irving would take much the same tack when it came to light that the February 1972 *Ladies' Home Journal* featured yet another book based on actual taped interviews with Hughes.[25] What were the chances? Irving's answer was to have his "Hughes" write a letter denouncing the *other* book as a hoax, buying time with McGraw-Hill's money.

While plagiarists regularly accuse others of plagiarizing them, hoaxers see hoaxes everywhere in order to shore up their own. Whenever Irving is confronted with other versions of events—whether through another book claiming to be an autobiography at the same time, or by Hughes himself through his lawyers or spokespersons seeking to stop Irvkind's efforts—his solution is to decry these others as lies. It's surprising how often the gambit worked. But remember: the hoax's makeup, as it were, isn't a lack of genuineness but a seeming excess of it.

Could Irving's failed "apocryphal autobiography"—the term is from the *New York Times*—also be the start of the celebrity *psychobiography* that dominated the decades to come? Subtitled a "memoir of Ronald Reagan," Morris's *Dutch* is a memoir of an imagined person, a projected double that by now should be familiar to students of the hoax; what saves it from being an outright hoax is Morris's admission of his fabrications in the face of Reagan's opaqueness. Yet is that all that separates nonfiction or fiction from a hoax: a confession before rather than after?

In a crucial way, Morris was simply following Reagan's lead—until recently, no other president has so blurred the line between reality and fiction. This, some might say, was Reagan's strength as the Great Communicator: an ability to project an ideal. But Reagan himself regularly quoted movie lines as gospel and at times seemed to conflate reality and screen, not simply as a form of the dementia that ultimately killed him but as a political expediency—and in ways that have grown only more familiar since. Critic

Michael Rogin explores such questions in his fascinating *"Ronald Reagan,"* *the Movie*, listing a few such screen gems:

> Reagan has not only hidden from his audience the filmic origins of his words to create the appearance of spontaneity but concealed those origins from himself as well. CBS's "Sixty Minutes" has traced the process by which Reagan first credited the line "Where do we find such men?" to the movie admiral in *Bridges at Toko-Ri*, then assigned that line to a real admiral, and finally quoted it as if he had thought of it himself. The president has inadvertently called his dog "Lassie" in front of reporters. He has told a mass audience about the captain of a bomber who chose to go down with his plane rather than abandon a wounded crew·member—"Congressional Medal of Honor, posthumous," concluded Reagan with tears in his eyes—only to have it revealed by a sailor who had seen the film aboard a World War II aircraft carrier that the episode was taken from Dana Andrews's *A Wing and a Prayer*. Reagan knew the Holocaust had happened, he told a gathering of survivors, because he had seen film of the camps.[26]

History as a movie: this is the forger's terroir, a double in the dark. "Movies have frequently used a mirror image to create a double of the self, a split of the ideal self from its dark reflection," Rogin writes. "But the screen also takes the place of a mirror."[27] Is one real, the other fake? Or is the ideal also unreal? President Reagan proved the perfect leader to further usher in our Age of Euphemism, conflating what we see, what we say, and what we believe. No wonder it would take an invention like *Dutch* to discover what was possibly real amidst the image.

The main requirement of any biography, of course, is that it tells of someone we presume to want to know. Such a notion has become central somehow to our national politics—"having a beer with" a president has become as important as whether she has humane policies or bold ideas. But the biographical hoax comes up against the issue that dogs our lives, in both the written and lived senses: can anyone ever be known? "It has taken me many years to get used to seeing myself as others see me," Reagan's own autobiography (quoted by Rogin) says. "Very few of us ever see ourselves except as we look directly at ourselves in a mirror."

Yet a great biography—try David Hajdu's *Lush Life* about composer Billy Strayhorn, or Mark Stevens and Annalyn Swan's *de Kooning*, or Valerie

Boyd's biography of Zora Neale Hurston—dispels falsehoods while getting to its subject, a slow but steady process the biographer lets us in on. This process can be fudged, sure, but can it be left out completely?

No one should write their autobiography until they're dead: Irving's epigraph from movie mogul Samuel Goldwyn, appended to the later, self-published editions of the *Autobiography*, indicates that the full import of a person's life is not usually revealed till after it's over. And perhaps not then—George Bernard Shaw declared while still a young man, "All autobiographies are lies. I do not mean unconscious unintentional lies; I mean deliberate lies. No man is bad enough to tell the truth about himself during his lifetime, involving as it must, the truth about his family and friends and colleagues. And no man is good enough to tell the truth in a document which he suppresses until there is nobody left alive to contradict him."[28] We might say such contradictions are those of autobiography itself, in which the living tell a far different tale than the dead.

You cannot legally libel the dead. Irving's (not-so-)original book took advantage of this fact, as he notes in *Project Octavio*. One passage describes the publisher's lawyers thanking the strange fortune that most of the outrageous stories happened to be about the dead, never suspecting this was by design. More importantly, Irving realized Howard Hughes was essentially "socially dead"—he had retreated not only from high society but also from human society. This realization also governs other hoaxes we've seen that wisely target those deemed socially dead, believed extinguishable, or soon to be—whether gay Indians, black Aborigines, or terminally ill kids.

It was exactly Hughes's wish for privacy that, like Elena Ferrante's pseudonymity, made a public target out of him. (Despite few calls for it, Ferrante's real identity was exposed during the finalizing of this book.) Hughes's billions also drew folks to him but let him withdraw further. This public–private paradox has become all of ours, upsetting millennia of human life in which our interior lives could remain that way. Through faked tapes, forged notes, false transcripts, and conscripted facts, *The Autobiography of Howard Hughes* heralded a new age in which there is no life worth leading that isn't public.

In such a time, anyone else can narrativize your life. The goal now, as realized by social media, seems to be to narrate your life before others do it for you—though, of course, such a life contains the secret wish to be caught up in a large media machine, to go viral, to appear on morning television claiming you never would've guessed anyone else would see something you purposefully posted online. To opt out as Hughes had is to court monstrosity.

At the same time Hughes himself has proved prescient in that his germophobia and love of all things organic has gone mainstream. "My eccentricities, if you look at them carefully, are just intelligent safeguards against the common dangers of life," fake Hughes tells Clifford, providing a modern mantra if ever was one. "Well, you must, by definition, be odd and eccentric and maybe even nuts if you're rich. . . . Artists are the closest to this, close to rich men like myself in this sense, because they have a highly developed sense of their own individuality and they don't mind telling the world to go take a flying fuck at a rolling doughnut, and I don't either. Because in my own way I suppose I'm an artist, too, as well as being rich."[29] Are we all now just pretending we're billionaires, as this passage does? That we're not just clients of the Billionaire's Club but the president of it? The faux documents the Hughes hoax created were warnings from a future that is now, when documents and photos and even presidential candidates continually surface unmoored, virtual, semipermanent, are hacked, and then disappear.

There are those who might not see this fraud as significant, or as a big enough change in our culture: in our digital world, nothing's original after all; words are just zeroes and ones, books mere texts. But these changeling autobiographies barely bear the trace of their making, absent the writer's hand or breath or body, the paper's fade and fold. Their sleekness is their rawest, and wrongest, quality. Case in point: not only were Elmyr's fakes faked, so was Clifford Irving's.

Irving, a free man now, summarizes what happened: "Ken Talbot was a London crook and bookmaker who, in 1991, reproduced and published my 1968 biography, *FAKE!* . . . His hardback edition includes a 'preface by Clifford Irving,' not a word of which I wrote; an introduction by Talbot himself that is mostly half-truths and lies; and a center color section of supposed De Hory paintings that Talbot busily tried to sell as genuine De Hory fakes of Matisse, Picasso, Modigliani, et al. I have no idea who painted them." Talbot renamed this forgery of a forgery *Enigma! The New Story of Elmyr de Hory, the Greatest Art Forger of Our Time*, managing to keep the exclamation point. Irving ends his story—actually an online review of *Enigma!* on Amazon.com—with a plug for his original *Fake!* "for sale at $5.99 on Kindle and Nook."[30]

Forgers seek a fortune, or forgiveness; a good writer seeks forever.

CHAPTER 13

Bakelite

Long familiar to art and poetry, the word *collaborator* took on a darker definition in the wake of World War II, coming to mean those who worked for and alongside the Nazis in occupied countries like France and the Netherlands. The Dutchman Han van Meegeren, the most famed forger of the first part of the twentieth century before Elmyr assumed the mantle, was a collaborator in both senses. Van Meegeren forged any number of painters through the 1920s and 1930s, especially Vermeer, who was then becoming a Dutch national treasure, one especially valued given his small output. Any new Vermeer was a revelation—and a remunerative one—earning its discoverer or identifier a small fortune and changing almost immediately the understanding of the Dutch artist's oeuvre.

Van Meegeren was undone not by wet paint, that typical giveaway for a forgery—he had innovated using the early plastic Bakelite, which withstood the time's initial toothpick tests, cooking up hard—but by selling one of his "Vermeers" to Hermann Goering during the war. When the war ended and the sale was discovered, Dutch officials arrested Van Meegeren for having sold a national treasure to Nazi occupiers; facing the death penalty for treason, he admitted that the painting was fake.

Being an unrepentant forger apparently beat being a Nazi collaborator. Van Meegeren also had to admit that the other Vermeers he'd painted and sold to the Netherlands' national museums were forgeries too. Like Piltdown Man, Van Meegeren's fakes meant to provide a "missing link"—here between Vermeer's known portraits and his few religious subjects. The most famous of these is *The Supper at Emmaus*, a depiction of Christ acquired for a huge sum on Christmas Day, 1937, and that went on to be the capstone of an important exhibition titled *Four Centuries of Dutch Art* the following year.[1] As it often does, the hoax played into questions of nation and race—Vermeer, like Shakespeare, was now a sign of national pride and just as often forged.

At his subsequent trial Van Meegeren furthered this idea, claiming his was not a faked national treasure but that his sale to Goering was a prank meant to spoof Nazi expertise. In an odd twist of fate, the fierce resistance leader who was Van Meegeren's principal investigator and captor quickly became his savior, setting him up with paints and easel to craft a new "Vermeer" as proof of his talent and, indeed, of Dutch ingenuity. Van Meegeren's 1947 trial became a circus with the forger at its center, one poll ranking him second in national popularity only to the prime minister.[2] None of this explains why he'd sold forgeries like the *Supper* to Dutch museums too.

Art historian Jonathan Lopez demonstrates in *The Man Who Made Vermeers* that despite his claiming he'd hoaxed Goering, Van Meegeren was a longtime Nazi sympathizer and fascist who was only too happy to see his work in the collection of one of the chief architects of the Holocaust and Holland's occupation. We should not underestimate the significance of Lopez's argument and evidence: many in war-torn Holland believed the fable, seeing Van Meegeren as essentially a trickster-hero, and such misperceptions continue to this day. The 1990 *Fake?* exhibition at the British Museum declared the sale to Goering "much to Van Meegeren's chagrin"; the title of Edward Dolnick's *The Forger's Spell: A True Story of Vermeer, Nazis, and the Greatest Art Hoax of the Twentieth Century* (2008) further indicates how desperately we might wish to see forgery as clever trickery.[3] Despite its being known at the time of the trial, no one seemed to pay much attention to the fact that a book inscribed effusively in 1942 by Van Meegeren to Hitler as "my beloved Führer" was discovered among Hitler's personal library.

Van Meegeren's Nazism is made all the more disturbing when Lopez reports that "not only was Van Meegeren an important player in an elaborate game of international deception in the 1920s and 1930s, but some of his disreputable associates later put their expertise to work laundering stolen Holocaust assets in the same way they had laundered fake pictures— through the art trade."[4] Goering himself had apparently traded 137 looted paintings for his "Vermeer."[5] The links between forgery, art theft, and the Holocaust still haven't been fully unpacked today, with up to a hundred thousand looted, stolen, or forcibly sold artworks yet unreturned. The recent revelation of over fourteen hundred "lost" masterpieces, much of them if not stolen then received under duress and till now hidden in an apartment in Belgium, points to the ways the war is still very much with us.

So too the case of the Hitler Diaries, whose discovery in 1983 was trumpeted as changing history. Two years before, veteran German reporter Gerd Heidemann brought the diaries to the attention of his long-time employer *Stern*, a popular magazine that might best be described as *Life*, *People*, and *Playboy* in one. (Like British tabloids it sometimes ran nudes.) Nicknamed the "bloodhound," Heidemann had also long been fascinated with the Third Reich; he bought and restored Goering's yacht, the *Carin II*, gifted to the Nazi leader as a present for his second marriage but named after his first wife. After the armistice, the boat became a spoil of war for British royalty, renamed the *Prince Charles*, before being inexplicably given back to Goering's widow in 1960.[6] Heidemann was enamored with the tawdry glamour and kitschy relics of the Nazi era as well as with Goering's daughter, Edda, with whom he promptly had an affair. The pair, and later Heidemann's third wife, Gina, would entertain former Nazi officials and even several SS generals onboard the restored vessel, reliving Germany's supposed past glory among Heidemann's growing collection. As Robert Harris details in the lively *Selling Hitler* (1986), it was the highest ranking of these Nazis, Karl Wolff—whom Heidemann would address by the same diminutive Himmler had used, *Wölffchen*—who served as a witness to Gina and Gerd's wedding. Wölffchen accompanied them on their honeymoon in search of fugitive Nazis in South America.

There was an uneasy nostalgia to all of this—including a lingering "grey market" in Nazi memorabilia, often fake, smuggled from the East to West Germany, where such propaganda remained largely illegal. In his obsessive hunting, Heidemann heard that a fellow collector had located one of Hitler's diaries, which he eventually saw; hearing there were more, he tracked the source to a Stuttgart dealer, Konrad Fischer. "Conny" claimed to have access to twenty-seven diaries found by farmers in what was now East Germany in the wreckage of Operation Seraglio—an actual failed flight from Hitler's last days that crashed near the Czech border. The transport was thought to have held a host of Hitler's personal documents, which Heidemann more than anyone believed to mean the diaries, and became convinced had survived. He would make a pilgrimage to the wreckage site and pose for pictures besides the homemade graves of the pilot and passengers.

The supposed diaries revealed less about Hitler's rise and fall than they provided proof of his persistent allure. The fervor the dozens of volumes stirred in Heidemann was shared by, or transmitted to, higher-ups at *Stern*, who kept the cache a secret in order to preserve a scoop; he skipped his editors and went straight to the publisher and moneymen. *Stern* would shell out nearly $5 million in deutsche marks for Heidemann to pass along to his source—a source, really Conny Fischer, whom he would not name, citing the danger of smuggling journals from the Communist East—making the Hitler Diaries one of the most expensive hoaxes in history. One scheme for delivering the journals meant a supposed East German general tossing them into Heidemann's open Mercedes. More often, they were secreted across the border in pianos.[7] Over the course of time, Fischer's price increased along with the number of diaries: "The 'Fuhrer' was increasingly communicative," wrote one of *Stern*'s editors, recollecting the events decades later. "The notebooks were growing fatter—and getting more and more expensive."[8] In the end, the Hitler Diaries numbered over sixty and covered 1932 to 1945—not accidentally, as *Selling Hitler* observes, exactly when the most details were known about the dictator and thus to exploit.

The desire of *Stern*'s higher-ups for secrecy meant that they didn't authenticate the diaries along the way. When at last they sought proof of the volumes' genuineness, it didn't help that the handwriting was compared to another forgery from the same source; or that the diaries' facts were also checked against the very book that had supplied them; not to mention that, as one critic observes, "authentication was sought only after large sums of money had been paid out."[9] This confirmation was conducted by former intelligence officer and Oxford historian Hugh Trevor-Roper, who had first verified Hitler's suicide in his authoritative *Last Days of Hitler* (1947). While skeptical at first, the don, newly minted as Lord Dacre, soon became enamored of the size of the find and staked his reputation on it.

To many, including Trevor-Roper, the goodly number of journals meant they had to be real. But it was exactly the scheme's combination of anonymity and lucrativeness that had encouraged the forgeries to proliferate. For Fischer was not just the dealer of the diaries but a prolific if petty forger, really named Konrad Kujau, who had grown up a refugee (much as Elmyr de Hory would claim to be). For over a decade Kujau had been supplying unscrupulous collectors a steady and unlikely amount of Nazi "memorabilia," from Hitler paintings to Hitler poetry. Forgeries always seem to include a faked poem—a way of establishing literary bona fides, both for the forger and the pretend subject. Heidemann was, like most forgery middlemen, skimming off the top; he used the funds to amass more Nazi relics, including the very Luger that Hitler was said to have employed in his suicide in the last days of the Reich, really another Fischer fake.

By the time of *Stern*'s announcement of the diaries' publication, Trevor-Roper had begun to have his doubts. Where his attestation for the *Times* the Saturday before would declare that the discovery meant "standard accounts of Hitler's writing habits, of his personality, and even, perhaps, some public events, may, in consequence, have to be revised," by the following Monday Lord Dacre waffled in front of the cameras. Bogarting the microphone, no less than the grandstanding Holocaust denier David Irving would deny the diaries' genuineness.[10] Only after the disastrous press conference would the still-defiant *Stern* team send the diaries off for chemical testing, blaming any doubts on jealousy: after all, once the material was verified, *Stern* and Heidemann stood to get very rich.

It took only two weeks for the laboratory to declare them "obvious fakes."[11] Fischer wasn't entirely careful—and clearly hadn't needed to be—using inexpensive and identical journals for the baker's dozen years of diaries. He also used cheap plastic lettering for Hiter's monogram on the covers, mislabeling them *F H* instead *A H*. In their rush to believe, no one seemed to notice what the Gothic letters really said—a close-up of the wrong initials can be found right there on *Stern*'s blockbuster cover.

The typical process of acquiring an archive goes: examination, authentication, payment, publication. The Hitler Diaries reversed this nearly exactly. What would have happened had the publishers not been so secretive and, at the same time, trusting? Why were such knowledgeable experts as Trevor-Roper so fooled? Many have described the team's "bunker" mentality—theirs was a shared delusion, a group hysteria whose underlying beliefs may prove most troubling. For not only were the forgeries "superficial," as the national archives declared them, but they were "grotesquely so"—*grotesk oberflächlich*. The fake entries meant both to fool readers and to rehabilitate Der Führer, making him reluctant to kill Jews and somehow not even aware of *Kristallnacht* or the Final Solution he had, in truth, enthusiastically ordered. Nostalgic for what never was, the diaries offered up a fake history—one especially suited to the conservatives who championed it, from Heidemann to David Irving (who unbelievably began to believe them real) to Rupert Murdoch and his *Sunday Times* that had first brought in Trevor-Roper as they considered syndication, at first pledging $3.75 million for the opportunity.

Instead of beastly, or bizarre, the diaries depicted Hitler as banal. That word keeps coming up in the most credulous outlets at the time of the case, including *Newsweek*, which had first been offered US rights—although they declined, their contemporary cover story wants it both ways, asking "Are They Genuine?" while announcing "How They Could Rewrite History." "The words, most of them, are banal and cryptic, the mundane jottings of an unlettered man who seems at times to be less an evil genius than a petty civil servant."[12] The banality the hoax couches itself in, much like science does for "science faction" or innocence does for the exoticist hoax, is designed to fool—to make the masterpiece more approachable, the insane "fact" more believable, unchecked like a mob's rage. In making Hitler boring, the diaries sought to make him not just believable but less of a monster.

It would be contemporary wishes, not the past, for which the diaries served as both time machine and "unauthorized autobiography." "This scandal could only have happened in a period in which Germans had fixated on Hitler as a way of ignoring the fact that the German population was complicit in the horrors of the Nazi era," one historian told the *New Yorker* thirty years later.[13] It seems clear that any forgery's complicity hides guilt; the forgery is believed not because it alters history but because we wish history were otherwise.

Heidemann would be sentenced to jail for fraud along with Kujau, who upon learning of the vast sum *Stern* gave Heidemann—far less than what Heidemann delivered to him—insisted Heidemann was involved. During the trial, Kujau enjoyed some of the same celebrity as Van Meegeren had during his, emerging from prison only to go into business crafting "genuine fakes" signed by him. Today, even these forgeries have been forged. In a further twist, Heidemann was later revealed to have been an agent for the Stasi, the East German secret police, igniting all sorts of conspiracy theories about the hoax's true origins.[14] Heidemann, living in poverty, boat presumably long sold, responded that he had actually been a double agent for the West. The hoax often is.

Is the hoax one more casualty of war? War, since at least the Civil War, often sits behind the modern hoax. Is this one reason why our modern hoaxes have become ones of horror? We certainly should not turn for answers to the forgers of paints or print, who claim it's all simply fun and games, especially when forgery has long been a brutal business tied to theft and death. In Van Meegeren's case, while one critic says that Christ's face in *Supper* was based on a photograph of Greta Garbo, calling the painting "a brilliant parody" that "anticipates postmodern ironic/iconic pastiche," Lopez more convincingly argues that "the new Vermeer hanging on the walls in Rotterdam was a subtle homage to Nazi image making. Of course, excitement and hoopla—welcome distractions during the grim economic situation of the 1930s—had kept a lot of people from seeing the scheming dictator in Berlin for what *he* was too."[15] Indeed, it was exactly the tale of a Dutch art collector persecuted by fascists that Van Meegeren used to lure a middleman to sell the *Supper* in the first place. This is the danger with the hoax and the forgery—time can turn an acknowledged "original" into mere pastiche, even ironic kitsch, pleading parody, evading painful facts and actual pain. The hoax matters because it distracts from what matters.

This fatal aspect of forgery suggests a question that lurks behind all this: is it not only the hoaxes themselves, but also the politics of the hoax, that remain hidden? Once we X-ray the forgery to see whatever's beneath—an underpainting that reveals the fakery—its ideology also happens to shine through.

PAINTED BIRDS

What the writer Jerzy Kosinski stands accused of isn't exactly hoaxing: though like forger Han Van Meegeren he was called a fraud, if for very different reasons; like Elmyr de Hory he was caught up in World War II and its aftermath; and like Clifford Irving, he crafted a dubious autobiography of someone who just might be him. Though always labeled fiction, Kosinski's semiautobiographical novel *The Painted Bird* (1965) has become a symbol of fakery though it is, in many places, true to life. Ambiguity marked its downfall—even its original publishing company seemed uncertain whether the book was a memoir or novel, a confusion Kosinski encouraged, or at least did not discourage. Soon the question would go from whether the book was entirely true, to whether any of it was.

Metaphorically speaking, Kosinski claimed to be painting from life but was caught *inpainting*—a term for going far beyond restoration to filling in an older painting in order to deceive, giving it an improved look or a famous signature to make it seem better than it is. Kosinski's *Painted Bird* appears far too touched up for contemporary tastes, taking what may have been there and making it far different from the original.

This marks an epochal shift. As we might recall, when Emily Dickinson's poems were first printed posthumously in the fruitful 1890s, spurring along modernism, her family and editors regulated the punctuation, smoothed over gaps, took out the dashes, gave the never-titled poems titles—and would never have considered the results anything but Dickinson. Such editorial interventions meant to rescue the so-called spinster poet's verses, refining them in preparation for publication; the second volume of *Poems* reproduced a "fac-simile" of her writing that undermined the editors' invisible hands given the manuscript's visible wildness. Decades later, when Thomas H. Johnson published his scholarly edition of Dickinson in 1955, he sought to represent exactly that, numbering the poems according to their composition and complete with her now-iconic dashes—the goal was to represent Dickinson's hand.[16] More recent editions of Dickinson have gone further, maintaining or re-creating the "facsicles" or small packets of poems that she sewed together, which earlier editors had promptly disassembled. From *fac-similes* to *facsicles*, the editor always faces such choices: How should the poems be organized? Or harder, how to represent the unrepresentable? The passion surrounding Dickinson continues: just as her archive has more or less finally come online, we discover and delight in *The Gorgeous Nothings*, an array of Dickinson pieces written and shaped on envelopes and scraps often excluded from the poems proper.[17]

All this means that Dickinson's vast output does not meet the unparalleled demand for her work, making the incentive for forgery quite high. The discovery of a new Dickinson poem that came to auction in the 1990s, right in the middle of our age's narrative crisis, was met with much excitement—experts were called, archives consulted, funds secured for bidding.[18] But the Dickinson turned out to be the latest forgery from Mark Hofmann, who would soon become notorious for selling forged Mormon documents pretending to be found artifacts. Raised Mormon himself, Hofmann knew exactly how to target the Church of Latter-Day Saints, which was among his biggest clients: he literally documented their fears, turning these into convincing forgeries like the "Salamander Letter" that contravened the religion's origin story with a Satanic twist. In debt, having forged the poem, fearing discovery, Hofmann would kill two people with letter bombs before a misfired explosive wounded him. Convicted of murder, he is still serving life in prison. Always dangerous, the forgery is too often a symbolic letter bomb waiting to wound.

An editor's choices of order and representation also face the artist—

especially the artist forged, as it were, during war. What to leave out, and how to render the mutilated world? World War II may have renamed Koskinki—his father changed the family from the more obviously Jewish Lewinkopf in order to survive—but the Cold War redefined him. His first two books, written under the pseudonym Joseph Novak, were nonfiction attacks on the communism of his native-born Poland after he fled to the United States. As his third book, but the first under his name, *The Painted Bird* soon became a sensation, garnering praise in hardcover and brisk sales in paperback.

As Kosinski's sensitive biographer James Park Sloan notes, *Painted Bird*'s original publisher was under the impression that the book was not just autobiographical but autobiography. How significant a few letters difference between those words; it's the same difference between *hearsay* and *heresy*. The difficulty for Kosinski became that he had traded in hearsay, telling and embellishing stories at parties of his childhood surviving the Nazi regime—it was one such occasion that first interested his publisher. Fine for a party, his embellished autobiography became part of his fiction's appeal, making its way into the marketing of the book, as well as into internal publishers' memos about the book. Some readers saw the book as a literary triumph; others as powerful, actual testimony.

Sloan compellingly re-creates this dilemma, one largely of Kosinski's own making. Kosinski let it be known to fellow Holocaust survivor and future Nobel laureate Elie Wiesel that the book was "in essence, autobiographical." As Sloan describes it, "The word that *The Painted Bird* was a chronicle of actual human suffering was the cue that Wiesel needed, and on Sunday, October 31, his review entitled 'Everybody's Victim' sanctified the book as an authentic Holocaust testament." Wiesel pronounced in the *New York Times*, "It is as a chronicle that *The Painted Bird*, Jerzy Kosinski's third book (but his first on this subject) achieves its unusual power."[19] Reviewers' use of *account*, *confession*, and *document* sealed the marketing of the novel, an ambiguity that Kosinski was only too happy to promote. Later he would take pains to say he removed all biographical info, though in truth he relied on it—a classic forger's trick.

Oddly, Kosinski would claim to Wiesel that he wasn't Jewish. Was he trying to cement the idea, left vague, of the book's protagonist as Gypsy (or Roma)? Certainly, to read interviews with Kosinski from the time is to see the ways he sought to shape his image early and often. This image was one of doubt, imagination, even nothingness: "There is a fleeting temptation to suggest that there is no Jerzy Kosinski, that he is a figment of his own vivid imagination, that, by all the rules of logic, he could not possibly exist," wrote Dick Schapp in the *New York Herald Tribune* in 1965. "But he does."

"The book is not literal," Kosinski told Schapp, "but it is almost all literal incidents, shown in a way not literal, improved, cut up, fitted into a pattern. I have used the stones of my life to build a new wall. I took the literal and turned it into something symbolic." This, I suppose, is what many writers do—but Kosinski goes further, collapsing his life, his learning English, and his fiction into a noble experiment. "Kosinksi taught himself English, first by listening to the radio, then by translating English-language poets—Shakespeare and Poe, for instance—into Polish and Russian and memorizing the poems," Schapp recounted, establishing Kosinski's embellished origin story. "'English is easy to learn,' [Kosinski] says, 'but almost impossible to master.' He would recite three versions of a paragraph into a tape recorder, then listen to the replay for the one that sounded best to his ear. When he wondered whether he was getting his meaning across, he would call a telephone operator, explain his predicament, read her a passage and ask if she understood it."[20] He remains a different kind of operator.

Elsewhere Kosinski insists on calling *Bird* a novel and referring to the protagonist as "the boy" yet turns around and says "*I* don't remember" when asked about incidents in the book. By calling the boy protagonist of *Painted Bird* "a modern Mowgli, a six-year-old Polish boy raised among Eastern European wolves in the jungle of World War II," Schapp inadvertently taps into the kinds of tropes that would come to dominate the more troubling Holocaust hoaxers to come, from Binjamin Wilkomirski's faked childhood, lost to his own memory, to *Misha*'s protagonist literally raised by wolves.

Was Kosinski guilty of promoting hearsay or heresy? Is it never being clear whether the unnamed "Boy" in the book is Jewish or what we'd today call Roma a sign of it being a metaphor-filled fiction? Or is ambiguity about something as devastatingly actual and painful as the Holocaust a form of betrayal? The Jews and Gypsies and gays and Negroes and others the Nazis sought to exterminate were not metaphors—though the "degenerate art" the Nazis simultaneously sought to excise was. It matters to us that we tell the truth of what happened in the Shoah in order that it not happen again; any ambiguity comes off as ambivalence. Perhaps this is what Adorno meant when he said that to write poetry after Auschwitz is barbaric: not that a poem cannot be written, but we don't now have the luxury of artifice, of language shaped—however artfully—much less faked.

To think of it another way: setting aside actual testimony and nonfiction, both of which must be truthful, how could a novel of the Holocaust, even one written by a survivor, *not* require imagination? The imagination remains a powerful tool of survival—one that can be hard to discuss and name. Daniel Mendelsohn in his damning critique of fake memoirs, including fake Holocaust books like *Misha*, starts by quoting an actual survivor:

> A Polish Jew who had survived the Holocaust, she'd been telling me how she and her young son had managed to keep a step ahead of the people who were hunting them down, and at the end of this stupefying tale of survival I'd looked up at her and said, "What an amazing story!" It was at that point that she flapped her spotted hand at me in disdain. "'Amazing story,'" she mimicked me, tartly. She fetched a heavy sigh. "If you didn't have an amazing story, you didn't survive."
>
> She was referring to literal survival, of course—survival at its meanest, most animal level, the mere continuance of the organism.[21]

Amazing, of course, still insists on true. The animal level of literal survival Mendelsohn mentions is one devoid of imagination, the very thing war takes away, and the Holocaust especially.

To conflate Kosinski, who came from the same city as Roman Polanski, with the fake memoir—which I've seen some do—is to miss the nuance of his novel, the way the boy's namelessness is only one more clue that he is not Jerzy Kosinski. But most people read "unnamed" as just another alias. It certainly doesn't help that in the first edition of *Painted Bird*, the boy, having survived, is given an italicized afterlife that looks remarkably like the author's:

> *The story of the boy, the Painted Bird of this book, does not end with his regaining the power of speech. He had become part of the society in which he found himself. It was against the pattern of his acquired habits at first, to cast off his feathers and to adjust to the increasing near-normality of postwar conditions. . . . The only escape from such pressure and limitation was flight, a journey across an ocean and beyond the confines of a continent where no wings could be spread. In this flight the Painted Bird again became himself.*[22]

Kosinski would remove these passages from later editions, attempting to shift the discussion from the boy's later life to the book's. But it's clear at least in the initial epilogue that the Bird and the book and the author are meant to be read as one and the same. The book's success largely rested on its authority as testimony, not necessarily on its literary merits, no matter if those are many.

Yet it would be this other side of the debate—*The Painted Bird* as literary achievement—that ultimately undid Kosinski. The Polish émigré regularly worked with translators, editors, and rewriters to craft his books, a fact that ended up as part of a notorious takedown in 1982 by the *Village Voice*. In the cover story "Jerzy Kosinski's Tainted Words," Geoffrey Stokes and Eliot Fremont-Smith eviscerated the author, saying he wasn't one. The two suggest Kosinski went past any modern notion of the translator in that his books, presumed written in English, were in fact translations at best (from his Polish) and completely ghosted at worst (written entirely by someone else). The article also charged that the CIA wrote his first two pseudonymous books.[23] The *Voice* piece accused Kosinski not only of fabricating events in his novel but also of fabricating Jerzy Kosinski.

I've never seen a prestigious writer's reputation so changed in so short a time. Despite a lengthy rebuttal of the *Village Voice* piece in the *New York Times* titled "17 Years of Ideological Attack on a Cultural Target," which convincingly argues that Kosinski had faced such accusations from Cold War Poland's state-approved and -sponsored newspapers ever since his first books, the damage was done. After decades of being considered among the elite of the time—hobnobbing with literary celebrities, appearing a dozen times on the *Tonight Show with Johnny Carson*, dining with the likes of Henry Kissinger, playing a bureaucrat in the historic epic *Reds*—his reputation quickly fell. He may have won the National Book Award in fiction for his second book, *Steps* (1968), and his best seller *Being There* (1971) was later made into an acclaimed film starring Peter Sellers, but Kosinski barely wrote again after the *Voice* attack.[24]

If anything, earlier articles such as "Being Jerzy Kosinski," the cover story of the *New York Times* magazine that depicted him shirtless in polo gear, only spurred on his downfall—a danger Sloan argues he courted. Trauma is a constant presence in Kosinski's unauthorized autobiography, not because of his dissembling but despite it. "Kosinski's was an exemplary twentieth-century life—a life entwined with both Hitler's and Stalin's; with the great totalitarianisms and American materialism; with sexuality unbounded and violence unrestrained; with instant celebrity and the life of the very rich; with extraordinary falseness and extraordinary authenticity," Sloan writes. "He was, if nothing else, a literary creator who probed the rules and the boundaries of literary creation, whose first and greatest creation was himself."[25] This sounds like the twenty-first century too, an era for which Kosinski's extraordinary falseness and banal authenticity may make more sense. Or at least be more familiar.

If clear forgeries like Van Meegeren's *The Supper at Emmaus*—once considered not only indisputably genuine but a masterpiece—can be revaluated and demoted to plain old fake, might the time be right to examine Kosinski's work as the clear fictions they now appear to be? A preview of Kosinki's possible revaluation is found in Eliot Weinberger's essay "Genuine Fakes," a terrific piece despite some factual errors of its own. Weinberger praises Kosinski as a forger, writing that "a forgery is an object without a creator, and human nature cannot bear anything without a narrative of its origin."[26] Do forgeries indeed last only a generation or two, and by 1982 Kosinki's time was up?

Unfortunately, any answer or restored praise would be too late to save Kosinski himself. In 1991, after attending and by most accounts seemingly enjoying a party thrown by friends and publishing insiders Nan and Gay Talese, Kosinski came home and killed himself by drinking, taking pills, and putting his head in a plastic bag—a technique suggested by the Hemlock Society to assure death. Like the ending of his literary career, it was overkill.

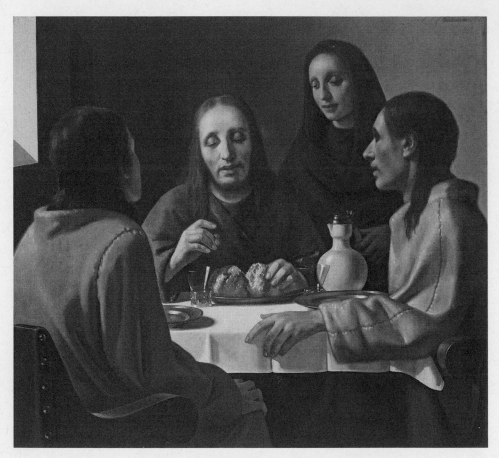

The Supper at Emmaus, a forged Vermeer by Han van Meegeren, ca. 1937.

CHAPTER 14

The Vampire's Wife

In art-world terms, Jerzy Kosinski stands accused of forging not just his books but also their provenance—not to mention his own. That magic word *provenance*, the story of how and where an artwork moved through time, has only gained in power over time: not only does provenance reveal how an artwork reached us, but it also symbolically connects us to its origins. To hold a Picasso in one's hands is not enough; we must know how it got here and show that the great man once touched it, and by implication, manage to touch him ourselves. By citing provenance, or the narrative of origin, we ultimately are doing that almost sacred work of tracing who begat whom, from "thence to the current owner" to "directly from the artist" as secular Creator.

The great art forgers of the last century spent as much effort forging provenance as aging canvases and perfecting paint—whether it was Van Meegeren's unlikely stories of discoveries of his "Vermeers," to the Hitler Diaries' wild backstories, to Elmyr de Hory and his crew's going from forging signatures to forging the very stamps and certificates of authenticity used by experts. In one case Elmyr's coconspirators got an aging artist to authenticate his own faked work. The forger regularly paints over the forgery's failures, which is to say, the genesis of almost any hoax; forgers cultivate a sense that the real crime is that they were not recognized for their own craft. But where the artist is busy making art and sacrifices, the art forger, like the fake journalist, is preoccupied with making up provenance—which is to say, faking history.

The argument from some quarters goes that if you enjoy a misattributed painting, what does it matter if it's real? This argument fails to understand that context is part and parcel of any art's pleasure. We remember when we first saw it and how, if lucky, we were able to get it. Do those who believe otherwise also think that if that diamond ring don't shine, it shouldn't matter when it turns out to be bullshit or shinola?

The problem with forgery is not that someone buys a fake and hangs it on the wall to enjoy. The problem is in what else forgery gets us to buy. Forgery aims to replace sight with belief: it isn't what you see, but what I say, the forger and the middleman says. Forgery is in essence Romantic, arguing that one's feeling about a piece is its main meaning. The wilder the story, the deeper the need to believe it. But believing shouldn't be our only form of seeing. As my Daddy the Doctor used to say: while it's good to get a second opinion, it's dangerous to ask around till you get the diagnosis you want. Yet the forgery is like a disease—one that after reading about it you suddenly have. With the hysterical hypochondria of the hoax, detection is everywhere, as is a mood of impending doom; the wise forger aims for the middle, to be noticed but not recognized. But rarely are forgeries left unsigned.

What's more, forgery can affect our sense of an artist's oeuvre, making the real unreal. Jonathon Keats's *Forged* relates the story of a collector who passed on genuine Dufys in favor of a forgery because the collector, accustomed to the forgeries already found in her collection, was looking for the forger's far more sure hand. When Elmyr declared that his hand in his Matisse forgeries proved steadier than Matisse's, he was right. This is not surprising: the original artist cannot ever be sure as she creates; the mix of hesitation, dread, and overconfidence that defines the artist is the ineffable difference in inventing and the copy. Let's call it the aura of art, as Walter Benjamin would. This aura, threatened and of course theoretical, adheres beyond the grave; it's what can make an older artwork feel alive.

In no way homage, the fact of the forgery actually manages to disparage the borrowed artist's art. Every fake Basquiat, for instance—eBay alone is rife with them, complete with certificates of authenticity straight from genuine computers—threatens to lessen our complex notions of Basquiat's work. We may begin to see his art brut skeletons and barbed-wire halos not as inspiring but as something anyone might do. This notion reproduces the kinds of clichés often said both about modern art and about Basquiat the "radiant child" early on in his career, seen as unaware of what he was doing, "savant or savage" as poet and critic Elizabeth Alexander so eloquently put it.[1] The stakes here aren't just about art but about history and denial. Art comes from struggle, often with and against truth—the true artist regularly endures rejections, accusations of being a phony, a fake, a poor imitation of her predecessors. This struggle often continues after the artist dies, the work of the once-dismissed sometimes gaining in perceived power and relevance, followed by what someone is willing to pay.

It is here where the forger enters, seeking to raise the dead like a price. Vampiric and monstrous, a Frankenstein of a different kind, forgery functions like the undead—becoming neither living nor gone, persistent, inexorable, hungry. It is also largely silent. Forgery, broadly defined, regularly engenders silence: Kosinski's boy is struck mute by his experiences in *Painted Bird*, something Kosinski suggested happened to him (though it didn't); Clifford Irving arrived in the United States to defend against charges of fraud and was struck with laryngitis; Howard Hughes's public silence also spurs on Irving's hoax in some ways, even if it was replaced by more silence in the end. Matching the mutism found in classic hysteria, silence is the hoax's boon companion.

A forgery ultimately changes, perhaps forever, what we expect the artist's work to look like. The forger's excuse, that the forgery is "just as good as" the real thing, ignores the ways forgery starts to erode our ability to tell not just what's good but what's real. And the real, sad to say, ain't always good. Every forgery aims to be not just another painting but a masterpiece.

STEPS

Sometimes it takes a sanctioned fake to remind us what's special about the real thing.[2] In 1979 writer Chuck Ross retyped all of Kosinski's award-winning *Steps* and submitted it to twenty-seven publishing houses and agents as if it was his own. Coming from an unknown writer, not from a recognizable name, *Steps* was universally rejected—even by Kosinski's own publisher. (Later Ross would do much the same with *Casablanca*, submitting it to dozens of movie studios, most of whom didn't recognize it, or more embarrassingly, said they thought its dialogue poorly done.)[3] The experts, in short, quickly proved they weren't.

Whether as a prank or pointed hoax, Ross's experiment wouldn't have been worthwhile had he not revealed it. He would go on to his own writing career, but you could say that the repudiation of Kosinski's reputation began right then. Ross's showing up of the publishing industry's fickleness and arguably slipping standards, several years before the *Village Voice* exposé of Kosinski in 1982, revealed what Kosinski must have feared: that his reputation was built not just on style but on testimony and backstory; and that the popularity of the author was merely a prop. As with plagiarism, the copy may perniciously suggest that not only is the work popular enough to be copied, but it also is highly copyable, ordinary, as unoriginal as the purposefully plagiarized work is.

Is forgery a form of praise? Not if you are the one lucky enough to receive it.

Kosinski might have said as much. He regularly sent two self-published pamphlets, *Notes of the Author of "The Painted Bird"* (1965) and *The Art of the Self* (1968), alongside copies of his first two books. Reading these essays now, it is hard to see them as anything but the kinds of apologia that regularly preface the hoax. "To say that THE PAINTED BIRD is nonfiction may be convenient for classification, but is not easily justified. . . . We fit experiences into molds which simplify, shape and give them an acceptable emotional clarity. *The remembered event becomes a fiction, a structure made to accommodate certain feelings.*" The frequent italics, and the "we" left unnamed, foreshadow what feels less like explication than justification, or obfuscation. "*It might be said that the writer takes from outside himself only what he is capable of creating in his imagination.*"[4]

All these permutations, or obfuscations, Kosinski came to call *autofiction*. This too he seems to have borrowed; most people credit Serge Doubrovsky with first coining the term in 1977, though Kosinski's early pamphlets certainly circled the notion. By 1989 Kosinski would employ *autofiction* as shorthand for a heady mix of autobiography and fabrication, authenticity and outlandishness he sought as an ideal—or justified as a necessary aspect of memory:

> I said [in the 1960s] that the writer incorporated the fragments of objective reality into a new literary dimension, but took from outside of himself "only what he is capable of creating in his imagination anyhow." Perversely, I can also take from outside things that in my fiction can exist as a fact of my life, since clearly I exist only as a fiction writer. My personality, a certain version of myself, and therefore one I sell as a storyteller—is it a one-to-one conversion? It is not, since no such transfer can take place in literature. Is it a revisitation of my life? No, it is not. Rather, it's a vision.[5]

If not quite the "auto-gothic" found in JT LeRoy, the prevaricating and baroque self-questioning here—not to mention the constant self-referential shifts from "the writer" to "I" to *Painted Bird*—indicate the slipperiness of Kosinski's performance and vagueness of his autofiction ideal. According to his biographer, autofiction's "deeper rationale is that all remembered human experience is, in one sense, fiction. This is not quite Faulkner's solution of 'lying one's way to the truth.' It is, more nearly, an argument that *there is no such thing as truth*."[6] In such a scheme little is out of bounds.

It is *autofiction*, far more than *faction*, that has lately emerged as a buzzword, spawning journals, conferences, and serious studies, in French no less. Its current usage might best describe the kinds of works that include the author as a character, bridging a line not so much between true/false as between author/narrator. In a 2014 essay that circulated widely online, Jonathan Sturgeon writes of "the induction of a new class of memoiristic, autobiographical, and metafictional novels—we can call them autofictions— that jettison the logic of postmodernism in favor of a new position." Such a position argues not simply for more fictionalized biographies like *Dutch* but that the self—any self—is a fiction. Mentioning Karl Ove Knausgaard's *My Struggle*, Nell Zink's *The Wallcreeper*, and the novels of Ben Lerner, Sturgeon asserts, "All of these novels point to a new future wherein the self is considered a *living thing* composed of fictions. . . . Fiction is no longer seen as 'false' or 'lies' or make-believe.' Instead it is more like Kenneth Burke's definition of literature as 'equipment for living.'"[7]

Sturgeon is not alone: any number of respected fiction writers—such as Rachel Cusk, who recently referred to fiction as "fake and embarrassing"— have found a growing impulse toward autobiography. In his increasingly important manifesto, *Reality Hunger*, the repentant fiction writer David Shields named this love of the nonfictional. As Cusk tells an interviewer for the *Guardian*, "I'm certain autobiography is increasingly the only form in all the arts. Description, character—these are dead or dying in reality as well as in art."

While I don't fully agree, it is important to note that this "dying" is not restricted to art but also applies to reality itself, which is rapidly changing—as reality does. It is exactly such changing realities I would argue that, ironically, stoke our hunger for realness. Or is it that while reality stays the same, its representations—what we call realism—change? "Once you have suffered sufficiently, the idea of making up John and Jane and having them do things together seems utterly ridiculous," Cusk argues. "Yet my mode of autobiography had come to an end."[8] In the midst of such a narrative crisis emerges this newfound *autofiction*, which can seem almost hyperreal.

With all this in mind you'd think anyone writing about autofiction would discuss Kosinski as a progenitor, if only as a cautionary tale. Yet rather conspicuously, Kosinski's name rarely comes up—likely because of the problems he raises in the narrative of autofiction's ascent. It does not help that Kosinski's defining autofiction was in defense of what turned out to be his last novel, *The Hermit of 69th Street: The Working Papers of Norbert Kosky* (1988), a mess of a book. Kosinski calls his main character Kosky, "Kosinski without the *sin*." In lieu of a plot, the book is obsessed with the number 69 and the initials *SS*—even the street of the title is a sexual innuendo. The text itself is interrupted by footnotes at the bottom of the page, an idea I love in theory but that here comes out as word salad, looking less like a polyglot bible than a teenager's poetry submission to a high school literary magazine.

In interviews Kosinski would reexplain—indeed, overelaborate—his theory of autofiction: "'Auto,' not for the automobile, but 'auto' for the parts which are mine—autobiographical or self-generated, so to speak. To a degree that also means nonfictional, as in the choices I would make. But at the same time the novel is also total 'fiction.' In autofiction, when I want to use somebody else who utilizes literary vehicles better than I, I use him or her to strengthen the text."[9] For Kosinski, the *auto* of autofiction, though not automatic, helps itself by hijacking other literary "vehicles"; it means autobiographical or self-generated or maybe true; it is anything at all.

Kosinski's notes and quotes and autofiction attempt to anticipate and answer his fiercest critics. Yet his quotes meant to support his notions of autofiction and originality tend to undermine them. *Hermit* quotes poet and essayist Muriel Rukeyser in bold (the regular, roman type is the narrator):

> **The Orgy is not a novel, and I hate the non-word "non-fiction." I have written other works grounded in fact: poems, biographies, films. . . . The Orgy is a book—whatever happened to that category?** . . . Music mixes. So does video and film. Why can't fiction mix?[10]

Hermit isn't so much quoting Rukeyser as conscripting her. Kosinski's boldface ellipses here cover a sin of omission: after "films," Rukeyser originally wrote, "*The Orgy* is entirely factual—even the dolphin—except that I drank the Irish before and after Puck Fair, which I was reporting on assignment for a documentary film director." But as "Jay Kay," yet another authorial stand-in, Kosinski conveniently leaves that out.

Perhaps Kosinski picks *The Orgy* for far different, unstated reasons—is it a way of slyly referring to places like Plato's Retreat, the notorious New York City sex club he frequented? The tell-alls about his visits indicate he usually headed right to the orgy room in order to watch. Certainly his book's form is not just promiscuous but downright orgiastic (and not in a good way). Yet in his book's very unreadability Kosinski had stumbled upon something like the chaotic plethora of information that passes for knowledge in our Age of Euphemism, a time in which social media may provide the ultimate *autofiction*.

DEATH AND DISASTER

What Kosinski created was a studio of style; if he had been his nearly exact contemporary Andy Warhol, also of Eastern European descent, we'd call it a Factory. The name of Warhol's Factory referred to the studio's post-industrial setting—and some might say the dehumanizing treatment of its workers. But the name also suggested his creative process, and its continuity with the studio system of the old masters, the very kinds of painters Van Meegeren would forge. But no matter the number of assistants, Warhol's art and films bear his stamp, if not his signature; till the estate stopped him, he would sign faked Warhols as if they were actually his own. Warhol saw authenticity as a trap, one he was only too happy to spring. It is ironically by fighting his distinctive commercial line from his original career as a successful illustrator—in making his process mechanical—that Warhol made art, which in turn became commercial. His true Factory was one of ideas.

No art-world ideas would save Kosinski. His analogous acts of inpainting and forging provenance are prosecutable crimes in the art world, not just an author's errors or a genre's blurred lines. His biographer describes Kosinski's process cinematically, the books being "produced" in a film sense; Kosinski's way of working in this scheme becomes another kind of studio (complete with casting couch, apparently). This movie metaphor seems to come closest to capturing his process—and is exactly what we do not trust about it. The hoax may make a good movie—almost every romantic comedy must include, besides the now-obligatory yoga-studio scene, an ongoing deception by one of the lovers—but we still like our authors to be writers, not "producers."

Yet Jerzy Kosinski's ultimate crime is not just against provenance or personae or the means of production *but against the very past*. What his methods showed was not his madness but our own—the idea, found online, that every personal detail, not just the author's, was simply material, novel fodder, less evidence than elements to be drawn from or downloaded or dictated, made our own. The past itself could be pillaged, one's very life and pain turned mere party talk. With his paid editors, unacknowledged translators, and ghosts in the publicity machine, Kosinski's work implied not a cosmic composer but the absence of one. His words could be anyone's.

To deemphasize the author just as he proclaimed himself one was to assert if not himself as a god then the universe as authorless. In a fashion, this was what Kosinski's most famous book, 1970's *Being There*, had done: Chance the gardener, the main character's original name, gets misheard as Chauncey Gardiner; he is a character so blank that people who encounter him attribute to him godlike qualities. Chance, indeed. It also turns out that, in structure, plot, and tone at least, Kosinski swiped *Being There* from a onetime famous Polish book he'd read when younger. But *Being There* isn't simply much plagiarized from the earlier Polish best seller; rather, as others have noted, Kosinski had modeled his entire persona—or is it being?—on the characters in it.[11] There's a sinking feeling that his fiction wasn't so much true as Kosinski wasn't all real. Kosinski's greatest forgery was his own story.

There is, in fact, a long tradition of self-impersonation in which someone is mistaken for him- or herself. As traced by Wendy Doniger in *The Woman Who Pretended to Be Who She Was*, self-impersonation occurs throughout world mythology and "Shakespeare, Wagner, Hollywood, and Bollywood": "Many cultures tell stories about people who pretend to be other people pretending to be them, thus in effect masquerading as themselves, impersonating themselves, pretending to be precisely what they are."[12] Someone dresses up as someone else (a boy, say) then must pretend to be herself at some point in the journey (a girl, say); or in cinema, the tradition of the facelift or amnesia, enacted in its most obsessive terms in *Vertigo*. The figure of self-impersonator might be described by the novelty song title my late mother-in-law loved: "I Am My Own Grandpa."

But self-impersonation presumes there's a self there to start with. The self-impersonation found in the hoax is not a means to discover the self, but a way of pretending to have one at all. As with dissociative identity disorder (once called multiple personality disorder), the question with the hoax and plagiarism is not having too many selves but not having a whole one. This dissociative crisis of the self has become cultural, our notions of a unified culture (which, it should be said, was always multiple) thrown into disarray, as witnessed by the fragments and factions exploited in the hoax.

This crisis of the self gets expressed best by the act of plagiarism. Though he didn't retype it word for word, hoaxer Binjamin Wilkomirski used elements of *The Painted Bird*—indeed the very idea—for his memoir of being a child survivor of the Holocaust. *Fragments* (1995) debuted to any number of prizes, garnering international respect and many translations, and earning its author invitations to speak in Israel, the United States, and beyond. Wilkomirski said he was born in Riga, Latvia, and wrote that when quite young he witnessed someone who could be his father shot dead; he pieced together memories that indicated he was sent to concentration camps across Europe, including Majdanek and Auschwitz-Birkenau, where he recalled enduring and seeing many horrors. After the war he ended up in an orphanage in Cracow. From there, he was adopted by a Swiss family and raised in Zurich with a new identity.

Though some early reviewers expressed reservations about Wilkomirski's reportedly recovered memories, the book was also praised and prized for bringing voice to the child survivors of the Holocaust who often had been separated from their families by war and death, and sometimes given new identities, even Christian ones. (If Kosinski had merely told of his actual past, he would likely be celebrated as a child survivor himself, having endured the war with his family living as Catholics.) Wilkomirski told a larger truth of child survivors of the Holocaust, a cause and community he was welcomed by; it turns out, in the end, to have been the very community on which he preyed.

For Wilkomirski was actually born Bruno Grosjean, a Gentile, in Switzerland, and then taken in by the Dössekker family, who adopted him. No shot father, no Jewish identity, no camps: "Wilkomirski" is not an identity, recovered or otherwise, but an invention conforming to the family drama of the orphan that often centers the fairy tale. Even this he took, if not from *Painted Bird*, then from Kosinski's essays about it: "THE PAINTED BIRD can be considered as fairy tales *experienced* by the child, rather than *told* to him," Kosinski would assert.[13] Wilkomirski would also make use of Kosinski's notorious "afterward" to *Bird*'s second edition in which he argues, "A person creates his own personal pattern out of his memories. These patterns are our individual little fictions. For we fit experiences into molds which simplify, shape and give them an acceptable emotional clarity. *The remembered event becomes a fiction, a structure made to accommodate certain feelings.*"[14]

Suspicions rising, the publishers of *Fragments* commissioned the investigator Stefan Maechler to find out the truth; the resulting tour de force *The Wilkomirski Affair: A Study in Biographical Truth* (2001) explores archives, experts, and relatives of the real Dössekker behind the hoax, coming to the inevitable conclusion that the author was indeed not who he said he was. Today Maechler's study appears in print alongside *Fragments*, the investigation's sheer length and sophistication overwhelming the flimsy forgery that prompted it.

By inventing himself as a child survivor, the hoaxer Wilkomirski channeled a broader Swiss guilt over the country's treatment of adopted and "illegitimate" children—not to mention Switzerland's official neutrality during the war, which led the country to rebuff many Jews seeking asylum at the border, turning them away to certain death. "To Bruno Dössekker, being a Jew was synonymous with the Holocaust," writes editor and author Elena Lappin. "Swiss history has nothing remotely similar to offer, nothing so dramatic to survive, or to explain to a man where he came from, or how he is."[15] In her searching and sympathetic "The Man with Two Heads," Lappin investigates Dössekker (whom I will refer to by his actual name whenever I mean the person, not the persona) shortly after his memoir was first questioned by Swiss journalist Daniel Ganzfried, whose own father had been in the camps. In unmasking *Fragments* Ganzfried named another, equally chilling problem facing other survivors and their children: "the idea Binjamin seemed to represent, the one-dimensional notion of the Holocaust survivor as victim." Ganzfried protests that Dössekker "spares us the task of thinking and the frightening experience of the failure of our human comprehension when it faces the fact of Auschwitz." As Lappin indicates, "Dössekker was not the only one to borrow Binjamin Wilkomirski's story; readers did too."[16] The fake memoir not only plagiarizes pain but performs it as it places it on a pedestal—along with we who sympathize, as if sympathy is enough.

What Wilkomirski forged, or what Dössekker's forgery of Wilkomirski offered, was hope. Writer Blake Eskin, whose family name had once been Wilkomirski, writes in his fascinating *A Life in Pieces* about meeting the man really named Dössekker at a family reunion, with the family wishing he were their cousin, and Dössekker of course pretending to be. He had already claimed to be the son of a man in Israel who had lost track of his wife and a son roughly Dössekker's age during the war, both presumed dead—could it now be that his son was alive, if not quite well? Eskin, like Ganzfried and Lappin, indicates the moral peril of this kind of fraud—after all, the would-be Wilkomirski sought to testify on behalf of others, quite literally, recording testimony for archival accounts of the Shoah. He also declared to have developed clinical, therapeutic treatments for survivors and other traumatized children based on the already controversial recovered memory movement; when he presented his theories at conferences serving as a clinical expert, he never mentioned that he alone was the case study he was discussing. Wilkomirski served as forger, fence, and mark all at once.

Silence must be broken, but can it be fixed? "I have no mother tongue, nor a father tongue either," *Fragments* begins. Later on, "Wilkomirski" writes that "the languages I learned later on were never mine, at bottom. They were only imitations of other people's speech." He means because of the Holocaust he's pretending to have experienced, but he could just as easily be describing the hoax, which claims no origins but is all imitation, derivativeness, bottomlessness. Dössekker means to copy not just Kosinski's mythic muteness, or the silence of the hysteric, but the very notion of a "Stepmother Tongue"—the title of a talk found on a copy of Kosinski's résumé tipped into *The Art of the Self*. His world is all symbolic stepmothers. But the fact remains that plagiarists, both of pain and of writing, and forgers, whether of identities or documents, remain dependent on the very documents they discount. Any hoax regularly proclaims itself a reliable record of a life that's without embellishment, its language mere documentary, *au naturel*—"I'm not a poet or a writer," the fake Wilkomirski writes—yet any document that reveals the hoaxers as phony they say does not matter.

Writing of Nobel laureate Elie Wiesel's memoir *Night*, scholar Ruth Franklin reminds us that there is in the memoir form—even in the Holocaust memoir—an element of artistic license and shaping. But this is not the same as untruth. "Like the translator who occasionally veers from the phrasing of an individual line for the sake of the work as a whole, the memoirist too must be at liberty to shape the raw materials into a work of art."[17] I couldn't agree more—it should be clear that my concern is not with fiction but untruth. The hoax is the very absence of truth, which usually means art is absent too—hoaxes regularly substitute claims of reality for imagination, facts for form, acting as if artifice is the antithesis of art. The toxic presence of Holocaust deniers helps us realize how sophisticated those critics who write about Holocaust literature, including its fiction, must be; and how troubling an outright Holocaust hoax is. Besides the cost to truth, and to lived and lost lives, a collateral yet not insignificant cost is to the idea of fiction. Would-be Binjamin Wilkomirski's case offers a different kind of denial.

The contemporary crisis of the self, and its emblem of self-impersonation, meets its height in the Holocaust hoax. This troubling phenomenon includes a book like *Angel at the Fence*, written by Herman Rosenblat, an actual Holocaust survivor whose true tale of survival in Buchenwald would have been inspiring on its own. Instead, he somehow felt he had to fabricate that he first met his wife through the camp fence; and that he survived by her throwing him apples over the fence and years later the two met on a blind date in the States. Before it was debunked, the story won a contest from Oprah Winfrey, who called it the "single greatest love story" she'd ever heard, and was sold as a children's book. The horror story must become a love story, an American tragedy with a happy ending. In his confession, Rosenblat said, "My motivation was to make good in this world. In my dreams, Roma will always throw me an apple, but I now know it is only a dream."[18] The author also contracted for a movie, which the producer claims still might happen. The self, all such efforts and self-impersonations suggest, is no longer enough.

HEARSAY

"He is like family to me even though I haven't met him yet—at least again," Laura Grabowski wrote a friend about the man she knew as Wilkomirksi.[19] Grabowski, with her cane, rare blood disorders from the camps, and story of being renamed and raised by a Christian family, began meeting with the Child Holocaust Survivors Group of Los Angeles in 1997. The first of its kind, the group had, since the mid-1980s, provided a powerful outlet for actual connection among survivors who often had been quite young during the war, and sometimes hidden or given new identities—in short, exactly the kind of group, formal or no, Dössekker pretended to belong to and that more or less accepted him.

Grabowski and Wilkomirski began corresponding, and he said he remembered her from Auschwitz-Birkenau, where both had lived. He recalled not just an earlier name of hers, but her blond hair. Though shy of giving out too much information about herself, Grabowski slowly warmed, Eskin writes, especially in an online group that provided a safe haven for survivors and scholars alike. Wilkomirski and Grabowski would soon meet thanks to the LA child survivors chapter, which sponsored his visit in 1998—the two would perform a duet, as well as her "'Ode to the Little Ones,' which she dedicated to the children who survived the Holocaust and also the one and a half million who didn't." Eskin describes the composition further: "It was a pastiche of '*Oyfn Pripetshok*,' other tunes with an Eastern European Jewish inflection, and the standard 'Try to Remember,'" selections many in the audience thought inappropriate.[20] Such a pastiche seems both telling and familiar, as both Wilkomirski and Grabowski were performing together in other ways.

Grabowski was really born Laurel Willson in Buckley, Washington, and had never been in a concentration camp or directly affected by the war. Her pastiche extended to her persona, the only thing actually adopted—she appears to have directly borrowed Grabowski's character from *Fragments* itself, reflecting the hoaxer's hoax back.

What's more, this wasn't Grabowski's first hoax. As Lauren Stratford she had a previous life as a different kind of survivor: starting with *Satan's Underground* in 1988, Stratford published a best-selling trilogy of books about her childhood Satanic ritual abuse; like the SRA movement, Stratford's confessions turned out to be entirely fabricated. The list of atrocities she endured, including three forced pregnancies that culminated in newborns sacrificed to the devil, grows as horrifying as it does unbelievable—the classic hoax move to inoculate against disbelief. "Stratford" appeared on talk shows ranging from evangelist telethons to *Oprah* (this last detail is widely reported, and still listed on the queen of daytime television's website, though nowhere viewable). Stratford as SRA victim used the language of the Holocaust, comparing "the SRA survivors' lack of evidence with the clandestine nature of Nazi atrocities," foreshadowing her future caper. This hoax was finally debunked by the Christian magazine *Cornerstone*, whose intrepid investigators would later also reveal Stratford's reincarnation as Laura Grabowski in 1999.[21]

There's terrible irony in these two fakers tricking each other, recognizing each other from false, or rather falsified, memories. Game recognizes game, I guess. The hoax is catching, till it catches up with you. This intertwining of lies and hoaxing and "evidence" is the harm the hoax has wrought—it is ultimately a problem wherein, as Grabowski wrote once, "For myself, the Holocaust is about individual suffering."[22] Such a view is not just solipsistic, but marks an epidemic of a self that isn't a self. Yet those who championed recovered memory and Satanic ritual abuse often invoked the Holocaust, saying it too wasn't believed; in criticizing such phenomena, Richard Ofshe and Ethan Watters convincingly argue that "the reasoning used to propagate and bolster the satanic-cult scare is the same sort of reasoning that is currently used by the so-called Holocaust 'revisionists,' who have, with growing efficiency, propagated the belief that it was a hoax."[23] Such a simplistic belief, shared by hoax and hoaxer alike, reduces all experience to suffering; and makes all suffering the same. Needless to say, focusing on individual suffering sidesteps the fact of planned, systematic genocide, which remains far more troubling, and true. Indeed, overwhelming suffering can prove hard to comprehend—the resulting disbelief allows room for the hoax to happen, and for any account to become hyperbolic and filled with hurt.

The hoax involving the Holocaust, especially once it's revealed, often becomes kitsch at best, schlock at worst. Survivor Ruth Klüger calls Holocaust fakes, once revealed, *kitsch*: "A passage is shocking perhaps precisely because of its naive directness when read as the expression of endured suffering; but when it is revealed as a lie, as a presentation of invented suffering, it deteriorates to kitsch. It is indeed a hallmark of kitsch that it is plausible, all too plausible, and that one rejects it only if one recognizes its pseudo-plausibility."[24] With kitsch, sentimentality predominates in a way distinct from campiness, which it sometimes resembles. While camp lies with the viewer and his or her pleasure (or his pleasure pretending to be her, or her him), kitsch remains with its very objects. Selection—or selectiveness—is part of camp's power. It dares you to get it, and if you can: then you're in. Campiness includes by excluding.

Kitsch, on the other hand, seeks to be inclusive, "for everyone"—it attempts to be appealing by being inoffensive. (Consider the garden gnome.) Yet kitsch isn't just filled with sentimentality but, like the forgery, filled with ideology: kitsch is the black lawn jockey, a myth of black servitude and death that signals not just racism but also racialized romance. One popular yet false origin story goes that lawn jockeys memorialize George Washington's horse trainer who froze to death rather than leave the horses untended—but there is often a false honorific note in kitsch, especially when it comes to race. Think, if we must, of approved Nazi art, disturbing in its blatant banality, but also the very idea of Aryan, a fabricated racial romance and past that exudes as well as excludes. Not to mention kills. As with the story of the Washington Redskins' name, with its made-up story of a fake Native that the mascot honors, this kitsch is a retrospective ideal.

Going past kitsch, the hoax as a whole is more typically schlock—a term that likely comes from the Yiddish for "evil" or literally "to strike."[25] A modern word, stemming from 1915 or so, *schlock* denotes a modern problem, much like the contemporary hoax, whose fake blood is meant to be believed.

Schlock one-ups both the mondo film that declares itself documentary and the exploitation film that tells a titillating yet moralistic story—as in the classic *Reefer Madness*—both of which can be read as kitsch or camp. Going past plausible into the outrageous and outlandish, schlock instead is the women-in-prison movie, not really attempting to cover up its thrills with morals; like the vampire movie, an auto-gothic, schlock prefers its blood bright red.

This is the breeding ground for the hoax. Much the way hoaxers such as JT LeRoy took up a so-called folk pornography in order to shock, schlock is a kind of *porno folklore* combining all manner of forces and forms, from fairy tale and tabloid-like headlines to drive-in horror. (I almost wrote "drive-thru.") It seems telling in Kosinski's case that one of the ideas he kept returning to was a potential book or screenplay, a collaboration called *The Vampire's Wife*—an idea that sounds like straight schlock if ever was.

The schlock of *Fragments* is found in its very assumptions of victimhood and pornographic blood. "The pact Wilkomirski implicitly demands of his readers is as follows," Maechler's exposé of *Fragments* notes. "You must read my text as a photographically exact copy of my remembered experience. I am no poet inventing stories. You will come to know the truth if you learn to read between the lines and surmise what is not said, for language is not my real mode of expression and I lack words for what is most essential. . . . Never forget: I come from a world divided into victims and villains, and I am among the most innocent of all victims." This pact is not only silent, so is the young "Wilkomirski" whom he turns mute as the hoax pretends to. What's more, Wilkomirski's fake memoir "explicitly offers many such lacunae," routinely employing silences, Maechler argues, for the reader to inevitably solve: "The moral pact leaves readers scarcely any choice but to fill these lacunae with their own sedimentary knowledge of the Shoah and to read the text as the genuine story of a survivor."[26]

The lacunae in the hoax we fill with longing.

HERESY

We often think of memory as purely personal, but memory is cultural too. The stories we tell ourselves lodge in our memory, and generate others; in this way cultural memory mirrors the process the individual undergoes. This is why narrative can be said to undergo a general crisis, as began in the 1990s and continues in our Age of Euphemism: the stories we tell ourselves fail to make sense, for a time, and we tend to make things up about the stories themselves. If the hoax is regularly about conflicts, one of these isn't just over history such as in Holocaust hoaxes, but over memory itself.

The late neuroscientist Oliver Sacks has written brilliantly of the vagaries of memory, noting that "frequently, our only truth is narrative truth, the stories we tell each other, and ourselves—the stories we continually recategorize and refine. Such subjectivity is built into the very nature of memory, and follows from its basis and mechanisms in the human brain. The wonder is that aberrations of a gross sort are relatively rare, and that, for the most part, our memories are relatively solid and reliable."[27] The stories Sacks tells do change: he describes his book *A Leg to Stand On* "as a sort of neurological novel or short story, but one which is rooted in personal experience and neurological fact."[28] Following on Charcot and Freud, this so-called neurological novel, like Capote's "nonfiction novel" *In Cold Blood*, means to tell the truth in a shapely fashion; it too faced critiques, not of factuality, but of being too literary. Sacks seeks nothing less in his reminiscences than a new science—or way of speaking of it—one that plagiarists and hoaxers would soon exploit. But the medical narrative has always proved literary, not to mention nostalgic: Breuer and Freud's famed *Studies on Hysteria* declared in 1895 that "the hysteric suffers mainly from reminiscences"; the hoax often does too.

In an essay written two years before his death in 2015, Sacks discusses his memoir of his wartime childhood in London that recounts two bombs landing in his backyard during the Blitz in London, one unexploded and one quite on fire. Speaking to his older brother after the book's publication, he learns that while the first was exactly right, he in fact wasn't actually there to see the second thermite bomb, never did feel what he vividly described as its "terrible, white-hot heat," nor saw his father and brothers try to douse the bomb with water and the resulting "vicious hissing and sputtering when the water hit the white-hot metal, and meanwhile the bomb was melting its own casing and throwing blobs and jets of molten metal in all directions." Rather, Sacks knew of the experience only from a letter from his eldest brother that "enthralled" him and had "taken it for a memory of my own."[29]

Memory is less a plagiarist or forger than a collaborator in the benign sense. It is social as well as individual, especially with early memories. As Stefan Maechler writes in a follow-up article to his exposure of Wilkomirski, "If memory is an act of construction, it does not depend only on the individual person but on the current context; it is not the action of an isolated person but a social practice." Maechler is in many ways sympathetic to the boy once called "Bruno Grosjean," forced by the state to be "moved from one foster family to another, thus being deprived of a person he could relate to": "Bruno Dössekker thus had very poor prospects for developing an autobiographical memory and for performing the task, difficult for all adopted children, of linking his biological and social origins in a meaningful way."[30] No wonder he would resort to now-discredited means of recovered memories, from visualization to rather suggestive hypnosis—Dösseker reenacted the history of the occult and psychodrama as the hoax often does, from multiple personality disorder to Satanic ritual abuse. "Wilkomirski" adopted what amounts to his third name as a way of adopting himself.

It is exactly these social aspects of memory that argue against Dössekker's outright fabrications. To remember is not (necessarily) to prove, but memory can, in the cultural realm, constitute a powerful antidote to official history, recalling humanity in the face of inhumanity, from slavery to the Shoah. "The truth is always something that is told, not something that is known," Susan Sontag writes. "If there were no speaking or writing, there would be no truth about anything. There would only be what is."[31] As Sacks puts it in his essay "Speak, Memory," "This sort of sharing and participation, this communion, would not be possible if all our knowledge, our memories, were tagged and identified, seen as private, exclusively ours. Memory is dialogic and arises not only from direct experience but from the intercourse of many minds." Its collective quality is all our responsibility, and to claim one's memories above all others is actually to do violence to memory, and its social pact. This is why the hoax matters so much.

The hoax uses memory's mysteries against it. The fake Holocaust memoir goes further, exploiting the gap between what we know and what we can understand or accept. "I wanted to know what other people had gone through back then," the man who would be Binjamin Wilkomirski wrote. "I wanted to compare it with my own earliest memories that I carried around inside me. I wanted to subject them to intelligent reason, and arrange them in a pattern that made sense. But the longer I spent at it, the more I learned and absorbed empirically, the more elusive the answer—in the sense of what actually happened—became."[32] Such a gap is not only exactly where Wilkomirski the hoaxer situates his tall tale, but also an idealized yet tragic place where the real Dössekker lives. Only in this way, his search for self—fragmented like a bomb, or false as the vampire's teeth—is our own.

FIVE

Hack

Heaven

❧{Of the journalist & the liar}❧

Beware of stories you want to be true, for whatever reason.
—BEN BRADLEE
A Good Life

FAKES
IN AMERICAN
JOURNALISM

BY MAX SHEROVER

PRICE TWENTY-FIVE CENTS

Fakes in American Journalism, 1914.

CHAPTER 15

Glass Ceilings

If anyone cared to notice, the likes of JT LeRoy, Binjamin Wilkomirski, and Jerzy Kosinski heralded a future in which folks were not necessarily famous for fifteen minutes but real for thirty minutes, minus commercials. The arrival of the millennium promised not so much the apocalypse as a proliferation of stories meant to be true, and not just hoaxes: the 1990s alone saw the advent of the memoir craze; that misnomer, reality television; the growing heights of gangsta rap; and, at the end of that decade, the nonevent and mass hysteria of Y2K, that supposed computer armageddon. All of these frequently unreliable narratives the hoax borrowed from or was inspired by, substituting the supposed self for the story.

I experienced this crisis in narrative firsthand around the same time, while editing *Let's Go: USA 1991* while I was in college. It was the first time I had spent long hours on a project whose ultimate goal was less art than accuracy; even then I thought the two could be related. The publishing manager of *Let's Go* that summer would later become known, and ultimately notorious: his name was Ravi Desai, and he went on ten years later to commit a series of large-scale hoaxes that I can still hardly wrap my mind around. His hoaxes cross all manner of fakery available to us, inventing a few new ones: from identity fraud to forgery; from publishing a fake online diary to bigamy; to committing what can only be called financial fabulism, promising several institutions to donate in the name of poetry millions of dollars that never materialized. Some of his exploits made the papers and others had many lives on the Internet; all garnered attention, and worse, led to pain for those who published, believed, or loved him.

Though headed for a business career, Desai had shifted to English for his senior year in order to write what Harvard calls a creative thesis, turning in a book-length manuscript of poems the year after I worked under him. To read Desai's 1991 manuscript, *Poison for a Cure*, as retained in Harvard's archives, is to discover that remarkable yet indescribable thing: promise. So you can imagine how devastated the entire office was the day Ravi called us all to a meeting where, voice cracking, he announced: *I have cancer.* We all sat stunned; a few cried. He was so young. After the meeting, some made their way to him, to console and comfort him. Others kept their distance, whether from fear or from uncertainty of just what to do.

Looking back we're left with a different kind of uncertainty. It seems inconceivable, but given all that came after, it seems clear we too were the victims of Desai's hoaxing. Hoaxes, after all, infect our sense of what's true—we come to mistrust not only others but also ourselves and our own instincts. I hate to think that the elegant poems in his thesis are somehow hoaxing too, but then hoaxing may be the last great undiagnosed addiction, poison instead of cure. To mimic the side effects of chemo, Ravi went so far as to shave his own head.

His eventual downfall is recounted in many places: from *Slate* magazine, which he duped not once but twice, first claiming under his real name that he worked for "Quantum, a hard-disk-drive manufacturer" and then using a false identity to file a story as a BMW executive; to *Poets & Writers*, which uncovered how his pledges of millions of dollars to several universities never came through.[1] Financial guru Jim Cramer's book *Confessions of a Street Addict* (2002) devotes several chapters to Desai's falsifying work at the pioneering stock-trading website start-up Cramer launched, not to mention Desai's apparent efforts to blackmail Cramer after he was discovered.

His was an emotional pyramid scheme. Much the way faux journalists Stephen Glass and Jayson Blair fabricated sources and deceived fact-checkers with fake receipts, business cards, and websites, Desai realized results were too often no more than what was claimed on paper—like any other forger, he is less a writer than a pusher of paper. Neither Desai on a small scale, nor Bernie Madoff on an almost unimaginable international one a few years later, appears as one person committing an unconscionable fraud but rather is symbolic of a larger cultural bankruptcy—a system already shaky, now shook. After his collapse with the start-up, Desai, according to Cramer, ended up driving a permanent wedge between Cramer and his longtime friend Martin Peretz, then owner of the *New Republic* (and partner in Cramer's new web venture, not to mention the best man at his wedding). Peretz was surely sensitive to such deceptions: shortly before Desai entered the scene, his magazine was revealed in 1998 to have played host to one of history's most notorious cases of falsified journalism in the form of Stephen Glass.

"When church and state are reconciled, the unconventional bit of religious lore is called heresy. When, however, ecclesiastical authority, either spiritual or temporal, wanes, apocryphal literature abounds," warns Curtis MacDougall in his classic *Hoaxes* (1940). "During periods in which science is largely a matter of academic concern to mathematicians and laboratory logicians, the masses are unconcerned except when some theorist is so rash as to question Holy Writ. When, however, the results of experimentation begin to become evident in everyday life, through technological developments, labor-saving devices and mechanical recreational facilities, no supposed discovery made possible by the microscope or telescope is too marvelous to be believed."[2] This sounds awfully familiar, describing what led to the Moon Hoax of 1835 or the hysteria of the fin de siècle as well as suggesting that widespread access to the Internet and other advances are one more culprit in the contemporary hoax.

Yet the Internet alone is not to blame. Our millennial crop of hoaxes—represented by JT LeRoy in novels, Margaret B. Jones in memoir, Tom MacMaster online, and in journalism by Stephen Glass and his vast fabrications—signals our age's narrative crisis a full century after the lyrical one that was modernism. There have been many recent responses to the current collapse of the sacred stories we tell ourselves: from fiction that looks like biography (what we've seen called "autofiction"); long-form journalism that abandons voice in favor of story (often just great writing); to reality television and the wild west of the Internet itself (including its impostor phenomenon known as "catfishing"). One would be tempted not to call this a crisis at all if it weren't for the proliferation of the hoax before and after the millennium, the post-factual present, embodying what philosopher Harry G. Frankfurt calls "the contemporary proliferation of bullshit."[3]

It isn't that the contemporary hoax provides "a different kind of truth" but that it offers far less. A whole lie would almost be welcome, but hoaxes won't extend us the courtesy of respecting the truth enough to betray it. Instead, we have become surrounded by the halfway, mealymouthed, politicking habit of bullshit. Frankfurt's *On Bullshit* reminds us of b.s.'s particular perniciousness:

"Both in lying and in telling the truth people are guided by their beliefs concerning the way things are. These guide them as they endeavor either to describe the world correctly or to describe it deceitfully," he writes. "Each responds to the facts as he understands them, although the response of the one is guided by the authority of the truth, while the response of the other defies that authority and refuses to meet its demands. The bullshitter ignores these demands altogether. He does not reject the authority of the truth, as the liar does, and oppose himself to it. He pays no attention to it at all. By virtue of this, bullshit is a greater enemy of the truth than lies are." The hoax is bullshit that believes its own bullshit, so much so that it starts to act like it doesn't stink—or worse, knows that in our current overwhelmed state, misinformation and information feel the same. It's all just denial. "One who is concerned to report or to conceal the facts assumes that there are indeed facts that are in some way both determinate and knowable. His interest in telling the truth or in lying presupposes that there is a difference between getting things wrong and getting them right, and that it is at least occasionally possible to tell the difference."[4]

The timing of this narrative and b.s. crisis may appear especially strange—for the 1990s were exactly when journalists such as Laura Hillenbrand, Susan Orlean, and Jon Krakauer were exploring a form in reaction to the showy "verbal pyrotechnics" of the New Journalism of the 1960s, one that "approached the craft of narrative journalism in a quieter way," as Wil S. Hylton writes in the *New York Times*. "They still built stories around characters and scenes, with dialogue and interior perspective, but they cast aside the linguistic showmanship that drew attention to the writing itself."[5] Such "New Narrative" writers, as I'll call them, are instead more invested in story and in staying out of the way.

But this New Narrative, or return to the old, left out something that the current crop of hoaxers, and even our politicians, have sensed and made use of: a need in the audience and the hoaxer to fill the facts with fancy, to trick the audience as badly as it sometimes thought it should be treated. This was distinct from the 1960s—though they brought us the New Journalism, the sixties didn't see a steady stream of hoaxes. The war then was for truth, not against it; the Vietnam War provided enough euphemism and bunk to go around. By the 1990s, if the New Narrative offered a solution for the narrative crisis, so did the hoax: sometimes we want a storyteller to boss us around. Judging by the attendant hoax's popularity, we crave the hoaxer's excuses as much as the story itself.

The hoax not only telegraphs the loss of story; it also appears a deep cause of such loss, less mourning it than almost literally making up for it. In journalism, where facts first get wedded to narrative, we can see up close this narrative crisis, which the hoax both represses and represents.

GLASS HOUSES

In a time often called "post-factual"—when press releases get repurposed by lazy reporters as articles, and terms like *advertorial* and *edutainment* are spoken with a straight face; when newspapers themselves are threatened, indeed menaced, with extinction; in the aftermath of a 2012 presidential campaign that saw "fact-checking" dismissed as optional, or a priggish liability; and when the 2016 president-elect has gone on record to argue that the sitting president was not American, by which he appears to mean, is too black—we cannot be too skeptical. No wonder President Donald Trump's most frequent word is "unbelievable"—in our Age of Euphemism, belief substitutes for truth, and truth is a commodity grown increasingly rare, a raw material no longer self-evident but made palatable by a writer, or a spin doctor, or by technology itself. Our devices will protect us from our own devices.

Apart from poets, those "unacknowledged legislators," to use Shelley's term, the reckoners of such a fallen, for-sale world have traditionally been reporters. The various forgers, frauds, and fabulists that journalism has endured in recent years have only hurt the idea of reporting as an essential part of democracy. The healthy skepticism that is the journalist's chief tool has lately succumbed to a contagious cynicism about journalism itself, if not an outright mistrust of the media as a whole. The First Amendment shall be last.

"Hack Heaven." "Ratted Out." "A Fine Mess." "Writing on the Wall." "Probable Claus." "Spring Breakdown." "State of Nature." "The Young and the Feckless." "After the Fall." The titles alone of pieces published by faux journalist Stephen Glass provide an unwitting, ironic indictment of their author. Several, and others, of these titles appear at the end of *Shattered Glass* (2003), the terrific biopic about his faking stories during his time at the *New Republic*. Five years after his lying spree was exposed, the movie used the titles as part of a framing device that implicates Glass's fantasias. Onscreen, they act almost as the refrain of a ballad, in which the opening and closing repetitions provide far different meanings given what's transpired in between. Though some were likely provided by clever editors, Glass's titles dare to expose the very lies they cover. Apart from money, and fame, the fabulist's true motive is a strange combination of getting away with it and getting caught, hinting all along.

Journalism is, we expect when we pick up or log on to a paper, the last bastion of "fact-checking"—information verified independently by outside sources. As iconic newspaper editor Ben Bradlee notes, the presumption readers and their editors have about reporters is not just neutrality but trustworthiness; the *Washington Post*'s profound history with the Watergate investigations under Bradlee only reaffirm this. Like Clifford Irving before them, both Glass and notorious *New York Times* fabulist Jayson Blair would fabricate not just stories but sources, exploiting the fact-checking feedback loop in which facts and quotes that cannot be independently or easily verified are provided by reporters themselves. Behind every fabulist is a frustrated forger.

Helping to diminish a venerable institution like the *New Republic* or the *New York Times* can lead to book deals: *The Fabulist* for Glass in 2003, *Burning Down My Masters' House* for Blair in 2004; Glass reportedly sold his book in the middle six figures. The desire, after the fact, for fabulists to consider their original fictions or late confessions as somehow radical and provocative is part and parcel of their initial delusions of grandeur. These authors aren't mere embellishers or aggrandizers, especially of the self; they indict the process and very idea of nonfiction, which finds its purest or at least most immediate form in reportage.

Upon hearing of Glass suing to be admitted to the California bar after he studied to be a lawyer, Adam L. Penenberg, original exposer of Glass's hoaxes, quipped that, like journalism, lawyering was yet another disgraced institution that couldn't be harmed by a confessed liar. But this quip only highlights the way Penenberg (now a journalism professor) remains concerned that a cleaned-up Glass hasn't really changed his ways. This is apparent enough in *The Fabulist*, a money-grabbing deal disguised as a novel that seemed designed to displace Glass's responsibility for what he did. A memoir might have been more welcome, though who would have believed it? As Penenberg notes in light of Glass's legal appeal,

Both in 1998 and in the present Glass has refrained from telling the whole truth. It took him more than a decade to provide a complete

list of articles he had fabricated, and only when pressed. He hid behind obfuscation when caught claiming he had worked with publications whose reputations he had besmirched to identify his published
falsehoods and blamed his harsh childhood for fueling his compulsion
to lie. When he was supposed to write fact he wrote fiction; with his
novel he wrote fiction and assumed the role of victim when he could
have written fact and told us what happened. Never has he fully come
clean. Are these the actions of a man who has rehabilitated himself?[6]

Glass's novel does feel less like a coded confession than a creeptastic evasion,
portraying those who found out his lies as somehow heartless. The opposite
of a roman à clef—a "novel with a key" made up of thinly veiled fiction—
The Fabulist is a *memoir de masque*. The feeling persists that even in fiction
Glass cannot tell the truth.

Ironically, Glass's very unreality makes his novel hard to read—or believe. "His stories were interesting only because they were purportedly true,"
Jonathan Chait writes. "The characters in his stories"—that is, his journalism—
"as in his novel, lack any depth or believability."[7] Hanna Rosin—the model
for Chloë Sevigny's character in the movie—would offer "a few guesses of
my own about why Steve so easily turned into 'the fabulist," including that
"Steve could so easily fabricate people because at some level he doesn't see
them as real, only as superficial extensions of himself. The characters in the
book have no existence except in relation to Steve; they are classified by
their level of loyalty to him."[8] *The Fabulist* manages to make all the other
people around the protagonist look bad, and "our hero, meanwhile, is a soul
repentant," Rosin writes. "He is humble, contrite. He is sad and afraid. He
sweats, he shakes, he is haunted by night terrors. And he's also a few shades
hipper than the original."[9] His book makes "Glass" better, unlike James
Frey, whose hoax meant to make him *worser*: no matter the direction, they
are meant to be made more interesting. The effect lets us know *The Fabulist*
is just an extension of Glass's hoax, or at least its fulfillment.

The book's protagonist (named "Stephen Glass" in a pretense of autofiction) plays the victim, as in this part of the opening:

Please don't misunderstand me: What I did was a terrible mistake—a
serious, damaging wrong—and they are correct to say so. However,
there are some individuals, journalists mainly, who think I should

always be ashamed, and perhaps always afraid, too. Because they are liberals, and have faith in rehabilitation, they never speak of it that way, but I believe they feel it profoundly. They cannot understand how after violating all their rules, fair and important rules, I go on living among them. If I am not punished further, what good is the salutary order they have imposed?[10]

Questions of rehabilitation and suffering are regularly posed by the journalist and the fabulist, over and over again. But there's no question of one thing: were you to find *nonapology* in the dictionary, it surely would have as its chief example a fiction disguising an autobiography from someone who, no sooner than he claims his lies to have been an accident, a mere "mistake," he then provides an incredibly big *but* (disguised here as *However*). Glass last resorts to the ultimate bogeyman, "They," providing the harbinger of a half-hoax world to follow.

One difficulty for Glass and his case is that, when arguing why he should be allowed to practice, his defenders resort to old, familiar narratives—a further sign of the narrative crisis that the hoax both captures and colludes with. One such narrative is "an awful childhood," in his case one of withheld love and high standards—a kind of prototypical immigrant story (though he's not a recent immigrant) that makes it as much American as anything. If his sob backstory sounds like something from a John Hughes movie, it might be because Glass hails from just outside Chicago, where most of Hughes's films are set.

Another familiar narrative, or defense strategy, is what twelve-step programs call "making amends"—Glass's apologies, we're told, consisted of *handwritten* letters to those he may have harmed. The fact of their being handwritten suggests to his defenders that somehow his inked-out words are more sincere than print. The irony here is that those who support Glass's bid to the bar seem not to understand that his "crime" did not just occur in print *but was the act of writing itself.* Glass must have sensed this: once he was discovered, he went so far as to employ a defense team to make sure that in any fessing up to fabrications he would not actually be admitting legal wrongdoing—all in order to prevent prosecution. Even his confessions are couched. Glass, in fact, did not admit most of his fictions until the eve of his book tour, and most of the rest only in his attempt to practice law. Could he still be said to have performed restitution? Need he? Is restitution more about *performing* these days?

The Supreme Court of California, which in January 2014 handed down a ruling against his being allowed to practice law, seemed to think so. In the compelling thirty-five-page ruling—almost as long as Glass's entire output as a fabulist—the judges noted that "it was not until the California State Bar moral character proceedings that Glass reviewed all of his articles, as well as the editorials The New Republic and other journals published to identify his fabrications, and ultimately identified fabrications that he previously had denied or failed to disclose." What's more, "many of his efforts from the time of his exposure in 1998 until the 2010 hearing, however, seem to have been directed primarily at advancing his own well-being rather than returning something to the community. His evidence did not establish that he engaged in truly exemplary conduct over an extended period."[11] The fact that only in 2015 did Glass begin paying back the fees to magazines that had paid him seventeen years before presumes that it's the magazines, not us readers, who need to be made whole.

No one wants gratuitous punishment or continued suffering, but then, suffering is actually the hoaxer's preferred métier. Long before being caught, modern hoaxers trade suffering the way Bernie Madoff traded fake shares—all in the name of "sharing." Afterward, suffering inevitably becomes the key character witness in the hoaxer's defense, from James Frey to Glass to Lance Armstrong, all of whom deny the suffering of others in the present while invoking and stressing their own past pain. The ultimate problem remains that admitting you hoaxed ultimately doesn't get you out of what you hoaxed about.

You may find gonzo the fact that I would rather read a collection of Glass's "collected stories"—that is, the false news stories he filed—than his novel. In that way, it reminds me of the *Complete Uncollected Short Stories* of the late J. D. Salinger, a book that doesn't exist—at least not yet—except in the pirated versions that circulate now and then, gathering all that he published in the *New Yorker* but would never let be reprinted during his lifetime.[12] While there's no comparison in terms of quality or of import, the *Uncollected Glass*—now mostly expunged from the record—tells us something about how fantasy often masquerades as fact, and tells us something about the very truths Glass's lies obscure. He is in this way a long-lost member of the Glass family who figure in—you might say make up—Salinger's beloved, as-yet-uncollected epic.

How then to measure the damage not just to those Glass lied to, personally and professionally, but also to his former profession that has suffered in his wake? Not to mention the truth itself?

IN BLACK AND WHITE

The hoax's addictive nature reflects not ease but discomfort with its subject. If no one fell for the hoax that would be one thing, but hoaxes are embraced for a time because they confirm what we suspect—but cannot know or, better yet, prove. When monologuist Mike Daisey embellishes stories about Apple computers on public radio, or Greg Mortenson his days in an Afghan village, the results are not meant to nuance the actual issue but to pretend they personally witnessed far worse. When a former soldier pretends to have witnessed the attack on the Embassy House in Benghazi, everything is not only *worser*, but he himself is badder—scaling walls, engaging in hand-to-hand combat, seeing the ambassador's death firsthand. The hoax's guns are always smoking, buoying up our worst suspicions without evidence or eyewitness. This is why it is so important that the journalist rely on and vet sources, plural, and that these sources are neither fabricated nor plagiarized. Doing so reaffirms the very idea of witnessing, of seeing and then saying.

The *New Republic* proves a central character in the history of the hoax, dating from early in the twentieth century. Some, surely its editors, might say it is because of the *New Republic*'s long-standing history but you'd be better off noting that it may be its position as both a political and a cultural magazine: the hoax too is deeply political. Especially as it wasn't part of a public trust like newspapers, the very mix of public and private has left the *New Republic* open to seeking out facts that fit its views rather than the other way around. In a time when public and private have become not just mixed but mixed up, the magazine would seem a fitting host for the hoax surprise party.

This is as true in our Age of Euphemism as it was in 1916 and the debut of the Spectra hoax, that fake modernist movement started by poets Witter Bynner and Arthur Davison Ficke just before the entry of the United States into the Great War. After what the late William Jay Smith describes in his irrepressible *The Spectra Hoax* as "ten quarts of excellent Scotch in ten days,"[13] Bynner and Ficke took on the persona of Emanuel Morgan and Anne Knish, respectively, publishing their mock poems first in the little magazines and the glossies. The story goes that when two prominent magazine editors saw the page proofs of *Spectra* on Bynner's desk in the house where he was staying, Bynner quickly managed to explain he had gotten an advance copy of the promising publication; promptly, the magazine asked him to review it. His November 1916 piece in the *New Republic*, reviewing his own hoax, is a paragon of self-parody: "Certainly their theory demands an art not stopping short with direct notation by the senses, but reaching connotation of all kinds. And they are ambitious, without being too solemn!"[14] Where Spectra was comedy masked as tragedy, using the solemnity of the *New Republic* against it, it would be ambition that came to dominate the journalistic hoax, its farce made over into fact.

Star reporter Ruth Shalit burst onto the scene at the *New Republic* a few years before Stephen Glass, whose "work" there has overshadowed her former star status. Shalit was just as instrumental in establishing the young neocon voice that the magazine came to be associated with, as well as the notion that gov jocks and pundits could themselves be the stars (though I confess I hadn't heard of her before working on this book).[15] After her first cover story at the *New Republic* in 1993—which the *Washington City Paper*, not unadmiringly, says "established Shalit as an attack-journalist *Wunderkind*"—Shalit's most infamous story two years later would be another cover story about affirmative action at the *Washington Post* after Ben Bradlee's tenure.[16] Her "Washington Post in Black & White" is marred by inaccuracies: both the publisher and the editor of the *Post* attacked Shalit, saying there were "somewhere between three dozen and 40" factual errors. What's more, the *Post* editor Len Downie's withering response accused Shalit of plagiarism, falsehoods, and "racial McCarthyism" while damning the entire *New Republic*. Downie's accusation of the magazine's "big lie propaganda" would be featured in the pages of *the New Republic* itself, along with a reply by Shalit and a further letter by the *Post*'s longtime publisher, Donald Graham, who called the *New Republic* "the last practitioner of de facto segregation since Mississippi changed."[17]

The strong response by the *Post*'s editors and publishers might be expected; more remarkable are the extensive critiques from others in the weeks after Shalit's piece on the *Washington Post* ran. "Journalistic Unabomber"; guilty of "racist chic": the names Shalit was called, and that she sometimes refers to herself by, indicate the extremity of the feeling about the issue as well as about her writing. "Many fellow reporters in town now regard Shalit as a careless ingenue at best and a pathological plagiarist at worst," the *City Paper*'s John Cloud reports.[18] In a contemporary interview in the *American Journalism Review*, Shalit reacts to being viewed in her words "as a hatchet woman who set out to take powerful people down a peg or two. This has been very sobering and chastening and, I think, in the long run, valuable because I've realized what it's like to be on the other side. I've realized what it's like to have my arguments mischaracterized. What it's like to have quotes taken out of context. What it's like to be misquoted." Shalit, however, was accused of not just getting quotes wrong but also facts. When reminded of this by her interviewer, Shalit has to admit again "there were several factual inaccuracies. The Post had two black reporters, not zero, on its national staff in 1972, and a couple of other errors of that degree, and one serious mistake."[19] There were many more than Shalit owns up to, but needless to say, knowing how many black reporters were at the paper early on might have been a good idea in a piece on affirmative action.

It also might have been a good idea to get the promotion of Milton Coleman right—the same "savvy city editor" in Bradlee's words who had sounded a warning on the Janet Cooke hoax over a decade earlier—to assistant managing editor for Metro News.[20] Shalit attributed his promotion to being merely race based, when by most accounts this appears patently untrue, if not outright insulting, to the longtime reporter. The "serious mistake" she glosses over involves Shalit incorrectly saying a city contractor had served time for corruption, when in fact he hadn't. His race seems the only place where race is unstated, merely implied, in any of the accounts.

Rather than a "derivative racist," as she labeled herself, Shalit would later proclaim herself pro-affirmative action—"If you go back and read the piece, I say that in a diverse society you need a diverse staff"—though the piece was widely read as saying quite the opposite. She may in fact be more in favor of it than the *New Republic*, which had no African Americans on staff in 1995. "We've had African American interns before," she protested, which in its tone deafness, might as well be *Some of my best blacks are my friends*. The *New Republic* may have had no racial difficulties simply because for decades it had been all-white. As the *Post* publisher Donald Graham writes of her article, "Ms. Shalit describes a place [the *Post*] where blacks and whites watch each other closely, where race becomes an excuse for some and a flashpoint for others. Sounds like America in 1995. Except, of course, for THE NEW REPUBLIC. (Motto: Looking for a qualified black since 1914)."[21]

Perhaps the most troubling aspect of Shalit as "derivative racist" is the derivative part. Not only is the racism unoriginal, but around the time of her cover story, Shalit admitted that she had not once or twice but three times plagiarized, claiming that the mistakes "came from having somebody else's words on my screen. From downloading Nexis searches as text files and then putting them onto my screen and later conflating them with my own notes. That is always a bad idea."[22] And a rather flimsy excuse. But Shalit isn't interested in her reputation, insomuch as she feels she can reinvent herself as much as she can change facts: "That's the nice thing about journalism. You can invent a new persona for yourself with every piece." In her case, self-regard matches self-invention; as Shalit continued under accusations of inaccuracy and even plagiarism, it would seem her concern is mostly with her star status, suggesting that "there are several ways you can learn those basic journalistic practices. One is to start in a small market covering the council and police and getting taken to the woodshed by your gravelly voiced editor when you don't get something right. Another, more unconventional way is to explode onto the scene, crash and burn, experience the sort of melodramatic thunderclap of denunciation from the journalistic community."

Shalit certainly takes a strange lesson from her errors. "What this has taught me is that whenever you go after journalists, especially one of the biggest, most powerful media institutions in the country, you've got to make sure your piece is triple riveted and that you've gone over every line, and you don't give them any weapons to use against you because they will," she says. It takes the interviewer, Alicia C. Shepard, to remind Shalit that it isn't just journalists that don't like inaccuracies; everyone deserves to be accurately rendered: "Any subject you tackle ought to be triple riveted." And quadruple checked. This isn't just for the subject's sake, but the author's—the author whose work does not feel riveted but rigged or riddled with errors soon loses the reader's trust. Shalit seems to confirm what certain readers suspect, but also what nonreaders fear—that all journalists have an agenda, one not always hidden.

This is exactly why we should remember Shalit's transgressions—because these days they would barely register as mistakes, much less fatal ones. She foreshadows our politics disguised as facts—predicting the online advocacy that regards facts as the only luxury that should be taxed; or perhaps as a consequence, that views anyone in the news or behind it as inherently suspect or corrupt. "The Washington Post in Black & White" actually led not just to a retraction, or recantation, or correction—all distinctions worth exploring—but to a lawsuit against the *New Republic*. Still, after the suit was settled, "Shalit was allowed to come back from leave for reasons that are a mystery even to the people who decided to keep her," the late, great David Carr reported. She had become a celeb reporter, featured in the magazines she once wrote for, making "the quintessentially '90s journey from media employee to media celebrity. One particularly perfervid profile of Shalit mentioned her in the same breath as Hemingway and E. B. White and suggested that we will all anxiously await her memoirs one day."[23]

What finally undid her was not actually getting caught. Shalit eventually resigned from the magazine in 1999 after continuing problems with sources and plagiarism: "She [Shalit] used then-Legal Times writer Daniel Klaidman's prose in a New Republic story about the young Turks in the Clinton administration. Less than a year later, she was discovered lifting the National Journal's Paul Starobin's language about presidential candidate Steve Forbes. There were two other instances from the same period of linguistic kleptomania," Carr would report.[24] Shalit's computer keyboard just seemed stuck on steal. "There are many who suggest that the problem was more split-personality than split-screen."[25] How to explain her continued theft yet continued high profile? Much like plagiarist Jonah Lehrer, Shalit remained scandal-proof for quite some time, preordained as a brand who sells.

Are some ships too big to sink? The title of an interview with her, and a common excuse that Shalit herself used—her youth—is posed as a question: "Too Much Too Soon?" Such an idea ironically is the same one that dominates her notion of affirmative action, demonized as promoting unqualified, which is to say black, candidates to positions they don't deserve. (Shalit relies on numbers to try to explain why there aren't more black journalists when, much like the misnomer *minority*, numbers fail to explain what are actually disparities of power.) Might some of what stoked her fame be the very affirmative action she indicts? In 1995 Shalit dismissed the prospect of her being hired because she was a woman, but after her resignation four years later she recognizes gender somewhat, all while insulting other women: "I think there is something more pruriently interesting in profiling a fallen woman, especially a young woman. There would have been less sadistic scrutiny if I had been a man or if I looked like Sarah McClendon. But then again, it probably cuts both ways."[26]

Shalit's admittedly well-written articles, with their smaller fabrications, just-so misquotes, and big plagiarisms, don't appear at first like other hoaxes until you realize they wrestle with race in much the way more pointed hoaxes do—seizing on panic and stoking it, expressing a country's anxiety, subtly or blatantly, over race and the workplace. The hoax, plagiarism too, almost always provides what we suspect but cannot prove: *Poof!* Here's magical proof, an abundance of evidence, actually masking stereotypes and clichés. Her mention of the "fallen woman" alone points out a theme that courses through American culture and history, one traditionally better expressed in the novel, where the fallen woman is often paired with blackness, either metaphorically (as in Hawthorne's "Black Veil" or in much of Hemingway) or with actual black characters (Melville, Twain, Harper Lee). Dark doubles abound.

Shalit remains linked with Glass, if only because Charles Lane, the *New Republic* editor who would fire Glass first, eventually edged out Shalit too. In the aftermath, according to Shalit, "It was 'Steve Glass, fabulist' and 'Ruth Shalit, plagiarist.' The rest of who I was and what I had done got dumped. And that was a drag, because if you stand back, there are good pieces with solid reporting, and that are true, by the way." True, though not necessarily all her own. "Shalit was a misdemeanor plagiarist, shoplifting prosaic passages that didn't merit coveting; it was her recidivism that set her apart," Carr writes. This alone is a misperception—like a minor heart attack, minor plagiarism is something that happens to someone else.

Shalit disdains Glass, calling him "a boring fabulist, the Milli Vanilli of journalism." Shalit is the Vanilla Ice (though *him* I prefer). She went from sampling the work of others to hawking herself as the ultimate franchise— then left journalism for a job in advertising. Shalit's Hot Tub Time Machine was set years ahead, managing to predict a time called Now when plagiarism and fame would be synonymous; when one's "samples" would become more and more obvious, whether a rapper or a writer, and when the self isn't just reporting the story, but is the story.

THE JOURNALIST AND THE MURDERER

Yet what if journalism is inherently unethical? Janet Malcolm opens her compelling *The Journalist and the Murderer* (1990) with just such a provocation:

> Every journalist who is not too stupid or too full of himself to notice what is going on knows that what he does is morally indefensible. He is a kind of confidence man, preying on people's vanity, ignorance, or loneliness, gaining their trust and betraying them without remorse. Like the credulous widow who wakes up one day to find the charming young man and all her savings gone, so the consenting subject of a

piece of nonfiction writing learns—when the article or book appears—
his hard lesson. Journalists justify their treachery in various ways according to their temperaments. The more pompous talk about freedom
of speech and "the public's right to know"; the least talented talk about
Art; the seemliest murmur about earning a living.[27]

Such temperaments, with their three excuses let's call them—freedom, art,
money—seem all the more prominent in the hoaxer than in the journalist.
Or in the con artist, whose delusions usually do not extend to the self.

Malcolm goes on to claim that what pains the proverbial human subject of a reporter, "what rankles and sometimes drives him to extremes of
vengefulness, is the deception that has been practiced on him. On reading
the article or book in question, he has to face the fact that the journalist . . .
never had the slightest intention of collaborating with him on his story but
always intended to write a story of his own." Malcolm calls this process *dehoaxing*. In doing so, she references the famous psychological experiment
from the early 1960s—about the same time Capote and the New Journalists
began experimenting with nonfiction as a fruitful form—in which subjects
in a study at Yale were told to shock someone in another room. Despite the
screams, and later, chilling silence from those supposedly hooked up to
the machine, "most subjects docilely continued giving shock after shock."
The point of what is called the Milgram experiment, named after the psy-
chologist who conducted it, may actually be obscured by its also being
known as the "Eichmann experiment," after the notorious Nazi—for what
the test revealed is not the extremes of evil but that ordinary people can be
coaxed to do terrible things in the face of authority.

The figures of the journalist and the murderer in Malcolm's book are
meant to have a troubled, symbiotic relationship; indeed, she suggests by her
very title that the relationship might be interchangeable, at least in terms
of ethics. Of course, Malcolm herself is a journalist, so her comparisons
only go so far.[28] But in seeing the slippery ethics of reporting on murder,
Malcolm's book is a clear descendant of Truman Capote's *In Cold Blood*—if
not in style, then in its being a book about writing, in much the same way
that in its enthusiastic, if at times critical, reception, *In Cold Blood* almost
immediately became about the ethics of Capote's work. *The Journalist and the
Murderer* signals the death of a kind of narrative surety whose demise would
lead directly to the hoax.

The specific journalist of Malcolm's title is Joe McGinniss, perhaps best known more recently for moving next door to Sarah Palin in order to write a book about her. In Malcolm's narrative he moved in closer, into the defense team for otherwise upstanding military man Jeffrey MacDonald, who stood accused of murdering his pregnant wife and their two daughters. Gaining unparalleled access, McGinniss betrayed him, according to MacDonald (and Malcolm would seem to agree), the journalist not only coming to believe MacDonald was guilty and not saying so but writing that the accused was a psychopath and that the Manson-style murders were his doing alone. McGinniss's best-selling book about the case, *Fatal Vision* (1983), falls squarely in the true crime genre; it was turned into a made-for-television movie, echoing the "magazine crime story" and other Lifetime channel fare with titles like *Who Is Clark Rockefeller?* or *Mother, May I Sleep with Danger?* However you feel about MacDonald's guilt—a hardly settled matter given that folks such as respected documentarian Errol Morris feel him innocent, publishing a 2012 book revisiting the case—Malcolm's book is chiefly about what she sees as the inherent betrayal in the process of a reporter gaining not the reader's but a source's trust.

One of the most fascinating parts of *The Journalist and the Murderer* concerns the shaping of spoken dialogue by journalists—the ways that quoting, *especially* when done right, requires some aspects of translation. Journalists are not court reporters—the news is not a mere transcription but a translation of the day's events and talk. This is why in writing *In Cold Blood*, using interviews Capote and childhood friend Harper Lee typed up only later, Capote's famed memory may actually have worked for him; and why journalistic notes and quotes prove as good as a tape recording, even in court. By the end of Malcolm's discussion and example, the idea of representing speech merely as recorded by a machine, rather than by a human, helps us understand that *not* to shape the speech of another has its own ethical problems. The goal is not to fix speech but to represent its essence and expression; to give some people, namely, the reporter, the only elegant speech and to reproduce every *um*, *ah*, pause, *you know*, or *et cetera* that a subject actually uses is not to do them any favors. It is actually to misuse the power of the press.

The difference between speech and a quote—between an experiment and a hoax; between a journalist and a murderer; between a cop lying to get a real confession and coercing a fake one—may make all the difference in the world. For Malcolm, "the point lies in the *structure* of the situation: the deliberately induced delusion, followed by a moment of shattering revelation. The dizzying shift of perspective experienced by the subject of the

Milgram experiment when he was 'debriefed,' or 'dehoaxed,' as Milgram calls it, is comparable to the dislocation felt by the subject of a book or article when he first reads it."[29] The distinction with *debunking* is worth considering: debunking would seem a public act, while *dehoaxing* is a personal, even private one. But with the hoax, what if the dislocating process of *dehoaxing* takes place not right away, upon reading something, but far later? Those readers who have spent months, years, or decades identifying with a piece of writing or art—in part because they believe it to be true—suddenly realize the hoaxer didn't even have the courtesy to tell her own story over theirs.

Unlike journalists, whom Malcolm suggests might tell their own story over their subjects' versions, hoaxers go further, telling the story of someone completely made up, who was not quite them. Such a feeling, if a feeling is what dehoaxing is, may prove familiar to anyone who has experienced racism in this country. In a strange way it provides my only metaphor—and merely a metaphor—for what it feels like to be mistaken not just for someone you are not but for *someone who doesn't really exist*. To be brutally called out your name; to be accused of being a criminal when you are a customer; to be accosted by an off-duty cop, or rather a security guard pretending to be one; to be misapprehended in ways often daily and sometimes deadly, is to experience dehoaxing.

What it means is that there is a story you did not know was being told, or tested, and if you'd known, maybe you'd have acted differently. Worse, you realize that you had trusted something untrue, unequal, put in place by powers beyond your control. You might feel led on, betrayed, lied to, having not only believed but also trusted that what was promised was actually true. The hoax, in such a view, is ongoing—in such a world, it is best to dehoax yourself before someone hoaxes, or rehoaxes, you.

JUKT

The film about the Stephen Glass affair, *Shattered Glass*, may feel "true" to viewers because much of it is—down to details like the filmmaker using word-for-word dialogue from the taped interview by the online journal that first questioned Glass. Though the truth is not simply a feeling, could it be an instinct that can be honed? Newshounds used to call this a *hunch*. That notion—that impulse at the start of a search—is one we must cultivate, rather than distract ourselves from.

The film presents Charles Lane's search for the truth with an almost

Old Testament fury: the hunch as hunt. As portrayed by Peter Sarsgaard, the *New Republic* editor emerges as a crusader for the facts—and the stand-in for the audience—all the more fervent after having been deceived. It is interesting to learn how writer David Plotz, a former friend of Glass married to Hanna Rosin, first viewed the film:

> Lane—the real Lane—has described the experience of watching it as something like being tickled. I know what he means. It was so unsettling to see the fake Steve acting *almost* like Steve did. . . . As with a tickling session, watching *Shattered Glass* made me so uncomfortable that I longed for it to stop, but I was so mesmerized that I never wanted it to stop. I became incapable of rational thought: I could concentrate only on my unease.
>
> That said I was alert enough to know that *Shattered Glass* felt true. It evokes the nerve-racking, jittery days in 1998 when Lane caught Steve.[30]

I can't help thinking the sensation he describes, from its odd pleasure to its unease, might be another way of describing *dehoaxing*. The truth, I think, can feel like that—primal, physical, unsettling.

The idea is almost something Glass would pitch. (It's the kind of thing Malcolm Gladwell would attempt to quantify in 2005's *Blink*.) Instead, as in the fake memoir, Glass appears to have pitched his pieces very much for their absurdity. The number of fake organizations (the Commission to Restore the Presidency to Greatness), phony bills of law and unconvened conventions (the First Church of George Herbert Walker Christ), crackpot stories and bullshit products (from a made-up Monica Lewinsky convention) found in his articles nearly boggle the mind in scope and audacity. Each is a mini-hoax. When he writes that he called into a radio show pretending to be a "bite expert" after the notorious Holyfield–Tyson fight—black gullibility being one point of the supposed stunt—no one at the publication, or in the public, seems to find that deception indicative of others. As writer Tom Scocca noted in the *Boston Phoenix*, "While everyone is marveling at the bold goofiness of Glass's inventions, what's much more disturbing is the way his fictions were constructed. Glass understood that even in the sober journalism practiced by the *New Republic*, articles make their impact with anecdotes, not facts; his stories, beyond the clear absurdities, are brightened up with improbably lively scenes and unusually good quotes. And anecdotes—even factually true ones—have a dangerous way of crowding out reality."[31]

The anecdote was Stephen Glass's method but also his madness. It allowed him to tell us a story with neither depth nor feeling, a mere factoid to be passed along like a virus. And what's wrong with going viral? Many such anecdotes are so unbelievable they are hard to believe, which is why, oddly, folks believe them. Who would make up such things?

"It's tough proving a negative. It is even tougher proving that something or someone does not exist,"[32] Adam Penenberg wrote right after the scandal. This is especially true because, as Buzz Bissinger reveals in his article "Shattered Glass," which inspired the movie, "He got away with his mind games because of the remarkable industry he applied to the production of the false backup materials which he methodically used to deceive legions of editors and fact checkers. Glass created fake letterheads, memos, faxes, and phone numbers; he presented fake handwritten notes, fake typed notes from imaginary events written with intentional misspellings, fake diagrams of who sat where at meetings that never transpired, fake voice mails from fake sources. He even inserted fake mistakes into his fake stories so fact checkers would catch them and feel as if they were doing their jobs."[33] Such true determination to be fake is truly hard to defend against.

The piece that undid Glass, "Hack Heaven," tells of a teenage computer hacker, Ian Restil, who electronically breaks into "big-time software firm" Jukt Micronics, posting "THE BIG BAD BIONIC BOY HAS BEEN HERE BABY." Perhaps the fact that Restil posted in practically poetic iambic pentameter should have been a clue to its phoniness. Rather than being prosecuted for such a transgression, Restil gets an agent and cuts a deal with the company, demanding absurd things like *X-Men* number one (well, who wouldn't?) and a Mazda Miata (not sure why), later celebrating his victory at a hacker convention. All of it was invented. And all of it really seems to be an allegory about how to break in somewhere and still be accepted—many of Glass's fabrications cannot help but be read as wishes to belong, but also to get caught.

How pedestrian and wonkish the things Glass invents are: newsletters and commissions, "super-agents for super-nerds." Given the preponderance of fake organizations in Glass—whether a National Assembly of Hackers, a crackhead Kenny Rogers fan club, or a church devoted to our forty-first president—Glass it would seem would do anything to be part of the club. Of course, in the light of day, it seems unbelievable that hackers, who live much of their lives as we all do, online, would have agents with business cards or assemble like the Avengers—much less have a printed newsletter. Running out of ideas, Glass simply names it "Computer Insider." The piece "Hack Heaven" has by my count at least six fake companies or legislative bills, practically one per paragraph. All the conventions are a sign of how conventional he is. Between the generic Center for Interstate Online Investigations, Computer Security Center, Uniform Computer Security Act, and Association of Internet-based Businesses (which might mean all businesses), his is a super-nerd's, not an X-Man's, view of heaven.

Across his career, and in his novel after, Glass casts himself as a *hacker*, a genius whose incursions get him not just noticed and flagged but also paid. "Hack Heaven" promotes while dismissing the idea that a break-in could lead to acceptance as well as money: "'The principal told us to hire a defense lawyer fast, because Ian was in deep trouble,' says his mother, Jamie Restil. 'Ian laughed and told us to get an agent. Our boy was definitely right.'"[34] Yet Glass is most of all a *hack*, meaning a writer who writes, and not always well, for money. Glass puts hacker Ian Restil in a Cal Ripken Jr. T-shirt not only as shorthand for his alleged home state of Maryland but also to borrow the Iron Man's greatness, his integrity, his lunch-pail performance that neither Glass nor the imaginary Restil share. Hackneyed, indeed.

It is not too much to say the Internet has caused a spike in hoaxes— its anonymity, its undiscerning false equivalence between things, and its subsequent obsession with Best Ofs and Top 31 lists would seem to welcome them. Certainly Glass's last piece appears to respond directly to the unease the Web has created, its narrative rift. But it is the Internet we can also thank for uncovering hoaxes. In this case, reporting by Penenberg for the online publication Forbes Digital Tool was responsible, including the good old-fashioned legwork of calling a number for Jukt Micronics, the supposed multinational web company that was really just a voice mailbox Glass had set up. Once the reporter discovered that dialing the same number at the same time from different phones yielded a busy signal—indicating just one phone line, rather odd for a reportedly major software firm—Penenberg realized the company too was a front.

The only question that remained was whether Glass was in on the hoax or was its victim. Victimhood in this case was, of course, a defensive position, one that Glass—with his catchphrase *Are you mad at me?*—would wield often and perhaps unconsciously.[35] After Penenberg's interviewing Glass made it quite clear that Glass was lying, Lane forced Glass to drive him to the site of the imaginary hacker convention, calling his bluff. Any speculation of his being rooked would give way to a "partial confession" and then the *New Republic*'s own investigation and correction "To Our Readers" in their June issue.

In our house, *Jukt Micronics* has become shorthand for just this kind of wishful, clearly fake, inelegant bullshit. Forget the fact that the Jukt Micronics website Glass crafted to cover his tracks was done in one night, and posted behind an America Online portal that no major company would use—the name doesn't at all sound real, has the clipped cadence of fakery. Or is it such an unmelodious name that it must be real? *Jukt*, pronounced "juked": behind it you can hear the idea of its homonym, meaning juked up, jazzed, tricked. Originally an African word, "jook" became "juke" as in the juke joint and jukebox; Glass deforms and defangs it to "Jukt," which is past tense, and passé, suggesting you done been "jukt" already.

CHAPTER 16

The Gingerbread Man

As goes "Hack Heaven," so goes Sandra Bullock in *The Net*, a great-bad thriller from around the same time as Stephen Glass's hoaxing. The 1995 film is filled with fear that no one might actually know us, whether from online anonymity to a mother with dementia; murder and identity theft ensue. Americans don't just have cultural, mass amnesia; we fear we have cultural Alzheimer's.

This condition has also corrupted the Internet itself. Trying to track down Glass's "originals" is harder than finding the fake folks in his articles. Most of Glass's fabrications have been taken down online, no doubt by prudent publishers and media outlets not just concerned about litigation or the propagating of Glass's lies, but presumably sick of the hoaxes' very existence. While certainly that beats leaving them up for the uninitiated to somehow repeat as fact, it would be nice if some were still up, accompanied by disclaimers—erasing the articles simply suppresses the incident rather than turning it into a moment of insight. Soon we will need to remember what we would all rather forget—let's hope not before we repeat it.

Online, we are all ghostwriters and spirit photographers. In that haunted place that is the Web, filled with dead ends, links "not found," and what a friend fruitfully called "digital litter," hoaxes are both overexposed and underexplored. The best treatment I believe for such hoaxes is to leave them asterisked with a correction, or better yet, to reproduce them contextualized in a casebook. (Some good example of this treatment are the Ern Malley, Spectra, Binjamin Wilkomirski, and Sokal hoaxes; published in a semiotic journal, the Sokal hoax managed to prove gravity didn't exist.) Then again, we maybe should let in the dopers to the Baseball Hall of Fame, their records and names simply asterisked to indicate what they are said to have done—or is it what baseball didn't do? Keeping them out doesn't change the record, or who holds one, much as we wish our heroes could be randomly tested beforehand for true heroism.

Though most often it means a writer pursuing only money, putting work ahead of work, there's yet another meaning of *hack*. A shortening of "hacker," it can also mean a taxi driver, someone who obtains a hackney license; like *livery*, a word sometimes still used for a hired town car in the city, hack goes back to the idea of a horse used for transportation. "Taxis and the Meaning of Work" was the title of Stephen Glass's first breakout piece, a cover story for the *New Republic* in 1996, the year after Ruth Shalit's own cover success. For years after his exposure it remained on the list of pieces Glass had not yet admitted as fabricated: this may be because of the prominence of the piece, as well as the subject, which is the changing face of race and work; it would seem too important to the idea of Glass or the magazine's reputation to be immediately repudiated.

The piece does a different kind of work. Reportedly encouraged by Martin Peretz, the magazine's owner and editor, the stated thesis of the piece is that recent immigrants to D.C. are replacing African American taxi drivers who previously dominated the field: "For decades, native-born blacks also accepted such risks in pursuit of upward mobility. Why don't they anymore?" It's a kind of once-typical *New Republic* affirmative action piece in reverse, with the point being the same: blacks are losing ground, aren't prepared to work and don't want to, can't quite cut it when they do. Oh, and they prefer drug dealing to cab driving, and chasing blondes to fares. As Glass writes, "It is what a 62-year-old black driver called the 'woo quotient': How fast can you get in someone's pants?"[1]

"The Meaning of Work" trades in Glass's typical, or stereotypical, anecdotes. Here's some of the *local coloreds* we meet: "Jim, the blonde-chasing limo driver"; "An equally tattered-looking 68-year-old black teacher" who's surprise surprise horny too, giving advice to a taxi class on "personal hygiene and its correlation with tips and sex" ("'If you're not clean,' he adds, 'you'll never get to touch her meters'"); and "Slippy—a 28-year-old black high-school dropout who has been a hack for one year." Such stock black characters, straight out of *D.C. Cab* starring Mr. T, are contrasted with Muslim and Arab immigrants—hardworking and religious, natch—

depicted as the perfect victims who, no matter what happens, consider themselves lucky:

> Sayed Farid, a short balding Pakistani driver, was robbed at knifepoint two years ago by a passenger who also ate Farid's lunch and dumped the hapless driver in a forest thirty miles outside Washington. Farid was back on the road the next day. He says he's lucky because he isn't Asad Alanan. Alanan, a dead ringer for Farid except that he's taller, points to his scarred ear, which was grazed by a bullet fired by a passenger annoyed that Alanan didn't have more cash on hand for him to steal. Then again, Alanan thinks he's lucky because he's not Ejay Eswan. Four months ago, a 17-year-old held a gun to Eswan's head while his girlfriend performed oral sex on the gunman. The couple then stole Eswan's money and, for kicks, locked him in his trunk. He was found fourteen hours later. Yet, believe it or not, Eswan, too, feels lucky, simply to be alive.

You're right, Steve, I don't believe it. Glass rides with an Imran "one night, around midnight"—the witching hour—when they pick up "the type of fare Imran would normally refuse," a young black man with headphones and, turns out, a potty mouth and a knife. After being robbed, Imran commiserates with his fellow cabbies, discussing a far more unbelievable Asian avenger:

> The conversation among Imran and his friends turns to the legend of Kae Bang, a Korean cab-driver-turned-vigilante who is to the D.C. cab community what Stagger Lee was to the Mississippi Delta. As Kae Bang's story goes, the cab driver was, one sticky summer night, bludgeoned on the head by three brick-wielding black teenagers. Bang quickly recovered and, using his martial arts expertise, struck back at the would-be thieves, hurting them badly. Everyone knows Bang's story, or at least a version of it—in some, he is a Chinese immigrant, in others he's hit with a pipe—but no one knows how to find him. Everyone knows someone who claims to have once met him, but those leads typically turn up just more names of other people who have supposedly met Bang. Bang is not registered to drive with any taxi company. While he is listed in the Maryland suburban phonebook, messages are never returned. Eventually I found him, due mostly to

luck. After hours of watching for him in a diner that he's rumored to frequent, I decided to head home. The cab I hailed was his.

"One night, around midnight" becomes Glass's own *Once upon a time*. This is almost genius, inventing a legend, then meeting him by chance; I'm only shocked Glass didn't just go all the way and call his imaginary, inscrutable Asian "Chop Bang." Reading the Glass piece makes clear that the religious and hardworking colored-person stereotype simply shifts over time—someone always occupies it—once it was black folks, here Muslim immigrants. For a while, the slot was assigned to "Hispanic voters," but in the wake of current anti-immigrant fervor, it seems to have shifted to Asians like Kae Bang.

Glass's piece—a cover story in all senses—remains one of the most race-baiting and racist pieces of writing I have read. As MacArthur "genius" grant winner Ta-Nehisi Coates writes, "The story was a whirlwind of spectacular 'gets' which could only have been executed by a crack reporter on his best day, or an outright liar willing to invoke every odious stereotype from Steppin [*sic*] Fetchit to Bruce Lee to Willie Horton. . . . What should not be forgotten is that one of the greatest fraud sprees in modern journalistic history, was aided and abetted by *The New Republic*'s belief in shiftless, dangerous blacks and the immigrant avenger Kae Bang."[2] The crime seems all the worse because it was maintained, and fact-checked, as nonfiction. Yet even had it been somehow true, Glass's "Meaning of Work" story still would have been racist: his is the very execution, as it were, of a strictly ideological premise, the opposite of what journalism is meant to do. "Work" is a not-so-subtle overabundance of evidence, proof less of black pathology than racist psychology.

By now I have grown more than frustrated, weary I suppose, to find yet another hoax centered on race. But this may be part of it too—revealed, or rather, exhausted, the hoax devolves to dreary kitsch. The racism unexamined, the generic people named Jim and James (two different characters, mind you), Turner and Slippy, all might be funny if they weren't seen then and yet and still as forms of truth. Like pop stars or black athletes, the figures in "Meaning of Work" go by first-names only—less a sign of heroic individualism than of types given no honorifics or last name, banal labels all the worse for their pretense.

Writer Paul Maliszewski also highlights Glass's banality: "Glass's wild inventions form a thin skin stretched over a fairly standard body of accepted truth and mainstream opinion. Glass's imagination is not, in other words, all that original. It is, in fact, crushingly banal."[3] Maliszewski should know—he too is a confessed hoaxer whose essay "I, Faker" reads like a how-to not just for the hoax but the confession after. "I must confess now. I must tell what I have done. I was a staff writer at a business newspaper. When called upon, I was an editor of sections on annuities, executive gift giving, and year-end wrap-ups. I was a hack and I knew it. What's more, I had come to see my hackwork as not just flimsy and inconsequential but damaging."[4]

Twelve years after his initial confession in 1997, Maliszewski published a book, *Fakers*, that takes up a by-now familiar cursory trip through several hoaxes—the Moon Hoax among them—without deep analysis. The majority of such books about hoaxes can come to seem so familiar as to remove the hoax's strangeness, their preset canons and tired taxonomies taking summary and paraphrase to their unnatural conclusions. Encyclopedias without being encyclopedic, more bric-a-brac than brilliant, such compendiums end up resembling the hoaxes they cursorily examine: *Look Ma, no notes!* Nor do they mention plagiarists, maybe because their techniques—poor sourcing and quotes without full, clear citation—resemble the plagiarist in practice if not exactly. One example, with the promising title *Impostors: Six Kinds of Liar*, contains endless quotes without any references to where they come from. Instead, we are given lists of sources, none clearer than the next, including fifteen older books about impostors that the author apparently drew from—seven from the early 1990s alone. No one asks, why this bombardment, much less why now?

The sheer vagueness of such casebooks starts to mimic the impostors they supposedly explore. This is especially disappointing in Maliszewski's case because after his initial confession he hoaxed again, creating a spurious website to spread gossip and, in classic hoax fashion, accusing others of hoaxes.[5] (This spurious site has since disappeared from the "Internets" so will not be spoken of again.) Like many other books about hoaxers, *Fakers* seems satisfied with what happened—rarely with how, and never with why. The why is hard: Why are all these banalities believed? Do we really think that little of each other? And why are all these white folks hoaxing about all these brown, yellow, and black ones? We have few other ways to say just how Americans remain divided, not only from each other but also schizophrenic about truth and race and detached from reality even though, or especially because, we refashion it daily.

It is instructive to see not how far Glass can go but how far readers go—or went—with him. "Glass's real trick was the way he appealed to his audience's prejudices," as the *Boston Phoenix* describes it. "His most colorful material usually involved people from outside the *New Republic's* readership: old folks in retirement homes, menial laborers, backwoods Christians. The behavior he described may have been improbable, but it conformed to stereotype. Old ladies doted, a bit battily, on obscure political figures; a limo driver plotted seductions; religious yokels ranted about the devil. . . . The stereotypes flattered the reader, making him or her privy to the inner workings of the common folk—as laid bare by a bright young lad with a Penn degree and an inquiring mind. The world, Glass assured everyone, was just as you imagined it to be, only weirder and more compelling."[6] He supplied things we imagined to be true because we wanted them to be, or feared they might be.

You can see this in an earlier piece from his days at the University of Pennsylvania paper, the *Daily Pennsylvanian*. Glass's 1991 piece is called "A Day on the Streets," implying not just a place I doubt he visited but a duration highly unlikely. The small header announcing "A Summer Times reporter spends 24 hours with a group of homeless men, learning what it really means to endure" is really more a pitch than a story. Practically everything and everyone in the story is known as something else—The Bottom ("also known as 'The Bucket of Blood'"), Red, Johnnie (reminiscent of "Frankie and Johnny")—indeed all are nicknames taken from African American culture, not to mention the fiction of Toni Morrison and John Edgar Wideman, a native of Philadelphia, where the action is meant to take place. (Stagger Lee waits in the wings.) Here's just part of Glass's piece, worth quoting at length:

> The Bottom is the area surrounding 40th and Lancaster—a crack haven where the homeless purchase drugs and get high in the crack houses and cheap hotels. The talk of the murder, however, soon dissipates (Johnnie says that death is an everyday occurrence for him and his friends). The topic of discussion moves onto graphic descriptions of the sexual favors that each man had purchased the night before. Two hours have passed, and T. has not returned from the liquor store. June and Johnnie go to find T., and more importantly, their money. . . . Johnnie is the leader of his "posse," a club of several dozen homeless people that has its own intricate rules and traditions. They used to meet at a clubhouse in a condemned home, but it burned down twice. All members of the club identify their alligiance [*sic*] by donning an

American Heart Association button and a Zenith Data Systems paint-ers' cap. Among the club's rules, foremost is the stipulation that "your word is your bond." No one ever goes into anyone else's bag of pos-sessions without permission, and food and booze is generally shared. Club members enjoy citing their hero, Kenny Rogers, as best express-ing the philosophy of surviving on the streets. Twice that day June and Johnnie sang "The Gambler," in chorus.[7]

Here, in prototypical form—which just happens to be stereotypical—are the tricks of Glass's trade, from the clichés with a twist (crackheads with a fan club, a Kenny Rogers one no less) to first names only (and some merely an initial).[8] Death warrants only a parenthetical aside. Lately this kind of hoax is not just something we fall for but a mode and mood we too easily fall into.

This piece as far as I know has been let stand. This far from the event, I cannot prove it is fake—*It's hard proving a negative*—but I've a good hunch. If it is (or rather, isn't) as it appears, the piece defies claims Glass has main-tained that he only started hoaxing late in his tenure at the *New Republic*. He maintained that "in early June 1996 he began fabricating material for publication" as recently as the 2014 Supreme Court of California ruling; such late dating means to shore up Glass's well-rehearsed narrative that he grew slowly unhinged, hoaxing incrementally, and is now repentant, wor-thy not only of forgiveness but of a job upholding the law. In truth he was a one-person narrative crisis.

"A Day on the Streets" isn't just an early example of his later rampant hoaxing; it provides a road map for it. Without "actual" names, who could verify such a story? But then again, who would ever want to? The desire for a Kenny Rogers club, for hookers and gigolos and crackheads who tour with the Grateful Dead selling acid, are details too good to be true but also to deny. These are nightmares not made real but made absurd, all the better for a college student in the bubble of a college experience that can feel set apart from the real world (but, of course, is real). He tells us what we want to fear. What's more, Glass gives his fellow students a pat on the back via Johnnie: "'If it wasn't for the college kids, I wouldn't be alive,' Johnnie says." It's Glass who's the "gigolo-want-to-be" in the story, pimping out homeless people to learn lessons, which overwhelmingly seem to be: Don't be home-less. Or black. Or I might make up whatever I want about you.

Why all these imaginary black people in all these journalistic hoaxes?

Or let's put it another way—why all these fantasies about black men who do not actually exist? It can start to seem like the figure of the black male is the exact "negative" being tried out, on trial, that no proof can confirm—the ultimate hoax. "Johnnie," Porterhouse, Uncle Tom, Mammy: all the fabricated black folks by Glass or Frey or a profound number of others conform to the dark double that's dominated white-authored American literature for centuries, yet without the charm or complication. Black bodies, especially male ones, get viewed as weapons—they are not allowed self-defense as society is not quite sure they have a self to defend.

It isn't that the black brute is just seen as a victim, because victims need be afforded innocence. Instead, Michael Brown's body lay in the street in Ferguson, Missouri, uncovered, for four hours in the August sun. Instead, black children aren't just tried as adults, but not allowed to even try. Instead, Trayvon Martin and Tamir Rice and—fill in the blank—are rendered deserving of death. The hoaxes that Glass and others perpetuated are ultimately forms of violence done to truth, much less invented and actual lives—Kenny Rogers's *You got to know how to hold 'em* provides a poor funeral song. What's worse, this shared delusion remains too familiar even in what Ralph Ellison calls "our most representative authors" of fiction, not to mention politics: "Too often what is presented as the American Negro (a most complex example of Western man) emerges an oversimplified clown, a beast or an angel."[9] As historian Leon Litwack writes in his tremendous study *Trouble in Mind* about violence in the Jim Crow South, "The Negro as beast became a fundamental part of the white South's racial imagery at the turn of the [twentieth] century, taking its place alongside the venerated and faithful Sambo retainer, and whites were perfectly capable of drawing on both to sustain their self-image. Blacks, after all, possessed a dual nature: They were docile and amiable when enslaved or severely repressed, but savage, lustful, and capable of murder and mayhem when free and uncontrolled."[10]

In his April 1998 article "The Vernon Question" for *George* magazine, Glass crafted his own admittedly invented black man—despite that he was at the same time real—in Vernon Jordan, President Clinton's chief adviser. Jordan had come a long way from segregated Georgia to sit in the halls of power in D.C., yet Glass relentlessly renders him as a stereotypical sexual dynamo, the black man whose limitless desire no clothes or fancy suit can contain. "Vernon Jordan—former civil rights leader, reputed ladies' man, longtime resident of Bill Clinton's innermost circle, and now the Target— briskly paces around the perimeter of his plush office. The six-foot-four, broad-shouldered, thick-necked man is vigorously wringing his hands. His steps are so forceful that a small trail of disturbed carpet has formed along his path." *Target*, the nickname Glass says the media coined but that he presumably invented, provides another hint that Glass had Jordan in his sights. "The Target Jordan bears little resemblance to his portrait that hangs outside the firm's twelfth-floor conference room"—the real portrait, Glass suggests, is the written one he's crafting of a man who "disturbs," who might not know his own strength (which is not to say power), and who is too smart or slick to lie.[11] Jordan is called "a Washington wise man" almost as an insult; his every success is a form of selling out. Jordan, in fact, is defined by his power, which is steadily eroded by Glass and his emphasis on details he can't possibly know and hasn't observed.

The six-page article appears as yet another attack piece in a "Sex in High Places" issue—filled with President Clinton's sex scandal, a feature titled "Monica's So-Called Life," and an excerpt from Elizabeth Wurtzel's *Bitch: In Praise of Difficult Women* (1998) about then–First Lady Hillary Clinton—in which you can see the stirrings of a new conservatism and neocon attitude that soon would spread. Even so, the Glass piece is particularly troubling, the president's infidelity somehow indicting Jordan: "The Lewinsky scandal is bringing a less attractive aspect of Jordan to the foreground: his penchant for lecherous behavior," Glass writes untruthfully, "a tendency that actually seems to have strengthened his bond with the president."[12] Jordan is pictured with white men of power, including past presidents Gerald Ford and George H. W. Bush—as well as glam white women such as Daryl Hannah and Famke Janssen, his costars in the film *The Gingerbread Man* (1998), here shown especially overexposed and pale—to connect him to something approaching Glass's own overexposure.

Glass describes Jordan as a phantom, saying, "No one seems to know for sure what he *does*," in a town where what you do is the same as who you are. In terms of work, he's all but called lazy. Invisibility extends to his speech: "To this day, when Jordan speaks to the press, he employs what he calls 'dead man's talk': If he is ever quoted, the offending reporter is cut off from Jordan's pipeline. The tactic pays off." So does Glass's, for a time—which is to smear Jordan as if he were dead, for dead men can't be libeled, much less sue. In a familiar kind of ventriloquism, Glass's anonymous sources—later shown to be fictional—disparage Jordan, claiming he is inappropriate with hostesses in restaurants. This mix of outrageous and seemingly believable—all while untrue—is the hoax's specialty, a fantasy in search of a fact.

Jordan considered a lawsuit, dropping the idea only after John F. Kennedy Jr., the publication's founder and editor in chief, reportedly wrote him an apology once Glass's rampant fabulism was revealed a mere month later. (No one indicates whether the apologies were handwritten.) The repeat racism of Glass's efforts indict him more than any suit or court case can. Admitting you hoaxed doesn't change *what* you hoaxed about, or why.

Glass's Jordan conforms to that familiar combo of angel and beast, lazy lawyer and invisible man; here speaks the language of racism, barely coded, euphemistic. Dead man's talk indeed—which may be another term for this deadly kind of hoaxing from which we're still trying to dehoax ourselves.

The two seeming contradictory sides of Uncle Tom and brute, angel and beast, were inextricably linked in a "fakelore of black inferiority" long used to justify harsh oppression for seemingly good Negroes, with whom violence was required to get their lazy bones to work; and in a "folk pornography" of black depravity that justified violence against them when they inevitably overstepped their bounds. This is what is known as a lose-lose. The results are a society in which "hate and fear transformed ordinary white men and women into mindless murderers and sadistic torturers" for whom lynching became a public ritual and police violence was always justified.[13] The destroying of black character also deforms the white one.

This is why, sixty years after Ellison was writing and only fifty years after the civil rights movement, it is so troubling to find supposedly legit articles like the one in the *New York Times* calling the late Michael Brown "no angel." This unfortunate phrase Kia Makarechi has traced across the entire *New York Times* online archives, finding it applied only to notorious killers, Nazis, or men of color.[14] This is not about truth but what Ellison names "a struggle over the nature of reality," a war often waged in the hoax—especially the journalistic one.

The hoax's words are its bonds.

QUARTER LIFE

One reason Stephen Glass's story—and his fabrications—have gotten by almost any measure the most attention of any modern hoax is because he is the so-called quarter-life crisis personified. By this I don't mean the relative youth of hoaxers from Ruth Shalit to Jayson Blair, though the quarter-life crisis is usually spoken of as occurring in a person's twenties; rather, I mean the quarter life of a relatively young nation dedicated to progress, often proud yet conflicted over its origins. This extended adolescence, let's call it, has provided one more incitement for America's hoaxes, passed down from Barnum's claiming to display George Washington's nursemaid to Washington, D.C.'s many journalistic fiascos. The hoaxes of the nation's capital, if not to say capitalism, express the anxieties of the end of a triumphant American Century, trumpeting ways of winning while worrying over authority, moral or otherwise. Glass, Shalit, and Blair prove predictors of the kinds of self-involvement and lack of accountability that would become the Internet's Wonder Bread and unmixed margarine. What had long been a part-time narrative crisis is now a full-time one.

Glass has also become central because most of his former colleagues are writers, and Glass has regularly and publicly reopened fairly fresh wounds—whether from lawyering up right away, the publication of *The Fabulist* in 2003, or trying to be a lawyer himself—giving former friends and onetime colleagues a chance, though not really a choice, to revisit the case. Almost from the instant of his unveiling, article after article by his erstwhile friends reveals that their dehoaxing is still ongoing years later.[15] "If they suspected Glass from a distance, surely those of us who worked with him every day should have sniffed him out," former *New Republic* colleague Jonathan Chait writes. "This seems intuitively sound, but in fact has it backward: It was our very proximity to Glass that made us susceptible to his fraud."[16] As is often the case, Glass's fraud was predicated on closeness—including a love of gossip and a firsthand knowledge of the rigors and loopholes of fact-checking, one irony being that Glass was a hard-ass when fact-checking others—but mostly, an intimacy in the writing. Not real intimacy, mind you, and never empathy, but the intimacy we've come to expect from the hoax—a close-up having become the same as being close.

You might also call his recent attempt at redemption another extension of his hoaxing—though Hanna Rosin sees it differently and has come to accept his having changed. For the centenary of the *New Republic* in 2014 (turns out weeks before it imploded, with much of the masthead leaving or forced out), Rosin met for a story with her former friend, whom she hadn't spoken to since those dehoaxing days in 1998. "If the first step of reforming yourself is acknowledging your sins," Rosin writes, "then Steve was determined to get an A-plus, along with extra credit. For example, I asked whether he had consciously made us his co-conspirators in the creation of fiction. I recalled him once asking me to help with his story about the non-existent Monica Lewinsky memorabilia convention. The story was dull but had a funny line at the end about a Monica Lewinsky sex doll. Were there any more details like that? I had asked, and he came to life, recounting various trinkets, including a condom named after her. I cheered him on, and thus together, we birthed a fabulous falsehood."[17] Oddly, the "fabulous falsehoods" sound confabulated in ways similar to his apologies—though of course only Rosin can say whether he is convincing. What she can't quite say is how the public trust might be restored. Still, Rosin indicates how we all might share blame in cheering on the hoaxers, confabulating with the fabulist in order to partake of the fabulous.

But if Stephen Glass is emblematic of our era it is in ways far beyond what he might wish, his former friends can imagine, or even Buzz Bissinger, who first wrote on the case, seems to think. "He is the perfect expression of his time and place," Bissinger writes of Glass, describing how "an era is cresting in Washington; it is a time when fact and fiction are blurred not only by writers eager to score but also by presidents and their attorneys, spinmeisters and special prosecutors. From one perspective, Stephen Glass was a master parodist of his city's shifting truths."[18] But Glass is more parrot than parodist. While Glass's hoaxes may at first appear absurd, outrageous, beyond belief, in another light they come across as rather pedestrian. This is purposeful, I think—it is this mix of hyperbole and ho-hum that really is the problem and Glass's sole genius.

The obvious full-on fake can prove easy to expunge; it is harder to erase the things he said about real people and the daily record that just by writing about he managed to alter. He not only gave us fictions and gross stereotypes but also cloaked them in ordinariness, which was his own. With Stephen Glass and no small number of other hoaxers, from Harvard plagiarist Adam Wheeler to phony Jonah Lehrer, we see the cultivation of a profound blandness that both covers up and enables the obviousness and extremity of their lies. Not quite the banality of evil, these hoaxers ultimately convey the evilness of banality. Their narratives and personae demonstrate a kind of ordinary extraordinariness, giving as much effort to being "regular" as to hoaxing so that this studied regular-guyness has become an integral part of the hoax.

This white-bread realness is another kind of drag show, complete with fake names and falsies but without the fun. It is this very khaki-ness that Buzz Bissinger, the legendary author of *Friday Night Lights*, with his new high-fashion outfits, his confessed shopping addiction, and now gender-bending appears to protest, raging, he says, "against the conformity that submerges us into boredom and blandness and the sexless saggy sackcloths that most men walk around in like zombies without the cinematic excitement of engorging flesh."[19] In contrast to the mythical black male—a perfect and usual suspect—the bland white kid performs being beyond suspicion, projecting a normality so normal it must be believed. That this "normate" persona regularly invokes and demotes blackness along the way is no accident.

Stephen Glass is emblematic of our era exactly because of his beseeching blandness. Not just his wild fabrications alone, but also the ways these inventions are married to a cultivated banality—something the hoax regularly employs as a form of "believability" but ultimately hopes to defeat or at least distract us from—have made his stories paradoxically mythic in all senses. "Hack Heaven," his hoax story about the Internet, worked at first because Glass's stories are the Internet distilled: near anonymous, virtual, viral, full of accommodating clichés and acronyms and aliases, all without clear source. "Overwhelmingly, what everyone remembers about my pieces are the fake things," he testified later.[20] If Glass hadn't invented his stories, we would have had to.

We have, in fact—many of the hyperbolic extremes and structural banalities found in Glass are now found in our daily interactions with our screens big and small, from text messages to news shows to Twitter to reality television. (And I like these last two.) "You're fake" is the biggest insult another contestant can launch at another on reality TV because the whole staged endeavor might topple if anyone ever noticed there are script supervisors. The reality these so-called unscripted shows—fully forged in the narrative crisis of the 1990s—convey is one overdetermined and experimented, controlled by their very chaos. It is now part of our politics.

What's more, like the Internet, a Glass article conveys the jumble of import and irrelevance provided by a Google search (or worse, whatever we searched with before Google). The effect can be simulated by watching more than a half hour of CNN's spin-off Headline News, in which one story follows the next without priority or hierarchy, and not in a revolutionary way: this happened, then this happened, our economy's collapsing, look over here, this dog was saved, this fire raged, this sister was shot, insert joke from late-night television, repeat. If you are trapped in a waiting room or hotel lobby, say, the first few minutes provide a willing distraction; by the time the cycle renews you realize how short the "top news" cycle is, and after that, how short life. Similarly, Glass's cultivated details, now revealed, stand as a hodgepodge of not just fact and fiction, but import and throwaway, factoid and cliché. Journalists call this *color*.

And Glass gives good color. Many of those writing after the fact cite this color as part of his meteoric rise and popularity in the newsroom and beyond—more than his faking notes, this faking of "human interest" is responsible for his writing getting through the gates. (Many oddly now say that he was not a good writer and required much editing, which may be mere hindsight talking.) But there's something else responsible for Glass's prominence, his being the height of the form, the hoaxer in charge: Glass's fabrications, his fall, and now his halfhearted seeking of forgiveness, predicted the storm to come. He was simply ahead of his time—a few years later, he could have hired not just an attorney or agent to defend and redefine him but a camera to follow him around.

Glass heralds a fundamental shift: one in which writing would be seen as content; in which the definition of self would not be citizen (as long as you could prove it) or voter (who might be suppressed) or even taxpayer (an identity mostly to be avoided) but consumer. It is a world in which the best thing to do after a devastating terrorist attack is shop, an ethos that regards culture not as something to which one might contribute or support but as a commodity to try and get as cheaply as inhumanely possible. When a book (I mean a physical copy of a book) costs one penny online, and the shipping $5.99, we have crossed into a place where words are not only devalued but not viewed as work.

Words can be abstract and now cut and pastable (paging plagiarism, please). The labor it took to make that physical object, the reporter's sweat, the writer's backache, the publisher's meetings, the bookstore's shelves, the binders and papermakers and designers: all are worthless. It is a fictional idea, this content. This is a "hack heaven," which can appear an awful lot like purgatory—one just as abstract and dwindling as the money paid to craft it.

It isn't Glass the person I mean to point to, but what he represents—or what he represented as true. Glass is only the first to alert us if we had bothered to notice that even people had become fictional. For millennia before then, we the people were nonfictions; now existence itself has become increasingly fractured, virtual, unreal. Glass's self-proclaimed gradual fabulism, which now seems highly unlikely—his moving from a made-up quote here and there to whole people and then whole stories fabricated—mirrors the euphemistic, post-factual world that was slowly coming and that suddenly we find ourselves in.

When *friend* is merely a verb, not a person; when apocalypses too are computer based and costly, like Y2K, then turn out to be mostly paranoia, or worse, marketing; when you can fall in love not with television or through television but *on* television through a series of dates you couldn't really afford in a rented mansion that seems specifically designed for reality TV, is a set really, a soft-core porn palace, and then wonder why it doesn't work when the cameras are off; when your first instinct at the sign of national tragedy is to tell your phone, not tell someone using that phone: then you have become as fictional as the world that you've created.

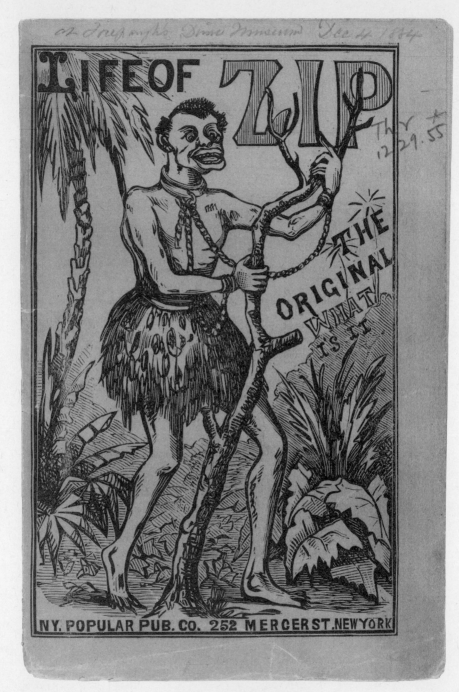

Life of Zip, pamphlet, ca. 1884.

Chapter 17

In Bad Blood

I remember when I first heard the name Susan Smith. It was October 1994 and I was in New York, visiting from Providence where I lived then; I recall overhearing on a store radio about two little white children in South Carolina being abducted in a carjacking by a black man. Instantly I said to the friend I was with: that don't sound right.

I wasn't a mind reader or prophet—it's simply that whatever code there is about behavior in the States, especially the South, would make such a scenario so unlikely as to be improbable, if not impossible. Not that people of all stripes can't do incomprehensible and cruel things to each other; but for a black guy seeking a simple theft to leave a mother alive and take her kids unknowingly, would be to invite a lynching of one kind or another. Even now. Despite the reported disbelief of the sketch artist, the mug shot of the fake perpetrator did lead to a sweep and a shakedown of local black males, much like in the Charles Stuart case in Boston after I had moved back to that area for college in 1989—he too had used a hoax black man to cover up his crime of killing his pregnant wife.

For Smith as for Stuart the deceit and danger were the same; for both, the phantom black man proved the perfect criminal for an imperfect crime. Beyond the horrific murders of their loved ones, Stuart's and Smith's crimes continued in their placing blame on those who cannot defend themselves because they don't exist. Certainly murder outweighs literary or journalistic mischief by quite a bit. However, the question remains as to why Stuart and Smith picked not just their real-life victims but such imaginary ones?

Doing so helped them continue the notion of themselves as victims. Victimhood is something hoaxers take to easily, martyrdom their bread and butter. The self-inflicted shot that Stuart claimed was from a carjacker proved prelude to his ultimate suicide once he was found out, revealing the level of suffering he was willing to concoct and endure after inflicting far more on his family and his wife's.

Luckily, in the years between Stuart and Smith, while there was a rush on the part of some to indict blackness more broadly, cooler heads saw through Smith's ploy relatively quickly.[1] Looking at the supposed abductor's literal profile now it is hard to believe anyone saw anything real in the artist's sketch, resembling nothing so much as those old phrenology textbooks demonstrating the inherent inferiority of the Negro based on skull shape. Both black men whom Stuart and Smith invented imply that not just these but all black people are phantoms, spooks you could say, invisible as the unnamed narrator of Ralph Ellison's *Invisible Man*. As both a freak and grotesque, the phantom Negro is a racial myth of the kind that once dominated headlines from the turn of the twentieth century to just before World War II: the "Giant Negro." As traced by the blog *Undercover Black Man*, giant Negroes filled the pages of papers across the nation, responsible for unlikely crimes and even some saving of lives—a giant Negro tackled the assassin who took President McKinley's life.[2]

Whether good or bad, denatured, displaced, even dissed, let's call this black figure the *disembody*—going further than the dissected black body of the nineteenth century, such a figure is not just black but blank, barely there. This is all the more true with the giant, seen as all body, physicality in extremis, excess made flesh. Smith's fake abductor is a bête noire—a black beast straight out of Stereotype 101, complete with knit cap, white lips, and one presumes, just out of frame, minstrel gloves. What does the "disembody" say about those who regularly invoke it?

Such invisibility is a problem not with being, but of seeing—as in the hoax. Foresight is rarely forensic; only hindsight removes the rose-colored glasses that most hoaxers assume we wear. The kind of sight I admire is the second sight shown in Cornelius Eady's *Brutal Imagination*, in which the imaginary black man Smith invented actually speaks. Eady's poems are testimonies from the invisible—haunted by this imaginary's voice and vision, which is clear and omnipresent, the speaker is the assassin Smith requires. He is her double, dark of course, enlightened by Eady's imagination.

Smith's imagined man is, after all, a "Composite"—not just as a drawing of a suspect, or the photo on the cover of Margaret Seltzer's hoax—but an unholy Frankenstein monster. He's the opposite of a *nondescript*—he's only a description, a disembodiment, a category come to life. To explore this predicament of the imagined, Eady's preface does the opposite of a typical hoax's not by claiming art but by specifying who's speaking. Eady also uses the voices of "Charles Stuart in the Hospital" and "Uncle Tom in Heaven," reminding us that Uncle Tom is a fiction who nevertheless has been made real, a threatening insult or imaginary role black folks might fall into:

> I watch another black man pour from a
> White woman's head. Fear
> He'll live the way I did, a brute,
> A flimsy ghost of an idea. Both
> Of us groomed to go only so far.[3]

What's almost more troubling than Smith's invention is how far it traveled: other people reported sightings of the imaginary black man. In the Stuart case, police arrested a perfect scapegoat (or black sheep) and quickly threw him in jail. Such phantom sightings indicate how quickly what we suspect can become manifest, made real: "I watch another black man roam the land, / Dull in his invented hide."[4] Eady manages to give voice to the ways such hoaxing can make "grown men," actual black people perceived as potential suspects, worry about their speech and ambition, for fear they might get conflated with just such a phantom. Being seen as a ghost doesn't mean you can't get killed.

Black Imaginations Matter: this "invented hide" too often hides real black inventions. What stories aren't being told in favor of these? Stowe's fiction, *Uncle Tom's Cabin*, is said to be based on an actual slave narrative by Josiah Henderson. But she's not alone—in the nineteenth century writers of the American Renaissance often turned to race explicitly (as in Whitman, Twain, Melville, Stowe, not to mention Douglass) and to blackness as an idea (Hawthorne, Poe) in ways that Smith can only envy. Eady continues that tradition while skewering it, matching Smith's typing with a brutal imagination—and honesty—of his own. The imaginary is an analog, after all, a dark mirror in which we all see ourselves—though perhaps not all of ourselves. Take Eady's "How I Got Born":

> When called, I come.
> My job is to get things done.
> I am piecemeal.
> I make my living by taking things.

The things the disembody takes are not lives but innocence—an idea that poetry seeks to understand, undermine, explore. Consider Eady's "My Heart":

> Susan Smith has invented me because
> Nobody else in town will do what
> She needs me to do.
> I mean: Jump in an idling car
> And drive off with two sad and
> Frightened kids in the back.
> Like a bad lover, she has given me a poisoned heart.
> It pounds both our ribs, black, angry, nothing but business.
> Since her fear is my blood
> And her need part mythical,
> Everything she says about me is true.

This truth, a halfway thing that stands in for a kind of whole, is what the hoax insists on. Like the "nonexistent man" that Smith invented and Eady imagines, the results can prove deadly.

In their evoking of race, the Smith and Stuart cases also suggest the specter and aftermath of violence familiar from Emmett Till and beyond—accusations such as theirs historically led to the demise of many a black person, excusing white mobs and others to visit their own sexualized violence on African Americans. Sex or its deformation, rape, was the accusation; race the unavoidable fact; lynching too often the result. Together they added up to the "folk pornography"[5] often carried in local newspapers, in which outrageous fictions often held violent sway over facts, much less the truth, in what must be the deadliest kind of hoax. Accounts of the accused's brutality masked the brutality of the violence it justified. The same folk porn threatens those videos of police killings of black lives now rampant on the Internet; the "disembody" regularly leads to dead bodies.

In the case of Smith, only smart investigators saved time, and more difficulty in the community, by ascertaining—and getting her to confess—that she had in fact killed her own children, letting her car roll into a lake with her two sons strapped in the backseat. It is almost too much to imagine.

The hoax often emerges as a reaction to the unimaginable. What actually happened proves hard to believe—which is not to say, hard to prove—and the hoax takes over. Whether in the case of Susan Smith or on a larger scale, honor killing or modern slavery or the troubling spate of recent fake

Holocaust memoirs, hoaxes replace actual, powerful experiences with fake ones that are tidier and tamer, yet wilder and *worser*. Facts overwhelm us; fantasy proves more relatable exactly because it is hard to believe: someone writes a book pretending to be both Jewish and having survived the Holocaust by traveling with a pack of wolves across Europe.[6] Whether the Holocaust or slavery or child abuse or addiction, the hoax takes the difficult and makes it easy to digest. It also makes actual messy history, both personal and public, at once more muddled than it really is while also far more simplex. The results give, for instance, Holocaust deniers only more fuel, even as many of the hoaxers claim to be identifying with the pain that they effectively plagiarize.

Rather than build up the truth, the hoax denies it as much as Holocaust deniers do, making reality as unreal as it may sometimes feel. Though built on disbelief, and overreliant on improbability, the hoax rarely trades in uncertainty. With the hoax, certitude is exactly what we should be wary of—borrowing from journalism a healthy skepticism that's perhaps its most important tool. What seems really lost lately in writing, whether hoax or otherwise, is a culture of accountability and a tradition of empathy.

This is a newfound, radical departure from the expansive yet intimate "I" of the nineteenth century—*I am the man, I suffered, I was there* or *Call me Ishmael* or *I'm Nobody, who are you?* Too many readers and writers confronted with Whitman's *Song of Myself* get only the self part. Today, like always, the best writers of our time, like Cornelius Eady, focus on the song as a form of self.

JIMMY'S WORLD

Before Glass or Smith's beastly black men, one of the biggest hoaxes contemporary journalism has ever seen was built around another imaginary, which is to say unreal, black male. In this case it was a sympathetic portrait, and not of a man but a young boy: Jimmy. If a more generic name has been dreamt up for a character, I don't know it. (First drafts apparently had him named "Tyrone.") But the article written by Janet Cooke about him, "Jimmy's World," went on to win a Pulitzer Prize for her and the *Washington Post* in 1981, and set off a chain of events that still resonate today.

To read *A Good Life*, the late Ben Bradlee's memoir of his distinguished run as editor of the *Post*, is chiefly to be impressed by his achievements and ethics. This includes his support for his reporters Bob Woodward and Carl

Bernstein, who uncovered Watergate—and ultimately changed the course of American history, effectively unseating a president and inadvertently feeding many a conspiracy theory. Bradlee not only steered the paper through the rough waters of Watergate but also left a wake that raised all boats, making journalists folk heroes in a country that desperately needed some.

It would have seemed at first that the *Post*'s profile would only continue to rise with the hiring and writing of Janet Cooke, a young reporter with a star résumé. Her front-page story "Jimmy's World" about a young heroin addict got widespread attention; that Sunday's issue shipped almost a million copies, with the news service syndicating the article to over three hundred papers around the world.[7] Mayor Marion Barry and others called for a search for the boy; the police offered a $10,000 award; even incoming First Lady Nancy Reagan weighed in, "How terribly sad to read it and to know there are so many others like him out there. I hope with all my heart I can do something to help them. Surely there must be a way."[8] Jimmy may have inspired Mrs. Reagan's campaign to urge us to "Just Say No" to drugs—and to appear on the hit show *Diff'rent Strokes* to say so.

There was only one problem with "Jimmy's World": the entire article turned out to be fabricated, with Jimmy not just a composite of actual people but also entirely nonexistent. Not that Cooke admitted it right away. Instead, one almost feels for her as the story becomes a sensation and then is nominated for a Pulitzer by the paper; she is perhaps the only person in history who hoped she wouldn't win. As Bradlee tells it, "On April 13, 1981, the worst happened: 'Jimmy's World' won a Pulitzer Prize."[9]

Certainly there were those at the *Post* who had doubted the story, especially after trying to take Cooke "to look for Jimmy's apartment and she couldn't find it. But their doubts were more about Cooke than about her story. No one ever suggested that Cooke concocted the entire story. Worse, none of us editors thought about the life and safety of the child. If we had insisted that a *Post* doctor examine Jimmy, we would have escaped disaster." Bradlee writes that Cooke was already "working on another blockbuster about a fourteen-year-old hooker and her twenty-year-old pimp, and this time Woodward, who topped the reporting chain from Cooke up, and Coleman insisted on meeting the hooker themselves. When those appointments kept getting canceled, we thought the hooker and the pimp were getting cold feet. It did not occur to us that she had invented them, too."[10] Cooke's planned, pulpworthy "blockbuster" article in progress indicates just how much she was giving up the goods, telling the clichéd stories the paper's readers—or at least its editors—wanted. File it under the other, politicized and sensationalist news hoaxes to come, from the craze about crack babies (now an admitted fiction) to political propaganda about "welfare queens": all are harbingers of how race and hoaxing go hand in hand.

It is only after Cooke won the Pulitzer—and after some good old-fashioned reporting—that the fabrication began to unravel. Jimmy could not be located, and neither could many of Cooke's credentials submitted to the *Post* as well as to the Pulitzer committee. Her former paper in Toledo proudly printed her bio and then pointed out the many discrepancies between it and the Pulitzer's bio, leading the *Post* to interrogate and ultimately expose her hoax.

It should be said that this, like most journalistic hoaxes, was ultimately discovered by other journalists. As Bradlee says in his memoir, "The fact is that the truth *does* emerge, and its emergence is a normal, and vital, process of democracy. If readers are generally too impatient to wait for the truth to emerge, that is a problem. It is our problem in the press. It is far easier and more comfortable for them to accept as truth whatever fact fits their own particular bias, and dismiss whatever facts misfit their biases."[11] Such biases are why objectivity became a standard in the first place, and, inasmuch as they threaten the accuracy I would advocate instead, I can see why objectivity remains necessary. As Bradlee notes, the presumption readers and their editors have about reporters is not just neutrality but trustworthiness. We need more these days, not less.

But there is another difficulty: the kinds of invisible bias that allow the most blatant aspects of the hoax to pass muster, even with other journalists. It's rather hard to believe Cooke's opening passed the smell test in the bullpen:

> Jimmy is 8 years old and a third-generation heroin addict, a precocious little boy with sandy hair, velvety brown eyes and needle marks freckling the baby-smooth skin of his thin brown arms. . . . He has been an addict since the age of 5. His hands are clasped behind his head, fancy running shoes adorn his feet, and a striped Izod T-shirt hangs over his thin frame. "Bad, ain't it," he boasts. "I got me six of these."[12]

The imaginary black man is to be feared; the mythic black boy to be pitied.

When uncovered and confronted, Cooke, as most hoaxers do, went on the defensive. A typical first line of defense is to cop to a lesser crime: with

Cooke, this meant admitting she never graduated Phi Beta Kappa from Vassar, leaving instead after one year. When pressed, she held her ground about the rest of her résumé and her story, as Bradlee recounts in a sentence that could be a line from a film noir:

> "It's true," she lied.

Interestingly, Cooke seems one of the rare instances of the hoaxer or plagiarist having lied only once, at least in print: "Janet Cooke had been at the paper close to two years, and after the 'Jimmy' disaster a careful examination of everything she had ever written for us revealed no other questionable facts."[13]

The same could not be said of her résumé. The paper had never checked her credentials, in part because they wanted her to be true; with a magna cum laude degree from Vassar and years of education and experience, including at the Sorbonne, Cooke was rare but not impossible, as Jimmy was. "Female Phi Beta Kappa graduates of Seven Sisters colleges who can write the King's English with style don't grow on trees, white or black."[14] She was, in that way, a real-life "literary darkling" to the institution that had exposed "all the president's men." Jimmy's World was a world away from N Street and Bradlee's world—"White reporters, much less white editors, don't circulate much in Jimmy's World," he'd say—and Bradlee was too willing to suspend his disbelief about what goes on over there. The piece might as well have been about Formosa or Australia or the moon.

Truth is, Jimmy's World does not exist. Reading Cooke's article reveals less the kinds of details that impressed editors from her initial notes—when the paper encouraged her toward the eight-year-old junkie angle—but rather bad dialogue and vague renderings. Much focuses on clichés of race—sandy hair, velvety brown eyes, baby-smooth brown skin—details not only formless but fetishizing, meant to entice us with Jimmy's "blackness" with a hint of race- and face-mixing. His sandy hair contrasts quite starkly with the large illustration that accompanied the piece, evoking something far more nefarious and definitively, visually black—with a large hand gripping Jimmy's Izoded arm. As the paper's ombudsman later wrote in an almost fourteen-thousand-word report on the Cooke case, citing the paper's responsibility, "Bradlee was later to find the full illustration so powerful in its horror that he insisted it run inside the paper."[15]

The picture's horror shares the modern hoax's. Bradlee notes the ways

Cooke "promised authenticity," then lists examples that appear now to be obvious hints: from Jimmy barely given a name by his mother ("I guess we got to call him something") to artier details ("Death has not yet been a visitor to the house where Jimmy lives. The kitchen and upstairs bedrooms are a human collage").[16] Bradlee finds authenticity where he knows not what's authentic. This does not mean that there aren't homes where addiction reigns, just that, like Jimmy's skin color, any such contrasts are meant to spur on the hoax's constant tension between what could be and what seemingly is. His sandy hair and skin also suggest a history that shadows slavery; Cooke mentions later, almost offhandedly, that Jimmy was the result of a rape of his mother. This, like Cooke's ventriloquizing someone calling drugs and black people close cousins, is repulsive.

Collage is a description not just of the heroin house but also of Cooke's method, which you could call an addiction: splicing together pat ideas about ghetto life with an arty sound track. These details are the very reasons *Post* editors should have doubted—they have a stock, cooked-up quality that clearly enacts the kind of details that are the real province of the hoaxer, especially the journalistic one. It all seems rather hackneyed now.

Cooke made herself Jimmy's metaphoric mother. She had to call her fabrication something: Why not a world? But Jimmy's is one without nuance, which isn't really news.

BEN'S WORLD

In *A Good Life*, Bradlee lists a number of other journalism scandals in the wake of Janet Cooke's—few if any of the names of these plagiarisms and fabrications have stuck in the popular imagination, suggesting that there are other reasons why the Cooke affair has persisted in the decades since as *the* main example of journalistic tomfoolery. One reason, of course, is Bradlee's previous fame and otherwise stellar record as the paper's editor during the Watergate scandal; his reputation is also due to his strong and sensible reaction to the Cooke affair itself, which could have sunk a lesser paper and editor, and did in many of the other cases he cites. (Hard to say how much of this is because none of the other papers' editors were portrayed by Jason Robards in a hit movie.) But there's also the frisson of race, both in the winning story and in Cooke herself, who is African American, that has allowed the affair to persist. Race, though obvious, is left merely implied in too many accounts of "Jimmy's World," becoming as hard to find as the fabricated boy in the story.

Most tellings, including Bradlee's, discuss the race of Cooke rather than of Jimmy—much less the writer's own. (Though Bradlee does discuss his own race, to his credit). As with fabulist Jayson Blair two decades after Cooke, much of the blame in any discussion gets assigned to affirmative action, as if a federal program somehow made liars out of its beneficiaries—who surely include the paper as well as any individual—rather than centuries of racism providing exactly the kind of blinders that made affirmative action necessary in the first place. And Jimmy, to some, believable.

The diversity Bradlee hoped to enhance by hiring Cooke could have helped prevent her scandal. Bradlee himself suggests as much in a retrospective look at the case in an interview with newsman Jim Lehrer; in his memoir he recalls that several of the other black reporters at the paper had serious doubts about the story almost from the start. It would seem the diversity problem they may have been trying to solve, had they solved it better, would have rooted out the fraud more easily—not because of some magical powers on the part of other black folks, but because of a range of experiences that may make it easier to say that just don't sound right, or to not fall for racial romance in lieu of reality.

In Bradlee's many terrific suggestions to counteract such a culture and hoax in the future, two stick out: "We must find a way to insure that everyone shares fears and doubts with their superiors as well as with their colleagues."[17] Having a range of voices can only help. But a top–down structure and culture at the *Post* further allowed Bradlee not to listen to those "below him" and beside him who could have helped along the way. "We share information down, better than we share it up," Bradlee admits. Indeed, the 1980s *Post* sounds much like the *New York Times* of the early "aughts" when Jayson Blair fabricated there. As anyone who's worked at anything like a hierarchical one-man show can attest, such an organization only leads to problems—if the little guy can't say something that ripples up the organization, or lead a call for change, it is far too easy for the emperor to remain naked.

Most urgently needed to be heeded: Bradlee's call to return to normal, stringent standards on sourcing. Bradlee writes that the paper has become careless, "losing sight of the Style Book injunction to seek maximum precision in the identification of sources, and to retreat from maximum identification with great reluctance." He means the *Post* but could mean newspapers in general. Eagerness can overwhelm accuracy—as the Internet well knows. We've perhaps gone well past this point when a presidential candidate can retweet racist sources and then denies accurate ones by others; where "fake news" is just an accusation leveled at facts one doesn't like.

Bradlee's memoir begins by acknowledging the place luck has played in his advancement and career. The "JFK" chapter begins, "Many of the most important events of my life seem to have occurred by accident. Like not getting off The Federal at the Baltimore train station for a job interview at the *Baltimore Sun*, and instead staying on to Washington for a job interview at *The Washington Post*. And like buying a house in 1957 in Georgetown on the north side of the 3300 block of N Street, NW, only months before the junior senator from Massachusetts and his wife bought a house on the north side of the 3300 block of N Street, NW. Our first contact as couples beyond handshakes came on a sunny Sunday afternoon walking slowly through Georgetown, wheeling baby carriages."[18] Anyone with a kid can attest to the fortuitousness of such meetings, of becoming friends with someone simply because they too have children and can share experiences and complaints, not to mention babysitters. But what black couple could have exchanged such handshakes in such a neighborhood in 1957? It isn't simply "luck" buying a house on the same street a young Jack and Jackie Kennedy would move to months later—others might call this *fortune*.

I don't mean to substitute handwringing about privilege for handshakes, merely to note that the future president Kennedy's career advances at the same pace as Bradlee's for many reasons, without a doubt talent but also often-invisible privilege. This in no way erases how Bradlee handled the aftermath of the Cooke scandal, and the way he writes, unflinchingly, of the things he and the paper did (and didn't do) to allow it to happen. Bradlee is a principled man, not a barely repentant liar like Cooke. But the fact remains that Bradlee hired Cooke, with her polish and pretend French, not just because she was different but because she appeared to be like him.

This idea is confirmed by Jill Nelson, the first black writer for the *Washington Post* magazine, which debuted in 1986. Nelson's 1993 memoir, *Volunteer Slavery*, recounts with verve, self-conscious black humor, and sardonic wit her time at the *Post*, painting a stark picture not only of race relations at the newspaper but also of Bradlee himself. Throughout the hiring process Nelson is well aware that she is being interviewed by the *Post* not just because she is a good freelance writer but in part because she is, as she says, "black and breasted." A self-defined race woman, she is also aware of the trade-offs in leaving her years of freelance in New York—often for the *Village Voice*—for what she calls *Cosby Show* stability in D.C. But she and her daughter have grown weary of her way-past-tired "Sixties class-suicide trip, of middle-class Mommy's vow of poverty in pursuit of the authentic Negro experience."[19]

This search for an "authentic Negro experience" is a refrain in the book (and its subtitle) and is a brilliant way of examining Nelson's wish not to be Mammy, but also to no longer be the militant version of herself she tried to cultivate in the 1970s by growing an afro that wouldn't quite take. "He's bad, therefore I am," she says of her "boyfriend who lived in the projects, had an African name, and could hardly read." Romance give way to reality when "one day, lounging in my parents' well-appointed apartment after filling himself up on their food, he said, 'You know what makes your 'fro so pretty? It's soft, 'cause you got that good hair.' Nowadays, I keep my hair cut short and try to avoid being either Malika or Mammy."[20] In many ways, the "authenticity" that Nelson signifies on here is the same problematic variety Bradlee found (and found desirable) in Cooke's "Jimmy's World"—a world Cooke herself was not familiar with. It's clear that while authentic ghettoness is welcome and indeed promoted in the pages of the paper, neither Malika nor Mammy would be welcome working at the *Post*, though Martha and her Vineyard would be.

For it is only when Nelson mentions that she grew up going to the Vineyard, where her parents own a house, that Ben Bradlee relaxes, realizing she's part of Ben's World: "The bond of the Vineyard makes me safe, a person like him. . . . The job is mine. Simply by evoking residence on Martha's Vineyard, I have separated wheat from chaff, belongers from aspirers, rebellious chip-on-the-shoulder Negroes from middle-class, responsible ones." In fact, when Bradlee mentions other black bourgeois families who summer there, he doesn't realize that Nelson in fact sees herself as more rooted than they are, not to mention apart: "The notion of myself as part of the black socialite scene I've spent a lifetime avoiding on and off the Vineyard strikes me as laughable. So does his evocation of the Bullocks, old Washingtonians, and former Mayor Walter Washington, who is married to a Bullock. The Washingtons, after all, don't own, they visit—an important distinction in Vineyard society."[21]

Volunteer Slavery describes the *Post* as its own closed society full of clueless colleagues, benign neglect, and an old-boy system in which, though hired by Bradlee for her perspective or at least her proximity, Nelson cannot easily get a piece in the paper or magazine—including what would have been an early piece on Oprah Winfrey as she first began national syndication. The problem is not that the paper's editors cannot imagine Jimmy's World but that they can't imagine Jill's. Nelson's upper-middle-class background is much of why she was hired, and yet violates the very narrative often invoked in the paper's pages, or seen through its clouded-over windows. Eventually the debut issue of the magazine featured a black rapper on the cover with the headline "Murder, Drugs and the Rap Star" and, inside, further articles about dangerous black men. The cover and contents of the first issue sparked citywide protests that lasted thirteen weeks, with protesters picketing outside the office and tossing purchased copies back on the steps of the paper. Often these were set on fire, the *Post* literally burned by the articles.

Nelson describes difficulty not just with times at the paper but also the very nature of objectivity. "If it's true that the only free press is the one you own, then it's not surprising that, at the *Washington Post* and elsewhere, objectivity is defined by the owners. Since those who run the *Post* are white men, objectivity, far from being 'independent of individual thought,' is dependent upon their experience—sensible or not. For most African-American journalists, working in mainstream media entails a daily struggle with this notion of objectivity. Each day we are required to justify ourselves, our community, and our story ideas. The more successful of us refashion ourselves in the image of white men. . . . Male and female, we make ourselves visually harmless. We are nonthreatening and never frivolous, always sensible, sensible, sensible."[22] Nelson provocatively sees "the Janet Cooke debacle" as an extension of "this syndrome taken to its ultimate conclusion," Cooke's artifice belonging not just to "Jimmy's World" but also to her attempt to fit in. "Much has been written about what Janet Cooke did, very little about why. Clearly, the sister had some severe ethical, moral, and psychological problems that caused her to mistake fiction for journalism, and self-hating journalism at that. But she was also an African-American female journalist at the *Washington Post*. It's not hard to imagine her nightmare: fighting it out with the other stars while the editors, for the most part, either stood by and smugly watched, or else egged their favorite on, she knew she would be outshone, discarded, and forgotten unless she did something—quick—to earn the notice and approval of the powers that be. What better than following the honored tradition of writing an exposé of pathological Negroes? After all, when you're black in corporate America, self-hatred often passes for being well-adjusted, competent, assimilated, and objective."[23] Objectivity here is defined not as a form of neutrality but as neutralizing a black self.

Whether we agree with Nelson or not, hers is a welcome voice. Nelson's appears from this vantage point as one of many post-soul memoirs from the early 1990s—Nathan McCall's *Makes Me Wanna Holler* (1995; also discussing his time at the *Post*), Lorene Cary's *Black Ice* (1992), Pearl Cleage's *Mad at Miles* (1990), and the work of Thulani Davis come to mind—that address similar concerns in a kind of Black New Journalism, substituting frankness for objectivity. These books seize the 1990s narrative crisis as an opportunity. Nelson seeks a fun, varied, tone, taking us into her confidence like we're one of her good girlfriends: she describes increasingly heavy drinking because of the stress of her job; she is gossipy and smart in portrayals of her divorce, love life, and single motherhood. If Zora Neale Hurston's *Their Eyes Were Watching God* innovated a narrator inherently black and female, Nelson imagines her audience being black and female too. Here's Nelson on her first-name-only sistergirl referred to only as Thulani: "We became friends because we discovered we could relax the racial vigilance, discard the 'correct' position, with each other. When we were together, our search for the authentic Negro experience was over: we were *it*. We'd talk about whoever we felt like dissing, get petty, whisper secrets, rant and laugh uproariously at confidences that to other ears would be seditious."[24] Involving the reader in the fold is part of the bitter and bitingly funny tone of the book.

Volunteer Slavery takes its title from a song and album *Volunteered Slavery* by Rahsaan Roland Kirk; his marrying of soul and jazz, interpolating "Hey Jude," finds its way in his title song:

> *Volunteered Slavery*
> *Has got me on the run*
> *Oh Volunteered Slavery*
> *Has got me havin fun*

Kirk's playful tone, all-important in jazz, is matched by Nelson. Her relaxed rebellion, her questioning of authenticity, her grievous gossip provides a relief from so-called objectivity that isn't really—jazz is but one example of self-expression that is also true. Nelson takes us into her *confidence* in all senses but the con artist one, establishing the necessary trust between writer and reader.

This trust differs from the confidence game, which, like the hoax, is often about power—the hoax is not just about wielding a power already held but also about expressing a profound wish for that power. What else explains the hoax's regularly replacing often-invisible privilege with a predictable narrative of all-too-invisible poverty? The problem at the *Post* appears to be one of being unable to imagine what hasn't been imagined already—how else to explain the steady recurrence, you could call it a relapse, of this despairing stereotype of "the authentic Negro experience" first provided by Cooke and years later by the magazine? You don't get noticed for writing an article about life *not* on the edge.

If it is a wish, the hoax is a wish corrupted. Where the fake memoir is a misguided attempt at redemption, just as often, Cooke, Smith, Stuart, Glass, and other hoaxers suggest things are as bad as we fear they are.

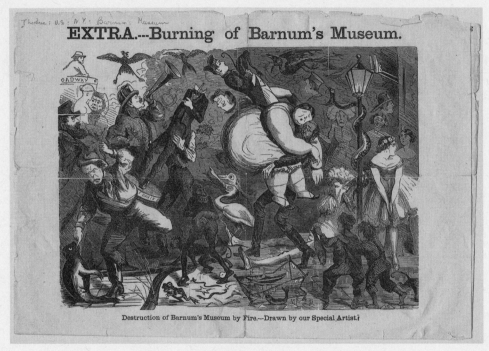

"Burning of Barnum's Museum," 1865.

CHAPTER 18

Burning Down

In the fateful, nearly unreal weeks following September 11, we may remember that the country, forever changed, mourned publicly and deeply. A veil had been torn away: people appeared that much more open, courteous, a kind word here, a nod there; our daily divisions disappeared and, New Yorkers all, we tended to greet strangers as fellow Americans, even kin, well met. In grief, many felt that overused word, *united*—though with United Flight 93, whose passengers fought back against its hijackers, that word had already taken on new meanings. The divisions the hoax exposes and exploits were gone, for a time.

Too quickly the fault lines would return. That autumn, headlines would soon and nearly continually bring threats of anthrax in the mail; everyone from newcasters to government offices to New York publishers regularly evacuated with anthrax scares or bomb threats. Grief gave way, as it will, to anger. We would eventually go to war, twice (not counting the many conflicts since). In such a tense climate an unknown sniper began a killing spree across D.C.—or properly, the Beltway—in October 2002.

The *New York Times* sent cub reporter Jayson Blair to the area to report on the random killings. (In an odd coincidence, the director of the biopic *Shattered Glass* indicates that he filmed early scenes for the movie—namely, those in which Glass pretended to show his editor where a nonexistent hacker convention was held in a Virginia hotel lobby—on the first day of the sniper shootings.) Blair's piece eventually ran on the front page, despite strong reservations from the paper's local bureau about his story's many anonymous sources and near-perfect quotes. To his fellow *Times* reporters Blair's seemed not just an unbelievable get but highly dubious; to his higher-ups, as journalist Seth Mnookin would later report, it was a terrific scoop.

Even those at the paper who already knew of Blair's spotty track record filled with corrections—including being caught writing about a September 11 benefit concert that he did not actually attend—never quite suspected just how much Blair was on a spree of his own. Plagiarizing and fabricating a slew of pieces that would eventually number at least half of the seventy-odd he would file for the front desk, Blair's actions, unchecked for months, would threaten to undo the achievements of the *Times*—including their unprecedented reporting right after the Twin Towers fell. The paper of record published pieces about every person killed in the September 11 attacks, amounting to the permanent version of the makeshift bulletin boards and notes posted downtown as people struggled to find loved ones. For his part Blair "pretended he had a cousin who had died in the Pentagon to avoid writing any 'Portraits of Grief,' the *Times*'s short, unbylined biographical sketches of the victims that collectively won a Pulitzer Prize. Blair seemed to bridle at the notion of doing work for which he might not get explicit credit."[1] As suspensefully recounted in Mnookin's *Hard News: Twenty-one Brutal Months at* The New York Times *and How They Changed the American Media*, the sniper story was actually Blair's redemption of sorts, after he had had numerous problems with news pieces, been disciplined, and sent to Sports. (Harder to fabricate scores and results, though Lance Armstrong might disagree.) Who exactly sent him, given such problems, to cover the D.C. shootings would eventually come to be of great import—especially as an email from an editor a year before had said unequivocally, "We have to stop Jayson from writing for the Times. Right now."[2] It would turn out that Blair filed many of his first-hand Beltway sniper stories not only while still in Brooklyn but also sometimes while sitting upstairs in the same building as the editors he was communicating with.

The most prolific fabulist since Stephen Glass, Blair was found out when another piece about the only soldier still missing in action in Iraq was learned to have been largely plagiarized from a small Texas paper. The article he stole from had actually been written by Macarena Hernandez, a former intern in the same diversity program at the *Times* that Blair had gone through; Mnookin reports she had been offered a position at the *Times* that she regretfully had to turn down because of a death in her family. In his 2004 memoir about the hoax and his downfall, *Burning Down My Masters' House*, Blair says he hadn't noticed the author was someone he once knew, which is rather hard to believe, especially as he himself describes calling the reporter afterwards to lie to her that he hadn't seen her piece though he'd clearly copied it. Hernandez didn't believe him—not least of which, as Mnookin relates, because Blair claimed any similarities must have been from getting similar translations from Spanish via the subject's daughter (and the missing soldier's sister). In fact, the soldier's mother spoke English. Blair was guilty of his own *typing* here, as it were—not to mention his cutting and pasting— assuming a subject's Latino last name meant she didn't speak English.

Blair not only plagiarized the story and then lied about it, he hadn't actually visited the mother of the missing soldier. She wasn't alone: those who ultimately cleaned up after Blair, rechecking his stories, would have the unenviable and distasteful task of calling up many a mourning parent or grieving spouse to confirm if a reporter they now suspected had lied had indeed been there to see them. Grief, anger, more grief.

Though Blair didn't write a novel like Glass had, Blair's memoir may suggest some revisions to the notion of confession-as-cure. To call Blair's *Burning Down* nonfiction is not to imply it's in any way objective or always accurate; turning nearly sinking "the Gray Lady" into a grandiose metaphor for burning down your masters' house assures that. In a preening preface, Blair does take great pains to emphasize that the "masters' house" in the title is plural possessive, suggesting serving or destroying many masters, but that too barely sticks. When faced with what he did, he balks, "I did not want to disappoint them with the truth."[3]

Though in no way unique, Blair's unusual stance as a black reporter at a major paper was matched by the Beltway snipers. Typical serial killer profiles and public speculation had it as a single white male shooter when it turned out to be two people—a man and an adolescent, both black—mirroring the haunting dyads of such crime sprees as recorded by nonfiction classics *In Cold Blood* and Dave Cullen's *Columbine*. The terrible random killings were accompanied by bizarre notes and, it just so happens, a black police chief, who would often talk to the snipers in what turned out to be coded ways via the media.[4] "Blair was not just *covering* the snipers' trial," Mnookin writes. "He was increasingly identifying with Lee Malvo, the teenage suspect. Within months, Blair was circulating drafts of a book proposal on the sniper story in which he discussed his own anger and frustration as an African American."[5] At the beginning of *Burning Down*, which is to say at the start of his undoing, Blair describes the book slightly differently—as an investigation into the legacy of American and, in Malvo's case, Caribbean, slavery—real deterministic, dysfunctional family stuff straight out of the clichéd Janet Cooke textbook. *In Cold Blood* it was not. The only twist would be a notion that Malvo is not just a dark double, like killer Perry Smith became for Truman Capote, but also somehow a folk hero to someone seeking to burn down the system that Blair believes made them both.

This folk hero angle is a rather easy one, as witnessed by Stephen Glass's invention of the stereotypical Asian avenger Kae Bang. Though brutality may understand only brutality, it does not justify it. This is yet one more problem with the hoax—rather than resist or merely represent the brutality of the world, it adds to it, victimizing the reader. Like the snipers themselves, or any sociopath, the hoaxer often impersonates not just a writer but a thoughtful, feeling person.

Blair's view of the young sniper quickly devolves from "outlandish" into overfamiliarity and overidentification. Blair would be taking on this view from the safety of his apartment, not on the ground where he might risk complexity, much less the field where he pretended to be. Indeed, the best critique of the "Malvo book" proposal is found in the words of Blair himself: "I had a term for stories that explored 'different' cultures as 'safari pieces,' where the word 'community' could easily be replaced with 'jungle' or 'reserve,' and the people could have just as easily been giraffes or cheetahs. . . . The subjects did not have to be black. They could be Asian, they could be Native American, and they could be white too, and all you need to see for proof of that was a *Times* story written from Staten Island, the borough that might as well not have been a part of the city."[6] Blair is right insofar as the safari piece, the island outlook of the travel liar, quickly become indistinguishable—all turns unfamiliarity into strangeness, every island into a zoo. Outlandished is the hoax's native land.

What to make of all these pseudo-explorations found in our desk-bound Age of Euphemism? The journalistic hoaxer, like the travel liar of the eighteenth century, finds "abroad" what he or she already thinks. Our current "desktop travelers" eschew sources even as they are deeply reliant on them—the hoax is a twice-told tale that, much like the travel liars, according to critic Percy G. Adams, commits "a type of plagiarism that seems to have been peculiar to travelers, a type that made some of them liars twice over, and a type that has turned out to be astoundingly effective."[7] The hoax not only makes false claims, it attempts to lay claim to those it describes, whether black kids or black reporters or others. This isn't just a claim to the truth but ownership over a rapidly changing world—one in which black folks have long provided an exemplar of unchanging reality since at least Barnum's day.

SNIPING

Blair was a modern spirit photographer, a ghostwriter who only pictured pain. It is beyond despicable the way he took death, loss, and a nation's grief for his fabrications; Blair plagiarized others' pain, lying not just about where he was but also about who other people were, including a dead soldier's family. Blair also fabricated who he himself was. "Several of the people closest to Blair during this time remarked later that Blair was something of a chimera; seemingly unable to develop a core personality of his own, he instead tried to become like the people around him," Mnookin writes. "In college, while writing about sexual abuse, he suddenly and publicly claimed he himself was a victim. When the space shuttle blew up, he said his father worked at NASA. When Illinois governor George Ryan pardoned all the prisoners on death row in his state, Blair said his uncle was on death row. After September 11, of course, he said he had a cousin in the Pentagon. And when Howell Raines married a Polish woman, Jayson Blair found a Polish girlfriend."[8] For Blair, pleasure is something else to imitate or fake.

In the opening chapter of *Burning Down*, Blair makes mention of this female friend, sometimes describing her as a girlfriend, sometimes indicating the two are just platonic: "I called her about my problems while she was reading the final pages of Ralph Ellison's *The Invisible Man*." Of course, no such book exists: Ellison's novel is called simply *Invisible Man*. Blair's *The Invisible Man* is no mere typo—he repeats the misnomer several times, including on the audiobook he reads himself (yes, an audiobook; and yes, I actually own the thing).[9] Not to be confused with H. G. Wells's 1897 science fiction classic *The Invisible Man*, Ellison's is a dystopian fictional autobiography of African American life by a speaker who is not only metaphorically "invisible" but unnamed, anonymity as a strategy. By mistaking Ellison's metaphor for Wells's horror, Blair does what the hoax has done for a century or more, going gothic—a way of seeming unbelievable yet conventional, the horror the hoax has become.

Then again, maybe both books are the same—at least to Blair, who in his ham-fisted memoir relies on the fictional, and sometimes fantastical. Between the two ideas of invisibility emerges a metaphor for Blair's experience and actions: not simply feeling invisible, sharing a condition implied by Ellison's title, but unwittingly becoming "*The* Invisible Man," some presumed affirmative action hero whose alter ego, like Superman's Clark Kent or Peter Parker's Spider-Man, is a mild-mannered journalist, for whom mental illness, sobriety, and racism are simultaneously kryptonite and a cause macabre. Just don't make him angry.

Does it bear asking why, excepting some key impostors, there aren't too many noteworthy black hoaxers other than journalists? Is it because rarely are black writers afforded such unerring authority, even today? It is hard to imagine a black writer claiming to ghostwrite and edit Howard Hughes's autobiography as Clifford Irving did on such little evidence as a handwritten letter, much less given a huge advance to do so. And just why do black journalists, both faux and actual, Blair and Jill Nelson, turn to slavery—violent or volunteer—as a metaphor to explain their situation?

Perhaps Blair repeatedly calls Ellison's novel out of its name, as the saying goes, because he is constantly, literally, disappearing. A key part of Blair's fraud is to say to photographers assigned to the locales he never visited that he just missed them, when in fact, "I lied about where I had been, I lied about where I had found information, I lied about how I wrote the story. And these were no everyday little white lies—they were complete fantasies, embellished down to the tiniest detail." Of course, in his lies that aren't quite white, Blair's mention of the snipers and "The Invisible Man" mean to paint himself as a folk hero, if not a super one—though flight is one power he doesn't seem to possess. "I lied about a plane flight I never took, about sleeping in a car I never rented, about a landmark on a highway I had never been on. I lied about a guy who helped me at a gas station that I found on the Internet and about crossing railroad tracks I only knew existed because of aerial photographs in my private collection. I lied about a house I had never been to, about decorations and furniture in a living room I had only seen in photographs in an electronic archive maintained by *Times* photo editors."[10] His was a fraud dependent on technology, marshaled less like "The Invisible Man" than Batman, utility belt filled with fake receipts, downloaded maps, and photo archives to cover his tracks.

As with James Frey or JT LeRoy the hoax can turn tough-guy talk into tall tale. Hoaxers build up not only themselves but also the problems they overcome, crafting large cartoon villains—jail, journalism itself—where there aren't any. That way they, or those like them, can play hero. Blair, as does many a hoaxer, confuses fabrication for fable.

Time to call: Ombudsman! An ombudsman's job sounds like one any writer might hope for: the *Washington Post* established the position in 1969, Bradlee writes, "to monitor the paper for fairness, accuracy, and relevance, and to represent the public in whatever strains might arise from time to time"; more to the point, the ombudsman can't be edited, or assigned, and can't be fired.[11] But at the *New York Times*, such a position did not exist—in part because as Mnookin notes, the paper considers all the editors there to serve the public interest. (Until 2017, the *Times* had a public editor who served much the same role as an ombudsman, a role specifically created in the fall of 2003 in the wake of Blair's scandal.) Yet, with the kinds of communication problems then found at the *Times*, any notion of sharing of information necessary for such stewardship, had become nearly impossible.

Once Blair's sniper story came up bad, an investigative team was assembled not just to cover the story but to uncover the truth. Their steady-handed actions will one day be studied, along with Mnookin's book and Bradlee's account of the Janet Cooke affair, to better understand a newspaper's internal and intensive reaction to a hoaxer, all with integrity. (*New Republic* editor Charles Lane reached for Bradlee's memoir in the height of the Glass mess.) What the team independently discovered was worse than anyone had suspected—not just carelessness but Blair's outright fraud in thirty-six of seventy-three stories. Their collective, ultimate "Correcting the Record" cover story from Sunday, 11 May 2003, opens this way:

A staff reporter for The New York Times committed frequent acts of journalistic fraud while covering significant news events in recent months, an investigation by Times journalists has found. The widespread fabrication and plagiarism represent a profound betrayal of trust and a low point in the 152-year history of the newspaper.

The reporter, Jayson Blair, 27, misled readers and Times colleagues with dispatches that purported to be from Maryland, Texas and other states, when often he was far away, in New York. He fabricated comments. He concocted scenes. He lifted material from other newspapers and wire services. He selected details from photographs to create the impression he had been somewhere or seen someone, when he had not.

And he used these techniques to write falsely about emotionally charged moments in recent history, from the deadly sniper attacks in suburban Washington to the anguish of families grieving for loved

ones killed in Iraq. . . . In the final months the audacity of the deceptions grew by the week, suggesting the work of a troubled young man
veering toward professional self-destruction.[12]

It wasn't just Blair's own self that was being destroyed—he violated trust not
only within the newsroom but also between writer and reader.

Seth Mnookin suggests Blair's deceptions threatened history itself. "Blair
was stitching his fraudulent accounts into some of the most heavily covered
stories of the day," he writes. "His 'reporting' had been featured on the front
page time and time again. It was moved on the *Times*'s newswires and
reprinted by other papers around the country. The *Times* is the paper of
record. What it writes is history. Blair had fabricated history."[13] Certainly
Mnookin is right in that Blair's daily audience, to put it in perspective, was
ten times that of the *New Republic*. But if Blair fabricated history, acting as
though it could be made up and was unverifiable—a common enough fear
and misperception these days—Glass turned fantasy into history, made our
fears print and almost bone. I'm not sure which is worse, but I believe actual
history can fight fake history. It does this all the time; it is why we still need
trained historians and not a History Channel that features alien autopsies.
But fantasy made real, now that's hard to fight—*it's hard proving a negative*.

While many of Glass's hoaxes pretended *not* to be about race, Blair pretended his implosion was *all* about race. Neither, we know, is true. Yet the
fabrications of Glass and Blair, Janet Cooke and company, have remained
so powerful and central to the conversation not necessarily because they falsified first drafts of history but because all touch on and exploit our darkest divisions, including race; all go even further, becoming parables of the
primal questions of human existence, namely, truth and death. After he
says he threatened suicide, Blair writes, unconvincingly, "I was not going
to keep fighting for a job that I didn't really want, for a position covering
something that mattered even less than the meaningless stories I had been
writing about lately. I wasn't going to fight for a job at a newspaper that had
disappointed my idealism, for a newspaper that I had allowed to take something very precious from me."[14] I'm not sure what the opposite of *meaningless*
is if not the deaths of people during war. Blair is no victim; his pathologies
excuse neither the paper's flaws nor his actions.

Daily news changes, evolves; it is truth, on a deadline. Just as important
as a hunch is our willingness to admit it was wrong, to change course and
say what we found anew. Especially when we are at our most disconnected,
virtual, and unverifiable, we need to fight the disembodiment and invisibility

that is its own inequality. What we need is not more immediate news—which we seem to crave, faster and faster—but more reliable information. We need less local color, or ideological coloring, and more depth; fewer people covering the same story than discovering a new one. We should write like no one is looking over our shoulder—except the future.

MASS DESTRUCTION

Beyond fantasy as history, and history turned into fantasy, journalistic hoaxes can be manipulated through anonymous or unidentified sources—this way, even reputable journalists can sometimes end up hoaxed. There has sprung up an entire world of unreliable, entertainment-driven media that have become more and more reliant on such unsourced material—that report rumor as fact and worse, dress it up in the clothing of inquiry. Tabloids print urban legends as fact; what should be called *fabloid* television's "Rumor Watch" and "True or False" segments allow fake news shows to repeat a rumor as they go on to debunk it. Such rumors-as-reporting have now become standard practice on more traditional television outlets, where recapping the Twitter feed has replaced the newswire, and morning shows have come to incorporate it all in a steady diet of diets, celebrity gossip, and pregnancy "baby bump" watches of those whose initial claim to fame is a sex tape, that rumor made flesh. And aren't pregnancies great—you get to report the insistent instantaneous weight loss after! It's a twofer.

The result is a culture kept constantly guessing, yo-yoing like its diets; or increasingly paranoid, the hoax a feeling grown familiar. This is bad enough, but there is a more pernicious way that a half-hoax culture has invaded not just our news but our politics, not just society but our science. The vaccine "debate," based on the bad science of an admitted liar, reveals how fast fears can trump facts, hedged over by Donald Trump and others in presidential debates; the denial of climate change (what Trump once called a hoax by "the Chinese") is belied not only by facts but illustrates how partisanship can overtake expertise. There aren't always two sides to every story.

And there needn't be outright fabrication to, say, take a nation to war, merely the repeated mention of anonymous sources by prominent news outlets. "What is still less obvious—and what the *Times* itself is struggling with—is how news organizations will address stories that are flawed because of something less nefarious than wholesale fraud," Mnookin writes. "The best example of this type of quandary is the *Times*'s own faulty coverage of both the hunt for weapons of mass destruction (WMD) in Iraq and the supposed ties between Iraq's former leaders and al-Qaeda terror-ists."[15] After months of seeming scoops that we know now were essentially press releases from the Bush administration, "Judith Miller began a run of stories that repeatedly took Bush administration and Iraqi exile claims about [Saddam] Hussein's WMD capabilities at face value. The problem was, those stories and others like them weren't breaking news, they were just broken."[16] All it takes is a focus on scoops and a lack of skepticism to let such stories happen.

The whole Miller incident brings up a question that may be lingering behind all this half-hoaxing that falls somewhere between outright deceiv-ing and spin as truth: Is the hoax always political? Is it a cloaked form of power? I think the news so to speak is worse than that. Like plagiarism, the hoax is not just a cloaked form of power; it is also panic about that power. The unfound and turns out unfounded "weapons of mass destruction" are some of the worst examples of a kind of gnawing, growing, euphemism and how influential and infectious it can be—but nowhere near the last.[17] *These are just words.*

How complex our networks of deception have become; "fake news" is a label the propagandist prefers for anything that cannot be spun. Declaring someone else is fake, like some extended feedback loop from reality TV, is the ultimate insult. Take soldier Jessica Lynch: she really was captured in Iraq and then rescued, but she was never shot or wounded as initially reported as a justification for that rescue; she soon later became used by military and news outlets as a sign of patriotism and heroism, the story distorted. Lynch later had to testify before Congress that she indeed wasn't the one who started such stories, yet to this day she is often blamed for them. Her being used in this half-hoax manner is something she has to fight, showing how the hoax, while often tied to politics and history, not only can remain beyond its subject's con-trol but also is something to which one can be subjected. Of course, Blair had filed many fabricated stories about Lynch in the course of his burnout.

Proving something doesn't exist is more than difficult; it can be deadly. A set of denials and lack of accountability can be costly, in money as well as lives. The hoax changes history and also the future. It's the worst kind of twofer: the hoax is ultimately a matter of life *and* death.

TRUE STORY

Michael Finkel must be the only former reporter at the *New York Times* thankful for Jayson Blair. If it weren't for Blair, Finkel, who was fired for fabricating a *New York Times Magazine* cover story in 2001, might be the most notorious of recent *Times* fabulists. Yet, despite Finkel's fabricating during the same time as Blair, Finkel doesn't merit a mention in Mnookin's book on the newspaper's collapse. Finkel recollects his hoaxing in the book *True Story*—a story not just about life and death but also about their modern correlatives, race and slavery.

For a piece on chocolate harvesters in West Africa, Finkel did in fact travel to the Ivory Coast to investigate and meet workers. To hear him tell it later, the question put before most Western reporters there is whether or not the chocolate trade led to slavery, though the truth was of course complex: while not exactly slaves, the laborers certainly worked in inhumane conditions, though they often had selected such a life, at least initially, believing promises of more. The story too had grown complicated because of the fact that the local human rights agency that served as most reporters' contact in the region both coached those they said had escaped those conditions and had a financial stake in their position, one to which reporters found themselves having to contribute.

Finkel, however, shifts the blame for his fabrication from himself to the editorial process, in which his first efforts at a story weren't seen as promising—not least of which because he had gotten scooped while he was overseas by other newspapers, including the *Philadelphia Inquirer* and the *Miami Herald*. These outlets reported on the "slave" story with the same skeptical angle Finkel was considering; he had even read similar kinds of stories while still in West Africa. Finkel says his editor told him to "go literary" and he chose to focus on a single protagonist, telling the story of one worker in particular.[18]

Mistaking literary for lie, on deadline and on drugs, Finkel fabricated the magazine cover story "Is Youssouf Malé a Slave?" Told with no quotes and in the close third person, as if a short story, the piece ticks off all the hoax boxes, yet surprisingly set off no alarms. There are things that the reporter cannot possibly have known: presumably these were suggested by interviews he had notes on, but the piece pretends he has fully embodied Malé's voice through his immersion with his subject:

> The man came to the village on a moped. Youssouf Malé watched him. A man on a moped was unusual. When visitors did come to Nimbougou, deep in the hill country of southern Mali, they were almost always on foot, or on bicycle. The man on the moped had come to sell fabrics, the flower-patterned kind from which the women in

Youssouf's village liked to sew dresses. Youssouf sat beneath a palm tree and watched. . . .

The man was not that much older than Youssouf, and already he owned a pair of genuine blue jeans. Maybe three people in Youssouf's whole village owned blue jeans. And on this man's feet—my goodness. On this man's feet was something that Youssouf had never before seen. In Nimbougou, people either wore flip-flops or plastic sandals or nothing. What this man wore on his feet looked to Youssouf like a type of house. Like a miniature house, one for each foot. Two perfect, miniature houses, painted white, with curved walls that rose to the man's ankles, with a fence up the front of each one made of thin rope. . . .

The man told Youssouf that he was old enough to get money. He said it was easy. All Youssouf had to do was leave Mali, where everybody was poor, and cross the southern border to the Ivory Coast, where everybody was rich. In the Ivory Coast, the man said, there were jobs and there was money, and Youssouf could find one of these jobs and earn some of this money, and then he could buy a pair of shoes.[19]

This immersion in another is of course the province of not just good but great fiction—and the nonfiction novel—and while the story turned out to be fiction it still ain't very good.

If its fabrications capture some of what we think of each other, the journalistic hoax does not use the uplift that the fake memoir ultimately insists on, but rather represents the downtrodden as downtrodden. The dispossessed are spoken for, not just about. Though providing more complexity than other hoaxes (an admittedly rather low bar), Finkel's hoax erases what it claims to reveal—it is significant that his character never speaks, or is quoted, a radical move in the abstract for journalism but one all too familiar for the hoax and for the treatment of those deemed not to have a voice. Ever abstracted, Finkel's made-up "Malé" is a boy through and through, able to see but barely to feel, able to do things—go to work in a field, to be disappointed in his living conditions—but never to act.

There are certainly fictional characters like that, from J. Alfred Prufrock to Willie Loman, trapped both by circumstance and by their own minds—an intelligence that knows enough to be paralyzed but not enough to do something about it. And, of course, such characters move us because they reflect people we may have met or fear we could easily become. But Finkel's is a close-up without real closeness. As a short story, especially so, it would have still had this defect. It is only as nonfiction, borrowing the intimate techniques of fiction, that such a piece could work at all: the perspective in all senses proved unusual for the *Times Magazine*, surely seen as a risk by the editors, but a worthwhile one. Yet such a point of view is a risk rarely taken with, for instance, a white celebrity—the assumption for those who at first thought this story was real was not just that Finkel should speak about or for or as Malé, but that he *could*.

Intimacy remains one of the hoax's best weapons: it is especially easy to speak for those we aren't exactly interested in hearing from. The piece has so many internal instances of mistranslation—fake Malé taking shoes as houses for feet, for instance—as to alert us to the difficulty not just of translation but to admit that Finkel's is a poor one. To make it plain: *The only way to understand this young black man's point of view is to make it up.* The only way to conjure empathy for someone we fear might be a slave is to conjure a made-up character pretending to be not just a slave but also a person.

For Finkel to quote from his subject, to render him with the dispassion and compassion given every other figure in almost every other form of journalism, new or otherwise, is too much to ask. Malé—whose name visually connotes both maleness and Mali, the country of his reputed origin—is a ventriloquist's dummy, the ultimate nondescript. We should be thankful, I suppose, that Finkel doesn't resort to the bad dialect that dogs the hoax memoir.

What's worse, there really is someone by the name Youssouf Malé, whom the reporter actually met—Finkel took that name to composite his own "Jimmy." His brazen deceit would begin to come unraveled because the piece ran with a photograph Finkel took of yet another young worker. As the image, names, faces, and voices of these actual people became enslaved to the writer's whims and career advancement, it is Finkel, not just this makeshift Malé, who emerges as a stock character, stuck somewhere between familiar travel liar and white abolitionist propagandist:

> They worked another row, and as everyone was waiting for Abdoul to finish, one of the older boys sat next to Youssouf and told him a story. He said that sometimes, when the work was too hard, a boy would try and run away from the plantation. When a boy tries to run, Youssouf was told, the owner and his family chase after him. People who grow up in the forest know the paths very well, and they can always catch

the boy. When they catch him, they bring him back to the plantation. They take off all his clothes. They tie his arms together and his legs together. They whip him with a tree branch until he is bloody from head to toe. Then they leave the boy outside, all night, still tied up, and the mosquitoes feast on him and the ants crawl into his wounds. The older boy admitted to Youssouf that he had never actually seen such a thing with his own eyes, but he had heard the story many times and was very sure it was true. Youssouf believed him.[20]

Finkel may be Youssouf Malé after all; more likely, he is the teller of the story, and we are Youssouf, an audience literally captive, listening, believing.

Why not try to capture what's really there? Or better yet, who? Why yet another literary darkling, a fake dark double as a way to express suffering when there is enough to go around? In some ways, because captivity captivates and repulses us, we can hardly believe it much less believe the ways we might be found complicit, whether through American slavery or the original Constitution's "three-fifths compromise lose," or in eating chocolate raised under unfair conditions. Slavery has regularly provided an occasion for hoaxes in the United States, if only because of its constant contradictions, rendered unreal. The mind boggles at the thought—but rather than think or write that thought, the hoaxer gives us something ultimately more palatable, even if it's a palate primed for pain. Finkel is an abolitionist on safari.

Then again, even this captivity Finkel makes *worser*. In the end the service organization that Finkel indicted in his piece discovered that the picture was not who it claimed, and, as the *Times* describes it, "Though the account was drawn from his reporting on the scene and from interviews with human rights workers, Mr. Finkel acknowledges, many facts were extrapolated from what he learned was typical of boys on such journeys, and did not apply specifically to any single individual. The writer says that he wrote this article without consulting his notes. (The article included no direct quotations.) The notes, which the editors have now read, reveal that contrary to the description of Youssouf Malé's year of work at the plantation, he spent less than a month there before running away."[21] Escape is the one thing the hoax cannot imagine, or report, settling instead for escapism—even if it's from reality into horror.

Once the fabrication was revealed, the editor of the *Times Magazine* told Finkel, "You're young. You have a long career ahead of you. But not here." As Youssouf Malé didn't really think or say at the end of Finkel's article, "He had seen some of the world, he said, and now he was finished."

TRUE CRIME

With its tangle of testimony and "as told to," with white mistranslation and authenticity, both Finkel's story and the ones he didn't tell bring us back to the slave narrative—the form critic Ben Yagoda calls the origins of the American memoir. These true stories did create a form, one that employed the techniques of narrative (as did Harriet Wilson's novel *Our Nig* around the same time) to tell of freedom and justice. It was this kind of strong narrative of survival and crime that figures like Truman Capote returned to when they went about creating the "nonfiction novel"; even he began to see one of the killers in the true-life case as his own literary darkling. In contrast, Finkel turns to truth and to fiction as a last resort, rather than employing improvisation and truth in ways the African slave did in the Americas, whether coded in the Negro spirituals or allegorized in the animal tales, seeking actual freedom through the imaginative act I call *storying*.[22]

Finkel's false Malé is unsophisticated, gullible, at least compared to the reporter with his reasonable doubts. "I am not a natural skeptic. I tend to believe what people tell me, especially if it confirms my expectations," Finkel wrote later about his time in Ivory Coast. "But there was clearly something wrong here. At that moment, I changed my tack—rather than searching for slaves, I was now looking for liars. And then, as if a code had been cracked, everything suddenly made sense."[23] If only it were that simple.

The day before the *New York Times* correction—and concurrent firing of Finkel—another article in the paper revealed that a man named Christian Longo, wanted by authorities for the murder of his wife and three children, was arrested in Mexico, where he'd fled and had adopted another false identity: Michael Finkel, *New York Times* reporter. This doppelgänger, in name at least, is Finkel's true darkling.

The coincidence of the murder and Longo's fabrication became the main subject of Finkel's *True Story: Murder, Memoir, Mea Culpa* (2006). It's hard to know which of those three subtitle ideas—or are they the same?— dominates the book and now a 2015 film starring James Franco as Longo and Jonah Hill as Finkel. Finkel's book employs many of the same cross-cutting techniques as *In Cold Blood*, switching between Finkel's own fabrications and Longo in the lead-up to the murders and his life on the lam.

Finkel soon writes to Finkel *faux* in jail and strikes up a correspondence: "I'd like to do this because at the same time that you were using my name, I lost my own—my firing, as I mentioned, was very public. During my firing, I was robbed of the two things that a freelance writer needs to survive—his name and his reputation. Both are now gone."[24]

The contrast becomes quite clear between Longo the murderer—and liar—and Finkel the fabricator, whose lies can only prove lesser by comparison. Certainly Finkel admits his own actions were problematic, and unethical; he takes his firing to heart, and throughout the book tries to connect and seek redemption by contacting the prisoner who stole, for a time, his not-so-good name. *Penance* after all is the root of *penitentiary*.

It is a hard trick and Finkel mostly pulls it off—except, perhaps unsurprisingly, in regards to his own actions. He builds up to them, waiting to tell us exactly what happened with his hoaxing much like he does building up to the murders:

> I've lied to strangers simply because it was exciting to lie, or because I wanted to impress them. Perhaps people who've spent time on the Internet pretending to be someone they're not can understand—that sense of risk, of power, of semi-illicit thrill. I *liked* lying. It could, for me, equal the escapist exhilaration of a drug.
>
> I always thought that my journalism was immune to such impulses. I wrote creatively at times; I condensed plots and simplified complications and erased some chunks of time, but I was sure I'd always stay within the boundaries of nonfiction: Reality could be shaped and trimmed, but it could not be augmented. I had no intention of ever breaking that rule. No intention, that is, until I sat down to write my chocolate-and-slaves story.[25]

It might as well be a chocolate-*as*-slaves story: both prove as addictive as hoaxing. Finkel also takes drugs, seemingly channeling fellow hoaxer James Frey in his actions and in his prose: "I stayed up for three days, virtually without rest, and my stomach went sour and my moods swung wildly and I puffed on marijuana when I felt out of control and popped sleeping pills to bring myself down and I never once changed my clothes and I cried without prompting and I finished the story, the entire story, and I felt it was as fine a piece of writing as I'd ever produced. But of course the story wasn't true."[26] And of course, at many stages between handing in his nontrue story and publication, he had many chances to take it back, rather than fool fact-checkers and lie to his editors and ultimately his readers, over and over. The opportunity for a *New York Times Sunday Magazine* cover story, his third that year, must have been irresistible.

Reading *True Story*, we might come to feel, as *New York Times* reviewer Sridhar Pappu does, that "*True Story* reads entirely too fast, as if Finkel were racing through Longo's story to arrive at his own apology. Like Finkel's composite African boy, Longo comes off not as a human being, but as a plot device meant to tell a story."[27] Finkel ends up much like Glass, effectively asking readers, *Are you still mad at me?*

By calling his book about two liars *True Story*, Finkel is presumably having us consider the colloquialism "true story," which folks sometimes say right before or right after a story that is patently, or seemingly, false—or at least has the air of an urban legend. Longo's ping-ponging between prosperity and poverty, between denial and despair and desperation, becomes a quintessential American story, though Finkel never quite describes it like that. Longo's story is American even in his heading to Mexico on the lam and changing his name: he makes it south of the border, where a certain kind of archetypal criminal, including *In Cold Blood*'s Perry Smith, seeks to flee. Mexico is a destination symbolizing not just freedom—from English too—but an inexpensive, outlaw liberty. Longo lives within the very hypocrisies of our age—on the one hand jealous and fearful and claiming religious faith; on the other having affairs, lying, enraged, slowly simmering. It is almost understandable that whenever Longo does get a little scratch, he embarks on a vacation the family cannot afford. Taking on Finkel's identity in Mexico, much like the lover he meets there, is less escape than escapism. He is the ultimate travel liar.

In his slavery story Finkel never gets close; with Longo he's far too close. He never really convinces us in the way that *In Cold Blood* does that this is not just an American story but a story about America. Longo's lies and unforgivable crimes of course outweigh the journalist's, no more so than when, at the time of trial, having for months maintained his innocence, or vied for insanity, Longo switches tactics and pleads guilty. Then, instead of telling the truth at last, Longo on the stand spins one last, elaborate, unbelievable, and unbelievably hurtful lie: that he only killed (and killed only) his wife after learning she had killed all their children, rather than drowning the two older children as he really did, having already brutally murdered his wife and smothered his baby. Longo is trying on different stories like identities—an innocent man, a wronged husband, someone who startled an intruder, a killer only out of "hysteria"—anything but the murderer he was.

In truth, after drowning his two oldest children by throwing them off a bridge, Longo went first to Starbucks, then to work. There he claimed to coworkers that his wife was an adulterer who had run off and left him high and dry. Longo then went and rented *Blow*, a mediocre "based on a true story" movie about a drug dealer in the 1970s played by Johnny Depp, which he claimed at trial he actually didn't finish watching—the only believable thing in his testimony.

I don't know why Longo's lying only compounds the murders—just like I don't know why the endless denials of a discovered hoaxer or take-no-prisoners actions of a disgraced athlete or the don't-send-me-to-prison testimony of a convicted and now admitted fraud only makes things far worse than if they just came clean, even when they eventually do. I think it is because we the deceived, or grieving, feel that these liars must think us stupid to fall for their tricks again. The lie, like the hoax maintained beyond chances to come clean, is an insult. The truth, however belated, is ultimately a form of respect, of admitting more than a mistake: it admits both the liar's and the lied-to's humanity. Sometimes, in the monstrous things people do to each other, hard truth is the only thing left—not to share, exactly, but to recognize as actually there, *fixed* and stable as a start to any possible repair.

The Truth has been hurt, badly. The Truth takes time to heal.

Longo was convicted within hours, his story clearly not believed by anyone in the courtroom, barely by Longo it would seem: he sent Finkel a thirty-seven-page letter justifying his testimony and trying yet a further tack, claiming that he told the truth in court but, "'Maybe this is the one time that I should have lied,' he wrote. 'Maybe in some way I took the cowardly course by not taking all of the blame.'" This gambit is as bad as they come.

Longo's story goes beyond *True Story*, the book and movie, or his trial. For a time, sentenced to death row, Longo wished to die—however, after authoring a couple of e-books, Longo has now become an activist seeking the dubious right to donate organs after his death (a practice outlawed, usually for ethical reasons involving killing people simply to harvest their insides). Finkel has written in *Esquire* of the troubling place Longo put him in when in 2009 he "asked if I'd be willing to help him formulate a plan to donate his body parts. I said, once I wrapped my mind around the idea, that it was something I could do, but first I needed to clear my conscience. If I was going to help him die, I had to hear the full story of the night his family was killed. Though he was convicted of the four murders, he had never fully confessed nor provided some essential details about his motivation and what actually happened. I needed to know he was completely guilty. Longo asked that I come to the penitentiary, where we could meet in person. He'd tell me everything, he promised, if I helped with his plan. Here was a chance, I believed, to extinguish Longo from my life forever. I admit I felt some relief. So I said yes." After fully confessing to the murders at last, Longo would go on to decide not to drop his appeals but to fight them to continue his campaign for the right to donate organs, as he detailed in a *Times* op-ed piece.

All these bodies, disembodied and disconnected, dead but barely buried. The end to Finkel's article about Longo's wish to live after denying his family theirs, is haunting: "It's odd. He [Longo] was the one person on earth I wanted to die, and instead I've helped to save his goddamn life."[28] Longo calls his newfound purpose, or scheme, his finale.

Longo's gambits—to live forever, in literature or in pieces, in lying about whether he should lie—prove extreme, but they are nevertheless familiar to those haunted by the hoax: by Stephen Glass saying he would say he'd made it all up if his editor wanted him to; by all those evasive hoaxers and even some readers who claim later on that the hoax's lies are truer than the truth actually is.

The Truth can be hard. It's never exactly invisible—though the Truth is a black man from Kansas. Everyone knows that. Or at least, anyone who's a basketball fan, for whom "the Truth" is the nickname of Paul Pierce, former University of Kansas Jayhawk and longtime Boston Celtic, ultimately traded. Though strong, the Truth always looks sickly, or tired, or weary—unless the Truth smiles at you. The Truth has a good smile. The Truth works hard and is hard work. The Truth can run better than you might think, can go deep with defenders in his face and beat the buzzer.

The Truth hurts, has literally been stabbed and survived. Still the Truth believes no matter the deficit, the Truth can come back, and win.

SIX

Unoriginal

Sin

On plagiary, murder, bad poetry & other crimes

On a chance we tried an important-looking door, and walked
into a high Gothic library, paneled with carved English oak,
and probably transported complete from some ruin overseas. A
stout, middle-aged man, with enormous owl-eyed spectacles,
was sitting somewhat drunk on the edge of a great table, staring with unsteady concentration at the shelves of books. . . .
"Absolutely real—have pages and everything. I thought they'd
be a nice durable cardboard. Matter of fact, they're absolutely
real. Pages and—Here! Lemme show you." . . . "See!" he cried
triumphantly. "It's a bona-fide piece of printed matter. It fooled
me. This fella's a regular Belasco. It's a triumph. What thoroughness! What realism! Knew when to stop, too—didn't cut
the pages. But what do you want? What do you expect?"

—THE GREAT GATSBY

Bell Studio, "Cannibal Fair Child," Philadelphia, Pa., ca. 1870.

CHAPTER 19

Blacker than Thou

It was never easy for me. I was born a poor black child . . .

The beginning of Steve Martin's *The Jerk* still makes me laugh with its twist on *Once upon a time*. The dissonance between what we know of the white comedian Martin, his relative success, and his obviously false declaration sends up not only the tragic showbiz biography but the corny black one: in both, the *worser*, the better. It also suggests his character's transformation, his overcoming—after all, he's clearly white now!—not to mention his current lot in which he's as smudged, bummy, apparently destitute. His isn't blackface, but his face half greased is certainly part of the effect—it's a familiar one, in other words, to black people used to watching white people only claim blackness as a "poor me" stance.

Now, why does this jerk remind me of Rachel Dolezal?

There's a long-standing American tradition of whites donning blackface, or redskins, or any other colored mask they pretend is a face. Those who wear blackface reduce blackness to skin in order not to be white. The implication, of course, is that black people are just miscolored or extra-dark white people. Many a joke told for my benefit in my Kansas grade school reinforced the same—*Know why black people's palms are white?*—though I'm not sure the term used was *people*.

But if you are white but truly "feel black," then why do you have to look like it?

I thought I'd nearly finished this book—filled with hoaxers and impostors, plagiarists and phonies—but as soon as I had sent a draft to my publisher, elated and relieved, Rachel Dolezal raised up her faux-nappy head. Now I have to take time to write about her too?

I can't decide if Dolezal, the woman revealed to have been merely pretending to be black, lecturing as such and even leading her local Oregon NAACP, is the natural extension of what I've been saying all along, or a distraction from this book's larger point: that quite regularly, faced with the paradox of race, the hoax rears its head. It turns out, I now know, it rears its rear too.

When Rachel Dolezal's fraud first broke, and was simply a joke on Black Twitter, I identified some of my favorite Twitter titles for the inevitable, anticipated memoir: "Their Eyes Were Watching Oprah" (that one's mine); "Imitation of Imitation of Life" (from Victor LaValle); "Blackish Like Me" (mine too). Now things done got serious.

When you are black, you don't have to look like it, but you do have to look at it. Or look around. Blackness is the face in the mirror, a not-bad-looking one, that for no reason at all some people uglify or hate on or wish ill for, to, about. Sometimes any lusting after it gets to be a drag too.

Every black person has something "not black" about them. I don't mean something white, because despite our easy dichotomies, the opposite of black is not white. This one likes European classical music; that one likes a little bit of country (hopefully the old stuff); this one is the first African American principal ballerina; this one can't dance. At all. Black people know this—any solidarity with each other is about something shared, a secret joy, a song, not about some stereotypical qualities that may be reproducible, imitable, even marketable. This doesn't mean there aren't similarities across black people or communities or, better yet, memory—just that these aren't exactly about bodies and not really about skin at all, but culture.

There is a long tradition of passing—of crossing the racial line, usually going from black to white. You could say it was started, like this country, by Thomas Jefferson.

One of the best things about being black is that, barring some key exceptions, it's not a volunteer position. You can't just wish on a dark star and become black. It's not paid either. It's more like a long internship with a chance of advancement.

I've never seen the TV show *black-ish* all the way through. (I hear it's quite good now.) From what I've seen, *Fresh Off the Boat*, another of ABC's offerings, seems a more accurate portrayal of the complexity of racial identity, even black identity. (This is despite the worries of its creator, chef and author Eddie Huang.) The young Asian immigrant who's the main character identifies with hip-hop in order to be both American and that misnomer, *non-white*. It's funny, and frequently brilliant: How do you become American?
   Is this the same as becoming black?

Traditionally, pretend blackness provided a shortcut to becoming white. This is true for Irish and Jewish immigrants, who adopted blackface in large numbers in the late nineteenth and early twentieth centuries, and soon assimilated; and for Northerners, for whom blackface helped them imagine themselves a nation since blackface's advent in the 1830s.
   Cue that effin caricature of Jim Crow dancing.

Like Rachel Dolezal, I too became black around the age of five. I first became a nigger at nine, so I had me a good run.

The problem isn't merely that Rachel Dolezal can wash off whatever she's sprayed on herself (it just don't look right), or that blackness is a choice, but that what she's wearing isn't just bronzer, but *blacker*: a notion that blackness is itself hyperbolic, excessive, skin tone only. Well, and wigs.
   This last, some black observers have praised.

Did Dolezal really fool those black folks around her? I have a strange feeling she didn't, that many simply humored her. You have to do this with white people, from time to time.

Black people are constantly recognizing and identifying those who look like secret black folks—many light-skinned people I know get identified as white by white people, but we know they're black. (This isn't passing, btw.)

Most look like one of my aunties. Knowing they are black, it is hard to see them another way.

It's one of the advantages of my folks being from Louisiana—there's plenty of folks who don't "look black" but are (which of course should make us stop and reevaluate what "looking black" is). Because of the one-drop rule, though begun as a controlling race law, black people themselves adapted and even invented and accepted a broader blackness. In general this has made black people—I am speaking for every single black person without exception here, of course—wary yet accepting.

Those surprised by a white lady darkening her skin and curling her hair haven't been out of the house or online in a while.

There was the rather white-looking bank manager in Athens, Georgia, who chatted me up one day and mentioned a couple of key black-striver things—a black sorority here, the Links there—that let me know she was black too. It was brilliant, and conscious but in no way calculated; hers was smart survival.

It was also a test to see if I was woke, or a striver, too.

Teaching a class about blackness doesn't mean you are black. Blackness ain't a bunch of facts to memorize, or a set of stock behaviors; nor darker skin color neither. It's like the jazz heads I've seen, often white, who can tell you every sideman on every session, but seem in the daylight unable to find the beat. The beat is there always; doesn't mean you can always hear it.

While black folks often hear the beat, and set it, doesn't mean when anyone else hears it, that she gets to be black.

Every church I know of had a white lady who arrived one day. Ours in Topeka did. After she hung around awhile, and proved she wasn't a tourist, "Mrs. Pete" was accepted and seen as part of the St. Mark's AME congregation, even singing in the choir (which was a high bar, as it were). But we never thought she was, or somehow became, black. *She's good people*, folks would say.

She did get herself a perm: I mean a white, curly one, instead of a straightened, black one; the fact that this clarification is necessary is just one more indication we're awfully mixed up. There's the joke: *You didn't get yourself a perm, but a temporary.*

There is this other, far rarer passing, which we may call reverse passing, of whites living as black. The most prominent I know of may be Johnny Otis— who was successful enough that many race women and men I know aren't aware he was actually born white. Or the Hall of Fame woman inductee, owner of a Negro League team who likely wasn't black herself. What's interesting is to compare what the black people around them thought, usually accepting them—not necessarily as what they said they were, but how they behaved. It isn't that they weren't judged, just that when they were, they weren't found wanting.

So when the killer [name withheld] walked into Mother Emanuel Church in Charleston one week after the Dolezal story broke, I am not surprised that the black worshippers there welcomed him. Welcome is an integral part of the African American Christian tradition; it is especially so in the African Methodist Episcopal one, begun over two hundred years ago when the Methodist Church prevented blacks, mostly freedmen and -women, from praying beside its whites, even pulling them off their knees during prayer.

How long did [name redacted] sit there waiting, in a prayer circle, deciding to deny the evidence of humanity before him? Nothing, it appears, could have convinced him not to kill blacks, who he believed—and spewed hate about—preyed on white people, especially women. One suspects he may not've known any women besides his family.

Thomas Jefferson hated black people but slept with one who bore his children, six of them. (*Misery is often the parent of the most affecting touches in poetry.—Among the blacks is misery enough, God knows, but no poetry*, he wrote in *Notes on Virginia*.) That Sally Hemings was also his wife's half sister neither stopped him nor made him reevaluate his stance toward black thought, which he saw and wrote of as an impossible paradox.

Jefferson had black heirs whom he, and for centuries his (sorta) white heirs and white defenders, denied. In our time, Strom Thurmond had him a black daughter out of wedlock; the only people surprised by this were the white voters he courted by vehement racist rhetoric. Of course, this behavior, demeaning blacks while desiring at least one, descends from slavery and is how we got most light-skinned folks who "look white" in the first place.

Why doesn't Rachel Dolezal seem to know that a white person can have a black child (see one-drop rule above)? (See Obama.) (See Hemings.) (See Jefferson.) See . . .

Being black is not a feeling. *I don't always feel colored.* Nor is it simply a state of mind. Blackness: a way of being.

After Rachel Dolezal had mumbled her way through various news shows looking like Gilly from *Saturday Night Live* and answered the question of whether she was black or not with *I don't understand the question,* the proximity in time of the murders in cold blood at Mother Emanuel makes clear that the two are not coincidental. Both are near-simultaneous misapprehensions not just of blackness but of whiteness too.

It would be one thing, I think, if in her house, to her pillow or family, Dolezal said she felt black. I imagine many white households across the country don blackface and grab banjos and have themselves a good ol' time when no one else is around. It's when that somehow translates to what she does, when she teaches black studies as if she's a black person—not a teacher, but a mind reader—that it becomes a problem. She wears the mask not to hide but to gain authority over the very thing she claims to want to be. How very white of her!

After the killings in Charleston, several things happened: Dolezal's story went back to merely being ridiculous. Talk shows moved on to something else and those who somehow willed Dolezal sublime retreated. Flags flew at half-staff—except the Confederate flag on South Carolina statehouse grounds. It took a black woman, Brittany Newsome, to climb up and take that down.

They gave the assignment to a black man to raise the "rebel flag" back up. Like Sally Hemings, he might not have minded, but he certainly couldn't have refused.

Soon the Confederate battle flag would be voted down by the state assembly, but flag sales would soar. Customers began to hoard them like guns once most major outlets suspended sales. Yet given the killer's postings of himself with Confederate flags and separatist mottoes, easy slogans like "heritage not hate" stood naked. The proof here only increased as a pro-flag rally brought out the American Nazi flag, side by side and even mashed up with the Confederate one.

In a place like the South that loves its tall tales, why do people take their Confederate stories hyperseriously? As gospel? *Everyone's a colonel*, someone joked about the South when I was at the University of Georgia, where I taught for five years.

It was my first job, and I was regularly thought by strangers at the university to be passing for a student (and not a grad student). *You look too young to be a professor*, surprised interrogators would say, usually after asking what year in school I was. (It's true I was only twenty-five, but had a book already and a degree or two.) After a while, I began to translate the comment about looking young to be a more polite way of saying what they couldn't: *You look too black to be a professor.*

Maybe blackness is only a look, one we're told cannot ever look back?

Far more interesting and provocative than a white mother in blackface would be a white mother with black children. Wouldn't that provide a much more complex identity than any blackface? You get the feeling that, for Dolezal, blackness equals hiding.

For the deaconess at church who had to make her way by cleaning white people's houses during the week, blackness don't mean hiding. Sunday meant rest, and a respite, wearing a different kind of white, black or grey hair crowned by lace.

Blackness too often veers between two poles in the public eye: opaqueness and invisibility. For [racist killer], blackness wasn't just opaque but conspicuous. It named an enemy and provided a uniform that allowed mass judgment—and mass murder.

Rachel Dolezal could be conspicuously outraged all the time, filing lawsuits, marching, because she didn't have to save any energy for just being herself.

Dolezal's drama didn't just start recently. The persecution complex, the past lawsuits (when she was white) against a historically black institution like Howard University no less, seem like the whitest thing ever. It's like when you are with a white friend and they experience racism, likely for the first time, alongside you: they usually go wild, protesting to no one and everyone; you shrug as much as shout. Some things are just part of the daily dose of being black. The cab will drive away with a white friend in it, door still open, rather than drive you too. It's dealing with blackness that black people have perfected—or at least gotten practiced at.

Racism's daily injustices are almost an inoculation against it. Almost.

Whenever I tell a white person about the injustices at the airport, or on the street, the daily snubs, or that my white neighbor's farewell to me as I was moving out of my apartment last year was *Goodbye, nigger* and that no one in the condos or the condo board, both painted white, did a thing about it, they too grow silent.

Part of grief, I've found, is silence. Protest too, at times. What the no-longer neighbor wanted from me most, I knew instantly, was a reaction. *Bye*, I said.

I've heard tell even Dolezal's paintings of black faces while in school as a white graduate student were actually plagiarized. Our Dolezal didn't just want to disappear into blackness, but disappear. For her, blackness was not a private thing, which ultimately may be where blackness best tells us what it knows. It is this private, shifting, personal blackness that cannot be borrowed. What can be: wigs, tanning booth, rhetoric.

Dolezal's righteous rage looks more like self-righteousness—or is it *other*-righteousness?

What no one seems to say is just how Dolezal's actions, over many years, conform to the typical hoaxer's: a constant shifting set of stories to explain her identity (it's complicated), an array of attempts not just to be someone else, as anyone might, but to be exotic, even in her birth (which she said was in a teepee or tipi). When asked directly on the teevee if she was born in a teepee, she answered, "I wasn't born *in* a teepee," emphasizing that maybe, just maybe, she could later say she was born near or under one. The hoaxer is always leaving the pretend teepee door ajar.

Dolezal also says she was abused, and claimed to have lived in South Africa. It is true that her actual parents did live there, but not with her, only her siblings—many of whom were actually adopted and black. She apparently earlier equated their alleged beatings (that several of them have denied) with slavery. Given her other disproven lies, abuse does not so much provide an explanation for her behavior as much as a distraction: true or not, like her making slavery a mere metaphor it would seem part of a scenario of victimhood, which to her is also, inherently, black.

Borrowed blackness and nativeness provides her, a plagiarist of pain, the ultimate virtual victimhood.

Finally the chief problem with racial impostors or blackface: it can be only, as James Weldon Johnson said of stereotypical black dialect, comic or tragic. Ultimately, it conforms to white views of "the blacks" themselves, offstage: as either a joke or a set of jailed youths and stooped old heads.

Even President Obama, who started up a Twitter feed weeks before the Dolezal incident, was inundated by racists posting pictures of nooses and equating him to a monkey or worse. It is only when one feels such stereotypes as real that one might find being in blackface freeing—not because you believe the stereotypes but because you want to establish other, corny ones.

Sinking feeling: blackfaced person always occupies a bigger public stage than a black one.

Standing back, maybe it's true: not that being black is only comic or tragic, but that too often white thinking or acting out about it, as demonstrated in Dolezal's hoax and the Charleston murders, remains only polarized: comic or tragic. Both are nullifying.

Amid the bewilderment and grief, for just a moment I wondered how onetime NAACP chapter leader Dolezal would've responded, as surely she would have sought to, had she not been unmasked. Where's our fearless leader now? I thought. Then I didn't think of her again.

I came out as black as a teenager. Before then, I was simply a boy. After, I was sometimes, still.

When President Obama broke into "Amazing Grace" at the funeral for the state senator killed at Mother Emanuel, it was mere hours after the Supreme Court declared gay marriage legal, and any barring of it as unconstitutional.

It was strange yet strangely fitting to hear him sing that song written by the reformed slaver while at sea. I like to think the enslaved people who took it over and made it a Negro spiritual were not the same kinds of *wretch* as its author.

Of course you can see why anyone would want to be black: being black is fun. Don't tell nobody.

This morning I woke from a "deep Negro sleep," as Léopold Senghor put it. I then took a black shower and shaved a black shave; I walked a black walk and sat a black sit; I wrote some black lines; I coughed black and sneezed black and ate black too. This last at least is literal: grapes, blackberries, the ripest plums.

CHAPTER 20

Professor Plum

Violent and violating, *plagiarism*, the term we now use to describe stealing another's language, is haunted by further crimes. The meaning of *plagiary*, as the act was first known, originally included theft not just of words but also bodies: taken from the Latin, *plagium* meant and still means in civil law "the crime of kidnapping," especially children; *plagiary* added the idea of stealing a slave, and of seduction, as well as being "a literary thief."[1] This final meaning is the one we are most familiar with today and provides the basis for plagiarism's biggest defense: what's the harm? "No, it isn't murder," starts Thomas Mallon's classic study of plagiarism, *Stolen Words*. But it isn't merely victimless: "Think how often, after all, a writer's books are called his or her children," Mallon continues. "To see the writer's words kidnapped, to find them imprisoned, like changelings, on someone else's equally permanent page, is to become vicariously absorbed by violation."[2]

The case of hoaxer "Clark Rockefeller" brings the connections between these different meanings of *plagiarism* into a sharp and bizarre focus. His crimes included not just the forgery of artworks and the theft of an entire family's identity and name, but also literal kidnapping—plagiary in its oldest form. Really a German immigrant named Christian Gerhartsreiter, "Clark" adopted the name Rockefeller after years overstaying a student visa in California, a state he left under a cloud of suspicion. He had, since coming to the United States as an exchange student and getting a quickie marriage to help cement his American residency, adopted the names Chris Gerhart, Christopher Mountbatten Chichester, Christopher Crowe, and, for good measure, Christopher Chichester Crowe Mountbatten. Moving in the 1980s to tony Greenwich, Connecticut, he claimed he worked as a producer of *Alfred Hitchcock Presents*—a nod perhaps to his *Vertigo*-like doubling—before talking his way into a job at a New York firm famous for selling junk bonds. His fake names and pretend old-money attitude would pave his way to Wall Street, where he was made vice president of a corporate bond department—as if he meant to mimic the double crosses, derivatives, and inflations of our time's would-be tycoons.

Those interviewed in *The Man in the Rockefeller Suit*, Mark Seal's tell-almost-all about the case, constantly return to the idea of the putative Rockefeller's accent. It was either highfalutin, or nonexistent, which may mean the same thing: "He spoke the most perfect English I can imagine," one of his ex-friends says. This is the ultimate privilege—to have one's accent be so dominant as to be invisible—also bringing to mind the "successful" plagiarist, whose theft goes unnoticed. At least for a time. Rockefeller's accent isn't so much meant to capture a high Boston accent as provide a stereotypical version of it; the more eccentric his behavior or unlikely his talk, the more people both believed and tolerated him: he was a Rockefeller after all. That the Rockefellers are from New York seemed to pass most he met by.

His parroting of privilege points out how much privilege is tolerated, its eccentricities expected, by those around the person with presumed power. Plagiarism too is a sign of power. All Rockefeller needed to convince people he went to Yale—or Harvard, or Princeton, Clark's story was ever changing—was a hat with the school's insignia.

Some of these questions of privilege and put-on come up in *Blood Will Out* (2014), Walter Kirn's sharp account of knowing "Clark," whom he met when he offered to drive a damaged, wheelchair-bound dog from Montana to Rockefeller's Manhattan. Even from their first phone call, Kirn thought Rockefeller terribly bizarre and beseeching—the heir said he could sing "any song I might name to the tune of the theme from *Gilligan's Island*"—and upon arrival, Clark is busy letting his current dogs lick his abstract expressionist masterpieces. The paintings, of course, turned out to be forgeries—fakes that the impostor Rockefeller used to convince people *he* was genuine. Not only did well-regarded museum curators trust the works were real, Kirn too chose to believe in their authenticity and that of their owner despite any initial reservations. The two men actually grew somewhat close in the aftermath of their divorces and custody cases, sharing a kind of Ivy League affectation as the midwestern-raised yet Princeton-educated Kirn makes clear.

Clearly modeled on *In Cold Blood* down to the front cover font, Kirn's book explores what it means to know, and kowtow to, someone who pretended to be somebody who then turns out to be no one.

Gerhartsreiter sought an extreme version of whiteness—a carte blanche, a check as blank as the one he claimed he gave his banker to buy art with. It was almost out of a novel, at least a plagiarized one. Someone who knew him describes Rockefeller as an embodiment of literary chicanery, "something out of the novel *Tom Jones* or a book by Joseph Conrad," or maybe the work of Truman Capote himself. Another of Clark's former friends seems to agree, saying to biographer Seal, "There is a phrase of Truman Capote's: 'a genuine fraud.' . . . It's a person who actually may be genuine, but built upon a fictional armature. I think all Americans are our own inventions. That's part of the allure of this country. And in some ways one has to see Clark as an archetypal immigrant who constructs a new life and a new persona, free of the constraints of the country he left behind."[3] Then there's his first name—and patented thick glasses that Kirn says "ought to come with a fake mustache attached"—that smacks of Clark Kent, the alter ego of the ultimate immigrant: Superman. For Gerhartsreiter, fictional armature was a form of armor, a superpower that he maintained for years at least until he got married and had a child, an adored daughter he nicknamed "Snooks"— she would be his kryptonite. His wife soon grew disenchanted with his controlling nature and spending and began divorce proceedings. After learning through private detectives that he wasn't exactly who she thought he was ("They couldn't tell me who I was married to") she left him and moved to England with their child at the end of 2007.

It was during his first scheduled, supervised visitation in late July 2008 that Rockefeller kidnapped his own daughter—*plagiary*, indeed. Knocking down the court-appointed monitor, he jumped into a chauffeured car with Snooks and drove off, setting off Amber Alerts across the region. He was arrested days later, posing as "Chip Smith" in Baltimore, after having purchased a boat, presumably for the two to set sail. In the search for him, federal investigators determined he wasn't who he said he claimed; after his arrest, suspicions arose that Gerhartsreiter may have also killed a couple from California during his time there. He had long been a person of interest in their disappearance, ending up back east with the missing couple's truck.

From immigrant to impostor, Gerhartsreiter's American story of re-invention is worthy of Gatsby, murder and all. Not only in a persona bigger than his past but in his invisible, invented accent, his case speaks of race and class, revealing how pretension to the latter can erase the former, well beyond the limits of nationality. Both the limo driver who inadvertently drove the getaway car and the realtor who sold him, on the lam, a condo in Baltimore compared his newfound accent to that of *Gilligan's Island*'s own Thurston Howell III. Kirn and his reporter buddy who sat daily at his murder trial would nickname Gerhartreiser "Hannibal Mitty"; "Gatsby the Ripper was our second choice." Rockefeller was as much a fiction as whiteness is: does being white let him act far whiter, richer, entitled? His pretentiousness is a cover for outright pretending, ostentation a way of avoiding suspicion.

What whiteness means for him is innocence—not just presumed but permanent. It calls to mind James Baldwin's *The Fire Next Time*, in which he's thinking of broader malfeasance: "It is not permissible that the authors of devastation should also be innocent. It is the innocence which constitutes the crime."[4]

The impostor not only remains unknowable but also reassures you there's nothing to know. In FBI custody at last in Baltimore in August 2008 after being a fugitive for several weeks, Rockefeller seemed unaware of the irony in describing how he first met his future (now former) wife at a party he threw to which guests came dressed like characters from the board game Clue. She came as Miss Scarlet, he Professor Plum: the point of the popular game is to solve a pretend murder. For Clark Rockefeller it would all seem a game, not just Clue but Trivial Pursuit. It is that late 1980s parlor-room staple that then-Christopher Chichester invites folks over to play near a mound of dirt—which, it has become clear since, was likely the newly dug grave of the son of the house's owner. "Clark was worse than a murderer and dismemberer and graveside board-game player," Kirn writes. "He was a cannibal of souls."[5]

This does not mean Clark acted alone—at least in the sense that like all plagiarists, he sees all others as mere texts, sources for borrowing. Unaware of how others create, or why they might bother, the plagiarist of words or identities sees others as coconspirators, or at the very least somehow complicit. "What a perfect mark I'd been," Kirn writes, pointing to another kind of troubling collaboration. "Rationalizing, justifying, imagining, I'd worked as hard at being conned by him as he had at conning me. I wasn't a victim; I was a collaborator. I'd been taught when I was young, and had learned for myself as I grew older, that deception creates a chain reaction: two lies protecting the one that came before, and on and on and on. Now I was learning something new; how *being* deceived, and not wishing to admit it, could proliferate into a kind of madness too."[6] In its serial nature, being plagiarized from in such a way surely feels both personal and despairingly impersonal, which tends to be the way serial killers view their victims. Obviously, would-be Clark Rockefeller is a sociopath, but such antisocial impulses also sit behind more ordinary plagiarism.

While the erstwhile Rockefeller is at last in jail, Kirn asks about the mysterious paintings. "Fakes," he answers. "All fakes, Walter. But very good ones."[7] It isn't just that the front of the painting was convincing: the back was meant to be beyond belief. One Rothko he had turned over and shown to Kirn, claiming that stains on the back were blood from the artist's suicide. The schlock of that fake blood from an actual artist and his very real suicide should give us pause. The plagiarist isn't just plagiarizing another artist's achievement but—again—his pain. The forger isn't just simulating suffering but adding to it.

That a revealed hoax devolves quickly into schlock shows just how precarious the hoaxer's privilege is. The unmasked charmer—whether impostor, forger, or ordinary plagiarist—becomes reviled, and the performance that once seemed sublime turns to instant kitsch. Not that this necessarily stops the inveterate plagiarist from continuing to push his craft. Or luck. In Rockefeller's case, even after he was caught, he continued to try to make others complicit: from jail, he asks Kirn one last favor, or is it a further collaboration? Would Walter go to Baltimore and retrieve some of his things from storage? He could also sell the forgeries, if he wishes. Kirn reports, "They were worthless in themselves, [Rockefeller] said, but perhaps their status as 'Clark Rockefellers' (he spoke the words flatly, without irony) would lend them appeal for a certain type of buyer."[8] Buying, selling, collaboration, favors: the forger and con artist, impostor and hoaxer, are always doing one and calling it the other.

The hoaxer is just another huckster, but where the con man is content with cold cash and the dealers of three-card monte have the decency to fold up their card tables and flee from those they've fleeced, figures like Rockefeller seek not just an audience but a coconspirator. To the hoaxer—whether impostor, plagiarist, or forger—pain isn't a side effect but the exact point. In the end, Kirn grows convinced that Clark "had killed for literature. To be a part of it. To live inside it. To test it in the most direct ways possible."[9] This must be any plagiarist's wish—to belong—even while confusing this wish with another's belongings. Clark's plagiarism is cannibalized, while also a form of cannibalism—he is in this way an incarnation of pop culture, which seemed to feed him in the ways that he's now feeding it.

Clark claimed he was a writer, but after much prelude and probing over the years, finally revealed the books he was asking Kirn to edit were, in Clark's words, "homages. They're reworkings. Amusing things to write, but I can't claim they're original."[10] They are, he says, adaptations from *Star Trek* episodes—and from *Star Trek: The Next Generation* at that. Such unoriginality extended to his beloved daughter: "Snooks, his daughter's pet name, was borrowed, lifted from the child of a family he'd known back in Connecticut."[11] Even the plagiarist's few pleasures are pilfered.

CHAPTER 21

Ghostbusters

Plagiarism is always aspirational. In a wish to have someone else take their place, or supply their words, plagiarists generally steal something better than they might write themselves. In this way, though it may seem an anxiety about status or a nervousness about originality, plagiarism paradoxically displays privilege—the belief that *I could've thought of it if I'd had enough time or desire*. This is one reason that while the hoax regularly refers to race, plagiarism is about class. But it isn't the class warfare those few "in favor" of plagiarism declare, seeing it as a radical recapturing or conceptual collage. The plagiarist is no Robin Hood of words. Rather, plagiarism is the very definition of work without work. *While hoaxers want to be someone else, plagiarists want someone else to be them.*[1]

In the novel *How Opal Mehta Got Kissed, Got Wild, and Got a Life* (2006), Kaavya Viswanathan details the aspirations of the main character, who seeks to get into Harvard, and by implication, realizes her own wish to become both a best-selling author and a polymath. A Harvard undergraduate herself, Viswanathan was marketed as many things in the run-up to the book's publication, especially as a young overachiever who resembles her title character. Despite the character's perfect scores and extracurriculars, when a Harvard interviewer asks Opal why she wants to go there and she cannot answer, he insists she pursue having fun or "getting a life" with the same kind of fervor with which she pursued perfection.[2] Opal's parents are also in on the project of making her more commercial, you could call it, with a schedule for getting busy in another sense, trading what they called

HOWGIH (How Opal Will Get Into Harvard) for HOWGAL (How Opal Will Get A Life). Dating and television, the American dream.

The review copy I tracked down of *Opal Mehta* has an extraordinary amount of supporting material—advance press, publisher statements, reviews, and copies of glossy magazine features—that first accompanied the book and continued to accumulate in the few weeks it was on the shelves. Focused on Viswanathan's backstory as a Harvard undergraduate—"The Six-Figure Sophomore" the *Boston Globe* would coo on 22 February 2006—the book's press packet purposefully confuses the author photo and front cover, Viswanathan and Opal: "One is a sophomore at Harvard, and one will do just about anything to get in. Meet Kaavya Viswanathan . . . and Opal Mehta." The sheer preponderance of evidence surrounding the book is actually reminiscent of the kinds of proof marshaled only after a plagiarist is discovered—usually listing the kinds of parallels between passages that ultimately indict the thief—not to mention the passages the plagiarist herself amasses, or the de rigueur excuses a plagiarist produces to say she isn't one.

The book's advance publicity had certainly helped, as *Opal Mehta* quickly climbed the best-seller list—unfortunately for Viswanathan, it was climbing right behind the latest of Megan McCafferty's series of young adult books that began with *Sloppy Firsts* and *Second Helpings*. Within days after the book was published in April 2006, the Harvard *Crimson* revealed that Viswanathan had plagiarized several portions from McCafferty. Reaching for thirds, Viswanathan helped herself to both of McCafferty's books to cook up her own. One similarity soon spread to a baker's dozen of exact wordings, and less than a fortnight later, after previously featuring the author in a fluff piece, the *New York Times* reported, "The *Crimson* cited 13 instances in which Ms. Viswanathan's book closely paralleled Ms. McCafferty's work. But there are at least 29 passages that are strikingly similar."[3] All this gives new meaning to the question posed in the press release: "How far would you go for that one thing you've always wanted?"

Why, when they steal, do plagiarists take from popular material? Why not stick to the obscure? Or is it that we only catch those plagiarists who become popular themselves? Most plagiarism cases, as with other hoaxes, include what amount to clues planted almost expressly to be found. In the midst of the mounting accusations, Viswanathan went on the *Today* show where anchor Katie Couric subtly undermined the book, asking the tough but obvious question just weeks after it had gotten published. I remember watching that episode at the time, cringing. Bravo for Viswanathan for keeping what appears to be a previously scheduled appearance; she's in full damage control, saying she's sorry and that it was unintentional. When discovered, many do what Viswanathan did at first: plead subconscious stealing. (Don't try this at your local Walmart.)

This is the first defense of the plagiarist: I only did it once, and by accident. The second defense is plagiarized from the first: I only did it once. Yet as Mallon reminds us, "Plagiarism is something people may do for a variety of reasons but almost always something they do more than once."[4] The "unconscious stealing plea" goes hand in hand with the idea of only doing it once—not simply that I did it just that one time, but rather, in that one instance too, I was so unconscious as to be blameless.

To rewatch the episode now is to see the hoaxer plead innocence in a way familiar enough that it may seem plagiarized from some clichéd script. Indeed, all this was happening within months of James Frey, "Nasdijj," and JT LeRoy implosions. Where the fake memoirist plays at suffering, the plagiarist, like the impostor, often performs innocence. In Viswanathan's case this doesn't mean just "not guilty" of the charges before her, but innocence as a permanent state—one feminine, youthful, American. Such enforced innocence—gendered and often raced—may explain why, in the press material of the young author, she is regularly referred to as a "starlet," a term usually reserved for cinema. No matter her actual age, a starlet performs youthfulness—and matching beauty. Such youthfulness quickly if quietly signifies newness, freshness, and originality in turn, an approachable prodigy.

The early notices and prepress frame Viswanathan as a "girl wonder" a century after the iconic figure's heyday. "A clever novel by a promising author . . . one of the hottest young talents in fiction," says the *Boston Globe*.[5] There's a sense too of the author as somehow a new invention: the "young adult" (or YA as it's known) Indian author; or more exactly, the Indian YA one. But by far the biggest suggestion of all is that the fictional Opal is true to life, a double who's her and not-her. Opal Mehta is plagiarized from Viswanathan.

I don't mean to substitute Freud's couch for the *Today* show's, yet we must be able to see the ways our culture's cult of innocence and youth is also the culture of plagiarism. Newness at all costs yields pressure not just on the potential author but also on the culture that cannot be honest about its recycling, much less its trash.

The *New York Times* reported on 25 April, "In an e-mail message yesterday afternoon, Ms. Viswanathan, 19, said that in high school she had read the two books she is accused of borrowing from, "Sloppy Firsts" and "Second Helpings," and that they 'spoke to me in a way few other books did.'" The reports continues, quoting Viswanathan as saying, "Recently, I was very surprised and upset to learn that there are similarities between some passages in my novel, "How Opal Mehta Got Kissed, Got Wild and Got a Life," and passages in these books." The press release goes on to reiterate that any borrowing was "unintentional and unconscious."[6] I didn't do it; Opal Mehta must have.

Is such a story believable on its poorly made-up face? How can Viswanathan recall and rewrite, word for word, a book she claimed to have forgotten she even read?

The first rule of influence is that there isn't any. The second rule of influence is that it is everywhere. In the case of *Opal Mehta*, it wouldn't matter for much longer which was which. For Viswanathan's book—a phrase we can no longer use—turns out to have filched from a number of other authors, including fellow writers of Indian descent Salman Rushdie and Tanuja Desai Hidier, who published a novel titled *Born Confused* (2002), dubbed "the first book with a US female teen desi heroine." *Desi*, to quote the contemporaneous, now-defunct website Sepia Mutiny, is "slang for the cultures of South Asia and the diaspora. It's similar to homeboy, paesano or boricua. Etymology: *deshi*, Hindi/Urdu for 'from the country,' 'from the motherland.' Pronounced 'they-see,' it's the opposite of pardesi, foreigner."[7] *Opal Mehta*'s publicity claims of being a new, original voice are not even true in terms of Desi culture.

While traditional print and television media was involved in the promotion and publicity of the book, as well as its downfall, its afterlife exists online alone. Online is also where Hidier writes of the case:

> Ironically I first saw firsthand these sections of *Born Confused* on the day Ms. Viswanathan was quoted in the *New York Times* as saying: "*I've never read a novel with an Indian-American protagonist. The plot points are reflections of my own experience. I'm an Indian-American.*" ... And so I was extremely surprised to find that the majority, though not all, of the passages in *Opal Mehta* taken from *Born Confused* are those dealing with descriptions of various aspects of South Asian culture (food,

dress, locale, even memories of India, etc.) and the way that culture is expressed in America; essentially every scene of *Opal Mehta* that deals with any aspect of South Asian culture in more than passing detail has lifted something from *Born Confused*.[8]

Hidier knows well that the marketing of both her book and Viswanathan's is predicated on their being this supposedly unusual thing, an Indian writer; but where Hidier embraces it, Viswanathan denies it at the same time she pleads it. How could she copy what doesn't exist?

The number of accusations increasing and evidence of plagiarism mounting, the publisher recalled the book, offering refunds. But why would Viswanathan not only plagiarize from, but also claim never to have read a book by fellow Desi authors, when her book is riddled with many of their exact words? The answer might be found in that Viswanathan could be telling the truth, inasmuch as she may not have exactly written *Opal Mehta* at all. Rather, the book may have been assembled by committee.

As the first feature in the *New York Times* mentions, Viswanathan got the offer to publish her book through a series of stand-ins and hirelings—the author's admission to Harvard too was due not just to some parental plan but to a, how we say, "college packager":

> Her parents were not immune to the competitive pressure, however. Because they had never applied to an American educational institution, they hired Katherine Cohen, founder of IvyWise, a private counseling service, and author of "Rock Hard Apps: How to Write the Killer College Application." At the time IvyWise charged $10,000 to $20,000 for two years of college preparation services, spread over a student's junior and senior years.
>
> But they did have limits. "I don't think she did our platinum package, which is now over $30,000," Ms. Cohen said of Ms. Viswanathan.
>
> Ms. Cohen helped open doors other than Harvard's. After reading some of Ms. Viswanathan's writing (she had completed a several-hundred-page novel about Irish history while in high school, naturally), Ms. Cohen put her in touch with the William Morris Agency, which represents Ms. Cohen. Jennifer Rudolph Walsh, who is now Ms. Viswanathan's agent, sold the novel that eventually became *Opal* to Little, Brown on the basis of four chapters and an outline as part of a two-book deal.[9]

The deal for *Opal Mehta* was reportedly for half a million dollars.

We may forgive the *New York Times* for rehashing the story as Viswanathan's was unraveling: "Ms. Walsh said that she put Ms. Viswanathan in touch with a book packaging company, 17th Street Productions (now Alloy Entertainment), but that the plot and writing of *Opal* were '1,000 percent hers.'"[10] Beware of people who say "1,000 percent"—they might not know just when to quit.

All this does bring up the problem of authorship—who quote-unquote wrote *Opal*? Is the packager responsible, presumably, for just the kinds of press the author garnered or for shaping the story? And what percentage do they take? (Presumably less than 1,000.) The book packager's very invisibility signals its power. "The relationships between Alloy and the publishers are so intertwined that the same editor, Claudia Gabel, is thanked on the acknowledgments page of both Ms. McCafferty's books and Ms. Viswanathan's."[11] This seems one key way book packagers differ from the ghostwriter, that figure paid to have his or her work officially plagiarized. Alloy with its series like *The Sisterhood of the Traveling Pants* functions in exactly the opposite manner: the author as an idea divorced from the writing; the author as owner. This is actually behind the charge, and the practice, of plagiarism—the plagiarist is she who claims she owns, borrows, and expands to fit another's words.[12]

The book packager's invisibility extends to the press packet for the book, authorless as the slang that peppers it. Rather than "about the author," we are told "The 411" on Kaavya Viswanathan. A glossary defines it this way: "411 (n.)—information. Usage: *I met this cute boy last night, but he left the party before I could get the 411 on him.*" An interview with her is called "Gettin' down with our flygirl," with *flygirl* defined as "a really hip and sexy chick." I'm not sure how outmoded 1980s slang terms like *flygirl* with origins in black, particularly hip-hop culture—other definitions listed include *crunk* and, more fittingly, *wack*—prove relevant, especially as written by corny publishing types. What was originally black slang now is seen as mere teenage talk. "Ms. Walsh, the agent, said: 'Knowing what a fine person Kaavya is, I believe any similarities were unintentional. Teenagers tend to adopt each other's language.'"[13] Black talk: the ultimate ghostwriter.

Where Viswanathan is portrayed as exceptional in all senses, Opal sets out to become ordinary. What *Opal Mehta*, the book and the titular character, seeks is not to be beyond category but well within it. This is how class often works in America—her ambition is like my eleventh-grade history teacher's in Kansas, who'd repeat to the entire classroom the wishful asser-tion, "We're all middle class here." Though Opal is certainly upper crust in the book, and Viswanathan well paid and well raised, Opal conveys a wish to emulate the American bourgeoisie, to be as middlebrow as the book itself. Only in this way can she "get a life"—by stealing her way into one. Part of its aspiration is assimilation.

At the same time there isn't any tradition that she knows of, Viswanathan says, promoting the idea that she is sui generis, without prece-dent. It is strange how Viswanathan wants to see herself as unique in her Indianness—is this another remnant of the book's spin cycle, whether by a company or her? For *Opal Mehta* to live, Indian American literature—indeed, Indian literature in English—must die. In contrast to the hoaxer whose bio is enhanced, with plagiarism the writing gets enhanced to match the extravagant bio. Despite the cliché suggested by the book's title, life of course is not something you get; you live it. When you're not wasting it.

To plagiarize another is to steal a bit of that person's soul—almost as much as soul music was stolen. It is also to steal, in other words, a cul-ture. Whether we think plagiarism a crime—the only crime in litera-ture to some—or at best a minor offense, all depends on if we're the ones being plagiarized. Or on whether we see writing as work. But why would Viswanathan steal her own culture? Why plagiarize in spirit and image, if not words, exactly those things that India-born Viswanathan may have ac-tually experienced? It's a puzzle—she seems to do so for ease, of course, but also perhaps as a way of becoming American, claiming an Americanness that, the book's plot seems to suggest, is always at a remove. There's a sense that Opal Mehta is somehow living a plagiarized existence, trying to own what doesn't belong to her: Harvard, full-blooded humanity, a "life."

Opal Mehta must become a type for Viswanathan to live.

I have said plagiarism is about class, but it's really race disguised as class. This is true of Viswanathan—not to mention Opal Mehta—who to some may come to represent the fast track that Harvard, or getting into it, has come to mean. When I was in school there, the saying went that the hard-est thing about Harvard was getting in; if at all true then, getting in has become only tougher, with just over two thousand students accepted from a pool of more than thirty-four thousand applicants for the class of 2016.[14]

Such pressure is the focus of *Conning Harvard*, a book by an editor at the Harvard *Crimson* about Adam Wheeler, who conned, copied, and inflated his way into several of the nation's finest schools. As *Conning Harvard* details, Wheeler started in 2005 with small but selective Bowdoin College, whose college application he completed almost entirely with plagiarized material; after two years, just as he was about to be exposed, he transferred to Harvard (while pretending to be transferring from MIT). At Harvard, he plagiarized papers and poems to obtain further grants and prizes. Only in 2009 did his bluff get called when he boldly applied for the prestigious Rhodes Scholarship to study at Oxford, and was on the verge of being named to the short list as well as being put up for the equally noteworthy Marshall Fellowship without having actually applied. A savvy professor recognized in Wheeler's application his colleague and best-selling Shakespearean scholar Stephen Greenblatt's work.[15]

Wheeler had in essence a four-year span of plagiarizing—he presumably could've graduated from somewhere legitimately by then. After withdrawing from Harvard the next spring while the university decided his fate, Wheeler continued his wheeling and wheedling, applying everywhere from Yale to Stanford—and getting in the latter—with false résumés, forged documents, and more plagiarized essays. In May 2010, Wheeler was arrested and indicted on twenty counts, from larceny to identity theft. Wheeler's is one of the few cases I know of plagiarism being prosecuted—he was considered, between grants, prizes, and financial aid, to have stiffed Harvard out of forty-five thousand dollars. (In contrast, Viswanathan would go on, like Stephen Glass did, to Georgetown University Law Center, which appears to have a fellowship for hoaxers.) If this is a drop in the bucket to Harvard, the richest university in the land, it might not be to another student whose place Wheeler was taking. His crimes go beyond plagiarism to include forgery of transcripts (a perfect SAT score, natch) and falsifying information such as his birthdate and his publishing record—in other words, outright fraud.

There's always, in these cases of Ivy League pretenders such as Clark Rockefeller, more than a mere financial wish—rather, there's a desire for the cultural capital such a school provides. Noted impostors like faker James Hogue, as detailed in David Samuels's *The Runner*, actually earned good grades after getting into Princeton under false pretenses; his desire seemed to be both to run track and to run from his past. Julie Zauzmer's *Conning Harvard* gives little insight into Wheeler's motives, though it is well versed on his methods. This may stem from Wheeler's being a cipher in that word's contradictory senses (though not its "fly" hip-hop ones): he's both *without a center* yet is *a key* essential to understanding our current culture of un-accountability. Not to mention of cheating.[16] His actions do seem particularly symbolic of the financial crash that was happening around this time, the kinds of bad mortgages and housing bubbles that made lenders and those who profited from them coconspirators at worse. Wheeler may be paying for all of our unoriginal sins—if so, forty-five large sounds cheap.

After denying the charges at first, Wheeler eventually pled out; the judge gave him probation with the understanding that he never represent himself as having attended any of the schools he was kicked out of, but Wheeler continued to apply for things using a fake résumé, including for an internship at the *New Republic* of all places. If any résumé is a display of puffery, Wheeler's is a remarkable dissertation on deceit: he claims to have been invited as an undergraduate to lecture at the National Association of Armenian Studies and to have given lectures at McGill University in Montreal titled "Cartography, Location, and Invention in *The Tempest*," which never happened either. He claimed to be working on two more books with one already under review at Harvard University Press; he also declared he had four volumes "coauthored" with Marc Shell—an actual professor of his—forthcoming or under review.[17] In reality these books Shell alone had written. Wheeler would not so much compare literature as conscript it to his purposes.

While all writers fall in love with different books and writers who influence them, few are faithful; great writers tend to go beyond a singular influence in that strange alchemy of many influences that creates originality. Plagiarists tend to be monogamous. They return to one or two texts to craft their plagiarisms. To get into Bowdoin, Wheeler plagiarized from a book of sample college essays compiled by *Crimson* editors that he would regularly return to; for his junior paper that won him a Hoopes Prize, Wheeler turned to a PhD thesis by a now-professor whose advanced ideas show up as if Wheeler's own.[18] Wheeler also regular used *Rock Hard Apps*—in an ironic twist, the very book written by the same woman hired by Viswanathan's parents to help get her into Harvard.

If Wheeler was faithful to anything, or anyone, it was to Stephen Greenblatt. Wheeler had already won poetry contests undetected with a poem by Pulitzer Prize–winner Paul Muldoon (his terrific "Hay")—there's always a fake poem in there somewhere—and plagiarized Harvard professors like Helen Vendler and even Harvard's president, Drew Faust. But again and again, he pillaged Greenblatt's works—not his best-selling writings on

Shakespeare but an in-house Harvard publication that proved Wheeler's go-to bible.

Shakespeare of course regularly, almost religiously, borrowed—especially plots—but his example only reinforces the difficulty of invention and reinvention, the difference between an idea and its elegant expression. (Generally speaking, it is only exact expression, not any shared idea, that gets called plagiarism.) Yet despite his use of *The Tempest* in one claim, Wheeler doesn't use his master's voice to curse with—merely to accumulate honors. Why would Wheeler dare steal from the very writers he was trying to impress? Why not fish further from home? This question comes up quite often with plagiarists, who tend not to go far afield when they steal. One reason may be because plagiarists crave being known to those they know; another is that plagiarism, like the hoax more generally, preys on and pretends to intimacy.

If a thief, Shakespeare was a thief of the highest order—though the fact that a writer who took many of his cues from others managed to perfect the English language still produces great anxiety.[19] This continued anxiety over Shakespeare's quality can be traced to the eighteenth century, when Shakespeare's name went from meaning just another good writer to the height of Western culture. This was also when the idea of originality as fundamental to literature took hold and was exactly when the West's notion of plagiarism took its modern form. "Originality—not just innocence of plagiarism but the making of something really and truly new—set itself down as a cardinal literary virtue sometime in the middle of the eighteenth century and has never since gotten up," Thomas Mallon writes.[20] Yet despite its emphasis on originality and attribution, the eighteenth century was an age not just of rampant hoaxes but also of plagiarism; in fact, it is exactly *because* of such a newfound need for originality that plagiarism and other hoaxes proliferated, providing an anxious expression.

Notorious William-Henry Ireland's "discovery" in 1794 of Shakespeare manuscripts emblematizes and takes advantage of Shakespeare's rediscovery by the eighteenth century as a whole—and the very kinds of anxious acquisition that would plague Wheeler. As his forgeries earned him not just acclaim but praise from an otherwise withholding father—he was literally named after another brother and feared he may not actually be his father's son—Ireland fils continued forging ever more boldly, including a full-length play, *Vortigern and Rowena*, which he claimed to have found before having written a word of it.[21] The play was only the latest discovery from a trunk like something clowns might climb out of, its unlikely trove including Shakespeare Folios; letters to Shakespeare's wife, Anne Hathaway (one contained a lock of the poet's hair); and "an early edition of Holinshed's *Chronicles*, the historical tales from which Shakespeare had cribbed so many of his plots—this one with marginalia in the playwright's own hand."[22] In other words, the very copy of the book Shakespeare would copy from. Though he publicly admitted his forgery in 1796 with a small pamphlet, *An Authentic Account of the Shakspearean Manuscripts, &c*, Ireland had to state again and again that he had hoaxed alone—and that his father, who stood to financially benefit, wasn't in on it. You can't get more anxious about originality than having to prove even your hoaxes are your own.

Our time is no different—again. Our Age of Euphemism's steady stream of plagiarism and increased attacks on Shakespeare's origins—not to mention our desire to get near him, or to say he wasn't who he said he was, with over seventy-seven people posited as him since the 1850s—reflect another anxious era.[23] Certainly the main through-line of the Shakespeare deniers, like other issues of plagiarism, centers on class. The thinking goes, how could Shakespeare not be learned in the most conventional sense? *I reckon our Will must've been an Oxford man.* All these debates about Shakespearean authorship, Shakespeare scholar and Harvard professor Marjorie Garber notes, are in many ways about ownership. Anxieties about Shakespeare's identity always reflect larger questions of who we are. It is not so much that scholars find ciphers in the plays and poems; rather Shakespeare proves a cipher for those people, and eras, who question him. Garber takes particular glee in noting how many of these earlier suppositions about Shakespeare come from scholars from Harvard.

Just as he uses Shakespeare, Wheeler returns over and over to Harvard publications put out by the university or edited by the *Crimson* to reinforce his Harvardness—stealing Harvard in order to reflect it back. There's this impostor syndrome found at Harvard that Wheeler taps into, through his writing and his case—a feeling of not being worthy of being there. *I feel like a phony, like I'm the only one who got in accidentally*, was an attitude I heard expressed more than once, the neat companion of *Catcher in the Rye*'s Holden Caulfield calling whatever and whomever he hates "phony." It is a feeling familiar to modern life—one that plagiarism particularly embodies. The Elizabethans got the Bard; we get Adam Wheeler plagiarizing papers about him.

How to extend tradition and not be overwhelmed by it? How to belong though you feel you don't? You can make the feeling of not belonging into a way of belonging; this is one definition of the writer. The plagiarist is more about *belongings*—about ownership and possession, which some euphemize isn't theft. This euphemism provides one more of plagiarism's clues and confessions.

Incredibly intimate, "plagiarism is a fraternal crime," as Mallon notes; "writers can steal only from other writers."[24] Along with what Mallon calls "a death wish," that notable, peculiar wish to be caught, plagiarists so want to belong to the company of other writers that they mistreat others' work. Why else would Wheeler steal from professors on the very same campus he doesn't quite share?

Within a year, Wheeler had violated parole and found himself sentenced to jail. There is little glee in the story really, though many have taken it a sign of Harvard's own bubble, delighting in its going *pop*. But unlike in some other famous cases—like William Street, depicted in the cult film *Chameleon Street*, who conned his way into Yale and later pretended to be a doctor, apparently even performing open heart surgery successfully— Wheeler never did do the work.

Wheeler wasn't just kicked out of Harvard; he was *expunged*. Anyone can get expelled, and any school can suspend you, but it takes real talent to get yourself expunged—this means not just being asked to leave or kept from graduating, but that the university destroys any record of the student having attended there. Such purges are rare enough that the only other one I know of is William Randolph Hearst, the model for *Citizen Kane* and the founder of yellow journalism. The reason: during exams, Hearst sent chamber pots to his professors with their names at the bottom; apparently not all were empty. His name only appears on campus at the Harvard Lampoon Building, where it's etched in the stained glass he helped pay for. The gap between prank and hoax, yellow journalism and far yellower plagiarism, is slim but sure.

As today's plagiarists reveal, the hoax has gone from Neverland to Hack Heaven, from flights of imagination and humor to a further version of hell. Dante's *Inferno* would place frauds and liars in the second-to-lowest circle, with falsifiers in the lowest portion of that, forced to forever scratch their skin. A hoaxer's skin is usually rather thin.

In the end, plagiarists and pilferers, "Opal Mehta" and Adam Wheeler and "Clark Rockefeller" don't just steal another's words or money or opportunities; they also steal experiences. (In contrast, professional ghostwriters who write college papers for a paper mill would seem to steal experience from the very people who paid the ghostwriters to have their experiences for them.) As Thomas Mallon puts it, "Anyone is relieved to come home and find that the burglar has taken the wallet and left the photo album. When a plagiarist enters the writer's study it's the latter—the stuff of 'sentimental value'—that he's after."[25] Both the subject and the strategy of plagiarism are sentimental, attached not just to the past but also to unearned emotion, which, rather than realize, the plagiarist copies verbatim.

The plagiarist would rather thank a stranger than cite one. The crime here is vast, and personal: Wheeler went so far as to copy another writer's personal acknowledgments.

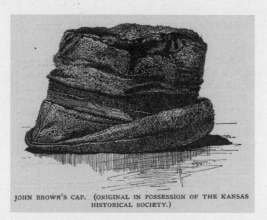

JOHN BROWN'S CAP. (ORIGINAL IN POSSESSION OF THE KANSAS HISTORICAL SOCIETY.)

John Brown's cap, ca. 1859.

CHAPTER 22

Michael Brown's Body

Plagiarism is about power. When the wife of the presumptive Republican presidential nominee, now First Lady Melania Trump, gave the capstone speech of the first day of the Republican National Convention in July 2016— after her warm introduction by the candidate himself and full reception by the crowd—Mrs. Trump spoke a bit stiffly, to be sure. Her discomfort with teleprompters gave her a shifty, side-to-side look, except when she paused at the places that the screens appear to have suggested. Like her presumed ghostwriters, teleprompters are proxies of a sort. But the machines provided something else: a mechanical ease with language, despite some forgivable stumbles and mispronunciations. (Mrs. Trump, as her speech mentioned, is originally from Slovenia, her immigrant status championed in a way her candidate husband would explicitly deny Muslims and Mexicans.) This ease, it appears now, was not her own, as large portions of the speech were directly stolen from Michelle Obama's 2008 impassioned speech at the Democratic National Convention—a speech that soon replayed on social and traditional media alongside the one we can hardly now call Mrs. Trump's.

Such side-by-side comparisons, typical when proving plagiarism, did not prove favorable to Mrs. Trump, not only because of the blatant theft or the bad look that's regularly euphemized as "optics," but also because of the difference in passion: Michelle Obama had the energy and delivery that came from saying things she believed. For the former model, the very same words in the same order became oddly detached, distant, vague. This is not accidental but is one of plagiarism's chief symptoms: love letters feel far less passionate when plagiarized. The stealing of heartfelt words doesn't result in heartfelt sentiment, and like a meal, isn't nearly as pleasant coming back up. I almost felt bad for her.

Twitter, especially Black Twitter, had a ball. The plagiarism was revealed there, in fact, discovered by out-of-work reporter Jarrett Hill (who one hopes has a job now). "It was kind of the same way that you hear a song you haven't heard in a long time but you know the lyrics to," he told *Politico*. "When Melania began saying, 'The height of your achievements is the reach of your dreams,' I finished it out loud to the screen, saying, 'and your willingness to work for them,'" he continued. "And then I immediately thought, oh my gosh. That's Michelle Obama. I know where that's from."[1] The best Mrs. Trump could hope for was something of a white cover of a black song; much was made of the way Mrs. Trump exactly parroted the First Lady's distinctive diction evoking the phrase "word is bond" that Black Muslims and hip-hop made popular: "That your word is your bond and you do what you say and keep your promise."[2]

Plagiarism isn't just the unacknowledged shifting of words; it is also the shifting of blame. The late-night, post-game political pundits who first commented on the theft seemed not to understand the plagiarism playbook: *Deny, deny, deny*. If that doesn't work, declare the plagiarism an innocent accident; imply plagiarism doesn't exist or if it does is not a big deal; if need be, the playbook ends with what passes as remorse, which can feel borrowed too. Such ideas, learned at plagiarism's feet, now apply to politics as a whole, in which denial in all senses is key.

A difficulty for the now first lady is that earlier that same day Melania Trump had said of the speech "I wrote it myself" with as "little help as possible." This may prove a white lie—a bit like a hostess saying she cooked everything when she merely heated dishes to specifications—to match her fashionable dress. Certainly it's a regular fib for politicians or celebrities, who merely hint at their ghostwriters, those paid to be plagiarized from— yet for Mrs. Trump, the claim exposes both the lie of the writing and the truth of the plagiarism. Even if she did write it, she didn't write it.

Eventually a speechwriter came forward to accept responsibility. Still the commentators made it seem as if plagiarism is a one-time thing, when it's more addictive than golf. Then again, plagiarists and their defenders tend to focus on *If* it is plagiarism rather than *How*, when *How* is all the pundits focus on. Far more interesting is *Why*.

There's always a lot of presuming with plagiarism, because plagiarism isn't just a display of power; it's also a nervousness about that power. The "help" Melania Trump speaks of appears now a bit more pointed—it can seem a euphemism for the black domestic, the ultimate helpmeet. For isn't the ultimate plagiarism the regular, sustained, daily theft of black ideas, music, style? Certainly many on Twitter saw it this way, prompting a hilarious stream under the trending hashtag #FamousMelaniaTrumpQuotes: including lyrics from Rihanna's "Work" as if they were Melania's own. *Nobody texts me in a crisis.* The humor is also the horror: demeaning is part of plagiarism's power, as Republican New Jersey governor Chris Christie made clear the next morning when he said that 93 percent of Mrs. Trump's speech was her own; this of course wouldn't fly at Kroger, paying for only 93 percent of the groceries at self-checkout. But plagiarism's meat and potatoes is saying that the original source isn't just stolen but not worth stealing; that plagiarism is not only normal but natural; that any rights to one's own words are fleeting, even fictional. "Michelle Obama doesn't own the English language," another Trump spokesman said—suggesting that Mrs. Obama not only doesn't own her own words but couldn't if she wanted to.

The double standard should be familiar, but has its own special twist: modern plagiarism is not about originality, but origins. Like Melania's supposed speech, it is a way to say not just that *this belongs to me* but that *I belong*—ironically finding oneself through using someone else's words, all the while never admitting so. Why else would her speechwriters, including Mrs. Trump herself, take from arguably the most popular first lady since Jackie O? It is almost like a spell meant to connect its sayer into "the source"—or a cloak of visibility that insists its source is all too invisible, unseen, beneath mentioning.

Plagiarism in this way behaves like racism (and vice versa): both "isms" feign respectability and invisibility; they also substitute a presumed privilege for real ability. The analogy is too close for comfort: like billions of black folks before them, the Obamas are one more black production to be maligned or made fun of while being made off with. For there is a larger plagiarism, however ecstatic it may be, that has stolen black cultural productions and artifacts—often literally—for centuries.

Certainly literature would grind to a halt if the folktale or folklore became subject to copyright. Yet black culture too often gets cited as a noble way of citation—or lack of it. Is this a justification for covering a song or is this a cover for larger cultural theft? Or is it that racism is a kind of plagiarism, stealing pain and pretending its practitioners are better—and greater—than they are? Like forgery, or any other noble vampire, plagiarism makes its living by hiding an ideology of ownership. While once it may've been original sin that often marked Western notions of innate evil, now this too is unoriginal, borrowed, rehearsed. As paranoid as our politics, plagiarism is not simply an anxiety about influence but an anxiety over anxiety.

In its serial nature, being plagiarized surely feels both personal and despairingly impersonal, even anonymous, the way serial killers view their victims. In this, it parrots modern writing itself: the originator of the phrase "anxiety of influence," Harold Bloom, says that writers want to kill their literary fathers; the plagiarist suggests that his or her ancestors never existed, all while being excessively obsessed with them.

Still, Jonathan Lethem's important essay, "The Ecstasy of Influence: A Plagiarism," is correct that influence isn't only or always anxiety. There is something profound in honoring and recasting our first loves, in paying homage while also reenacting them. Reciting a source can be a way of saying I know it well enough it is *practically* my own. Memory has a way of making something ours. Such premasticated pleasures are to be found in Lethem and in pop art, as well as in blues, jazz, hip-hop.

Yet African American forms, regularly reached for as examples of art that riffs and recycles, have not a lesser but a different standard of originality. The figure in Ralph Ellison's essay "The Little Man at Chehaw Station" knows the tradition, and can quiz you on it when you least expect it. In hip-hop, from the very beginning one of the worst things to be accused of is being a "biter"—called out for stealing if not someone's style then words. Though the beats were sometimes shared, they were as often fiercely guarded by their makers as well as their discoverers; it is an imperative not just to copy the tradition but to know it cold. Especially when doing a standard or transforming an old song, you must make it new:

Blues and jazz musicians have long been enabled by an "open source" culture, in which preexisting melodic fragments and larger musical frameworks are freely reworked. Technology has only multiplied the possibilities; musicians have gained the power to *duplicate* sounds literally rather than simply approximate them through allusion. In '70s Jamaica, King Tubby and Lee "Scratch" Perry deconstructed recorded

music, using astonishingly primitive pre-digital hardware, creating
what they called "versions." The recombinant nature of their means of
production quickly spread to DJs in New York and London. Today our
endless, gloriously impure, and fundamentally social process generates
countless hours of music.[3]

Of course, this paragraph from Lethem's now-famous essay isn't exactly
Lethem's doing. A patchwork self-consciously and seamlessly made up from
other sources—and a bravura performance—Lethem's medium is his message, borrowing to enact his point about the possibilities of recasting as a
form of creativity. Lethem's essay ends with a "key" to indicate "the source
of every line I stole, warped, and cobbled together as I 'wrote' (except, alas,
those sources I forgot along the way)."[4]

The key indicates that the above inset quote contains lines from a book
by Kembrew McLeod and refers to another book by him, *Owning Culture*;
segues through Joanna Demers's *Steal This Music*; and pirouettes with parts of
William Gibson's "God's Little Toys." A quilt too is taken from other sources,
but is a new thing—an aesthetic sharing a bed with the blues. Yet despite
what the others quoted in "Ecstasy" claim, the blues are not some open source
culture. Not only does this apply recent digital thinking to an analog situation, it fails to understand oral culture, a culture without exact ownership *but
not without originality*. The point of blues is transformation as a form of participation, found in the repeated—but not exactly—verses. If you don't bring
it, you can't take it: the cutting contest, the riff, the boxing ring not as open
source but statement and counterstatement, revision as crucial to vision.

Blues music has proved less "open source" than outsourced. Both terms
are mere euphemisms for theft. In describing a recording by Muddy Waters,
Lethem's "Ecstasy" turns out to contest the very notion of "open source":
"In 1941, on his front porch, Muddy Waters recorded a song for the folk-
lorist Alan Lomax. After singing the song, which he told Lomax was titled
'Country Blues,' Waters described how he came to write it. 'I made it on
about the eighth of October '38,' Waters said. 'I was fixin' a puncture on a
car. I had been mistreated by a girl. I just felt blue, and the song fell into my
mind and it come to me just like that and I started singing.'" This elegant,
inward-turning paragraph, originally from Siva Vaidhyanathan's *Copyrights
and Copywrongs*, goes on to say that "in nearly one breath, Waters offers five
accounts: his own active authorship: he 'made it' on a specific date. . . . After
Lomax raises the question of influence, Waters, without shame, misgivings,

or trepidation, says that he heard a version by [Robert] Johnson, but that his mentor, Son House, taught it to him. In the middle of that complex genealogy, Waters declares: 'This song comes from the cotton field.'"⁵ Setting aside the problematic Alan Lomax—who took credit for Lead Belly's songs such as "Goodnight, Irene" and then, after helping secure his freedom, employed him as a chauffeur and had him sing in prison stripes—Muddy Waters isn't actually giving alternate versions of the earlier iterations of the song taught him by Son House. Instead, he's admitting its multiple tributaries. The artist—even the black one—takes influence from everywhere, from a flat tire to a no-good woman, from a lowdown feeling to a downhome blues. The river of song has many tributaries; it is "Muddy," after all.

Muddy Waters sees story and the song as the same, joined by struggle. It is the difference between quoting and appropriation, between a source and a siphon. I should say I believe that in his own work Lethem is trying to recognize these various tributaries—Lethem's essay, and the very idea of ecstasy, is dependent if not on struggle then at least transformation. This is clear in the key to "Ecstasy": "Nearly every sentence I culled I also revised, at least slightly—for necessities of space, in order to produce a more consistent tone, or simply because I felt like it."⁶ Lethem reveals that everything in the essay is taken from somewhere else, but also that he has made everything here his own. By crafting a "plagiarism" he renders plagiary not as a crime or an activity, but a form, an object, an art. Such "plagiarisms" are revolutionary exactly because he names what he's up to. The name of the game is revelation.

By not properly quoting or not claiming influence, plagiarists have more or less implied they alone—not the works they reportedly love—are orphaned. As a result, plagiarism doesn't just express anxieties of paternity but is both patronizing and paternalistic. That is its form of power: plagiarism asks us, *What have you got to lose?* Plagiarism, the ultimate dog whistle.

The fact that plagiarism has recently begun to plague poetry, that most personal and sometimes private of arts, indicates the depths of the plagiarism crisis. Over the past few years, English-language poetry has been rocked by a series of plagiarists—usually after they won prizes whose monetary amounts were significant.⁷ The tens of thousands of dollars in question, from the United States to Australia, are more than what would put Harvard plagiarist Adam Wheeler in jail.

In England, one Christian Ward seemed neither as charitable nor as careful as his name, ingesting and exactly copying a series of poets—claiming at first a one-off mashup, then slowly being forced to admit he'd done it several times. Winning so much with another's words, Ward makes the idea of a poetry agent almost viable.[8] Ward is not only a serial plagiarist but he also fits that familiar hoaxer profile of a perpetrator who feels put upon, a poet who purposefully misconstrues poetry, an apologist who's terrible at apologies. He relates he's "written somewhere between 5 to 600 poems over the last eight/nine years. I intend to write more. I do not believe I should have to throw away several years worth of work over isolated incidents which I deeply regret. I am not, for the record, a compulsive plagiarist who gets a rush from doing it. I'm not that person. Please believe me."[9] Of course, many, many more infractions—not so isolated—came to light soon after. Whether we believe this prodigious claim of work, or claim of prodigious work, hinges on that key word, *written*.

Two American poets plagiarized by Ward, Paisley Rekdal and Sandra Beasley, have written beautifully on how it felt to be stolen from, using the same weapons used against them: words. Ironically, in the same issue of the *New York Times* as Beasley's rebuttal, the *Sunday Magazine* details the fabrications of a European scientist who, as the tagline had it, fudged evidence in order to fit what he wished to prove, rather than actually settling for what the results revealed. The problem in both cases is the same: a mishandling of sources, a shading of evidence. The hoax not only results when charlatanism or racism meets science but also seeks to make hoaxing into a science.

In her open letter to Ward, Rekdal uses the word *bemused* to describe her feelings upon finding out she'd been stolen from, as was British poet Helen Mort: "That's a word Helen Mort used to describe what you did to her when you took her poem 'The Deer' and passed it off as your own. Helen Mort is clearly a very good poet, because that word 'bemused' exactly describes much of what I feel too: a heady mix of anger, resentment, amusement and bewilderment, even a touch of embarrassment as well. But though anger falls first on that list of nouns, it is not, in fact the first emotion that I feel. To a certain extent, I feel more pity than anger, mixed with the chagrin of feeling that what you've done really isn't that far away from what so many writers do and have done, what we flirt with continually in our own work." Yet Rekdal is quite clear on just how cribbing is not collage:

> You took my poem. You took *all* its language, changed only the tense, and added ten words. Ten words, out of a poem containing 125. And

then you muddied the line breaks, and you put your name on it, and you published it as your own. . . . I'm interested in "uncreative writing." But you didn't do that.

You clearly aren't a conceptual poet and you weren't sampling language in any of the collage-type ways you now cite from poor, put-upon Eliot: you understood you wanted the poem to reflect an individual voice that comes from the particular imagination of a single author. You aren't conceptual: you're Romantic. And how do I know this?

Because you fucking added your own line breaks and words.

Rather than conceptualism, plagiarism constitutes defacement of another's experiences. It isn't merely a modern replica, but a defaced romanticism—in short, a gothic—that Ward is guilty of. Despite their protests, the "uncreative writing" as practiced by the so-called conceptual poets remains awfully Romantic too, centered as it is on a sole genius able to conceive it. The thief's recognizing the stolen property's value doesn't make him the owner.

Ward's parasitic plagiarism threatens to take over not just Rekdal's experience but her process and very memories:

It wouldn't even surprise me to know that you didn't like the poem. No, I don't feel flattered by or angry about your decision to plagiarize me. I feel angry that I'm having to write this, in some pathetic attempt to get you to apologize. I feel angry that you made my poem worse. In this, I admit, my emotions are entirely egotistical, circling around and around the drain of my own self-loathing and self-regard, the particular pains I took over my work to make it sound original and beautiful, the particular disgust with which I am forced to regard it, broken and clunky with your new line breaks, the poem less mine now than some sort of monstrous palimpsest that only limply resembles the sounds of the original.

Plagiarizing another's pain, making things *worser*—this is what it means to shortcut the writing process, shortchanging both the writer and the reader. Those rhythms, lost—those little choices that, when plagiarized, add up to large losses. What Rekdal puts her finger on (and raises a middle finger to) is the violence of the act—the "monstrous palimpsest" is no mere inert thing, or rather, has been rendered so, stilled, a Frankenstein, that monster equated with its maker. "The side effect of my writing process is that I memorize all my work, so that whatever poem I write lingers inside me, like a bell still vibrating after the sound has passed. And now that sense, those sounds, that particular pleasure of making—which is the only reward we ever get in poetry, Christian—is gone. So thanks for that."[10]

Are truths spoken through someone else's mouth still truths? Too soon they can devolve to clichés: much as too-familiar platitudes (*Everything happens for a reason*) fail to be comforting in the face of death, such recyclings come off as bad ventriloquism, or a crappy cover song, derivative and distracting. *It is what it is.* It's also dishonest in a way that sentimentalism can be too. This might help explain why the most devastating critique Rekdal offers of—and to—her plagiarist is to call him "Romantic." By this I believe she means both the Romantic notion of originality (which changing words implies) and the loosey-goosey notion of inspiration (which plagiarism betrays); she also recalls the ways that many of the Romantic poets were plagiarists themselves. Just as the Enlightenment was accompanied by hoaxes, the Romantic era's deification of originality was accompanied by plagiarism, often by the very same original geniuses who'd invented it.

Our current crop of plagiarists fully embody plagiarism's paradox: though some of them claim to be anti-Romantic or postmodern in their efforts, declaring nothing is original, they rely deeply on the Romantic notion of the author as all-powerful, originating force. By recognizing her plagiarist as Romantic, Rekdal also indicts the postmodern or "conceptual poetry" defense that believes that plagiarism, I dunno, liberates words from enslavement by their masters—content wanting to be free, after all—when really all such ideas do is shift the author further up the line, not freeing the work but placing the rampant plagiarist's imprint and authorship above all others. This is the romance of the vampire. Plagiarists in the end are less liberators than plantation owners, the most grotesque American gothic of all.

The hoax is not just a coded confession but a corrupted one: in pretending to have written something, the plagiarist claims ownership of someone else's words as well as of a nonexistent self. The news might be worse: the self these days isn't simply make-believe, which can be fruitful; lately it has shrunk, been prepackaged, boiled down to mere feelings—especially fear—and to the basic body. The modern hoax, plagiarism included, substitutes the gross for the truly grotesque; seeks memorability over memory; even its freaks are mere fakes. The hoax suggests the self isn't just small, or pretend, but alien. It is exactly such absence, such phony hokiness, ironically, that may be enough to lead someone to abuse another's words. For if the self is derivative why wouldn't the work be too?

That the hoax devolves into schlock or kitsch once exposed is indicative of how far from the glorious sublime hoaxers, whether impostor, forger, or plagiarist, actually are. The hoax also, like the gothic, may end up a mood, a hysteric symptom erupting forth—a faked disease cloaking real unease—to remind us of our unprocessed beliefs and irrepressible fears. But the hoax is a representation of repression, a mock sublime, where the gothic is a sublime suppression. Plagiarists might put us in mind of the visitor to Gatsby's "high Gothic library," that place where the books need not be real to impress— that's their only function—but somehow are. They are illusions made actual.

As in forgery, or Gatsby's Gothic library, plagiarism makes its living by hiding an ideology of ownership. To soothe or suffer loudly this sin, plagiarism also reaches—as the hoax often does—for our time's chief emblem of ruin: race. Modern plagiarism does this not so much through "the native" or the newcomer as the hoax does, as, first, through invoking the most American of forms, blues and jazz—and then through the most troubling American invention, lynching.

These words, written some time ago, went from supposition to prophecy as self-described conceptual poet Kenneth Goldsmith kicked off 2015 by "repurposing" the autopy for Michael Brown, the young man killed by a Ferguson, Missouri, policeman just months before, and reading it at a Brown University conference. Yet another of our time's Emmett Tills, Michael Brown's shooting in August 2014, and the uprisings that followed in protest revealed continued fissures in American culture and its conception of race—the very milieu the hoax feels most comfortable in.

Just as being a construction hasn't prevented race from having serious, if not deadly, effects, plagiarism oddly behaves like racism. And just as race, like originality, is a relatively modern concept doesn't mean that it hasn't had huge effects on Western thought. Is it that racism is a kind of plagiarism, stealing pain and pretending its practitioners are better, and greater, than they are? As with racists, plagiarists maintain an air of inevitability, constantly anxious over their practices' inexorable, if drawn out, end. "Plagiarism is necessary, Lautréamont insisted. Progress implies it," Goldsmith writes. His manifesto on "the purposes of repurposing" in *Poetry* magazine repurposes theories he has been floating for a number of years: that this essay appeared on the heels of his Brown performance in an issue otherwise dedicated to the Latinx and African American BreakBeat poets, reveals both the misconception and preconception that the poets needed authenticating; and the harder truth, that Goldsmith needed these hipper poets not to appear completely out of it. While I'd agree with Goldsmith that "authenticity is another form of artifice," his subsequent maxims—"It is possible to be both inauthentic and sincere" and "The moment you stand up in front of people, you are no longer authentic"—seem justifications before the fact of his borrowing of Brown. Goldsmith's appearance onstage, his deracinated text, in a process he was first to label "uncreative writing," is meant to be shorn of any details, just the facts, ma'am—or bossman.

But the facts, particularly of what happened to Brown's body, are exactly what's at issue. While *John Brown's Body lies a-mouldering in the grave, but his soul goes marching on,* Michael Brown's body lay in the Missouri heat for hours. John Brown had fiercely fought to keep Kansas free in ways that Missourah did not; the long-standing situation in Ferguson, Missouri, as reported by a devastating federal investigation after the shooting, revealed widespread corruption and questionable practices that kept black people in what amounts to a sharecropper system, fines and late fees and arrests and policing outpacing any original infraction like traffic tickets. This was slavery by another name. As such, even long before his death, Michael Brown's brown body didn't even belong to him—for Goldsmith and the police state that "repurposed" it, the body of Big Mike Brown was a happenstance, an accident, a text to be traded or erased. Or owned.

This ownership is integral to plagiarism, and to Goldsmith's manifestos on conceptual poetry: "Our writings are now identical to writings which already exist. The only thing we do is claim them as our own." Plagiarizing pain, Goldsmith makes much of the autopsy being publicly available; but while trying to start conversations about literary ownership, conceptual poets fail to see that their infraction is not copyright but wrongheadedness; the issue is neither legal nor literary but ethical and moral. Just as admitting you hoaxed doesn't get you out of what you hoaxed about, stealing, no matter how sanctioned, does not get you out of what you steal. "Conceptual writing is political writing; it just prefers to use someone else's politics."[11]

In reading and reusing a black boy's autopsy while Brown's graduation picture looked down on him from a projection screen rather than a tree, Kenneth Goldsmith reenacted centuries of black bodies on display, abstracted but not abstract, an example to all. The belabored black body becomes merely a body of work, while the very name "conceptual" implies that its white interpreters are not only necessary but necessarily all mind. "The idea is much more important than the product." But what if the idea is bad? Or better yet, dangerous bullshit?

Afterward, Goldsmith wants it many contradictory ways at once: to say he didn't alter the text, just that he performed what's already there; to say that of course he changed it some, he had to; and to say that it was merely a performance. "The document I read from is powerful," Goldsmith posted online during the uproar. "My reading of it was powerful. How could it be otherwise?"[12] These are the pomo plagiarist's reasonings: that mine is just a document; that mine is altered slightly and thus mine; that I'm the one and only; and that it's all just a show anyway, a game almost. But Goldsmith's reading of the reworked autopsy ended with Brown's genitalia, the source of ongoing fascination and fear: "The remaining male genitalia system is unremarkable."[13]

All this becomes all the more problematic around black bodies, which are not texts—or rather, too often become disembodies, mere numerals, marked statistics, not even metaphors. "The Body of Michael Brown" effectively said that Brown was nobody but a body.

Goldsmith might seem an outlier if another chief architect of conceptual poetry, Vanessa Place, hadn't caused an uproar around the same time for retweeting all the instances of *nigger* in Margaret Mitchell's novel *Gone with the Wind*. The widespread outrage over Place's ongoing project came after a concerned white person petitioned to get her removed as a writing conference judge—an anonymous online group called the Mongrel Coalition, much like the Guerrilla Girls before them, then took on the whole of what they term "gringpo" (as in "gringo poetry").[14] With the white "avant-garde" under fire for its racism and exclusion, the experimental movements that consider themselves its inheritors have not been helped by their reactions almost to the man (and almost always a man) comparing any critiques to Nazism and lynching. One defender managed to compare petitioners against Vanessa Place to Michael Brown's police shooter.

The white avant-garde dismisses metaphors as passé then resorts to similes—racialized ones they themselves enact. Race, after all, is a script, and it can be hard, if you ain't dehoaxed yourself, to borrow from its structures without also borrowing its subterranean tellings and coded confessions. The theories of derivativity are so familiar, much like justifications for American slavery or the theft of Native lands, which is to say, always after the fact and ultimately not based on fact. Even the story of a whites-only avant-garde fails to reckon with the avant-garde's Asian influences and actual black past—in modernism and postmodernism alone, whether through the Jazz Age or bebop prosody or experimental free jazz—not to mention its polyvalent present.

For her part, Place says she hoped her project would get her sued for copyright infringement by the Mitchell estate—an outcome that seems rather unlikely, especially given her small number of online followers. In truth, the main person the estate sued for infringement was black writer Alice Randall for writing *The Wind Done Gone* (2001), an unauthorized satire—is there another kind?—that took on the original's problems with race by further developing its black characters, rather than merely and literally reproducing it, as Place did. (If we think the race problem lies with Place only, the second authorized sequel to *Gone with the Wind* is about Mammy's past, filled with dialect by its white writer. This despite the fact that Randall's book had already imagined the black perspective on Tara plantation.) Echoing W. E. B. Du Bois's famed formulation about the color line, Goldsmith opines, "If you're not making art with the intention of having it copied, you're not really making art for the twenty-first century."[15] Goldsmith indeed regularly dj's as Kenny G, his name riffing on the white musician whose horn is the heights of what one of my white friends calls "wazz." It is tempting to see "Kenny G" this way too, but Goldsmith is more the Michael Bolton of the poetry world—the very Bolton who has had to settle out of court for stealing melodies from black folks.

Pretending plagiarism is not about power but about performance, not about origins but about the question of originality, not about texts but about ideas, is part of plagiarism's power. This too is not original. It is, however, in some ways ingenious: where else could conceptual poets, in one fell stoop, take up themes of ownership, theft, and death, except through the black body?

This extends to excuses too: plagiarists or their defenders inevitably reach for lynching to describe how they feel treated when revealed. After being caught for his prize-winning plagiarism of Helen Mort—changing only the gender of the deer in the poem—Ward offered up an apology to the *Guardian*: "I have made several stupid mistakes during my time as a poet and there is simply no excuse for plagiarism. This behaviour is unacceptable and I shouldn't have let questionable morals and a lack of conscience govern the way I acted during this incident. I'm sorry." Quickly, however, he becomes the wounded party: "Now, I would also like to bring up how I was treated in this affair. I have been bullied, victimised and abused by a number of 'poets' who thought it was necessary to act like a lynch mob."[16] Is lynching now merely a metaphor for feeling slightly uncomfortable? And why is "poets" in quotes?

Similarly, in an otherwise balanced view of the Australian plagiarism cases, Toby Fitch of the *Guardian* writes, "I don't condone plagiarism, but it would be a great shame if, in our rush to lynch a couple of plagiarists and their misguided ideas of 'patchwork,' 'sampling' and 'remixing,' we forget to remember why poetry needs experimentation."[17] *My work was so bad, Your Honor, I was left no recourse but to steal*, is the plea. Bad poetry can get better, and often doesn't know just how bad it is; half-bad seems to know it, and often seeks to get good by taking someone else's work. It's a different kind of hack.

In the case of Brad Vice, this lynching was literal—or at least a reference to a literal lynching. (There is, I want to stress, no other kind.) Vice's short story collection *The Bear Bryant Funeral Train* originally won the Flannery O'Connor Award for Short Fiction and was slated to be published by the University of Georgia Press in 2005—however, just upon publication, a librarian noticed striking similarities to Carl Carmer's *Stars Fell on Alabama*, a best-selling nonfiction book that's remained something of a near classic since its publication in 1934. Vice had copied numerous scenes verbatim; many more reveal slight shifts that reek of plagiarism far more than exact copying or "uncreative writing" might.

The University of Georgia Press rescinded the award and pulped the book; very few copies of that first edition survive. From the one that has come into my possession, it's clear *Funeral Train*'s first edition never hints at its debt to Carmer's book. But Vice's plagiarism is more than a lack of acknowledgment, as the entire idea is lifted, untransformed really, from Carmer.

Vice has since reissued the book with a small press, complete with an introduction by him that provides any number of by-now familiar plagiarism excuses, including homage. These reasonings are found as part of the 2007 second edition's packaging itself, which has left behind poor Flannery and her southern imprimatur for a kind of mishmash: "THE BEAR BRYANT FUNERAL TRAIN IS NOT A REAL DOCUMENT," the new back cover boldly announces; "IT IS A COMPUTER-GENERATED FILM MADE TO LOOK LIKE A DOCUMENT." The new back cover even reprints the starred *Kirkus* review the book received before the plagiarism was revealed, as if the revelation never happened.

Such misquoting is not just taking another's words—and work—for one's own, but also using those words for a purpose for which they were never intended. No one likes feeling misquoted, either by the newspaper or by a spouse in the heat of an argument: we often spend more energy fighting mischaracterizations by others than we might missteps we ourselves made. Vice's "not a real document" is a chorus of proof meant to shore up Vice himself. And just why isn't the Truth enough?

Seventy years after Carmer's original, Vice faces the dilemma that if he assumes we haven't read the original, then he's a plagiarist; if he assumes we have read it, and know his sources, then *Funeral Train* isn't so much filled with examples of reckless borrowing as it appears nowhere near as good or interesting as its source material. This is the true mark of the plagiarist—not simply the lack of credit but that the plagiarized work is fresh and exciting only if you haven't read the original. In stark contrast, the modern collagist or jazz riff or postmodern mashup is all the *more* enjoyable if you know the originals. These other forms don't hide, but pay homage to, their origins.

Vice's reissue, much like eighteenth-century forger William-Henry Ireland's career switch from forging Shakespeare to writing gothic romances, also shifts what once felt like classicism to something tinged with ruin. Critic Benjamin Franklin Fisher's description of Ireland's "Gothic and other novels of a violent, hectic prose style" and their "page after page filled with exclamations, short, jerky sentences, and asterisks—all stock devices for engendering emotional upheaval in a reader"[18] could easily apply to Vice's book, its exclamations and asterisks starting on the back cover and spreading inward into the body of the book. This transformation from classic to gothic takes place in acts of plagiarism more broadly: classic material stolen by the plagiarist quickly becomes a scene, and emblem, of ruin.

The opening of Carmer's original book also echoes the gothic in its southern form: "Alabama felt a magic descending, spreading, long ago. Since then it has been a land with a spell on it—not a good spell, always. Moons, red with the dust of barren hills, thin pine trunks barring horizons, festering swamps, restless yellow rivers, are all part of a feeling—a strange certainty that above and around them hovers enchantment—an emanation of malevolence that threatens to destroy men through dark ways of its own."[19] The result in *Stars Fell* is something of a folklore of Alabama, touching on key if now overdetermined southern themes, from music to drinking to the Ku Klux Klan, all with an outsider's eye. "I have chosen to write of Alabama not as a state which is part of a nation, but as a strange country in which I once lived and from which I have now returned."[20] What once was true or at least nonfiction for Carmer becomes in Vice fiction, unoriginal and overdetermined. Vice most prominently conflates a Klan rally that Carmer actually witnessed into a fictionalized one at which he places legendary football coach Bear Bryant. He means to suggest something about the South yet Vice conspicuously leaves out the separate lynching that's central to Carmer—while it's strange to critique something that Vice *didn't* plagiarize, it does indicate something of the problem with plagiarism. Just as conspicuous as what you do steal can be what you don't.

Carmer, in contrast, comes clean in his author's note—right where a hoax usually starts hedging its bets. He writes that he has chosen to hide his hosts in ways his hosts fail to hide the black folks who work for them, now in harm's way:

> All of the events related in this book happened substantially as I have recorded them. It has been necessary in a few instances to disguise characters to avoid causing them serious embarrassment (for instance my hosts during the lynching). I have also taken the liberty of telescoping time occasionally—since I have attempted to select significant occurrences which took place over a span of a half-dozen years.[21]

The note too is a telling (or not telling, as it were) part of the book's southernness. The lynching is an "embarrassment," presumably as much for what the hosts—and our narrator—didn't do as what they did. This same complicit politeness caused the hosts to allow a leader of the lynch mob to use their phone. Surely it wasn't mere embarrassment the hosts would have suffered if their fellow whites found out they did not cooperate.

The silence Carmer cultivates in his author's note is like that surrounding the lynching itself. While his telescoping of events is acceptable in that he tells us what he's up to—we been warned—his "disguising" lingers and looms large as you read the lynching chapter, especially given the fact that people in the real lynch mob don't cover their faces at all. The effect of the lynching is much like that of plagiarism, a far less serious crime but one that, once discovered, also results in a sense of public spectacle and private shame.

Not all hoaxes are witch hunts—but all witch hunts have an element of the hoax. A false narrative, a coerced confession: such things the hoax and witch hunt share. More troubling, the most innocent of hoaxes plays into the very things witch hunts and lynch mobs feed—those divisions and taboos that threaten to undo us. The hoax means to make good on its threats.

Reading Carmer now, I can't help thinking not just how Vice has stolen Carmer's words, but the way both landscapes were actually stolen from Native Americans. "Being property once myself / I have a feeling for it": poet Lucille Clifton's lines recognize the ways southern and American masks are Native and black long before they became white hoods (and white hoods'). The theft of black stories is only slightly better than blackness being left out of too many American ones. While Carmer does insist a southern story includes a black and Native one, he still describes the preachers at a "midnight babtizin" as having "gorilla-like arms," much like the sheriff of the lynch mob says, after burning down a supposed hiding place, that they found no "apes in the ashes."[22] Such a familiar fire fuels the white southern story too often.

If adding in citations attempts to resolve the act of stealing, admitting plagiarism still does not get you out of *what* you've stolen. It is hard, in such a context, to view stolenness as somehow without consequences, even for the thief. Or to leave lynching merely a metaphor, when like the past, it is not even past.

But there's another thing. Lynching, like plagiarism, is a ritual connected to power. It is in this way the opposite of hysteria, or rather, a reaction to it: where the hysteric is by definition out of control, a suffering rooted in the mind that affects the body, the lynch mob like the witch hunt marks a mass hysteria that's a constant if sometimes submerged part of the body politic. The mob regularly locates deviance or crime in another body, whether black or brown or red, male or female or in between or beyond, as long as it's judged impure; the lynch mob's monstrous act means to defeat such scapegoated monsters. Analogous to the folk pornography of lynching, replete with descriptions in the paper that we might extend to the totems of lynching—severed genitals, the lynching photograph—the hoax exhibits a pornographic folklore of violent untruth. It seeks fame, and to defame. This is all the more chilling for plagiarism's ritualistic qualities, its rehearsed behaviors that, like folklore, get retold and reinhabited by those who seek to define morals by policing bodies. It is this reaching after race that is the hoax's true addiction.

When Vice changes Carmer's section title "Tuscaloosa Nights" to "Tuscaloosa Knights," the result suffers from being obvious. Others have asserted the opposite, that obviousness is what protects Vice from critique— yet such obviousness after the fact is exactly what makes Vice's book less than enjoyable. In Carmer, the shoes of the Klan members are clear give-aways, despite their hoods: "'Look,' [Knox] said, can you see their shoes? They tell a lot.'" When Vice changes Carmer to a female narrator and Knox to Pinion and, then has him say,

> "Look." Pinion pointed at the Klansmen. "You see their shoes?
> Invisible empire, my ass. I know every one of them sum'bitches.
> Every one."

he seems only to have added cursing. Full of distortion, overdubbed dialogue would seem to travel to its new context worse than other plagiarism does—speech not only has an expiration date but is so delicate as to be damaged by the plagiarist's rough handling.

Vice asserts over and over that he's somehow disconnected from what he did. "In graduate school, where I wrote many of these stories, I felt caught between two worlds—the world of ideas and the world of commercial publication." Talk about a curse! Vice does apologize in his introductory "Aims and Acknowledgments," less for what he did than "for any offense my methods may have caused the University of Alabama Press, the University of Georgia Press, or the family of Carl Carmer." But what exactly is his method? "I weave direct passages from Carmer's text into 'Tuscaloosa Knights,' because my story is meant to look and feel like Carmer's world. But my 'Tuscaloosa' is an alternate universe, a virtual re-creation, a postmodern commentary on the primary text. The aim was to suggest the nature of absurdity and madness—not only the madness of the hateful white supremacists, the madness of the escaped mental patients, or the madness for football, but also the mad casualness of Carmer as he and his political companion stroll to the cross burning as if it were an outing to the state fair or a sporting event, an event of trivial entertainment. To do this, I reinvent already existing characters, recast them in different roles, and tell a new story containing parts of an old story."[23] Vice has mistaken Carmer's method for madness—it is exactly the "trivial" nature of how Carmer's compatriots discuss the cross burning that indicts it. Like plagiarism, it is a sign of privilege, the oldest story in the "borrowed," long-overdue book.

The fact that Vice has a "primary text" at all seems the issue. For literature, we too easily forget, plagiarizes life.

YOUNG AMERICA. RAVELS

Young America, performer with the Ravel Family troupe, ca. 1850s.

The Age of Euphemism

Once I thought I would include in this book a hoax of mine own. I had a fake name picked out and everything, a bit of prank or Easter egg as a thank-you to those readers who went on this journey through the finite jests found in the hoax. It would be much like the fake entries in encyclopedias meant to catch plagiarists—unique by design, such an entry, if it appears in another book, proves the whole thing was nabbed—a hoax for us hoax catchers to find.[1] But no, I realized, that would defeat the point: to tell the truth about those who weren't just telling it slant but who also sought to make slants seem like truth.

Spin, say-so, hooey, fiddle, Mickey Mousing, jazzed.

Truth be told, I realize now I could never compete with the ways that the half-hoax world I worried over and wrote against has given way to a full-time one, *fact-check* gone from a rare word to a dirty one. It isn't just plagiarists who have become less and less concerned with fact-checking, I suppose, but too many of us.

Esquivalience, dating from the late nineteenth century, means "the willful avoidance of one's official responsibilities." According to the *New Oxford American Dictionary*, the term likely comes from the "French *esquiver*, 'dodge, slink away.'" Except—the entry is bunk, purposefully made up to trap anyone who copied the dictionary. (The ploy worked.) Its "inherent fakeitude is fairly obvious," the creator declared when the entry was discovered in 2005. "We were trying to make a word that could not arise in nature."[2]

Today's hoaxes rely less on human nature or collective memory than cultural amnesia. We quickly erase hoaxes once exposed, excising the monstrous palimpsest, because as with any witch hunt or obvious fake, afterward we can't quite explain why we ever believed the outrageous thing in the first place. The resulting dehoaxing leads to outrage. For the hoax reminds us, uncomfortably, that the stories we tell don't just express the society of the self, they construct it.

Till now, we've spoken of our millennial narrative crisis as if the stories we tell could be separated from the self who tells them. But now it must be said that just as our technology often outstrips its users, so have our contemporary stories, more and more, outstripped the self. The recent plagiarism plague and its corresponding confessions surf the sea change I call the Age of Euphemism.

Euphemisms for sale: *Homemade. All-Natural. Artisanal. Post-factual.*

Our Age of Euphemism differs from Barnum's Age of Imposture in that, while imposture merely masks, euphemism misunderstands and misspeaks, going so far as to spite its own face. Part of the pleasure of the nineteenth century's painted woman or confidence man was finding oneself fooled, scammed, diddled, entertained; the humbug and the audience often proved unlikely yet likable collaborators. This pleasure is mostly gone from the hoax, the mask replaced with a face in pain—or at least pretending to be.

It would be the end of the 1960s, with its growing or rather revealed social divisions, that the modern hoax as we've come to know it truly resurrected, egged on by and egging on the Age of Euphemism. Between Nixon and Vietnam, assassinations and Charles Manson, Howard Hughes and his faked autobiography, it was reality that proved unreal. The Vietnam War—filled with newspeak, including whether it was a war at all—suggested as much. In her dispatches from the so-called conflict, writer Mary McCarthy wrote of "verbiage" and the ways that "napalm has become Incinder-jell, which makes it sound like Jello." As she put it, "The resort to euphemism denotes, no doubt, a guilty conscience—or the same thing nowadays— a twinge in the public-relations nerve."[3]

Or is euphemism an extension of a Nixon-like reframing, or refusing, of the truth? Does the age first deepen with nicknaming, as President Reagan did, a speculative, highly destructive national defense system "Star Wars," after a fiction—and a science fiction no less—as if it's all just make-believe? Or does euphemism peak in the first Gulf War, with its video-game images of battle glimpsed mainly from television? War, as war often has, spurred on hoaxes from spirit photography to the Cottingley fairy hoax, the *War of the Worlds* radio show to *The Embassy House* hoax about the Benghazi attack.

Other euphemisms for war include *homemade*. See *Rawson's Dictionary of Euphemisms and Other Doubletalk*: "The 'homemade mines' (President Ronald Reagan's words) that were deployed in Nicaraguan harbors in 1984 actually were company-made (by the CIA). See also *company* and *home*."[4]

These days we're experiencing a flood—not of facts but factoids, not of truth but truthiness. In an age where reality is something experienced on television, where we've substituted the tragic for tragedy—that is, tales of what can go wrong instead of ideas of right and wrong—we've become especially vulnerable. Untruths spread faster and faster, at the click of a mouse, spawning whole faux movements like birthers and truthers, billionaire populists and the alt-right, whose euphemistic names describe exactly what they do not believe. We've even had seemingly unreal presidential candidates like Donald Trump refer to these reactionary subterranean ideas directly and obliquely, claiming to see crowds of Muslims, in New Jersey no less, cheer for the fall of the Twin Towers on 9/11.[5] (There are those who even claim the Towers didn't fall, despite the literal and symbolic wreckage they left, but were a controlled demolition.)[6] Such conspiracy theorists go beyond denying facts to arguing that a certain number of dead children doesn't warrant being called "a massacre." This is euphemism not as avoidance but insistence; the ease of their being disproved does nothing to lessen belief.

Conflict, collateral damage, friendly fire.

The self was always made up of others, but now it seems the self is only others. Almost any hoax, from plagiary to forgery, treats other people only as raw material to be molded, made up, made use of, and made off with. Rather than Rimbaud's dictum that "I is an other," rather than identifying with the work of art or empathizing with the other, the hoax maintains the exoticist mantra: *The others are all mine.* One is the self as multitude, the other is the multitude as colonies from which money, labor, and language itself may be extracted.

Or maybe the hoax marks the dissolution of the self? Plagiarism enacts this theft quite succinctly, parroting another's pain as much as words. This is the chief problem with the modern hoax's focus on pain over pleasure: it shifts our attention away from those stolen from, masking their actual hurt while strip-mining away the joy the published person might have felt. Pretend "victims" should not distract us from the real victims in our midst.

The idea of violation is frequently mentioned by those who are plagiarized from—a state we don't have a word for (plagiarizee?), as if that state too has had its words removed from it. In his fascinating 1997 book *Words for the Taking*, Neal Bowers writes of being plagiarized by someone calling himself "David Sumner." Bowers's account is a detective story, not least of which because it leads to his hiring a private investigator to track down Sumner, really named David Jones: "For a brief time Nancy [his wife] and I tried to convince ourselves that pursuing Jones would only push him farther along some obscure escape route. But just when we were about to turn luminous with generosity, other plagiarisms of my poems came to light. There seemed no end to them, especially now that friends and total strangers across the country were looking for anything with the name David Sumner attached to it. With each new instance, I cared less about the Joneses' dilemma. The only thing I required was an admission of David Jones's guilt, the one thing he seemed determined never to give me."[7]

Bowers gives us a further insight into how it feels to be stolen from. In his pursuit of truth, Bowers discovers that Jones the teacher was expelled from teaching after being tried and convicted for sexually molesting young girls in his second-grade class. We share Bowers's discomfort and outrage upon learning Jones is guilty of not just plagiarism but *plagiary*, with its original meaning of "kidnapping," especially children: "He was an unrepentant copyist, but he had turned a corner and undergone a loathsome transformation. The fact that he claimed to have found me through my poems, actually to have chosen me because of some affinity he felt with me and my work, brought back my original feelings of violation and intensified them."[8] Almost as disturbing, Jones's sociopathic behavior in stealing from Bowers and other poets, including Sharon Olds, means he's up to "more than literary larceny. Many of Jones's published poems, including nearly all of those we know to have been plagiarized, are about parents or parent-child relationships. . . . Collectively these poems represent the father as negligent, noncommunicative, diseased and dying, domineering, or simply absent."[9] Like most plagiarism, Jones's has daddy issues.

Undertaker, funeral director, mortician, thanatologist.

Whenever euphemism leaps or seeps in, there's an opportunity for the hoax, marking and exploiting the schism between "official" language and the vernacular, the politician and the constituent, the self that commits the crime and the self that seeks to get out of it—or that cannot believe it. *Believe me, folks.* Ours is not a Gilded Age, as Mark Twain labeled the end of the nineteenth century, so much as a blinged-out, bedazzled one.

Wherever found, *euphemism* still suggests its Greek roots, meaning both "fair of speech" and also "fame"—especially as fame seems to have overtaken all speech lately, not to mention fairness. If euphemism began to flow in the late 1960s, the millennium seems to have brought on a deluge. Our current era's embrace of truthiness and "faction"—of fact meeting fiction—is a sign of our own fragmented, factionalized culture, before and after the millennium. Take 2013 for instance, called by CNN "the Year of the Online Hoax"; the *Washington Post* would ask a year later, "If 2013 was 'the year of the viral hoax' what then should we call 2014—a year slightly older, slightly wiser, and even more full of moronic shenanigans?"[10] By the end of 2015, the very *Washington Post* column meant to track such online fakes was suspended because readers (or whatever we are online) seemed not to care if an article was real or not.[11] Spurred along by technological advances—whether terrifying, like napalm; neutral, like the computer; or nebulous, like the Internet—our Age of Euphemism only increased the anxieties the hoax both speaks of and covers up. It's become hard to say which came first, the narrative crisis or the hoax.

Intelligence briefings. Enhanced interrogation. Casualties.

"The dishonesty of words illustrates the dishonesty of America's wars. Since 9/11, can there be any doubt that the public has become numb to the euphemisms that regularly accompany US troops, drones, and CIA operatives into Washington's imperial conflicts across the Greater Middle East and

Africa? Such euphemisms are meant to take the sting out of America's wars back home. Many of these words and phrases are already so <u>well-known</u> and well-worn that no one thinks twice about them anymore," writes William J. Astore in the *Nation*. "As euphemisms were deployed to cloak that war's bitter and brutal realities, over-the-top honorifics were assigned to America's embattled role in the world. *Exceptional, indispensable*, and *greatest* have been the three words most commonly used by presidents, politicians, and the gung-ho to describe this country."[12]

In 2016, *post-truth* overtook *alt-right* as the word or phrase of the year, when both are not only euphemisms but synonyms.[13]

Our cultural Alzheimer's is not simply a slow, inevitable, organic forgetting—rather social and cultural amnesia is employed by the likes of Donald Trump to signal nostalgia. This is a forced forgetting in which the most immediate facts are displaced and denied in favor of older ones that claim a long neglected past, a newfound Neverland. This nostalgia goes hand in hand with the conspiracy theories that describe the present only in terms of pain—terms the hoax made fast friends with. What Donald Trump the candidate promised was not freedom for but freedom *from*.

The narrative crisis of the Age of Euphemism responds more and more to the simultaneous rise of autobiography, whether unreal or "unauthorized," and the self in its most limited form: the confession. Invented by Saint Augustine, practiced during the Enlightenment by influential hoaxers like Psalmanazar and William-Henry Ireland, the pressure of such bald narratives of self don't necessarily lead to more honesty—indeed, as they typically emerge as an admission of a life of sin, they bear an anxious relation to the truth. Is the deceiver's confession to be believed? Redeemed?

The confession has now become the dominant form of our Age of Euphemism—it could be said to have caused it, suffused as it is with the language of addiction and recovery, trauma and memory and regret. With the plagiarist, confession becomes not only complicated, to say the least—is a plagiarized apology real?—but also necessary, as if the misdeed of the plagiarism is matched only by its misguided confession, which it is not complete without. Rather than in our fictional tales of a split self, a dark double, these days our horrors, real or imagined, must be expressed as autobiography, theft, or both—so much so we must now confess that we're addicted to confession.

Confession is a big part of the plagiarist's job description, extending the misdeed—often euphemized as "borrowing" or "oops"—further into the realm of the self. It isn't simply the plagiarist's text that's corrupted but the author, whose confessions are hardly apologies, or complete; rather, the plagiarist regularly revels in deceit, and may use any admission to deceive all the more. The tragedy is in the telling, and the plagiarists' confessions can hardly conceal their glee at all their indiscretions, which come to include the confession itself.

Though the means of such confession may have changed since Saint Augustine or Coleridge's unoriginal *Biographia Literaria*, his largely plagiarized autobiography, by definition all plagiarism awaits discovery of its stolen texts, half-hoping to be found out. Players gonna play; haters gonna hate; cons gotta confess: the only question is whether they do so after, or before, in the stolen texts themselves. Though they regularly speak of a utopia where no one owns words, plagiarists secretly think of ruin, that other eighteenth- and nineteenth-century preoccupation. Not only did learned people in those centuries visit actual ruins, they would invent simulated ones both in Europe and America. We have our own in Nashville's re-creation of the Parthenon, built for the 1897 Tennessee Centennial: not meant to be permanent but kept due to its popularity, the facade eroded such that the very replica of the ruin as it had originally stood had to be rebuilt. Again.

The replicated ruin's desire to travel back in time is part of plagiarism's problem: the plagiarist thinks, If only this fragment, this ruin, this form raided from others like a grave, were alive! (The actual artist or author thinks that all her sources are alive already; the memorialist wishes to honor the dead as dead.) Playing mad scientist the plagiarist seeks to raise the dead. And these reanimated corpses walk and are difficult to put to rest—as with hoaxes, they live on in our archives and history, our textbooks and lore, and especially online, replacing and erasing what they claim to honor.

Malarkey, blather, blarney, tosh, twaddle.

This infringing on the past, this perversion of research and the scientific method, is what links Spiritualism and ghostwriters, pseudospirituality and the conspiracy theories of the present day. These may be represented by *Report from Iron Mountain: On the Possibility and Desirability of Peace* (1967), an intentional hoax that pastiched official government jargon so effectively that, years after it was revealed to be a put-on—before the Pentagon Papers and Watergate paranoia it preceded and seemed eerily prescient of—some still believe it. Just as its claim that peace was bad for the country at first fueled (and parodied) a radical left, by the 1980s its fake, made-up committee-speak was being passed around as gospel by fringe right-wing survivalist groups. As noted in a recent reprint, these groups had gone so far as to republish *Iron Mountain* without the permission of the author, Leonard C. Lewin; it would take a court injunction to stop such pirating. But book piracy sounds almost romantic now, as romantic as plagiarism wishes it was.

Drawing from the language of recovery, both postmodernism and contemporary confession share the idea that whatever you claim, you are. Recovery, rehab, rehash: the stories being told, the confessions plagiarists don't often offer, those that all other hoaxers do, are American too.[14] In her 1994 memoir, writer Carolyn See describes how "those people in AA in the late forties and early fifties can be said to have reinvented American narrative style. All the terrible, terrible things that had ever happened to them just made for a great pitch."[15] If this meant baseball, not just Hollywood, the pitches would also come from stolen signs: it has long been acknowledged that much of Bill Wilson's Big Book—the nickname given by "friends of Bill" to the 1939 book *Alcoholics Anonymous* that founded and outlines the organization—borrows, if not outright plagiarizes, ideas from other books.

One of these includes Richard Peabody's *The Commonsense of Drinking*. Richard "Dick" Peabody came from a prominent Boston Brahmin family whose pedigree Clark Rockefeller could only envy. Peabody's esteemed ancestors included a governor of Massachusetts (and whose name in Massachusetts resonates as much as would-be Clark Rockefeller's did); his first marriage was officiated by an uncle who had also married future president Franklin Delano Roosevelt to future first lady Eleanor Roosevelt.[16] First delivered as a paper in 1930, Peabody's is a learned, even philosophical book by a man confronting not just recovery but also the thinking of Freud and Menninger, and a postwar generation whose drinking Prohibition had only fueled. The Lost Generation in many ways lived lives plagiarized from the same social script: "Bill's Story," a chapter in the Big Book, could have been written by any number of that cohort; for this generation, returning home from the front lines with undiagnosed post-traumatic stress, drinking provided both a sport and an unhealed wound. Though he managed to maintain his "cure," Peabody would die in 1936 at the age of forty-four, likely in no small part because of his past drinking.

It is hard to overstate the ways in which, though he didn't invent drinking, Peabody was crucial to inventing the modern idea of how to stop. The influence of *The Commonsense of Drinking* on AA is widely acknowledged; many of its ideas and its exact phrasing can be found in the first edition of AA's "Big Book." What's more, most of our now commonly held ideas about drinking originate with Peabody: describing drinking as a disease, rather than a moral failing, in which alcoholism is never completely cured; seeing oneself as an alcoholic while sober; and the very idea of telling your own story as a way of healing. So states the foreword to the first edition of *Alcoholics Anonymous*: "It is important that we remain anonymous because we are too few, at present to handle the overwhelming number of personal appeals which may result from this publication. Being mostly business or professional folk, we could not well carry on our occupations in such an event. We would like it understood that our alcoholic work is an avocation."[17] Avocation, affliction, anonymity: the bounds of the organization and its talking cure, while Freudian, trace further back, at least to Augustine's *Confessions*. No matter one's religious beliefs, "The thing was," Carolyn See writes, "you could change your life. You could remake your life. But you had to go by the Book."[18] Perhaps it is this biblical quality of the Big Book, also seeking to be Good, that let its makers feel comfortable quoting, borrowing, and using the work of others. This too is awfully American.

In any life raft, the instructions are first to go even as you make use of them. Now the hoax, married to confession, caught in the narrative crisis, has replaced drink as our national addiction and substituted loss for feeling lost.

Esquivalience.

In 1978 noted science writer David Rorvik published a book announcing that he had witnessed, even assisted in, the production of the first human clone. Many a science fiction writer had explored cloning before, but *In his Image: The Cloning of a Man* was sold as nonfiction. The "his" purposefully, distractingly lowercase, *In his Image* has all the hintings of a hoax. The book, after all, comes with a disclaimer from the publisher: "The author assures us it is true. We do not know." As if that weren't enough, a "Note on Obfuscation" follows, written by Rorvik, inadvertently confessing his book's technique while he seeks to conceal it: "Throughout I have sought an accommodation of the truth and the protective untruth consistent always with the basic course of events."[19] Rorvik's cloning shares the same shrouding in secrecy as that of other hoaxers, who insist their story is true but refuse to say how or why.

Proof is as important to science as doubt, which in turn sparks the search for proof. But today, surrounded and overwhelmed by information and misinformation as we are, has the nature of proof not only changed but eroded? And, if so, has this erosion given us more leeway to make things up—or, worse, not to recognize when we do? Must we now call this *disinformation*, purposefully misleading as it is? In Rorvik's case, a multi-million-dollar lawsuit ruled the book a hoax, with the publisher settling out of court, though this didn't stop Rorvik from keeping up his cloning claim. The contemporary hoax remains fraught with eugenicism and pseudoscience, so much so that we could say it is a fake science itself. As a pseudoscience, the hoax means to measure and provide hierarchies, ascribing order that's only opinion; tries to influence what's natural with the eugenicist goal of improvement over all else; or claims degeneration of society and self. It too creates its own lingo, *English-ish* as euphemism that's a substitute for insight. The result seeks to establish the self as superior, quantifying pain while qualifying it.

Unlike the prodigy as an ancient sign of wonder, the clone is a sign not of God's power but of that misnomer, Man's. The clone offers the ultimate double—one for our own time just as Jekyll and Hyde or multiple personality disorder had for theirs—a mutant, an animated genetic anomaly, the freak further medicalized. The clone is a double who's genetic rather than robotic; unlike the spirit photograph or earlier hoaxes, this double is physical rather than psychic. The idea had long been with us at the sideshow in the figure of conjoined twins, often people of color, from the original "Siamese twins" Chang and Eng or in Millie-Christine, born a slave but who died free. The freedom of the uncanny double is matched by the twins' literal attachment and by the clone's immortality: if done right, after all, one could simply clone oneself (or cloneselves) endlessly. But the clone also represents a crisis in confidence and creativity, like the hoax does—rather than the freedoms of the freak or the powers of the mutant, the clone may mean the end of imagination, less generative than degenerative. The clone is a kind of making—much less the art of making love—gone wrong.

Commerce, diddle, intercourse, freak, make out, pork. Locker-room talk.

The very Age of Euphemism may indeed be a euphemism—we could easily name ours the post-factual era, or the time of truthiness, or the misinformation age—but the term *euphemism* does help us name the increasing distance between what we mean and what we say. This rift is central not just to plagiarism but in our age's very derivativeness. The articulators of our era's "theory of derivativity" can be found forcefully in many quarters, including a young German, Helene Hegemann, whose prominent debut novel about the Berlin club scene was discovered to be largely stolen verbatim: "There's no such thing as originality anyway, just authenticity," she said afterwards almost reflexively.[20] It does not matter that I happen to believe exactly the opposite, for hers is less an excuse than a prediction: a spate of plagiarism by German public officials has led to several resignations by cabinet members, revoked degrees, and the exposing of the German political system's frequent quickie doctorates.[21] Or is plagiarism, and its euphemism, always political, echoing the arena where the very term *bunkum* was born?

Hoover hog, Texas turkey, penguin, pork barrel.

"The term 'pork' originated in the days of plantation slavery in the South in the years before the Civil War via which, on special occasions, slave owners would put out salt pork in big barrels at a certain time on an announced day, and their slaves would rush to grab what they could," *Rawson's Dictionary* reminds us. "The Oxford English Dictionary (1989) describes 'pork-barrel' politics as 'appropriations secured by congressmen for local projects.'"[22]

The Age of Euphemism has its modern inheritor to P. T. Barnum: none other than our own Donald J. Trump. The Donald is a showman—and now the U.S. president—one powerfully aware of media, by turns defiant of and dependent on it in ways that only reinforce the spectacle's power. Trump too bears other similarities to Barnum: both endured and employed bankruptcies; both also ran for office (Barnum unsuccessfully); both planted fake news stories as a matter of course. Trump also watched the burning down of his symbolic American Museum, which is to say, his casino. Though even Barnum did not think to start a fake university or pretend to be his own publicist, or place fake magazine covers in his many properties. For Barnum humbug had to deliver a proper, popular show no matter what got people in the door; it was the crowds that were catered to, not the other way around.

Trump's symbiotic, indeed parasitic, relationship to the press—banning journalists and jurists, who nevertheless dutifully report on him—reveals the feeling is mutual. The hoax aided by the penny press becomes the candidate no one took seriously, empowered by a news cycle that is both too fast and too slow to engender fact-checking. Or for the facts to matter.

Like one showman said of his pitch for fake African exhibits, we the audience "were subjected to 'fact' which had no relation whatsoever to the truth."[23] Indeed, Trump's team has trumpeted "alternative facts" as a thing. The worst of it is that Trump too exploits deep-seated social divisions, ones that, despairingly, echo the very same ones of race and difference on which the history of the hoax has long relied. Little has changed in the century or two since Barnum—race and ruin, devolution and descent, dangerous city life and a noble, now-gone American past become fodder for and are fed by the huckster. Only the stakes are even higher. Trump's sideshow of a presidential campaign also depended on the body, seeking to make the extraordinary—from alleged sexual assaults on women and beauty queens, to financial ones on businesspeople and the tax code, to verbal attacks on personhood and bodies deemed unfit, to confessions to the same—quite ordinary. The lame excuse of "locker-room talk" is the new ballyhoo. The sideshow has now taken over center stage.

Barker, inside talker, bunkum, rube.

Elections have always been circuses. But days before Donald Trump's inauguration and the far bigger crowds in protest against him a day later, Ringling Bros. and Barnum & Bailey circus announced it was closing.[24] People had begun to feel uncomfortable watching elephants, so the circus removed them from the acts; but once the elephants were gone from the Greatest Show on Earth people decided they didn't want to see it: the elephant in the room is that what people say they want, and what they are willing to pay for, are often at odds.

Literally and *like* are just two words whose meanings in American speech have morphed until euphemistic: one by becoming its opposite, the other becoming meaningless. *Literally* is literally used only when the thing described hasn't happened ("My head literally exploded") or hopefully won't. *Like* is an in-between word used to fill a pause but to express how things no more simply are, but merely resemble.

The hoax is a way of saying without saying, as euphemism also does. Or it's a way of not saying while saying a whole lot of nothing. Either way, euphemism does its nefarious work by seeming innocent—just like *Caucasian*, not only the banalities of a pretend whiteness but also the way whiteness pretends it is not constructed. It is much like the notion of Trump as a self-made man.

Real estate maintains perhaps the most euphemisms: *cozy* for tiny, *quaint* for old, *character* for decrepit. Even *Realtor* is a euphemism, making use, as *Rawson's Dictionary of Euphemisms* says, of the fact that the suffix "-or" just seems fancy; an "advisor" is far better than an "adviser"; a Realtor better than a real estate developer who settles one of the nation's largest lawsuits for housing discrimination.[25] The practice was long-standing enough in the family business that not only were Trump's father and Trump sued by the Justice Department, but also Woody Guthrie wrote lyrics about the practice way back in 1951: *Beach Haven is Trump's Tower / Where no black folks come to roam, / No, no, Old Man Trump! / Old Beach Haven ain't my home.*[26]

Redlining, gerrymander, urban, inner city. Members only.

The hoax is a sign of the poverty of our language surrounding race and helps perpetuate the same. You could go so far as to say the hoax is racism's native tongue. They both are things that don't really exist but that stay with us despite our disbelief, revealing more than is meant.

The hoax's haunting history of race was invoked by the likes of candidate Trump familiar as a figure of horror: fake Indians, Mexican rapists, violent Negroes and their neighborhoods, invisible Asians. These are the very same persistent fictions that the pseudoscience of the nineteenth century poured forth, trickled down, and traded up to our present day. Such exoticist behavior crosses place and even race, enacting a system of otherness for which blackface or brown, yellowface or red, has become a crucial ritual. The point of blackface is not imitation; the point of the hoax is not accuracy: the objective is to present the deeply subjective as objective, and racism as history or science. Or entertainment.

What strikes watchers most may be Trump's relationship to the truth—which may at times seem as rocky and riotous as any other hoax we've known. It isn't so much that President Trump is a liar—that epithet he regularly employs for others, while by every standard lying himself—as he's a bullshitter. This prevalence of bunk goes beyond even Barnum's; Barnum did at least display actual people. Trump instead relies on phantoms, on the ghosts not just of truth but of actual people: dead Muslim soldiers, desirous women, professional protesters, the blacks. Instead of *nondescripts* we today have *illegals*, racism as euphemism.

Sure, Joice Heth was not 161 years old as Barnum claimed, but he could then claim to be as shocked as anyone else when it was revealed to be a hoax dissected before our eyes. Trump frequently dissects himself and more importantly the process of spin, debate decorum, flouting the rules of polite society, if not the Constitution. Barnum's humbug insisted that it be entertaining, it need not be true; Trump asserts that no facts need be entertained if he says they're true. Trump at his rallies issued decided falsehoods, then used the words "believe me" or "unbelievable" as if that made what he said true; the fact that he could say either "bigly" or "big league" in ways we could argue over means that, as he said in a debate of his opponent, *These are just words*. This is the utter underlying—and lying—statement of our Age of Euphemism.

A confession: whenever anyone asked me what I was working on when I started this book, I lied; usually I said I was writing a book about liars. But as we should know by now, hoaxers aren't liars, exactly—a liar has some relation to the truth, shady and shattering, but not always seeking the way the hoax does, to gain our trust. Liars often lie to escape getting caught; the hoaxer lies as a form of escapism, all the more pernicious in that it pretends to be real. Bunk doesn't care if it's real or not—it just expects you to accept it.

Trump's are old-fashioned Barnum statements. Where Barnum makes everyone an expert, Trump suggests everyone's an amateur, even him. Or a celebrity. This is seen as honest.

A poorer propaganda, the hoax is actually all the more effective for appearing amateurish. Plagiarism does much the same. If I were a true plagiarist, it seems to say, wouldn't I have made my theft less obvious? If I were lying, wouldn't I lie better? Why lie about lying?

Trump signals a far more troubling mind-set—one in which the truth isn't so much absent or contested as it doesn't matter. This is both deeply cynical and strangely hopeful—a wish that maybe no one will notice. Or not mind if they do.

The truth is, he was right.

Alt-right. Alternative facts. White lies.

This strategy, if we can call it that, is also spectacularly modern and of the moment—Trump is calling on old ideas of public versus private while relying on the absence of either in our 24-7 news and conspiracy cycle. What he says in the "privacy" of a ten-thousand-person rally doesn't count outside it. If he can deny or divert before the facts are checked, what does it matter if he's inconsistent or indeed inconstant? In the afternoon candidate Trump tells Mexican television that he'll work with Mexico if elected, by the evening he's urging the most anti-Mexican rhetoric to a crowd of jeering thousands. It is the truth itself Trump conscripts as *nondescript*.

To call this a swindle is almost to admire it. The effort is so complete, its effects and hubris so unapologetic, and it must be said now, effective—from not releasing taxes to admitting to a billion dollars in debt (which his supporters termed "genius" or "good business") in one year, to lawsuits over a bunk university, to a fake charity and even a faux hairdo—as to suggest not the half-hoax but a full-bore one.

Most hoaxes have at least a wink about them, or a slight break in the facade; the Donald has a dictator's distemper and lack of self-awareness, which is to say there is neither mask nor man, and maybe not even money. Everything is always the most and best and biggest—except for hands—which goes for hotels, wine, racism, and misogyny too, O my! *No one respects women more than me. I'm the least racist person you know.* This seems the apotheosis of the modern hoax in which extremes replace expertise. It isn't for us to judge; no one can, much less a judge. Or journalist. Or woman.

What Trump really heralds is a time when there are no more experts.

If there is little to admire in bunk like Trump's, there's much to wonder at when you consider the collective aspect of such an unlikely endeavor. He ran a campaign and now rules by asserting his own amateurism as expertise, as well as by belittling the kinds of heroes and experts we have typically admired, from soldiers to POWs, scientists to artists, journalists to mothers. The best way to commit a hoax now is to claim you've spotted one.

I preferred "fake news" when it was simply called propaganda. These days it is not so much belief that inspires the crowd—though it never was exactly in Barnum's day either, reliant on wonder or plain curiosity. Whether that's falsely claiming the sitting president is un-American, or continuing to lie that voter fraud is widespread in an election you won (when voter suppression was far more likely), Trump the former reality TV star, beauty pageant owner, birther, and casino bankrupter provides neither simple entertainment nor distraction, but the comfort of the crowd filled with a wildness that seems peculiarly American.

What have you got to lose?

As I am writing this, the world is covered in haze. In this instance it's leftover from wild fires far away; how the smoke travels, and lingers. Its persistence gives a sense of the fabled "Year without a Summer" two hundred years ago that changed the climate as well as literature. You could say that 2016 gave us an election without a winner (or a popular winner who didn't win). The haze is here to stay: either way, the smoke gets in your hair and eyes. How to see past it?

Driving back home, smoke still in the air, book almost done, a sign in bold on a roadside motel: AMERICAN OWNED. *American*, now the ultimate euphemism.

Once I hoped that the twenty-first century would find us in the tail end of this narrative crisis and the Age of Euphemism. Figures that we've traced, with us since our nation's inception—the self-made man, the girl wonder, the inventor, the improviser—have now given way to or been revealed as euphemisms for the impostor, the spy, the forger, the plagiarist, the vampire, all of whom lie about pain and race, which they conflate as the same thing. All these selves across time are invented—or imagined—but only some of them are real.

    With the hoax more broadly, this is all the more troubling because what the hoax says about us isn't true—just as what plagiarism says about itself is untrue—or rather, is only true of our gullibility and misplaced trust. We collaborate with the hoax, and collude with it; the hoaxer just gets there first, making unwilling coconspirators of us all.

    I hate being right about this.

All along I'd hoped this book would have a happy ending. To be able to say that though we've experienced a tsunami of hoaxes, the tide has crested and now we're on the other side. Smooth sailing from here on out? At least no more drowning? This wish seems to me now particularly American, re-alizing what William Howells told Edith Wharton—or at least what we think he said—*What the American public always wants is a tragedy with a happy ending.*

It's not to be. The half-hoax world seems in no danger of ending—unless it's to give way to the complete-hoax one. This is the world we've made; one that we can only hope from here on out is not merely made up.

What if truth is not an absolute or relative, but a skill—a muscle, like memory—that collectively we have neglected so much that we have grown measurably weaker at using it? How might we rebuild it, going from chronic to bionic? The facts are on our side; let's hope the fictions once again will be too.

Funk, hokum, blue devils, the trap, the blues.

"Young America," baby elephant declared "the first known to have been born in captivity, in the world," 1880.

Acknowledgments

This book began as a slim meditation about a few hoaxers I've known and ended up a deeply researched story of an idea—or the opposite of an idea, namely, feelings faked into facts. Along the way, there are many to thank: Emory University, where a sabbatical first helped me see what the book could be and whose Rose Library provided an important home; Beloit College, where the Mackey Chair helped me find this book's early structure, with many odd volumes of rare hoaxes arriving in the mail almost daily; and the MacDowell Colony, where an emergency residency helped me rewrite the first of many drafts of the haunted whole. Thanks to Princeton University, where I spent a special semester as the Holmes Chair lost in writing, teaching, archives, and snow. Though I finished the bulk of the book before becoming its director, the Schomburg Center for Research in Black Culture continues to remind every day me how an archive can tell the truth.

Thanks to Rob McQuilkin, my agent, who championed the book and always keeps the reader in mind; and to my Graywolf editors, Fiona McCrae and Jeff Shotts, who believed in the book and saw it through many passes, Jeff's green pen enhancing all the way and Fiona's steady hand highlighting the themes. Thanks too to Katie Dublinski, managing editor, who helped through the incredibly thorough copy edit (and to the copy editor, who—sorry, *whom*—I don't know, but who performed the herculean task). All are stars. Thanks to those who published or podcasted bits of the book, often in earlier forms: *Virginia Quarterly Review*, *Tin House*, Princeton's lecture series, *Bookforum*, *Kenyon Review*, and *The Fire This Time* anthology. I couldn't have finished this book without the heroic team of Aaron Goldsman and

Sarah Harsh, my Emory grad students who undertook fact-checking a book with a lot of facts to check: *Mazel & Slainte.*

I especially need to thank my wife, Kate, and son, Mack, who endured my having to hole up and write in what often felt like any waking moment; thanks to their good humor, good advice, and goodness. I couldn't have done it without you. Thanks to Colson Whitehead, Natasha Trethewey, Elizabeth Alexander, Mom, departed Dad, and my brothers and sisters in the struggle. Thanks to my Emory colleague Ben Reiss, whose scholarship and friendship inspires. Thanks to my favorite librarians, including those at Harvard's Houghton Library who helped with many of the images at the end, especially Matthew Wittman, who directed me to and through the rich Harvard Theatre Collection. Thanks to old friend Regan Huff, who helped me with tracking down a key title, and Nancy Kuhl and the Beinecke, for providing images of one of Prokosch's "butterfly books." A special thanks to Harvard's Kate Donovan, who goes above and beyond, and shares the belief that libraries are for people not just books—an idea that keeps me on my toes. Also thanks to Birmingham (twice), Princeton, Memphis, Nashville, Asheville, and Oxford, Miss., for stolen moments that helped complete this project. Thanks finally to Richard Eoin Nash, dedicatee of this book and the first to suggest that Barnum should not be buried in the book as he once was. Thanks for helping me see what all this could be.

Notes

1. The Age of Imposture

1. Some dispute—or misquoting—surrounds this quote. Most sources list this as Howells's statement, amending it to "what they want in the theater," I believe, because the theater provided the original occasion. However, Robert M. Dowling's "Sad Endings and Negative Heroes: The Naturalist Tradition in American Drama," in Keith Newlin, ed., *The Oxford Handbook of American Literary Naturalism* (2011), attributes the quote exactly as I have it here and to Wharton instead of Howells (see 427–28), citing in turn R. W. B. Lewis, *Edith Wharton: A Biography* (1975), 172. I have stuck with the quote as I first heard it, from Howells and without the theater, as confirmed by the website of The Mount, Wharton's Berkshires home: "The first stage adaptation of Edith Wharton's bestselling novel *The House of Mirth* was not a success. In *A Backward Glance* when Wharton describes the reaction of William Dean Howells, who had come at her invitation to see the performance, she writes of "the lapidary phrase in which, as we left the theatre, he summed up the reason of the play's failure. 'Yes—what the American public always wants is a tragedy with a happy ending'"; www.edithwharton.org/film/a-tragedy-with-a-happy-ending.

2. P.T. Barnum, *The Life of P.T. Barnum*, 234–35.

3. Indeed, one turned out to be African American. See Bogdan, *Freak Show*, 178–87.

4. Barnum, *Humbugs*, 7.

5. Lepore, "A Nue Merrykin Dikshunary," in *The Story of America: Essays on Origins*.

6. Quote apparently from George Henry Evans in *Workingman's Advocate*, thinking about Matthias. Found in Goodman, *The Sun and the Moon*, 74.

7. Ibid., 154.

8. Barnum, *Humbugs*, 7–9.

9. Ibid., 19–20, 21.

10. These include three exposés and one account of the trial. Several, such as Barnum's *Humbugs*, also impugn Joseph Smith and Mormonism, which was still controversial and seen as a hoax. (Many a religion can be seen so by nonbelievers.) Certainly it is true that before Smith discovered the tablets he was known for using lenses for "scrying," often for gold, which was illegal in many states, including New York. But as Simon Worrall notes in *The Poet and the Murderer*, Smith's was not only one of America's homegrown religions; it also included America in its foundational narratives, in which Christ visited the New World after the resurrection.

11. Goodman, *The Sun and the Moon*, 73.

12. Ormond Seavey, introduction to Locke, *Moon Hoax*, vii.

13. Goodman, *The Sun and the Moon*, 13.

14. Ibid., 10. See page 146 for when the comet was first sighted.

15. Locke, *Moon Hoax*, 7–9. Herschel's father was also a famed figure in England.

16. Ibid., 26.

17. Ibid., 31.

18. Ibid., 36–37.

19. Reiss, *The Showman and the Slave*, 147.

20. Locke, *Moon Hoax*, 44–45.

21. See Goodman, *The Sun and the Moon*, for more details on these and other cultural productions stemming from the Moon Hoax.

22. Seavey, *Moon Hoax*, xxiii–xxiv.

23. Poe, "Diddling Considered as One of the Exact Sciences," in *Poetry, Tales, and Selected Essays*, 607. Originally written in 1843; published in 1845.

24. Ibid., 608.

25. Poe, "The Unparalleled Adventure of One Hans Pfaall," in *Poetry, Tales, and Selected Essays*, 952.

26. Poe, "Letter to Mr. —— ——," *Poetry, Tales, and Selected Essays*, 16.

27. Goodman, *The Sun and the Moon*, 236.

28. Seavey, *Moon Hoax*, xxxii.

29. Poe to John Pendleton Kennedy, 11 September 1835, quoted in ibid. Seavey here is quoting from Arthur H. Quinn's 1941 critical biography of Poe.

30. Poe, note to "The Unparalleled Adventure of One Hans Pfaall," in *The Works of the Late Edgar Allan Poe*, ed. Rufus Wilmot Griswold (New York: Redfield, 1849), vol. I, 46–51. Reprinted in Seavey, *Moon Hoax*.

31. *New York Herald*, 5 September 1835, quoted in Seavey, *Moon Hoax*, xx.

32. Poe, quoted in Seavey, *Moon Hoax*, xxxii.

33. Some say *hoax* may be a corruption of the word *hocus*, but given that both words emerge around the same time, and even the same decade, of the eighteenth century, this seems unlikely. Like *mystification, humbug* too can be narrowed down

as dating from the 1750s. See Julia Abramson, *Learning from Lying*, for her definition of mystification: "Among the multifarious forms of literary deceit, mystification has a unique history and a singular purpose that reflects its origins during the century of Enlightenment. In Paris during the 1750s conservative thinkers invented the verb 'mystifier' along with its substantive cousin 'mystification' to describe pranks played on members of their own social circle. Subsequently, liberal philosophes appropriated the neologisms and inflected them to suit their own aims. Mystification may have begun with deception, but in the hands of the philosophes it led to discovery. In mid-eighteenth-century France, masks, imposture, and illusion flourished alongside the scientific and philosophical inquiry that aimed to reveal hidden causes, communicate knowledge, and promote critical reasoning. A similar tension between transparency and stratagem characterizes itself. The practice evolved both to trick and to teach, achieving its own synthesis of these contradictory movements" (12–13). *Humbug* is defined by the *Oxford English Dictionary* as "a thing which is not really what it pretends to be; an imposture, a deception, fraud, sham," or in its obsolete first meaning, "a hoax; a jesting or befooling trick; an imposition."

34. Poe, "Mystification," *Poetry, Tales, and Selected Essays*, 260–61.

35. Ibid., 254–55; emphasis added.

36. Ibid., 130.

2. The Freaks of Dame Fortune

1. Lindberg, *The Confidence Man in American Literature*, 3.

2. Goodman, *The Sun and the Moon*, 183.

3. Ibid., 221.

4. Goodman, *The Sun and the Moon*, 221, quoting from the *Sun* for 16 September 1835.

5. "Great Attraction Just arrived at Concert Hall" handbill, 1835. From the author's collection.

6. Paull, *Literary Ethics*, 149.

7. Eric Fretz, "P.T. Barnum's Theatrical Selfhood and the Nineteenth-Century Culture of Exhibition," in Garland Thomson, *Freakery*, 97–98. Fretz is here thinking of critic Jay Fliegelman.

8. Ibid., 98.

9. Barnum, *Humbugs of the World*, 24–25.

10. Ronald E. Ostman, "Photography and Persuasion: Farm Security Administration Photographs of Circus and Carnival Sideshows, 1935–1942," in Garland Thomson, *Freakery*, 126.

11. [Barnum,] *The Life of Joice Heth*, 5. Pamphlet issued anonymously.

12. Ibid., 9. Thanks to Ben Reiss for making this point about Barnum's opportunistic "abolitionism" far more eloquently in his *Showman and the Slave*.

13. Consult Reiss, *The Showman and the Slave*, for the ramifications of Heth as automaton.

14. The eventual schism between the kinds of maids and between North and South, white and black might best be symbolized by the two film versions of *Imitation of Life*: the first, black-and-white one (1934), which I love, and the color (or colored) remake from 1949. In both films, the mammy nurtures not just her own daughter—or as Toni Morrison's *Bluest Eye* (1969) points out with its similar namesake, Pecola—but everyone else's. In the remake, daughter Peola—who will ultimately pass for white—is not actually colored but in blackface (call it light-brownface) and the mother is no longer a figure like that played by Louise Beavers in the first film, meant to invoke Aunt Jemima. (Besides having to take a class to learn her supposedly native "dialect," Beavers had to be padded to play a mammy.) In both versions, it is only death that wakes the white-wishing daughter out of her reverie. First brilliantly played in 1934 by light-skinned black actress Fredi Washington, the daughter's hysteria before and after her mother's death black audiences would read as less a protest against blackness than one against racism. (We'll further explore hysteria as female protest soon enough.) It is only in death that the family is made whole, the daughter who passes for white brought home to her mother's homegoing too late. Is it that death proves a poor imitation of life, the viewer wonders, or blackness?

15. Agassiz's trip is described in numerous places; for example, Avery F. Gordon, *Ghostly Matters*, 185. We will return to Agassiz in chapter 8, "The Time Machine."

16. The term *freakery* I take from the title of Rosemarie Garland Thomson's noted anthology *Freakery: Cultural Spectacles of the Extraordinary Body*.

17. One of the most fascinating essays in Garland Thomson's collection *Freakery* reconsiders Michael Jackson and his often purposeful freakiness. From Bubbles the Chimp to his hyperbaric chamber and Neverland Ranch, his various acts can seem a way of humbugging taking over from where Ripley's "Believe It or Not" left off. And yet, such freakery had its dark, gothic side that, despite what his hit song says, depended deeply on a dichotomous view of blackness and whiteness.

18. Gould, "Poe's Greatest Hit," reprinted in *Dinosaur in a Haystack* (2011). Elizabeth Alexander, *The Venus Hottentot* (1990), 6–7.

19. The *Oxford American Dictionary* traces the origin of *bunkum* thus: "Etymology: < *Buncombe*, name of a county in N. Carolina, U.S. The use of the word originated near the close of the debate on the 'Missouri Question' in the 16th congress, when the member from this district rose to speak, while the house was impatiently calling for the 'Question.' Several members gathered round him, begging him to desist; he persevered, however, for a while, declaring that the people of his district expected it, and that he was bound to *make a speech for Buncombe*. (See Bartlett, *Dict. Americanisms*)." Other sources say he had to speak *to* Buncombe.

20. Contemporary play bills from the American Museum make clear the "is" is lowercase—the way I've quoted it throughout, emphasizing the *It*-quality the performer is meant to have.

21. Cook, ed., *The Colossal P. T. Barnum Reader*, 211–12, quoting from *New York Mercury*, 8 December 1860.

22. Sellers, *Mr. Peale's Museum*, 16. The only other time I've seen *nondescript* in relation to a person concerns another black figure, "Nichodemus the Nondescript," in his inscription on a cabinet card in the Harvard Theatre Collection. I can locate little on Nichodemus (or Nicodemus), though given the cabinet card format and from the one reference I found, it appears he worked at the end of the nineteenth century and well after What is It?; surely his using nondescript in his stage name is an attempt to capture some of Barnum's magic. See John William Ballantyne, *Manual of Antenatal Pathology and Hygiene*, vol. 2 (1905).

23. Sellers, *Mr. Peale's Museum*, 18.

24. Handbill, Harvard Theatre Collection, Houghton Library, Harvard University. These handbills were printed by the New York Herald Company.

25. As found on the Lost Museum Archive's What Is It? page: http://chnm.gmu .edu/lostmuseum/searchlm.php?function=find&exhibit=what&browse=what. As the website describes it, "The exhibit claimed to prove that Africans descended from monkeys and thus merged supposedly objective scientific findings about evolution with ongoing antebellum debates over racial definition, the morality of slavery, and sectional politics."

26. *Life of Zip, the Original What is It* (ca. 1884), Harvard Theatre Collection, 3–5. The cover reads *Life of Zip* with the title pages saying "History of Zip, the Original 'What is It?'"

27. Bogdan, *Freak Show*, 133, 142. Thanks to Chris Myers for pointing out Johnson's last words. See also an interview with his sister found in Colin Campbell, dir., "Wild West Tech: Freak Show Tech," History Channel, 21 December 2004.

28. Cabinet card found in Theatre Collection, Houghton Library, Harvard University.

29. Frost, *Never One Nation*, 63–64.

30. *Biographical Sketch of the Circassian Girl, Zalumma Agra*, [3].

31. I first came across Blumenbach in Gregory Fried, "A Freakish Whiteness: The Circassian Lady and the Caucasian Fantasy," Mirror of Race website, 15 March 2013 (with updates); http://mirrorofrace.org/circassian. See also Frost, *Never One Nation*, and Painter, *History of White People*, who devotes a chapter, if not the whole book, to Blumenbach's legacy.

32. Painter, *History of White People*, 79.

33. Sarah Lewis, "Mickalene Thomas on Beauty," in *Mickalene Thomas: Origin of the Universe*, ed. Lisa Melandri, 8. I want to thank Lewis for first drawing my attention to the Circassian Beauty; no doubt her forthcoming work will illuminate these ideas further than I might here.

34. Frost, *Never One Nation*, 57.

35. Painter reminds us that the term *odalisque* "derives from the Turkish *odalk*, meaning 'harem room.' Georgian, Circassian, and Caucasian were interchangeable names for the figure. Each term refers to young white slave women, and each carries with it the aura of physical attractiveness, submission, and sexual availability—in a word, femininity. She cannot be free, for her captive status and harem location lie at the core of her identity." Painter, *History of White People*, 48.

36. Frost, *Never One Nation*, 67.

37. A headline from the *New York Times* for 5 December 2013 may illustrate the confusion: "Winter Games, Caucasian Misery." Jahar Tsarnaev, who actually was in the same high school class as my stepdaughter, may illustrate the strange power of racism. By all accounts a rather assimilated kid, part of the multiculturalism of Cambridge, he listened to hip-hop and smoked pot like many another teenager. He became "radicalized," they say, under the influence of his older brother; upon his capture, photos of him with his big mossy hair almost conjure the Circassian Beauty across the centuries, as well as its conflict: many protested his being placed on the cover of *Rolling Stone*, seemingly glamorized. Later tried and sentenced to death, his changing view of race seems to have affected even his voice: he now speaks with an accent and appears not as fluent in English as he unmistakably once was.

38. Gould, *Mismeasure of Man*, 117.

3. Splitfoot

1. In 1866 Barnum's *Humbugs of the World* would have called many movements we consider religions fake. Of course, all religions appear absurd to nonbelievers, with their rituals and reckoning with the supernatural—this is one reason why for the most part I don't discuss religious hoaxes, even those that can be decidedly proved false in their origin. The most heinous religious-related hoax, *The Protocols of the Elders of Zion*, is not only anti-Semitic and fake but plagiarized from an entirely other set of menacing pseudodocuments justifying prejudice. Reprinted by the likes of Henry Ford in the twentieth century, it could be said to be the most powerful of hoaxes, further proof that the hoax is not only about cultural fissures but also about life and death.

2. Letter from Mary Lincoln to Charles Sumner, near Chicago; in Turner and Turner, *Mary Todd Lincoln*, 123.

3. Braude, *Radical Spirits*, 2.

4. Horowitz, *Occult America*, 54, quoted in Stephen Mansfield, *Lincoln's Battle with God* (2012), 157.

5. [Wilson], *Our Nig*, 70–73. With introduction by Foreman. Many thanks to Professor P. Gabrielle Foreman for personally and fortuitously making me aware of Wilson's spiritualism, as well as the writing of Randolph. Her introduction to *Our Nig* is a tremendous discussion not just of Wilson but also of nineteenth-century literary and political issues.

6. Stephen Mansfield mentions this as an aside in his Christian-themed *Lincoln's Battle with God*: "A friend of the Lincolns later attributed Mary's involvement in spiritualism to Elizabeth Keckly [*sic*], the freed slave who served the First Lady as seamstress and confidante. There may have been some racism in this" (155).

7. Gates's 2011 edition of *Our Nig* incorporates some of Foreman's discoveries, noted earlier in note 5, especially investigating Wilson's spiritualism. Henry Louis Gates Jr. and Richard J. Ellis, introduction, *Our Nig; or, Sketches from the Life a Free Black*.

8. Wilson, *Our Nig*, 72.

9. Ibid., 85.

10. See the introduction and appendix to the Gates and Ellis edition; also Foreman's Penguin reissue.

11. Barnum, *Humbugs of the World*, 110. Braude's principles in *Radical Spirits* remain useful here: "Some may object that self-identification is insufficient evidence that a person is a Spiritualist, that frauds and charlatans must be distinguished from genuine inquirers. I see no reason to make retrospective judgments on this question. It concerns me only insofar as it concerned nineteenth-century Spiritualists. If someone was judged to be a fraud by contemporary coreligionists, I take that view into account. Any further judgments on my part would be comparable to judging the miraculous origins of any religion" (8)—something that professed Christian Barnum most certainly did.

12. The Amazing Randi—more recently following the tradition inaugurated by Barnum and realized by Houdini of being both an illusionist and debunker—describes how "the public confessions had done nothing to dampen the belief in the Fox sisters or the movement they had started. The believers expressed their regret at the fact that the sisters had been forced into lying, and spiritualism continued as if the confessions of the Fox sisters had never happened." Notably, "the oldest spiritualist group still in existence," the National Spiritualist Association of Churches, was founded in 1893—*after* the confessions. Randi, "Fox Sisters," in *An Encyclopedia of Claims, Frauds, and Hoaxes of the Occult and Supernatural*, 102.

13. *New York Daily Tribune*, 13 April 1869, 8; quoted in Kaplan, *The Strange Case of William Mumler*, 182. These days Mumler's photographs can be appreciated for their historic and aesthetic values, if not quite their spiritual or documentary ones. Though recent studies like Chéroux et al.'s *The Perfect Medium* or Kaplan's *The Strange Case of William Mumler* take pains to remain neutral regarding whether the pictures are faked or not, the plethora of confessed fakes found in those volumes, not to mention those debunked by the likes of famous magician Houdini, should make it clear.

14. Douglas, *Feminization of American Culture*, 207.

15. Harris, *Humbug*, 80.

16. In the Bible such beings, if they can be called that, as angels are beyond

human concern in ways that Tony Kushner manages to dramatize in his epic *Angels in America*.

17. Christian writer Tim Challies first coined the genre "heaven tourism" on Challies.com, 18 June 2012; www.challies.com/articles/heaven-tourism.

18. Chéroux et al., *The Perfect Medium*, 26–27. The original album is found at the College of Psychic Studies, London.

19. William H. Mumler, *The Personal Experiences of William H. Mumler in Spirit-Photography* (1875). Reprinted in Kaplan, *Strange Case of William Mumler*, 110.

20. See Gates and Ellis, introduction, *Our Nig*, expanded edition, li. Also see Appendix I, xxxii–iii.

21. See Braude, *Radical Spirits*, for more on this, especially the introduction.

22. Conan Doyle recounts the story in his original *Strand* article, and he uses the girls' real names in *The Coming of the Fairies*.

23. Poet Robert Duncan was adopted into a theosophist family as a child. See Peter Washington's *Madame Blavatsky's Baboon* for a lively account of "spiritual science" from Swedenborg on—much the same territory, though from a necessarily different perspective, as Conan Doyle's *History of Spiritualism* (volume 1).

24. Conan Doyle, *The New Revelation*, front cover. Doyle's son died in 1918 of influenza-related pneumonia two years after being wounded in the Battle of the Somme.

25. *Strand* magazine, December 1920, 463–68, illustrated. See also Conan Doyle, *Coming of the Fairies*, 13.

26. Conan Doyle, *Coming of the Fairies*, 57–58.

27. Ibid., 53.

28. Ibid., 24–25. .

29. Ibid., 55.

30. May Bowley quoted in ibid., 22.

31. Ibid., 65.

32. See Donald E. Simanek, "Arthur Conan Doyle, Spiritualism, and Fairies," for details on the 1977 revelation; www.lhup.edu/~dsimanek/doyle.htm. Simanek also contains links to Joe Cooper's interview with the cousins in which they confessed to the hoax. See Joe Cooper, "Cottingley: At Last the Truth," *Unexplained*, no. 117 (1982): 2338–40; www.lhup.edu/~dsimanek/cooper.htm.

33. Cooper, "Cottingley."

34. "It was clear that at the last it was the character and surroundings of the children upon which the inquiry must turn, rather than upon the photos themselves." Conan Doyle, *Coming of the Fairies*, 33.

35. Emily Tennyson writing to Edward Lear, quoted in Phyllis Rose, "Milkmaid Madonnas: An Appreciation of Cameron's Portraits of Women," *Julia Margaret Cameron's Women*, 13. The quote also appears in Colin Ford, *The Cameron Collection: An Album of Photographs by Julia Margaret Cameron Presented to Sir John Herschel* (1975).

36. Bernstein, *Racial Innocence*, 4.

37. See Wark, *Charles Doyle's Fairyland*, and Baker, *The Doyle Diary*, for more on Doyle père's work and life.

38. Conan Doyle, *Coming of the Fairies*, 55, 58.

39. Quoted in Cooper, letter from Frances Griffiths, 9 November 1918; www .lhup.edu/~dsimanek/cooper.htm.

40. Conan Doyle, *Coming of the Fairies*, 58.

41. Conan Doyle's assertions are found in *The Edge of the Unknown* (1930). A reliable reference and images on the case can be found in Randi's *Encyclopedia of Claims, Frauds, and Hoaxes* and in Donald E. Simanek's online article "Arthur Conan Doyle, Spiritualism, and Fairies"; www.lhup.edu/~dsimanek/doyle.htm. Profiting off grief was matched by the profits the girls never received from their photographs, for the theosophist movement that believed and popularized them claimed the copyright of the Cottingley photos as their own. See the Museum of Hoaxes' account of the contested copyright; http://hoaxes.org/photo_database /image/the_cottingley_fairies.

4. Bearded Ladies

1. Maynard, *Was Abraham Lincoln a Spiritualist?*, vii.

2. MacDougall, *Hoaxes*, 164. A picture of the fake John Wilkes Booth's mummy, another hoax, can be seen on 165.

3. Ellery Sedgwick, "The Discovery," *Atlantic*, December 1928; www.theatlantic .com/magazine/archive/1928/12/the-discovery/304443. The whole of the case is usefully summarized by Katie Bacon in the November 2005 *Atlantic* (www.theatlantic .com/magazine/archive/2005/11/an-atlantic-scandal/304449), itself a preview of Joshua Wolf Shenk's recounting in his afterword to *Lincoln's Melancholy*.

4. Quoted in Edward Weeks, *My Green Age*, 255.

5. Sandburg, *Abraham Lincoln: The Prairie Years*, 113.

6. Sedgwick, "The Discovery."

7. Fehrenbacher, "The Minor Affair," in *Lincoln in Text and Context*, 258–59.

8. Paul Angle, who wrote the ultimate exposure, published in the *Atlantic* in April 1929, quoted in Weeks, *My Green Age*, 256.

9. Fehrenbacher, "The Minor Affair," 266–68.

10. As pointed out by Katie Bacon in the *Atlantic*, Shenk's afterword in his book *Lincoln's Melancholy* makes the point about Lincoln now becoming the province of professional historians after the Minor affair: "The Minor affair ended up ushering in the third era of Lincoln studies. First the story had been controlled by Lincoln's friends (and their ghostwriters). Then the popular historians had taken over. Now the reins passed to professional historians, a burgeoning group emerging from new Ph.D. programs (a creation of the late nineteenth and early twentieth centuries). University-trained historians tended to look askance at the amateurs who had come

before them. For the professionals in the Lincoln field, the Ann Rutledge story was a perfect example of what had gone wrong. For years they had been aching to knock it down, and the *Atlantic Monthly* threw a hanging curve" (230–31).

11. Thompson, *A Curious Man*, 145. Ripley's widely syndicated newspaper column and then empire began in a career as a cartoonist, first signing as Rip or Ripley; by 1913 he had enough success that the New York *Globe* had him change his name from LeRoy to Robert, which he was only too happy to do. As Thompson indicates, "'LeRoy' apparently wasn't masculine enough for a sports cartoonist/reporter"; it is ironic that by the end of the century, "LeRoy" would be adopted by Laura Albert exactly because of its masculine connotations in naming her literary creation JT LeRoy—though perhaps equally absurdly, in the end the name also proved not "masculine enough."

12. First quoted in Jill Lepore, "The Oddyssey: Robert Ripley and His World," *New Yorker*, 3 June 2013, 63. Lepore's is a rather critical review of Thompson's *A Curious Man*, with the added benefit of a portrait of *New Yorker* writer Geoffrey T. Hellmann, who first profiled Ripley in 1940.

13. Fiedler, *Freaks*, 16. See Rosemarie Garland Thomson's *Extraordinary Bodies* on this medicalization. Critic Robert Bogdan's *Freak Show* also describes how the freak, once a figure of wonder or speculation, soon became medicalized, made merely ill and curable.

14. Paul Semonin, "Monsters in the Marketplace: The Exhibition of Human Oddities in Early Modern England," in Garland Thomson, *Freakery*, 73. Another essay in this essential volume dates the sideshow's heyday as occurring from 1840 to 1940. Garland Thomson herself discusses this change in the "extraordinary body."

15. Garland Thomson, *Extraordinary Bodies*, 58. I cannot overstate the import of this book on me and on the now-established field of disability studies.

16. Geoffrey T. Hellmann, "Odd Man—I," *New Yorker*, 31 August 1940, 20.

17. Bogdan, *Freak Show*, 3.

18. Susan Stewart, *On Longing*, 109.

19. Virginia Woolf, "Mr. Bennett and Mrs. Brown," in McNeillie, *The Essays of Virginia Woolf*, vol. 3, *1919–1924*, 421.

20. Letter by Horace de Vere Cole, quoted in Dalya Alberge, "How a Bearded Virginia Woolf and Her Band of 'Jolly Savages' Hoaxed the Navy," *Guardian*, 4 February 2012. See also the later account by one of the other participants, Adrian Stephen, *The "Dreadnought" Hoax*. Quentin Bell's biography of his aunt states that Adrian also made use of the *Aeneid* in Latin as "Swahili." Bell, *Virginia Woolf*, 157.

21. Bell, *Virginia Woolf*, 159. Bell misstates the date as 10 February 1910 on 157.

22. Stephen, *"Dreadnought" Hoax*, 22–23; emphasis added.

23. Ibid., 37. In the surviving fragment of an otherwise lost recounting of the hoax, Woolf writes: "We heard afterwards that one result of our visit had been that the regulations were tightened up; and that rules were made about telegrams that

make it almost impossible now to repeat the joke. I am glad to think that I too have been of help to my country." Reprinted in Bell, *Virginia Woolf*, 214–16.

24. Coleridge, "Kubla Khan," *The Major Works*, 102–4. Includes the poem and his famous headnote about composition, though the story of his writing being interrupted by a visitor from Porlock after taking an "anodyne" is at best embellished and at worst poor cover for writing in an opium haze.

25. Both the *Dreadnought*'s cultural import as "a public symbol, located at the intersection of cultural and political contexts," and the details of the telegram, may be found in Blyth, Lambert, and Rüger, *The Dreadnought and the Edwardian Age*; see Blyth's introduction and chapter 2, Rüger, "The Symbolic Value of the *Dreadnought*," 9–11. The topic of Ethiopianism deserves more than I can manage here, but may be explored by reading, among other things, contemporary poems such as *The Harp of Ethiopia*, by Maurice N. Corbett (1914), or Randall K. Burkett's fine writing on the topic.

26. The photographs also refer to a previous smaller-scale hoax when Adrian Stephen and the mastermind Horace de Vere Cole dressed in blackface to pose as "The Sultan of Zanzibar and his suite" and hoaxed the mayor of Cambridge while they were at university.

27. Jeremiah 13:23. The title *The Leopard's Spots* (1902) would adorn the first of racist Thomas Dixon's KKK trilogy, whose sequel would give us modern cinema in *The Birth of a Nation*; the phrase also would supply the title to William Stanton's tremendous rebuttal to "scientific attitudes toward race in America," the very pseudo-science that had fueled Dixon.

28. Rush quoted in Martin, *The White African American Body*, 41–43. This was actually the sympathetic view, not shared by Thomas Jefferson, to whom the fellow Philosophical Society member first put his theories in a 1797 letter.

29. One critic refers to the synthesized author as "Macphossian." See Ruthven, *Faking Literature*.

30. From the third stanza of Coleridge's "Monody on the Death of Chatterton":

> I weep, the heaven-born Genius so should fall,
> And oft in Fancy's saddest hour my soul
> Averted shudders at the poison'd Bowl.
> Now groans my sickening Heart, as still I view
> The Corse of livid hue;
> And now a Flash of Indignation high
> Darts thro' the Tear, that glistens in mine Eye!
> Is this the Land of song-enobled Line?
> Is this the Land, where Genius ne'er in vain
> Pour'd forth her lofty strain?

Coleridge, "Monody on the Death of Chatterton," 1794; http://spenserians.cath.vt.edu/TextRecord.php?action=GET&textsid=35278.

31. "Forgive, neglected shade! my pensive lay, / While o'er thy tomb I hang my rural wreath." Yearsley, "Elegy on Mr. Chatterton," *Poems on Various Subjects*, 145. The "milk-woman" phrase is from a letter from an early supporter, Hannah More, to a patron, introduction, [vii].

32. Holmes, *Coleridge: Early Visions*, 63.

33. "George Psalmanaazaar," *An Historical and Geographical Description of Formosa*, 150, 145, 156.

34. See Percy G. Adams, *Travelers and Travel Liars*, for more on Psalmanazar's influence on Rousseau. For Rousseau's import more generally, consult any number of sources, including Yagoda, *Memoir*, and Daniel Mendelsohn reviewing Yagoda in the *New Yorker*.

35. Psalmanazar, *Memoirs of* ****, 3.

36. John Matthew Gutch, *Caraboo: A Narrative of a Singular Imposition* (1817), 21–22 and 9–10.

37. Consult Martin, *The White African American Body*, 7. Martin discusses the Bartholomew Fair and Barnum's later exhibition of White Negroes and white Moors.

38. As quoted in ibid., 22, taken from *Notes on the State of Virginia*, 70.

39. Jefferson quoted in Rogers, *Delia's Tears*, 114–15. Rogers provides a solid introduction to race and the White Negro.

40. Adams, *Travelers and Travel Liars*, 80–81.

41. Ibid., vii.

42. Stagl, *History of Curiosity*, 207. Stagl's study of travel literature has a useful chapter on Psalmanazar.

43. Even Prohibition, historian Lisa McGirr convincingly argues in *The War on Alcohol*, while remaining only a mild suggestion for certain elites, was enforced severely and unevenly for the poor and communities of color—providing an excuse for groups like the then-fading Klan to enact vigilante justice. What's more, the rule of law is one that would continue in societal crackdowns such as the War on Drugs of the 1980s, which also affected these same communities unequally.

44. Bogdan, *Freak Show*, 224. The entire chapter is useful for understanding what Bogdan calls the "aggrandized" presentation of freaks.

45. For a terrific summary of the Jazz Age that Fitzgerald named, consult Ann Douglas's *Terrible Honesty*, especially the epilogue and bibliographic essay. Douglas argues that "the 1920s resembled what earlier generations had considered an event rather than what was usually defined as an epoch; they were a phenomenon too momentous and unique to be easily subsumed into the neighboring historical landscape. Today, we think in discrete decades almost as naturally as we thinking months and years. . . . The idea of the decade as a special, marketable package was, in fact, largely a 1920s invention" (481).

46. Douglas's thesis is a complex one, but she does suggest ways in which sen-

timentality was tied to progressive causes, in contrast to Calvinism. Oddly, she doesn't much mention temperance, and McGirr doesn't mention Douglas's thesis at all.

47. Patricia Lockwood as quoted in Jesse Lichtenstein, "The Smutty-Metaphor Queen of Lawrence, Kansas," *New York Times Magazine*, 28 May 2014.

48. Early on, Barrie had enlisted the sons of the Llewelyn-Davies family who would inspire his fairy tale to playact and photograph a proto–Peter Pan story, *The Boy Castaways of Black Lake Island* (1901). This "best and rarest of this author's works," as Barrie playfully put it, consisted of two copies; one was promptly lost by the boys' father, who was jealous of Barrie's relationship with their mother. Consisting of photographs with captions and titles, *Castaways* already introduces some of the figures that would become part of Peter Pan's mythology, including a dog integral to the action. Barrie would name his dog, the model for *Peter Pan*'s Nana, Luath, after a character from the eighteenth-century hoax epic *Ossian*. See *The Annotated Peter Pan* for images and the story of the *Boy Castaways*. See 16–17 for the genealogy of the dogs and the origins of the name Luath.

49. See *The Young Visiters*. For a recent appreciation of this novel (and the source of the quote from the *New York Times*) consult Alice Bolin's "Daring Daisy Ashford, the Greatest Ever Nine-Year-Old Novelist," *Paris Review*, 8 July 2013; www.theparisreview.org/blog/2013/07/08/daring-daisy-ashford-the-greatest-ever -nine-year-old-novelist.

50. Ashford, *The Young Visiters*, 37.

51. All accounts indicate how devastated Follett was by this split, as witnessed by a precocious letter to her father in March 1928, in which she calls her mother by her first name: "In the desiring of a divorce from Helen (and I shouldn't have let her give it to you, anyhow) how is it possible that this answer which 'rang clear as a bell' in your mind was the *right* one?" This letter can be found on the quite good Farksolia website dedicated to Follett, written by her "half-nephew," which provides a reliable resource on her life and work; www.farksolia.org/1928-03-07 _wilsonfollett. Opal's revival is in part due to a piece by Paul Collins in *Lapham's Quarterly*, originally Winter 2011 but itself revived in 2015.

52. Michelle Dean, "Opal Whiteley's Riddles," *New Yorker*, 23 August 2012; www.newyorker.com/books/page-turner/opal-whiteleys-riddles.

53. Weeks, *My Green Age*, 114. As a returning veteran and student at Harvard, Weeks helped oversee a Harvard *Advocate* parody of the *Atlantic* in 1920, including "a take-off of a Sedgwick discovery, which in our eyes was a fake: 'The Diary of Opal Whiteley.' . . . No one could have invented a better subject for derision; we called our version 'The Story of Isette, the Journal of a Misunderstanding Heart' by 'Isette Likeley.'"

54. Whiteley, *The Story of Opal*, 143.

55. Bogdan, *Freak Show*, 224.

56. Ralph Thompson, Books of the Times column, *New York Times*, 6 January 1941. Thompson also quotes the poem in the previous sentence.

57. Bogdan, *Freak Show*, 212.

58. The *New Yorker* still has the most reliable account of the Lowell case in a three-part article on Simon and Schuster. Colcord's correction to Hellman's article ran later in a letter to the *New Yorker*, 11 November 1939, 79–80.

59. In many ways, Lowell did embody her made-up last name, sublimating the "mill-girls" of Lowell, Massachusetts, which, Ann Douglas reminds us, was founded by Francis Lowell as "shrewdly semi-utopian." Douglas describes "mill-girls" as the Seven Sisters before their time: "Originally lured by relatively high wages and good living conditions, these girls came from farms all over New England and the central Atlantic states. Bright, ambitious, literate, they were . . . rather like the girls from the same area who would be going to Mount Holyoke and Vassar in the next generation." Douglas, *Feminization of American Culture*, 69–70.

60. As Albee's artist statement has it, found online in 2013, "Author Lincoln Colcord (1883–1947) exposed it [*Cradle of the Deep*] to be a complete fabrication (Lowell grew up in Berkeley with her mother) and a major scandal followed. My father, Parker Bishop Albee Jr., is a historian and a specialist on Colcord (who in fact grew up on a ship) and possesses Colcord's personal scrapbook. This contains Colcord's research on Lowell before the scandal as well as documentation, clippings and correspondences he collected after she was exposed. I collaborate with my father for performances using the scrapbook and projected archival footage of Lowell with her father. During a live Skype with my father, he shows Colcord's scrapbook page by page as we discuss and debate the story of Lowell and Colcord. My Lowell-based work includes photography, sculpture, performance, video and scent. Examples of the photo-based work from the project include a photograph of my father's sun-damaged first edition copy of Lowell's autobiography, his water-stained copy of a satirical book based on Lowell's, and an enlarged jpeg of Lowell in Brazil in 1966, sourced from Wikipedia."

61. F.S.N., "The Screen," *New York Times*, 9 August 1934; www.nytimes.com /movie/review?res=9C04EED9153FE53ABC4153DFBE66838F629EDE.

62. "Adventure Girl," *New York Times*, 9 August 1934.

63. Anne Colby, "Meet the Grandmother of Memoir Fabricators," *Los Angeles Times*, 14 March 2008. Katsoulis calls her "the true progenitor of the phoney genre" (*Telling Tales*, 166). Katsoulis's account of Lowell paraphrases rather aggressively, far beyond borrowing from, the three-part story on Lowell's publisher, Simon and Schuster, by Geoffrey T. Hellman in the *New Yorker*. See "How to Win Profits and Influence Literature—III," *New Yorker*, 14 October 1939.

64. Quoted in obituary, "Joan Lowell Is Dead in Brazil; Author and Adventure Seeker," *New York Times*, 15 November 1967.

65. Lowell, *Cradle of the Deep*, 232.

66. Details and useful illustrations found in *The Annotated Peter Pan*. I should say Neverland is not alone in this—across the Atlantic at the same time, the comic strip *Little Nemo in Slumberland* also filled its fantasy with cannibalistic natives, visually blackfaced—one would be kidnapped and become a regular who, when not silent, speaks gibberish.

5. Cowboys & Aliens

1. Grifters, as Maurer indicates, don't need to steal—the goal is not to trick, strictly speaking, but to gain the utter confidence of the mark, often by confirming the mark's less savory suspicions: *Everyone cheats or lies*, the mark wonders, *why shouldn't I? Especially if I can get rich in the process.* Greed feeds the con just as the hoax is fed by hubris, both of the hoaxer and his or her audience. This could be one of the hoaxer's chief defenses, but the hoaxer typically does the opposite, asking, *Why would I lie about such a thing?*, whether that thing is surviving Hiroshima or child abuse or AIDS. Just as the grifter seeks to make that company literal, in the form of "the store," misery loves company and the fake memoir seeks ours.

2. Luc Sante, introduction to David W. Maurer, *The Big Con*.

3. See Bogdan, *Freak Show*: "Most notable was the incorporation in the Barnum and Bailey Circus of 1894 of a 'Great Ethnological Congress of Savage and Barbarous Tribes,' a display of 'primitive' people rivaling that in Chicago" (50).

4. Jonathan D. Martin, "'The Grandest and Most Cosmopolitan Object Teacher': *Buffalo Bill's Wild West* and the Politics of American Identity, 1883–1899," *Radical History Review* 66 (1996): 23–123.

5. Letter signed "Grey Owl" addressed to "The Editor, Charles Scribner's Sons," dated "June 3rd 1984" and found in the Scribner's archive, Princeton University. This letter was important enough that it was typed up by Scribner's from Grey Owl's handwriting, likely for editorial eyes.

6. Lovat Dickson, *Half-Breed* (1939), recounts the details of Grey Owl's life—he starts with the story of Grey Owl on tour.

7. National Film Board of Canada website; www.nfb.ca/film/beaver_people.

8. Bogdan explains in *Freak Show*: "That word [gaffs] was reserved for fakes who pretended to be born with anomalies" or extraordinary bodies, rather than self-made fakes such as tattooed men (235). Besides, all freaks, he argues, had some element of fraud: "Words like *freak* did not have the deep stigmatizing and discrediting meaning that they have today. The great majority of exhibits were troupers, amusement world showmen, and in that world the outsider was held in contempt. . . . Life was about tricking the rube, and making money. The exotic and aggrandized presentations of the freak show were abundantly fraudulent. The most important criterion for judging the appropriateness of the word *freak* was, most likely, whether it was good for business" (271–72).

9. Barrus, *Mineshaft*, 4–5 and back cover.

10. Fiedler, *Waiting for the End*, 134.

11. Cooley, *Savages and Naturals*, 25.

12. Gilda Williams, "How Deep Is Your Goth?," in *The Gothic*, 14. Williams makes clear the difference between the Gothic and other related terms: "Generally anti-intellectual and unscientific, the Gothic can spill easily into related terminology, particularly the uncanny but also the grotesque, the abject and horror—yet 'Gothic' retains its unique, evocative power."

13. Mark Edmundson, *Nightmare on Main Street*, quoted in Williams, *The Gothic*, 30.

14. Fiedler, *Waiting for the End*, 132.

15. See Stryker, *Queer Pulp* (2001), one of many books on the highly collectible gay and lesbian paperbacks of the 1950s and 1960s.

16. Amory, *Song of the Loon*.

17. Ibid., [4].

18. Barrus, *Genocide*, 3–4.

19. Burkett and Whitley, *Stolen Valor*, 165.

20. See the original unmasking of Nasdijj in Matthew Fleischer, "Navahoax," *LA Weekly*, 23 January 2006. For more about Barrus postexposure, including the *Esquire* article and solicitation, consult Andrew Chaikivsky, "Nasdijj," *Esquire*, 29 April 2006.

21. Yipes: http://prairiemary.blogspot.com/2007/08/anywhere-anywhere-by-tim -barrus.html.

22. Thanks to Native American scholar Gina Valentino for her thoughts on blood quantum.

23. It seems rather undeniable given that one of the main characters in Alexie's story, a storyteller himself, is called Thomas Builds-the-Fire. Where Alexie's character's name is, of course, invented and inventive—it tells its own story—it is also a name first and not a mere label as Nasdijj's "Tommy Nothing Fancy" is.

24. Fleischer, "Navahoax." As the *LA Weekly* continued to reveal, even the original reviewer of *The Blood Runs Like a River Through My Dreams* from the *New York Times*, Ted Conover, had come to believe he too may have been fooled—especially after receiving an angry note from Nasdijj protesting what was in essence a positive review. This was a preview of things to come.

25. Sherman Alexie, "When the Story Stolen Is Your Own," *Time*, 29 January 2006.

26. Barrus, *The Blood Runs Like a River Through My Dreams*, 6.

27. Ibid., 2.

28. The comic, as penned by actual comic writers, nevertheless remains interesting—it makes far more explicit and visual the parallels with alien invaders who treat conquered earthlings like European settlers treated Native Americans.

29. Barrus, *The Blood Runs Like a River Through My Dreams*, 3.

30. Ibid.

31. Ibid., 15.

32. Chaikivsky, "Nasdijj".

33. Barrus, *Geronimo's Bones*, 244–45.

34. Chaikivsky, "Nasdijj."

35. Fiedler, "Race—the Dream and the Nightmare," *Commentary*, 1 October 1963; www.commentarymagazine.com/articles/race-the-dream-and-the-nightmare.

36. Ellison, "Change the Joke," in *Collected Essays*, 108.

37. The ad for the Keep America Beautiful campaign debuted on Earth Day 1971; www.adcouncil.org/Our-Work/The-Classics/Pollution-Keep-America-Beautiful -Iron-Eyes-Cody.

6. Blood Nation

1. William Faulkner, "The Art of Fiction, no. 12," *Paris Review*, 12, Spring 1956. Interviewed by Jean Stein.

2. This is not to say that Karr's *Liar's Club* and Susanna Kaysen's *Girl, Interrupted* (1993), which jump-started the memoir form—or even Cohen's *Loose Girl* for that matter—are false. Rather, as indicated by their very titles, even accurate memoirs like *Liar's Club* and Geoffrey Wolff's *The Duke of Deception* discuss family members who themselves are con artists in ways well suited for even the accurate memoir.

3. Karr, *The Art of the Memoir*, 84.

4. Hemley, *A Field Guide for Immersion Writing*, 3.

5. Steve Almond, "The Heroic Life: A Brief Inquiry into the Fake Memoir," *Rumpus* (online), 20 April 2011; http://therumpus.net/2011/04/the-heroic-lie-a-brief -inquiry-into-the-fake-memoir.

6. Nathan Rabin, interview with Stephen Colbert, Onion AV Club, 25 January 2006; www.avclub.com/article/stephen-colbert-13970. The fact that the idea of "truthiness" began with Colbert's on-air alter ego and that his interview definition is taken from a conversation that happened apparently out of character only re-inforces this point. A version of this quote also appears in Maggie Nelson's *The Art of Cruelty*.

7. The Seltzer cover was designed by Honi Werner. "The New Face of America," *Time* magazine special issue cover story, 18 November 1993. The cover announces: "Take a good look at this woman. She was created by a computer from a mix of several races. What you see is a remarkable preview of . . . The New Face of America."

8. "An American Tragedy," *Time* cover, 27 June 1994. *Newsweek* published the original, unaltered mug shot on its cover.

9. Daniel Mendelsohn, "Stolen Suffering," *New York Times*, 9 March 2008. Mendelsohn reminds us about the perils of such over- and misidentification. "Ms.

Seltzer has talked about being 'torn,' about wanting somehow to ventriloquize her subjects, to 'put a voice to people who people don't listen to.' . . . While these statements want to suggest a somehow admirable desire to 'empathize' with the oppressed subjects, this sentimental gesture both mirrors and exploits a widespread, quite pernicious cultural confusion about identity and suffering. We have so often been invited, in the past decade and a half, to 'feel the pain' of others that we rarely pause to wonder whether this is, in fact, a good thing."

10. Read more: www.oprah.com/oprahshow/Oprahs-Questions-for-James/7# ixzz24bFDQCJq.

11. Frey, *My Friend Leonard*, 3.

12. Ibid., 4.

13. Ibid., 5.

14. *Nanook* is still seen by some as a documentary, as an online essay for the definitive Criterion Collection indicates. Though the film "transcended the travelogue, as the picturesque became a real and respectful portrait," in fact, it "is full of faking and fudging in one form or another. Observers (starting with John Grierson) would come to accuse Flaherty of ignoring reality in favor of a romance that was, for all its documentary value, irrelevant. The family at the film's center was not at all. These were photogenic Inuit, cast and paid to play these roles. The characters' authentic clothes were actually a nostalgic hybrid; the Inuit had started to integrate Western wear some time previously. This integration was in fact quite general: igloos were giving way to southern building materials, many harpoons had been replaced by rifles, many kayak paddles by motors. The seal that appears to be engaging Nanook in a delightful tug of war is actually dead; Nanook is in fact being pulled around by friends at the other end of the rope, standing just off camera. During the famous walrus hunt the hunters desperately asked the filmmaker to stop shooting the camera and start shooting the rifle. For his part, [director] Flaherty pretended not to hear, and kept filming until the prey was taken in the old way." Dean W. Duncan. *"Nanook of the North"* [1922], Criterion Collection/ 11 January 1999; www.criterion.com/current/posts/42-nanook-of-the-north.

15. Seltzer, *Love and Consequences*, 120–21.

16. Ibid., 121.

17. Stepto notes that in slave narratives the other voices' "primary function, is, of course to authenticate the former slave's account; in doing so, they are at least partially responsible for the narrative's acceptance as historical evidence"; *From Behind the Veil*, 3.

18. Seltzer, *Love and Consequences*, 1–2.

19. This video, uploaded by Harry Allen's "Media Assassin" organization on 29 April 2008, can be seen on YouTube: www.youtube.com/watch?v=RVxs5t2wyzs; accessed 21 October 2016.

20. Robert Lowell, quoted in Meyers, *Robert Lowell: Interviews and Memoirs*, 291.

21. "A Million Little Lies: Exposing James Frey's Fiction Addiction," *Smoking Gun* (online), 4 January 2006.

22. This "therapeutic" idea of feeling over fact is discussed in Maggie Nelson's *Art of Cruelty* in a chapter that also considers Frey. Despite her otherwise frequent wisdom, Oprah herself has embraced such pop psychology as Rhonda Byrne's *The Secret* (2006), with its notion that you can remake reality simply with your attitude—coming dangerously close to embracing notions simultaneously about fate (everything happens for a reason) and wishful thinking ("It is very true that the way you think creates reality for yourself," Winfrey once put it to Larry King). Such paradoxical stances are echoed by Frey—even in the idea of "secrecy" as a value—in his two "memoirs," in which overcoming is fundamental to their structure. Yet memoirists like Frey never manage to mistake the *Oprah Winfrey Show*'s motto of searching for "your own truth" as a search for facts.

23. Karr, *Art of Memoir*, 84–85.

24. Ebersole, *Captured by Texts*, 6–7.

25. We can see this in the "white Indian" of Katniss, the protagonist in *The Hunger Games*. The films make use of many different racial and cinematic tropes, from Affrilachia to Cleopatra to Katniss's dyed-blond companion who is doubly marked white and, we're told, weaker; the books mark Katniss, a foil who's described as olive-skinned and dark-haired. Her image in the movie version—dark haired, tracking the land with bow and arrow, enflamed—is symbolically Native. Like the other white Indians, she is the so-called noble savage often used to characterize the Native here made flesh and familiar. But which part is noble, what savage? Where does the white begin and the Indian end?

26. Carter, *The Education of Little Tree*, 123.

27. Ebersole, *Captured by Texts*, 7.

28. Almond, "Controversial Author and Cultural Icon Found Dead," *Virginia Quarterly Review*, Writers on Writers issue, September 2006, 136.

7. Lost Boys

1. Recorded in Anna Broinowski's documentary *Forbidden Lies*.

2. See Rana Husseini, *Murder in the Name of Honor*.

3. The incorrect details of Khouri's book are recounted in many places, perhaps found most easily in *Forbidden Lies*.

4. Karr, *Art of Memoir*, 89.

5. Krakauer, *Three Cups of Deceit*, 7.

6. David Oliver Relin, introduction to Mortenson, *Three Cups of Tea*, 3–4.

7. Taken from "Update on Amina" from *Gay Girl in Damacus* blog. The post ran in April 2011; accessed June 2011. The blog now appears to have been taken down.

8. Eyder Peralta, "Man Behind Syrian Blogger Hoax: Something 'Innocent . . . Got Out Of Hand,'" NPR.org, 13 June 2011.

9. [MacMaster,] "A Thousand Sighs, and a Sigh: An Arab American Education." Unpublished ms, unpaginated [3].

10. Louys's book also inspired the Daughters of Bilitis, the first lesbian rights organization in the United States, founded in 1955.

11. Quoted in Mark Memmott, "Another Supposedly Lesbian Blogger Turns Out to Be a Man," NPR.org, 14 June 2011.

12. Description of Facebook page from CBS News online, 14 June 2011.

13. Ibid. This quote is from the audio version of the story, and is slightly altered to reflect that.

14. From the *Gay Girl in Damascus* blog, now defunct. Quoted in NPR story, Eyder Peralta, "'Gay Girl in Damascus': A Personal Friend Sifts Through What's Real," NPR.org, 9 June 2011.

15. [MacMaster,] "A Thousand Sighs, and a Sigh."

16. Iain McCalman, "The Empty Chador," *New York Times*, 4 August 2004.

17. Brooks, *Sons of Clovis*, 11.

18. See Roslyn Poignant, *Professional Savages* (2004), for the story of the Aborigine showpeople, and Bogdan, *Freak Show*, for details on the Wild Australian Children.

19. Carey, *My Life as a Fake*, 19. Though the Ern Malley story is found in many places, the fullest account is Heyward, *The Ern Malley Affair*.

20. As if to make the contrast clearer, an outline of the mainland United States is overlaid with that of Australia; other editions depict a black hand and white hand shaking, in a pastiche of civil rights iconography from thirty years before.

21. Katsoulis's *Telling Tales* (144) gives the figure as $1.7 million though I've seen figures as high as $1.8 million with none lower than $1.6.

22. Marlo Morgan, *Mutant Message Down Under* (Harper Perennial, 2004), xvii. Tenth anniversary edition. The earlier self-published edition simply has "the message" in the last sentence. Unless otherwise noted, all quotes from *Mutant Message* come from the tenth anniversary edition.

23. Lejeune, "The Diary as 'Antifiction,'" in *On Diary*, 203.

24. In striking contrast, B. Wongar's books are littered with an excess of Aborigine words—this is not necessarily a problem, yet in a book like 1993's *The Last Pack of Dingoes* with its romanticized extinctions, such words appear italicized, an excess that reinforces not just the pseudonymous author's unfamiliarity but the words' foreignness. "B. Wongar," *The Last Pack of Dingoes* (Pymble, Australia: Angus & Robertson/HarperCollins, 1993).

25. Morgan, *Mutant Message*, xix.

26. Morgan, *Mutant Message Down Under*, 45–46.

27. Kevin Young interview with Les Murray, "International Poets in Conversation"; poetryfoundation.org/features/audio/detail/76750.

28. McCalman, "The Empty Chador."

29. Morgan, *Mutant Message Down Under*, 45.

30. Ibid., 52–53.

31. Ibid., 90.

32. Ibid., 91–92.

33. *Mutant Message from Forever* advertises "10 Messages of Aboriginal Wisdom" including "1. Express Your Individual Creativity"; "3. Before Birth You Agreed to Help Others"; and "5. Entertain/Inner-tain."

34. Rolls and Johnson, *Historical Dictionary of Australian Aborigines*, 65–66.

35. Morgan, *Mutant Message*, 115.

36. Ibid., 61.

37. The monkey book is by Marina Chapman, and has all the markings of the hoax, complete with a childhood claiming not to remember her name, her parents, or her village. The book certainly centers on race and trauma such as kidnapping, prostitution, orphans, the Colombian mob, and, of course, monkeys. See NPR for an account of the controversy: www.npr.org/sections/13.7/2014/06/08/319104905/the -girl-who-was-raised-by-monkeys.

38. Morgan, *Mutant Message Down Under*, 63.

39. Ibid., xviii.

40. Healy, *Forgetting Aborigines*, 200.

41. Rose, *Dingo Makes Us Human*, 2.

42. Morgan, *Mutant Message Down Under*, 147.

43. Ibid., 162.

44. Showalter, *Hystories*, 191. See especially the chapter titled "Alien Abduction."

45. "Most abductees are female; most aliens are male. Of the seventy-six cases studied by Mack, forty-seven were women, and in some ways their narratives re- semble those of childhood sexual abuse or satanic ritual abuse. Alien perpetrators, however, do not belong to this world. Moreover, they are benignly motivated; ab- ductees often see themselves as the chosen heralds of a superior intergalactic race." Showalter, *Hystories*, 195.

46. Ibid., 196.

47. Morgan, *Mutant Message Down Under*, 73.

48. The full text of *We of the Never Never* is available on Project Gutenberg (www.gutenberg.org/etext/4699). Here's the fuller preface: "Distinct in the fore- ground stand:

"The Maluka, The Little Missus, The Sanguine Scot, The Head Stockman, The Dandy, The Quiet Stockman, The Fizzer, Mine Host, The Wag, Some of our Guests, A few black 'boys' and lubras, A dog or two, Tam-o'-Shanter, Happy Dick, Sam Lee, and last, but by no means least, Cheon—the ever-mirthful, ever-helpful, irrepressible Cheon, who was crudely recorded on the station books as cook and gardener.

"The background is filled in with an ever-moving company—a strange medley of Whites, Blacks, and Chinese; of travellers, overlanders, and billabongers, who passed in and out of our lives, leaving behind them sometimes bright memories, sometimes sad, and sometimes little memory at all.

"And All of Us, and many of this company, shared each other's lives for one bright, sunny year, away Behind the Back of Beyond, in the Land of the Never-Never; in that elusive land with an elusive name—a land of dangers and hardships and privations yet loved as few lands are loved—a land that bewitches her people with strange spells and mysteries, until they call sweet bitter, and bitter sweet. Called the Never-Never, the Maluka loved to say, because they, who have lived in it and loved it Never-Never voluntarily leave it. Sadly enough, there are too many who Never-Never do leave it. Others—the unfitted—will tell you that it is so called because they who succeed in getting out of it swear they will Never-Never return to it. But we who have lived in it, and loved it, and left it, know that our hearts can Never-Never rest away from it."

The book has sold over a million copies.

49. Dumbartung Aboriginal Corporation, "Mutant Message Down Under Campaign," www.dumbartungaboriginalcorporation.org/first_report_on_mutant _message.html.

50. This apology and its aftermath are recounted in numerous sources, including the *Seattle Times*; see the following note.

51. Deloris Tarzan Ament, "Fact or Fiction? Whichever, Her 'Message' Strikes a Chord," *Seattle Times*, 23 September 1994. Morgan's local paper was early to question the story; see Elaine Adams, "A Tale Told Down Under: Truth or Fiction? Ooota, Magic Oil and a Chosen Mutant: Writer's Story Is Fraught with Inaccuracies, Experts Say," *Kansas City Star*, 28 June 1992, A1, A12, A13.

52. There are other significant fictions now left out: the author bio shrank considerably to simply say Morgan "is retired and lives in Missouri," whereas the original states, "Marlo Morgan regards herself as an average American female. She was married, raised a family, divorced, and worked full time while earning her doctorate degrees. The most valuable education she has received, did not come from the universities and clinics but instead took place during a four month walkabout, barefoot, in the blazing desert of Australia." See Marlo Morgan, *Mutant Message Down Under*, first edition [n.d.]. Morgan was later proved not to have *any* advanced degrees, much less several. Shaky or shaded facts like this caused a small New Age publisher to drop the book after optioning it for reprint before HarperCollins did.

8. The Time Machine

1. I. F. Clarke, "The Tale of the Future: Its Origins and Development," in *The Tale of the Future*, 3.

2. *What We Know about Waino and Plutano, the Wild Men of Borneo; with Poems Dedicated to Them* (New York: Damons & Prets, Printers, ca. 1870s). Different edi-

tions with the same name bear different text (and illustrations), though often the same frontispiece, which gives the duo's approximate ages.

3. Walker's hard-to-find books often start with a search for gold or for treasure, but usually not before a preface or poetic "proem" that makes his fantasy's intertwining of empire and sexual conquest explicit: "From her stone-wrought, stone-quarried cities she [Australia] calls, from her barren interiors made prolific by underground water, where even her loneliest places whisper 'Abide here and I will enchant and teach you how to use me,' she returns no barren answer, often a golden or silver one." From William Sylvester Walker, preface, *The Silver Queen*, 7. Almost every Walker book bears a prose preface (*Silver Queen*) or a poem as "prologue" (*Wombat*) or "Introductory" (*At Possum Creek*), signed "Coo-ee" or "The Author"; such apparatus sits quite outside the story. Several volumes can be viewed digitally at the Colonial Australian Popular Fiction Archive: www.apfa.esrc.unimelb.edu.au/biogs/E000015b.htm.

4. Tilley, *White Vanishing*. "The cultural history of Australia has long been gloomily fascinated with the figure of the lost child," wrote one critic in the 1950s; Tilley has noted in *White Vanishing* the ways this also applies to the lost adult (203).

5. Walker, *Silver Queen*, 21 and 31. *Silver Queen* finds in fantasy what his book's prefaces—a kind of anti-disclaimer—explore in Coo-ee's poetry. Take this, from the prologue to Walker's *Native Born*:

> Hark, and listen! There 'tis echoed, cries from other lands!
> Where brave swarthy races burn with loyal pride.
> Why then hesitate, Great Britain?—unto you they stretch their hands;
> And by you they stood before—and for you they died!
>
> 'Tis the Greater Britain rising! 'Tis the spirit of the age!
> And from town and country we are all aware
> That this clarion call is ringing; and thy children raise the gauge.
> We are *one*—Our mother wants us—We are there.

Whenever he speaks of "Australia's first-born" or "The Spirit in the Australian 'Native' Rose" Walker's own quotation marks indicate he means something non-Indigenous and even mutated. Also consider a blog from *Wormwood* magazine that describes Walker's last book, a serial never gathered in book form: "His last work appears to have been a lost race novel that was published in *The Queenslander* in 1924–25 with the unlikely title of *Koi; or, The Thing Without any Bones*. It traces the efforts of an Australian adventurer and bushman, Mark Payton, and his love interest, the rich, beautiful and ambitious Brenda Sardrou, to foil the machinations of the evil German Jew named Solomons, an international spy, self-made millionaire and dabbler in the occult. Solomons is the direct descendant of Ben Suleiman, who two thousand years earlier led an expedition out of Mesopotamia to northern Australia where he established a new civilisation based on Egyptian magical beliefs. Koi is the

Soul Shadow, a disembodied spirit that attaches itself to a living person and only de-parts during sleep, sickness and death to wander in other places—aboriginal descen-dants of the ancient race are accompanied and aided by their Koi. Solomons plans to return to northern Australia and set himself up as ruler of the revived kingdom—a European invasion of the Commonwealth, no less! Heady stuff: a spectacularly over-the-top fantasy." See James Doig, "A 'Lost' Lost Race Serial": http://wormwoodiana .blogspot.com/2009/09/lost-lost-race-serial.html.

6. Walker, *From the Land of the Wombat*, [ii]. This and several other Walker titles may be viewed through the National Library of Australia (NLA) "Trove" website: http://trove.nla.gov.au/book.

7. Gould, *Mismeasure of Man*, 43.

8. Ibid., 42.

9. This story of Agassiz and racist science may be found in many places, in-cluding classic studies such as William Stanton's *The Leopard's Spots*, or more re-cently in Louis Menand's *The Metaphysical Club*.

10. Menand, *Metaphysical Club*, 99. Gould tells of how, in keeping with racial-ist theories of degeneration and recapitulation, "Several school boards prescribed [Longfellow's] the *Song of Hiawatha* in early grades, reasoning that children, pass-ing through the savage stage of their ancestral past, would identify with it." Gould, *Mismeasure of Man*, 143.

11. Emerson, "Race," in *English Traits*, 30. The introduction to the 1966 reprint of this volume by Howard Mumford Jones is telling: "The chapter on race is puz-zling. Emerson's terminology is confused and inconsistent. Sometimes by 'race' he means mankind in general, sometimes one or more of the three or five or eleven 'fixed' races his authorities [including Blumenbach and Humboldt] told him about, sometimes a particular racial strain (Caucasian, Celt, Saxon), sometimes an almal-gam of various racial stocks that is tagged by the name of one among them. . . . Nor, though he uses all the terms, does he discriminate carefully among Teutons, Germans, Scandinavians, Norseman, Northmen, Danes, Saxons, and Normans" (xix). Such confusion is actually part of the fiction—or hoax—of race and white-ness itself.

12. Emerson on the Scottish and Irish found in "Race," in *English Traits*, 34; on the Normans and Saxons, see "Ability," in *English Traits*, 48.

13. "Scandinavian" quote found in Emerson, 42; emphasis added. Emerson on "the blonde race," ibid. The term *Aryan* as an "imagined, superior race," Nell Irvin Painter reminds us, was first turned from linguistic to racial by Gobineau in his "pes-simistic" *Essai sur l'inégalité des races humains* (1853–55)—just a year before Emerson's *English Traits*—but didn't gain traction until it was reprinted in the early twenti-eth century. Painter first directed me to Emerson and his status as what she terms "the philosopher king of American white race theory." See Painter, *History of White People*, 195–97. On "ruling passion," see Emerson, "Truth," in *English Traits*, 70.

14. Writing in 1966, Mumford Jones tries reconciling Emerson's contradictory race theories in which he "unconsciously transferred his bewilderment to his manuscript": "These infelicities should not, however, obscure his central point, which is that we are dealing not with the Mediterranean world but with the world of the North, a world that contains an island called Britain anchored like a ship off the coast of Europe. On this island various racial strains were amalgamated by force of environment, circumstance, and time to produce a people called the English, whose survival value has been and is extraordinarily high." *English Traits*, xx.

15. Taken from Agassiz's major statement on the separate races, including his essay "The Diversity of Origin of Human Races" (1850) as quoted in Gould, *Mismeasure of Man*, 46, and discussed in Stanton, *Leopard's Spots*, 104–10.

16. See Rogers, *Delia's Tears*, 76–77.

17. See Alan Trachtenberg for images and a discussion of the Agassiz photographs, shot by J. T. Zealy. Trachtenberg, *Reading American Photographs*, 52–60.

18. Rogers, *Delia's Tears*, 76–77.

19. Agassiz's reaction is now quoted in many places, beginning with Stephen Jay Gould, who was the first to translate it fully: "The standard *Life and Letters*, compiled by Agassiz's wife, omits [the last sentence] in presenting an expurgated version of this famous letter. Other historians have paraphrased them or passed them by. I recovered this passage from the original manuscript in Harvard's Houghton Library and have translated it, verbatim, for the first time so far as I know." Agassiz, letter to his mother, 2 December 1846, trans. Stephen Jay Gould, more fully excerpted in Gould, *Mismeasure of Man*, 44–45.

20. Stanton, *Leopard's Spots*, 28. Stanton is a terrific start to the study of race science, and someone I first read on race and science in a course with Professor Nathan Huggins. Other studies of the history of race include Gould's *Mismeasure of Man* and Menand, *Metaphysical Club*, both of whom recount the "American Golgotha" nickname.

21. Menand, *Metaphysical Club*, 102.

22. Gould, *Mismeasure of Man*, 28–29.

23. Ibid., 55–56.

24. Menand, *Metaphysical Club*, 107.

25. Stanton, *Leopard's Spots*, 100; and Menand, *Metaphysical Club*, 109.

26. Menand, *Metaphysical Club*, 141.

27. Steers, *Hoax*, 159. The hoax was no doubt committed by its "discoverer," Charles Dawson. See Miles Russell, *Piltdown Man: The Secret Life of Charles Dawson and the World's Greatest Archaeological Hoax* (2003).

28. Menand, *Metaphysical Club*, 138.

29. For more on this topic, consult Chamberlin and Gilman, eds., *Degeneration*. See the conclusion, 291, and Nancy Stepan, "Biology and Degeneration: Races and Proper Places," in Chamberlin and Gilman, *Degeneration*.

30. For more on this topic, consult Chamberlin and Gilman, eds., *Degeneration*, 1985. See the conclusion, 291, and Nancy Stepan, "Biology and Degeneration: Races and Proper Places," 97–120.

31. For more on degenerate art, consult Barron, ed., "*Degenerate Art*" and the sequel of sorts, Peters, ed., *Degenerate Art*, especially the chapter on degeneration by Peters.

32. [Croly and Wakeman], *Miscegenation*, 1.

33. Ibid., 64. See also Barnum, *The Humbugs of the World*.

34. Personal thanks to China Miéville for the Borges quote; it can be found referenced in Margaret Atwood's introduction to *The Island of Dr. Moreau* in her book *In Other Worlds* (150). Much of the information of Devo and their beginnings I first encountered in the bookseller Division Leap's noted Cleveland catalog in their description of *Jocko-Homo Heavenbound*, by B.H. Shadduck (1925). Further information can be found in the Criterion Collection extras of *Island of Lost Souls*, which features a short documentary with interviews with Devo members Mothersbaugh and Gerald Casale as well as a glimpse of their short 1976 film about De-evolution.

35. NASA website, "All About Mars"; http://mars.nasa.gov/allaboutmars /mystique/history/1800.

36. Wells, *War of the Worlds*, chapter 1; 279 in the Barnes & Noble Classics Series edition, *The War of the Worlds and Other Novels* (2012).

37. Koch, *The Panic Broadcast*, 67.

38. Quoted in Schwartz, *Broadcast Hysteria*, 76.

39. Koch, *The Panic Broadcast*, 28.

40. Ibid. *The Panic Broadcast* reprints articles from many of the newspapers that appeared the day after the hoax.

41. Gould, *Mismeasure of Man*, 64, quoting from Franklin's *Observations concerning the Increase of Mankind* (1751).

42. See J. Tithonious Penand: www.thehumanmarvels.com/willie-and-george -muse-the-men-from-mars. Beth Macy's 2016 book on the twins, *Truevine*, explores their lives further. Thanks to her for the image of the pair.

43. Hemley, *Invented Eden*, 25–26.

44. Nance, *Gentle Tasaday*, ix–x.

45. Hemley, *Invented Eden*, 187.

46. Ibid., 120.

47. Gould, *Mismeasure of Man*, 53.

9. The Heart Is Deceitful

1. Bogdan, *Freak Show*, 187. See also Garland Thomson, *Extraordinary Bodies*, on the term "Nig Shows."

2. Louise Linton, *In Congo's Shadow: One Girl's Perilous Journey to the Heart*

of Africa (2016). An excerpt appeared in the *Telegraph* (UK), which sparked international outcry. In Britain, the book was pulled and an apology issued after the outcry, which trended on Twitter under #LintonLies. www.latimes.com/books/la -et-jc-louise-linton-memoir-20160706-snap-htmlstory.html. www.dailymail.co.uk /news/article-3675169/Actress-accused-inventing-parts-memoir-nightmare-gap -year-Zambia-one-local-says-thing-missing-Tarzan-Mowgli.html.

3. JT LeRoy [written by Laura Albert], "Flower Hunting in the Congo," in Hicklin, *The Revolution Will Be Accessorized*, 190.

4. "LeRoy" expressed the poster-boy idea as a fear, telling *Vanity Fair*, "I quit writing for two years because I didn't want to be the poster boy for the dysfunctional-memoir bullshit." See "Strange Innocence," interview with Tom Waits, *Vanity Fair*, July 2001; www.maryellenmark.com/text/magazines/vanity%20fair/925E -000-021.html.

5. Mary Ellen Mark, preface, *Indian Circus*; www.maryellenmark.com/text /books/indian_circus/text001_icircus.html.

6. See Bogdan, *Freak Show*, 195–99, and Holtman, *Freak Show Man*, 188, for information on Charlie Lucas and the show.

7. See Arbus, *Hubert's Museum Work*. The Jungle Creep (also named "Hezekiah Trambles") appears in Arbus's photoessay "The Vertical Journey: Six Movements of a Moment within the Heart of the City," *Esquire*, July 1960. See *Diane Arbus Magazine Work*, 8, which also includes the unpublished "Hubert's Obituary; or, This Was Where We Came In" (1966), 80–81.

8. *Diane Arbus Magazine Work*. The phrase "privileged exile" is from Arbus, "The Full Circle," *Harper's Bazaar*, November 1961. Found in *Diane Arbus Magazine Work*, 16.

9. *Diane Arbus Magazine Work*, 81.

10. John Nova Lomax, "Coal Miner Mother of a Mess," *Houston Press*, 25 August 2005. Lomax's article appeared before LeRoy's full unmasking: www.houstonpress .com/music/coal-miner-mother-of-a-mess-6548530.

11. Stephen Beachy, "Who Is the Real JT LeRoy? The True Identity of a Great Litarary Hustler," *New York*, 10 October 2005. Beachy published the article with *New York* after a Los Angeles outlet that commissioned it wouldn't run it.

12. "JT LeRoy," "Uncle Walt, Parlez-Vous Français?," *New York Times*, 25 September 2005.

13. This remarkable number was taken at the time of writing from the official Livestrong website, whose timeline indicated that in 2005 alone "the Foundation sells more than 55 million wristbands." Accessed 4 September 2014, www.livestrong .org/who-we-are/our-history/milestones.

14. Lance Armstrong, *Every Second Counts*, 156; quoted in United States Anti-Doping Agency, *Report on Proceedings under the World Anti-Doping Code and the USADA Protocol* (2012), 55.

15. Ibid.

16. Ibid.

17. Warren St. John, "The Unmasking of JT LeRoy: In Public, He's a She," *New York Times*, 9 January 2006; www.nytimes.com/2006/01/09/books/09book .html?_r=0. St. John is characterizing Beachy's take.

18. Albert, quoted in Nathaniel Rich, "Being JT LeRoy," Encounter interview with Albert, *Paris Review* 128 (Fall 2006): 156–57. Thistle doesn't succeed with what Beachy writes is "a new Speedie, Jennifer Hall, an actress who starred on HBO's *Unscripted*," itself a show about actors playing versions of themselves trying to make it as actors.

19. Jack Boulware, "She Is JT LeRoy," Salon, 8 March 2006; www.salon.com /2006/03/08/albert_3.

20. Albert, "Being JT LeRoy," 153.

21. Ibid.

22. Quoted in Nancy Rommelmann, "The Lies and Follies of Laura Albert, a.k.a. JT LeRoy," *LA Weekly*, 20 February 2008; www.laweekly.com/arts/the-lies -and-follies-of-laura-albert-aka-jt-leroy-2152091. Thanks to her for directing me to details of the case.

23. Quoted in Warren St. John, "Figure in JT Leroy [*sic*] Case Says Partner Is Culprit," *New York Times*, 7 February 2006. LeRoy is frequently reported as not having the "R" capitalized, but the books all spell it "LeRoy."

24. Beachy, "Who Is the Real JT LeRoy?" Though hard to track down, *Cyborgasm 2: Edge of the Bed* (Passion Press, 1999) can be sampled here: www.cduniverse.com /search/xx/music/pid/1231434/a/edge+of+the+bed+-+cyborgasm+2.htm. The short preview gives a sense of the scenario.

25. Albert, quoted in Rich, "Being JT LeRoy," 158. The accounts of who this image is taken from vary; Albert claims, "My publisher paid to use a photograph of a teenage boy who looked a lot like JT and got permission to run it as the author photo" (160).

26. St. John, "Unmasking of JT LeRoy," clarifying article: http://query.nytimes .com/gst/fullpage.html?res=9B06E1DC133EF936A1575AC0A9639C8B63&page wanted=4.

27. Tad Friend, "Virtual Love," *New Yorker*, 16 November 2001.

28. Acocella, *Creating Hysteria*, 29, 31.

29. Hustvedt, *Medical Muses*, 15.

30. Didi-Huberman, *Invention of Hysteria*, 19.

31. Ibid., 115. "Charcot's 'genius' was . . . not simply to arrive at a description of all this, but to calibrate it into a general type that can be called 'the great hysterical attack,' examples of which can be further qualified as 'complete and regular'" (ibid.).

32. André Breton's phrase proves all the more important as Breton had trained as a physician under an apprentice to Charcot. Quoted in Hustvedt, *Medical Muses*,

210. Originally in Louis Aragon and André Breton, *La Revolution Surréaliste*, no. 11 (March 1928).

33. There are many histories of hysteria, including those written by Acocella, Hustvedt, Showalter, and Didi-Huberman. These "attitudes" are most easily found in Hustvedt's *Medical Muses*, where they appear in photographs reprinted from Désiré Bourneville and P.-Marie-Léon Regnard, *Iconographie photographique de la Salpêtrière* (1878). The "hysterical wink" is pictured in Didi-Huberman, *Inventions of Hysteria*, 131, taken from the *Nouvelle Iconographie* (1889).

34. Showalter, *Hystories*, 49.

35. See Hustvedt, *Medical Muses*.

36. Acocella, *Creating Hysteria*, 3.

37. Albert, quoted in Rich, "Being JT LeRoy," 152.

38. Ibid., 154. Later, when she hears Madonna is reading *Sarah*, Albert says, "My God, Madonna's in my world. It was an incredible feeling. . . . It was like running over a joyful spot that gave me energy. She's in my world, she's in my world, she's in my world." Ibid., 165.

39. "Sybil: A Brilliant Hysteric?" *New York Times*. A RetroReport video on the case, with useful interviews and summaries with some of the participants and critics; contains some of the therapy session; www.nytimes.com/video/us/100000003250377 /sybil-a-brilliant-hysteric.html.

40. Showalter, *Hystories*, 164.

41. Ofshe and Watters, *Making Monsters*, 69.

42. See Beck, *We Believe the Children*, for an in-depth discussion of the case and the phenomenon. Consult PBS for a brief overview and outcomes of several cases, as well as confirmation of the trial's length and expense; www.pbs.org/wgbh /pages/frontline/shows/fuster/lessons/outcomes.html.

43. According to Ofshe and Watters, "Such stories of murder and rape have not gone unheeded by law enforcement officials. Police departments across the country have aggressively investigated stories of murderous satanic cults. They have questioned thousands of people, excavated for bones, and hunted high and low for ritual sites. Nothing has turned up that would indicate the existence of a widespread cult network. Even most promoters of recovered memory therapy admit that no compelling evidence of such cults has been found. Special Agent Ken Lanning of the FBI has looked into more than three hundred such cases and found no evidence that rings of child-murdering satanic cults exist. 'Until hard eveidence is obtained and corroborated, the public should not be frightened into believeing that babies are being bred and eaten, that 50,000 missing children are being murdered in human sacrices, or that Satanists are taking over America's day care centers or institutions,' Lanning wrote in his *Investigator's Guide to Allegations of Ritual Child Abuse*" (*Making Monsters*, 180).

44. Satanic ritual abuse (SRA) too caused a kind of nationwide paranoia, being

cited in court along with "expert testimony" much like in many a forgery case—or more hauntingly, the way the devil and "spectral evidence" were cited in the Salem witch trials. Ours is all a New Jerusalem, Salem its namesake and its progenitor, in which Satan is shorthand for policing outsiders, femininity, the unfamiliar. The lives such testimony would ruin would include the mid-1990s case of the Arkansas youths known as the West Memphis Three, chronicled in three installments of HBO documentaries called *Paradise Lost: The Child Murders and Robin Hood Ridge*. Almost more stunning than the literary and folklore references in the titles, places, and alleged causes in the film's very title—from Milton to Robin Hood—are the ways the film helped free the accused after eighteen years of wrongful conviction and even death row. It would seem they were targeted as much for being "goths" or outsiders as for any evidence. Though in some ways an expression of difference, of a dark sublime, the gothic here is also a way of policing that difference.

The hoax acts much the same way, at least in LeRoy's case. The ruination of lives from the overdiagnosis and disturbing practices of MPD is enough to indict it. It is now more commonly called dissociative disorder, and the kinds of treatment techniques prolific in the 1980s and 1990s—when LeRoy was taking shape, it should be noted—are discouraged. But MPD, SRA, and alien abduction all appear to be another fin de siècle manifestation of the gothic, a way of representing ruination itself.

45. Showalter, *Hystories*, 203.
46. "Sybil: A Brilliant Hysteric?," beginning at minute 5:53.
47. Showalter, *Hystories*, 167.
48. Dr. David Spiegel, in "Sybil: A Brilliant Hysteric?"
49. Showalter, *Hystories*, 19.
50. Ibid., 145.

10. Eve Black

1. The real "Eve" passed away during the writing of this book. As reported in the *New York Times* on 5 August 2016: "The patient whose story the book and movie purported to tell, Chris Costner Sizemore, actually had a much grimmer time of it. Her new marriage turned out to be not an ending at all; she endured a fragmented identity until the mid-1970s, seeing several psychiatrists after Thigpen and Cleckley, until, in the care of a Virginia doctor, Tony Tsitos, her personalities—not three but more than 20, it turned out—were unified." www.nytimes.com/2016/08/06/us/chris-costner-sizemore-the-real-patient-behind-the-three-faces-of-eve-dies-at-89.html?smprod=nytcore-ipad&smid=nytcore-ipad-share. The "Sixty Minute Man" detail appears in Thigpen and Cleckley, *Three Faces of Eve*, 63.

2. Thigpen and Cleckley, *Three Faces of Eve*, 1. Chris Costner Sizemore, "Eve" herself, would go on to publish many volumes of Eve writing as Evelyn Lancaster,

from *Strangers in My Body: The Final Face of Eve* (1961) to *I'm Eve* (1977) to *A Mind of My Own* (1989), an account, she says, "at last . . . about my wellness" but capitalizing on the then-raging MPD phenomenon.

3. Acocella, *Creating Hysteria*, 33.

4. JT LeRoy [Laura Albert], *Sarah*, 1. The book uses British-style 'inverted commas' instead of double quotation marks for dialogue.

5. John Nova Lomax, "Coal Miner Mother of a Mess," www.houstonpress .com/music/coal-miner-mother-of-a-mess-6548530.

6. Marc Smirnoff, "Anatomy of a Hoaxing," *Oxford American*, Winter 2006, 4–11. This lengthy editor's note is defensive in all the worst ways.

7. Bakhtin, *Rabelais and His World*, 317. Emphasis added.

8. O'Connor, "The Grotesque in Southern Fiction," in *Mystery and Manners*, 44.

9. Bakhtin, *Rabelais and His World*, 308. It matters here whether the grotesque is merely "negative" and satirical, commenting on the world, or whether it creates a world without hierarchy. For what Rabelaisian grotesque seeks is a world without highest orders at all, but a thrilling connectivity that developed in, and helped develop, the Renaissance, whose cultural body was one constantly rejuvenating. "In the grotesque concept of the body a new, concrete, and realistic historic awareness was born and took form: not abstract thought about the future but the living sense that each man belongs to the immortal people who create history" (ibid., 167).

10. See the Marjorie Strum film, *The Cult of JT LeRoy* for the powerful reactions by trans teens and twenty-somethings.

11. Ayelet Waldman, "I Was Conned by JT LeRoy," 11 January 2006; www .salon.com/2006/01/11/jt_leroy. Waldman writes, "I went along with it happily, once even listening for an hour or so as he played taped portions of his sessions with his therapist, Dr. Terrence Owens. I never really understood why JT wanted me to hear these unbelievably boring sessions. I assumed back then that it was because we had talked a lot about mental illness and he wanted me to understand the depth of his experience. In retrospect, knowing that JT does not exist, I think those tapes are a marvel. Someone actually went to the trouble of producing elaborate two-person recordings. And for what? What was the point? They were clearly meant to provide evidence of authenticity, and perhaps playing them for me was a dress rehearsal for a bigger, more important audience." Note Owens appears to be real (and appears in Strum's *The Cult of JT LeRoy*).

12. Albert, quoted in Rich, "Being JT LeRoy," 146–47.

13. Rommelmann, "The Lies and Follies of Laura Albert, a.k.a. JT LeRoy."

14. Ibid.

15. Stoker, *Famous Impostors*, 12.

16. Albert, quoted in Rich, "Being JT LeRoy," 145.

17. Stoker's *Famous Impostors*, like many other studies, has a whole section devoted to women pretending to be men—never do they mention the opposite. You'll

note I don't equate such gender crossings with the hoax, and don't include them here just as I don't discuss racial passing: these are more often than not less impersonations than self-defense. The topic is one worthy of further study.

18. Albert, quoted in Rich, "Being JT LeRoy," 148.

19. Leslie Fiedler, introduction to Cott, ed., *Beyond the Looking Glass*, xiv.

20. LeRoy, *Sarah*, 112–13.

21. Fiedler, introduction, xv.

22. Even *Peter Pan*, with its boy who won't grow up and lost boys who have fallen out of their prams, has long held an attraction for grown-ups, largely because it was rather grown already—George Bernard Shaw called *Peter Pan* "really a play for grown-up people." See A. S. Byatt, introduction to Lang, *The Pink Fairy Book*, ix.

23. Manohla Dargis, "The Harrowing Tales of the Deceitfulness of Hearts from a Highly Deceitful Author," *New York Times*, 10 March 2006; emphasis added.

24. Anthony Lane, "Telling Tales," *New Yorker*, 13 March 2006; emphasis added. The review continues: "Her cover—the one indication of brilliance in the entire farcical business—has been blown for good, and if that stops a few weepy nineteen-year-olds from filling their blogs, or, worse still, their début novels, with first-person reports of the sun shadows that ripped into their flesh, so much the better. As for Asia Argento, she gets off lightly, for the simple reason that there is no such thing as a cinematic hoax."

25. Quoted in Alan Feuer, "At Trial, Writer Recalls an Alter Ego That Took Over," *New York Times*, 21 June 2007.

26. Quoted in ibid.

27. Author's collection. Other of LeRoy's signatures look quite different from this one. The use of "left-handed" or "childlike" writing is a device actually familiar from the "recovered memory" and MPD movements. See Ofshe and Watters.

28. Far more interesting, courageous, and true is the real life and the fantasy work of the writer Samuel Steward. He too adopted many personas, but they were not impersonations, as he would become all of the things he pretended to be: he pretended to be a hustler, but he really did pick men up and wrote stories of them as Phil Andros; he ended up, as Phil Sparrow, actually being a tattoo artist for the Hell's Angels, a dangerous profession at best but certainly edgy for someone who was never really closeted, who in fact refused to be. He was, as the title of Justin Spring's fascinating biography about him has it, a *Secret Historian*, providing an invaluable record of gay life over his lifetime—keeping extensive, detailed records and even DNA of his sexual encounters from everyone from an aging Rudolph Valentino to Thornton Wilder, author of *Our Town*, with whom he had a lengthy relationship. His life and art provide a remarkable documentation of gay life before and after Dr. Kinsey (whom he worked with). Although he died in humble circumstances, he certainly was not abject.

29. This footage is viewable on several sites, including YouTube, and is currently downloadable on the Moth's site: http://themoth.org/posts/stories/my-avatar-and-me. Laura Albert has her own site now: lauraalbert.org.

30. See Colin Moynihan, "Asia Argento and Others Are Angry about Being in JT LeRoy Documentary," *New York Times*, 11 September 2016; www.nytimes.com/2016/09/12/movies/asia-argento-and-others-are-angry-about-being-in-jt-leroy-documentary.html?_r=0.

31. Ferrante, "Without Keeping a Safe Distance," in *Frantumaglia*. Thanks to Lili Loofbourow, who first pointed me to Ferrante's interview via a post on Twitter.

32. Lejeune, *On Autobiography*, 30.

11. Butterfly Books

1. Wilson, *Modern Book Collecting*, 191. Wilson's chapter on fakes mentions Prokosch, one of the few studies to do so.

2. See Robinson, ed., *The Original Frankenstein*. The editor here has even changed the authorship to "(with Percy Shelley)."

3. Shelley, *Frankenstein*, 95.

4. Sady Doyle, @sadydoyle Twitter feed, 25 November 2015. A great example of how Twitter isn't just for memes. Storifyied as "Sady Doyle on Mary Shelley"; https://storify.com/kellyoyo/sady-doyle-on-mary-shelly.

5. Carey, *My Life as a Fake*, [ii].

6. "U.S. representatives of the Frankenstein story make visible, and further transform, the complex representations of New World slavery already refracted in the novel." Young, *Black Frankenstein*, 8.

7. This publication includes Eliot's "Cape Ann" and "Usk."

8. The Danowski Poetry Library at Emory University's Rose Library holds this particular copy.

9. Harold Strauss, "A Strange and Haunting Tale Set in Central Asia: Frederic Prokosch, in *The Seven Who Fled*, Writes a Memorable Novel of Spiritual Adventure," *New York Times Book Review*, 29 August 1937, 3.

10. See Freind, *Scubadivers and Chrysanthemums*, for the best summary of the Yasusada case, and its issues, where the facts and both sets of issues are recounted.

11. [Kent Johnson,] "Appendices: A Few Words on Araki Yasusada and Tosa Motokiyu," *Doubled Flowering*, 125.

12. Ibid., 10.

13. Ibid., 48–49.

14. Quoted by Bill Freind, ed., in *Scubadivers*, 8. Originally in Chang et al., "Displacements," *Boston Review* 22.3–4 (1997), 34. bostonreview.net/archives/BR22.3/Chang.html.

15. Chang et al., "Displacements." Perloff in her cogent defense of the poems argues that "Kent Johnson has thus found a perfect recipe for a new Orientalism,

conceived in the best American tradition of Emerson's doctrine of 'natural' hi-eroglyphic language, Pound's Cathay, and most recently, Kenneth Rexroth's *Love Poems of Marichiko*." Rexroth's poems were once pitched as translations from a Japanese woman, but I don't think that makes them a hoax—the gesture is by now a familiar one that doesn't so much define the hoax as it is one the hoax borrows from.

16. David Wojahn, *Strange Good Fortune*, 161.

17. Ibid., 130.

18. Kent Johnson and Javier Alvarez, eds. *Also, with My Throat* . . . , 3.

19. Eliot Weinberger, "Can I Get a Witness?," *Scubadivers*, 21. Weinberger's was one of the first to call the poems fake in print, even before the APR supplement. Perloff makes a similar point in her essay on the hoax.

20. In his review of *Doubled Flowering*, Forrest Gander's complex argument does anticipate the charge of cliché japonisme: thinking of the poems, he writes, "I do not think that they add up to a kind of joke, as some critics have argued, by seducing North American readers with their Orientalist exoticism, by fooling us into liking them for all the wrong reasons, or by taking advantage of our desire for Western clichés of Japanese and Chinese writing. Clearly, though, the poems do make jokes, setting up puns, proposing anachronisms, making purposeful factual and typographical mistakes and juxtaposing versions of translations from classical Japanese poetry, novels, Hiroshima literature and Zen manuals with formal concerns—dissonance, collage, ellipsis, fragmentation—associated with literary modernism. But the book does not merely 'play into the residual guilt of contemporary American readers' or serve mainly to poke fun at the American market for 'authentic' witness poetry by parodying it, as Marjorie Perloff has suggested. Sentimental references to kimono sleeves soaked with tears, to moon and hair and perfume may seem parodic, but they occur often enough in the poems of the imperial anthologies and, to a lesser degree, in the Manyoshu, and Yasusada always complicates such images. John Solt, a professor of Japanese culture at Amherst College argues that Yasusada 'plays into the American idea of what is interesting about Japanese culture . . . and gets it all wrong, adding Western humor and irony.' But I think he misses the point, too." See Forrest Gander, *Nation*, 13 July 1998. Reprinted in *Jacket* online magazine; jacketmagazine.com/04/ganderyasu.html.

21. Alexie, ed., *Best American Poetry 2015*, 167.

22. http://jezebel.com/if-youre-a-white-man-who-cant-get-published-under -your-1729280567.

23. One positive result of the hoax was the number of people writing about #ActualAsianAmerican writers. Consult Zhang on Buzzfeed (www.buzzfeed.com /jennybagel/they-pretend-to-be-us-while-pretending-we-dont-exist#.tr13m VbGOW) and the Asian American Writers' Workshop (http://aaww.org/after-yi -fen-chou). As *Jezebel* points out, the ratio is still 9 to 1 whites to people of color

published across literary magazines. This is true despite the inarguable renaissance in black poets and poets of color. Unfortunately, editorial numbers for people of color are far worse: 1 to 9 would appear to be the actual number, not the ratio.

24. Quoted in Murray et al., *Forging a Collection*, 62.

25. Wilson, *Modern Book Collecting*, 196. Wilson offers one of the few discussions of Prokosch's forgeries.

26. [Frederic Prokosch as] "Gertrude Stein," *Lily* (Paris, 1969). Thanks to Nancy Kuhl and the Beinecke Rare Book and Manuscript Library at Yale University, who provided images of the library's copy of this rare publication.

27. Greenfield, *Dreamer's Journey*, 338. Poe, *Narrative of Arthur Gordon Pym*, chapter 17.

28. Harold Strauss, "*The Skies of Europe* Is a Novel of the Years Before Chaos," *New York Times Book Review*, 10 August 1941, 1.

29. Greenfield, *Dreamer's Journey*, 290.

30. Soderholm, *Fantasy, Forgery, and the Byron Legend*, 41–42. Lamb's letter as Byron imitates him spot on:

> Once more my Dearest Friend let me assure you that I had no hand in the satire you mention so do not take affront about nothing but call where I desired—as to his refusing you the Picture—it is quite ridiculous—only name me or if you like it then but this note & that will suffice . . . My Dearest Friend take care of xxxxxxxx [crossed out].

The gambit worked for Lamb, and the two were together, at least for a time. She did not get the portrait, however.

31. Consult the Modern Library edition of *Frankenstein* (1993) for a discussion of the novel's textual history. This 1993 edition takes from the revised 1831 edition. Kinnell's phrase "malaise à trois" comes from his terrific poem "Shelley" found in *Strong Is Your Hold* (2006).

32. Sims, ed., *Dracula's Guest*, 45. Headnotes to selections of Byron and Polidori provide useful summaries of the events of that summer and *The Vampyre*'s publication; more detail is provided by Davenport-Hines in *Gothic* and by Antiquarian Booksellers' Association of America member L.W. Currey's description of a copy for sale.

33. Quote from a letter by the would-be Major Byron, quoted in Farrer's *Literary Forgeries*, 187.

34. Mayo, "Vampyrism," in *Popular Superstitions*, 35.

35. Quoted in Greenfield, *Dreamer's Journey*, 98–99.

36. Taken from a 1963 letter to John Radcliffe Squires; quoted in ibid., 17.

37. See de Villiers, *Opacity and the Closet*.

38. Acton, *Memoirs of an Aesthete*, 7–8. This edition is also known as *More Memoirs of an Aesthete*, being the second volume of his memoirs; the first *Memoirs* cover the years 1904–69, overlapping somewhat.

39. Gore Vidal, "The Collector," *New York Review of Books*, 12 May 1983. Review of *Voices*.

40. Singer, "On the Courage to Be Old-Fashioned," *Book World*, 14 January 1968, 6. Quoted in Greenfield, *Dreamer's Journey*, 19.

41. Barker had actually worked on the sequel to Carter and Pollard's original *Enquiry*, updating its evidence.

42. Having already uncovered Chatterton's Rowley as a hoax, the critic Edmond Malone, in *An Inquiry into the Authenticity of Certain Papers and Instruments Attributed to Shakespeare* (1796), dissected the Ireland fakes. It also was a response to the father Samuel Ireland's *Miscellaneous Papers and Legal Instruments under the Hand and Seal of William Shakespeare*, which sought to authenticate and advertise the alleged finds, which he stood to profit from handsomely. Often credited with starting Shakespeare studies, and helping to establish the order of the plays, Malone's scholarship still is admired today—but back then he was among the first to say something was rotten in the Irelands' Denmark.

43. See Carter and Pollard, *An Enquiry into the Nature of Certain Nineteenth Century Pamphlets*. While the *Enquiry* points clearly at Wise, later books have also indicted Harry Buxton Forman, eventual comptroller, as party to the forgeries. See John Collins, *The Two Forgers: A Biography of Harry Buxton Forman & Thomas James Wise* (New Castle, DE: Oak Knoll Books, 1992).

44. Carter and Pollard, *Enquiry*, 76.

45. Prokosch, *Voices*, 66. Referenced by Vidal's review.

46. Eric Naiman, "When Dickens Met Dostoevsky," *Times Literary Supplement*, 10 April 2013; www.the-tls.co.uk/tls/public/article1243205.ece. A great piece of literary investigation. A 10 July 2013 follow-up in the *Guardian* has Stephen Moss interview the hoaxer, A. D. Harvey, whose aliases have included "Stephanie Harvey, Graham Headley, Trevor McGovern, John Schellenberger, Leo Bellingham, Michael Lindsay, Ludovico Parra and of course Janis Blodnieks"; www.theguardian.com /books/2013/jul/10/man-behind-dickens-dostoevsky-hoax.

47. Quoted in Naiman, "When Dickens Met Dostoevsky."

12. Spruce Goose

1. Keats, *Forged*, 3–4. Keats would go on to take Jonah Lehrer to task for his bad science in a key review of *Proust Was a Neuroscientist*, Salon, 20 November 2007.

2. Peter Schjeldahl, "Fakery," *New Yorker*, 8 November 2013; www.newyorker .com/culture/culture-desk/fakery.

3. Keats, *Forged*, 3. Also consult the British Museum's groundbreaking exhibition called *Fake?* (Like Irving's *Fake!* the subject seems to draw out exclamations, interrogations, and bold punctuation.) The 1990 show and catalog explored the ways fakes tell us about ourselves, and how beliefs change.

4. Friedlander, *On Art and Connoisseurship*, 259.

5. Ibid.

6. Israel, *Can You Ever Forgive Me?*, 50.

7. Friedlander, *On Art and Connoisseurship*, 261.

8. Keats, *Forged*, 5.

9. Irving, *Project Octavio*, 34.

10. I tracked down and bought a record that contains the press conference in its entirety: *Howard Hughes Press Conference* (Anaheim, CA: Mark 56 Records, 1972). "Actual voice recording taken from a telephone news conference January 7, 1972. A Documentary narrated and interviewed by Wayne Thomis, aviation editor for the Chicago *Tribune*." But the audio clip can be found at www.history.com/speeches /howard-hughes-breaks-his-silence#howard-hughes-breaks-his-silence (accessed 2 June 2015). Transcript by the author.

11. In Welles, *F for Fake*.

12. The term *film essay* is regularly applied to Welles's last film, and used by him in the interviews gathered in Biskind, *My Lunches with Orson*.

13. Biskind, *My Lunches with Orson*, 107.

14. See the bibliography under Fay, Chester, and Linklater and under Irving for these full titles. The authors assure readers in a note that despite their track record of admitted lies they should now be believed because if caught misrepresenting anything, they are at risk of perjury and more hard time. It is the ultimate antidisclaimer.

15. Frederik was later shot dead in 1994 in a mysterious, possibly drug-related, assassination while living in the Philippines—a story unto itself.

16. Irving, *Project Octavio*, 141.

17. Keats, *Forged*, 127.

18. Irving, *Project Octavio*, 148–49.

19. Ibid., 145.

20. Irving, *Project Octavio*, 40. As mentioned, this book, except for a final update on the court case and jail sentences, reprints nearly exactly *What Really Happened*, a mass-market Grove paperback. If not for the quality of the writing, you could call it a quickie book—but it is not the first on the Hughes affair, an honor that would go to *Hoax*, written by British reporters Fay, Chester, and Linklater and published even earlier, in 1972.

21. Irving's fascinating *60 Minutes* interview (and a follow-up years later) can be found as one of the extras on Criterion Collection's *F for Fake*. The quote also appears in Keats, *Forged*, 129. Irving had turned to espionage in previous books, including *The Thirty-Eighth Floor* (1965), his novel of international intrigue with a black protagonist. Irving here attempted to place Huck and Jim's symbolic raft into international waters, even naming the hero—"an American and a member of the Negro bourgeoisie," as the book flap has it—John Burden.

22. As reported and maintained by Edward Champion's website Reluctant Habits, at least as maintained in 2012–13.

23. Kingsley Amis had previously used "Robert Markham" as a pseudonym for authoring *Colonel Sun*, his 1968 Bond novel after Fleming died. Amis's Bond novel came after publishing the *Bond Dossier* (1965), and being on the forefront of James Bond studies that, like the Baker St. Irregulars before them with Sherlock Holmes, take their hero seriously while not themselves. (Q. R. Markham seems to be just the opposite.) At the same time it is true too that the traditional spy novel, even in Ian Fleming's initial vision, was regularly built on borrowed goods, cracked codes, stolen plans: "Ian Fleming was taken to court for plagiarism, and settled, and that he sometimes refashioned premises and ideas from other writers," author Jeremy Duns writes. "In *You Only Live Twice*, James Bond's philosophy is quoted as 'I shall not waste my days in trying to prolong them. I shall use my time.' As John Pearson revealed in his 1966 biography of Fleming, this line was Jack London's, and Fleming used it without attribution." See Jeremy Duns, "Highway Robbery: The Mask of Knowing in Assassin of Secrets," Dun's blog, Thursday, 10 November 2011. http://jeremyduns.blogspot.com/2011/11/highway-robbery-mask-of-knowing-in .html?showComment=1321259953379#c563057237791226662. Perhaps most importantly, and far different from Markham, Duns writes that "by merging the existing two schools of spy fiction, the heroic and the believable, Fleming forged an entirely new kind of spy thriller." See "Cold Male," Duns's blog, 16 December 2016; http://www.jeremy-duns.com/blog/ Duns would interview Rowan days before he was exposed; even for this friendly Q & A, Rowan plagiarized several responses.

24. Rowan's confessions appear places: most immediately after the incident in "Confessions of a Plagiarist," The Fix, 30 November 2011; www.thefix.com /content/confessions-plagiarist and later in Quentin Rowan, *Never Say Goodbye* (2012).

25. See Robert P. Eaton, "Meet Howard Hughes," *Ladies' Home Journal*, February 1972, 46–60. The article too bears Hughes's signature beneath his declaration "These notes are for your eyes only. I authorize you to edit them and arrange to have them published as my memoirs." The genuine book Irving blocked is *My Life and Opinions*, by Howard Hughes, an authorized biography edited by Robert P. Eaton that bears a rather strange preface by Robin Moore that opens: "I am constantly asked if the books I have written and edited—*The Green Berets*, *The French Connection*, *The Khaki Mafia*, *The Happy Hooker*—are authentic. This is a journalist's ultimate compliment. The autobiographies and biographies, and special interview stories of some of the world's most mysterious men sometimes strain credulity."

26. Rogin, *"Ronald Reagan," the Movie*, 7–8.

27. Ibid., 6–7.

28. Shaw, quoted in Yagoda, *Memoir*, chapter 8.

29. Irving, *Hoax*, 122.

30. Clifford Irving, review of *Enigma*, Amazon.com, accessed 21 August 2016:

www.amazon.com/gp/pdp/profile/A1VKDHDZBRHQRK/ref=cm_cr_dp_pdp.
This appears to be the actual Irving, now an author again active on Amazon, both
as a reviewer and in selling e-books and reprints.

13. Bakelite

1. The phrase *missing link* is used by a curator in a short documentary about
the case, found on the Boijmans Collection's website: http://collectie.boijmans.nl
/en/object/101464/The-men-at-Emmaus/Han-van-Meegeren.

2. The poll detail comes from Peter Schjeldahl, "Dutch Master," *New Yorker*, 27
October 2008, who provides a useful capsule review of the case (and of the Jonathan
Lopez book, quoted later in this chapter).

3. Jones, *Fake?*, 238. See also Dolnick's *The Forger's Spell*.

4. Lopez, *The Man Who Made Vermeers*, 3, 19–20. Lopez also indicates that
"for a forger, the appeal of facism, is its full Nietzschism mode, ultimately goes for
deeper than mere soreheadedness. What is a forger if not a closeted Übermensch,
an artist who secretly takes history itself for his canvas, who alters the past to suit
his present needs?" (8).

5. Peter Schjeldahl, "Dutch Master," *New Yorker*, 27 October 2008. For an in-
depth account of the looting of Europe's treasures, seek out Lynn Nicholas, *The
Rape of Europa: The Fate of Europe's Treasures in the Third Reich and the Second World
War* (1995).

6. See Harris, *Selling Hitler*, and Alistair Reid's particularly accurate film of
the same title for details of the case. For reference to the yacht, see Harris, *Selling
Hitler*, 57.

7. These smuggling details are featured in Reid's film *Selling Hitler* and in
Sally McGrane, "Diary of the Hitler Diary Hoax," *New Yorker*, 25 April 2013; www
.newyorker.com/books/page-turner/diary-of-the-hitler-diary-hoax.

8. Former *Stern* editor Felix Schmidt, quoted in McGrane, ibid.

9. See Steers, *Hoax*, 90.

10. See Steers, *Hoax*, for a capsule account of David Irving. Here's his bio
from the Southern Poverty Law Center website (accessed 2016): "David Irving was
once treated with great respect for his historical tomes on World War II and Nazi
Germany. But since the 1980s, he has cultivated a reputation as the world's most
prominent Holocaust denier, a status he cemented by suing Penguin Books and
American scholar Deborah Lipstadt for libel in 2000 after Lipstadt wrote that he
was a denier and a pro-Nazi ideologue. In a dramatic judgment, Irving lost his
case and most of the considerable amount of money he made over the years selling
his books. That, and his 2006 stint in an Austrian prison for denying the existence
of gas chambers at Auschwitz, have made Irving a hero in extremist circles. Any
reputation he once had as a real 'historian' has been wrecked"; www.splcenter.org
/fighting-hate/extremist-files/individual/david-irving.

11. See "Hitler's Forged Diaries," *Time* cover story, 16 May 1983, for the laboratory's language quoted here.

12. *Newsweek*, "Hitler's Secret Diaries," 2 May 1983, 50–60.

13. McGrane, "Diary of the Hitler Diary Hoax."

14. John Hooper, "'Hitler Diaries' Man Was a Spy," *Guardian*, 29 July 2002; www.theguardian.com/world/2002/jul/29/books.humanities.

15. Lopez, *The Man Who Made Vermeers*, 141. See also Weinberger, *Karmic Traces*: "As an original van Meegeren it is a brilliant parody which, in one startling gesture, both delivers the last laugh and anticipates postmodern ironic/iconic pastiche: van Meegeren clearly copied the face of Jesus from a photograph of Greta Garbo" (59).

16. This is an important distinction; it is no accident that in the interim between 1891 and 1955 the very idea of translation had changed, largely adopting Ezra Pound's injunction to render a new poem in English. In a sense, Johnson's edition, still the definitive one, was a bit like the practice of reprinting an original alongside its modern translation—it sought to show us the workings of a mind far more modern than even the fin de siècle could accept. All this would seem foreshadowed by the 1892 "Second Series" of her poems, which includes as a frontispiece a "Facsimile of 'Renunciation'" in her hand—soon resulting in a renunciation of another kind.

17. Emily Dickinson, *The Gorgeous Nothings*, ed. Jen Bervin (New York: New Directions, 2013).

18. Simon Worrall, *The Poet and the Murderer*, gives an account of the auction and subsequent murders and trial.

19. Sloan, *Jerzy Kosinski*, 223; Wiesel, quoted in ibid.

20. Dick Schapp, "Stepmother Tongue," *New York Herald Tribune Book Review*, 14 November 1965, 6. Found in Tom Teicholz, ed., *Conversations with Jerzy Kosinski* (1993).

21. Mendelsohn, "Stolen Suffering."

22. *Painted Bird*, first edition, 269 and 272. Thanks to James Park Sloan's study for directing me to this epilogue.

23. Geoffrey Stokes and Eliot Fremont-Smith, "Jerzy Kosinski's Tainted Words," *Village Voice*, 22 June 1982.

24. Kosinski's cohort of 1969 National Book Award winners included John Berryman for the second installment of *The Dream Songs* and Norman Mailer, nominated in two categories for *The Armies of the Night: History as a Novel, The Novel as History*. Winning the now-defunct category "arts and letters," *Armies* in its very subtitle—not to mention its category—demonstrates that Kosinski's ambiguities are as much a product of his time, concerns shared by New Journalism and the nouveau roman. Even Berryman's book is a disguised autobiography of "Huffy Henry," who himself appears in blackface. It was a time of masks.

25. Sloan, *Jerzy Kosinski*, 6.

26. Weinberger, *Karmic Traces*, 57. Weinberger significantly mistakes the book later typed up by the prankster (Chuck Ross, whom he leaves unnamed), naming it *Painted Bird* when significantly it was *Steps*. See note 13 for chapter 14.

14. The Vampire's Wife

1. Consult Elizabeth Alexander's catalog essay in *Two Cents: Works on Paper by Jean-Michel Basquiat and Poetry by Kevin Young* (1995). Reprinted in Alexander, *The Black Interior* (2004) as "A Black Man Says 'Sorbet.'"

2. In the spring of 2015, an art museum in London commissioned an artist who plans to replace one of its Old Master paintings with a copy "Made in China," borrowing a technique from art thieves in order to question the public's eye. While museums sometimes do this to discourage potential thieves—there are Mona Lisa copies traded for the original at different times, for security reasons—this sanctioned fake means to combat the way, as the artist puts it, "When you walk into a collection with a large amount of paintings, it's very easy to gloss over everything quickly and to take it all in as a kind of vista."

3. Thanks to the online Museum of Hoaxes for pointing out the later *Casablanca* experiment; hoaxes.org/archive/permalink/casablanca_rejected.

4. Kosinski, *Notes of the Author on "The Painted Bird,"* 11 and 12.

5. Jerzy Kosinski, "Society and Disorder," in *Oral Pleasure*, 167. From an interview originally appearing in 1989.

6. Sloan, *Jerzy Kosinski*, 217.

7. Jonathon Sturgeon, "2014: The Death of the Postmodern Novel and the Rise of Autofiction," *Flavorwire*, 31 December 2014; flavorwire.com/496570/2014-the-death-of-the-postmodern-novel-and-the-rise-of-autofiction. While I do agree with Sturgeon that "although critics will endlessly retread tired discussions . . . concerning fiction vs. reality (and therefore the exhausted conversation about "realism"), that isn't really what's at stake here," I don't know if the self as a made thing is the same as a fiction. Rather, as I hope the latter part of this book has made clear, this is actually a sign of our current narrative crisis.

8. Kate Kellaway, "Rachel Cusk: 'Aftermath Was Creative Death. I Was Heading into Total Silence," interviewed in *Guardian*, 24 August 2014.

9. Kosinski, "My Private Fantasy," in *Oral Pleasure*, 156.

10. Kosinski, *Hermit*, 226.

11. See Sloan, *Jerzy Kosinski*.

12. Doniger, *The Woman Who Pretended to Be Who She Was*, 3.

13. Kosinski, *Notes of the Author*, 19.

14. Maechler, *The Wilkomirski Affair*, 242

15. Elena Lappin, "The Man with Two Heads," *Granta: The Magazine of New Writing* 66 (Summer 1999): 65. Franklin and others point out what we might call

survivors' guilt regarding what it took to survive the Holocaust: "'The worst—that is, the fittest—survived,' [Primo] Levi wrote also in *The Drowned and the Saved*. 'The best all died.' What he meant, as he had already written repeatedly, is that it was impossible to survive in Auschwitz without resorting to theft, to trickery, even to collaboration—at the very least, to selfishness and deception. . . . This is hardly a moral judgment; no one can fault survivors for the ferocity of their will to survive. And it is also not universally true: Levi's writings are full of evidence of the help he received from others, from the non-Jew Lorenzo who brought him extra portions of soup to his partnership with his friend Alberto Dalla Volta, with whom he shared 'everything.'" Franklin, *A Thousand Darknesses*, 143.

16. Ganzfreld, quoted in Eskin, *A Life in Pieces*, 114. Lappin, "The Man with Two Heads."

17. Ruth Franklin, *A Thousand Darknesses*, 78.

18. Motoko Rich and Joseph Berger, "False Memoir of Holocaust is Canceled," *New York Times*, 28 December 2008; www.nytimes.com/2008/12/29/books/29hoax .html?pagewanted=1&_r=1.

19. Eskin, *A Life in Pieces*, 98.

20. Gary Mokotoff from the board of the Jewish Book Council stateside told Eskin he always saw *Fragments* as "historical fiction" rather than strictly accurate. Mokotoff also names the difficulties with such historical fiction, even with a view of memory as "little fictions": "[*Fragments*] reminded me of Martin Gray's book [*For Those I Loved*], which was also a Holocaust memoir that was exposed as fiction. It worried me, because today you will find references to that book only on revisionist websites. These kinds of pseudo-memoirs may do real damage to survivors, by rendering each Holocaust memoir suspect." Mokotoff wrote to the council after it gave *Fragments* the prize in memoir—even though "it would never have won in the Holocaust category," he notes, with its more rigorous standard of fact, he was concerned enough to protest the prize—but was ignored.

21. Bob and Gretchen Passatino, a married pair of evangelical journalists, wrote both articles in *Cornerstone* along with editor Jon Trott. See "Lauren Stratford: From Satanic Ritual Abuse to Jewish Holocaust Survivor," *Cornerstone* 28 (1999); www.answers.org/satan/laura.html. Also Gretchen and Bob Passantino and Jon Trott, "Satan's Sideshow," *Cornerstone* 18 (1989): 23–28; www.answers.org/satan /stratford.html.

22. Quoted in Eskin, *A Life in Pieces*, 216. Despite her faking the nature of her suffering, whether satanic or Sybil, *Cornerstones* isn't wrong to say that "Laurel's emotional distress is real."

23. Ofshe and Watters, *Making Monsters*, 202.

24. Quoted in Maechler, *The Wilkomirski Affair*, 280–81.

25. *Webster's* has it as "perhaps from Yiddish *shlak* evil, nuisance, literally, blow"

with the *O.E.D.*'s 1982 entry tracing schlock from the "Yiddish, apparently < *shlogn* to strike."

26. Maechler, *The Wilkomirski Affair*, 276 and 280.

27. Oliver Sacks, "Speak, Memory," *New York Review of Books*, 21 February 2013.

28. Oliver Sacks, *A Leg to Stand On*, x–xi.

29. Oliver Sacks, "Speak, Memory."

30. Stefan Maechler and Moira Moehler-Woods, "Wilkomirski the Victim: Individual Remembering as Social Interaction and Public Event," *History and Memory* 13, no. 2 (Fall/Winter 2001): 70.

31. Sontag, "From *The Benefactor*," *Susan Sontag Reader*, 10.

32. Wilkomirski, *Fragments*, 147.

15. Glass Ceilings

1. See *Slate* author page for Desai (www.slate.com/authors.ravi_desai.html) and Jack Shafer's "Who Is Robert Klingler? On the Trail of the Man Who Duped Slate," *Slate*, 12 March 2002; www.slate.com/articles/news_and_politics/press _box/2002/03/who_is_robert_klingler.html.

2. MacDougall, *Hoaxes*, 147.

3. Frankfurt, *On Bullshit*, 64.

4. Ibid., 59–60, 60–61.

5. Wil S. Hylton, "The Unbreakable Laura Hillenbrand," *New York Times*, 18 December 2014; www.nytimes.com/2014/12/21/magazine/the-unbreakable-laura -hillenbrand.html?_r=0.

6. Adam L. Penenberg, "Lessons from Serial Fabulist Stephen Glass on How Not to Reboot a Career," *Fast Company*, 14 December 2011; www.fastcompany.com /1800761/stephen-glass-lawyer-fabulist.

7. Jonathan Chait, "Rememberance of Things Passed," *Washington Monthly*, July/August 2003.

8. Hanna Rosin, "Glass Houses," *Slate*, 21 May 2003. www.slate.com/articles /arts/books/2003/05/glass_houses.html.

9. This and the Rosin quotes that follow come from Hanna Rosin, "Glass Houses."

10. Glass, *The Fabulist*, 3.

11. "In re Stephen Randall Glass on Admission," Supreme Court of California, 27 January 2014; www.courts.ca.gov/opinions/documents/S196374.PDF.

12. Copies of this book sometime appear, as in a 1974 piracy. The cataloging of a copy in the Manuscript, Archives, and Rare Book Library at Emory quotes Bixby saying it's "a piracy, believed to have been produced in California. Salinger's law-yers were successful in suppressing most of the edition"—G. Bixby, in *American Book Collector*, May/June 1981, 30.

13. William Jay Smith, *The Spectra Hoax*, 31.

14. Witter Bynner, "The Spectric Poets," *New Republic*, 18 November 1916. Thanks to Smith's directing readers to this review.

15. Such a development of self-as-story the tremendous film *Broadcast News* (1987) would predict. In depicting the struggle between reporting facts and the fabrication of feelings—faking or at least enhancing a reaction to a moving date rape story by the handsome, ambitious, airheaded reporter played by William Hurt—the movie reveals how faking can sometimes barely harm the faker. Not everyone gets his comeuppance.

16. John Cloud, "Baby Ruth," *Washington City Paper*, 20 October 1995. Ruth Shalit, "Race in the Newsroom," *New Republic*, 2 October 1995, 20–37.

17. The number of inaccuracies comes from "Defending the Family," an interview by Alicia C. Shepard with Leonard Downie Jr., *American Journalism Review*, 1 December 1995. Howard Kurtz, "A Diversity of Opinions," *Washington Post*, 21 September 1995. See also "Race in the Newsroom: An Exchange" between Downie, Shalit, Graham, and the editors, *New Republic*, 16 October 1995. Even a casual search reveals a not-quite-invisible yet insistent fixation on affirmative action that persists in the *New Republic* even today. As recently as 2012, the magazine continued to run articles by a wide range of authors with titles such as "Race to the Flop: The Problem with Affirmative Action." Jeffrey Rosen wrote an article titled "Is Affirmative Action Doomed?" in 1994; eighteen years later he still was looking, as evidenced by his article "An Affirmative Action Solution Even Conservatives Should Love" (10 October 2012). Online at least, in 2012 several articles recycled images of African Americans at the same protest with cardboard signs scrawled with slogans like "I Believe in Affirmative Action" as if they were homeless people selling roses and newspapers for change at an off-ramp. It seems a bit too coincidental that the one pro–affirmative action protester featured alongside many articles looks a lot like President Obama while a headline announces "President Obama's Affirmative Action Problem and What He Should Do about It."

18. Cloud, "Baby Ruth." The epithets applied to Shalit appear in any number of sources; I first encountered them in an interview with Ruth Shalit by Alicia C. Shepard; Alicia C. Shepard, *American Journalism Review*, December 1995, but they are also all over the "Race in the Newsroom" exchange.

19. Shepard, "Too Much Too Soon?," interview with Ruth Shalit, *American Journalism Review*, December 1995.

20. Bradlee, *A Good Life*, 437.

21. Donald Graham, "Race in the Newsroom: An Exchange," letter to the editors of the *New Republic*, 16 October 1995, 17.

22. Shepard, "Too Much Too Soon?" Subsequent comments between Shepard and Shalit are from this interview.

23. David Carr, "Goodbye to All That," *Washington City Paper*, 9 April 1999; www.washingtoncitypaper.com/articles/17092/goodbye-to-all-that. All subsequent quotations from Carr in text come from "Goodbye."

24. Carr does praise Shalit, saying after returning of leave, "Her version of donning sackcloth meant crawling under the wing of the *New Republic*'s literary editor, Leon Weiseltier, and taking occasional turns as culture babe in the back of the book. She did good work—much of it about the wrongly accused, it should be pointed out—and it seemed to be her own. But people who work at the magazine say she was still a nightmare to fact-check and remained confused about the gravity of what she did for a living."

25. Shalit, quoted in Carr, "Goodbye."

26. Ibid.

27. Malcolm, *The Journalist and the Murderer*, 3.

28. It should be said that the book also echoes Malcolm's being sued by source for libel in her earlier book, *In the Freud Archive*, a case that took over twelve years to conclude. As a 1994 *Village Voice* article by Robert Boynton has it in a teaser, "Janet Malcolm's Journalistic Relationship with Analyst Jeffrey Masson Seemed as Intimate as Romance. No Wonder Their Recent Libel Trial Felt Like a Divorce." Malcolm eventually won the suit.

29. Malcolm, *The Journalist and the Murderer*, 4–5.

30. David Plotz, "Me and Stephen Glass," *Slate*, 30 September 2003. It should be said that Plotz has now written that he feels Glass should be admitted to the bar.

31. Tom Scocca, "Faking It," *Boston Phoenix*, 21–28 May 1998.

32. Adam L. Penenberg, "Lies, Damn Lies and Fiction," Forbes Digital Tool, 11 May 1998; www.forbes.com/1998/05/11/otw3.html.

33. Buzz Bissinger, "Shattered Glass," *Vanity Fair*, September 1998.

34. Stephen Glass, "Hack Heaven," *New Republic*, 18 May 1998; penenberg. com/story-archive/hack-heaven.

35. Bissinger, "Shattered Glass": *"Are you mad at me?'* That was something Glass said incessantly. The slightest look or gesture could send him into a panic of self-doubt. Certain friends advised him to stop asking the question; others found that it called forth their protective instincts. Glass's would-be parent surrogates wanted only to help make this terribly insecure boy, who would describe a story he wrote as a 'piece of shit,' feel better about himself."

16. The Gingerbread Man

1. Stephen Glass, "Taxis and the Meaning of Work," *New Republic*, 5 August 1996. Buzz Bissinger is the source for the idea of Peretz's encouraging the piece.

2. Ta-Nehisi Coates, "On the Cheapness of Life," *Atlantic*, 20 September 2010. www.theatlantic.com/national/archive/2010/09/on-the-cheapness-of-life/63172 /#bio. After September 11, Peretz would say of Muslims that their lives were cheap,

even to them; but in that prelapsarian world before the Twin Towers fell, when Glass wrote "Work," invented immigrant religiosity beat native blackness hands down. In "*The New Republic:* An Appreciation," 9 December 2014, Coates sums up: "If one were to attempt to capture the 'spirit' of TNR, it would be impossible to avoid the conclusion that black lives don't matter much at all."

3. Paul Maliszewski, *Fakers*, 89.

4. Maliszewski, "I, Faker," in *Fakers*, 1. "I, Faker" first appeared in the *Baffler*, then in *Boob Jubilee*, an anthology of the magazine's best pieces; there, the company he worked for is actually named.

5. More on the fake website (what Maliszweksi calls "satirical") appears in a 2009 interview on Bookslut.com: www.bookslut.com/features/2009_03_014155.php.

6. Tom Scocca, "Taking It," *Boston Phoenix*, 26 May 1998.

7. Stephen Glass, "A Day on the Street," *Daily Pennsylvanian*, 6 June 1991.

8. As reported by Buzz Bissinger in *Vanity Fair*, "At *Harper's*, Glass would be dismissed from his contract after a story he had written about phone psychics, which contained 13 first-name sources, could not be verified." Bissinger, "Shattered Glass," *Vanity Fair*, 5 September 2007; www.vanityfair.com/magazine/1998/09 /bissinger199809.

9. Ralph Ellison, "Shadow and Act," *Collected Essays*, 80.

10. Leon Litwack, *Trouble in Mind*, 302. The "fakelore" term is from Albert Murray's *OmniAmericans* (1970); the "folk pornography" from Jacquelyn Dowd Hall's *Revolt against Chivalry* (1993).

11. Stephen Glass, "The Vernon Question," *George*, April 1988, 88.

12. Ibid., 90.

13. Litwack, *Trouble in Mind*, 284.

14. Kia Makarechi, "Besides Michael Brown, Whom Else Does the New York Times Call 'No Angel'?" *Vanity Fair* online, 25 August 2014; vanityfair.com/online /daily/2014/08/michael-brown-no-angel-new-york-times?mbid=social_twitter.

15. After watching the movie *Shattered Glass*, David Plotz says as much in *Slate* magazine (where he once served as editor), finding a dissonance between actor Hayden Christensen's portrayal of Steve and "Our Steve," who "was a lovely, winning, hilarious, endearing person. Christensen's Steve is not. He's got all the Glass tics—the endless apologies, the constant helpfulness, the excessive ingratiation— but while Steve made them endearing, Christensen makes them only creepy. Our Steve rubbed off on all of us, made us think that life could be luscious and fun." Then again, Plotz realizes, "Maybe this Steve is the real one. Maybe Steve was creepy in his insecurity; maybe he was constantly manipulating us emotionally, and maybe we were too stupid to notice." Plotz "Steve and Me," *Slate*, 30 September 2003.

16. Jonathan Chait, "Remembrance of Things Passed: How My Friend Stephen Glass Got Away with It," *Washington Monthly*, July/August 2003; www.unz.org /Pub/WashingtonMonthly-2003jul-00041.

17. Hanna Rosin, "Hello, My Name Is Stephen Glass, and I'm Sorry," *New Republic*, 10 November 2014; www.newrepublic.com/article/120145/stephen-glass -new-republic-scandal-still-haunts-his-law-career.

18. Bissinger, "Shattered Glass."

19. Buzz Bissinger, "My Gucci Addiction," *GQ*, April 2013.

20. State Bar hearing, as detailed in the Supreme Court of California ruling, 3.

17. In Bad Blood

1. This doesn't mean that some black men weren't picked up in a sweep— including Smith's ex-mother-in-law's husband. *Jet* magazine had this covered; see the 7 August 1995 issue: books.google.com/books?id=QD0DAAAAMBAJ&pg =PA64&lpg=PA64&dq=susan+smith+suspect&source=bl&ots=mvaotjrD6v& sig=weM8m6Ii5b7bmPTnJZUkEhrIKng&hl=en&sa=X&ved=0ahUKEwj30v -Pnp_PAhXD6iYKHXuvD-wQ6AEIOzAI#v=onepage&q=susan%20smith%20 suspect&f=false.

2. See "Attack of the GIANT NEGROES!!" 10 July 2007: http://undercover blackman.blogspot.com/2007/07/attack-of-giant-negroes.html.

3. Eady, "Uncle Tom in Heaven," in *Brutal Imagination*, 27. To call the imag- ination and not honesty brutal is to admit that all imagination has a degree of vio- lence, whether rendering ideas apart and reconstituting them (as William Carlos Williams insisted in *Spring and All*); or worse, that words themselves contain traces of their violent wrenching from the throats of others (metaphorically in Margaret Seltzer, and actually in Smith). The imagined speaker's voice contains a vernacular that is a living language instead of the zombie-like black dialect found in so much supposed art, not to mention the hoax. The imagination, the poems know, is a thing that itself can speak—and even if conjured for nefarious reasons, can in the end be of use to a poet as gifted as Eady, to counter the oppressions and denials of black iden- tity and imagination on the imagination's own terms. To fight liars by lighting fires.

4. Ibid., 26.

5. Thanks to Leon Litwack's *Trouble In Mind*, 304, for pointing me to this idea from Jacquelyn Dowd Hall's *Revolt against Chivalry*, 150–51. And thanks to Kate Tuttle, my wife, for first mentioning the term to me.

6. *Misha: A Mémoire of the Holocaust Years*. Turned out to be faked by a non- Jewish Belgian really named Monique De Wael.

7. Ben Bradlee, *A Good Life*, 442.

8. As quoted in Bill Green, "The Players: It Wasn't a Game," *Washington Post*, 19 April 1981. "Much later, after Ronald Reagan was elected president, Donnie Radcliffe of The Post's Style staff sent a copy of the story to the nation's first-lady- to-be. Radcliffe thought it would be useful information as the Reagans prepared to come to Washington."

9. Bradlee, *A Good Life*, 442.

10. Ibid. In other accounts, including a PBS interview with Jim Lehrer for the documentary *Free Speech*, Bradlee describes these as only after the fact. *Free Speech* transcript (originally aired 19 June 2006). www.pbs.org/newshour/bradlee/transcript _cooke.html.

11. Bradlee, *A Good Life*, 432.

12. Janet Cooke, "Jimmy's World," *Washington Post*, 28 September 1980. Part of this opening appears in Bradlee, *A Good Life*, 436.

13. Ibid., 447.

14. Ibid., 439.

15. Green, "The Players." Jimmy's portrait was done by "historical portraitist" Michael Gnatek Jr. His obituary in the *Washington Post* says, "In September 1980, Mr. Gnatek was assigned by *The Post* to make a drawing to accompany 'Jimmy's World,' a story about an 8-year-old heroin addict by then-*Washington Post* reporter Janet Cooke. In several meetings with the artist, Cooke became emotional, Mr. Gnatek's family said, as she described 'Jimmy' and the sordid world in which he lived. When she saw Mr. Gnatek's shadowy black-and-white portrait of a thin, wide-eyed boy, she told Mr. Gnatek, 'That's exactly what he looked like.'" *Washington Post*, 11 October 2006.

16. Bradlee, *A Good Life*, 436–37. Quotes in parentheses are from Cooke's "Jimmy's World."

17. Ibid., 450.

18. Ibid., 449 and 204.

19. Nelson, *Volunteer Slavery*, 13–14. For more on Nelson, Nathan McCall, and other black journalists, as well as alternative notions to objectivity, consult Calvin L. Hall, *African American Journalists: Autobiography as Memoir and Manifesto* (2009).

20. Nelson, *Volunteer Slavery*, 18–19.

21. Ibid., 6. One sign of the nearsightedness: Bradlee, though embarking on a magazine, had never even heard of *Essence*, by then well established and certainly the liveliest and most literary of the black glossies. Compare the interview experience of Peter Maass in the Intercept: https://firstlook.org/theintercept/2014/10/22 /a-ben-bradlee-story-thats-not-fucking-charming.

22. Nelson, *Volunteer Slavery*, 85–88.

23. Ibid., 87–88.

24. Ibid., 56–57.

18. Burning Down

1. Mnookin, *Hard News*, 116.

2. "Correcting the Record," *New York Times*, 11 May 2003. This email came in April 2002, well before Blair was assigned to the sniper story that fall.

3. Blair, *Burning Down*, 7.

4. Strangely enough, the killers' blackness was sensed even before being re-

vealed by none other than my late cousin (who was my parents' age), who said she thought the sniper was black as soon as one disclosed note taunted "Mr. Policeman"—a black phrasing, she felt, and one that appears in this case to have been taken from a song. Fascinating how language might provide clues to crimes, for language is one of the crimes itself in these cases—as in the hoax.

5. Mnookin, *Hard News*, 123.

6. Blair, *Burning Down*, 345.

7. Adams, *Travelers and Travel Liars*, 17.

8. Mnookin, *Hard News*, 124.

9. Oddly enough, another book about a hoaxer, David Samuels's *The Runner*, has the same error—though in listing "*The Invisible Man*" as one of the books Princeton impostor James Hogue had on a reading list in his college application, it's not clear if the mistake is Samuels's or Hogue's.

10. Blair, *Burning Down*, 1.

11. Bradlee, *A Good Life*, 438–39.

12. "Correcting the Record; Times Reporter Who Resigned Leaves Long Trail of Deception," *New York Times*, 11 May 2003. "This article was reported, written [by] Dan Barry, David Barstow, Jonathan D. Glater, Adam Liptak, Jacques Steinberg. Research support was provided [by] Alain Delaquérière and Carolyn Wilder." The *Times* journalists "have so far uncovered new problems in at least 36 of the 73 articles Mr. Blair wrote since he started getting national reporting assignments late last October."

13. Mnookin, *Hard News*, 162.

14. Blair, *Burning Down*, 27.

15. Mnookin, *Hard News*, 240.

16. Ibid., 240–41.

17. The newly named public editor of the *New York Times* wrote a nearly fifteen-hundred-word piece after the WMD debacle. What's worse, the WMD seems like a focus handed down from editor Howell Raines in the same kind of top–down culture that had doomed the *Post* during Cooke and still seems prominent at too many outlets to mention. As one former *Times* editor, who worked on Miller's stories, says, "My sense was that Howell Raines was eager to have articles that supported the war-mongering out of Washington." The quote is from "former investigative editor Doug Frantz" to Mnookin. See Mnookin, *Hard News*, 243.

18. Michael Finkel, *True Story*, 178–81.

19. Michael Finkel, "Is Youssouf Malé a Slave?," *New York Times Magazine*, 18 November 2001.

20. Ibid.

21. From the *New York Times*, 21 February 2002:

> **Editors' Note:** An article in The Times Magazine on Nov. 18, headlined "Is Youssouf Malé a Slave?" described the experience of an

adolescent West African boy in Mali who left his home village and sold himself into service on a cocoa plantation in Ivory Coast. The article described his year hacking weeds in the fields, earning a total of $102, and his decision against staying a second year. It reported on two organizations that helped him return home, and it asked whether they were exaggerating the plight of youths like Youssouf. One agency mentioned was a branch of the human rights organization Save the Children Canada, in the Malian city of Sikasso. The article was illustrated with photographs, including one taken by the writer, an uncaptioned full-page image of a youth. On Feb. 13, the writer, Michael Finkel, informed The Times that an official of Save the Children had contacted him to say that in investigating the case, the agency had located the boy in the picture, and that he was not Youssouf Malé. The editors then questioned the writer and began to make their own inquiries to verify the article's account. The writer, a freelancer, then acknowledged that the boy in the article was a composite, a blend of several boys he interviewed, including one named Youssouf Malé and another, the boy in the picture, identified by Save the Children as Madou Traoré. Though the account was drawn from his reporting on the scene and from interviews with human rights workers, Mr. Finkel acknowledges, many facts were extrapolated from what he learned was typical of boys on such journeys, and did not apply specifically to any single individual. The writer says that he wrote this article without consulting his notes. (The article included no direct quotations.) The notes, which the editors have now read, reveal that contrary to the description of Youssouf Malé's year of work at the plantation, he spent less than a month there before running away.

The note goes on almost twice as long as I have here.

22. For a fuller discussion of the African slave's resistances and what I call the *storying* tradition, including codes in the spirituals and the animal tales, consult my previous study *The Grey Album*. For more on the slave narratives as memoir, consult Yagoda's *Memoir*.

23. Finkel, *True Story*, 25.

24. Ibid., 43.

25. Ibid., 13, 178.

26. Ibid., 181.

27. Sridar Pappu, "'True Story': Murder He Wrote," *New York Times*, 29 May 2005.

28. Michael Finkel, "How I Convinced a Death-Row Murderer Not to Die," *Esquire*, 21 December 2009.

20. Professor Plum

1. *Oxford English Dictionary*, 3rd ed., June 2006; online version June 2012. See also Mallon, *Stolen Words*, 10–11. Samuel Johnson in his famous dictionary (1755)—the eighteenth century was, as Thomas Mallon's classic study *Stolen Words* reminds us, "hot for attribution"—defines plagiary as "The Crime of literary theft. Not used. *Plagiary* had not its nativity with printing, but began when the paucity of books scarce wanted that invention.—Brown." As Sir Thomas Brown indicates, via Johnson (and thence Mallon), plagiarism actually preceded printing.

2. Mallon, *Stolen Words*, x, xiii–xiv.

3. Seal, *The Man in the Rockefeller Suit*, 259. Note that I have not yet been able to locate this quote in Capote's oeuvre.

4. Baldwin, *The Fire Next Time*, 5–6.

5. Kirn, *Blood Will Out*, 162. I once tried playing this game with some old and new friends, and right out of the gate, in lieu of *Sophie's Choice* someone came up with *Sophie's Options*. Game over; no topping that one.

6. Kirn, *Blood Will Out*, 202.

7. Ibid., 174. How good were these fakes? Kirn even suggests that so-called Rockefeller may even have been "Mister X," the mysterious supplier involved in the 2013 art-world forgery case of Pollocks and others mentioned above that shuttered one prestigious gallery and involved hundreds of million of dollars worth of faked paintings—all authenticated by experts and sold by a broker who has admitted to the fraud. By all accounts, Rockefeller's fakes were good enough to fool experts from the country's major museums. Though a Chinese painter, paid relative peanuts, is now suspected of actually rendering the convincing Pollocks, it does make a fascinating story. Consult Patricia Cohen and William K. Rashbaum, *New York Times*, "One Queens Painter Created Forgeries That Sold for Millions, US Says," 15 August 2013. One painting's signature was misspelled "Pollok." Also Michael Kaplan, "Inside the $80M Scam . . . ," *New York Post*, 24 January 2016.

8. Kirn, *Blood Will Out*, 202.

9. Ibid., 186.

10. Ibid., 154.

11. Ibid., 187.

21. Ghostbusters

1. Thanks to my good friend Richard Nash for providing the exact phrasing of this idea.

2. My own Harvard interview faced a strange version of the immigrant dilemma: my interviewer, a graduate and former hippie turned lawyer, asked about my blackness. *You don't seem black* is less a confession than an accusation and an exclamation of relief.

3. Dinitia Smith, "Harvard Novelist Says Copying Was Unintentional," *New York Times*, 25 April 2006.

4. Mallon, *Stolen Words*, xiii.

5. Quoted by Little, Brown press kit. Originally from David Mehegan, "How Kaavya Viswanathan Got Noticed, Got an Agent, and Got a Monster Two-Novel Contract," *Boston Globe*, 22 February 2006.

6. Smith, "Harvard Novelist Says Copying Was Unintentional."

7. Sepia Mutiny ran from "7/30/ 2004 to 4/1/2012" according to the blog homepage. Luckily it is well archived, including the FAQs page, which is both funny and smart (and where this definition of *desi* comes from); http://sepiamutiny.com/sepia /faq.php. Sepia Mutiny also has a fascinating rehash of the Ravi Desai case, including some rather harsh comments. "The many lives of Ravi Desai"; http://sepiamutiny .com/blog/2005/03/24/the_many_lives.

8. Emphasis added. This and the earlier quote about the "first" are from "Tanuja Desai Hidier on Born Confused & Opal Metha" (2006); www.desiclub.com /community/culture/culture_article.cfm?id=265 (now defunct).

9. Smith, "A 'How to Get into College by Really, Really Trying' Novel," *New York Times*, 6 April 2006.

10. Smith, "Harvard Novelist Says Copying Was Unintentional."

11. Quoted in Motoko Rich and Dinitia Smith, "First, Plot and Character. Then, Find an Author," *New York Times*, 27 April 2006. During the incident we hardly hear from Alloy—their very name implying fabrication or at least a mixed product—though they share the book's copyright and presumably the movie deal signed with DreamWorks before publication. But as Rich and Smith report, "Even officials at Random House, the parent company of Ms. McCafferty's publisher, said they did not consider Alloy responsible. 'Most relationships with packagers and book producers have been relatively free of the kinds of problems cited in the coverage of this story,' said Mr. Applebaum, the spokesman, 'and beneficial for all concerned.'"

12. Of course, the beloved Nancy Drew books were also produced by a book packager, the Stratemeyer Syndicate, which published them under the shared pseudonym "Carolyn Keene." Thirty-three Nancy Drew books were actually penned from 1930 to 1953 by one Millie Benson, an aviatrix who later served as columnist for the *Toledo Blade* well into her nineties. Spunky and spirited, she died after writing at her desk. Benson's relative anonymity—it was only in her eighties that she revealed having been one of the shapers of the girl detective—suited her just fine. Once unmasked, Benson is quoted as saying about the belated attention, "I'm so sick of Nancy Drew I could vomit"; Patricia Leigh Brown, "Conversations/Mildred Benson: A Ghostwriter and Her Sleuth; 63 Years of Smarts and Gumption," *New York Times*, 9 May 1993. The story of the ghostwriters of Nancy Drew is also featured in a recent book. But where Keene was the writer as ghostwriter, anonymous and happily

so, Alloy, with series such as *The Sisterhood of the Traveling Pants*, functions in exactly the opposite manner: the author as an idea divorced from the writing; the author as owner. This is actually behind the charge, and the practice, of plagiarism—the plagiarist is she who claims she owns, borrows, and expands to fit another's words.

13. Smith, "Harvard Novelist Says Copying Was Unintentional."

14. Elizabeth S. Auritt, "Harvard Accepts Record Low of 5.9 Percent to the Class of 2016," *Harvard Crimson*, 29 March 2012.

15. See Zauzmer, *Conning Harvard*.

16. These days, all the surveys and studies tell us plagiarism and cheating run rampant on campus, not to mention piracy of music and images; far worse, most students who admit to cheating don't even consider it that. The numbers Zauzmer reports in *Conning Harvard* are startling: "In a 2010 survey of more than 40,000 high school students, 80 percent said that they had copied someone else's homework, and 59 percent said that they had cheated on a test in the previous year. Moreover, 25 percent said at the end that they lied on that very survey" (4). It is in such a context that plagiarism is a sign less of aspiration than privilege.

17. The résumé is still viewable online, and is also included in *Conning Harvard*, where it appears annotated as it apparently was in an edition of the *Crimson*.

18. See *Conning Harvard*.

19. Of course, what is and isn't in the Shakespeare canon has shifted over the centuries, and is an argument still very much with us: in his account of attempting to authenticate "Funeral Elegy by W. S." as by Shakespeare, so-called literary detective Don Foster (who would go on to help correctly identify the Unabomber) relates not just the textual process but also the politics that ensue. Don Foster, "Looking into Shakespeare," in *Author Unknown: Tales of Literary Detective*. The title page has a different subtitle, "On the Trail of Anonymous," which appeared on the hardcover edition, suggesting both Foster's correct assessment of the anonymous author of *Primary Colors* and his broader search for often unknown authors. For a detailed account of the "Funeral Elegy," consult Foster's *Elegy by W. S.* (1989). In his lively *The Shakespeare Wars*, Ron Rosenbaum dissects Foster's claim (and attacks Foster's techniques), not just telling the story of how the poem has been discredited definitively but also speaking of Rosenbaum's initial impulse (which he published) that the "Funeral Elegy" didn't sound Shakespearean. He also describes, and takes great glee in, Foster's recantation. All these accounts remain fascinating because of their academic and cultural jockeying for what can and can't be Shakespeare.

20. Mallon, *Stolen Words*, 24.

21. Ireland's actions are recounted widely, in everything from MacDougall's *Hoaxes* to Stewart's *Boy Who Would Be Shakespeare* to more academic studies, including Rosenblum's *Practice to Deceive*. Ireland also would fabricate his own origins, providing a deed gifting property from Shakespeare to an earlier William-Henry Ireland, who, the forgery claimed, had saved Shakespeare from drowning in the

River Thames. Not yet eighteen, Ireland's hoax would unravel in front of everyone during a sold-out performance of *Vortigern*, half the audience rooting for him, the rest mocking and laughing. The tipping point may have been the well-known lead actor, John Kemble, who, convinced of the play's counterfeit nature, played his line "And when this solemn mockery is o'er" for laughs. Some say that Kemble wanted to schedule the opening for April Fools' Day. Yet MacDougall's *Hoaxes* relates that the affair was "popularly called 'the immoral hoax of Ireland' or 'Ireland's sin,'" indicating the high stakes involved.

22. Stewart, *Boy Who Would Be Shakespeare*, 83.

23. "Since the 1850s, 77 people have been suggested as the likely author, with Francis Bacon, Edward de Vere—the 17th Earl of Oxford—and Christopher Marlowe the most popular candidates, and Queen Elizabeth I among the most outlandish," the London *Guardian* reports. Not only was Shakespeare prolific, but so too the number of others claimed to have written as him. See Dalya Alberge, "Shakespeare Scholars Unite to See off Claims of the 'Bard Deniers,'" *Guardian*, 30 March 2013; www.theguardian.com/culture/2013/mar/30/shakespeare-scholars-silence-doubters (accessed 8 January 2015). As the *Guardian* describes, the 2013 book *Shakespeare Beyond Doubt*, written by twenty-two scholars (including scholars of other writers accused of being Shakespeare), tries turning the tide: "The academics feel the anti-Shakespeare campaign has intensified lately, and that the elevation of Shakespeare authorship studies to master's degree status has been the final straw. Three eminent experts on Bacon, Oxford and Marlowe are among the Shakespeareans who demonstrate in a series of essays precisely why only Shakespeare could have written his plays and poems, apart from his collaborations." See Shakespeare's Beehive website and George Koppelman and Daniel Wechsler, *Shakespeare's Beehive: An Annotated Elizabethan Dictionary Comes to Light*, 2nd ed. (2015), for details on Shakespeare's possible dictionary.

24. Mallon, *Stolen Words*, 237. In this postscript Mallon also provides suggestions for preventing plagiarism (or at least its recidivism), including publicizing plagiarism. This seems to have worked at least in part with Wheeler, whose name was recognized by several he later tried to defraud.

25. Ibid.

22. Michael Brown's Body

1. See www.politico.com/media/story/2016/07/rnc-melania-trump-plagiarism-jarrett-hill-004680.

2. For an overview of "word is bond," from the idea's biblical origins to its hip-hop heyday, consult *Slate* (www.slate.com/blogs/lexicon_valley/2016/07/19/your_word_is_your_bond_history_and_origins_from_matthew_to_hip_hop.html) or just listen to some Wu Tang.

3. Jonathan Lethem, "The Ecstasy of Influence: A Plagiarism," in *The Ecstasy of Influence*, 96. The essay first appeared in *Harper's* in 2007.

4. Ibid., 112.

5. Ibid., 96.

6. Ibid., 112.

7. Plagiarist poets Andrew Slattery and Graham Nunn were both revealed to have plagiarized their "own" poems both on the same day: Friday, 13 September 2013. Stealing everyone from Emily Dickinson to Sylvia Plath, Slattery "has won or been commended in more than 30 poetry prizes in Australia and Britain," reports the *Sydney Morning Herald*; he "received thousands of dollars in poetry prize-money, and two Australia Council grants in 2008 and 2010, each worth $15,000." Susan Wyndham, "Plagiarism the Word That Cannot Be Uttered," *Sydney Morning Herald*, 13 September 2013; www.smh.com.au/entertainment/books/plagiarism -the-word-that-cant-be-uttered-20130913-2tpha.html#ixzz2n1IntanX.

8. Many of these uncoverings were the work of Ira Lightman, regularly now called a literary sleuth (and who was plagiarized from himself), and a flashpoint and key researcher in the field. Lightman seems to have some sympathy for Ward, though it may be belied by the numbers when he says, "The plagiarism was a sideline, two dozen or so, among a few hundred poems. He wrote daily, which I admire, and which improves the technique. It annoyed me that people would say that they'd bet every Christian Ward poem was a plagiarism. It's not true. He never gathered a plagiarism into a collection published in his name. They were all in magazines and competitions." "The Write Out Loud interview: Ira Lightman," 9 June 2013, Write Out Loud; www.writeoutloud.net/public/blog entry.php?blogentryid=37078.

9. Both quotes referenced in the Write Out Loud website, "Christian Ward's Plagiarism 'Mistakes': Is This No. 4?," www.writeoutloud.net/public/blogentry .php?blogentryid=33701.

10. Paisley Rekdal, "On Plagiarism: An Open Letter to Christian Ward," *Anapessimistic* blog, 15 January 2013; http://paisleyrekdal.blogspot.com/2013/01/on -plagiarism-open-letter-to-christian.html.

11. Kenneth Goldsmith, "I Look to Theory Only When I Realize That Somebody Has Dedicated Their Entire Life to a Question I Have Only Fleetingly Considered," *Poetry*, April 2015. Goldsmith's *Poetry* essay, reprinted in part from an essay titled "Postlude: I Love Speech," in Marjorie Perloff and Craig Dworkin, *The Sound of Poetry/The Poetry of Sound* (2009), had the ironic timing to appear within weeks of the "Michael Brown" controversy and in the same issue featuring the "BreakBeat Poets," mostly young poets of color.

12. Goldsmith's Facebook post about the controversy, quoted in Priscilla Frank, "What Happened When a White Male Poet Read Michael Brown's Autopsy as Poetry," Huffington Post, 17 March 2015; www.huffingtonpost.com/2015/03/17 /kenneth-goldsmith-michael-brown_n_6880996.html.

13. Ibid.

14. See gringpo.com and twitter.com/gringpo.

15. Goldsmith, "I Look to Theory," quoting Cory Doctorow.

16. As reported by the website Write Out Loud: "Christian Ward's Plagiarism 'Mistakes': Is This No. 4?"

17. Toby Fitch, "Plagiarism Scandal Has Revealed an Ugly Side of Australian Poetry," *Guardian*, 23 September 2013; www.theguardian.com/commentisfree/2013/sep/23/australian-poetry-plagiarism.

18. Fisher, introduction to Ireland, *The Abbess*, x.

19. Carmer, *Stars Fell on Alabama*, xxiii.

20. Ibid., xiv.

21. Ibid., xii.

22. Ibid., 26, 185.

23. Vice, *Bear Bryant Funeral Train*, 16–17.

Coda. The Age of Euphemism

1. "Hoax of mine own." See Ezekiel 29:3: "Speak, and say, Thus saith the Lord GOD; Behold, I *am* against thee, Pharaoh king of Egypt, the great dragon that lieth in the midst of his rivers, which hath said, My river *is* mine own, and I have made *it* for myself." Regarding "copyright traps": http://mentalfloss.com/article/24027/quick-10-10-fictitious-entries.

2. Henry Alford, "Not a Word," *New Yorker*, 29 August 2005; www.newyorker.com/magazine/2005/08/29/not-a-word.

3. Mary McCarthy reports from Vietnam, *New York Review of Books*, 20 April 1967.

4. Entry for "homemade" from H. Rawson, *Rawson's Dictionary of Euphemisms and Other Doubletalk* (Chicago: Hugh Rawson, 2002). Retrieved from https://proxy.library.emory.edu/login?url=http://search.credoreference.com.proxy.library.emory.edu/content/entry/rawdeod/homemade/0.

5. Max J. Rosenthal, "A Brief History of Donald Trump's 9/11 Controversies," *Mother Jones*, 9 September 2016. This false Trump claim was investigated and proved false by the *Washington Post* and others. It also makes little sense given how many victims of the Twin Towers commuted from New Jersey; www.motherjones.com/politics/2016/09/brief-history-donald-trumps-911-controversies.

6. This false conspiracy theory is largely based on the fact that World Trade Center Tower 7 fell later owing to fire; www.dailymail.co.uk/news/article-2056088/Footage-kills-conspiracy-theories-Rare-footage-shows-WTC-7-consumed-fire.html.

7. Bowers, *Words for the Taking*, 110.

8. Ibid., 114–15.

9. Ibid., 122.

10. Year of the Online Hoax, CNN; www.cnn.com/2013/12/03/tech/web/web-hoaxes-2013. Year of the Viral Hoax, *Washington Post*; www.washingtonpost.com

/news/the-intersect/wp/2014/12/18/the-15-worst-internet-hoaxes-of-2014-and
-where-the-pranksters-are-now.

11. "What Was Fake on the Internet This Week: And Why This Is the Final Column," *Washington Post*, 18 December 2015; www.washingtonpost.com/news/the-intersect/wp/2015/12/18/what-was-fake-on-the-internet-this-week-why-this-is-the-final-column.

12. William J. Astore, "All the Euphemisms We Use for 'War.'" *Nation*. 15 April 2016; www.thenation.com/article/all-the-euphemisms-we-use-for-war.

13. www.nytimes.com/2016/11/16/arts/post-truth-defeats-alt-right-as-oxfords-word-of-the-year.html.

14. As Ruth Shalit would say, "I am a recovering Nexisholic," referring to her allegedly confusing her notes with online LexisNexis searches as the source of her plagiarism. Even in what is surely a joke, Shalit's joking sheds light on the very ways confession gets mixed with addiction when it comes to plagiarism. Shalit quoted in Cloud, "Baby Ruth."

15. Carolyn See, *Dreaming: Hard Luck and Good Times in America* (1996). Issued as a Random House e-book in 2011. Thanks to Ben Yagoda's *Memoir* for first leading me to this quote.

16. All were the subject of an exhibition I curated based on their lives and the Black Sun Press called *Shadows of the Sun* that ran at Emory University from 2011 to 2012. Peabody wedded the former Mary "Polly" Phelps Jacobs, who would later shock Boston by having an affair with and then going on to marry fellow blueblood Harry Crosby, the nephew of financier J. P. Morgan; renamed Caresse (the shocks kept coming), she and Harry would help found the Black Sun Press, one of the centers of Paris expatriate life. See Geoffrey Wolff, *Black Sun* (New York: New York Review of Books, 2003). Originally 1976. If Caresse Crosby's two husbands were unalike in temperament, they both shared the destructive love of drink that doomed many of their Lost Generation. Their lives together, and Caresse's life after Harry's suicide in 1929, could fill yet another book, and just might.

17. "Foreword to the First Edition," *Alcoholics Anonymous: The Story of How Many Thousands of Men and Women Have Recovered from Alcoholism* (New York: Works Publishing, 1939). "Preface to the first edition" is most easily found at www.aa.org/bigbookonline/en_fre.cfm.

18. See, *Dreaming*, 57.

19. David Rorvik, *In His Image*, 11.

20. Nicholas Kulish, "Author, 17, Says It's 'Mixing,' Not Plagiarism," *New York Times*, 11 February 2010.

21. Harriet Torry, "Another German Minister Felled by Plagiarism Claims," *Wall Street Journal*, 11 February 2013; "Former German foreign minister latest to face plagiarism charge," Reuters, 29 September 2013.

22. The list is taken from *Rawson's Dictionary* and refers in part to euphemisms for

foodstuffs (such as "Hoover hog" for armadillo). For a definition of "pork/pork-barrel politics," see D. Watts, *Dictionary of American Government and Politics* (2010). Retrieved from https://proxy.library.emory.edu/login?url=http://search.credoreference.com .proxy.library.emory.edu/content/entry/eupamgov/pork_pork_barrel_politics/0.

23. Lewiston quoted in Holtman, *Freak Show Man*, 190. See Bogdan, *Freak Show*, 195. Lewiston the showman seems at least a bit retrospectively embarrassed by his "Darkest Africa" act from 1933: "Who could question what I had to say? Wasn't I the great 'Major' Lewiston, one of the foremost authorities on Africa? If anybody knew what he was talking about, it was I. Since that time, I've often wondered how many arguments my 'facts' generated. Even those who didn't actually pay to see our show were exposed to some of the so-called African lore which was pure hokum." Holtman, *Freak Show Man*, 190.

24. Christopher Mele, "Ringling Bros. and Barnum & Bailey Circus to End Its 146-Year Run," *New York Times*, 28 August 2016; www.nytimes.com/2017/01/14/us /ringling-bros-and-barnum-bailey-circus-closing-may.html?_r=0.

25. Jonathan Mahler and Steve Eder, "'No Vacancies' for Blacks: How Donald Trump Got His Start, and Was First Accused of Bias," *New York Times*, 28 August 2016; www.nytimes.com/2016/08/28/us/politics/donald-trump-housing-race.html ?_r=0.

26. Woody Guthrie, "Old Man Trump," http://woodyguthrie.org/Lyrics/Old _Man_Trump.htm. Guthrie would even nickname his home at Beach Haven "Bitch Haven." See Will Kaufman, "Woody Guthrie, 'Old Man Trump' and a Real Estate Empire's Racist Foundations," *The Conversation*, 21 January 2016; https:// theconversation.com/woody-guthrie-old-man-trump-and-a-real-estate-empires -racist-foundations-53026.

Annotated Bibliography

To write about hoaxes in full, to go beyond the shallow clichés you find repeated nearly every April Fools' Day—*Truth is stranger than fiction! Sometimes, people lie*—is to track down the books that often contain them. More often than not, because of their very falsehoods, no matter how popular at the time, the hoax in print form is pulled, pulped, expunged, banished to the Phantom Zone. I am tempted to say, as the hoax *Mutant Message Down Under* does, "I have saved you a trip to the public library by including important historical information. I can also save you a trip to Australia." But who'd want to be saved from either? Readers might be surprised to learn that hardest actually to find are the more recent hoaxes: so many of them end up pulled before being published or are Internet-based that their disappearance is the surest sign of their existence. Finding the hoaxes as close as possible to their original form—books and articles and websites and films—helps us view the hoax not from afar but up close.

Hoaxes, Plagiarisms, Confessions, Early Exposés, and Firsthand Accounts

Alexie, Sherman, ed. *Best American Poetry 2015*. New York: Simon & Schuster, 2015. Contains hoax poem by pretend Asian poet.

Anahareo. *Devil in Deerskins: My Life with Grey Owl*. Edited by Sophie McCall. Winnipeg: University of Manitoba Press, 2014. Originally published 1972.

"Ashe, Penelope" [pseudonym for a host of writers from *Newsday*]. *Naked Came the Stranger*. New York: Lyle Stuart, 1969.

Barker, Nicolas. *The Butterfly Books: An Enquiry into the Nature of Certain Twentieth Century Pamphlets*. London: B. Rota, 1987. A forensic account of Prokosch's forgeries.

Barnum, P. T. *The Humbugs of the World*. London: John Camden Hotten, 1866.

The American edition bears the subtitle *An Account of Humbugs, Delusions, Impositions, Quackeries, Deceits and Deceivers Generally, in All Ages*. New York, 1866.

[Barnum, P. T.]. *The Life of Joice Heth, the Nurse of Gen. George Washington (the Father of our Country,) Now Living at the Astonishing Age of 161 Years, and Weighs Only 46 Pounds*. New-York, 1835.

Biographical Sketch of the Circassian Girl, Zalumma Agra; or, "Star of the East." Chicago: Evening Journal Book and Print, 1868.

Bowers, Neal. *Words for the Taking: The Hunt for a Plagiarist*. New York: W.W. Norton, 1997. Firsthand account of Bowers's poetry being plagiarized by someone calling himself "David Sumner."

"Boyd, William." *Nat Tate: An American Artist, 1928–1960*. Cambridge, UK: 21 Publishing, 1998. Fake biography of a purposefully fake artist by a real writer who was later tapped to write the next James Bond novel.

Bradlee, Ben. *A Good Life: Newspapering and Other Adventures*. New York: Simon & Schuster, 1995. Contains a firsthand account of the Janet Cooke debacle.

[Bynner, Witter, and Arthur Davison Fricke.] *Spectra: A Book of Poetic Experiments by Anne Knish and Emanuel Morgan*. 1916.

Bynner, Witter. *Light Verse and Satires*. New York: Farrar, Straus Giroux, 1978. Introduction by William Jay Smith. This volume of *The Works of Witter Bynner* contains the whole of *Spectra*, plus selections from the virtually impossible-to-find *Pins for Wings* in the voice of Emanuel Morgan.

———. *The Selected Witter Bynner: Poems, Plays, Translations, Prose, and Letters*. Edited by James Kraft. Albuquerque: University of New Mexico Press, 1995. Contains a range of the poems, including the Spectra hoax, as well as "The Story of the Spectric School of Poetry," originally in the serial *Palms* (March 1928).

Carter, Asa. *The Education of Little Tree*. New York: Delacorte Press, 1976.

Carter, John, and Graham Pollard. *An Enquiry into the Nature of Certain Nineteenth Century Pamphlets*. London: Constable; New York: C. Scribner's Sons, 1934. About the famous Thomas Wise forgeries, setting the standard for such investigations (despite its casual racism).

Chapman, Marina. *The Girl with No Name: The Incredible Story of a Child Raised by Monkeys*. With Vanessa James and Lynn Barrett-Lee. New York: Pegasus Books, 2012. All the markings of the hoax, complete with a childhood claiming anonymity and near amnesia, combined with vivid tales of being raised by monkeys.

Conan Doyle, Arthur. *The Coming of the Fairies*. Argument for the veracity of the faked "Cottingley fairy" photographs.

Cramer, James. *Confessions of a Street Addict*. New York: Simon and Schuster, 2002. Contains account of hoaxer Ravi Desai.

[Croly, David Goodman, and George Wakeman]. *Miscegenation: The Theory of the Blending of the Races, Applied to the American White Man and the Negro*. New York: H. Dexter, Hamilton, 1864. A hoax actually published in 1863.

Daniel, Jane. *Bestseller! The $33 Million Verdict, the 20-Year Hoax, the Truth behind the Headlines.* Gloucester, MA: Laughing Gull Press, 2008. The publisher of *Misha* tells her side of many stories. Not as entertaining as it should be.

The Darkening Ecliptic. Poems by Ern Malley. Paintings by Sidney Nolan. Preface by Robert Melville; introduction by Elwyn Lynn. Australia: R Alistair McAlpine, [1974]. One of a thousand copies.

Defonesca, Misha [Monique De Wael]. *Misha: A Mémoire of the Holocaust Years.* Boston: Mt. Ivy Press, 1997. A fake memoir with the most confusing array of copyright holders in history.

Dickson, Lovat. *Half-Breed: The Story of Grey Owl.* London: Peter Davies, 1939. The outing of Grey Owl by his publisher, appearing a year after his death.

Dwyer, David. *Ariana Olisvos: Her Last Works and Days.* [Amherst:] University of Massachusetts Press, 1976. Poems in voice of Olisvos, first submitted as if actually written by the "92-year-old woman poet" to a feminist magazine, which printed them; the book bears a description of the case and rebuttal by the magazine as part of its acknowledgments.

Eskin, Blake. *A Life in Pieces.* London: Aurum Press, 2002. A thoughtful, personal account of the Wilkomirski affair.

Fay, Stephen, Lewis Chester, and Magnus Linklater. *Hoax: The Inside Story of the Howard Hughes–Clifford Irving Affair.* New York: Viking Press, 1972. Precedes Irving and Suskind's own account by a few months.

Fehrenbacher, Don E. *Lincoln in Text and Context: Collected Essays.* Stanford, CA: Stanford University Press, 1987. Contains the most complete and concise account of the hoax Lincoln letters.

Felt, Ivan, and Harris Conklin [Jonathan Lethem and Chris Sorrentino]. *Believeniks! 2005: The Year We Wrote a Book about the Mets.* New York: Doubleday, 2006. A hoax/prank by friends and fiction writers, who gave their alter egos backstories and even a backlist.

Finkel, Michael. *True Story: Murder, Memoir, Mea Culpa.* New York: Harper Perennial, 2006. Fabricator Finkel describes the strange coincidences of his name being used by a murderer on the lam, whom he later befriended. This paperback edition has an updated epilogue.

Fishman, Steve, John Homans, and Adam Moss, eds. *New York Stories: Landmark Writing from Four Decades of "New York" Magazine.* New York: Random House, 2008. Terrific anthology that in many ways includes the day-to-day workings of the New Journalism, including Tom Wolfe's coining the "Me Decade" and Nik Cohn's hoax that spawned the film *Saturday Night Fever.*

Ford, Corey. *Salt Water Taffy; or, Twenty Thousand Leagues Away from the Sea. The Almost Incredible Autobiography of Capt. Ezra Triplett's Seafaring Daughter by June Triplett.* New York: G.P. Putnam's Sons, 1929. Hilarious parody of Joan Lowell's *Cradle of the Deep.*

Freind, Bill, ed. *Scubadivers and Chrysanthemums: Essays on the Poetry of Araki Yasusada.* Bristol: Shearsman Books, 2012. Critical essays, including the first exposés, denials, and accounts of the Yasusada hoax; with works by Eliot Weinberger and Marjorie Perloff.

Frey, James. *A Million Little Pieces*. New York: Nan A. Talese/Doubleday, 2003. Subsequent editions contain brief note about the book's fabulism.

———. *My Friend Leonard*. New York: Riverhead Books, 2005. The paperback has a note about the book's non-nonfictionness, plus several afterwords.

Galluzzo, Leopoldo. *Altre scoverte fatte nella luna dal Sigr. Herschel*. Naples: L. Gatti e Dura, 1836. Italian portfolio of prints imagining not just the lunar surface inspired by the Moon Hoax but also balloon travel there. The Smithsonian holds a copy.

George, William, and Richardson Wright, eds. *Feodor Vladimir Larrovitch: An Appreciation of His Life and Works*. New York: Authors Club, 1918. A hoax/ prank by the Authors Club, complete with illustrations of dried flowers once placed on the fake author's grave.

Gladwell, Malcolm. "Something Borrowed." *New Yorker*. 22 November 2004. "Should a charge of plagiarism ruin your life?": the tagline of Gladwell's account of being plagiarized almost verbatim by a playwright indicates his answer.

Glass, Stephen. *The Fabulist: A Novel*. New York: Simon & Schuster, 2003.

Grey Owl [Archibald Belaney]. *The Tree*. London: Lovat Dickson, 1937. "Illustrated by Grey Owl."

———. *A Book of Grey Owl: Selections from His Wild-Life Stories*. Toronto: Macmillan of Canada, 1971. Reprint of second edition (1941) "by Grey Owl—trapper, guide, blood-brother of the Ojibway, and master storyteller." Author's copy has photograph of "Grey Owl" tipped in.

———. *The Men of the Last Frontier*. London: Country Life; New York: Scribner's, [1931].

———. *Pilgrims of the Wild*. London: Lovat Dickson & Thompson, 1935.

———. *Sajo and the Beaver People*. New York: Scribner's, 1936. A children's books with illustrations by the faker. A fascinating account of the publishing is found in the Scribner's archives at Princeton University.

Gravel, Fern [James Norman Hall]. *Oh Millersville!* Muscatine, Iowa: Prairie Press, 1940. The coauthor of *The Mutiny on the Bounty* crafts what one critic calls "mildest of hoaxes."

Hamilton, Tyler, and Daniel Coyle. *The Secret Race: Inside the Hidden World of the Tour de France*. New York: Bantam Books, 2013. With a new afterword by the authors added after Armstrong's confession of doping to Oprah Winfrey.

Harris, Max, ed. *Angry Penguins*. Ern Malley issue, Autumn 1944 [published May 1944]. First publication of the hoax poet Ern Malley.

Hicklin, Aaron, ed. *The Revolution Will Be Accessorized: "BlackBook" Presents Dispatches from the New Counterculture*. New York: Harper Perennial, 2006. Includes the last of JT Leroy's fabrications.

Howard Hughes Press Conference. Anaheim, California: Mark 56 Records, 1972. LP recording of press conference Hughes gave denouncing the Clifford Irving hoax once and for all.

Ireland, William-Henry. *The Abbess: A Romance. In Four Volumes.* Originally London: Printed for Earle and Hemet, 1799. (Reprinted New York: Arno Press, 1974, with an Introduction by Benjamin Franklin Fisher IV.) A novel by the Shakespeare forger.

————. *The Confessions of William-Henry Ireland. Containing the Particulars of His Fabrication of the Shakspeare [sic] Manuscripts; together with Anecdotes and Opinions (Hitherto Unpublished) of Many Distinguished Persons in the Literary, Political, and Theatrical World.* London: Printed by Ellerton and Byworth for Thomas Goddard, 1805.

Irving, Clifford. *Fake! The Story of Elmyr de Hory the Greatest Art Forger of Our Time.* New York: McGraw-Hill, 1969.

————. *Clifford Irving: What Really Happened; His Untold Story of the Hughes Affair.* New York: Grove Press, 1972. A Zebra Book. This mass-market paperback (*"For the First Time! His Own Story!"*) was later reissued as *Project Octavio*, then further revised into *The Hoax* (1981) under Irving's sole authorship. Later still, *The Hoax* was turned to a decent if not entirely accurate 2007 film with Richard Gere starring as Irving.

[Irving, Clifford.] *Enigma! The New Story of Elmyr De Hory; The Greatest Art Forger of Our Time.* Retold and presented by Ken Talbot. London, ON: ONT, 1991. A piracy of sorts of Irving's *Fake!*

Irving, Clifford, with Richard Suskind. *Project Octavio: The Story of the Howard Hughes Hoax.* London: Allison & Busby Ltd., 1977. This is a later hardcover version of the book *What Really Happened,* with a few final paragraphs of update on the case.

Israel, Lee. *Can You Ever Forgive Me? Memoirs of a Literary Forger.* New York: Simon & Schuster, 2008. Lively firsthand account of Israel's three "trimesters" of forgery.

"Johnson, Anthony Godby." *A Rock and a Hard Place.* Foreword by Paul Monette. Afterword by Fred Rogers. New York: Crown, 1993. Forgery of a dying boy later fictionalized by Armistead Maupin.

Johnson, Kent [as Araki Yasusada]. *Doubled Flowering: From the Notebooks of Araki Yasusada.* New York: Roof Books, 1997.

Johnson, Kent, compiler. "Araki Yasusada: Partial Bibliography." 1998. http://www.lang.nagoya-u.ac.jp/~nagahata/yasusada-bib.html Includes a list of "Kent Johnson" publications, including in *Ironwood* journal under yet another pseudonym.

Johnson, Kent, and Javier Alvarez, eds. *Also, with My Throat, I Shall Swallow Ten Thousand Swords: Araki Yasusada's Letters in English.* By Tosa Motokiyu. Continuation of the Yasusada hoax, with this iteration calling "Motokiyu" the creator of the "fiction"; in all likelihood, Motokiyu, like Yasusada, is Johnson's own creation.

Jones, Margaret B. [Margaret Seltzer]. *Love and Consequences: A Memoir of Hope and Survival.* New York: Riverhead Books, 2008.

Jordan-Smith, Paul. *The Road I Came: Some Recollections and Reflections concerning Changes in American Life and Manners since 1890.* New York: Crown Publishers, 1993. Originally Caldwell, Idaho: Caxton Printers, 1960. Memoir by the long-time literary editor of the *Los Angeles Times*, including a discussion of his short-lived "Disumbrationist" hoax as Russian painter "Pavel Jerdanovitch."

Keane, Walter. *The World of Keane.* [No place:] Creative Books, 1983. A largely imagined memoir by the "fence" and marketer behind the Keane children-with-big-eyes paintings, taking credit for years for his wife Margaret's work.

Khouri, Norma. *Forbidden Love: A harrowing true story of love and revenge in Jordan.* Sydney: Bantam Books, 2003. This retitled edition of *Honor Lost* became a best seller in Australia.

———. *Honor Lost: Love and Death in Modern-Day Jordan.* New York: Atria Books, 2003.

Kirn, Walter. *Blood Will Out: The True Story of a Murder, a Mystery, and a Masquerade.* New York: Liveright, 2014. Nonfiction account of the author's friendship with impostor "Clark Rockefeller."

Knoop, Savannah. *Girl Boy Girl: How I Became JT LeRoy.* New York: Seven Stories Press, 2008. Memoir by the sister-in-law of Laura Albert she recruited to play LeRoy in person.

Knox, Cleone [Magdalen King-Hall]. *The Diary of a Young Lady of Fashion in the Year 1764–1765. By Cleone Knox. Edited by her Kinsman Alexander Blacker Kerr.* A novel purporting to be an eighteenth-century diary.

Koch, Howard. *The Panic Broadcast: Portrait of an Event. With an Introductory Interview with Arthur Clarke and the Complete Text of the Radio Play "Invasion from Mars."* Boston: Little, Brown, 1970. Includes the radio play that started the panic, plus an account of the newspaper responses to Orson Welles's version of *War of the Worlds*.

Krakauer, Jon. *Three Cups of Deceit: How Greg Mortenson, Humanitarian Hero, Lost His Way.* New York: Anchor, 2011.

Landis, Floyd, with Loren Mooney. *Positively False: The Real Story of How I Won the Tour de France.* New York: Simon Spotlight Entertainment, 2007. This is indeed positively false, though it means to say the testing was.

Lehrer, Jonah. *How We Decide.* 2009. Pulled and pulped for inaccuracies.

———. *Imagine.* 2012. Pulled and pulped for plagiarism and inaccuracies.

Leroy, J.T. *Meteors: A story from* The Heart Is Deceitful Above All Things. New York: Bloomsbury, 2001. Offprint pamphlet, a preview or giveaway for the novel.

LeRoy, JT [written by Laura Albert]. *Harold's End.* San Francisco: Last Gasp, December 2004.

———. *The Heart Is Deceitful Above All Things: Stories.* New York: Bloomsbury, 2001. My copy is signed; by whom, I don't know.

———. *Sarah.* New York: Bloomsbury, 2000. The cover describes it as "a novel by JT LeRoy A.K.A. Terminator." Signed on a laid-in piece of paper.

LeRoy, JT, guest editor. "Introduction: Better than Anything I Could Say." *Da Capo Best Music Writing 2005*. Cambridge, MA: Da Capo Press, 2005.

LeRoy, JT [as "Terminator"]. "Baby Doll." *Close to the Bone: Memoirs of Hurt, Rage and Desire*. Laurie Stone, ed. New York: Grove Press, 1997.

Locke, Richard Adams. *The Moon Hoax; or, A Discovery That the Moon Has a Vast Population of Human Beings*. Boston: Gregg Press (division of G. K. Hall), 1975. Introduction by Ormond Seavey. Originally printed by William Gowans, 1859.

Locus Solus. No. II (Summer 1961). "Special Collaborations Issue." Paris. Early reprinting of two Ern Malley poems.

Louys, Pierre. *The Collected Works of Pierre Louys*. Includes *The Songs of Bilitis*, purported to be poems by Bilitis, a Sappho-like figure claimed from the sixth century; caused a scandal upon its first publication.

Lowell, Joan. *The Cradle of the Deep*. New York: Simon & Schuster, 1929. This "unghost-written autobiography," as the book's flaps have it, turned out to have been a hoax.

———. *Gal Reporter*. New York: Farrar and Rinehart, 1933. The sequel to the first hoax, involving another supposed seafaring trip with the author's father.

———. *Promised Land*. New York: Duell Sloan & Pearce, 1952. Perhaps a truer book about Lowell's later life in Brazil with a husband.

Macpherson, James. *Ossian's Fingal*. Poole [UK]: Woodstock Books, 1996. Introduction by Jonathan Wordsworth. Useful introduction to, and faithful facsimile of, the entire 1792 version of the Ossian hoax poem *Fingal* that included Hugh Blair's contemporaneous "Dissertation on the Poems of Ossian, the Son of Fingal." Blair's defense of Ossian is not to be confused with Macpherson's "Dissertation concerning the Poems of Ossian," also found in this 1792 edition.

Macpherson, James, trans. *The Poems of Ossian*. With notes and with an introduction by William Sharp. Edinburgh: John Grant, 1926.

Maechler, Stefan. *The Wilkomirski Affair: A Study in Biographical Truth*. New York: Schocken Books, 2001. Translated from the German by John E. Woods. The definitive account of Binjamin Wilkomirski's hoax, "Including the Text of *Fragments*."

Maliszewski, Paul. *Fakers: Hoaxers, Con Artists, Counterfeiters, and Other Great Pretenders*. New York: New Press, 2008. This book begins with "I, Faker," a confession of the author's own hoaxes, though not all of them.

Maliszewski, Paul, guest editor. *McSweeney's* 8 (2002). Special issue on "the themes of fact and fiction, hoax and prank, truth and its variations."

Malley, Ern [James McAuley and Harold Stewart]. *The Darkening Ecliptic*. Australia. Angry Penguins, 1944. Published after the revelation of Malley as a hoax.

Markham, Q. R. [Quentin Rowan]. *Assassin of Secrets*. Novel withdrawn by publisher after discovering Rowan had plagiarized virtually all the book.

McCabe, Joseph. *Is Spiritualism Based on Fraud? The Evidence Given by Sir A. C.*

Doyle and Others Drastically Examined. London: Watts, [1920.] An account written by a skeptic who engaged Conan Doyle in a public debate.

Messinger, Jean Goodwin. *Hannah: From Dachau to the Olympics and Beyond.* Windor [CO]: White Pelican Press, 2005. Further hoaxing.

Morgan, Emanuel [Witter Bynner]. *Pins for Wings.* [New York:] Sunwise Turn, 1920. Found in the Stuart A. Rose Manuscript, Archives, and Rare Book Library, Emory University, as part of the Raymond Danowski Poetry Library.

Morgan, Marlo. *Mutant Message Down Under.* New York: Harper Perennial, 2004. Tenth anniversary edition.

———. *Mutant Message Downunder.* Lee's Summit, MO: MM Co., [n.d.] First, self-published edition.

Morris, Lloyd. *The Young Idea: An Anthology of Opinion concerning the Spirit and Aims of Contemporary American Literature.* New York: Duffield, 1917. Author's edition of 150 copies. With a study of the Spectrists before they were exposed.

Mortenson, Greg. *Three Cups of Tea: One Man's Mission to Promote Peace, One School at a Time.* New York: Penguin, 2006. See also Jon Krakauer, *Three Cups of Deceit: How Greg Mortenson, Humanitarian Hero, Lost His Way.* Mortenson's book was once subtitled *One Man's Mission to Fight Terrorism, and Build Nations, One School at a Time.*

Nasdijj [Tim Barrus]. *The Blood Runs Like a River Through My Dreams.* New York: Houghton Mifflin, 2000. Hoax written by a "pretendian." With two sequels.

———. *The Boy and the Dog Are Sleeping.* New York: Ballantine Books, 2003. Second in the hoax trilogy.

———. *Geronimo's Bones: A Memoir of My Brother and Me.* New York: Ballantine Books, 2004. "In *Geronimo's Bones,* award-winning author Nasdijj has written a love song to his brother, Tso—short for The Smarter One." Downhill from there.

Partington, Wilfred. *Forging Ahead: The True Story of the Upward Progress of Thomas James Wise, Prince of Book Collectors, Bibliographer Extraordinary, and Otherwise.* New York: G.P. Putnam's Sons, 1939. Well-written and lively account of the most famous forger of the nineteenth century.

Parfrey, Adam, and Cletus Nelson. *Citizen Keane: The Big Lies behind the Big Eyes.* Port Townsend, WA: Feral House, 2014. About Walter Keane's forgeries.

Poe, Edgar Allan. *The Narrative of Arthur Gordon Pym of Nantucket.* New York: Modern Library, 2002. Originally 1838. Poe's only novel, which borrows extensively from Lewis and Clark, among other texts.

———. *Poetry, Tales, and Selected Essays.* New York: Library of America, 1996. Includes the essay "Diddling Considered as One of the Exact Sciences," which is useful for the study of how and how not to hoax.

Prokosch, Frederic. *Voices: A Memoir.* London: Faber & Faber, 1983. Heavily fictionalized "memoir" accompanying his forgery of his "butterfly books."

Psalmanaazaar, George. *An Historical and Geographical Description of Formosa, An Island Subject to the Emperor of Japan. Giving an Account of the Religion Customs,*

Manners, &c. of the Inhabitants. . . . London: Robert Holden & Co. Ltd., 1926. Fascsimile reprint. Originally 1704.

Psalmanazar, George. *Memoirs of ****: Commonly Known by the Name of George Psalmanazar; a Reputed Native of Formosa. Written by himself in order to Be Published after His Death.* 1765. Reprinted: https://itun.es/us/SVmoC.

Randi, James. *An Encyclopedia of Claims, Frauds, and Hoaxes of the Occult and Supernatural.* New York: St. Martin's Press, 1995. "James Randi's Decidedly Skeptical Definitions of Alternate Realities." Randi is an inveterate hoax spot-·ter, having discovered the initial source of the Cottingley fairy photographs.

Reynolds, Quentin. *The Man Who Wouldn't Talk.* New York: Random House, 1953. "The heroic true short of 'the gentle spy'" that turned out to be fake.

Rorvik, David. *In his Image: The Cloning of a Man.* Philadelphia: J.P. Lippincott, 1978. Hoax of the first human clone by a supposed science writer.

Rowan, Quentin. *Bethune Street and Other Writings.* New York: iUniverse, 2007. Self-published; contains some early plagiarism.

———. *Never Say Goodbye.* Portland, OR: Yeti Books, 2012. Memoir including an account of Rowan's plagiarism.

Samuels, David. *The Runner: A True Account of the Amazing Lies and Fantastical Adventures of the Ivy League Impostor James Hogue.* New York: New Press, 2008. Based on a 2001 *New Yorker* article of the same title.

Seal, Mark. *The Man in the Rockefeller Suit: The Astonishing Rise and Spectacular Fall of a Serial Imposter.* New York: Viking, 2011. The first book-length account of impostor "Clark Rockefeller."

Seiffert, Marjorie Allen. *A Woman of Thirty. And Poems of Elijah Hay.* New York: Alfred A. Knopf, 1919. A gathering of poems by "Elijah Hay," Seiffert's Spectra hoax persona, too little discussed.

Sinclair, Upton. "Pavel Jerdanovitch." *Money Writes.* New York: Albert & Charles Boni, 1927. An account of the Jordan–Smith hoax in Sinclair's "study of American literature from the economic point of view."

Smith, William Jay. *The Spectra Hoax.* Ashland, OR: Story Line Press, 2000. Originally 1961. Includes the full text of *Spectra* from 1916.

Stephen, Adrian. *The "Dreadnought" Hoax.* London: Hogarth Press, 1936. Account by one of the members of the hoax twenty-four years after it took place; published by the author's sister, Virginia Woolf, also a participant in the hoax.

Tomar, Dave. *The Shadow Scholar: How I Made a Living Helping College Kids Cheat.* New York: Bloomsbury, 2012. Confession of a term-paper ghostwriter.

Van Pallandt, Baroness Nina. *Nina.* New York: Popular Library, 1973. Account of the Howard Hughes hoax by one of the players.

Vice, Brad. *The Bear Bryant Funeral Train.* Montgomery, AL: River City Publishing, 2007. Reissue (and reordering) of the original University of Georgia Press edition, which was withdrawn and pulped after plagiarism was discovered.

Viswanathan, Kaavya. *How Opal Mehta Got Kissed, Got Wild, and Got a Life: A*

Novel. New York: Little, Brown, 2006. Withdrawn by the publisher after extensive plagiarism discovered.

Welford, Theresa M. *The Paradelle: An Anthology*. Los Angeles: Red Hen Press, 2005. With an introduction, "A Brief History of the Paradelle," by Billy Collins. Anthology of poems in a fake form Collins invented that many took seriously.

Whitely, Opal. *The Story of Opal; The Journal of an Understanding Heart*. Boston: Atlantic Monthly Press, 1920.

Wilkomirski, Binjamin. *Fragments: Memories of a Wartime Childhood*. Translated from the German by Carol Brown Janeway. New York: Schocken, 1996.

Wise, Thomas J. *A Bibliography of the Writings in Prose and Verse of Elizabeth Barrett Browning*. Folkestone and London: Dawsons of Pall Mall, 1970. Originally 1918. Includes Wise's own forgeries of Barrett Browning's books.

Zauzmer, Julie. *Conning Harvard: Adam Wheeler, the Con Artist Who Faked His Way into the Ivy League*. Guilford, CT: Lyons Press, 2012. With additional reporting by fellow Harvard student Xi Xu.

Popular Literature, Critical Studies, and Art

Three kinds of hoaxes, six types of liar, seven deadly unoriginal sins: even many of the reliable academic studies on the hoax fall back on taxonomy; while mimicking science this tends to keep the unruly, factitious form of the hoax far more regulated than it actually is. If taxonomy, the hoax has far more in common with cryptozoology. Those who wish to reduce the hoax to mere taxonomy try to resolve the paradox of our being affected by things that are patently untrue and deceptive by displacing blame from our beliefs onto categories or even the hoaxers themselves. The majority of what follows are items that have contributed to the field, and to my own study, but also for the sake of completeness includes a number of less-than-stellar compendiums of compendiums.

Abramson, Julia. *Learning from Lying: Paradoxes of the Literary Mystification*. Newark: University of Delaware Press, 2005.

Acocella, Joan. *Creating Hysteria: Women and Multiple Personality Disorder*. San Francisco: Jossey-Bass, 1999. Brilliant dissection of the hysteria surrounding multiple personality disorder, Satanic ritual abuse, and recovered memory—and their political implications.

Acton, Harold. *Memoirs of an Aesthete, 1939–1969*. New York: Viking, 1971.

Adams, Percy G.. *Travelers and Travel Liars, 1660–1800*. New York: Dover, 1980. Originally published by the University of California Press, 1962.

Alexander, Elizabeth. *The Venus Hottentot*. Charlottesville: University Press of Virginia, 1990.

Alexie, Sherman. *Smoke Signals*. New York: Hyperion, 1998. Introduction, screenplay, and notes.

Amory, Richard. *Song of the Loon*. San Diego: Greenleaf Classics, 1966.

Arbus, Diane. *Hubert's Museum Work 1958–1963.* New York: Phillips de Pury, 2008. Catalog pulled for reasons detailed in Gibson's *Hubert's Freaks,* listed below.

Diane Arbus Magazine Work. New York: Aperture, 2005.

Armstrong, Lance, with Sally Jenkins. *Every Second Counts.* New York: Broadway Books, 2003.

Ashford, Daisy. *The Young Visiters.* New York: George H. Doran, 1919. With preface by J. M. Barrie. Many suspected Barrie of authoring this novel by a nine-year-old, but the adult Ashford went on to publish several other novels.

Atwood, Margaret. *In Other Worlds: SF and the Human Imagination.* New York: Random House, 2011.

Baker, Michael. *The Doyle Diary: The Last Great Conan Doyle Mystery. With a Holmesian Investigation into the strange and curious case of Charles Altamont Doyle.* New York: Paddington Press, 1978.

Bakhtin, Mikhail. *Rabelais and His World.* Translated by Hélène Iswolsky. Cambridge, MA: MIT Press, 1968.

Baldwin, James. *Giovanni's Room.* New York: Dial Press, 1956.

Barnum, P. T. *The Life of P. T. Barnum.* New York: Redfield, 1855.

Barrie, J. M. *The Annotated Peter Pan: The Centennial Edition.* Edited by Maria Tatar. New York: W. W. Norton, 2011. *Peter Pan* has a long bibliographic history, starting as a character in *The Little White Bird* (1902); then the well-known play; next, *Peter Pan in Kensington Gardens* (1906, reprinting the excerpt from *White Bird*), and then as a novel called *Peter and Wendy* (1911), which is reprinted in this *Annotated* edition, and better known (and eventually published) as simply *Peter Pan.*

Barron, Stephanie, ed. *"Degenerate Art": The Fate of the Avant-Garde in Nazi Germany.* Los Angeles: Los Angeles County Museum of Art; New York: Harry N. Abrams, 1991.

Barrus, Tim. *Anywhere, Anywhere.* Pound Ridge, NY: Knights Press, 1987.

———. *Genocide: The Anthology.* Pound Ridge, NY: Knights Press, 1988.

———. *Mineshaft.* Cleveland, Ohio: Magcorp/Ram Books, 1984.

———. *My Brother, My Lover: A Novel.* San Francisco: Gay Sunshine Press, 1985.

Beck, Kathrine. *Opal: A Life of Enchantment, Mystery, and Madness.* New York: Viking, 2003.

Beck, Richard. *We Believe the Children: A Moral Panic in the 1980s.* New York: PublicAffairs, 2015.

Bede, Elbert. *Fabulous Opal Whiteley: From Logging Camp to Princess of India.* Portland: Binfords & Mort, 1954. This scarce book pitched to young people tells Opal's story from the perspective of a newspaperman who covered Opal locally before her national fame.

Bell, Quentin. *Virginia Woolf: A Biography.* New York: Quality Paperback Book Club, 1992. Originally 1972. Contains a brief account of the "Dreadnought hoax" and a surviving fragment of Woolf's only account of the hoax, originally given as a talk in 1940.

Berlin, Isaiah. "The Counter-Enlightenment." *Against the Current: Essays in the History of Ideas*. New York: Viking Press, 1980.

Bernstein, Robin. *Racial Innocence: Performing American Childhood from Slavery to Civil Rights*. New York: New York University Press, 2011.

Billinghurst, Jane. *Grey Owl: The Many Faces of Archie Belaney*. Vancouver/Toronto: Greystone Books, 1999. An illustrated biography.

Biskind, Peter, ed. *My Lunches with Orson: Conversations between Henry Jaglom and Orson Welles*. New York: Metropolitan Books, 2013.

Blair, Jayson. *Burning Down My Masters' House: My Life at the New York Times*. New York: New Millennium, 2004.

Blyth, Robert J., Andrew Lambert, and Jan Rüger, eds. *The Dreadnought and the Edwardian Age*. Farnham, UK: Ashgate, 2011.

Bogdan, Robert. *Freak Show: Presenting Human Oddities for Amusement and Profit*. Chicago: University of Chicago Press, 1988. The definitive book on the subject, and one of the foundational texts of disability studies.

Braude, Ann. *Radical Spirits: Spiritualism and Women's Rights in Nineteenth-Century America*. Boston: Beacon Press, 1989.

Brooks, David. *The Sons of Clovis: Ern Malley, Adoré Floupette and a Secret History of Australian Poetry*. St. Lucia: University of Queensland Press, 2011. Though I came to it late in my writing, this dense study argues the connections between Malley and Floupette, an earlier *Symboliste* hoax.

Browder, Laura. *Slippery Characters: Ethnic Impersonators and American Identities*. Chapel Hill: University of North Carolina Press, 2000.

Brunvald, Jan Harold. *Encyclopedia of Urban Legends*. New York: W. W. Norton, 2001. Useful entries, including one distinguishing urban legends from hoaxes.

Bryant, Howard. *Shut Out: A Story of Race and Baseball in Boston*. Boston: Beacon Press, 2002. Has a great, detailed summary of the Charles Stuart case and an overall sensitive account of Boston's racial divides.

Burkett, B. G., and Glenna Whitley. *Stolen Valor: How the Vietnam Generation Was Robbed of Its Heroes and Its History*. Dallas: Verity Press, 1998. The "Rambo" and "Would I Lie to You?" chapters are especially edifying.

Burton, Sarah. *Impostors: Six Kinds of Liar*. London: Viking, 2000. Cover tag line reads "True Tales of Deception." A surfacey recounting, sans notes.

Bynner, Witter, and Kiang Kang-Hu. *The Jade Mountain: A Chinese Anthology. Being Three Hundred Poems of the T'ang Dynasty, 618–906*. Translated by Witter Bynner from the texts of Kiang Kang-Hu. New York: Knopf, 1929.

Capote, Truman. *In Cold Blood: A True Account of a Multiple Murder and Its Consequences*. New York: Vintage Books, 1994. Originally published 1965, after first being serialized in the *New Yorker*.

Carmer, Carl. *Listen for a Lonesome Drum: A York State Chronicle*. New York: Farrar & Rinehart, 1936. Includes account of famous "Cardiff Giant" hoax.

————. *Stars Fell on Alabama*. New York: Farrar & Rinehart, 1934. Illustrated by Cyrus LeRoy Baldridge. Plagiarized by Brad Vice.

Carey, Peter. *My Life as a Fake*. New York: Random House, 2003. Fictionalized account of the Ern Malley hoax, using the original, as it were, Malley poems.

Cassuto, Leonard. *The Inhuman Race: The Racial Grotesque in American Literature and Culture*. New York: Columbia University Press, 1997.

Chamberlin, J. Edward, and Sander L. Gilman, eds. *Degeneration: The Dark Side of Progress*. New York: Columbia University Press, 1985.

Charney, Noah. *The Art of Forgery: The Mind, Motives and Methods of Master Forgers*. London: Phaidon, 2015.

Chatwin, Bruce. *The Songlines*. New York: Penguin Books, 2012. Introduction by Rory Stewart.

Chéroux, Clément, Andreas Fischer, Pierre Apraxine, Denis Canguilhem, and Sophie Schmit. *The Perfect Medium: Photography and the Occult*. New Haven, CT: Yale University Press, 2005. Definitive English-language version of catalog for exhibition that traveled to the Metropolitan Museum of Art in 2005; largely responsible for the revival of spirit photography as historical and aesthetic topic.

Clarke, Gerald. *Capote: A Biography*. New York: Carroll & Graf, 2005.

Clarke, I. F. *The Tale of the Future: From the Beginning to the Present Day*. London: Library Association, 1972. "An Annotated Bibliography."

Cohen, Kerry. *Loose Girl: A Memoir of Promiscuity*. New York: Hyperion, 2008.

Cole, Sonia. *Counterfeit*. London: John Murray, 1956. Fascinating overview of forgery.

Collins, Suzanne. *The Hunger Games*. New York: Scholastic, 2008. Postapocalyptic source for movies of the same name.

Cook, James W., ed. *The Colossal P. T. Barnum Reader: Nothing Else Like It in the Universe*. Urbana: University of Illinois Press, 2005.

Cooley, John. *Savages and Naturals: Black Portraits by White Writers in Modern American Literature*. Newark: University of Delaware Press, 1982.

Conan Doyle, Arthur. *The Case for Spirit Photography*. New York: George H. Doran Company, 1923. "With corroborative evidence by experienced researchers and photographers."

————. *The History of Spiritualism*. Vol. 1. New York: George H. Doran Company, 1926. With chapters on the Fox Sisters.

————. *The New Revelation*. New York: George H. Doran Company, 1917.

Cott, Jonathan, ed. *Beyond the Looking Glass: Extraordinary Works of Fairy Tale and Fantasy*. New York: Stonehill Publishing, 1973.

Crane, Hart. *Complete Poems & Selected Letters*. New York: Library of America, 2006. Includes "Black Tambourine," later published by forger Frederic Prokosch.

D'Agata, John, and Jim Fingal. *The Lifespan of a Fact*. New York: W. W. Norton, 2012. Fascinating reconstruction of the editing of a nonfiction piece by D'Agata, and its decided fictions.

Davenport-Hines, Richard. *Gothic: Four Hundred Years of Excess, Horror, Evil, and Ruin*. New York: North Point Press, 1998.

de Villiers, Nicholas. *Opacity and the Closet: Queer Tactics in Foucault, Barthes, and Warhol*. Minneapolis: University of Minnesota Press, 2012.

Didi-Huberman, Georges. *Invention of Hysteria: Charcot and the Photographic Iconography of the Salpêtrière*. Translated by Alisa Hartz. Cambridge, MA: MIT Press, 2003.

D'Israeli, Isaac. *Curiosities of Literature*. 2nd ed. 3 volumes. Boston: Lilly, Wait, Colman, and Holden, 1834. Reprinted as *Curiosities of Literature by Isaac Disraeli, with a View of the Life and Writings of the Author by His Son the Right Hon. B. Disraeli*. New York: A. C. Armstrong and Son, 1881. Four volumes in three. From the fourteenth corrected London edition. A popular work whose publishing history spans the first part of the nineteenth century.

Doniger, Wendy. *The Woman Who Pretended to Be Who She Was: Myths of Self-Imitation*. New York: Oxford University Press, 2004.

Dorfles, Gillo. *Kitsch: The World of Bad Taste*. New York: Bell, 1969. Includes foundational essays by Hermann Broch and Clement Greenberg.

Drake, William. *The First Wave: Women Poets in America, 1915–1945*. New York: Macmillan, 1987. With a useful study, and one of the only studies, of Marjorie Allen Seiffert, including her pseudonym as Angela Cypher.

Douglas, Ann. *The Feminization of American Culture*. New York: Farrar, Straus and Giroux, 1977.

Eady, Cornelius. *Brutal Imagination*. New York: Putnam, 2001. Includes the title poem in the voice of the imaginary black man Susan Smith said killed her children.

Ebersole, Gary L. *Captured by Texts: Puritan to Postmodern Images of Indian Captivity*. Charlottesville: University Press of Virginia, 1995.

Ellison, Ralph. *The Collected Essays of Ralph Ellison*. Edited by John F. Callahan. New York: Modern Library, 2003.

Emerson, Ralph Waldo. *English Traits*. Edited by Howard Mumford Jones. [1856] Cambridge, MA: Belknap Press of Harvard University Press, 1966.

Ewick, David. *Japonisme, Orientalism, Modernism: A Bibliography of Japan in English-Language Verse of the Early 20th Century*. 2003 (online): http://themargins.net/bibliography.html.

Farquhar, Michael. *A Treasury of Deception: Liars, Misleaders, Hoodwinkers, and the Extraordinary True Stories of History's Greatest Hoaxes, Fakes, and Frauds*. New York: Penguin, 2005. General overview with basic bibliography.

Farrer, J.A. *Literary Forgeries*. London: Longmans, Green, 1907. A terrific "survey" of the field, now largely forgotten. With an introduction by Andrew Lang.

Ferrante, Elena. *Frantumaglia: A Writer's Journey*. Translated by Ann Goldstein. New York: Europa Editions, 2016.

Fiedler, Leslie A. *Freaks: Myths and Images of the Secret Self*. New York: Simon and Schuster, 1978.

————. *Love and Death in the American Novel*. Rev. ed. New York: Stein & Day, 1966.

————. *Waiting for the End*. New York: Stein and Day, 1964.

Fish, Laura. *Strange Music*. London: Jonathan Cape, 2008. A novel of Elizabeth Barrett Browning and Jamaica, personifying her poem "Runaway Slave."

Follett, Barbara Newhall. *The House without Windows; & Eepersip's Life There*. New York: Knopf, 1927. Well-received debut novel by the nine-year-old author.

————. *Voyage of the Norman D; as told to the cabin-boy*. New York: Knopf, 1928. Even rarer follow-up, about a sea journey with her mother, published when she was thirteen years old.

Foster, Don. *Author Unknown: Tales of a Literary Detective*. New York: Henry Holt, 2000.

Frankfurt, Harry G. *On Bullshit*. Princeton, NJ: Princeton University Press, 2005. A useful introduction.

Franklin, Ruth. *A Thousand Darknesses: Lies and Truth in Holocaust Fiction*. New York: Oxford University Press, 2011.

Friedlander, Max. *On Art and Connoisseurship*. Boston: Beacon Press, 1942. Foundational text not read nearly enough. Includes the essay "On Forgeries."

Frost, Linda. *Never One Nation: Freaks, Savages, and Whiteness in U.S. Popular Culture, 1850–1877*. Minneapolis: University of Minnesota Press, 2005.

Frost, O. W. *Joaquin Miller*. New York: Twayne, 1967.

Fruman, Norman. *Coleridge, the Damaged Archangel*. New York: George Braziller, 1971. A full account of (and assault on) Coleridge's plagiarisms.

Gaige, Amity. *Schroder*. New York: Twelve, 2013. A novel based on the life of "Clark Rockefeller."

Garber, Marjorie. *Shakespeare's Ghost Writers: Literature as Uncanny Causality*. New York: Metheun, 1987.

Gibson, Gregory. *Hubert's Freaks: The Rare Book Dealer, the Times Square Talker, and the Lost Photos of Diane Arbus*. Orlando, FL: Harcourt, 2008.

Gillman, Susan. *Blood Talk: American Race Melodrama and the Culture of the Occult*. Chicago: University of Chicago Press, 2003.

Goodman, Matthew. *The Sun and the Moon: The Remarkable True Account of Hoaxers, Showmen, Dueling Journalists, and Lunar Man-Bats in Nineteenth-Century New York*. New York: Basic Books, 2008.

Gordon, Avery F. *Ghostly Matters: Haunting and the Sociological Imagination*. Minneapolis: University of Minnesota Press, 1997.

Gould, Stephen Jay. *The Mismeasure of Man*. Revised and expanded. New York: W.W. Norton: 1996. Originally 1981.

Greenfield, Robert M. *Dreamer's Journey: The Life and Writings of Frederic Prokosch*. Newark: University of Delaware Press, 2010. Only comprehensive look at Prokosch.

Gribbin, John, with Mary Gribbin. *Einstein's Masterwork: 1915 and the General Theory of Relativity*. New York: Pegasus Books, 2016.

Hagedorn, Jessica. *Dream Jungle*. Fictionalized account of the "discovery" of the Tasaday peoples in the Philippines.

Hall, Jacquelyn Dowd. *Revolt against Chivalry: Jessie Daniel Ames and the Women's Campaign against Lynching*. New York: Columbia University Press, 1993.

Hammond, Brean, ed. *Double Falsehood*. The Arden Shakespeare. A critical edition, with crucial intro, of play attributed to Shakespeare and written in collaboration. London: Metheun Drama, 2010.

Harris, Neil. *Humbug: The Art of P. T. Barnum*. Boston: Little, Brown, 1973.

Harris, Robert. *Selling Hitler: The Extraordinary Story of the Con Job of the Century—the Faking of the Hitler "Diaries."* New York: Pantheon, 1986. Definitive and lively.

Healy, Chris. *Forgetting Aborigines*. Sydney: University of New South Wales Press, 2008.

Hemley, Robin. *A Field Guide for Immersion Writing: Memoir, Journalism, and Travel*. Athens: University of Georgia Press, 2012.

———. *Invented Eden: The Elusive, Disputed History of the Tasaday*. Lincoln: University of Nebraska Press, 2006. With a new afterword by the author.

Heyward, Michael. *The Ern Malley Affair*. London: Faber & Faber, 1993. Terrific account of Australia's fake poet laureate.

Holmes, Robert. *Coleridge: Early Visions*. New York: Pantheon, 1988. First volume of Holmes's brilliant biography, including early discussions of Coleridge's plagiarism continued in part two.

———. *Coleridge: Darker Reflections, 1804–1834*. New York: Pantheon, 1999.

Holtman, Jerry. *Freak Show Man: The Autobiography of Harry Lewiston as told to Jerry Holtman*. Los Angeles: Holloway House, 1968. Important resource by a consummate sideshow man.

Horowitz, Mitch. *Occult America: White House Séances, Ouija Circles, Masons and the Secret Mystic History of Our Nation*. New York: Bantam Books, 2009.

Husseini, Rana. *Murder in the Name of Honor: The True Story of One Woman's Heroic Fight against an Unbelievable Crime*. Oxford: Oneworld Publications, 2009. Journalist credited with highlighting honor killings; includes account of Khouri's *Forbidden Love* hoax.

Hustvedt, Asti. *Medical Muses: Hysteria in Nineteenth-Century Paris*. New York: W. W. Norton, 2011. Great overview of Charcot and the Salpêtrière, with a focus on the women patients themselves.

Irving, Clifford, and Herbert Burkholz. *Spy: The Story of Modern Espionage*. New York: Macmillan, 1969.

Jackinson, Alex. *The Romance of Publishing: An Agent Recalls Thirty-Three Years with Authors and Editors*. New York: Cornwall Books, 1987. His history in publishing includes various Howard Hughes projects and "That Book by Clifford Irving."

Jaher, David. *The Witch of Lime Street: Séance, Seduction, and Houdini in the Spirit World*. New York: Crown, 2015. A fairly good overview of the spiritualism vogue of the 1920s (though without a footnote in sight).

Jolly, Martyn. *Faces of the Living Dead: The Belief in Spirit Photography*. West New York, NJ: Mark Batty Publisher, 2006.

Jones, Mark, ed. *Fake? The Art of Deception*, London: British Museum Publications, 1990. What's with titles called *Fake* and their love of punctuation? *Pranks!* too.

Juno, Andrea, and V. Vale, eds. *RE/Search #11: Pranks!* San Francisco: Re/Search Publications, 1988. An interesting take on related phenomena.

Kaplan, Louis. *The Strange Case of William Mumler, Spirit Photographer*. Minneapolis: University of Minnesota Press, 2008.

Karr, Mary. *The Art of Memoir*. New York: HarperCollins, 2015. With a terrific manifesto against fake memoirs.

Katsoulis, Melissa. *Telling Tales: A History of Literary Hoaxes*. London: Constable, 2009. Published in the United States as *Literary Hoaxes: An Eye-Opening History of Famous Frauds* (New York: Skyhorse, 2009).

Keanie, Andrew. *The Oxford Handbook of Samuel Taylor Coleridge*. Oxford: Oxford University Press, 2009. 435–454. Solid overview of the arguments around Coleridge, including "Coleridge and Plagiarism."

Keats, Jonathon. *Forged: Why Fakes Are the Great Art of Our Age*. New York: Oxford University Press, 2013.

Keevak, Michael. *The Pretended Asian: George Psalmanazar's Eighteenth-Century Formosan Hoax*. Detroit: Wayne State University Press, 2004.

Kenner, Hugh. *The Counterfeiters: An Historical Comedy*. Normal [IL]: Dalkey Archive Press, 2005. With drawings by Guy Davenport.

Kerr, Howard, and Charles L. Crow. *The Occult in America: New Historical Perspectives*. Urbana: University of Illinois Press, 1983.

Kinney, David. *The Dylanologists: Adventures in the Land of Bob*. New York: Simon & Schuster, 2014. The vagaries of obsessive Dylan fans, including those who chart the sources of *Chronicles*, his memoir that may be a mashup—a fact I'd heard about already from my Dylanologist friends.

Kooijman, Jaap. *Fabricating the Absolute Fake: America in Contemporary Pop Culture*. Amsterdam: Amsterdam University Press, 2008.

Kosinski, Jerzy. *The Art of the Self: Essays à propos "Steps."* New York: Scientia-Factum, 1968.

———. *The Hermit of 69th Street: The Working Papers of Norbert Kosky*. New York: Seaver Books, 1988.

———. *Notes of the Author on "The Painted Bird": 1965*. New York: Scientia-Factum, 1967. Self-published pamphlet "written in English as an appendix to be translated for the German-language edition of *The Painted Bird*." Source of many of the questions surrounding the autobiographical claims of the novel.

———. *Oral Pleasure: Kosinski as Storyteller*. Edited by Barbara Tepa Lupack and Kiki Kosinski. New York: Grove, 2012.

———. *The Painted Bird*. Boston: Houghton Mifflin, 1965. A novel of the Holocaust. First edition contains an afterword, later removed, that more strongly suggested an autobiographical nature. This should not be confused with the "Afterward" that appears in the current paperback editions.

———. *Steps*. New York: Vintage, 1988. Originally 1968.

Kurz, Otto. *Fakes*. 2nd rev. and enlarged ed. New York: Dover, 1967. "The *definitive* work on art fakes in English"—meaning the book, not the fakes, are in English.

Lang, Andrew, ed. *The Pink Fairy Book*. London: Folio Society, 2007.

Lehman, David. *The Big Question*. Ann Arbor: University of Michigan Press, 1995. Includes review and recounting of the Ern Malley poetry hoax.

Lejeune, Philippe. *On Autobiography*. Edited and with a foreword by Paul John Eakin. Translated by Katherine Leary. Minneapolis: University of Minnesota Press, 1989.

———. *On Diary*. Translated by Kathy Durnin. Manoa: University of Hawai'i Press, 2007.

Lepore, Jill. *The Story of America: Essays on Origins*. Princeton, NJ: Princeton University Press, 2012.

Lethem, Jonathan. *The Ecstasy of Influence: Nonfictions, etc.* New York: Vintage Books, 2012. Influential title essay first appeared in *Harper's* in 2007.

Lewis, Jim. *Sister: A Novel*. St. Paul, MN: Graywolf Press, 1993. Beautiful book plagiarized by Quentin Rowan (even before he became "Q. R. Markham").

Lewis, Robin Coste. *The Voyage of the Sable Venus*. New York: Knopf, 2015. Poems.

Lindberg, Gary. *The Confidence Man in American Literature*. New York: Oxford University Press, 1982.

Litwack, Leon. *Trouble in Mind: Black Southerners in the Age of Jim Crow*. New York: Vintage, 1999.

Lopez, Jonathan. *The Man Who Made Vermeers: Unvarnishing the Legend of Master Forger Han van Meegeren*. Boston: Mariner Books, 2009. Sophisticated study.

Loxton, Daniel, and Donald R. Porthero. *Abominable Science! Origins of the Yeti, Nessie, and Other Famous Cryptids*. New York: Columbia University Press, 2013.

MacDougall, Curtis D. *Hoaxes*. Rev. and expanded ed. 1940. New York: Dover, 1958. The most comprehensive and reliable account of hoaxes from antiquity to World War II, as well as their causes.

Macintyre, Ben. *Operation Mincemeat: The True Spy Story That Changed the Course of World War II*. London: Bloomsbury, 2010.

Malcolm, Janet. *The Journalist and the Murderer*. New York: Vintage Books, 1990.

Mallon, Thomas. *Stolen Words: The Classic Book on Plagiarism*. San Diego: Harvest Book/Harcourt, 2001. Originally published in 1989, this edition revised with an afterword about the Internet.

Mansfield, Stephen. *Lincoln's Battle with God: A President's Struggle with Faith and What It Meant for America*. Nashville: Thomas Nelson, 2012.

Martin, Charles D. *The White African American Body: A Cultural and Literary Exploration*. New Brunswick, NJ: Rutgers University Press, 2002.

Maupin, Armistead. *The Night Listener: A Novel*. New York: HarperCollins, 2000. Based on the case of "Anthony Godby Johnson."

Maurer, David W. *The Big Con: The Story of the Confidence Man.* Introduction by Luc Sante. New York: Anchor Books, 1999. Originally published in 1940.

Max, D. T. *Every Love Story Is a Ghost Story: A Life of David Foster Wallace.* New York: Viking Penguin, 2012.

Maynard, Nettie Colburn. *Was Abraham Lincoln a Spiritualist? or, Curious Revelations from the Life of a Trance Medium.* Philadelphia: Rufus C. Hartranft, 1891. Ends with nearly twenty pages of "Spirit Poems" dictated through Maynard's mediumship.

Mayo, Herbert. *Popular Superstitions and the Truths Contained Therein, with an Account of Mesmerism.* Philadelphia: Lindsay and Blakiston, 1852.

McGirr, Lisa. *The War On Alcohol.* New York: W.W. Norton, 2015.

Melandri, Lisa, ed. *Mickalene Thomas: Origin of the Universe.* Santa Monica, CA: Santa Monica Museum of Art, [2012]. With essay by Sarah E. Lewis.

Menand, Louis. *The Metaphysical Club: A Story of Ideas in America.* New York: Farrar, Straus and Giroux, 2001.

Mendelsohn, Daniel. *Waiting for the Barbarians: Essays from the Classics to Pop Culture.* New York: New York Review Books, 2012. See especially the foreword and "But Enough about Me (The Memoir Craze)."

Meyers, Jeffrey, ed. *Robert Lowell: Interviews and Memoirs.* Ann Arbor: University of Michigan Press, 1988.

Miss Morning Glory [Yone Noguchi]. *The American Diary of a Japanese Girl.* Illustrated by Genjiro Yeto. New York: Frederic A. Stokes, 1902. The first novel ever published in English by a Japanese American writer, an influential figure on Western modernism. With a rare sequel, *The American Letters of a Japanese Parlor-Maid.*

Mnookin, Seth. *Hard News: Twenty-One Brutal Months at the New York Times and How They Changed the American Media.* New York: Random House, 2004. A terrific account of coverage by the *Times* and the paper's well-earned Pulitzers after the World Trade Center attacks, and its subsequent difficulties during the Jayson Blair affair.

Moore, Marianne. *Becoming Marianne Moore: The Early Poems, 1907–1924.* Edited by Robin G. Schulze. Berkeley: University of California Press, 2002.

Murray, Timothy, et al. *Forging a Collection: The Frank W. Tober Collection on Literary Forgery.* Newark: University of Delaware Library. A fascinating overview of an archive of literary forgeries, from Thomas Wise to Prokosch.

Nance, John. *The Gentle Tasaday: A Stone Age People in the Philippine Rain Forest.* New York: Harcourt Brace Jovanovich, 1975. Foreword by Charles A. Lindbergh.

Nelson, Jill. *Volunteer Slavery: My Authentic Negro Experience.* Chicago: Noble Press, 1993. Memoir of her time at the *Post* under Bradlee in the late 1980s.

Nelson, Maggie. *The Art of Cruelty: A Reckoning.* New York: W. W. Norton, 2011.

O'Brien, Geoffrey. *Dream Time: Chapters from the Sixties.* New York: Penguin Books, 1988. A great book, plagiarized by Quentin Rowan (a.k.a "Q. R. Markham").

O'Connor, Flannery. *Mystery and Manners: Occasional Prose.* Selected and edited by Sally and Robert Fitzgerald. New York: Farrar, Straus & Giroux, 1970.

Ofshe, Richard, and Ethan Watters. *Making Monsters: False Memories, Psychotherapy, and Sexual Hysteria*. Berkeley: University of California Press, 1994.

Painter, Nell Irvin. *The History of White People*. New York: W. W. Norton, 2009. Essential overview of the science and history of race.

————. *Sojourner Truth: A Life, a Symbol*. New York: W. W. Norton, 1996.

Paull, H. M. *Literary Ethics: A Study in the Growth of the Literary Conscience*. London: Thornton Butterworth, 1928. An important, wide-ranging study, especially on forgers, piracy, and "a dubious licence in fiction."

Peters, Olaf, ed. *Degenerate Art: The Attack on Modern Art in Nazi Germany 1937*. Munich: Prestel, 2014. Printed for the eponymous exhibition at Neue Galerie New York, 2014.

Plimpton, George. *Truman Capote: In Which Various Friends, Enemies, Acquaintances, and Detractors Recall His Turbulent Career*. New York: Anchor Books, 1998. An oral history in the tradition of Jean Stein's *Edie* (1982).

Poignant, Roslyn. *Professional Savages: Captive Lives and Western Spectacle*. New Haven, CT: Yale University Press, 2004.

Powell, D. A., and David Trinidad. *By Myself: An Autobiography*. New York: Turtle Point Press, 2009. A brilliant, brief tour de force made up of parts of other, acknowledged autobiographies.

Prokosch, Frederic. *The Asiatics*. New York: Farrar, Straus & Giroux, 2005. Introduction by Pico Iyer. A novel; originally 1935.

Rainey, David. *Ern Malley: The Hoax and Beyond*. [Bulleen, Victoria, Australia]: Heide Museum of Modern Art, 2009. Catalog recounting the hoax and featuring the art and literature it influenced.

Rawson, Hugh. *Rawson's Dictionary of Euphemisms and Other Doubletalk*. Chicago: Castle Books, 1995.

Reiss, Benjamin. *The Showman and the Slave: Race, Death, and Memory in Barnum's America*. Cambridge, MA: Harvard University Press, 2001.

Robinson, Charles E., ed. *The Original Frankenstein*. New York: Vintage, 2008.

Rogers, Molly. *Delia's Tears: Race, Science, and Photography in Nineteenth-Century America*. New Haven, CT: Yale University Press, 2010. Further reading (and images) of Agassiz's commissioned photographs of racial types, which is to say, enslaved Africans in South Carolina in the 1860s.

Rogin, Michael. *"Ronald Reagan," the Movie, and Other Episodes in Political Demonology*. Berkeley: University of California Press, 1987.

Rolls, Mitchell, and Murray Johnson. *Historical Dictionary of Australian Aborigines*. Lanham, MD: Scarecrow Press, 2011.

Ronson, Jon. *So You've Been Publicly Shamed*. New York: Riverhead Books, 2015. Among other things, traces the aftermath, Ronson feels unjustly, of Jonah Lehrer's self-inflicted implosion.

Rose, Deborah Bird. *Dingo Makes Us Human: Life and Land in an Australian Aboriginal Culture*. Cambridge: Cambridge University Press, 2000.

Rose, Phyllis. *Julia Margaret Cameron's Women*. Chicago: Art Institute of Chicago, 1998. Includes the essay "Milkmaid Madonnas: An Appreciation of Cameron's Portraits of Women."

Rosenbaum, Ron. *The Shakespeare Wars: Clashing Scholars, Public Fiascoes, Palace Coups*. New York: Random House, 2006. Especially fascinating on the controversy over the now-discredited Shakespeare "Funeral Elegy."

Rosenblum, Joseph. *Practice to Deceive: The Incredible Story of Literary Forgery's Most Notorious Practitioners*. New Castle, DE: Oak Knoll Press, 2000. This book contains an excellent, comprehensive bibliography based on the forgers discussed, especially older English ones, from Wise to Byron.

Ruthven, K. K. *Faking Literature*. Cambridge: Cambridge University Press, 2001. Study and argument of "literary forgeries" as literature. Terrific, definitive bibliography (also reprinted in *Jacket* online magazine).

Said, Edward W. *Orientalism*. New York: Vintage Books, 1979. Classic study.

Sandburg, Carl. *Abraham Lincoln: The Prairie Years*. New York: Blue Ribbon Books, 1926.

Schmidt, Michael. *Lives of the Poets*. New York: Knopf, 1999. Useful overview of English and American poetry.

———. *The Novel: A Biography*. New York: Belknap Press, 2014.

Schwartz, A. Brad. *Broadcast Hysteria: Orson Welles's "War of the World" and the Art of Fake News*. New York: Hill and Wang, 2015.

Schwartz, Hillel. *The Culture of the Copy: Striking Likenesses, Unreasonable Facsimiles*. New York: Zone Books, 1996.

See, Caroline. *Dreaming: Hard Luck and Good Times in America*. Berkeley: University of California Press, 1996.

Sellers, Charles Coleman. *Mr. Peale's Museum: Charles Willson Peale and the First Popular Museum of Natural Science and Art*. New York: W.W. Norton, 1980

Shaffer, Andrew. *Literary Rogues: A Scandalous History of Wayward Authors*. New York: Harper Perennial, 2013. "A wildly funny and shockingly true compendium of the bad boys (and girls) of Western literature," ending with James Frey.

Shelley, Mary. *Frankenstein; or, The Modern Prometheus*. New York: Modern Library, 1993. Text of the novel's third, corrected edition from 1831.

Shenk, Joshua Wolf. *Lincoln's Melancholy: How Depression Challenged a President and Fueled His Greatness*. Boston: Mariner Books, 2005. Ends with an afterword about Lincoln historiography, including the "Minor affair."

Showalter, Elaine. *The Female Malady: Women, Madness and English Culture, 1830–1980*. New York: Pantheon, 1986.

———. *Hystories: Hysterical Epidemics and Modern Media*. New York: Columbia University Press, 1997. Useful overview of various modern "epidemics," including Satanic ritual abuse and multiple personality disorder.

Sims, Michael, ed. *Dracula's Guest: A Connoisseur's Collection of Victorian Vampire Stories*. New York: Walker, 2010.

Sloan, James Park. *Jerzy Kosinski: A Biography.* New York: Dutton, 1979.

Smith, Donald B. *From the Land of Shadows: The Making of Grey Owl.* Saskatoon, SK: Western Producer Prairie Books, 1990.

Soderholm, James. *Fantasy, Forgery, and the Byron Legend.* Lexington: University Press of Kentucky, 1996.

Sontag, Susan. *A Susan Sontag Reader.* New York: Farrar, Straus and Giroux, 1982.

———. *Illness as Metaphor* and *AIDS and Its Metaphors.* New York: Picador, 2003. Originally 1977 and 1988, respectively.

Stagl, Justin. *A History of Curiosity: The Theory of Travel 1550–1800.* London: Routledge, 1994.

Stanton, William. *The Leopard's Spots: Scientific Attitudes toward Race in America 1815–59.* Chicago: University of Chicago Press, 1960.

Steers, Edward, Jr. *Hoax: Hitler's Diaries, Lincoln's Assassins, and Other Famous Frauds.* Lexington: University Press of Kentucky, 2013. Cogent summaries of six hoaxes, the best being the "Piltdown Man" hoax.

Stewart, Doug. *The Boy Who Would Be Shakespeare: A Tale of Forgery and Folly.* Cambridge, MA: Da Capo Press, 2010.

Stewart, Susan. *On Longing: Narratives of the Miniature, the Gigantic, the Souvenir, the Collection.* Durham, NC: Duke University Press, 1992.

Stoker, Bram. *Famous Impostors.* New York: Sturgis & Walton, 1910.

Stryker, Susan. *Queer Pulp: Perverted Passions from the Golden Age of the Paperback.* San Francisco: Chronicle Books, 2001.

The Stuart B. Schimmel Forgery Collection & Other Properties. Auction catalog for Bonham's, 23 May 2012 auction, Knightsbridge, London. Useful images and stories about many literary forgeries, including "original" manuscripts from William Ireland to Thomas Wise.

Sueyoshi, Amy. *Queer Compulsions: Race, Nation, and Sexuality in the Affairs of Yone Noguchi.* Honolulu: University of Hawai'i Press, 2012.

Sussman, Robert Wald. *The Myth of Race: The Troubling Persistence of an Unscientific Idea.* Cambridge, MA: Harvard University Press, 2014.

Teicholz, Tom, ed. *Conversations with Jerzy Kosinksi.* Jackson: University Press of Mississippi, 1993.

Thigpen, Corbett H., and Hervey M. Cleckley. *The Three Faces of Eve.* New York: McGraw-Hill, 1957. Medical history written by the doctors for the first popularized multiple personality disorder case.

Thompson, Neal. *A Curious Man: The Strange and Brilliant Life of Robert "Believe It or Not!" Ripley.* New York: Crown Archetype, 2013.

Thomson, Rosemarie Garland. *Extraordinary Bodies: Figuring Physical Disability in American Culture and Literature.* New York: Columbia University Press, 1997.

Thomson, Rosemarie Garland, ed. *Freakery: Cultural Spectacles of the Extraordinary Body.* New York: New York University Press, 1996.

Tilley, Elspeth. *White Vanishing: Rethinking Australia's Lost-in-the-Bush Myth.* Amsterdam: Rodopi, 2011.

Trachtenberg, Alan. *Reading American Photographs: Images as History, Mathew Brady to Walker Evans*. New York: Hill and Wang, 1989.

Trethewey, Natasha. *Thrall*. New York: Houghton Mifflin Harcourt, 2012.

Turner, Justin G., and Linda Levitt Turner, eds. *Mary Todd Lincoln: Her Life and Letters*. New York: Knopf, 1972.

Walker, William Sylvester ("Coo-ee"). *At Possum Creek*. London: J. & J. Bennett, 1915.

———. *From the Land of the Wombat*. London: John Long, 1899. With illustrations by J. Ayton Symington. Short stories set in Australia.

———. *Native Born: A Novel*. London: John Long, 1900.

———. *The Silver Queen: A Tale of the Northern Territory*. 2nd ed. London: John Ouseley, 1908. "Lost-race novel" set in Australia.

———. *What Lay Beneath: A Story of the Queensland Bush*. London: George Bell & Sons, 1909.

Wark, Robert R.. *Charles Doyle's Fairyland*. San Marino, CA: Huntington Library, 1980. Color plates and catalog of the nineteenth-century "fantasy art" and fairies of Charles Doyle, Arthur Conan Doyle's father.

Washington, Peter. *Madame Blavatsky's Baboon: A History of the Mystics, Mediums, and Misfits Who Brought Spiritualism to America*. New York: Schocken, 1995.

Weeks, Edward (Ted). *My Green Age*. Boston: Atlantic Books/Little, Brown, 1973. A terrific and lively memoir by a World War I vet and editor at the *Atlantic*, who also served as the U.S. agent for the expatriate Black Sun Press.

Weinberger, Eliot. *Karmic Traces, 1993–1999*. New York: New Directions, 2001.

Weinstein, Debra. *Apprentice to the Flower Poet Z.* New York: Random House, 2004. A roman à clef whose narrator works for "the Flower Poet" of the title, who plagiarizes from her.

Williams, Gilda, ed. *The Gothic*. Cambridge, MA: MIT Press, 2007.

[Wilson, Harriet E.]. *Our Nig; or, Sketches from the Life of a Free Black in a Two-Story White House, North*. With an introduction by P. Gabrielle Foreman. Originally 1859. New York: Penguin Classics, 2009.

———. *Our Nig; or, Sketches from the Life of a Free Black*. With an introduction by Henry Louis Gates Jr. and Richard J. Ellis. Expanded edition. New York: Vintage Books, 2011. Originally 1859. Rediscovered and first reprinted by Gates in May 1983.

Wilson, Robert A. *Modern Book Collecting*. New York: Knopf, 1980. Useful chapter discusses *Lily* by "Gertrude Stein" as forged by Prokosch.

Wojahn, David. *Strange Good Fortune: Essays on Contemporary Poetry*. Fayetteville: University of Arkansas Press, 2000. Chapter considering the Yasusada hoax.

Worrall, Simon. *The Poet and the Murderer: A True Story of Literary Crime and the Art of Forgery*. New York: Dutton, 2002.

Yagoda, Ben. *Memoir: A History*. New York: Riverhead Books, 2009. Ends with a discussion of certain false memoirs.

Yearsley, Ann. *Poems on Various Subjects. A Second Book of Poems on Various Subjects* by Ann Yearsley, a Milkwoman of Clifton, Near Bristol, Being Her Second Work. London: Printed for the Author and sold by G.G.J. and J. Robinson. 1787. Includes what may be the first poem on Chatterton, "Elegy for Mr. Chatterton." Reprinted in the Revolution and Romanticism series (Oxford: Woodstock Books, 1994).

Young, Elizabeth. *Black Frankenstein: The Making of an American Metaphor.* New York: New York University Press, 2008.

Young, Kevin. *The Grey Album: On the Blackness of Blackness.* Minneapolis: Graywolf Press, 2012.

Young, Kevin, curator. *"Democratic Vistas": Exploring the Raymond Danowski Poetry Library.* Stuart A. Rose Manuscript, Archives, and Rare Book Library, Emory University, Atlanta, 2008. Includes entries on and images of the Spectra Hoax.

Films

in color, unless otherwise noted

Richard Attenborough, dir. *Grey Owl.* Canada, 1999. Stilted biopic of the famed faker, starring Pierce Brosnan.

Warren Beatty, dir. *Reds.* United States, 1981. With Jerzy Kosinski starring as an early Soviet bureaucrat.

Anna Broinowski, dir. *Forbidden Lies.* Australia, 2007. Documentary on hoaxer Norma Khouri, author of *Honor Lost* (aka *Forbidden Love in Australia*).

Sophie Deraspe, dir. *A Gay Girl in Damascus: The Amina Profile.* Canada, 2015. 84 minutes.

John Frankenheimer, dir. [Richard Stanley, dir., uncredited.] *The Island of Dr. Moreau.* New Line Cinema, 1996. 96 minutes.

Alex Gibney, dir. *The Armstrong Lie.* 2013. Documentary on Lance Armstrong, from the director who followed Armstrong on his 2009 comeback.

Samantha Grant, dir. *A Fragile Trust: Plagiarism, Power, and Jayson Blair at the "New York Times."* 2013. Documentary premiered on PBS in May 2014.

Angelo Guglielmo, dir. *The Woman Who Wasn't There.* Germany, 2012. 65 minutes. A documentary about notorious 9/11 impostor "Tania Head."

Lasse Hallström, dir. *The Hoax.* Miramax, 2006 [released 2007]. Fictionalized version of the Howard Hughes hoax.

Alex Holmes, dir. *Stop at Nothing: The Lance Armstrong Story.* 2014. 104 minutes.

Nunnally Johnson, dir. *The Three Faces of Eve.* 1957. Black and white, 91 minutes. Joanne Woodward rightly won an Oscar for her depiction of a woman with "multiple personality disorder."

Henry Joost and Ariel Schulman, dir. *Catfish.* Supermarché, 2010. 87 minutes. Documentary that named a phenomenon and spawned an MTV show.

Erie C. Kenton, dir. *The Island of Lost Souls.* 1932. Black and white, 70 minutes. With Charles Laughton and Bela Legosi.

Baz Luhrmann, dir. *The Great Gatsby.* Warner Bros. 2013. 143 minutes.

Jesse Moss, dir. *Con Man: The True Story of an Ivy League Impostor.* 2001. Documentary as part of the Cinemax Reel Life series; story of James (Jim) Hogue, with interviews by David Samuels.

"Henry Paris" [Radley Metzger], dir. *Naked Came the Stranger.* 1975. Hard-core adaptation of the hoax novel.

Herman C. Raymaker, dir. *Adventure Girl.* 1934. Black and white, silent with voiceover, 69 minutes. Joan Lowell, star and narrator. Despite most accounts, the film appears to be based on her book *Gal Reporter* (and not *Cradle of the Deep*, as invariably cited).

Alistair Reid, dir. *Selling Hitler.* 1991. Fascinating and vivid five-part miniseries retelling the story behind the fake "Hitler Diaries," based on the Robert Harris book of the same name.

Gary Ross, dir. *The Hunger Games.* Lionsgate, 2012. 142 minutes.

Patrick Stettner, dir. *The Night Listener.* 2006. 91 minutes. Based on Armistead Maupin's novel.

Marjorie Sturm, dir. *The Cult of JT LeRoy.* USA, 2014.

Dan Taylor, dir. *The Island of Dr. Moreau.* American International Pictures, 1977. Starring Burt Lancaster, Michael York, and Barbara Carrera.

Orson Welles, dir. *F for Fake.* 1972. Filmic "essay" rereleased as Criterion Collection no. 288 in 2005.

FIJI CANNIBALS.

"Fiji Cannibals [Fiji Jim and Wife Annie]," 1883.

Illustration Credits

Page x: Charles Eisenmann studios, "Ashbury Ben The Leopard Boy" and "Old Zip Barnum's What is It?" cabinet card, 1885. Courtesy of Harvard Theatre Collection, Houghton Library, Harvard University. TCS 7.

Page 2: Salvatore Fergola, *Scoperte fatte nella luna dal Sigr. Herschell.* Napoli: Lita. Fergola Largo S. Gio. Maggiore No. 30, [between 1835 and 1849]. Italian translation and images from the Moon Hoax. Library of Congress Prints and Photographs Division. Call number: PR 13 CN 1964:R01, container 37, no. 9 (B size)

Page 6: "Great Attraction Just Arrived at Concert Hall." Handbill for Joice Heth exhibition, 1835. Author's collection.

Page 62: [Houdini and the ghost of Abraham Lincoln], lantern slide, circa 1925. Library of Congress Prints and Photographs Division. Lot 7426.

Page 94: Opal Whiteley costumed as an "Indian," 1918. Opal Whiteley papers, Special Collections & University Archives, University of Oregon Libraries, Eugene, Oregon. AX 097, Box 9a.

Page 116: Grey Owl Indian Craft Supplies catalog, 1956. Author's collection.

Page 138: "Are They Ambassadors from Mars." Photograph of the Muse Brothers, 1926. Courtesy of Beth Macy.

Page 188: Louis McQuaid, photographer, "Sideshow of Darkest Africa, Strange People from Africa exhibit," Century of Progress World's Fair (Chicago), 1933–34.

Courtesy of Robert Langmuir African American photograph collection, Stuart A. Rose Manuscript, Archives, and Rare Book Library, Emory University. MSS1218, Box 7.

Page 210: Désiré Bourneville and P-Marie-Léon Regnard, Plate XXXVI, "Attaque: Crucifiement." *Iconographie photographique de la Salpêtrière (service de M. Charcot)*, vol. 2. Paris: Aux bureau de Progrès Médical/V. Adrien Delahaye & Co., 1878. Courtesy of Houghton Library, Harvard University.

Désiré Bourneville and P-Marie-Léon Regnard, Plate XIV, "Léthargie: Hyperexcitabilité Musculaire." *Iconographie photographique de la Salpêtrière (service de M. Charcot)*, vol. 3: Hystéro-Épilespsie. Paris: Aux Bureau de Progrès Médical/V. Adrien Delahaye & Co., 1879-80. Courtesy of Houghton Library, Harvard University.

Page 228: "Circassian Beauty with Standing Man." Author's collection.

Page 232: Cigarette card, Kimball Company, ca. 1890s. Author's collection.

Page 252: "Con Man of the Year: Clifford Irving by Elmyr de Hory," *Time* magazine cover, 21 February 1972. Author's collection.

Page 284: Han van Meegeren, *The Supper at Emmaus*, ca. 1937. Collection Museum Boijmans Van Beuningen, Rotterdam. Reproduced by permission of the Museum Boijmans.

Page 304: Max Sherover, *Fakes in American Journalism*. Brooklyn, N.Y.: Free Press League, 1914. Author's collection.

Page 342: *Life of Zip: The Original What is It?* New York: Popular Pub. Co., ca, 1884. Courtesy of Harvard Theatre Collection, Houghton Library, Harvard University. Thr 1229.55 (3).

Page 348: "Burning of Barnum's Museum," 1865. Courtesy of Billy Rose Theatre Division, The New York Public Library. New York Public Library Digital Collections. Accessed July 9, 2017. http://digitalcollections.nypl.org/items/12a88d90-3449-0131 -77ab-58d385a7b928

Page 380: Bell, Photographer, "Cannibal Fair Child," carte-de-visite, ca. 1870. Courtesy of Harvard Theatre Collection, Houghton Library, Harvard University. TCS 20 & 21.

Page 410: John Brown's cap. (Original in possession of the Kansas Historical Society) [p. 515]," The Miriam and Ira D. Wallach Division of Art, Prints and Photographs: Print Collection, The New York Public Library. New York Public Library Digital Collections. Accessed July 10, 2017. http://digitalcollections.nypl.org/items/510d47dd-d5f5-a3d9-e040-e00a18064a99

Page 430: Charles D. Fredricks & Co., 587 Broadway, New York, "Young America [John H. Haslan]," carte-de-visite, ca. 1850s. Courtesy of Harvard Theatre Collection, Houghton Library, Harvard University.

Page 448: A. W. Rothengatter & Co., "The MOTHER Elephant, 'HEBE,' and her BABY, 'Young America,'" carte-de-visite, Philadelphia, 1880. Courtesy of Harvard Theatre Collection, Houghton Library, Harvard University.

Page 534: C. L. Weed Star Photograph Gallery, "Fiji Cannibals [Fiji Jim and Wife Annie]," carte-de-visite dated "at Dime Museum 13 November 1883" on verso. Courtesy of Harvard Theatre Collection, Houghton Library, Harvard University. TCS 20 & 21.

Index

KEVIN YOUNG is the author of a previous work of nonfiction, *The Grey Album: On the Blackness of Blackness*, which was a *New York Times* Notable Book, a finalist for the National Book Critics Circle Award for criticism, and the winner of the Graywolf Press Nonfiction Prize. He is also the author of ten books of poetry, including *Blue Laws: Selected & Uncollected Poems 1995–2015*, which was longlisted for the National Book Award; *Book of Hours*, which won the Lenore Marshall Poetry Prize from the Academy of American Poets; and *Jelly Roll: a blues*, which was named a finalist for both the National Book Award and the Los Angeles Times Book Prize. He is the editor of many books and anthologies, including *The Collected Poems of Lucille Clifton 1965–2010* and *The Best American Poetry 2011*.

Young is the director of the Schomburg Center for Research in Black Culture, part of the New York Public Library, located in Harlem, USA. Elected into the American Academy of Arts and Sciences, he is also the poetry editor at the *New Yorker*. For more information, visit his website: kevinyoungpoetry.com.

The text of *Bunk* is set in Adobe Caslon Pro.
Book design by Rachel Holscher.
Composition by Bookmobile Design & Digital Publisher Services,
Minneapolis, Minnesota. Manufactured by Friesens on acid-free,
100 percent postconsumer wastepaper.

BARNUM'S AMERICAN MUSEUM

Cor. Broadway and Ann St., opposite St. Paul's Church.

P. T. BARNUM .... PROPRIETOR AND MANAGER
JOHN GREENWOOD, Jr .... ASSISTANT MANAGER
E. F. TAYLOR .... Director of Amusements

Admittance to the whole Museum, the Picture Gallery, the Natural History Department, the Happy
Family, and the Cosmorama Room, as well as the entertainments in the Lecture Room ......25 Cents
Children (under ten years) ....15 Cents each
Tickets for Parquet or first Balcony seats, in the Lecture Room ....15 Cents extra
For Children (under ten years) ....10 Cents
Morning Visitors admitted to the Afternoon Performance Free.

☞ LAST WEEK

But one of the great, roaring, barking

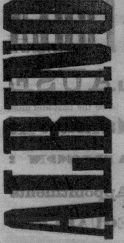

BLACK SEA-LION

The mighty King of the Ocean, the long-supposed fabulous NEPTUNE,
the most MAJESTIC, TERRIFIC, though yet docile, inhabitant of the
great Deep, the most interesting creature alive.

☞ LAST WEEK

But one of

The Extraordinary and Wonderful

ALBINO FAMILY

WHITE NEGROES, OR MOORS,

From Madagascar, consisting of a **Husband, Wife and Child,** all with pure
White Skin, Silken White Hair and Pink Eyes. They were born of **Parents perfectly Black.** They will be seen here but two weeks longer.